GEORGE LANSBURY

At the Heart of Old Labour

GEORGE LANSBURY

At the Heart of Old Labour

JOHN SHEPHERD

OXFORD
UNIVERSITY PRESS

OXFORD

UNIVERSITY PRESS

Great Clarendon Street, Oxford OX2 6DP

Oxford University Press is a department of the University of Oxford.
It furthers the University's objective of excellence in research, scholarship,
and education by publishing worldwide in

Oxford New York

Auckland Bangkok Buenos Aires Cape Town Chennai
Dar es Salaam Delhi Hong Kong Istanbul Karachi Kolkata
Kuala Lumpur Madrid Melbourne Mexico City Mumbai Nairobi
São Paulo Shanghai Taipei Tokyo Toronto

Oxford is a registered trade mark of Oxford University Press
in the UK and in certain other countries

Published in the United States
by Oxford University Press Inc., New York

© John Shepherd 2002

The moral rights of the author have been asserted
Database right Oxford University Press (maker)

First published 2002
First published in paperback 2004

British Library Cataloguing in Publication Data
Data available

Library of Congress Cataloging in Publication Data
Data available

ISBN 0-19-820164-8
ISBN 0-19-927364-2 (Pbk.)

1 3 5 7 9 10 8 6 4 2

Typeset in Minion by
Jayvee, Trivandrum, India
Printed in Great Britain
on acid-free paper by
Biddles Ltd.,
King's Lynn, Norfolk

In Memory of

My Parents

Vi and Sam Shepherd

Preface

By any measure, George Lansbury was a remarkable and engaging figure in late nineteenth- and twentieth-century British politics. He was also an exceptionally active politician and tireless campaigner for a host of causes in this country and abroad. While he was 'the most lovable figure in British politics' in the 1930s, his reputation dwindled after the Second World War. No full-scale study has appeared since 1951, when his son-in-law, Raymond Postgate, published *The Life of George Lansbury*. At a time of renewed interest in Labour politics and history, it seems appropriate to attempt a fresh assessment of George Lansbury's life on the left and his contribution to modern democratic politics.

In consequence, writing a new life of George Lansbury has been a fascinating and challenging project—far greater than was originally anticipated. I am taking a self-denying ordinance—prompted by acute embarrassment—in not revealing how long it has taken me to complete a book that has left me with an enormous number of debts to individuals and organizations.

To my good fortune, my interest in George Lansbury received enthusiastic encouragement from members of the Lansbury family, who provided unlimited access to papers in their possession and answered my interminable enquiries. At the same time, I have enjoyed full academic freedom to write whatever I wished. I am most grateful to Angela Lansbury and Peter Shaw for warm hospitality at their Santa Monica home at the start of my research, access to papers, and for putting me in touch with British members of their family. I owe an enormous debt to the late Esme Whiskin, who opened up family papers in Exeter and Dorset and shared her extensive memories of her grandparents and their family. She was always full of life and greatly encouraging. Sadly, Esme will not see the final version, but she did receive copies of my interim writings about George Lansbury.

I am also most indebted to other members of the Lansbury family for generous hospitality, friendship, and unfailing help over many years: Kate Geraghty and Anthony Broad; Billy Geraghty; Sean Geraghty; Alison and Bob Higgs; Brenda and Terry Lansbury, the late Peter Thurtle, and Nigel Whiskin. I would also like to thank Professor John Postgate and Mary Postgate for generous hospitality, access to the Raymond Postgate Papers in their possession, and assistance with my enquiries about Lansbury's first biographer. My thanks also to Chris Sumner, for generous help with information about his family and for providing a recording of the BBC radio programme on the Poplar Rates Rebellion.

This research first saw the light of day after my part-time doctoral studies, when I was greatly encouraged to pursue this line of enquiry by my supervisor, Professor Eric Hobsbawm, and my two examiners, Professors Peter Clarke and

Kenneth O. Morgan. Since then, they have been unfailing in their help and support in their many different ways. I am also grateful to the late Dr Henry Pelling, who encouraged me to write about George Lansbury and followed my progress with interest.

I benefited enormously from the knowledge and insight of those who knew George Lansbury in the 1930s. I am most grateful for memorable interviews with the following: the late Baroness Barbara Castle of Blackburn; Professor Lionel Elvin; The Right Hon. Michael Foot; Jack Jones OM; the late Lord Douglas Jay; Angela Lansbury; Professor John Postgate; the late Lord Donald Soper; the late Peter Thurtle; the late Esme Whiskin.

Expert assistance has always been available at a number of institutions, where I have been a frequent visitor. I would like to thank: Dr Angela Raspin; Sue Donnelly, and Conor Hartnett at the British Library of Political and Economic Science; Stephen Bird, Phil Dunn, and Janette Martin at The Labour History Archive and Study Centre, The John Rylands University Library, University of Manchester; Chris Lloyd, Malcolm Barr-Hamilton, Harry Watton, and David Rich at Tower Hamlets Libraries Local History and Archives; Bill Noblett, Anne Toseland, and Tim Nicholas, Cambridge University Library. I am also most indebted to Bill Hether-ington of the Peace Pledge Union for expert guidance on pacifism and conscientious objection; Dr Lesley Hall at the Wellcome Trust for her kind advice on birth-control and abortion collections. I am very grateful to Dr Sara Tyake and staff at the Public Record Office for invaluable help over many years.

I have also received generous assistance from the staff of many libraries, record offices, and other organizations in this country: Albert Hall; the Bodleian Library; Borthwick Institute of Historical Research, York; British Library; British and Foreign Schools Society Archives Centre; Cleveland County Council Library; Churchill Archives; Cumbria County Council Archives Department; East Surrey Library; London Metropolitan Archives; Madame Tussaud's; Marx Memorial Library; Middlesborough North East Archives; Robinson Library, University of Newcastle; Newspaper Library Colindale; Redhill Library; the Religious Society of Friends in Britain Library; John Rylands Library, Manchester; Sydney Jones Library, University of Liverpool; the Theosophical Society in London; The Royal Archives, The Royal Collection, Windsor; University of Leeds Adult Education Centre; Woolwich Local History Library; Working Class Movement Library. My particular thanks go to Bill Morris and Karen Livingstone at the Transport and General Workers' Union for expert assistance and kind hospitality. Libraries and their staff in other countries who also receive my sincere appreciation for their help include Boston Public Library; Brisbane State Archives; International Institute of Social History; John Oxley Library; Mills Memorial Library, McMaster University; Historical Society of Pennsylvania, South Carolina University Library; Theosophical Society, Adyar, India.

I wish to thank the History Division of Anglia Polytechnic University, Cambridge, where I am now Senior Research Associate, for a financial contribution towards research expenses; and the British Academy for a research grant that allowed me to visit Australia in 1996.

I am grateful for the permission of HM Queen Elizabeth II to quote from copyright material in the Royal Archives. I am also indebted to the following institutions and individuals for their permission to use copyright material; Professor John Postgate and British School of Political and Economic Science (Lansbury Papers); the late Esme Whiskin Lansbury (Lansbury Papers); Professor John Postgate (Raymond Postgate Papers); Angela Lansbury (Lansbury Papers); the late Peter Thurtle (Thurtle Papers); Bodleian Library (Attlee and Ensor Papers); National Museum of Labour History (Labour Party Papers); British Library of Political and Economic Science (Beveridge Papers, Passfield Papers, and Webb Local Government Collection); University of South Carolina (Allen Papers); Durham University Library (Lawson Papers).

I am also grateful for permission from the Keeper and Director of Public Records to quote from Crown copyright material at The National Archives; from the Special Collections Librarian to use the Trevelyan Papers at the Robinson Library, Newcastle University; from the Home Office to see files on Lansbury's political activities before their official release; and the Trades Union Congress for the use of Tolpuddle Martyrs Centenary photographs. I would like to acknowledge that the Ramsay MacDonald Diaries were 'meant as notes to guide and revive memory as regards happenings and must on no account be published as they are'. In line with Ramsay MacDonald's wishes, I have only used small extracts from his diaries. Every effort has been taken to trace copyright-holders and to avoid infringement of copyright. I apologize unreservedly to any copyright holders who have inadvertently been overlooked.

I have made research visits in Britain, Australia, Holland, and the United States. I would like to thank the following for their generous help and hospitality: Professor Philip Bagwell and Rosemary Bagwell; Kelly and Reg Chapple; Jenny and John Childs; Thelma and Malcolm Daggett, Heloise and Alan Downe; Ive and Fred Elliott; Pat Perry; Carol Probert; Dr Sal Richardson and Ken Richardson; Sue Lusted; Viv and Ian Matthieson.

Considerable secretarial and technical assistance was received while completing this book. I am grateful to Joan Haddock who typed many chapters; to Tony Ing, and Mike Haddock, who invariably solved my computer failures; and to Bruce Robertson, University Photographer at Anglia Polytechnic University, Cambridge, for photographic assistance. Louise Shepherd and Peter Foulds also provided magnificent technical support at the crucial eleventh hour. I also wish to thank Dr Juliet Vale for her expert and valuable copy-editing and her unfailing good humour during the final stages of preparing the text.

My thanks go to Lady Cass, Paul Holmes, and fellow justices at Cambridge Magistrates Court, in particular George Brewster, David Gillett, Rosemary Gardiner, and other members of the editorial committee of the Court Bulletin; also John Yates and fellow magistrates at Epping and Ongar Magistrates Court, for their support. I also wish to thank Mr John Scott who restored my sight at a vital time.

I have been fortunate to receive invaluable help from learned colleagues, and I would like to thank Professor Philip Bagwell, Dr Eugenio Biagini, Professor Peter

Clarke; Dr Peter Cunningham, Dr Phil Gardner, Peter Gathercole, Dr Bobbie Wells, Dr Rohan McWilliam, Dr Huw Richards, Dr Alastair Reid, Professor Jonathan Schneer, Dr Peter Searby, Dr John Shaw, Dr Chris Southgate, Dr Paul Tyler, Dr Maggie Walsh.

I would also like to thank Kevin Bonnett, Libby Cull, Mary Hope, Diane Tucker, Sean Lang, Nick Kinloch, Mike Murphy, Dr Boyd Hilton, Dr Peter Hoare, Dr Paul McHugh, Professor John Pollard, David Weigall, Dr Leonardo Castillo, Patrick Chaplin, Janet Howes, Dorothy Kendall, Rosemary Taylor, Philip Mernich, Jean Plaister, Peter Smith, Jill Theis, Earl De La Warr, Dr Malcolm Chase, Mark Govish, Elizabeth Crawford, Eryl McNally MEP, John Beresford, Beverley Harding and Stephen Lees.

My research has benefited greatly from opportunities to present papers about my research at universities and learned societies. I am most indebted to members of the History Society, Anglia Polytechnic University, Cambridge; St John's College Graduate Seminar, Cambridge University; the Politics and History Society, Salford University; the Postgraduate History Seminar at Huddersfield University; Cambridge Labour Party; South Cambridgeshire Labour Party; East London History Society; History Society, Hills Road Sixth Form College, Cambridge; Cambridge Branch of the Historical Association; The Society for the Study of Labour History Conference organized by The Dictionary of Labour Biography and The University of Manchester Communist Biographical Project.

I am most grateful to Ivan Howlett for an invitation to contribute to the BBC Radio 4, 'Making History' programme on the eightieth anniversary of the 'Poplar Rates Rebellion' and for subsequent help, particularly with access to the BBC Sound Archives recordings; and also to Greg Neale, *BBC History Magazine*; Martin Sheppard, The Hambledon Press; Mark Seddon, *Tribune* and the Editor of *The Times Higher Education Supplement* for publishing my articles on George Lansbury.

Many learned colleagues and friends have generously read and commented on the work in progress. I owe an incalculable debt to Professor Chris Wrigley, who read and commented on the complete typescript and has provided invaluable counsel and friendship over many years. I am also most grateful to Professor Philip Bagwell, Professor Keith Laybourn; Dr Huw Richards, Dr Janet Shepherd, and Professor Pat Thane, who read substantial parts of the work, for their expert comments. I alone am responsible for any errors or omissions that remain.

At Oxford University Press I have been most fortunate in my two editors who have given me matchless guidance and constant encouragement throughout this project. I would like to thank Dr Tony Morris and Dr Ruth Parr for their unfailing patience and support. I am also most grateful to Kay Rogers for her understanding and assistance in progressing the book to publication.

My last debts are most important to me. I am especially grateful to my daughters, Emma and Louise Shepherd, for their constant help and encouragement. Together, we have supported Arsenal Football Club through triumph and disaster. My appreciation goes also to other family members for their assistance and interest: Doug, Karen, Carrick, and Findlay Livingstone; Debra, Eleanor-May, and Cllr Stephen

Wade; Jessica Livingstone; Bob, Sandra, and Sarah Shepherd; Sue and Colin Drummond; Dan Shepherd and Patrick Murphy; Peter Foulds.

My wife, Dr Janet Shepherd, has lived with this project for a considerable time and has read every word. I am deeply grateful for her unflagging support and wise counsel throughout—especially in the final stages, when she put her own research on hold. Without her help, this book would not have been finished.

The book is dedicated to the memory of my parents, Vi and Sam Shepherd, who worked hard and sacrificed much so that their children could have a better future. Born in the East End before the First World War they were part of the generation of working people that George Lansbury fought for throughout his political life.

Contents

Contents

List of Illustrations

Abbreviations

BLPES	British Library of Political and Economic Science
BSP	British Socialist Party
BUF	British Union of Fascists
CAP	Clifford Allen Papers
COS	Charity Organization Society
CPGB	Communist Party of Great Britain
CU	Conservative and Unionist
CUB	Central Unemployed Body
ECC	Economic Committee of the Cabinet
EFF	Election Fighting Fund
ELES	East London Ethical Society
ELFS	East London Federation of Suffragettes
FSDC	Free Speech Defence Committee
Hansard	*Hansard's Parliamentary Debates*, 5th series
ICWPA	International Class War Prisoners' Aid
IFOR	International Fellowship of Reconciliation
ILP	Independent Labour Party
ITGWU	Irish Transport and General Workers' Union
JCP	Jane Cobden Papers
JRMP	James Ramsay MacDonald Papers
LCC	London County Council
LGB	Local Government Board
LLRU	London Liberal and Radical Union
LPCF	Labour Party Correspondence Files
LPLF	Labour Party Letter Files
LRC	Labour Representation Committee
NAC	National Administrative Council
NCF	No Conscription Fellowship
NEC	National Executive Committee
NJC	National Joint Council
NLF	National Liberal Federation
NLWF	National Left-Wing Movement
NUWCM	National Unemployed Workers' Committee Movement
NUWSS	National Union of Women's Suffrage Societies
OMS	Organization for Maintenance and Supplies
PBMA	Poplar Borough Municipal Alliance
PLP	Parliamentary Labour Party
PP	Passfield Papers
PPU	Peace Pledge Union
RA	Royal Archives
SCL	Socialist Christian League

SDF	Social Democratic Federation
SDP	Social Democratic Party
SIOT	'Socialism in our Time'
SLP	Socialist Labour Party
SSAU	Soldiers', Sailors' and Airmen's Union
SSIP	Society for Socialist Inquiry and Propaganda
TGWU	Transport and General Workers' Union
THLLH&A	Tower Hamlets Libraries Local History and Archives
TUC	Trades Union Congress
UDC	Union of Democratic Control
WBCG	Workers' Birth Control Group
WFL	Women's Freedom League
WLGC	Webb Local Government Collection
WLL	Women's Labour League
WSPU	Women's Social and Political Union

1
Labour's Everyman, 1859–1886

On 23 April 1930 a group of figures appeared on the Northumberland horizon walking slowly in the brilliant sunlight along Hadrian's Wall. Included in the party were officials of local antiquarian societies, civil servants, businessmen, and newspaper reporters. In the midst was the Cabinet minister from Whitehall: a large-framed seventy-year-old man, with white hair and ruddy face adorned by mutton-chop whiskers, attired in an old alpaca suit and bowler hat. Instantly recognized wherever he went, he possessed an unmistakable ringing voice, in which he greeted everyone as his friend.

At Housesteads, the official retinue stopped to concentrate on the silent stones. Characteristically, the minister conversed warmly with the eighty-one-year-old keeper of the fortification, Thomas Thompson, before pondering the moral and political dilemma revealed by the threat of extensive quarrying to the Roman Wall.

As the Cabinet minister in the second Labour government responsible for national monuments and historic sites, George Lansbury was steeped in British history. However, he recognized that 200,000 tons of quarried stone provided the possibility of permanent employment in a region blighted by the inter-war Depression, but only at the expense of one of the most striking and beautiful stretches of the ancient monument.[1]

In Britain today, George Lansbury is probably remembered best, not as the First Commissioner of Works, but as the humanitarian and Christian pacifist leader of the Labour Party, apparently out of touch with the *realpolitik* of European affairs in the 1930s. Lansbury's unilateralist conscience was increasingly in conflict with his role as party leader as Labour faced up to rearmament in the face of the threat of international Fascism. In an encounter memorable in British politics at the 1935 Labour party conference at the Dome in Brighton, the pugnacious trade union boss, Ernest Bevin, drove the pacifist George Lansbury from the leadership in a brutal speech, sharpened by accusation and betrayal of party loyalty.

In an active life, which extended from Victorian Britain to the Second World War, George Lansbury was a passionate supporter of more minority causes and organizations than any other contemporary politician. In his crusades for social justice and the underprivileged, he twice suffered imprisonment for his political

---

[1] 'Ancient Monuments and Historic Buildings' file, PRO, WORK 14 /1257 184682. George Lansbury was known affectionately during his life-time as 'G. L.' (or, simply, 'George' to those who were close to him). In this book he is mostly referred to as 'Lansbury'.

beliefs and also surrendered his parliamentary seat in the women's cause. After a rapturous reception for Lansbury at a mass rally of the unemployed in Hyde Park, Clem Attlee, his successor as party leader and future Labour Prime Minister, wrote to his pacifist brother, Tom: '[W]e tell him he is almost a Gandhi'.[2] Yet, in some quarters, Lansbury's actions provoked criticisms of sentimentality and lack of realism, captured in the famous phrase attributed to the Liberal MP, Augustine Birrell: 'the trouble with Lansbury is that he will let his bleeding heart run away with his bloody head.'[3]

By contrast, Fabian historian, Margaret Cole, remembered George Lansbury as 'the *friendliest* person she had ever met'. She recalled his tireless endeavours for ordinary people and included a random list of twelve organizations associated with the socialist pioneer: 'all struggling bodies, all chronically hard-up for cash, all working for the 'underdog'. However, Dame Margaret chose Lansbury among her fifteen 'makers of the labour movement' only eight years after his death, as she felt his memory was already fading.[4]

Today it is difficult to comprehend the unparalleled affection ordinary people felt in this country and beyond for the Labour pioneer. Lansbury fully merited A. J. P. Taylor's description as 'the most lovable figure in modern politics', a view common among his contemporaries across the political spectrum.[5] He enjoyed a friendship of nearly thirty years with Edward Aubrey Hastings Jay, the Municipal Reform candidate who defeated him at Woolwich in the 1907 London County Council (LCC) election.[6] Lansbury achieved all the elective offices in political life from poor law guardian to Cabinet minister and party leader and was most naturally at home among 'the common people', as could be observed at Hadrian's Wall in 1930. In the words of his son, Edgar: 'For him "the common people" are coalmen, dustmen, porters, postmen, navvies, bricklayers, clerks, sailors, soldiers, shopkeepers, grocers, engineers, carmen, chauffeurs, the unemployed and their wives. Company directors, stockbrokers, statesmen, archbishops, and experts in

---

[2] Clement Attlee to Tom Attlee, 7 Feb. 1933, Attlee Papers, fo. 55.

[3] P. Snowden, *An Autobiography*, i, 1864–1919 (1934), p. 258.

[4] M. Cole, *Makers of the Labour Movement* (1948), pp. 269–87. To Sophie Brown, from a politically active Stepney family, Lansbury was her favourite speaker at the annual Hyde Park Rally. 'I knew he was the MP for Bow, but with his white hair and pink cheeks he was my idea of God, Father Christmas, a favourite uncle and a hero all rolled up into one.' P. Preston, *Tired and Emotional: The Life of Lord George-Brown* (1993), p. 29. I owe this reference to Chris Wrigley.

[5] A. J. P. Taylor, *English History, 1914–1945* (Oxford, 1992), p. 191 n. 3. Lansbury was a close friend of Taylor's father, Percy, and like others on the political left, such as Arthur Henderson, a regular visitor to the Taylor family household in Southport. A. J. P. Taylor, *A Personal History* (1983), pp. 52–3, 56; A. Sisman, *A. J. P. Taylor: A Biography* (1995), p. 38. A. J. P. Taylor might never have become a famous historian. He could have joined the law firm of his uncle Harry—W. H. Thompson, leading left-wing solicitor to the Poplar councillors during the 1921 Rates Rebellion. Later, Taylor considered the possibility of a post as an inspector in the Office of Works when Lansbury was First Commissioner of Works. K. Burke, *Troublemaker: The Life and History of A. J. P. Taylor* (New Haven, 2000), pp. 35, 68–9, 84–5.

[6] The late Douglas Jay recalled that he and his father, Edward, visited George Lansbury in Manor House Hospital in Hampstead after the Labour leader's serious accident in 1934. I am grateful for an interview with Lord Jay at Minster Lovell, 15 Sept. 1995. See also D. Jay, *Change and Fortune: A Political Record* (1980), p. 16.

general may be common, but they are not the common people.'[7] Unlike some socialist leaders, Lansbury avoided the infamous 'aristocratic embrace' throughout his political career. He did not seek personal wealth or social status. Above all, he practised in his public and private life the Christian principles which inspired his socialism, pacifism, internationalism, and support for women's rights. An unbridled passion for social justice and unshakable belief in democracy sustained Lansbury's lifetime of public service in local government and on the national stage.

Many of his contemporaries testified that George Lansbury was also a pragmatic politician of considerable skill and experience. In a memorable phrase Harold Laski, one of the leading British intellectuals of the twentieth century, recalled that George Lansbury 'was not a clear thinker, but had a heart which reached beyond the stars'. He added: 'Contact with Lansbury was a great education. He was absolutely straightforward, absolutely democratic, and entirely fearless. He always meant every word he said, and it never occurred to him to say less than he meant.'[8] Laski dismissed the charge that Lansbury had 'no taut intellectual doctrine to preach'. Instead, the English philosopher proclaimed that only by meeting Lansbury was it possible to know the meaning of a 'passionate conviction for a great ideal'. 'Send him to a meeting, and you find the audience feeling that, with just one more effort, they may be on the high road to the promised land,' Laski declared.[9]

Though most of his political life was spent in the British Labour party, Lansbury first joined the Gladstonian Liberals, as did most of the early socialist leaders. As a party agent, he masterminded three election victories before his conversion to socialist propagandist in the 1890s. In the Labour party he was first its popular but stormy petrel, often in opposition to the Labour leadership of Ramsay MacDonald. Lansbury led the famous, or infamous, 'Poplar Rates Rebellion' of 1921. Thirty Labour councillors went to gaol and 'Poplarism' entered the political vocabulary as the symbol of local defiance of central government.[10] Then, after the catastrophic 1931 general election defeat, at the nadir of Labour's political fortunes, Lansbury became party leader, almost by default. In Parliament, the people's politician from East London proved indefatigable in rallying the forty-six opposition Labour MPs against the National Government and in raising the morale of the labour movement throughout the country.

During his lifetime, George Lansbury published an autobiography of sorts in 1928, followed by a second book of recollections seven years later.[11] In his article 'What I Should Like to Read about Myself', in *The Listener* 'auto-obituary' series that asked contemporary figures to attempt a self-assessment for posterity, Lansbury suggested that 'He was proud to belong to the common people, had no class

---

[7] E. Lansbury, *George Lansbury, My Father* (1934), p. 1; Taylor, *A Personal History*, pp. 52, 56.

[8] H. J. Laski, 'Why I Am a Marxist', *Nation*, 14 Jan. 1939, p. 59.

[9] For this portrait of Lansbury, see Harold Laski's 'Introduction' to G. Lansbury, *My Life* (1931 edn), pp. ix–xv.

[10] For the Poplar Rates Rebellion, see N. Branson, *Poplarism, 1919–1925: George Lansbury and the Councillors' Revolt* (1979).

[11] George Lansbury, *My Life* (1928); id., *Looking Backwards and Forwards* (1935).

prejudice and found himself after a few minutes as much at home with royalty as with a docker'.[12]

Lansbury's almost unique ability to strike a genuine chord of sincerity and honesty in all who heard him speak was intertwined with a magical sense of the theatrical, perhaps seen at its best in the Poplar Rates Rebellion. This street- and prison-drama, as orchestrated by Lansbury, evoked the memories of the popular clamour surrounding 'Wilkes and Liberty!' in the eighteenth century, although these two politicians were otherwise as different as proverbial chalk and cheese.[13]

In 1951 Raymond Postgate published the official biography, *The Life of George Lansbury*, the only full-scale study to have appeared to date.[14] Postgate married Lansbury's daughter and secretary, Daisy, and was also Lansbury's close associate as foreign editor of the *Daily Herald* and assistant editor of *Lansbury's Labour Weekly*.[15] A former Communist party member, Postgate was further to the political left than his father-in-law, whom he respected and admired. He drew on personal knowledge and family recollections, as well as the main Lansbury archive now located at the British Library of Political and Economic Science. In his foreword Postgate mentioned the missing Lansbury papers—some thirty boxes of papers which he had handed over to the government authorities during the Second World War on the assurance of their return, once a dozen or so Cabinet documents had been extracted. Since then, attempts to resolve the mystery of these Lansbury papers, which were never retrieved, have proved as elusive and unsuccessful as the search for the Holy Grail.[16]

In 1963 Ronald Blythe produced a spirited piece on George's pacifism.[17] Ten years ago, two short studies appeared. Bob Holman's *Good Old George* viewed Lansbury's story from a Christian socialist perspective. Jonathan Schneer's study in the Manchester University Press series 'Lives of the Left' chose a thematic approach and broke new ground in examining the importance of the women's franchise question in Lansbury's career.[18]

Raymond Postgate's biography was generally welcomed on publication in 1951, though the author readily admitted that he had 'not concluded this *Life* with a formal estimate of George Lansbury's place in history'. In the tradition of historical works of nearly fifty years ago, the book lacked footnotes to indicate the sources

---

[12] *The Listener*, 22 July 1936.

[13] During the Poplar Rates Rebellion in 1921, Lansbury attempted to edit the *Daily Herald* from Brixton Prison, citing John Wilkes and W. T. Stead, previously imprisoned newspaper editors, as historical precedents.

[14] Keir Hardie's son-in-law, Emrys Hughes, who knew George Lansbury, compiled a short biography that was never published. See draft of *George Lansbury* (1955), Emrys Hughes Papers, Dep. 176 box 6 No. 8.

[15] For an excellent history of the *Daily Herald*, see H. Richards, *The Bloody Circus: The Daily Herald and the Left* (1997).

[16] For the correspondence between Raymond Postgate and the authorities, see PRO, CAB 21/2393/132346.

[17] R. Blythe, *The Age of Illusion: Glimpses of Britain between the Wars, 1919–1940* (1986), pp. 237–57.

[18] B. Holman, *Good Old George: The Life of George Lansbury* (1990); J. Schneer, *George Lansbury* (1990). For entries on Lansbury in biographical dictionaries, see below, Bibliography, D. 5.

consulted. In the intervening years, the private papers of many of Lansbury's contemporaries have become available. Sound and film archives are now accessible, as well as government documentary sources previously closed to historians.

George Lansbury was a remarkable figure in twentieth-century Britain and a substantial politician, who spent much of his life in the Labour party after an association with most of the groups on the left in British politics. For more than ten years, Lansbury was active in the Social Democratic Federation (SDF)—'on the whole the best organiser the Social Democratic Federation ever had', according to its Marxist founder H. M. Hyndman. As a Marxist candidate Lansbury twice fought the parliamentary seat of Walworth in South London, the location of Labour party headquarters in the late twentieth century. In 2000 a plethora of publications marked the centenary year of the founding of the British Labour party.[19] With the eightieth anniversary of the Poplar Rates Rebellion in 2001 and the seventieth anniversary of Lansbury's accession to the national party leadership in October 2002, the time appears appropriate to undertake a fresh and critical evaluation of the political life and career of 'Labour's Everyman'.

Clem Attlee first came across George Lansbury in the socialist movement around 1903. He called him 'Lansbury of London', a reference to Lansbury's close lifelong identification with the East End, although his actual birthplace was in Suffolk.[20] The details of his early life are somewhat sketchy and must be reconstructed largely from the recollections he shared in his autobiography in 1928 and from his other writings.[21] For the years up to 1884–5, Lansbury's published memoirs remain the principal source and Postgate drew heavily upon them in his biography after the Second World War.[22]

According to George Lansbury's own accounts, he was convinced he 'first saw the light of day' on 21 February 1859 in a toll-house outside Halesworth, a small East Anglian market town, on the then turnpike road to Lowestoft. He first visited his place of birth as an adult in 1922 and again in August 1934 when he signed a photograph of himself outside the building, adding for his family the words '"Toll House" Cottage I *was* born in February 21 1859'.[23] The documentary evidence possibly suggests otherwise. His birth certificate gives the date as 22 February 1859 and the

[19] For the Labour party, see B. Brivati and R. Heffenan (eds.), *The Labour Party: A Centenary History* (2000); K. Jefferys (ed.), *Leading Labour: From Keir Hardie to Tony Blair* (2000); K. Laybourn, *A Century of Labour: A History of the Labour Party, 1900–2000* (2000); D. Tanner, P. Thane, and N. Tiratsoo (eds.), *Labour's First Century* (Cambridge, 2000). For George Lansbury, see J. Shepherd, 'A Pioneer, by George' *Tribune*, 12 May 2000.

[20] *Observer*, 30 Dec. 1951; see also Attlee's review of Edgar Lansbury's *George Lansbury* in *Daily Herald*, 6 Mar. 1934.

[21] Lansbury, *My Life*, esp. pp. 15–43; see also Lansbury's recollections in *Looking Backwards and Forwards*. His son, Edgar, included interesting details of family life in the 1890s, though the earliest details must have been drawn from his parent's recollections: E. Lansbury, *George Lansbury*.

[22] Parts of *My Life* were serialized in *New Leader* in late 1927–early 1928, including some additional information not used in Lansbury's book. J. R. Clynes reviewed the autobiography on 5 Oct. 1928. For further Lansbury reminiscences, see also *Graphic*, 30 Nov. 1929.

[23] Lansbury, *My Life*, p. 15; photograph of George Lansbury's toll-house at Mells, Suffolk, in the possession of the author (courtesy of the late Esme Whiskin).

place as 'Thor.fare [*sic*], Halesworth', the town's main street, where the local history society placed a plaque in 1993 on what was considered the appropriate building, number 14, The Thoroughfare.[24] However, two Suffolk historians, Michael and Sheila Gooch, believe the Lansbury family 'moved into Halesworth sometime between 21 February and 10 March [the date of registration of Lansbury's birth] and that Mrs Lansbury decided not to confuse matters by telling the Registrar about this'. If this is correct, it is impossible now to explain why she decided to do this.[25]

George Lansbury was the third child of the seven boys and two girls born to Anne (*née* Ferris) and George Lansbury. Anne came from Radnorshire in Wales and his father from Warwickshire. They married at an early age, after eloping, and his mother did not revisit her Radnor home at Clyro for several years, by which time she had her own young family, including George aged seven years.

Lansbury said very little about his father, except that he had three brothers and two sisters and worked as a timekeeper supervising railway navvies for Thomas Brassey and Partners, the railway construction firm. George senior died in 1875 and the sixteen-year-old Lansbury appears to have replaced his father as the principal wage-earner in the family.[26] By this time, the Lansbury family had finally settled in Bucks Row, an Irish community in Whitechapel in the East End, after an unsettled and peripatetic existence. As a result of their father's railway work, they had moved around Kent and London—from Penge near Sydenham to Greenwich, and then to Bethnal Green.

The details of George Lansbury's schooling are equally sketchy. Like many working-class children, before elementary schooling became compulsory and free towards the end of the nineteenth century, his education was limited and interrupted. At the age of eleven he worked for a year, first in an office in Coram's Fields in Bloomsbury, to which he walked each day from Whitechapel, and then for Dakin Wright and Co., a local coal merchants. In Sydenham his first school was in the front room of a cottage—clearly one of the surviving 'dame-schools'—where he learnt his alphabet and simple calculations, literally at the feet of 'an old lady with a big granny cap'.[27] For a while, he also went to a similar establishment in Greenwich and later 'a private school' in Whitechapel. In Lansbury's childhood, 'dame-schools' offered working-class families basic schooling that was cheaper and more

---

[24] General Register Office, London, Certified copy of an entry of birth certificate [of George Lansbury], BXB 463802.

[25] George Lansbury was baptized at Halesworth church on 13 Mar. 1859, when his parents' address was given as Halesworth. The earlier baptismal record for his brother, James, on 10 October 1858 shows them living at nearby Wenhaston. According to Mrs Heather Philips of Wenhaston, her great-grandfather Robert Clarke, recorded by the 1861 census as the toll-gate keeper living with his family at 106 Halesworth Road, Mells, moved the Lansbury family into his toll-house at the time of Lansbury's birth. Unfortunately, if the story of the toll-house is correct, there remains the difficulty of the photograph taken in 1934, as the toll-house was demolished when the turnpike trust was terminated in 1872. For details of Lansbury's birth and baptism, see M. Gooch and S. Gooch, *The People of a Suffolk Town: Halesworth, 1100–1900* (Halesworth, 1999), pp. 146–8.

[26] Thomas Brassey was the grandfather of Muriel, Countess De La Warr, George Lansbury's friend and political associate many years later.

[27] Lansbury, *My Life*, p. 20.

flexible regarding attendance than the state-sponsored education provided for the majority of the population. For historians of education, these private establishments are 'the lost elementary schools of Victorian England', only rediscovered in recent times.[28] In East London the Lansbury family attended St James the Less School in Sewardstone Road, Bethnal Green, followed by Birkbeck School in Cambridge Road, Whitechapel. Lansbury's final school, to which he returned after his first spell of manual work, was St Mary's in Whitechapel, where he was under the guidance of an influential head teacher, Michael Apted, and where his mother paid a weekly fee of 4*d.* for each child.

Lansbury later believed his education was no more than that achieved in Standard Three in the late 1920s, a basic literacy and numeracy, but he was fired by a love of British history, taught by 'a kind old man' at the Whitechapel private school. 'I have never met his like since', Lansbury noted happily in his memoirs.[29]

At the same time, there were stirrings of political consciousness in the young Lansbury, which give an indication of later instincts and interests. East End schooling, where he sang revolutionary songs with enthusiasm with his Irish peers, brought him his first contact with the Irish Question in the form of Fenianism. His recollections show his mother and grandmother to have been the dominant influences of his early years. His grandmother awakened his interest in mid-Victorian radical causes and introduced him to the *Reynolds* newspaper. As a young man, Lansbury continued to read papers avidly, particularly *The Times, Daily News, Standard, Echo,* and *Reynolds* on Sundays.[30] An even more evocative memory of an early general election remained with Lansbury throughout his political life. In 1868 his mother took him and his brother to the political hustings at Greenwich, where the future Prime Minister, William Gladstone, was campaigning and where the Lansburys encountered anti-Semitism among the throng, directed against David Salomons, the candidate standing for Jewish political emancipation.[31] As part of their religious upbringing, Anne Lansbury hurried her young family at once to the local Primitive Methodist chapel, for a dose of 'fire and brimstone', at the slightest hint that they had attended the meetings organized by Charles Bradlaugh and his fellow atheists on the nearby Bonner Fields.[32] However, unlike most labour leaders with a religious affiliation and background in the Nonconformist tradition, Lansbury later joined the Church of England and remained a steadfast Anglican for virtually all his life.

Lansbury was also becoming aware of the unacceptable face of nineteenth-century capitalism, witnessed at first hand, both in the death of hard-grafting railway navvies killed in tunnel collapses and from mixing with railwaymen and other industrial workers in East London.[33] Even so, and though money was a recurrent problem, particularly in his later career, Lansbury gives no indication of extreme and grinding poverty in his early childhood. He did not suffer the degradation of

---

[28] For a pioneering survey of this previously unknown sector of schooling, see P. Gardner, *The Lost Elementary Schools of Victorian England* (1984).

[29] Lansbury, *Looking Backwards and Forwards*, p. 27; id. *My Life*, pp. 32–4.

[30] Lansbury, *My Life,* p. 40.   [31] Ibid. p. 25.   [32] Ibid. p. 28.   [33] Ibid. pp. 17, 35–6.

the workhouse or the scourge of sudden unemployment, which haunted the child-hood memories of contemporary working-class pioneers, including Will Crooks and Keir Hardie.[34]

In Whitechapel two vital events occurred which were to be of fundamental sig-nificance to George Lansbury's life. At St Mary's School he met the young Elisabeth Jane Brine, 'Bessie', the daughter of Isaac Brine, a local sawmill and timber-yard owner, and his wife, Sarah.[35] They began 'walking out together', but did not marry for five years. It was a long engagement, in part because her parents at first strongly disapproved of their better-educated daughter marrying the sturdy Whitechapel contractor, whose only merit appeared to be his physical strength in loading twice as much coal as the next man. Among the earliest correspondence is Lansbury's furiously scribbled five-page outpouring in 1877 to his closest friend in the Whitechapel Band of Hope, Wait Chester Sewell. In the tense atmosphere, boiling up for months as the two young people determined to marry, Lansbury's Christian indignation finally broke out in a blazing family row in defence of Bessie, after Mr and Mrs Brine's unwarranted attacks on their sixteen-year-old daughter's moral standards. Relations with Isaac Brine were uneasy for a number of years and Lans-bury continued to think of him as 'this great hulking Lancashire bully of a father'.[36]

Bessie and George, aged nineteen and twenty-one respectively, were married at the Whitechapel parish church, by Revd J. Fenwick Kitto, on 29 May 1880. It was the beginning of a lifetime's partnership between George and Bessie Lansbury that was to last over fifty years. As Lansbury publicly acknowledged, the importance to his political career of their marriage and the stable home base in Bow, that was a haven to all, was incalculable. He was frequently away from their home on political engagements in every part of Britain and abroad. Bessie shared George's political and religious convictions and was a staunch supporter of the Bolshevik Revolution. Her dedication to work for the socialist cause by remaining at home in Bow to look after their growing family, which appears to have been her decision, was an important factor in Lansbury's early support for the women's question in British politics.[37]

Together, Bessie and George Lansbury had joined the Whitechapel church in 1875, where the Anglican minister, Revd J. Fenwick Kitto, later vicar of St Martin's, was of supreme influence. At the age of sixteen, Lansbury experienced a spiritual and moral renaissance, tantamount to a religious conversion. Bessie and George

---

[34] For Crooks's experience of the workhouse, see G. Haw, *From Workhouse to Westminster: The Life Story of Will Crooks, M.P.* (1907), ch. 2, and for Keir Hardie's experience of childhood destitution, see K. O. Morgan, *Keir Hardie: Radical and Socialist* (1975), p. 5.

[35] According to the 1891 and 1901 censuses, Bessie was the eldest of their four daughters and two sons.

[36] George Lansbury to Wait Sewell, 27 August 1877, LP, vol. 1, fos. 8–11. See also J. A. Murray MacDon-ald's offer twenty years later to intercede on Lansbury's behalf: 'I wish you would let me go down and speak to Mr Brine . . . you ought to yield something to him, even though what you are yielding to may be prejudices.' Murray MacDonald to George Lansbury, 5 Aug. 1895, LP, vol. 1, fo. 262.

[37] Members of the Lansbury family confirmed Bessie's attitude in interviews with the author. See also Lansbury's plea 'to working men . . . including trade unionists and Socialists' for economic and social, as well as political, equality in gender relations in two draft articles, 'Our Wives' (n.d.) [1899–1900], LP, vol. 1, fos. 314–18.

were active participants in the life of their church, joining the local Band of Hope in the Ragged School building in Chicksand Street, where Bessie played the harmonium and her husband often led the bible-reading and discussion groups in the Whitechapel Young Men's Association. The roots of his future Christian socialism can be traced to this time, as well as his personal moral code as a total abstainer and non-smoker who was vehemently opposed to gambling.[38] However, George Lansbury was never a killjoy, approving for example of Sunday observance *and* sport on the Lord's Day.[39] He later told those reading his reminiscences: 'Don't imagine I was a goody-goody boy, most certainly I was not.'[40]

In earning his living, after his initial experience at eleven of the world of employment, Lansbury had a succession of manual jobs from the age of fourteen, including working in a charcoal factory and as a checker on the Great Eastern Railway. In 1875, on the death of his father, George and his brother James took over the family contracts for unloading coal at Whitechapel Arches on to barges at Thames Wharf, Blackwell. There he almost lost his life in an industrial accident with a hand-winch, one of four occasions he mentioned when he came close to death.[41] After their partnership ended in 1883, Lansbury for a time enjoyed running a coffee-bar and gymnasium, attached to the Whitechapel church, a business 'devoted to literature, politics, temperance and religion'.[42]

Lansbury's contemporaries did not fail to notice his passion for self-improvement of Smilesian proportions. From Australia, Thomas Tilbrook, raised in the same part of the East End as Lansbury, congratulated the new MP on his return to Parliament in the December 1910 general election. Tilbrook ruefully acknowledged the benefits of learning Victorian values in early life:

You deserve to be a member of parliament—from your boyhood days you sought to help your fellows. I knew you when you first came to London. I was born in Bucks Row myself and am about your own age . . . you and your [family] were familiar figures in that street [Court Street] . . . you went the right way and I went the wrong; you sought anything that would improve your character and mind, I sought the company of the little Irish boys at the top of Queen Ann Street, you went to St Mary's Sunday School, I played rounders with the said boys instead. You went to the lad's institute, I went to the Pavilion Theatre almost nightly. I learned to drink beer, you escaped, thank God, otherwise you would not be in the proud position you are tonight.[43]

The young Lansbury's life was not 'all work and no play'; his recollections display a fervent passion for cricket, as a player and spectator. From *c.*1875, he often heaved coal all night so that during the day he was free to go the Oval, Lords, or Princes (a now-defunct venue) to marvel at English cricketing heroes, or

---

[38] For a time, as editor of the *Daily Herald* he refused to carry racing tips in the paper.
[39] Lansbury, *Looking Backwards and Forwards*, p. 43.   [40] Ibid. p. 27.
[41] The other three occasions were: almost drowning as a child, experiencing a hurricane in the Indian Ocean, and his accident at Gainsborough, when Labour party leader in 1934. Lansbury, *Looking Backwards and Forwards*, pp. 63–7.
[42] Lansbury, *My Life*, p. 44.
[43] Thomas Tilbrook to George Lansbury, 26 Dec. 1910, LP, vol. 4, fos. 161–3.

to watch the Australian team on tour, such as 'the demon bowler, Sporfforth [who] . . . [N]obody seemed to be able to stand up to'.[44]

Earlier, issues of diplomacy and politics arising from the Franco-Prussian War of 1870 caught his imagination and sympathy, particularly for the working-class Communards. Though only eleven, his political views developed through an association with the Irish working-class radical, John Hales, the controversial secretary of Marx's First International, who taught him about working-class solidarity. At this time Lansbury also attended the meetings of mid-Victorian radicals, George Odger, Randal Cremer, George Howell, and Capt. Maxse. But the prevailing influence on the political adolescence of the young Christian radical was the towering figure of the Liberal politician, William Gladstone. Lansbury and his brother walked from Whitechapel to Blackheath to hear the 'Grand Old Man' and again at the Newman Street Hall, off Oxford Street. Between the ages of sixteen and eighteen, Lansbury worked at night and during the day was present in the Strangers' Gallery in the House of Commons to hear 'the great speeches of Gladstone and Bright' and their opponents. In 1878, as Macdermott's jingoistic chorus,

> We don't want to fight, but by jingo if we do
> We've got the ships, we've got the men, we've got the money too,

resounded across London, war fever gripped the capital. Gladstone 'with voice and pen' roared against Disraeli's imperialism over the Eastern Question. On 24 February George Lansbury, present at the huge peace-meeting in Hyde Park, assisted Charles Bradlaugh's escape from the mob. Later that day, he was a helpless spectator as the hostile crowd of more than ten thousand broke the windows of Gladstone's house in Harley Street until a detachment of mounted police arrived.[45]

Sixty years later, Lansbury still retained powerful memories of Gladstone, recalling with affection that he heard most, if not all, of Gladstone's speeches on the Eastern Question:

But Mr. Gladstone was entirely different from any other politician I have known. He was much older in years than most of those he acted with, but was the youngest in body, soul and spirit . . . I can hear his voice and see him now; though nothing I can write will convey to a reader the tremendous emotional effect of his words . . . that word alone ['inspired'] gives the impression that was left on the mind of the eighteen year old boy who was listening to him.[46]

During the Bulgarian agitation, from the House of Commons Gallery and at outside gatherings, the idealistic young Lansbury had witnessed this Christian statesman proclaim individual liberty, freedom for subject peoples, and the community

---

[44] Lansbury, *Looking Backwards and Forwards*, pp. 32–5. For 'the Demon', Frederick Robert Sporfforth, and other Victorian cricket heroes, see S. Rae, *W. G. Grace: A Life* (1998).

[45] Lansbury, *My Life*, pp. 40–3, J. Morley, *The Life of William Ewart Gladstone*, ii, *1872–1898* (1906), p. 182; H. C. G. Matthew, *Gladstone, 1878–1895* (1995), p. 38.

[46] In 1935 Lansbury quoted at length one of Gladstone's memorable speeches (on 7 May 1877) on the Eastern Question. Lansbury, *Looking Backwards and Forwards*, pp. 83–8. For other eye-witness accounts (by W. E. Forster and A. J. Balfour) on Gladstone's 2.5-hour-long *tour de force*, see Morley, *Life of William Ewart Gladstone*, ii, pp. 173–6.

of mutual interests of different social classes, which made up Liberalism. It was a heady mix that left an indelible mark.

In April the following year, George Lansbury was a patient at Poplar House, Redhill, described as 'a convalescent home or hospital', after a breakdown in his health.[47] There, among the Surrey hills, a complete rest was ordered for the over-worked and overwrought twenty year old, though there were visits from his mother, Anne, and from the Revd and Mrs Kitto, as well as letters from an equally distressed Wait Sewell. Lansbury's letters to one of his closest friends reveal a deep religious and moral crisis, which had taken him to the brink. Part of Lansbury's personal suffering was the extent to which others depended heavily upon him, even at this relatively early age. At this time of depression and self-guilt, Lansbury derived intense spiritual comfort from his unbending Christian faith, but doubted his friend Wait's capacity to resolve his own difficulties to do likewise. Writing, often in a puritanical tone, Lansbury confessed:

Since I have known what the love of God is tho I really can't comprehend one half of his great goodness to me yet Since I have known that my salvation depends on Him & that my chance of meeting my friends in Heaven is all a free gift from him I have been worried to know whether I should ever meet you & Bessie there.[48]

Lansbury recovered, though it is not clear how long he stayed at Poplar House. A year later there were happier times as Bessie and George finally married and spent a short honeymoon near Coleston in East Anglia. In 1881 Anne died at about the same time as Bessie and George's daughter, Bessie was born. At the age of twenty-two Lansbury, who now had the additional responsibility of two younger siblings, as well as his own family, became unsettled once more. He investigated the possibility of becoming the manager of a Board school after giving up the coal contract part-nership with his brother. However, the promise of an outdoor life in a young coun-try of opportunity was one reason Bessie and George finally decided to emigrate to Australia. They raised the necessary capital by selling their wedding presents and, like many others from the British Isles in 1884, prepared to sail from Plymouth for Australia.

On 20 May, 1884, after a grim train journey from Waterloo to Plymouth, George and Bessie Lansbury, with their young family, departed for Australia on the steamship, the *Duke of Devonshire*—a four-masted converted cargo boat, one of thirty-three vessels of the British India Steam Navigation Company transporting emigrants destined for Queensland that year. Their disastrous attempt to find a new life in the main migrant colony of Australia was a major landmark for George and

---

[47] Poplar House was owned by the Revd Kitto and the patients appear to have paid for admission. See George Lansbury to Wait Sewell, 26 Apr. 1879, LP, vol. 1, fo. 20. Nearby at South Park in Reigate, his wife ran 'Mrs Kitto's Free Convalescent Home', a twenty-eight-bed establishment for the poor of East London ('no eligible person ever kept out of it on ground of poverty'). *The Annual Charities Register and Digest* (1902), p. 158. I am grateful to Maggie Lewis Vaughan and Rosemary Lynch at Redhill Public Library for information about the Revd Kitto's ownership of Poplar House.

[48] George Lansbury to Wait Sewell, 21 Apr. 1879, LP, vol. 1, fo. 19. See also George Lansbury to Wait Sewell, 18, 26 Apr. 1879: ibid. fos. 17–19.

Bessie. In terms of the great migrations of the nineteenth century, the Lansbury family was a solitary statistic in the great flood of humanity from the British Isles that peopled the distant regions of the globe. Nearly a quarter of all emigration from England and Wales before 1930 took place in the fifteen years between 1879 and 1893.[49] Of these emigrants more than 1.6 million, chiefly from Britain and Ireland, took the long, arduous, and expensive route to Australia.[50] Between 1860 and 1900 around 250,000 left Britain and Europe in search of a new life of prosperity and opportunity.[51] Queensland, where successive governments continued to recruit and subsidize migration, remained the most popular colony for emigrants, served by three disembarkation ports at Rockhampton, Townsville, and Brisbane, the main point of entry for the new arrivals after their sea voyage. George and Bessie decided to emigrate to Queensland as numbers peaked in the mid-1880s.

In his memoirs Lansbury devoted a chapter to his family's traumatic experience in Australia. He explained his reasons for leaving Britain, his memories of the six-week voyage and the painful process of seeking work in Queensland. Instead of the new life and freedom from British economic depression promised to emigrants in the 1880s, he and his family discovered the fear and deprivation of unemployment. Although their stay in Australia in 1884–5 was relatively brief, it was to be extremely important in the formation of Lansbury's political ideas and values.

According to Postgate, Lansbury's reasons for emigrating were the tempting employment opportunities on offer to British workers. Bessie and George were enticed to a 'Promised Land' in Australia by the free emigration propaganda issued by the Queensland Agent-General for Emigration as part of the drive to recruit British men as labourers and single women as domestic servants. This literature was readily available in British libraries, post offices, schools, and railway stations.[52]

In 1880 the colonial government of Queensland actively sought British emigrants, particularly from rural communities, to assist in the future development of the colony. Besides free literature and advertisements in the London, national, and provincial press, the Agent-General employed a successful former emigrant, George Randall, as the government's chief emigration lecturer. Assisted by a network of local agents, he made extensive tours of the British Isles, in search of 'ideal migrants', who were offered various forms of assistance, including free passages. More enquiries resulted about Queensland than any other Australian colony.[53] No evidence exists that Lansbury met Randall, who concentrated on rural areas outside London, but the attractions outlined by the Queensland government were clearly discussed by George, Bessie, and their friends in Whitechapel church. In particular, the Revd Kitto, a formidable religious and moral influence, was a convincing

[49] D. Baines, *Migration in a Mature Economy: Emigration and Internal Migration in England and Wales, 1861–1900* (1985), pp. 58–9, 206.

[50] E. Richards, 'Annals of the Australian Immigrant', in E. Richards, R. Reid, and D. Fitzpatrick, *Visible Immigrants: Neglected Sources for the History of Australian Immigration* (1989), p. 7.

[51] H. R. Woodcock, *Rights of Passage: Emigration to Australia in the Nineteenth Century* (1986), p. 328.

[52] R. Postgate, *The Life of George Lansbury* (1951), ch. 3.

[53] J. Camm, 'The Hunt for Muscle and Bone: Emigration Agents and Their Role in Migration to Queensland during the 1880s', *Australian Historical Geography*, 2 (1981), pp. 7–29.

advocate of emigration and, as chairman of the East End Emigration Committee, clearly influenced Bessie and George's decision to emigrate.[54]

There was one other crucial reason for leaving Britain. From the early 1880s, Lansbury became thoroughly disillusioned with the pernicious and competitive nature of late Victorian capitalism. Fifty years later he recalled that 'it was freedom we desired—most of all freedom from competition . . . It was little short of heaven to think of—a place where a man could earn his living without injuring a competitor or linking himself up with (the) sweating (trades). The idea sustained us through-out the long journey'.[55]

The Lansbury party consisted of George (twenty-five years old), Bessie (twenty-three) and their daughters, Bessie (three), Annie (two), and baby son, George, as well as Lansbury's eleven-year-old brother, Harry. In all, the SS *Duke of Devonshire* carried 556 passengers, mainly English, Scottish, and Irish emigrants bound for the three Queensland ports.[56] The voyage lasted six weeks via Malta, Port Said, the Suez Canal, and Aden. Lansbury recorded that he went ashore at Malta and again at Colombo, where he had a row with a Dutchman who was bullying women loading coal onto the steamship. In the Indian Ocean their vessel was trapped in monsoon conditions for nearly a week. The final leg of the journey was through the Torres Strait, eventually arriving in Brisbane in July 1884.

More than forty years later, George still recalled their appalling voyage. In particular, Bessie suffered dreadfully from recurrent bouts of sea-sickness throughout the voyage. Conditions on board were cramped, food was inadequate, and the Lansbury family survived because two members of the crew shared their rations.[57]

Unknown to the Lansburys and hundreds of other British migrants tempted to sail to a new life of better opportunities and relative prosperity, the Queensland government altered its emigration policy in November 1883 to restrict numbers and limit assistance, including food rations previously allocated to migrants for the journey.[58] In contrast to the expected land of economic opportunity and freedom from class distinctions promised by the emigration agents, the Lansburys found themselves in colonial Brisbane, Queensland's capital city with its distinct class, status, racial, and gender divisions. They soon discovered that the majority of migrants to Queensland came from manufacturing and urban centres in Britain, whereas the colony had a pastoral economy.[59] In Brisbane, George and Bessie met fellow Londoners who had emigrated earlier—an army of unemployed who

---

[54] See *Echo*, 24 Feb. 1886.   [55] Lansbury, *Looking Backwards and Forwards*, p. 48.

[56] According to the SS *The Duke of Devonshire* passenger list, George Lansbury's brother, Harry, travelled as steerage. The Lansburys' baby in arms was inaccurately recorded as 'Henry' (instead of 'George', who later 'died young'). Immigration Department Immigrant Passenger Lists, 1883–5, Queensland State Archives, Z 1961, pp. 108, 110–11.

[57] Lansbury, *My Life*, pp. 45–9.

[58] James F. Garrick to Colonial Secretary, 2 Feb. 1885 (enclosing *General Report for 1884*), Letter Book of the Agent-General from Queensland, Queensland State Archives, AGE/G623, fos. 106–10.

[59] For a recent study, see B. Thorpe, *Colonial Queensland: Perspectives on a Frontier Society* (1996). For Brisbane, see also R. Lawson, 'Class or Status? The Social Structure of Brisbane in the 1890s', *Australian Journal of Politics and History*, 17–18 (1971–2), pp. 344–59.

thronged the quayside and city streets. It was a totally different picture from that portrayed in the Queensland emigration propaganda. In 1884, Australia's fourth-largest city was inundated to bursting-point with the newcomers from abroad. Typhoid fever was endemic there and another epidemic, as in 1883, threatened.

On their arrival Bessie and George experienced the atrocious facilities provided for incoming travellers, especially the Immigrants Home in William Street that was reminiscent of a British workhouse and had caused a public outcry in the city.[60] The rented accommodation they eventually found in a rudimentary Brisbane 'humpy' in Fortitude Valley was no better. After eight weeks of unemployment, which virtually drained their savings, Lansbury took up stone-breaking, then a job at a slaughterhouse, which he finally gave up as he would not work on Sundays. His next job was eighty miles away on a farm at Harrisville, near Ipswich, which the Lansburys reached, complete with their American organ in packing-case, after a long, monotonous railway journey.

The extent of Lansbury's anger is revealed in the surviving letters he sent home to his friend, Wait Sewell.[61] He complained about his employer who kept him in permanent debt by forcing him to purchase food from the farm:

... and now I am about 40 miles up the bush under the worst old tyrant it has ever been my lot to meet up with ... none of these farmers will employ men unless they agree for a term of 6 months, 12 months or so on as well they promise you all manner of good things till the agreement is signed and then you may as well be a slave.[62]

Lansbury was threatened with imprisonment if he severed his contract, but eventually broke free to return to Brisbane to work on Eagle Farm, followed by ten days laying out the Brisbane Cricket and Sports Ground before the arrival of the English national cricket team. His last job was as a parcel delivery man at Joowong, outside Brisbane, until his family's ill-health and Lansbury's own disillusion with Australia, finally caused them to leave the country. Bessie's father, Isaac Brine, sent £100 for the return fare to England.[63]

Eighteen months after leaving Britain, Bessie and George Lansbury arrived back in London, penniless. Their Australian experience was clearly a watershed and launched George Lansbury into British politics determined to expose the scandalous iniquities of the emigration business, for which he largely blamed the colonial government of Queensland.

Throughout everything, however, Lansbury remained a devout Christian with his personal faith and belief in God intact. He wrote to Wait: 'I am fully persuaded with

---

[60] H. Woolcock, 'Immigrant Health and Reception Facilities', in Brisbane History Group, *Brisbane in 1888: The Historical Perspective* (1988), pp. 71–82.

[61] Collections of migrant letters have been used recently to reconstruct lives of the poorest groups of emigrants, hitherto lost to posterity, who left their homes in Britain and elsewhere to seek out new prospects on the other side of the world. See D. Fitzpatrick, *Oceans of Consolation: Personal Accounts of Irish Migration to Australia* (1994). For pioneering work on the USA, see C. Erickson, *Invisible Immigrants: The Adaptation of English and Scottish Immigrants in Nineteenth-Century America* (1972).

[62] George Lansbury to Wait Sewell, 16 Sept. 1884, LP, vol. 28, fo. 14.

[63] Lansbury, *My Life*, pp. 59–60; Postgate, *Lansbury*, p. 29.

S. Paul that nothing in this world can ever separate us from the love of our Gracious Lord. Farras Early days & Boyd Carpenters Prophets of Christendom [probably books sent to Australia by Wait] have done much to strengthen my faith.'[64]

Despite direct experience of unemployment for the first time in his life, on his return, Lansbury was still prepared to work within the existing capitalist framework. He soon became a loyal Gladstonian Liberal party-worker by joining his local association. As he recalled, except for a former Irish Land Leaguer, a fellow worker on the farm at Harrisville, Lansbury had no contact with the emergent Australian trade union and labour movement, which became organized mainly after his departure.

The main impact of Lansbury's Australian experience on his ideas and political values was seen in his increasing awareness of the appalling social and economic conditions faced by emigrant women in the late nineteenth century. He witnessed himself the degrading conditions under which the women and girls worked and lived, with many forced into prostitution in order to survive.[65] This was particularly evident in his letter to Sewell in March 1885:

Another statement that I heard over and over again thrust down the throats of the people was that those who had sisters or grown up daughters could not do better than send them out here . . . Now I distinctly say that girls are not wanted here the streets are foul day and night and if I had a sister I would rather shoot her dead than see her brought out here to this little hell upon earth . . . I don't wonder the girls go on the street for besides sending out hundreds of girls unprotected the Emigration people send out hundreds of single men who thrown upon their own resources go into all kinds of vice and crime.[66]

On both long journeys to and from Australia, daily care of the Lansbury children was literally in George's hands as prolonged illness overcame Bessie each time. He later recalled: 'I came back home a rebel, and I am still a rebel against the present man-made poverty and destitution. I also came home a feminist, convinced that human society will only be redeemed and purified by the conscious co-operation of men and women.'[67]

In England, Lansbury discovered unsuspecting working-class families still being encouraged to emigrate. His bitter experience in Australia hurled him into a political campaign in London to press for government action. Emigration to Australia and Canada offered no panacea for Britain's economic distress. But emigration remained a matter of controversial debate in this country. The governing class sought an immediate remedy for unemployment and for the growing social unease particularly associated with the organization by the Social Democratic Federation (SDF) of the unemployed and the public disturbances in London and other cities in the winters of 1886–7.[68] In the severe winter of 1885–6 Lansbury campaigned

---

[64] George Lansbury to Wait Sewell, 16 Sept. 1884, LP, vol. 28, fo. 14.
[65] The main accounts of the Lansbury family's emigration to Australia in 1884–5 can be found in *My Life* and in *Looking Backwards and Forwards*.
[66] George Lansbury to Wait Sewell, 1 Mar. 1885, LP, vol. 1, fo. 21.
[67] *Graphic*, 30 Nov. 1929.
[68] P. S. Bagwell, *Outcast London: A Christian Response: The West London Mission of the Methodist Church, 1887–1987* (1987), ch. 1.

vigorously against 'the swindle that had been practised on him and thousands of other emigrants' generated by the misleading publicity and appeals in Britain for emigration funds. For three months he organized meetings every Thursday evening on the frozen ground of the Mile End waste, the traditional open space for outdoor political gatherings in the East End.[69] Lansbury's campaign, including his letters to the *Echo*, revealed the work of the successful agitator. Typical of his style was his speech at St Martin's Club, Maidment Street at Mile End. There, supported by Wait Sewell, Lansbury with the authority of a former emigrant condemned the economic and moral inequities of 'the emigration fraud'. Quoting from several Brisbane newspapers, he exclaimed that: 'as a Christian he felt that a great crime was committed by sending navvies out to Queensland, to live, as their own papers admitted, in the most perfect state of heathenism'. He really thought the 'Social Purity people at home might take the matter up . . . how was it that, in the richest city in the world [London] . . . there should be so much starvation'.[70]

Lansbury's guiding hand was behind the increasing pressure for accurate information on the true state of emigration. Wait Sewell joined a newly formed committee and benefited from the comprehensive data Lansbury supplied on conditions in Queensland.[71] In February 1886 Lansbury challenged the appeal by Capt. Andrew Hamilton for donations to the East End Emigration Fund, managed by Lansbury's old religious mentor, the Revd J. F. Kitto.[72] A few days later, during an important conference on emigration in the theatre at King's College on the Strand, with the Bishop of Bedford in the chair, the meticulously prepared Lansbury confidently brushed aside the defensive arguments of the Agents-General of the Colonies.[73]

Finally, Lansbury's campaigning reaped some dividend when the government acted on the question of emigration. In Parliament, on 5 April 1886, Under-Secretary of State, Osborne Morgan, announced that 'Her Majesty's Government are making arrangements for the establishment of an "Emigrants Information Bureau" in connection with the Colonial Office where intending emigrants may obtain full and trustworthy information as to the state of the labour market in the various colonies'.[74]

At twenty-seven, George Lansbury was now established once more in Britain with Bessie and their family after a bitter experience in Australia. In Bow, Isaac Brine provided work for his son-in-law as a veneer-dryer at his sawmill and timber yard and a family home in a small cottage on the same site. Lansbury's campaigning

---

[69] Postgate, *Lansbury*, p. 30. For Lansbury's account, see his letter to the *Echo*, 27 Feb. 1886.

[70] *East London Observer*, 30 Jan. 1886.

[71] For Wait Sewell's role in the agitation in 1886, see *East London Observer*, 2 Jan. 1886; George Lansbury to Wait Sewell, 30 Jan. 1886 [wrongly dated], LP, vol. 1, fo. 26; and Sewell's letter to the *Echo*, 22 Feb. 1886.

[72] *Echo*, 24, 27 Feb. 1886.

[73] 'Conference on Emigration' [27 Feb. 1886], LP, vol. 1, fo. 47; *Echo*, 27 Feb. 1886.

[74] *Parliamentary Debates*, vol. 304, 5 Apr. 1886, cols. 735–6. For the Emigrants' Information Office, opened 11 Oct. 1886 at 31 Broadway, Westminster, see 'Papers relating to the Emigrants' Information Office', *Parliamentary Papers*, lvii, 1887 (Accounts and Papers, 9) (C. 5078), pp. 667–74.

on the emigration issue took place after his daily work. It was to be a springboard into greater activity in East London and beyond. In the coming months and years, the young Radical with a passion for social justice found that Brine was also sympathetic to his son-in-law's growing political interests as Lansbury joined his local Liberal party in 1885. The arrival of a new working-class leader, with a flair for adept organization and a finger firmly on the political pulse, also did not go unnoticed among the more radical Liberal leaders in London.

2
Liberal Politics, 1886–1892

In 1886 the opening of the Emigrants' Information Office by the government, after the successful emigration conference in London, demonstrated George Lansbury's notable political expertise. This soon attracted the attention of the local Liberal party bosses. Samuel Montagu (later Baron Swaythling), Liberal MP for Whitechapel, who was at the emigration conference to observe Lansbury's political credentials at first hand, saw an important representative of the working class who could be usefully recruited to the Liberal fold. On leaving the King's College conference he told him, 'You must let me get you into the House of Commons. You are just the sort of man we want there.'[1]

There was some point to Montagu's remark that, apparently, the young conference organizer from the East End took to be mere pleasing flattery. George Lansbury would certainly not have been amiss then in the House of Commons as a Liberal MP in the labour cause. In the 1880s, faced by the rise of mass politics, the Gladstonian Liberal party was increasingly compelled to respond to the demands of organized labour for improved representation and social reform. Increasing the number of labour members within the Liberal ranks in Parliament was a key issue in working-class politics. After the 1885 general election twelve new labour MPs met together at the TUC office in Buckingham Street, near the Strand, to walk proudly together to Westminster for the state opening of Parliament.[2] Thereafter, with no qualms, they took their places on the Liberal benches as a distinct Lib–Lab grouping. The august TUC secretary, Henry Broadhurst MP, a former stonemason, became the first working man to hold government office upon his appointment to Gladstone's short-lived administration in 1886.[3] In the twenty-five years before the advent of the modern Labour party, the main path to Parliament for working-class politicians, albeit at times strewn with difficulty or sheer hostility in local associations run by businessmen and industrialists, lay with the Liberal party.[4] However, despite highly regarded Liberal connections, George Lansbury eventually chose the more arduous route to Westminster as a socialist candidate.

---

[1] Lansbury, *My Life*, pp. 63–4.   [2] *English Labourer's Chronicle*, 30 Jan. 1885.
[3] For Henry Broadhurst, see H. Broadhurst, *Henry Broadhurst MP Told by Himself* (1901).
[4] For the Lib–Lab MPs, see J. Shepherd, 'Labour and Parliament: The Lib.–Labs. as the First Working-Class MPs, 1885–1906', in E. F. Biagini and A. Reid (eds.), *Currents of Radicalism: Popular Radicalism, Organised Labour and Party Politics in Britain, 1850–1914* (1991), pp. 187–213. For one example of a troublesome local association, see J. Brown, 'Attercliffe, 1894: How One Local Liberal Party Failed to Meet the Challenge of Labour', *Journal of British Studies*, 14 (1975), 48–77.

During his winter campaign, which brought him into contact with the political left during the unemployed riots in London, Lansbury did not join the socialist camp, notwithstanding the bitter experience of his Australian venture. Despite the presence of the prominent member of the SDF, John Burns of Battersea at his emigration conference, Lansbury remained true to his political roots, an ardent Radical prepared to give unflagging voluntary assistance to the Gladstonian cause. In the East End Lansbury joined the ranks of the Bow and Bromley Liberal and Radical Association and, with his reputation for political organization, soon became a leading light in the local party.

The party, of which Lansbury became a member in 1886, was a coalition of different sections and competing interests: Liberals, Whigs (soon to depart), Radicals, Nonconformists and temperance people, the 'Celtic fringe' of Welsh and Scottish nationalists, London progressives, and labour adherents. After the 1886 crisis over Irish Home Rule and the secession of the Birmingham Radical Joseph Chamberlain and the Whig aristocrats, which ripped the Liberals apart, the citadels of the central party organization came under the control of the remaining Radicals drawn from the ranks of the middle class. From 1886 Irish Home Rule was the single great cause which bound together the diverse, and somewhat ill-disciplined, interest groups which sheltered under the umbrella of the Gladstonian leadership.[5] For a while, in his late twenties, Lansbury found a political home among the progressives who attended the London Liberal and Radical Union (LLRU). However, he soon began to question the basic tenets of his Liberalism and his party membership. Personal loyalty to Gladstone, however indelible, was then insufficient to hold him in the Liberal ranks.

In July 1886, Samuel Montagu invited Lansbury to be his election agent, at a salary of £3 per week, for the general election campaign.[6] Lansbury's first professional assignment in the Liberal cause met with outstanding success, as he again displayed his flair for organization. Though his party suffered national defeat, Montagu was one of the few Liberal members to increase his majority.[7] He immediately tried to retain his agent's services, but lost Lansbury again to the Isaac Brine timber business.

Montagu continued to assist the various causes Lansbury campaigned for in the following years as a voluntary worker with his local Liberal and Radical Association in Bow and Bromley. In due course, in the House of Commons, in a memorable encounter, the Member for Whitechapel made the seemingly irresistible offer, which Lansbury again rejected, of paid employment at £5 per week plus a parliamentary

---

[5] For the different interest groups in Liberal party politics, see D. A. Hamer, *Liberal Politics in the Age of Gladstone and Rosebery* (1972); M. Barker, *Gladstone and Radicalism: The Reconstruction of Liberal Policy in Britain, 1885–1894* (1975).

[6] *East London Observer*, 3 July 1886.

[7] In two straight fights, Montagu's majority went up from 381 to 587, while the Tories defeated the sitting Liberal MP in neighbouring Bow and Bromley, one of the five out of seven seats which were captured. *East London Observer*, 3, 10 July 1885.

seat at the first opportunity, with Montagu's added incentive 'You can preach all the socialism you like: all I ask is support for the Liberal party, which is the best instrument even for your socialism'.[8]

In Samuel Montagu, George turned down an influential and powerful patron. Founder of one of the most celebrated merchant banks of the nineteenth century, Samuel Montagu and Co. of Leadenhall Street and Broad Street, the future Baron Swaythling was a millionaire Jewish philanthropist and foremost figure of the Anglo-Jewish community. As a foreign exchange banker, he helped to establish London as the clearing-house centre of the international money market. Montagu was an ardent Gladstonian Liberal and, like Lansbury, an admirer of the 'Grand Old Man'. A generous contributor to party funds, the Whitechapel MP was closely associated with radical causes, including universal suffrage and support for trade unionism, as well as charitable work for his poor constituents.[9]

Even so, after the experience suffered by his family in Australia, Lansbury could not risk the uncertainty of an MP's career in the days before payment of members' salaries. For Lansbury the central issue was not, however, a matter of personal advancement nor one of family security, but a fundamental question of principle. By this stage, the important first inkling was there that he no longer saw his future as a Radical but as a Socialist, a commitment he made increasingly clear as similar parliamentary offers came his way.

In 1886 the Liberal MP for Bow and Bromley, W. S. Robson, was defeated at the polls and the local association adopted John Archibald Murray MacDonald as the new prospective parliamentary candidate. A well-heeled middle-class Scot with progressive ideas, Murray MacDonald was a product of Toynbee Hall and brought with him a reputation for being active in working-class causes in the East End. His analysis of the poverty endemic in his prospective constituency convinced him he should support the eight-hour day through parliamentary legislation.[10] He soon became a close political associate and personal friend of George Lansbury.[11]

In Bow and Bromley, the Liberal and Radical Association, open to 'Progressivists of all shades of opinion', adopted an advanced programme entitled 'The New Liberalism': 'Home Rule for Ireland, One Man One Vote, Eight-Hours' Labour Day, taxation of land rents, improved working-class housing, free education and local control of licensing'. In a single phrase, George Lansbury and his fellow East End Liberals summed up their Radical philosophy as, 'We work for a Happier, a more Moral, and a more Equal Life for all'.[12]

---

[8] Lansbury, *My Life*, pp. 74–5.

[9] *The Times*, 13 Jan. 1911. For Baron Swaythling, see also B. Wasserstein, *Herbert Samuel: A Political Life* (1992), pp. 3–8.

[10] For more on J. A. Murray MacDonald's progressive stance, see J. A. Murray MacDonald, 'The Case for an Eight-Hour Day', *Nineteenth Century*, 27 (1890), pp. 553–65; id., 'The Liberal party and Imperial Federation', *Contemporary Review*, 77 (1900), pp. 644–55. See also *The Times*, 17 Jan. 1939.

[11] For some examples of their personal friendship, see J. A. Murray MacDonald, 29 July 1890, 17 Jan. 1894, LP, vol. 1, fos. 112–13, 192–3.

[12] *Coming Times*, newscutting (n.d. [1890]) in LP, vol., 1, fo. 34. See also 'Mr MacDonald's Address to the Electors', in *Coming Times*, Sept. 1889.

To achieve this state of affairs, George Lansbury was prepared to work hard himself in his father-in-law's sawmill and timber yard at Bow and to serve his local community first as local party agent (and later as an elected guardian, councillor, and, finally, Member of Parliament). In this capacity, he lived with his family in one of the most deprived areas of East London. Working as a veneer-dryer from 7 a.m. to 7 p.m., Lansbury earned a weekly wage of 30s. He and his young family of four lived in a small cottage next to the timber yard in St Stephen's Road, at the poorer end with five pubs, where their neighbours scraped a living by making matchboxes, shirts, and brushes.[13]

After serving as a ward secretary in his local party, Lansbury was appointed general secretary of the 'Council of 400', the main council, which governed the four ward committees of the local association. His talents extended to publicity and journalism and, with William Hoffman, a fellow Radical, Lansbury established a monthly penny paper, *Coming Times*, distributed in Bow and Bromley and neighbouring Mile End.[14] It only survived for about two years but sheds useful light on Lansbury's activities in the local party, as well as his changing views on Liberalism as he began to embrace socialist values and ideas.[15]

In 1888, the newly formed 'Society for Promoting Women As County Councillors' selected the two London constituencies of Bow and Bromley and of Brixton for its first two women candidates. In January 1889 Jane Cobden and Lady Margaret Sandhurst were the first two women returned to the London County Council, following the Local Government Act which created the new tier of local administration.[16] Murray MacDonald engaged Lansbury to act as Jane Cobden's election agent for the LCC campaign.[17]

Jane Cobden was the younger daughter of the mid-Victorian free-trader, Richard Cobden, and featured this fact in her contest. There is, however, only a brief mention of this election in the Lansbury memoirs and no account of the specific part he played. Postgate added little about the contest, except to state that Lansbury was pressed to stand, once Jane Cobden's opponents had challenged her election in the law courts.[18] In fact, George Lansbury's effective stewardship of Jane Cobden's campaign was one of his early political achievements and another notable triumph he pulled off for the Liberal party. More important for Lansbury, it marked a significant stage in the evolution of his political ideas, especially in relation to the women's question and party politics in the late nineteenth century.

What George Lansbury brought to Jane Cobden's campaign, which is well illustrated in his surviving correspondence with her, was the consummate skill of a hard-working and talented party agent, sensitively aware of local East End

[13] See D. Postgate, 'A Child in George Lansbury's House', *The Fortnightly*, Nov., Dec. 1948.
[14] *Coming Times*, July 1889.
[15] For more on *Coming Times*, see Schneer, *George Lansbury*, pp. 17–20.
[16] For more on 'The Society for Promoting Women as County Councillors' (eventually renamed the 'Women's Local Government Society'), see P. Hollis, *Ladies Elect: Women in English Local Government, 1865–1914* (1987), pp. 306–17.
[17] J. A. Murray MacDonald to Mrs Mallett, 24 Jan. 1889, JCP.
[18] Postgate, *Lansbury*, p. 37.

conditions. On 12 December Lansbury wrote to the new candidate to announce that the executive of the Bow and Bromley Liberal and Radical Association had decided in her favour, by fourteen votes to three, and recommended her to the 'Council of 400' as the only official Liberal candidate.[19] Before her selection Lansbury had already advised her on the vital issue left unsettled by the new legislation, that of whether it was legal for women to stand for election and to serve on the new County Councils.[20]

Within days, Lansbury was quickly off the mark, dispensing detailed guidance about planning the campaign to suit an East End electorate with an emphasis on radical concerns, as well as his recommendation to go 'straight for social reform'. He gently pushed her to distribute her election address before Christmas. 'There are one or two matters people feel strongly about & if you are in favour of them it would be well to emphazise them. I mean the housing of the poor, smashing the letting of contracts to sweaters, equalisation of poor rate, upholding the right to outdoor meetings, control of the police, . . .' he advised.

His last suggestion for Jane Cobden's address—'Blackwall Tunnel which is a purely local matter & the one thing which gives Mr Cook [the independent Liberal candidate standing against her] such power down here'—demonstrates Lansbury's local knowledge. A river tunnel for access to employment north and south of the Thames was a long-standing demand by working people. His fellow Labour pioneer, Will Crooks, lobbied successfully on the same issue some years later.

The timely reminder to Jane Cobden to expect a disappointingly low attendance at her next meeting before Christmas was more the shrewd advice of the local agent in tune with the behaviour of fellow East Enders than, as has been suggested, a principle of domestic feminism in his organization of election campaigns: 'It is very near Christmas and Christmas comes once a year in the East End and every father and mother has to take the children to see the shops, and Friday is pay day for some men and it will be chosen for this purpose.'[21]

From letters to his candidate it is clear that Lansbury was meticulous about all aspects of running the campaign, from the *minutiae* of day-to-day organization to the grander sweeps of electoral strategy and tactics. His hard work gathered together local temperance workers—temperance was a central Liberal article of faith and one of Jane Cobden's strong points. Throughout the campaign he busied about inviting prominent Liberal women and men to speak, while not forgetting publicity, hall-bookings, envelopes, and a thousand and one other necessary items.[22] Firm guidance was also offered to Miss Cobden that she speedily form 'a definite opinion in the matter of payment of members', to be ready for a likely campaign question.[23] Three days before Christmas, Lansbury gave Jane Cobden the

[19] George Lansbury to Jane Cobden, 12 Dec. 1888, JCP.
[20] George Lansbury to Jane Cobden, 9 Dec. 1888, ibid.
[21] George Lansbury to Jane Cobden, 20 Dec. 1888, ibid. Cf. Schneer, *George Lansbury*, pp. 74–5.
[22] George Lansbury to Jane Cobden, 20, 21, 27 Dec. 1889, JCP.
[23] George Lansbury to Jane Cobden, 14 Dec. 1888, ibid. Murray MacDonald also recommended that the 'local option' was a key card to be played: 'it will be well to say something about it. There is a very

crucial news that he had consulted the local Returning Officer 'informally' to discover that her nomination as a woman candidate would be accepted.[24]

However, all was not trouble-free and smooth sailing with the Cobden campaign. At one point there was an unfortunate and embarrassing mix-up over the amount to be paid to the party agent for his excellent services, including a query about the usual 'win bonus' for a successful election. In the end a private apology from Murray MacDonald cleared up the confusion.[25]

Polling day on 19 January 1889 brought an overall Progressive victory in London with 73 out of the 118 seats captured, as well as a successful conclusion to the efforts to return the first women to the new County Council. In the Bow and Bromley division, Jane Cobden finished second in the poll of four candidates with 2,045 votes, over 300 votes ahead of her two defeated male rivals. Lansbury advised on the distribution of a short address of thanks and added: 'I am so glad to think it was people of my class who rallied to your support.'[26] Elsewhere, the Brixton division returned Lady Sandhurst while the number of women increased to three when Emma Cons was elected in the aldermanic contest, after the new body assembled.

What followed next was an extended legal challenge by their Conservative opponents to the new women members on grounds of the legality of their election and their qualification to serve as county councillors. Lady Sandhurst lost in the High Court and again on appeal as her opponent took her County Council seat.[27] Jane Cobden suffered no immediate challenge, but decided to attend meetings of the County Council as a silent and non-voting member. Under a legal anomaly, after a year of such inactivity, her position would then be safe. Even so after February 1890, her opponents still brought writs, with a penalty of possible fines, to challenge the rights of the two women members to act as normal county councillors. As before, Lansbury was unfailing in Jane Cobden's support, working imaginatively to bring publicity to her case by arranging rallies and assuring her of local backing if any fine was imposed. In particular, he took the matter successfully to the LLRU.[28] Finally, he even recommended that she prepare boldly for the ultimate sacrifice of imprisonment rather than admit defeat, though the fiery Emma Cons probably first thought of going to Holloway as a martyr in their cause.[29]

---

strong local option party in the division.' Murray MacDonald to Jane Cobden, 9 Dec. 1888, ibid. For Jane Cobden's election address, with only an opening reference to women's issues, see *East London Observer*, 29 Dec. 1889.

[24] George Lansbury to Jane Cobden, 24 Dec. 1889, JCP.

[25] J. A. Murray MacDonald to Jane Cobden, 26 Jan. 1889, JCP; J. A. Murray MacDonald to Mrs Mallett, 24 Jan. 1889, ibid.; L. J. Mallett to George Lansbury, 25 Jan. 1889, LP, vol. 1, fos. 36–7. Jane Cobden's committee noted Lansbury's 'charge for his services is even less than the very low figure originally agreed upon . . . under these circumstances . . . a bonus of three guineas instead of the two guineas originally proposed . . . [C]ertainly no one could have worked harder or have deserved it better.' Mrs Mallett to Jane Cobden, 25 Jan. 1889, JCP.

[26] George Lansbury to Jane Cobden, n.d. [*c.*19 Jan. 1889], JCP. The result was: W. Hunter, civil engineer, 2,109; J. Cobden, 2,054; E. R. Cook, soap manufacturer 1,722; J. H. Howard, timber merchant, 1,060.

[27] For the case of *Beresford Hope* v. *Sandhurst*, see Hollis, *Ladies Elect*, pp. 310–12.

[28] George Lansbury to Jane Cobden, 7, 24 Jan., 18 Feb. 1890, JCP.

[29] George Lansbury to Jane Cobden, 14 Mar. 1890, JCP.

The successive waves of opposition to the three new county councillors revealed the prejudice surrounding women in late Victorian politics, even where advancing numbers of female members on school boards and as poor law guardians had been secured. In contrast to the formidable barriers preventing the winning of the parliamentary suffrage, progress had been achieved to some extent in the previous twenty years in local government, as it was often regarded as an extension of the domestic sphere of home and family to which women were naturally relegated. In fact, Jane Cobden opened her energetic election campaign, in the main fought on radical and local questions rather than on feminist lines, with the strategy of underlining the specific and unique contribution women representatives could bring to municipal affairs:

It will be well here to enumerate a few of the chief duties which will fall to the work of the county councillors, laying greater stress upon those which in my opinion, it will be most desirable that *women should take part in*. They are these: maintenance of industrial and reformatory schools . . . pauper lunatic asylums . . . for these two departments alone . . . a woman's knowledge and powers of observation should be brought to work . . .[30]

Jonathan Schneer has rightly pointed to the significance of George Lansbury's organization of Jane Cobden's LCC campaign in the evolution of his understanding of the women's question, emphazising though that this was a very different proposition from the later feminism of the Edwardian women's suffrage movement that endeavoured to remove the distinction of gender. In Schneer's view, Victorian feminism had the more limited objective of extending women's role only within their natural domestic sphere. Male politicians and electors might object less to women's participation in local government, since the new county councils were perceived as governing those areas of life traditionally associated with wives and mothers.[31]

However, at times, feminist strategy was not as singular or as clear-cut as suggested. Mrs Humphry Ward's celebrated *Appeal against Suffrage* in 1889, with Beatrice Potter among her co-signatories, immediately earned a stern rebuke from Liberal campaigner Millicent Garrett Fawcett that included examples of feminists actively breaching the walls separating the public and domestic spheres.[32] Moreover, achieving what was politically possible at the time, by seemingly accepting that women's natural capabilities were limited to the realm of municipal affairs, was a subtle strategy adopted by feminists gradually to undermine the whole ideology of separate spheres in politics and life. Whatever George Lansbury's exact position on the women's question at this time, it is difficult to believe he accepted a limitation of women to local government, even in the late 1880s. Clearly though, his active involvement in Jane Cobden's cause was another massive stepping-stone in his own political development towards the eventual placing of gender above social class on his socialist agenda.

[30] *East London Observer*, 29 Dec. 1888 (emph. added).
[31] Schneer, *George Lansbury*, p. 73.
[32] Mrs H. Ward, 'An Appeal Against Female Suffrage', *Nineteenth Century*, June 1889; M. G. Fawcett, 'Female Suffrage: A Reply', ibid. July 1889.

Jane Cobden was an independent and determined campaigner in her own right, as demonstrated in 1891 by her decision to sit out her first year silently at the Council to retain her seat. Eight years older than George Lansbury, she formed an effective partnership with her local agent. It would be wrong to describe Lansbury as the sole architect of her successful election campaign or the prevailing voice in its legal aftermath. In the end, among considerable confusion about the legality of serving as a county councillor, Jane Cobden too lost her court case, with her appeal dismissed in April 1891 with a reduction in the penalty from £250 to £5. Only action by Parliament to change the law could resolve the position of women on county councils. Here, the Liberal leadership failed miserably and deliberately to support attempts to pilot sympathetic private Members' bills through Parliament. Lansbury wrote in outrage once more to the *Pall Mall Gazette* to urge that, 'surely those who are in earnest about the enfranchisement of women will not be content to be a mere appendage of the Liberal party. Let them shake themselves free of party feeling and throw the energy and ability . . . [into] securing . . . the full rights of citizenship to every woman in the land.'[33]

Nevertheless, it had been Jane Cobden who, on discovering through her political contacts that the Liberal chief whip Arnold Morley had conspired to persuade Members to stay away from the House, angrily demanded that Lansbury take the matter up in the press and guided his pen.[34] Here was a further disheartening experience, to set beside the others, to undermine the morale of the loyal partyworker.

Leaving one party to join another is a major step and one not taken lightly by committed politicians. If, on the central planks of Gladstonian Liberalism, Irish Home Rule, and free trade, the Bow and Bromley Liberal and Radical Association remained steadfast, as well as showing a progressive attitude towards labour and social questions, why did George Lansbury finally break with the Liberal party and turn decisively towards the Social Democrats?

The decline of the Liberal party and the rise of the Labour party constitute one of the major questions of British history debated during the last thirty years of the twentieth century. British historians remain keenly divided over the nature and timing of this major change in the British party system and have expended a considerable amount of pen and ink debating rival explanations for the changes in the nation's voting behaviour and party loyalties.[35]

---

[33] *Pall Mall Gazette*, 1 June 1891.

[34] Jane Cobden to George Lansbury, 28, 29 May 1891, LP, vol. 1, fos. 120–1.

[35] For an excellent analysis of this debate, see K. Laybourn, 'The Rise of Labour and the Decline of Liberalism: The State of the Debate', *History*, 80 (1995), pp. 207–26. There is an extensive literature on this subject; essential sources include: P. F. Clarke, *Lancashire and the New Liberalism* (1971); K. O. Morgan, 'The New Liberalism and the Challenge of Labour: The Welsh Experience, 1885–1929', in K. D. Brown (ed.), *Essays in Anti-Labour History: Responses to the Rise of Labour* (1974), pp. 159–82; C. Wrigley, 'Liberals and the Desire for Working-Class Representatives in Battersea', ibid., pp. 126–58; K. Laybourn and J. Reynolds, *Liberalism and the Rise of Labour, 1890–1918* (1984); D. Tanner, *Political Change and the Labour Party, 1900–1918* (1990); E. F. Biagini and A. J. Reid (eds.), *Currents of Radicalism: Popular Radicalism, Organised Labour and Party Politics, 1850–1914* (1991).

Lansbury himself gave some clear reasons for the transfer of his political allegiance even many years before the publication of his autobiography in 1928. His
most comprehensive answer can be found in a series of articles in *Labour Leader*, in
which prominent socialists examined the origins of their political faith. Lansbury
claimed he was not aware of socialism until he came into contact with various
socialists in London in the late 1880s. In 1912 he declared that his analysis of social
conditions led inexorably to certain political conclusions:

Liberalism would progress just so far as the great capitalist money bags would allow it to
progress, and so I took the plunge and joined the SDF . . . [adding] I cannot say that at this
time [1892] I was a Socialist, or rather a Social-Democrat, in what Hyndman or Quelch would
call the full sense of the word, but I joined the SDF because I felt that they stood in England
for revolt against present conditions, and for a reorganized society which would be built up
by the efforts of the workers themselves.[36]

In 1912 Lansbury's analysis applied equally to women, whose cause he championed
since he felt as strongly about inequalities of gender as about inequalities of social
class. By this time social and political justice for women was the dominant issue in
his socialism. 'I have also come to see what we call the Woman Question is of very
greatest importance for the future of our society, he declared.'[37]

In the 1880s contact with prominent and influential socialists, including William
Morris, Henry Mayers Hyndman, Eleanor Marx, John Burns, Tom Mann, and
Henry J. Burrows, provided George Lansbury with a new network of political associates, as well as the opportunity to analyse human society through a different set of
political lenses. But this was only part of why he left the Liberals. Steadily, as we have
already partly seen, he became convinced in the late 1880s by a number of experiences that the Liberal party was no longer his political home.

Trafalgar Square was the traditional meeting-place in the capital for public
demonstrations, as well as a gathering-place each night for the unemployed and
destitute of 'Outcast' London. In 1886–7, by employing heavy-handed law-
enforcement methods, banning access to Trafalgar Square, and arresting leading
figures in the demonstrations, the authorities provoked a populist campaign in
London. The London radical clubs and socialist groups combined against coercion
in Ireland and for the defence of free speech in Britain.

The mix of traditional radical causes and current economic distress struck a stri-
dent chord and raised grave concerns in the heart of the metropolis. Most notable
of the disorderly scenes, widely reported in the press, was the riot in the club-land
of Pall Mall and St James in February 1886 and 'Bloody Sunday' in November 1887,
followed by the arrest of Burns and Cunninghame Graham.[38] Thousands witnessed
the spectacle of Linnell's cortège—comprising 120,000 people and stretching one
and a half miles in length—the greatest procession since the funeral of the 'Iron

---

[36] G. Lansbury, 'How I Became a Socialist', *Labour Leader*, 17 May 1912.   [37] Ibid.
[38] For the politics surrounding Trafalgar Square, see R. Mace, *Trafalgar Square: Emblem of Empire*
(London, 1976), pp. 160–95; K. D. Brown, *John Burns* (1977), pp. 20–35.

Duke' thirty-five years before. It filed from central London to Bow cemetery—close to Lansbury's home and place of work—where William Morris movingly uttered the graveside eulogy at the martyr's funeral.[39]

The extent of Lansbury's direct involvement in these events is not clear. He does not appear to have been present on 'Bloody Sunday' but was certainly at the demonstration in Trafalgar Square on 6 February 1886, though he did not follow the crowd as the police dispersed the demonstrators towards Pall Mall.[40] His radical ideas would have been pushed sharply leftwards by the political demonstrations that disturbed the city and the government, as well as the industrial disputes in the East End in the following years.

In 1887 Lansbury arranged for a deputation of East End working-class radicals financed by Sir Samuel Montagu to visit Ireland to examine conditions there at first hand. Not only did he discover the horror of evictions but he also noted that the poverty of Irish peasantry was largely caused by the exodus of the country's wealth to London financiers:

I think the finishing touch to my education was seeing the Irish Question just as it was . . . the realisation that the tenants on the Drapers Estates of one of the City of London companies really earned the rent which helped to pay for the great City banquets . . . for the building of the People's Palace in East London . . . I saw much clearer than any theoretical political economy could have taught me that without these tenants and their labour there would be no rent, no dinners, no People's Palace.[41]

The way in which he described his first visit to Ireland, where he saw 'foul housing conditions' in Dublin, before journeying north to Belfast, Newry, Carrickfergus, Londonderry, and other Irish towns reveals that this eye-opening experience made 'a big impression' on him. Everywhere the deputation went, its members were under close supervision by 'police in uniform and police in plain clothes, spies and informers'. His consequent unease led to a close scrutiny of the political values and practices of Liberalism in Britain.

Back home, Lansbury witnessed further outbursts of working-class militancy in the heart of the East End, associated with the Match Girls' Strike, the Gasworkers' Dispute, and the London Dock Strike, which convulsed the capital and beyond in 1887–9. As a radical, he found himself drawn in from the periphery of these struggles of 'New Unionism', but mentioned no direct involvement with Annie Besant's celebrated organization of the match-girls, a classic example of the struggle of the downtrodden with whom he identified. The massive Bryant and May Fairfield Road factory, owned by doctrinaire Liberal employers and operated by a previously unorganized workforce of over a thousand women and girls, was virtually a stone's throw from the Lansbury home. He must have been shaken by the sensational

---

[39] Alfred Linnell was killed on 'Bloody Sunday'. *Commonweal*, 24 Dec. 1887; W. J. Fishman, *East End, 1888: A Year in a London Borough among the Labour Poor* (1988), pp. 3–4.

[40] Lansbury, *My Life*, p. 87; see also Lansbury, *Looking Backwards and Forwards*, p. 69. For contemporary reports, see *Echo*, 8, 9, 16, 18, 20 Feb. 1886.

[41] *Labour Leader*, 17 May 1912.

publicity, brought about by the appalling moral and health conditions of the casual female labour force, that the three-week dispute attracted far beyond the East End.[42]

In the London Dock Strike, run by the central strike committee from Wade's Arms at Poplar, Lansbury joined the local committee and participated in door-to-door collections every Saturday to raise funds to support starving dockers. As a result, Will Thorne became a new ally and in May 1889 Lansbury joined the Bromley East branch of the newly formed Gasworkers' Union. It was to be an enduring political relationship and alliance. Lansbury became a trustee of the Union and attended Labour party annual conferences from 1920 as one of its official delegates.[43]

Lansbury's association with the Gasworkers' Union was of more immediate significance, as it brought him into contact with the East End stalwart, Charlie Sumner. Together they organized assistance for the 'bass-dressers' in their dispute with their employers. Open-air meetings were organized outside the gasworks in St Leonard's Road, Bromley, under the auspices of the Bow and Bromley Liberal and Radical Association and chaired by Jane Cobden.[44]

His connection with Will Thorne and the Gasworkers' Union also provided Lansbury with an entry to the popular agitation in 1890 for the legal eight-hour day, the key issue in working-class politics at that time. The Gasworkers, who had secured an eight-hour day for 80,000 men in East London during the previous year wished to defend their better working day through parliamentary legislation. The union was part of the coalition of socialists, trade unionists, and radicals which organized the first May Demonstration in Hyde Park held on Sunday, 4 May 1890 and attended by around 250,000 people. The Gasworkers' Union sent Lansbury as a delegate to the Legal Eight-Hour Day Committee in the process of arranging the vast procession and rally. In Hyde Park he spoke from the second platform, alongside the socialist Cunninghame Graham and Irish nationalist, Michael Davitt. These activities brought him into direct contact with leading Marxists, Eleanor Marx and Edward Aveling, one of many examples at that time of co-operation on the left which blurred the distinctions between popular radicalism and the emergent forms of socialism. Throughout all this political activity, Lansbury was still nominally a Liberal party agent, though one faced with an intellectual and ideological quandary.[45]

[42] The match-girls had also been on strike in 1886. Fishman, *East End, 1888*, pp. 119, 270, 284–8.

[43] Lansbury, *My Life*, pp. 69–71. For the London Dock Strike, see also T. McCarthy, *The Great Dock Strike, 1889* (1988); J. Lovell, *Stevedores and Dockers: A Study of Trade Unionism in the Port of London, 1870–1914* (1969), ch. 4. For Lansbury's membership of the National Union of General and Municipal Workers' delegations at Labour party conferences, see Labour Party, *Reports of the Annual Conference* (1920–9).

[44] *Coming Times*, Sept. 1889.

[45] For the role of the Gasworkers in the Eight-Hour Working Day Demonstration, see *People's Press*, 19 Apr., 10 May, 1890. For the 'Monster Labour Demonstration . . . in Hyde Park', see *Daily Chronicle*, 5 May 1890. George Lansbury is mentioned briefly in *People's Press*, 10 May 1890. On continuities between popular radicalism and socialism in the late 19th cent., see J. Lawrence, 'Popular Radicalism and the Socialist Revival in Britain', *Journal of British Studies*, 31 (1992), pp. 175–7.

In his capacity as a Liberal party agent George Lansbury took up the eight-hour cause with enthusiasm, an aim shared by his parliamentary candidate, Murray MacDonald, who had made the improvement of social conditions a central proposal of his address to the electors of Bow and Bromley. Besides the usual Liberals' nostrums of Irish Home Rule, reform of the House of Lords, the administration of the state, the liquor laws, and disestablishment of the Church, Murray MacDonald shared some of the increasing unease of his party agent, though he did not draw the same political conclusions:

What is it that is at the root of the acknowledged evils of our social system? I answer without hesitation—An oppressive and demoralising poverty at one end of the social scale and at the other end an equally oppressive and demoralising wealth . . . How is this to be solved. No one can as yet give a complete or finally satisfactory answer to this question . . .[46]

As a fairly advanced Radical, Murray MacDonald proposed reform of the Land Laws—a traditional remedy—alongside other measures. He was among the newer voices of those in the Liberal party prepared to respond favourably to demands for greater working-class representation that would sanction parliamentary intervention in traditional relations in industry and commerce in order to secure improved social conditions. Lansbury acknowledged the help of his wealthier Liberal associates but added, 'though men like Montagu, Murray MacDonald, and Corrie Grant were very kind, my mind continually took me towards the Socialists'.[47]

By 1890 George Lansbury was convinced that only a revolutionary solution, and not piecemeal political reforms, would eradicate poverty and inequalities of wealth, as well as provide social justice for the working people of Britain. His decision had been reached through reading socialist literature, contact with socialist activists, and listening to the great set debates of the 1880s, between Henry Mayers Hyndman and Henry George, the American land-reformer, and between Hyndman and the atheist Charles Bradlaugh.[48]

At this time, attitudes within the national Liberal party organization conspired to destroy the constructive work of Murray MacDonald and others at local level to retain the services of Lansbury, the enthusiastic and adroit party-worker. The machinations inherent within the party caucus system in the late nineteenth century severed Lansbury's political association with Liberalism and pushed him into the ranks of the Social Democratic Federation. As he explained himself:

My final break with Liberalism really took place after a controversy with Lord Morley, . . . one of the great leaders of the Liberal party. I argued with him that if the Government could fix rents in Ireland and so indirectly fix the income of the tenants, there was no logical

---

[46] *Coming Times*, Sept. 1889.   [47] Lansbury, *My Life*, pp. 71–2.

[48] Lansbury was not part of W. T. Stead's famous survey of the reading habits of forty-four Labour and Lib–Lab MPs: 'The Labour Party and the Books that Helped to Make It', *Review of Reviews*, 33 (1906), pp. 568–82. In 1928 Lansbury recalled the influence of the Bible; William Morris, *News from Nowhere*; Robert Blatchford, *Merrie England*; Marx, *Das Kapital*; and Engels, *English Socialism: Utopian and Scientific*, as well as poetry, *Reynolds's Newspaper*, novels, and historical works 'such as Greene's History of The English People'. Lansbury, *My Life*, pp. 33, 37, 77, 79.

reason why industrial wages and hours should not also be fixed by Parliament. I found that the Liberal party, with him as its spokesman, were quite willing to adopt principles for dealing with poverty in Ireland which they were quite unwilling to adopt in this country . . .[49]

In fact, Lansbury's explanation in 1912 somewhat abbreviated this major turning-point in his political life. Towards the end of 1889, Lansbury succeeded in persuad-ing the LLRU Council to adopt a resolution of only a limited form of statutory eight-hour day for all government and municipal employees, rather than the wider legal eight-hour day campaigned for by a combination of socialists, radicals, and trade unionists in 1889–90.[50] Lansbury proposed only a relatively moderate meas-ure to put before the annual conference of the National Liberal Federation (NLF) at Manchester in December 1889 but, if agreed to, it would mean parliamentary inter-vention in the economy.

On 14 November, at the LLRU meeting at the National Liberal Club, Lansbury in a 'forcible address' about inequalities of wealth ('much applauded') argued: '. . . it was no use giving people all the privileges it was proposed to give them unless you gave them time in which to enjoy them. Eight hours a day was a necessary limit and it was desirable that London should set an example to the rest of the community . . .'. With only sixteen opposing votes, Lansbury's resolution was carried:

That . . . the London Liberal and Radical Union is of the opinion that the time has arrived . . . that no Government nor Municipal employee shall be required to work more than eight hours a day or to receive less than the standard rate of wages; and . . . shall be allowed . . . right of combination . . .[51]

This successful resolution provoked considerable opposition within the ranks of Gladstonian Liberals, even in the more radical parts of London and exposed the deep divide within the party between those impatient to take up a more advanced line on social policy in the metropolis and the provincial Liberals' fixation on Irish Home Rule. In particular John Morley, close political associate, friend, and future biographer of William Gladstone, staunchly opposed parliamentary intervention, especially on the eight hours' question. Morley disliked developments in London, 'this chaotic monster of a city', particularly socialism and radicalism. In his own constituency of Newcastle, he was under pressure from socialist candidates who campaigned with success on the eight hours issue in municipal elections. He faced a crisis in his career and political thinking.[52]

Five days after the meeting of the LLRU, Morley addressed the Eighty Club at St James Hall in London on Liberalism and social reforms. He made a direct attack

[49] Lansbury, 'How I Became a Socialist'.
[50] For the divisions within the eight-hour movement, see C. Wrigley, 'May Days and After', *History Today*, 40 (June 1990), pp. 35–41.
[51] *Daily News*, 15 Nov. 1889.
[52] For Morley's opposition to 'Eight Hours' legislation, see D. A. Hamer, *John Morley: Liberal Intellect-ual in Politics* (Oxford, 1968), pp. 230, 243, 254–62; Wrigley, *Arthur Henderson*, pp. 12–16.

on the proposal that 'nobody is to be employed more than eight hours continuously, or 48 hours in a week, either in Government works or in municipal bodies':

Well, I would like to ask one or two questions. What business has Parliament to prescribe to the people of Manchester . . . Birmingham, or . . . Newcastle, the terms on which they shall employ their men? . . . is the good workman to be paid for eight hours what he gets now we will say for nine?[53]

Morley went on to ask whether overtime would be prohibited and how the Secretary of State would know that a majority in a particular trade favoured legislative restriction of hours. He concluded: '"I want workmen of this country to consider the question [of a statutory eight-hour day] . . . and as they make up their minds, so it will be the business of Parliament to legislate, but speaking absolutely for myself . . . I shall not vote for it." (Cheers)'[54]

Lansbury responded next day in a letter from 105 St Stephen's Road, Bow, to the Liberal *Daily News*. He pointed out that Morley had misunderstood the nature of the eight-hour proposal and added: 'Mr Morley should also remember the chief reason for an eight hours' day is that more men and women would get employment, and that the labour market would be steadier . . .'[55]

Yet Lansbury also found the weight of the Liberal national press against him. Stung by comments in his letter about the newspaper, the *Daily News* entered the lists against the working-class champion of the eight-hour day. The Liberal organ argued even a limited measure would be extended by parliamentary means and interfere with natural economic processes. 'But what does the triumph of the Dockers, the lightermen, and the bakers . . . prove? Surely . . . the intervention of the State is unnecessary and combination ensures victory . . . Mr Lansbury's argument may easily be turned against himself . . .'.[56]

Murray MacDonald was a sympathetic supporter of George Lansbury, congratulating him on his successful LLRU resolution and journeying with him (he offered to pay Lansbury's expenses) to the NLF conference at Manchester.[57] Attended by William Gladstone at the start, the NLF was the 'annual parliament' for Liberal representatives from different parts of the country. But the possibility of parliamentary legislation in the national economy and interference in the relationship between employers and workmen provoked a crisis in the Liberal party. Murray MacDonald found the workings of the northern caucus, the bedrock of provincial Liberalism, prevented any consideration of the resolution from the radicals of the metropolis. Lansbury later described the scene in his own words:

Sir James Kitson presided over a huge gathering in the Free Trade Hall. Pressure of all kinds was brought to bear on me . . . not to move the resolution; Sidney Webb and H. W. Massingham both wrote agreeing the resolution was a good one but . . . we must wait till the iron and coal-masters of the North had been won over.[58]

---

[53] *Daily News*, 21 Nov. 1889. [54] Ibid. [55] Ibid. 22 Nov. 1889. [56] Ibid.
[57] J. A. Murray MacDonald to George Lansbury, 15, 16, 22 Nov., LP, vol. 1, fos. 81, 89, 93–5.
[58] Lansbury, *My Life*, pp. 72–3.

Lansbury added that he was a delegate and entitled to be heard, 'but the caucus said otherwise'; when he attempted to mount the conference platform, the chairman, Sir James Kitson, 'rang a bell'. What happened next was decisive and had ominous echoes of events much later in Lansbury's career. 'One half of the audience supported me, the other half tried to howl me down. After a few minutes I was gently but firmly pushed down the steps and thus ended my connection with Liberalism', he recalled.[59] As might be expected, the *Daily News* largely ignored this incident in Manchester, including only a brief reference, similar to that in the *Manchester Guardian*, in its main report of the NLF proceedings. It stated tersely: 'Mr Murray MacDonald wished to add a rider with reference to the eight hours question but the CHAIRMAN ruled that no new question could be introduced to the question.'[60]

On his return Lansbury wrote immediately to the *Pall Mall Gazette* to protest about the lack of democracy in the party organization. 'No delegate has been allowed to ask a question; no delegate has been allowed to move any amendment to the cut-and-dried proposal of Messrs. Kitson, Schnadhorst and co.', he complained.[61] In his own paper, which previously reported his successful resolution with the front-page headline 'London reformers endorse the Eight Hour's Movement!', he put a brave face on his brusque rebuff, though bitter disappointment seeped through as he attempted to explain his rejection at Manchester. None the less, in the end he readily admitted that working men had little to 'hope for from either of the great political parties'.[62]

Whatever happened at the conference hall in Manchester, Lansbury had fallen foul of the caucus system, controlled by middle-class élites, and so distrusted by working-class politicians from George Howell onwards. Over thirty years later he gave a longer account that included the pressure put on him to withdraw his resolution even before he reached Manchester:

I reckoned without the wire-pullers. No sooner was my motion sent in than all sorts of influences were brought to bear to induce me to withdraw . . . intrigue and chicanery during the weeks that passed between the meeting in London and the so-called conference in Manchester, convinced me there was nothing of real worth to be gained from the Kitsons, Illingworths and their like.[63]

However, George Lansbury continued his work as a loyal party agent for a while in Bow and Bromley. Earlier, Murray MacDonald had attempted, albeit unsuccessfully, to keep the young party worker within the Liberal party by encouraging Lansbury to visit the Warwickshire constituency to consider becoming the political successor to the sitting Liberal MP, P. H. Cobb, about to retire at the next election.[64] On his return, Lansbury explained why he declined these opportunities to join the Liberal ranks at Westminster: he could only contest a parliamentary seat as a socialist, independent of the Liberal party—which is what he did. After the

[59] Ibid.; *Daily Herald*, 13 Jan. 1923.
[60] *Daily News*, 5 Dec. 1889; *Manchester Guardian*, 5 Dec. 1889.
[61] Schneer, *George Lansbury*, p. 14.   [62] *Coming Times*, Dec. 1899–Jan. 1890.
[63] *Daily Herald*, 13 Jan. 1923.   [64] Lansbury, *My Life*, p. 74.

Manchester NLF débâcle, and the failure of the parliamentary Liberals to support Prof. Stuart's Bill on women county councillors, he remained with his own candidate, Murray MacDonald to steer his election campaign in 1892. MacDonald's successful return to Parliament was Lansbury's third triumph for the Liberal party, but his last. The day after the victorious poll, accompanied by around twenty working-class fellow workers, George Lansbury left the Gladstonian party he had served since 1886. These former Liberals now turned themselves into the Bow and Bromley branch of the SDF.[65]

[65] In 1892 Murray MacDonald defeated the sitting Tory MP, Sir J. C. Colomb, in a straight fight and was returned with a majority of 423. Three years later, when Lansbury was no longer his election agent, he lost the seat to the Conservatives. For the 1892 election result, see *East London Observer*, 9 July 1892.

3
Socialist Propagandist, 1892–1903

In the 1930s, George Lansbury looked back on a long life, spent mostly in the labour movement, in which he 'tried to fight the good fight'. In a private note to his family, he set out his simple personal philosophy in near-visionary terms, a universe for ordinary people based on love and service for one another, inspired by an enduring Christian faith. He recognized he would leave 'very little wealth in the ordinary sense in which men use that word' but, instead, 'a wealth of love and high endeavour which in a tiny way I have enjoyed with others'.

His only direct reference to his politics was to declare himself 'a convinced out and out socialist, one who accepts as true, literally and eternally true, Love is the only true law of life. Seeking the good of all, learning through service is the one way to the goal of human happiness.'[1] For over fifty years, from the first day he left the Liberal party immediately after the 1892 election to join the SDF, George Lansbury was simply a socialist, a steadfast faith he believed in and practised as a way of life for the rest of his days.

George Lansbury can be counted among the early apostles of this new faith in late nineteenth-century Britain. For William Morris, Robert Blatchford, Annie Besant, Keir Hardie, George Lansbury, and others, their new way of life was defined as 'the religion of socialism', a term in common currency in the 1880s and 1890s. Socialism was about a new and better world to replace the dark satanic mills of Victorian capitalism. That said, for those who believed in and worked towards building the new Jerusalem, the ethical and moral dimension of human behaviour was as important as an economic analysis of what was wrong with contemporary industrial society. Robert Blatchford believed he first used the phrase in 1885:

If you want socialism to be a religion, you must widen your definition of socialism. You must draw out all the ethical and spiritual implications of these desires and efforts for a juster social order . . . Socialism is a step—a long step indeed, but still only a step—to the realisation of a new social ideal . . . [A] new conception of life is taking shape . . .[2]

Throughout most of his life George Lansbury was a Christian socialist in thought and action. His religion remained the bedrock of his life and provided the important source of his political belief and active service for his community. However, at the start of the 1890s, a largely forgotten decade when George Lansbury lost his

---

[1] This statement was first composed in 1932 and re-dated in 1938 without any changes. George Lansbury to his family, 3 Mar. 1932 and Aug. 1938, Esme Whiskin Papers.

[2] R. Blatchford, *The Labour Prophet* (Apr. 1897), quoted in S. Yeo, 'A New Life: The Religion of Socialism in Britain, 1883–1896', *History Workshop Journal*, 4 (1977), p. 5.

religious faith, he was inspired by a different ideology. During these early years of his political education, it can truly be said that George Lansbury owed more to Marx, and his disciples, than the simple and lasting Christianity that later inspired his socialism.

In 1921, from his cell in Brixton Prison during the Poplar Rates Rebellion, George Lansbury described how, thirty years before, the influence of William Morris had revealed to him the possibility of a new life based on a different set of values:

in the columns of *Commonweal*, in pamphlets, lectures and speeches [he] made me realise that there was something more to be thought of than Acts of Parliament and State Bureaucracy . . . surely what we strive for is a society of free men and women bound together by ties of comradeship and communal well-being as pictured by Morris in his wonderful book, *News from Nowhere . . .*[3]

As an active young Liberal party worker in the years of the so-called 'Great Depression' of the 1880s and 1890s, Lansbury witnessed the daily struggle for survival that was the lot of so many residents of the East End. Nor should we forget that in Queensland he and his family had also suffered the unremitting effects of burgeoning capitalism for the first time. William Morris's revolutionary socialism survived him in his writings, poetry, and journalism to inspire others in the twentieth century, from G. D. H. Cole to R. H. Tawney, Harold Laski, Clem Attlee, and Barbara Castle.[4] Similarly, Morris's contribution to Lansbury's socialist awakening was immense. Two events, among many, were particularly important and can be recalled. In 1895 Lansbury shared the same election platform with Morris, the visionary craftsman-designer and poet, who journeyed to Walworth to support his SDF parliamentary candidature.[5] Morris's final political speech in 1896 was to second Lansbury's resolution of international greetings at the Federation's New Year meeting at Holborn town hall.[6] Instead of the horrors and ugliness of industrialism, the vision of a new and beautiful society, where 'fellowship is life', was seminal. It fired the imagination and captured the intellect of George Lansbury among many others in contact with Morris.[7] Watching sparrows from his prison cell on that twenty-fifth anniversary of Morris's death, Lansbury wrote that 'his conception of what life would be when men and women are free from [satisfying] material needs . . . is what appeals to me . . . the day must come when human beings will see the folly of fighting to exist, and will co-operate to live'.[8]

However, in 1892 Lansbury chose to join the SDF in London and not the Socialist League founded in 1884 by Morris, after he broke with the Federation. By the early 1890s the League had crumbled and left only an anarchist rump. In the

[3] *Daily Herald*, 3 Oct. 1921.
[4] In a memorable address to the Cambridge Labour party in 1996 on the centenary of the death of William Morris, Baroness Castle showed that his influence on her was as bright and powerful as in her socialist youth sixty years before.
[5] E. P. Thompson, *William Morris: Romantic to Revolutionary* (1977), p. 619.
[6] F. MacCarthy, *William Morris: A Life for Our Times* (1994), pp. xvi–xix, 645–6.
[7] For an important article on this subject, see C. Wrigley, 'William Morris, Art and the Rise of the British Labour Movement', *The Historian* (2000), pp. 4–10.
[8] *Daily Herald*, 3 Oct. 1921.

intellectual ferment of British socialism from the mid-1880s to mid-1890s, new parties and sects proliferated. The roll call is impressive: the Fabian Society (1884); the SDF (1884); the Socialist League (1884), the Scottish Labour Party (1888), and the Independent Labour Party (ILP) (1893). In 1889 the First International was established to unite the socialists of different countries. May Day was first celebrated in Britain on 4 May 1890.[9]

Originally founded as a radical body in 1881, three years later the Democratic Federation was translated into the SDF, the first main socialist organization in Great Britain. Until 1916 the Federation (and its later political configurations) were closely identified with its founder and leader, Henry Mayers Hyndman, the former Tory representative of the upper classes famously described as 'a gentleman, cricketer and stockbroker leading the toiling masses towards revolution in a top-hat and frock-coat'. However, the early years saw serious factional disputes, including the doctrinal row and personality clash with Eleanor Marx and Edward Aveling in 1884, which split the Federation apart. Hyndman's abrasive character, his inability to collaborate except with those he saw as his inferiors, as well as his quasi-Marxist views, drove prominent figures, most notably William Morris, out of the organization. For many contemporaries, and some modern historians, Hyndman embodied the SDF.[10]

The wealthy Hyndman had studied at Trinity College, Cambridge, and converted from Conservatism to Socialism after reading Marx's *Capital* in French. However, his *England for All* (1883) borrowed freely from Marx and Engels and provoked a famous split with Marx, followed by a debilitating feud with Engels over the years. Traditionally, the domineering Hyndman has been depicted as nationalistic, anti-Semitic, against co-operation with trade unions, and hostile to women in politics. According to Robin Page Arnot, 'the evil genius of the Socialist movement' prevented the Federation benefiting from its pioneering start as the main Socialist party.

None the less, despite its founder's faults and idiosyncrasies, the Federation was less centralized and more open to debate than previously recognized by many historians, as its branches in different parts of Britain often ignored autocratic leadership from London. If the Federation had been cast irredeemably in Hyndman's mould, it is doubtful whether Lansbury would have joined it. In fact, he remained for ten years, to become an unpaid SDF delegate, poor law guardian, and parliamentary candidate, as well as the official national organizer for a year. Lansbury did not move to his more natural home of the ILP until *c.*1904. What the Federation provided for a cohort of working-class politicians—such as Tom Mann, John Burns, Will Thorne, all future labour leaders—was a socialist training-school and an apprenticeship in political theory and practice. Indeed, the list of names of those

[9] For the international history of the first May Day, see E. J. Hobsbawm, 'Birth of a Holiday: The First of May', in C. Wrigley and J. Shepherd (eds.), *On the Move: Essays in Labour and Transport History Presented to Philip Bagwell* (1991), pp. 104–22.

[10] E. J. Hobsbawm, 'Hyndman and the SDF', in id., *Labouring Men: Studies in the history of labour* (1971), pp. 231–8.

labour figures whose early political lives were in contact at some point with this Marxist party is almost endless, and ranges from Ramsay MacDonald to Margaret Bondfield, Selina Cooper, and Ernest Bevin.[11] George Lansbury was a prime example of one who honed his political skills in his Federation days.

'It may be that Hyndman was the greatest political influence upon George Lansbury' was Postgate's estimation of this shaping force on his subject's political mind, a possibility suggested by the inclusion of the Federation leader as one of 'those truly great ones' in Lansbury's autobiography.[12] Hyndman is first mentioned there briefly as early as 1875–7, when Lansbury walked with his brother Jim from Whitechapel to Blackheath to hear Gladstone, who read aloud at the meeting from a letter sent by the upper-class socialist.[13] Lansbury later attended the public debates between Hyndman and the American land-reformer, Henry George in the 1880s. Only weeks before he left for Australia in 1884, Lansbury crammed into a packed St James Hall in London for the famous encounter on 18 April when the radical and atheist, Charles Bradlaugh, and the socialist, Henry Hyndman, debated the question 'Will Socialism Benefit the English People?'. The predominantly radical audience that night gave Hyndman a hostile reception, but his exposition of socialism as a solution to the pernicious nature of capitalism, with its inherent defects and recurrent crises, planted some fertile ideas firmly in the young Lansbury's mind. With penetrating clarity, Hyndman argued that capitalism created extreme wealth for the few but subjected the many to an abject poverty in a harsh struggle for daily survival in Victorian Britain. No one needed to work long and inhumane hours. '[T]hree or four hours work a day is more than sufficient to cover comfort and luxury for every man', Hyndman asserted. Later Lansbury recalled that 'on each occasion [I] found myself theoretically on the side of Hyndman'.[14] More than that, Hyndman's arguments, and his very words that night, can be found in subsequent Lansbury speeches.[15]

It was not altogether surprising that in 1892 George Lansbury chose to form the Bow and Bromley branch of the SDF instead of joining one of the other Socialist groups. The political strength of the Federation lay in the leadership of Hyndman, his executive and control of *Justice*, all metropolitan based and London focused. In the capital, the Federation played an important role in promoting independent labour politics in the upsurge of 'new unionism' in 1889–92 after the London Dock Strike. Federation influence can be seen in increased membership of the LCC and of the London Trades Council. By the end of the 1890s there were over forty London branches, with an active membership in the local labour parties of East London. In 1898 in West Ham, a working-class alliance formed by a mixed Labour–Socialist

---

[11] M. Crick, *The History of the Social-Democratic Federation* (Keele, 1994), p. 297.
[12] Postgate, *Lansbury*, p. 32; Lansbury, *My Life* (1928), p. 2.
[13] Lansbury, *My Life*, p. 40.   [14] Ibid. p. 72.
[15] For the *Bradlaugh* v. *Hyndman* debate, see W. L. Arnstein, *The Bradlaugh Case: Atheism, Sex and Politics among the Late Victorians* (1983), pp. 271–5. For Hyndman's 'three or four hours a week' repeated by Lansbury eleven years later, see *Todmorden Advertiser and Hebden Bridge Newsletter*, 29 Nov. 1895.

group briefly gained control of the local council.[16] In Lansbury's own words, what attracted him in the early 1890s was that the Federation 'stood in England for revolt against present conditions, and for a reorganised society, which would be built up by the efforts of the workers themselves'.[17] From the late 1880s, Lansbury was aware of the Federation's campaigns on behalf of free speech, the unemployed, and independent representation on municipal bodies. Here was an organization which offered opportunities to work for political democracy and the socialist beliefs he had been moving towards.

Nevertheless, the Federation was more of a sect than a political party of national standing, despite its presence in Lancashire, Yorkshire, and other parts of Britain. In London small-scale workshop and domestic manufacture formed the dominant mode of production rather than the large industrial factories of the North with aggregations of the working population.

The consequent weakness of trade unionism and the sharp divide between skilled and unskilled were among the barriers to organizing a political party with mass proletariat support. In these circumstances, the Federation's main objective had been to advance revolutionary socialism by 'making Socialists' through political agitation and education, though an alternative strategy of contesting elections for Parliament and the reformed municipal authorities was also being tried by the time Lansbury joined.[18] Within a year, Lansbury himself was successfully returned as the SDF candidate for the poor law guardians' elections in Bow and Bromley, a position he held with different political affiliations for over thirty years.

Within the Federation, Lansbury rapidly became well known for his tireless energy and political skills. Invitations to speak in different parts of the country flooded in, initiating the socialist propaganda work for which he was to be so well known and beloved among ordinary people for the remainder of his life. Lansbury travelled around Britain from John O'Groats to Land's End, speaking in villages, townships, and cities. His wife and family—in their early thirties they had five children—did not see a great deal of him. Nearly all his weekends were sacrificed to the socialist movement. Back in Bow, Bessie was left to cope with the usual tensions and problems of a growing number of young children.

On a Saturday after work Lansbury caught a late train to speak at an evening meeting, often in the North of England. Edgar Lansbury later remembered with some poignancy that his father always carried a large red flag, which he waved out of the carriage window to his young family when his Great Eastern express train passed close to the family home in Bow.[19] During these weekends, three more engagements would usually follow on the Sunday before Lansbury caught the night train back to arrive at a London terminus in the early hours. As no fees were taken for this work, Lansbury was faced with a long walk home to Bow, but always Bessie was 'waiting up with a first-class breakfast and a nice big fire'.[20] His selfless political

[16] D. Tanner, *Political Change and the Labour Party*, p. 177.
[17] Lansbury, 'How I Became a Socialist'.
[18] Crick, *History of the Social-Democratic Federation*.
[19] E. Lansbury, *George Lansbury*, p. 34.   [20] Lansbury, *My Life*, p. 76.

activity, and the support of his family, appears saint-like or apocryphal now. But it definitely took place; and it was typical of those early pioneers who displayed the missionary zeal of converts to a new faith. In an era before radio and television, many people in distant parts of Britain had the opportunity to hear George Lansbury and meet him, which in part explains his personal popularity and the remarkable affection in which he was held by so many.

George Lansbury acknowledged the effect of his political activity on family life and the extent of the sacrifices required by those who supported him. He certainly was not a neglectful or uncaring husband and father—indeed, he was completely the opposite:

The only person who has paid for this work is my wife, so if any thanks are due to me for this sacrifice of time and energy, the thanks are due to her and no one else, because she has borne the loneliness of life without any regret, feeling sure the work we were trying to do was for the good of mankind . . . How she managed things is a mystery: our family kept growing, but my wages were for a long time only thirty shillings a week.[21]

None the less, on the personal and private matter of birth-control, George Lansbury held traditional Victorian values for many years until he changed his views in the 1920s, when his daughter Dorothy and her husband Ernest Thurtle were prominent in the birth-control movement in the Labour party.[22] Otherwise, during his time in the Federation, he appears to have said little about women's rights. The 1890s were hardly years of quiescence. The Women's Franchise League had been formed in 1889. Socialists, such as Caroline Martyn, Katherine St John Conway, and Edith Stacey, were prominent public speakers on feminist issues. On the political Left, the decade also witnessed two *causes célèbres* which highlighted male attitudes to gender—the notorious Edith Lanchester Case and the sexual scandal involving Dora Montefiore and George Belt.

On franchise reform, Lansbury publicly backed the official Federation line of support for universal adult suffrage. However, the socialist construction of the central women's question relegated it to a matter of conscience rather than one of declared party policy. As a consequence, within the Federation, this attitude permitted a free reign to the misogyny of Belfort Bax and others. Their views appeared to dominate the organization, despite the pioneering feminism of SDFers, Dora Montefiore, Mary Gray, and Rose Jarvis. In 1894, on the vexed question of 'socialism versus feminism', a new voice emerged to challenge the ragbag of male prejudice in the columns of *Justice* that stereotyped women in traditional roles. Inspired by the poetry of the American democrat, Walt Whitman, Marion Hansen, only in her early twenties, wrote powerfully on the essential contribution women had to make to socialism. She thereby gave a glimpse of how her influence was to play on Lansbury's attitude to the women's question a decade later.[23]

---

[21] Ibid.   [22] See below, Ch. 18.

[23] K. Hunt, *Equivocal Feminists: The Social Democratic Federation and the Woman Question, 1884–1911* (1996); C. Collette, 'Socialism and Scandal: The Sexual Politics of the Early Labour Movement', *History Workshop Journal* (1987), pp. 103–11. For Lansbury's support of universal adult suffrage, see his Political

George Lansbury's time in the SDF broadly coincided with the complete loss of his religious faith. To the dismay of Revd J. Fenwick Kitto, he left the Anglican Church to join the Ethical movement in London. Lansbury said very little about these secularist years in his life, particularly at that time.[24] Alf Watts, his comrade in the Federation, is the source for reconstructing the circumstances in which Lansbury temporarily gave up the Church. For the first time, Lansbury studied left-wing tracts and mixed regularly in socialist circles, where many were free-thinkers and atheists drawn from the secularist tradition in metropolitan London. Two contemporary works were especially influential on his thinking. As Watts revealed: 'Many of his [Lansbury's] friends and fellow workers had already become Socialists and his reading of *Robert Elsmere* and Tolstoy's *What I Believe* helped him to sweep away some of the cobwebs of religious bigotry from his understanding.'[25]

Both books circulated widely in England and the USA and achieved enormous readerships. In *Robert Elsmere* (1888), Mrs Humphry Ward paralleled much of the Victorian crisis of faith suffered by Lansbury in her portrayal of a young Church of England clergyman who loses his religion in an intense, intellectual, and personal crisis.[26] Lansbury never mentioned this novel in his writing, but readily acknowledged the influence of Tolstoyan ideas in questioning the central beliefs of conventional Christianity. He confessed he tried to model his own life on the Russian writer and moral philosopher.[27]

For several years there was another set of influences on his thinking and behaviour. 'Give Your Life a Moral Purpose' was the philosophy of the East London Ethical Society which the Lansburys joined c.1890. Bessie and George were among the early members of this East London group, their names included in the list of subscribers.[28] By 1898 they were well-established members. 'The religion of morality without theology' was what attracted people, albeit in some cases temporarily, to the ethical movement in late Victorian England.[29] Ramsay MacDonald and, perhaps surprisingly, Murray MacDonald moved in ethical circles for a while.

The East London Ethical Society (1890) was one of a number of British ethical societies established after 1886 under the influence of an American humanist, Dr Stanton Coit. Its first public meeting in February 1890 was in a dancing-saloon in Mile End Road. The society moved four years later to a corrugated-iron hall it built in nearby Libra Road in Old Ford. The winter programme of meetings included

Action Commission Report at the 1896 International Congress, Labour History Archive, BAR 6/15/13. For Marion Coates's challenge, see *Justice*, 16, 30 June; 7, 28 July 1894.

[24] For the time when Lansbury 'left the Church' and his children 'attended the Ethical Sunday School in Bow, organised and conducted by the prince of preachers, F. J. Gould', see Lansbury, *My Life*, p. 77.

[25] *Social Democrat*, Jan. 1900.

[26] B. Lightman, 'Robert Elsmere and the Agnostic Crisis of Faith', in R. J. Helmstadter and B. Lightman (eds.), *Victorian Faith in Crisis: Essays on Continuity and Change in Nineteenth-Century Religious Belief* (1990), pp. 283–307.

[27] Lansbury, *My Life*, p. 9. For Tolstoy, see A. N. Wilson, *Tolstoy* (1988), pp. 316–17, 320–5.

[28] East London Ethical Society, *First Annual Report* (1890) [copy in THLLH&A].

[29] For this description by the secularist Labour MP Harry Snell, see H. Snell, *Men, Movements, and Myself* (1936), p. 160.

lectures and discussions on philosophical, moral, and historical themes, and summer gatherings were held in Victoria Park. The society's membership comprised predominantly artisans and clerks. Among the leading local lights were Zona Vallance, daughter of an East End doctor, and an agnostic London School Board teacher, Frederick J. Gould, who ran the Libra Road Sunday School. Those sixty-or-so young members included the four small daughters of Tom Mann, 'a staccato, emphatic orator with pointed moustache and revolutionary menace', and several of the Lansbury children. At the Ethical Sunday School, there was story-telling with humanist themes on personal and social conduct, as well as several trips a year away from an East End environment to museums, Westminster Abbey, the Tower of London (London) Zoo, and the popular Epping Forest. Education was an important aspect of ethicist thinking.[30] The Sunday School must have been popular, too. After cheerfully attending the Ethical Sunday School for many years, one Lansbury daughter, a convinced free-thinker, hid under the bed in anger rather than attend church when her father eventually regained his Christianity.[31]

Among the reasons which drove Lansbury, hitherto a devout Christian of almost puritanical dimensions at times in his youth, into the ethical movement was the official attitude to the casual poor and dispossessed displayed by the Church. What especially disillusioned Lansbury were the local clergy, who believed firmly in a vigorous administration of the relief of poor families in the East End, the line adopted by many in the influential Charity Organisation Society (COS) opposed to any collective response to social need in East London.[32] Interviewed at his sawmill as part of the famous massive survey of London undertaken by the social investigator, Charles Booth, Lansbury was of the opinion that of the local ministers 'there is no one of any influence in the whole of Bow. And as for Bromley there is certainly no one there.' In fact, he believed that those on the political left in the East End had greater influence over the people: 'Nowadays it is rather a case of Victoria Park against the Church and the Park has the advantage.'[33]

When not campaigning in the provinces, Lansbury could be seen regularly in Victoria Park, the traditional venue for recreation, particularly on Sundays, for families from the East End. Over the years, the Park was used for rallies and meetings of all shades of political and religious opinion. Most of the main figures on the political left in London in the 1880s and 1890s addressed large gatherings there: from Henry Hyndman, John Burns, Annie Besant, and William Morris to Ben Tillett, Tom Mann, and George Bernard Shaw. In Victoria Park, as crowds congregated, 'The Forum', as it was known in common parlance, played an important part in the life and culture of the East End, where working people engaged in intellectual discussion and intense political debate on contemporary issues. In 1886 Morris wrote to his daughter Jenny: 'Eastward Ho to Victoria Park . . . It is a rather pretty place

---

[30] F. J. Gould, *The Life-Story of a Humanist* (1923), pp. 76–8. For the East London Ethical Society, see G. Spiller, *The Ethical Movement in Great Britain* (1934), pp. 56–61; for the Ethical movement, see I. D. MacKillop, *The British Ethical Societies* (Cambridge, 1986).
[31] Postgate, *Lansbury*, p. 55.   [32] Holman, *Good Old George*, pp. 33–4.
[33] Charles Booth Papers, B. 178, p. 115.

with water (though dirty) and lots of trees. Had a good meeting, spoke for an hour in a place made noisy by other meetings near, also a brass band not far off.'[34]

Victoria Park was literally a stone's throw from the Lansbury home. By the 1890s, when Lansbury was not campaigning somewhere in the provinces, his booming voice propagated the socialist message of the class struggle and the inherent contradictions of capitalism there, as it did in halls and street-corners throughout Britain, to all and sundry. On these occasions in Victoria Park, his children busied around him selling the latest issue of *Justice* and Blatchford's *Merrie England*. Some years later, another associate of the Lansbury family, Sylvia Pankhurst, drilled her suffragette army in its wide-open spaces.[35]

In Bow, political life centred on the weekly meetings of the Bow and Bromley SDF branch held in the club-room established by Annie Besant for the match-girls. This arrangement began the long political association between George Lansbury and Annie Besant, which continued after her conversion to theosophy and her departure from Britain to India in 1890. At the time their political alliance was a remarkable turn-around in events and demonstrates some important development in Lansbury's thinking on politics and religion. Previously, Lansbury held serious misgivings about the Fabian socialist, on account of her well-publicized views on atheism and birth-control. During the exciting London School Board election of 1888, when Annie Besant headed the poll in the Tower Hamlets Division in a spectacular victory, Lansbury worked hard as the local Liberal agent for Annie's opponent, Revd J. F. Porter.

At this time the SDF branch in Bow and Bromley comprised about forty members, probably all 'Labour aristocrats'. Lansbury's recollections afford some valuable glimpses into the community and fraternity of branch life. Earlier religious associations were not all entirely lost and some lingered in aspects of branch organization and activity:

We were all in good jobs, all very enthusiastic, and convinced that our mission was to revolutionise the world. Our branch meetings were like revivalist gatherings. We opened with a song and closed with one, and often read together some extracts from economic and historical writings . . . every Saturday we ran dances—humorously telling our critics we were going to dance into Socialism . . . We ran an economics study class under comrade Hazell and weekly struggled with *Das Kapital* and Engels's *Socialism Utopian and Scientific.*[36]

Bessie and George's fellow members of the SDF were a cheerful and enthusiastic group, and Lansbury's memoirs provide details of otherwise-unsung heroes of the branch. Among the intellectuals was E. E. Metivier, keeper of the branch records and tireless organizer of meetings—'another blackcoated proletarian' who kept the red flag flying in newspaper columns. On one occasion he enticed William Morris, the artist Walter Crane, and others to campaign successfully against the demolition

[34] Cited in C. Poulson, *Victoria Park: A Study in the History of East London* (1978), pp. 97–101.

[35] On 21 May 1887, the Socialist League arranged a 'No Coercion' rally on Ireland. Original pamphlet in the William Morris Gallery, Walthamstow, cited in P. Mernick and D. Kendall, *A Pictorial History of Victoria Park London E3* (1996), pp. 50–1.

[36] Lansbury, *My Life*, pp. 78–9.

of the ancient Norman Bow church, most probably for aesthetic and environmental reasons. Two closer friends were Alf Augustus Watts, 'A. A.', described as 'a compositor, tall and lean, as befits one whose work [is] at times when the midnight oil is burned'. Lansbury found him 'full of book learning . . . learnt Marx's *Das Kapital* backwards and forwards', painstaking erudition which the autodidactic socialist put to effective use to explain the theory of value and the materialist conception of history to George and Bessie.

The down-to-earth and unconditionally loyal Charlie Sumner was a totally different character: a hard-working and hard-living local chemical-worker and stalwart of the National Union of Gasworkers. He 'knew nothing of economics according to books but . . . had a clearer conception of right and wrong than most experts'. Unlike Lansbury, who abhorred alcohol and drunkenness, Sumner 'liked a tankard of beer or glass of whisky and never concealed the fact'. However, Lansbury readily acknowledged that he 'might well have taken to drinking strong liquor' himself, if subjected to Charlie's 'seven twelve-hour days a week for 30s'.[37]

Some political connections were still maintained by Lansbury outside the Federation. After his breach with the Liberal party, Samuel Montague and Murray MacDonald kept friendly relations with him over a number of years, despite the Federation's vigorous opposition to Liberalism. The personal warmth between the Liberal MP and his former election agent meant that Lansbury consulted Murray MacDonald on confidential aspects of his career and its important effects on his family, long after he had left the Liberal party. It was an unusual friendship across the social and political divide, but one that was important to Lansbury. Murray MacDonald was pleased when Lansbury decided to stand for the local Board of Guardians and in 1893 he also wrote warmly about the possibility of co-operation on the unemployment question in Parliament with the Independent Labour Member for nearby West Ham, Keir Hardie, who had been of direct assistance to Lansbury in his candidate's campaign the previous year.[38] Lansbury continued to consult Murray MacDonald, who was now Liberal MP for Bow and Bromley, at many points of his political career.[39]

By the following year Lansbury himself was drawn into another of those public feuds which had characterized the early years of the Federation. His involvement gives an indication of the position he was beginning to hold in the London organization. In 1894 George Lansbury intervened in the acrimonious correspondence in the radical London paper, the *Star*, between the former executive member of the SDF, John Burns MP, and Henry Mayers Hyndman. The central allegation being touted by Burns, who by this stage had moved close to the Liberal party, was that the Federation was in alliance with the Tories against him in his Battersea constituency. George Lansbury, as the SDF candidate for Walworth, took up the challenge made by H. W. Lee, secretary of the Federation, that Burns 'either . . . prove his statements

---

[37] Ibid. pp. 78–9, 171–2.
[38] J. A. Murray MacDonald to George Lansbury, 24 Nov. 1893, LP, vol. 1, fos. 192–3.
[39] J. A. Murray MacDonald to George Lansbury, 27 Aug. 1895, LP, vol. 1, fos. 265–6. See also, J. A. Murray MacDonald to George Lansbury, 17 Jan. 1894, ibid. fo. 198.

or withdraw them'. Yet Lansbury twisted the knife with an accusation of disloyalty. Burns was no longer a socialist, but directly associated with those he had previously condemned—whose government was now in brutal conflict with the workers: 'The ordinary workman does not understand the difference between killing miners in Yorkshire [at Featherstone in 1893] by law and doing the same thing in Ireland [in the early 1880s] or in Trafalgar Square [in 1887].'

Over the years, constant calumny surrounded the head of the former socialist agitator and leader of the unemployed in 1886–7, and organizer of the London Dock Strike of 1889, for his traitorous desertion of the ranks of his social class. As 'Labour's Lost Leader', Burns associated increasingly with the Liberals and eventually became the first working man to hold a Cabinet post in the December 1905 government.

Lansbury's onslaught, spiced with some venom, heralded future conflict, particularly once he entered Parliament and challenged Burns directly about poor law policy. It also explains the personal animosity between the East End socialist and the future President of the Board of Trade. In 1894 Lansbury took Burns to task for his personal aggrandisement and attacks on other Labour leaders and warned that 'retribution . . . will justly fall on any public man who uses the tomahawk and the scalping knife with which to carve his way to power'.[40]

By now Lansbury was one of the leading spirits in the Federation in London. In 1895 the SDF decided to contest its first parliamentary by-election at Walworth, caused by the death of the Liberal MP, William Saunders, and chose Lansbury to represent the cause.[41] As it happened, Lansbury was to fight the seat twice within a few weeks, as the general election in 1895 was called shortly after the by-election was settled.

In the 1890s Walworth was one of the two constituencies in Newington, a poorer, largely residential district that straddled the part of South London between Camberwell to the west and Southwark to the east. In neighbouring Newington West the local Liberal MP, Capt. Cecil Norton, was a staunch Liberal with a professed interest in Labour questions, but in Walworth itself the electors had more often returned a Conservative Member in the years between 1886 to 1894. Lansbury gave the impression Walworth was promising territory for a socialist candidate. Up to polling day he declared that he expected to take the seat. Privately he could not have been so optimistic about a three-cornered contest. Murray MacDonald told him to fight on: 'I can understand your feelings about your own candidature. But you have put your hand to the plough, and you will have to go resolutely through with the work'. Three days later MacDonald tactfully declined to speak on a Federation platform. As he told his old friend, his 'judgement' was with Reade, but his 'personal feelings' were with Lansbury.[42]

Considerable support for the Lansbury candidature was, however, available

[40] *Star*, 25 Jan. 1894.
[41] For George Lansbury's account of his first parliamentary election, see Lansbury, *My Life*, pp. 110–11; Lansbury, *Looking Backwards and Forwards* (1935), pp. 76–82.
[42] J. A. Murray MacDonald to George Lansbury, 3, 6 May 1895, vol. 1, fos. 238–9, 240–1.

from those on the political left. Hyndman, Harry Quelch, the editor of *Justice*, Keir Hardie, and William Morris all spoke on his behalf. Dr and Mrs Pankhurst campaigned for him, another glimpse of the growing importance of the women's question in his politics.

He was, however, open to the charge that as a Socialist candidate in a three-cornered contest, he would split the progressive vote, thereby giving victory to the Conservative candidate, James Bailey.[43] Within two hours of the close of polling, the announcement of the result swept away any remaining illusions that Lansbury might have retained about victory:

James Bailey (Con.)	2,676
Col. Colquhoun Reade (Lib.)	2,105
George Lansbury (Socialist)	347
Majority	571

Despite achieving a paltry vote, within a few weeks Lansbury was back again in Walworth to fight the seat in the 1895 general election. As required of all candidates under the Federation red flag, Lansbury put forward the Marxist programme of the Social Democratic Federation: 'The socialisation of the Means of Production, Distribution and Exchange, to be controlled by a Democratic state in the interests of the entire community, and the Complete Emancipation of Labour from the Domination of Capitalism and Landlordism, with the establishment of Social and Economic Equality between the Sexes.'

But on this occasion he compiled his own election address, and his inclusion of a poem by Russell Lowell brought a wrathful inquiry by Hyndman as to whether 'the electors were a lot of fools or sloppy sentimentalists'.[44]

Lansbury's brief descriptions of his two election campaigns in 1895 provide an insight into the problems faced by a working-class candidate who 'used to tramp from Bow to Walworth night after night to do the canvassing and propaganda'. *Justice* supported his campaign with enthusiasm, noting 'the returning officer's fees are banked, and the money will, therefore, be forthcoming', but his election expenditure was the lowest by far of the three candidates.[45] The official return for the general election contest reveals that Lansbury spent £60 on his campaign, compared to £563 for the re-elected Bailey and £343 for the Liberal Russell Spokes.[46]

Lansbury finished bottom of the poll in the by-election on 14 May 1895, with 6.8 per cent of the votes cast. Six weeks later, at the general election, in another three-cornered contest, he secured only 203 votes, just 3.8 per cent of the poll. The other three SDF candidates fared little better, including H. M. Hyndman defeated at Burnley; all four candidates totalled fewer than 4,000 votes each.

---

[43] *South London Press*, 4, 18 May 1895; *Justice*, 11, 18 May 1895; *The Times*, 6–11, 13–15 May 1895; *Manchester Guardian*, 8–11, 13–15 May 1895.
[44] Lansbury, *My Life*, p. 111.   [45] *Justice*, 11 May 1895.
[46] 'Return of charges made to Candidates at the General Election of 1895 in Great Britain, and Ireland by Returning Officers, specifying the Total Expenses of each Candidate', *Parliamentary Papers*, lxvii, 1896 (Accounts and Papers, 19) (HC 145).

Before the general election, Lansbury had produced a challenging and well-argued public critique of the Liberal ministry.[47] The government's abject failure to implement urgent social and political reforms, including the Newcastle and London programmes which they had announced, confirmed Lansbury's total disenchantment with Liberalism. According to the thirty-six-year-old SDF candidate, only a new political party committed firmly to socialism could provide radical solutions for the unemployed, the aged, and the sick. 'The workers, who for fifty years have looked to the middle-class Liberal party for help, are gradually deserting it, and forming themselves into a compact body for the working out of their own salvation', he announced.[48]

The dismal 1895 results for the SDF, which demonstrated that considerable political work had still to be undertaken, provided Lansbury with his next role in British politics. Already a well-known voluntary propagandist within the Federation ranks, for twelve months he became its full-time salaried national organizer and most important asset.

Hyndman had recruited an activist of note for the Federation and gave the business arrangements his careful personal attention. He reassured Lansbury that he had made the right decision to leave his employment at the family sawmill:

From my point of view the great thing is to see that your salary is always paid up in advance. I put this very strongly on Tuesday week as I know that nobody can work his best until his bread and butter at any rate is secure. I quite understand and appreciate your disinclination on the one hand to give up business and working gratuitously for the SDF, and on the other hand to accepting any pay from the organisation.[49]

Despite this reassurance, Lansbury had hesitated in becoming the full-time, paid worker for the Federation in uncertain political times, since he and Bessie had a young and growing family. Hyndman also made it abundantly clear what would be expected from the new officer. 'It will be a very great mistake if you overdo your voice. What we need now is organisation and discipline more than agitation and I think also it is necessary that the funds should be better seen to', he declared.[50]

Lansbury's Federation post took him all over the country and extended his work for the socialist cause. Audiences ranged in size from small gatherings in villages to larger demonstrations and meetings in town-centres. There was scarcely a part of Britain he did not visit, whether to start a new branch or to give help to revive an ailing one. Hyndman declared him 'on the whole the best organizer the Social-Democratic Federation ever had'.[51] His contributions to *Justice* in the form of monthly reports, articles, and other jottings of his activities provide valuable insights into SDF politics, particularly at branch level.

During late November–early December 1895, Lansbury undertook a two-week tour of Lancashire, addressing sixteen meetings in nearly as many towns. Typical of his work was the meeting on 26 November 1895 at Todmorden, following the

[47] G. Lansbury, 'A Socialist View of the Government', *National Review*, 25, June 1895, pp. 564–70.
[48] Ibid. p. 569.   [49] H. M. Hyndman to George Lansbury, 25 Aug. 1895, LP, vol. 1, fo. 267.
[50] Ibid.   [51] H. M. Hyndman, *Further Reminiscences* (1912), p. 283.

opening of a new Socialist Room at the SDF club in Brunswick Street, Bortons, Walsden. Comrade George Lansbury, national organizer of the SDF and by then newly endorsed Parliamentary candidate for Bow and Bromley, delivered a lecture on the shortcomings of capitalism and the benefits of socialism. His talk opened with a denunciation of conventional party politics practised by their opponents, the Liberals and Tories, as part of the modern competitive capitalist system. 'He did not care whether they called themselves Liberals or Tories . . . they were owned and controlled by someone else', he declared. In his critique of capitalism, Lansbury was prepared even to acknowledge the existence of benign employers but added that 'if their employers were angels . . . they would still have to do shady things or otherwise go to the wall, owing to the iron law of competition.'[52] His audience was also told about the inevitability of recurrent crises and the final collapse of capitalism, as well as the next evolutionary stage when the working class would live in a socialist society. Lansbury put forward a promising prospect: 'the time had arrived for the working classes to seize political power and use it to overthrow . . . the competitive system . . . and establish in its place state co-operation . . .'[53]

Wherever George Lansbury travelled, he preached the gospel of social democracy derived, at this point in his political life, from the scientific analysis of Marxism. Marxist stock in trade, such as the surplus value of labour and the materialist conception of history, was translated into everyday terms to explain what could be achieved to overcome poverty, unemployment, and similar social evils inherent in capitalism. In typical Lansbury fashion, which was to become the hallmark of his performances on public platforms for the next forty years, his main message expressed in simple unmistakable language—on this occasion, that 'society could be transformed from competition to social democracy . . . The only enemy they had to fight was capitalism, and the only way . . . by joining hands together . . . [socialism] was the highest and noblest ideal of society'—was repeated again and again.

Typically, at the end there was a final flourish. At Todmorden, Lansbury gave a clarion call for solidarity, preceded by a prediction of the shortened working day he had heard uttered by Hyndman many years before: ' "about three hours work per day would keep them at a standard of comfort none of them dreamed of at the present time. The only enemy they had to fight was capitalism, and the only way they could fight it was by joining hands together." (Applause)'[54]

Back in London there was other valuable work to be undertaken to improve Federation organization. In October–November 1895, *Justice* published four articles by Lansbury with detailed guidance on improving branch organization. His recommendations included the appointment for each branch of branch secretary, weekly chairman, librarian, treasurer, six visitors (to collect subscriptions), assistant officers, and committee, as well as the use of a prominent meeting-place in the centre of the division. Meetings should be at least once a week, as every member possessed 'some special talent which is needed in the work of a branch'.[55] In London

---

[52] *Todmorden Advertiser and Hebden Bridge Newsletter*, 29 Nov. 1895.
[53] Ibid.   [54] Ibid.   [55] *Justice*, 12 Oct. 1895.

he advocated large-scale meetings 'instead of wasting the time and energy of our lecturers on small audiences of twenty or twenty-five people, most of whom are Socialists'. Open-air meetings were the most effective training-ground for new speakers and propaganda work throughout the country.

However, this particular phase came to an unexpected end. In 1896 his father-in-law, Isaac Brine, died and Lansbury resigned as national organizer to return home to manage the family sawmill and timber yard. Lansbury remained an active member of the Federation and on the executive from 1895 for some years. At the 1896 International Socialist Congress in London he had to try to placate delegates, angered by the admission of anarchists, before presenting a report on political action.[56] His attention to local matters in the East End did not waiver. In 1898, during the severe water famine that hit the East End during the summer, he led an important deputation to Westminster to raise serious concerns about the incompetence and corruption of the London water companies.[57] As we shall see, he was also willing to stand again in the parliamentary cause at the next election on his home territory of Bow and Bromley.

As Keith Laybourn has shown, after 1884 the SDF was at the heart of the abortive 'socialist unity' debates conducted at various times on the most effective means to promote and advance socialism in Britain.[58] The debates intensified after the severe reversal of political fortunes for the socialists that gave a derisory total of around 40,000 votes at the 1895 general election to thirty-two candidates for the ILP and SDF. After the catastrophic defeat of all twenty-eight ILP candidates, including Keir Hardie, the ILP decided on a change of political strategy, switching to the idea of the 'Labour Alliance'—active co-operation between socialist groups and the trade union movement, although this was to be somewhat short of unity.[59]

The SDF continued its policy of 'making socialists' and campaigning on specific issues, such as unemployment. But, following its costly involvement in the Southampton by-election of 1896, where Lansbury had been involved as national organizer, the SDF also considered including working with trade unions as part of its overall political strategy. The by-election had one other important outcome in the divisions between George Lansbury and Ramsay MacDonald, who unsuccessfully contested Southampton in the 1895 general election but withdrew from the subsequent by-election. An angry MacDonald stated: 'I think in the past there has been too much street corner shouting on the part of the socialist . . . there will be no united Socialist party in the country so long as the Social Democratic Federation continues its present attitude.'[60]

---

[56] Y. Knapp, *Eleanor Marx: The Clouded Years, 1884–1898* (1976), pp. 656–64; C. Tsuzuki, *Life of Eleanor Marx, 1855–1898: A Socialist Tragedy* (1967), pp. 284–6.

[57] *Justice*, 1 Oct. 1898. To increase the water supply, Lansbury also pressed the Bow Vestry to sink various 'Abyssinian Wells' (*sic*), including one in the grounds of the Poplar workhouse. George Lansbury to Chairman of Bow Vestry, 6 Sept. 1898, Lansbury Collection, THLLH&A.

[58] K. Laybourn, 'The Failure of Socialist Unity in Britain, 1893–1914', *Transactions of the Royal Historical Society*, 6th ser., 4 (1994), pp. 153–75.

[59] Morgan, *Keir Hardie*, p. 89.

[60] *Bristol Evening News*, 22 Feb. 1896, quoted in *Justice*, 31 March 1896.

On the left, different schemes were advanced to unite or 'fuse' socialists in one party with a common cause in British politics. As national organizer, Lansbury pointed out that

for at least fourteen years there has been such a party in existence . . . It is a National Socialist Society which shall take political action . . . altogether face the convenience or otherwise of the two great factions, a Society to be managed and controlled by its members . . . Well, this is exactly what the SDF has been and is.[61]

Nevertheless, in 1897–8, the debate over 'fusion or federation' revealed differences between the leadership and the rank and file in both political organizations. At the 1896 and 1897 ILP conferences, delegates pressed for negotiations to be renewed with the SDF. Lansbury was one of the SDF team (with Hyndman, Quelch, Lee, and Barwick) that met Hardie, MacDonald, Mann, and Russell Smart in 1897.[62] Towards the end of 1898 the debate had fizzled out, as revealed by the published correspondence between the ILP and SDF secretaries, John Penny and W. H. Lee. The SDF, at its annual conference in Edinburgh, 'instructed the Council of the SDF to use every effort to bring about the fusion of the two Socialist organisations', following an earlier majority vote of the two organizations in favour of fusion. But the vote was never implemented and delaying tactics by the ILP leadership, principally Hardie supported by Bruce Glasier, scotched the snake.[63]

None the less, within the next two years events occurred which shaped the remainder of Lansbury's life. His religious faith began to return, and he was restored to Christianity and the Anglican Church. On 27 and 28 February 1900 the two-day conference on Labour Representation, convened by the Parliamentary Committee of the Trades Union Congress (TUC), opened in London. In 1900 it was an event of historic importance, though barely noticed in the middle of the South African War by the British press.

At the conference 129 delegates, representing 568,177 members of over sixty trade societies and the Fabian Society, ILP, and SDF, gathered in the Memorial Hall in Clerkenwell, the scene of many important meetings in the labour world. George Lansbury was not present on this august occasion, and the Federation delegation consisted of Harry Quelch, H. R. Taylor, James MacDonald, and M. Judge. Will Thorne led a thirty-strong group of representatives of the Gasworkers and General Labourers, Lansbury's union since 1889.[64]

As we shall learn, George Lansbury stood in the general election of 1900 as the SDF candidate for Bow and Bromley endorsed under the auspices of the Labour Representation Committee (LRC). The new body represented the effective and permanent alliance of trade unionists and socialists which had been envisaged for some time. It marked the arrival of the Labour Party, the name adopted in 1906, in which Lansbury was to spend the rest of his political career.

Within a year, however, the SDF made the disastrous decision to secede from the

---

[61] *Justice*, 5 Oct. 1895.   [62] Ibid. 17 Aug. 1897.   [63] Ibid. 27 Aug. 1898.
[64] *Report of the Conference on Labour Representation Held in the Memorial Hall, Farringdon Street, London EC on Tuesday, the 27 February, 1900* (1900).

new party. Disappointed over this outcome, and exasperated by the splits within the Federation and its attitude to organized religion, in *c.*1903 George Lansbury left the SDF to join the ILP, another step on his route to the modern Labour party.[65]

George Lansbury's years in the ranks of the Federation, which Postgate quickly passes over in his biography, should not be underestimated or ignored. As the Christian Pacifist leader of the Labour party in the desolate years after 1931, George Lansbury displayed the political skills largely gained from his experience as the national organizer for the SDF. Sixty years after his death, the modern Labour party may not realize, or may wish to forget, that for more than ten years its most popular leader was the leading light of the Marxist SDF and its salaried national organizer. Three times Lansbury ran as an SDF parliamentary candidate, including the two contests at Walworth—the location of John Smith House, the former headquarters of the modern Labour party.

[65] For the splits within the SDF, see Crick, *History of the Social-Democratic Federation*, pp. 97–102; C. Tsuzuki, 'The "Impossibilist" Revolt in Britain', *International Review of Social History*, 1 (1956), pp. 377–97.

4
The People's Guardian, 1893–1914

'Abandon hope all ye who enter here' was George Lansbury's verdict as a newly elected guardian after his first memorable visit to the workhouse in Poplar High Street in 1893 revealed its formidable Bastille-like environment. Sick and aged, mentally deficient, lunatics, babies and children, as well as the able-bodied and vagrants, were all crowded together in the single institution which was the hated symbol of the Victorian poor law. Throughout his life Lansbury was more popularly linked with the battle to end working-class poverty, destitution, and unemployment than any other cause. By 1929, when the local authorities assumed responsibility for poor law administration, no one was more identified than Lansbury with the various crusades to reform and ultimately abolish the horrors of the Victorian system, which had cast a long shadow over social provision during the nineteenth and twentieth centuries.

From 1893 George Lansbury, the people's politician, held the office of poor law guardian continuously for over thirty-five years with a single objective. As he put it: 'From the first moment I determined to fight for one policy only, and that was decent treatment for the poor outside the workhouse, and hang the rates!'[1] This famous clarion call epitomized the pioneers in the East End labour and socialist movement who saw themselves as guardians of the poor, rather than guardians of an infamous poor law. Their fame, or notoriety, derived from their uncompromising use of every legal loophole in the poor law administration to defend the living standards of the working-class community they came from and defiantly represented. In 1921 Lansbury's mobilization of the unemployed and dispossessed, first seen in their lobbying the local guardians in the 1890s, produced the celebrated propaganda triumph of the Poplar Rates Rebellion, whereby thirty councillors deliberately went to prison in a defence of their local community. 'Poplarism' with its roots in the pre-war action of the Poplar guardians was added to the political vocabulary in the 1920s and became the symbol of local defiance of central government.

In the late nineteenth century the Poplar Board of Guardians covered the three civil parishes: Bow, Bromley St Leonards, and All Saints, Poplar, an area of East London that coincided with the Metropolitan Borough of Poplar established in 1889. Within these boundaries were two parliamentary constituencies: in the northern part, Bow and Bromley and, to the south, Poplar itself. This district was part of the East London investigated during Charles Booth's massive seventeen-volume

---

[1] Lansbury, *My Life*, p. 133.

survey of poverty, industry, and religion.[2] He described the predominantly working-class area as:

Poplar, a huge district, consists of the subdivisions of Bow and Bromley as well as Poplar proper. Bow includes Old Ford and Poplar itself includes the Isle of Dogs—transformed now into an Isle of Ducks. In all it is a vast township, built, much of it, on low marshland, bounded in the east by the River Lea and on the south by a great bend in the Thames. In North Bow and the outlying parts there is a great deal of jerry building . . . among the early troubles of these streets are fevers . . .[3]

In effect, the East End was a city of 2 million inhabitants within the imperial metropolis of London, by then the largest conurbation in the world. However, the term 'East End' was easy to portray, but difficult to define exactly. In 1902, a cockney cab driver admitted to his fare—the visiting American novelist, Jack London—that he didn't know where the 'East End' was. According to Bill Fishman it was the geographical district bordered by the City of London to the west, the River Lea to the East, Hackney and Shoreditch to the north. The River Thames marked out its southern limits. It was a cosmopolitan area, dominated by the Thames and its shipping trade, and with a long history, resplendent with tradition and custom. Over the centuries, successive waves of immigrants—French Huguenots, Irish peasants, and many other nationalities—had settled among the residents of East London, contributing to its many trades. In the late nineteenth century, large numbers of Jews—fleeing political persecution in Eastern Europe—arrived in England and joined established Jewish communities. Many put down roots in the East End in Whitechapel, Mile End, and Stepney.

As Peter Ackroyd has written, the East End was always known as the home of the working poor. By the late Victorian period, what were termed as 'the dirty trades', processing or manufacturing noxious substances, such as chemicals, dyes, and paint, had located in Bow, Old Ford, and Stratford to the east, and were cheek by jowl with match-making and clothing and furniture manufacture. Larger enterprises included the Beckton gasworks and the expansive docklands that made London the largest port in the world.

Perceptions of human distress allied to heathen immorality in the East End attracted social investigators and religious missionaries, and led to the establishment of middle-class university settlements to tackle its poverty, social deprivation, and associated wickedness. A fashionable image of the 'East End', encapsulated in the title of 'The Bitter Cry of Outcast London'—Andrew Mearns's celebrated pamphlet—evoked a picture of slums, chronic unemployment, and destitution, as well as notorious crimes in gas-lit alleys and courts, such as the 'Jack the Ripper' murders. In reality, though the lives of the inhabitants of East London had interested Dickens and Mayhew, this 'East End' was the creation of later writers,

---

[2] For Booth's survey, see D. Englander and R. O'Day (eds.), *Retrieved Riches: Social Investigation in Britain, 1840–1914* (1995).
[3] C. Booth (ed.), *Life and Labour of the People of London*, i, *East, Central and South London* (1892), 71.

novelists, and journalists around the 1880s, among them Walter Besant, George Sims, and Arthur Morrison.[4]

As a political heartland, the East End gave Lansbury his identity along with others who spoke for and served their neighbourhoods, such as another son of Poplar, Will Crooks.[5] They represented a cluster of varied districts and distinct communities that belied popular perceptions drawn from the late Victorian press and literature. As Booth's immense social survey also demonstrated, there was a different side to Cockney life, besides the poverty, violence, and criminality, that included theatres, music halls, and traditional fairs and festivals.

By the late nineteenth century, this part of London was clearly associated with the working class, radicalism, and the threat of potential public disorder. In the previous twenty years or so before 1893 an inexorable exodus of wealth denuded the East End of propertied and professional groups. Instead, the East End, close to Westminster and to the financial centre of the City, was like a dagger at the heart of the government of the capital, whose respectable citizens boarded up their windows during the unemployed disturbances of 1886–7.

Most of the characteristics of 'Outcast London' were endemic in Poplar: chronic unemployment, poor housing and extremes of poverty and destitution.[6] Perhaps not as poor as the destitute inner East End districts administered by the guardians of St George's in the East, Whitechapel, and Stepney, nevertheless, Poplar contained a high percentage of the casual poor below the poverty-line. Only a small number of craftsmen and skilled artisans, as well as a few middle-class residents made up the remainder of the inhabitants. In 1906 Lansbury told the Davy Inquiry that the well-heeled ship-owners and monied merchants connected with the docks, the major industrial and commercial heart of Poplar, had fled the East India Dock Road to move outside the district. As Lansbury so famously put it at the time of the Rates Rebellion, the community of Poplar he represented as guardian, councillor, and later MP was populated by only one social class—the working class.

After the First World War, the Labour party swept to power in Poplar and dominated municipal affairs to the exclusion of other political parties. From 1922 the two constituencies consistently returned Labour MPs to Westminster. But in pre-war party politics the political left consisted at first of two main groups who ran candidates for the board of guardians and other local bodies: the Poplar Labour League and the Bow and Bromley branch of the SDF. Founded in 1891 by local new

---

[4] This brief description of the East End (broadly represented since 1965 by the Boroughs of Tower Hamlets and Newham) draws heavily on W. J. Fishman, *East End, 1888: A Year in the Life of a London Borough among the Labouring Poor* (1988); P. Ackroyd, *London: The Biography* (2000), pp. 675–84; A. Palmer, *The East End: Four Centuries of London Life* (1989); P. J. Keating, 'Fact and Fiction in the East End', in H. J. Dyos and M. Woolff (eds.), *The Victorian City: Images and Reality*, ii (1999), pp. 585–602; J. Schneer, *London, 1900: The Imperial Metropolis* (New Haven, Conn., 1999).

[5] J. Lawrence, *Speaking for the People: Party, Language and Popular Politics in England, 1867–1914* (Cambridge, 1998), pp. 237–9.

[6] For a classic study, see G. S. Jones, *Outcast London: A Study in the Relationship between Classes in Victorian Society* (1971); for two important accounts of Poplar, see P. Ryan, '"Poplarism", 1894–1930', in P. Thane (ed.), *The Origins of British Social Policy* (1978), pp. 56–83; F. Bedarida, 'Urban Growth and Social Structure in Nineteenth-Century Poplar', *London Journal*, 1 (1975), pp. 159–88.

unionists and progressive clergy the Poplar Labour League, a broadly Lib–Lab body active in progressive politics, within four years returned working class representatives to most of the local bodies. The first notable victory was the election of Will Crooks to the London County Council in 1892. The League raised a voluntary wages fund to support its rugged champion of the working class and son of Poplar, who became its first Labour mayor in 1901 and two years later triumphed in the famous Woolwich parliamentary by-election.

The local branch of the SDF which George Lansbury and his fellow ex-Liberals started was the other left-wing group to contest local elections, but with a more militant socialist stance than the League. In the pre-war period these two groupings, sometimes in conflict over social policy on unemployment, provided an influential and dominating minority presence on municipal bodies in Poplar. In *c.*1903 Lansbury and others broke away from the SDF to start a local branch of the ILP which eventually affiliated to the Poplar Labour Representation Committee and Trades Council, the beginnings of a strong local Labour party.

Poplar was one of the districts where an emergent socialism combined with a strong radical tradition in municipal politics. Alliances formed on the left among radical and socialist groups who shared a common approach to the municipal problems of housing, unemployment, poverty, and destitution. The creation of the LCC in 1889 had led to a revival of London radicalism and the establishment of the Progressive Party, usually of Radicals, advanced Liberals, and Labour, to contest local elections on a programme of municipal and democratic reform. As Pat Thane has shown, in London particular successes were achieved by such alliances in local government in Battersea, West Ham, Woolwich, and in Bow and Bromley with the Poplar Labour League.[7] At times Lansbury was willing to co-operate with local Liberals in municipal affairs and his political association and personal friendship with J. A. Murray MacDonald, the Liberal MP for Bow and Bromley from 1892 to 1895 was an individual example of this progressive alliance.

In 1893 there was a similar alliance when George Lansbury, veneer-dryer, and William Purdy, a local bricklayer, stood as the SDF and Liberal candidates respectively for the guardians' elections in the parish of Bow with a comprehensive twelve-point programme of reform. Despite some improvements at the end of the century, such as the provision for the aged poor and children, after sixty years the Victorian poor law still remained the last refuge for the destitute in society and was held in dread by working people. In some places outdoor relief was given, but this was subject to attempts to curtail or abolish it by the Local Government Board, the government body responsible for the central regulation of the poor law administration.

When Lansbury became a poor law guardian, pauperism had lost none of the traditional stigma attached to it. Poor relief and medical treatment were normally only available in the workhouse, and entering it was akin to committal to prison in

[7] P. Thane, 'Labour and Local Politics: Radicalism, Democracy and Social Reform', in E. F. Biagini and A. J. Reid (eds.), *Currents of Radicalism: Popular Radicalism, Organized Labour and Party Politics in Britain, 1850–1914* (1991), pp. 248–52.

Victorian society. Families were broken up on entering the workhouse; conditions inside were dreary and austere, if no longer cruel. Oakum-picking, stone-breaking, and other menial tasks were still commonplace for the inmates. There was no greater stigma in Victorian society than the pauper's funeral.

To turn the workhouse into an 'agency of help instead of a place of despair', Lansbury and Purdy proposed a more humane treatment of the poor in their Federation manifesto: the abolition of pauper dress, better workhouse conditions, and improved medical facilities. In particular, the taint of pauperism would be removed from the welfare and education of very poor children. Old age pensions for the aged poor were also advocated, fifteen years before their introduction. An eight-hour working day and trade union wages were stipulated for firms that took on any contracted work from the guardians.

There were long-standing political objectives as well: principally, the demand that Lansbury hammered away at for years for the equalization of the rates throughout London to share the cost of relief and thereby benefit the poorer East End districts afflicted by a greater incidence of pauperism. In the 1890s guardians' elections remained antiquated affairs, and hardly democratic, with ballot papers delivered to the homes of ratepayers and collected by hand. Also included, therefore, were proposals to reform this electoral system by the abolition of *ex officio* members, plural voting, and the property qualification for candidates.

Lansbury also firmly believed that the responsibilities of guardians extended beyond dealing with paupers to the provision of work for the able-bodied unemployed outside the workhouse. He was to pursue this conviction with great energy and dedication. But the proposal to establish labour colonies 'for the treatment of the habitual casual and repression of the loafer', included in his 1893 manifesto, also reveals a hard line attitude towards the work-shy, characteristic of even those on the progressive left in late Victorian politics.[8]

George Lansbury later recalled 'I was first elected in 1892, when I was thirty-three years of age', but he actually became a guardian a year later. He was the fourth candidate returned in the St Mary Stratford ward in Bow, with 1,109 votes, in the guardians' elections of April 1893, but the Liberal, William Purdy, was not elected.[9]

The Poplar Board comprised twenty-four guardians, but Lansbury and Crooks led a minority of five Labour and Socialist members whose influence was out of all proportion to their numerical representation. The Poplar Board consisted of chemists, doctors, clergy, undertakers, house agents, and a representative of the London and India Dock Company. Most were freemasons, for whom Lansbury reserved some sharp criticism about cronyism and abuse within the poor law system:

You scratch my back and I'll scratch yours was the kind of policy where jobs and contracts were concerned . . . You see, the slum owner and agent could be depended upon to create the

---

[8] Election of Guardians Leaflet, Parish of Bow, Programme of the Bow and Bromley Branch of the Social Democratic Federation, LP, Apr. 1893, vol. 1, fo. 186.

[9] *East End News*, 14 Apr. 1893.

conditions which produce disease: the doctor would then get the job of attending the sick, the chemist would be needed to supply drugs, the parson to pray, and when, between them all, the victims died, the undertaker was on hand to bury them.[10]

The *East London Observer*, the oldest local newspaper in the East End and a critic of the new Socialist and Labour members, argued that by regular attendance the group dominated the Board and exerted an undue influence over other Radical guardians:

There are five Labour members, . . . eight members . . . opposed to the advanced policy . . . three members who were elected on . . . a Radical ticket . . . consistently (support) the Labour members . . . and . . . three members who vote sometimes one way and sometimes the other . . . thus . . . a determined faction, though small could influence the Board; and this is exactly what the Labour party has done.[11]

Despite some initial setbacks, such as the failure to secure evening meetings at 6 p.m., Lansbury and Crooks achieved a considerable number of important and mainly non-contentious reforms of the local poor law along the lines of Lansbury's manifesto.[12] In Lansbury's own words 'with their assistance [the new master and matron] and good advice from Mrs Crooks and Mrs Lena Wilson [one of the first women SDF guardians in the country elected to the Poplar Board in 1894], we revolutionized the place from top to bottom'.[13] Pauper clothing was abolished, a varied and improved diet introduced, and greater freedom allowed to inmates, particularly in terms of temporary leave for the aged poor. Irregularities in the administration of the workhouse were investigated, local officials prosecuted and then pensioned off.[14]

Lansbury took a particular interest in the welfare and education of pauper children, as well as in improving family life in general, in municipal politics. By 1900 he reported to the Bow and Bromley branch of the SDF on the developments in Forest Gate District School to which Poplar children were sent. Lansbury worked closely with Lena Wilson to persuade the Board to abolish the school uniform, pension off the teacher of tailoring, and appoint new teaching staff for tailoring, boot-making, and other vocational subjects. The diet was also improved and according to a delighted George Lansbury, the benefits displayed in the on-field performances by the boys' football club.[15] Within a few years the use of Forest Gate was abandoned. Poplar guardians removed their children to the newly constructed Shenfield School near Brentwood in the Essex countryside. Many of the surviving photographs show Lansbury surrounded by children—and not only his own large family of children and grandchildren. Children and their street songs—'Vote, vote, vote for Mr Lansbury'—featured in his many election campaigns. Much of his later work as First

---

[10] Lansbury, *My Life*, pp. 134–5.   [11] *East London Observer*, 15 Dec. 1894.
[12] Ibid. 3 May 1893.   [13] Lansbury, *My Life*, pp. 135–8.
[14] For Lansbury's efforts to transform the management of the Poplar workhouse, including an unforgettable clash with the chief officer over the inmates' oatmeal porridge, riddled with rat- and mice-droppings, see Lansbury, *My Life*, 136–7.
[15] Ibid. 17 Feb. 1900.

Commissioner of Works centred on his sincere desire to improve recreational facilities for children and families. This genuine affection is well illustrated in an oft-mentioned Lansbury story. When Queen Mary arrived at Shenfield, regarded as a model poor law school, the children swept past the distinguished visitor to greet instead their beloved George Lansbury.

The editorial comments of the *East London Observer* notwithstanding, not all was plain sailing over poor law policy, even within the ranks of the Labour members on the Poplar Board. In April 1895 Lansbury, who had been chairman from January, was defeated by ten votes to six for the chairmanship.[16] In early 1895 the working-class representatives on the Poplar Board of Guardians were bitterly divided, ostensibly over the opening of the stone-yards for the relief of the unemployed. In the severe winter of 1895 Lansbury was in favour of the policy, but was sternly opposed by Crooks and Mercer who wanted to grant outdoor relief without work. Lansbury denounced Crooks in the strongest terms in public:

Now . . . my writing this article is not so much to attack individuals as it is to call attention to the policy pursued by the Progressive and Labour men . . . I have worked with Will Crooks for two years in Poor Law work . . . he is a most dangerous reactionary force. In the East End he is trying the same game of bluff as his god Burns is playing . . . the Progressive Labour men are no longer labour representatives, they are servants of those who find the money . . . to some of us, myself especially, it is very unpleasant . . . what I have said here about other men . . . but . . . our cause is superior to all persons . . . it is [hoped] that this short article will have the effect of either driving Crooks and Mercer clean away [to the enemy] or making them see the error of their ways . . .[17]

Lansbury's outburst in *Justice* against the popular Will Crooks may appear out of character, when his reputation for humanitarianism is considered. But on poor law matters, he remained a militant socialist.

As an active municipal politician, the demands were considerable, varied, and unending. The list of the official positions Lansbury held in connection with the poor law alone gives an indication of the calls on his time. By 1906 he had been a member of the Poplar Board and its committees continuously for thirteen years, as well as Poplar councillor since November 1903. He was chair of the Works Committee (in 1903–6), the Schools Committee (since 1895), and the Farm Committee (from January 1904). He was a frequent visitor to the labour colonies established by the Poplar guardians at Laindon and Hollesley Bay to resettle unemployed East End workmen back on the land. Several times he was a delegate at the annual conference of poor law guardians, as well as serving on the Central (Unemployed) Body (CUB) in London. Lansbury also wrote on social policy and led deputations to Whitehall. As his reputation spread in poor law circles, invitations soon followed to give evidence to official inquiries and commissions.

Lansbury's political work was underpinned by his strong belief in democratic participation and public accountability to those who elected him. His passionate commitment towards the local community was clearly evident at his first annual

---

[16] Poplar Board of Guardians, Minutes, 22 Apr. 1895. [17] *Justice*, 23 Mar. 1895.

poor law conference, attended by delegates from Boards of Guardians throughout England and Wales. In November 1893 the two-day Central Conference was held at St Martin's Town Hall in Charing Cross under the chairmanship of the powerful Conservative MP for South Leicestershire, Albert Pell. The Local Government Board regularly lauded his Brixworth Board of Guardians as a model union, an example of impressive financial stringency and strict relief policy. Pell brought the conference forward six weeks to consider the Local Government Bill, particularly the proposals to remove virtually all qualifications for the office of guardian and abolish plural voting at elections.[18]

At the conference Thomas Mackay's paper on the impact of these changes articulated widespread fears about future working-class influence on the boards and at guardians' elections, were the bill to become law. Mackay, author of *A History of the English Poor Law*, was the hard-line Secretary of the COS in St George in the East, one of the poorest areas of the East End, and a leading advocate of the abolition of outdoor relief. The rampant George Lansbury was unable to restrain himself and picked up the cudgels for a cause he believed in:

The extraordinary statements . . . [about] the working classes made it imperative on me to come on this platform and contradict them . . . you have been told that if the bill passes you will have working men members . . . Well, you have already got working men . . . [as] guardians. I am a member of the Poplar Union, and I am a working man on that board . . .[19]

This declaration of his proletarian credentials was swiftly followed by Lansbury's proposal for salaried guardians. To the consternation of the volunteer guardians present, he also denounced corruption in the system:

I am an advocate for the payment of Poor Law guardians—(cries of 'No, no,' and 'Oh')—and for the payment of any other man who performs a public service . . . I say that the boards of guardians . . . get paid in a very roundabout sort of manner. (Cries of 'Oh' and interruption). They find jobs for their friends . . . (Uproar.)

The CHAIRMAN: Order, order. (Cries of 'Shame.') Please give everybody a fair hearing. (Interruption.)[20]

At his first conference Lansbury publicly and proudly identified himself as a working-class member of an overwhelmingly middle-class assemblage. His direct assault was hardly surprising, in view of the concerns he heard expressed around him. On this first occasion George Lansbury's parting shot was to remind the delegates that democracy had come at last to the Boards of Guardians: ' "you have heard this morning . . . how the working men of the country will administer the Poor Law . . . the Poor Law will be administered not for the benefit of classes but for the benefit of the whole community." (Interruption . . .)'[21]

The next day Lansbury was back to point out the scourge of unemployment in Britain and to challenge the assembled guardians to develop a wider perspective on

[18] A. Brundage, 'Reform of the Poor Law Electoral System, 1834–94', *Albion*, 7 (1975), pp. 206–11.
[19] *Report of the Twenty-First Central Poor Law Conference, 8–9 November 1893*.
[20] Ibid.   [21] Ibid.

the causes of poverty in late Victorian Britain. 'There is an unemployment problem, which if you do not grapple with it, other people will, and in a more rough-and-ready manner than the guardians'—a direct reference to the Federation's strategy of organizing the unemployed and the possibility of social disturbances again in British cities.

When Lansbury next addressed the annual Central Poor Law Conference, held in the Council Chamber of the Guildhall in London in 1896, his theme was a familiar one—that greater attention should be given to providing for the unemployed within the Victorian poor law system. Underpinning his contribution was a burning denunciation of the capitalist system:

You are obliged to have a reserve of labour under the present system. If the Poor Law is to be of use at all, it should be used to organise the labour of those men in an intelligent manner. . . . if it is right . . . to provide for the army reserve men it is still more right for the State to provide for the dock labourer . . . out of employment by the adoption of electrical machinery. (Laughter) It is all very well to laugh at this; but nowadays you see the electric crane going up, by which men, even on the shady side of forty, are displaced.[22]

Lansbury's contribution to the proceedings ended on a strong note of humanity and passion: 'Remember what you would be if you were out of work, brought up in a slum . . . [in] such a place as Whitechapel, or . . . Manchester, Liverpool and other places. You cannot expect flowers to grow unless you tend them properly . . . human beings you expect to flourish and be good in the slum . . .'[23]

In 1897 Lansbury presented his first published paper to the Central Poor Law Conference in London setting out his views with great clarity and authority.[24] By this time he was well known in official circles as a poor law guardian of advanced views with a controversial and outspoken style. He had already given evidence to the Royal Commission on the Aged Poor in 1894, at which he told the Prince of Wales and his fellow commissioners that he would abolish the workhouse for the aged poor and introduce old age pensions. Pressed on the fate of those who wilfully wasted a pension, he advocated the use of prison.[25] In 1895 his evidence to the Parliamentary Select Committee on Distress from Want of Employment showed Lansbury to be a well-informed expert witness with a comprehensive view of the poor law system, poverty, and unemployment. On each occasion during those years his analysis of poverty and unemployment was underlined by a Marxist critique of the shortcomings of capitalism. His most comprehensive exposition was to the Campbell-Bannerman Select Committee on 11 June 1895, when he concluded that only a collectivist approach would permanently solve contemporary economic problems: 'I know this will seem a big order here, you cannot hope . . . to [solve] . . . unemployment . . . without a complete reorganization of our industrial system . . . the

---

[22] *Report of the Central Poor Law Conference, 3–4 March 1896.*   [23] Ibid.
[24] G. Lansbury, 'The Principles of the English Poor Law', read at the Central Poor Law Conference, 9 Mar. 1897. *Report of the Twenty-Fifth Annual Central Poor Law Conference, 9–10 March 1897.*
[25] Report of the Royal Commission on the Aged Poor, *Parliamentary Papers*, xiv, 1895 (Reports from Commissioners, Inspectors and Others, 1) (C. 7684). For Lansbury's evidence, see ibid. QQ. 13,797–14,053.

only solution of the unemployment question is for the community to take over and control industries of the country, and for use instead of profit.'[26]

Unemployment in the late nineteenth and early twentieth centuries was a major and chronic problem which, as Lansbury noted, local authorities, poor law unions, and private charity could not solve. From the 1880s the terms 'unemployment' and 'unemployed' first entered the political vocabulary and the Board of Trade started to collect regular statistics of the number of those out of work. While local authorities tried temporary relief works, the organized labour movement proposed different solutions, particularly the demand for a statutory eight-hour day. Labour leaders, such as George Lansbury, Will Crooks, and Keir Hardie, were also strong advocates of starting labour colonies for re-training the urban unemployed, the most popular remedy at the time.

Labour colonies represented the practical expression of a utopian desire to return to the land, a possible panacea for the ills of the capitalist system with its industrial crises and trade depressions. Their history went back to Robert Owen and even earlier pioneers of rustic communities of co-operative living. From the 1880s there was a revival of interest in these colonies to provide opportunities for the unemployed in agricultural and horticultural training, including market-gardening and fruit-growing, with the possibility of permanent resettlement on the land or emigration to the Empire. But some social reformers, including Charles Booth, envisaged labour colonies of a totally different order, which would provide a reformatory function to deal with the problem of the habitual vagrant and loafer in society. Most famous was the scheme promoted by William Booth of the Salvation Army, which opened the Hadleigh colony in Essex, where some of the Poplar unemployed went.

In 1904, under pressure especially from groups on the left, the Conservative President of the Local Government Board, Walter Long, summoned a conference of all London guardians for 14 October. The SDF campaigned for Parliament to be recalled for an autumn session to deal with unemployment, but only a number of boards, including Poplar, passed the SDF resolution. At the guardians' conference, Long successfully opposed Lansbury's attempt to secure the passage of this resolution. However, Lansbury pulled off a publicity coup instead by announcing that the industrialist Joseph Fels from the United States of America had offered to lease land in Essex at a peppercorn rent to the Poplar guardians for the establishment of a labour colony.

Joseph Fels was the American millionaire who used his fortune made out of the manufacture of naptha soap in Philadelphia to promote his radical ideas about social reform and politics. A disciple of the American land-reformer, Henry George, Fels became an ardent advocate of establishing colonies as a remedy for unemployment. In Britain he promoted three experiments, starting with the

---

[26] Third report from the Select Committee on Distress from Want of Employment. Proceedings, Minutes of Evidence, Appendix, *Parliamentary Papers*, ix, 1895 (Reports from Committees, 3) (HC 365), Q. 10,408. For Lansbury's evidence, see QQ. 10,401–10,517.

Mayland Small Holdings scheme in Essex.[27] In the summer of 1903 Fels was introduced to George Lansbury at the beginning of what was to become a close and successful partnership. Fels was a prime example—he was probably the first—of a
number of wealthy philanthropists who, totally convinced by Lansbury's selfless
dedication to worthy causes, poured thousands of pounds into his campaigns and
crusades. In funding Lansbury's 1906 parliamentary contest at Middlesbrough,
Fels provided one of the most important contacts in Lansbury's political career.
Marion Coates Hansen, sister of Fels's business associate, Walter Coates, became
Lansbury's election agent and thereby an important influence in bringing Lansbury
into the Edwardian women's movement. In May 1907 Fels also answered Lansbury's appeal to assist the exiled Lenin and his Bolsheviks, short of travel expenses
in London after the Fifth Congress of the Russian Social Democratic Labour Party
in the Brotherhood Church off Southgate Road in Islington.[28] Lansbury later wrote
to Mary Fels:

Business and money-making must have compelled much of his attention, but it never
entered into his conversation round their table . . . Usually we talked of how the lot of the
toiling masses might be brightened and bettered. Our talks ranged from Single Tax and
Anarchy, to Landlordism and Bureaucracy. To listen to him was like listening to one who
had seen a great light . . .[29]

By this point, the work of the Poplar Board of Guardians had become part of the
popular agitation of the unemployed movement in early twentieth-century Britain.
Lansbury played an important part in the 'Right to Work Campaign', becoming
treasurer of the newly formed National Right to Work Council in November 1905,
thereby strengthening his links with leading socialists in the labour movement.[30]
Lansbury had become established as the leading advocate of establishing labour
colonies to solve the economic depression by the permanent resettlement of unemployed workmen on the land. He had raised the question of labour colonies ten
years before he met Fels on first joining the Poplar guardians, who then promoted
the idea under his influence. In 1895 the guardians applied for permission to purchase a 280 acre farm in Essex but discovered that the Local Government Board
would only agree to the use of nearby land for additional workhouse accommodation. In 1903 a second attempt also failed to establish a 'country workhouse' for the
Poplar unemployed, when the local workhouse was overcrowded.

As José Harris has noted, George Lansbury's attitude to labour colonies at first
appeared uncertain. His first election manifesto in 1893, as we have seen, proposed
the 'formation of Labour colonies for the treatment of the habitual casual and
repression of the loafer'. In the 1895 parliamentary by-election at Walworth he

---

[27] For Joseph Fels, see A. P. Dudden, *Joseph Fels and the Single-Tax Movement* (1971); Mary Fels, *Joseph Fels: His Life and Work* (1920).

[28] For the story of Fels's loan, which Lenin repaid after the Bolshevik Revolution in 1917, see A. P. Dudden and T. H. von Laue, 'The RSDLP and Joseph Fels: A Study in Intercultural Contact', *American Historical Review*, 61 (1955–6), pp. 21–47.

[29] George Lansbury to Mary Fels, 30 June 1914, Joseph Fels Papers.

[30] K. D. Brown, *Labour and Unemployment, 1900–1914* (Newton Abbott, 1971), pp. 63–4.

denied he was in favour of 'pauper colonies or in anyway perpetuating the workhouse system'. In the same year, he told the Campbell-Bannerman Select Committee on Unemployment that he advocated 'self-supporting' colonies, if there was no free competition. In his paper at the 1897 central poor law Conference he acknowledged that 'drunkards, incapables and loafers are to be found in the ranks of the unemployed' but informed the delegates: 'I do not wish to be mis-understood. I do not wish for penal settlements, for you will never drive out wickedness by wickedness, you cannot do good work with the devil's tools.'[31]

Under Lansbury's guidance the Poplar guardians proposed a type of labour colony, more on the lines of earlier utopian projects, which would instruct unemployed men in agricultural and horticultural skills and thereby place them back in the labour market either in this country or abroad. Lansbury saw farm colonies as self-sustaining communities living and working on a co-operative basis—an alternative to the capitalist mode of production in early twentieth-century Britain. With Fels's financial support, the Poplar colony was established by the purchase of Sumpners Farm at Laindon, near Basildon, in Essex, which Fels leased to the East End guardians at a peppercorn rent. From 5 March 1904, 200 men were engaged at Laindon in fruit-growing and market-gardening. Eventually the 100 acre site included dormitories, kitchens, a dining-hall, laundry, and a small reservoir.[32]

A second project was started at Hollesley Bay in Suffolk, where Fels purchased an agricultural training college for gentlemen on a 1,300 acre estate for £40,000 and made it available on a similar interest-free arrangement for the CUB. The main purpose was the training of selected men for work on co-operative smallholdings with the prospect of earning an independent livelihood. Initially, a number of un-employed men from Poplar with their families were settled in cottages on the estate.

Laindon and Hollesley Bay attracted the attention of politicians and social reformers, who made pilgrimages to inspect the colonies in large numbers. Among the visitors were Henrietta and Samuel Barnett, early pioneers of back-to-the-land settlements. Henrietta Barnett, who was later involved in the establishment of Hampstead Garden Suburb, noted the beneficial effects on the 335 residents.

The CUB for London was established under the Unemployed Workmen Act (1905) to operate the legislation with regard to the urban unemployed in the capital. George Lansbury and Will Crooks were among its leading members, though the CUB was largely recruited from the middle-class, business, and professional groups and its meetings were held in the daytime. Lansbury became the chairman of the Working Colonies Committee, which instituted a number of temporary works at Osea Island, Letchworth Garden City, and Fambridge, as well as the permanent colonies in which Lansbury was directly involved.[33] In November 1905, at the first

---

[31] Cited in J. Harris, *Unemployment and Politics: A Study in English Social Policy, 1886–1914* (1972), p. 139.

[32] *The Poplar Labour Colony . . . Opened by the Poplar Board of Guardians*, June 1904; for a less sympathetic view, see 'What Poplar Owns!', *Poplar's Local Municipal Review*, Dec. 1911. (Copies in THLLH&A, Farm Colonies file.)

[33] Central (Unemployed) Body, *Report of Working Colonies Committee: For the Period Covering 12th December, 1905, to 30th June, 1907.*

meeting of the CUB, Lansbury met the chairman, Henry Russell Wakefield, vicar of St Mary's, Bryanston Square, with whom he was soon to serve on the Royal Commission on the Poor Law formed in 1905. Other members included C. H. Grinling, socialist pioneer and editor of the *Woolwich Pioneer*, who in 1907 was responsible for Lansbury's candidature for the LCC. The main figure with whom Lansbury formed a working alliance was William Beveridge, journalist, influential social reformer, and later architect of the Beveridge Report, the basis of the twentieth-century welfare state in Britain.

Unlike other alliances with Joseph Fels and, to some extent, his co-operation with Beatrice Webb on the 1905 Royal Commission, the partnership of Beveridge and Lansbury was a somewhat uneasy one. Beveridge was suspicious about 'Poplarism' and Lansbury did not like middle-class associates of Toynbee Hall. Moreover, both men took a different view on labour colonies. Beveridge, who instead favoured labour exchanges, saw their main purpose as a temporary base for those displaced by the labour market, whereas Lansbury regarded the colonies as permanent communities, which could offer an alternative type of society to industrial capitalism. But a practical compromise prevailed, as each man supported the other's specific hobby-horse.[34]

Unfortunately the change of government at the end of 1905 brought forward an old foe and an opponent of labour colonies: John Burns became President of the Local Government Board (LGB) in the incoming Liberal administration. The hero of the London Dock Strike of 1889, Burns became the first working man to hold Cabinet rank on the grounds that 'the confidence of the labouring chaps to the next Liberal Government will be enormously promoted by the inclusion of John Burns in the Cabinet'.[35] However, the former socialist agitator, imprisoned after the events of 'Bloody Sunday' in Trafalgar Square, was no longer a friend of Labour some thirty years later. Moreover, he was determined to prove it.

After an initial inspection of the Suffolk scheme, when he walked the several miles to Hollesley Bay from the nearest town of Woodbridge, he duly authorized its purchase by the Central (Unemployed) Body, after judging 'the whole place fit for a doubtful experiment'.[36] But, with its President hostile to the idea of labour colonies, the Local Government Board soon declared Hollesley Bay *ultra vires*. Those sent from Poplar were limited to stays of only sixteen weeks, whereas Lansbury planned to establish permanent smallholdings on the estate. By 1907 this ruling, and the departure of C. H. Grinling, his principal supporter on the Colonies Committee, effectively ended the project, as far as the chairman was concerned. Disillusioned by the lack of support on the Colonies Committee—'half the committee is not interested . . . except to see that I do not get my way'—he told Beveridge that he was 'only waiting for Burns' reply, and if . . . small holdings are off, then I'm off too'.[37] Lansbury resigned his chairmanship in 1907 and eventually left the

---

[34] J. Harris, *William Beveridge: A Biography* (1977), pp. 122–5.
[35] Jack Pease to Herbert Gladstone, 6 Dec. 1905, Gainford Papers, fo. 82.
[36] Diary 18 Apr. 1906, John Burns Papers, BL, Add. MS 46,324.
[37] Lansbury to Beveridge, 11 Jan., 1 Feb. 1907, William Beveridge Papers.

Central (Unemployed) Body in 1908. But at the next government inquiry Lansbury did not mince his words: 'No; my description of Hollesley Bay is a glorified work-house. I think it is a shocking waste of time and money to be sending men all that way merely for sixteen weeks and then letting them come back to London . . . '[38]

In 1907 Lansbury launched a bitter attack in the columns of *The Times* against John Burns over the Hollesley Bay colony. Lansbury claimed Burns had 'deliber-ately misunderstood and misinterpreted the whole experience, and [appeared] to be desirous of wrecking it by compelling the committee to run it on lines contrary to those which it had in mind'. He also repeated the accusation first made in 1894 of a betrayal of loyalties by the former socialist. To become the first working-class Cabinet minister, Burns had 'carved his way to power, as someone once said of Disraeli, by the unsparing use of the scalping knife and tomahawk'. He had outlived his early faith and 'stepped from the ranks of the workers and become one of the bitterest opponents of all those principles and ideas by the preaching of which he obtained place and power'.[39] This was not the end of their public feud, which took on even greater force, once Lansbury was returned to Westminster after the December 1910 general election.

Outside Parliament, another strategy used by George Lansbury to attract public and government attention to the plight of the unemployed was the mass deputation of working women to Westminster. Thirty years before, the march of poor working women in the West End made the Chancellor of the Exchequer, Robert Lowe, aban-don his plans for a tax on match-boxes. Lansbury first employed this technique in the 1890s to urge the East End unemployed men to attend the meetings of the guardians and other local bodies in large numbers to lobby for the provision of work. In December 1905 he took part in the Right to Work Demonstration held in the Leicester Palace in Ramsay MacDonald's constituency. Lansbury referred to the propaganda value of the unemployed marches, especially of the working women in London in arousing public opinion.

After an earlier march of about a thousand working women to Westminster, on 6 November 1905 Lansbury, Crooks, and others, in conjunction with the London Trades Council and the Poplar Trades and Labour Representation Committee, organized a large-scale demonstration of several thousand women. To lobby for government action on unemployment, about four thousand Poplar women, wives of navvies, dockers, and casual labourers, joined contingents from West Ham, Shoreditch, Bethnal Green, Walthamstow, Edmonton, Paddington, and South-wark. They travelled by train and tram-car to assemble on the Embankment before marching with babies and young children to Whitehall. At the LGB offices Lans-bury and Crooks headed a deputation with representatives from the Central

[38] Second report (on Afforestation) of the Royal Commission appointed to inquire into . . . Coast Ero-sion, the Reclamation of Tidal Lands, and Afforestation in the United Kingdom, ii pt 1, *Parliamentary Papers*, xiv, 1909 (Reports from Commissioners, Inspectors and Others, 6) (Cd. 3240), Q. 16,085. For Lansbury's evidence, see QQ. 15,855–16,997.

[39] *The Times*, 2 Apr. 1907; for Lansbury's defence of the labour colony, see 'Hollesley Bay Labour Colony', *The Commonwealth*, 7 July 1907.

Workmen's Committee to interview the Conservative Prime Minister, Arthur Balfour. The women's march achieved little but sympathy from the prime minister—Crooks said Balfour's speech of despair 'was unworthy of a twopenny-halfpenny statesman'—but the whole exercise was flamboyantly stage-managed and attracted a great deal of public and press attention.[40] However, Lansbury's earlier request to ask Queen Alexandra to receive a similar delegation of unemployed women in October 1905 was rejected after Edward VII had met a gang of the Poplar unemployed at the official opening of the Aldwych–Kingsway junction.

In 1906 the Poplar Board of Guardians was subjected to detailed scrutiny of its activities by an official investigation launched by the Local Government Board—a portent of the classic confrontation fifteen years later between the Poplar councillors and the central government over the 'Rates Rebellion'. At the Local Government Board, Burns inherited a government department responsible for the central administration of the Victorian poor law and staffed by entrenched Conservative officials schooled in the principles of the Poor Law Amendment Act of 1834. Most notable were Sir Samuel Paris, its ageing Permanent Head and the reactionary Chief Inspector, J. S. Davy. Both men and their officials applied prudent economy and uniformity to poor law administration, particularly where boards of guardians had departed from the 'principles of 1834' which underpinned the Victorian system. A number of unions were under scrutiny—at West Ham several councillors and officials were eventually prosecuted and imprisoned—but Poplar was the most famous and attracted most national publicity.

In running their Board, the Poplar guardians gained a reputation for municipal extravagance, especially in terms of lavish expenditure on outdoor relief. Newspaper placards carried headlines of 'champagne and oysters'. On 19 March 1906, Beatrice Webb cast a cold and disapproving eye over the way contracts to the value of £50,000 to £100,000 were settled by the Poplar guardians. In her words, they were 'about thirty [of] a rather low lot of "doubtful" representatives of Labour with a sprinkling of builders, publicans, insurance and other "agents"'. She noted:

The procedure was utterly reckless. The tenders were opened at the meeting, the names and prices read out; and then, without any kind of report of a committee or by officials, straight away voted on. Usually the same person as heretofore was taken, nearly always a local man—it was not always the lowest tender, and the prices were, in all cases, full, in some cases obviously excessive. Butter at 1s. 2d. a lb, when the contracts ran into thousands of pounds' worth, was obviously ridiculous! Milk at 9d a gallon, the best and most expensive meat, tea at 2s. 8d.[41]

What Beatrice Webb criticized as 'reckless' conduct in awarding contracts others, critical of the Poplar guardians, termed 'municipal extravagance'. She did not note that Crooks, Lansbury, and their fellow Labour guardians were in a minority on the Poplar Board but able to exert a controlling influence. Beatrice Webb witnessed the origins of 'Poplarism' that flowered in the 1921 Poplar Rates Rebellion.

---

[40] *Daily Graphic*, 7 Nov. 1907; *The Times*, 7 Nov. 1907.
[41] B. Webb, Diary, 19 Mar. 1906. See also *The Diary of Beatrice Webb*, iii, ed. N. Mackenzie and J. Mackenzie (1984), pp. 33–4.

These Labour councillors were determined to be guardians of the poor and acted accordingly in the best interests of their people. Disturbed by what she saw and did not understand, she added the following observations about Crooks and Lansbury:

Will Crooks sat in the chair and did nothing to check the recklessness. Considering that he has had twelve years' experience of the businesslike and careful procedure of the LCC in matters of contracts, it is gravely to his discredit that the Poplar guardians are as they are. If there is no corruption in that Board, English human nature must be more naively stupid than any other race would credit. Is Will Crooks (as John Burns asserts) a corrupt politician? Or merely a demagogic sentimentalist? Even Lansbury, by constitution a thoroughgoing sentimentalist, and with no other experience of public affairs, protested, and was clearly ashamed of the procedure.[42]

Again, Beatrice Webb's acerbic observations were somewhat wide of the mark, especially in connection with Lansbury's 'no other experience of public affairs'. He had been a poor law guardian and local employer for over twelve years.

The Poplar Borough Municipal Alliance (PBMA), backed by the Industrial Freedom League, laid the principal charge of extravagance and bribery against the Poplar guardians in 1904 and handed the LGB an early opportunity to investigate the goings-on at Poplar, as well as other boroughs. The Alliance, formed in 1903 by Gilbert Bartholomew, chairman of the Bryant and May match firm, was a powerful coalition of political and business interests—Conservatives, orthodox Liberals, and local shopkeepers. In Poplar it replaced the ratepayers' organization of the 1890s and contested local elections as the principal opposition to the socialist and labour members of the Poplar Board of Guardians.[43]

The Davy Inquiry lasted twenty days and was conducted in the Board Room of the guardians' offices in Upper North Street in Poplar between 7 June and 26 July 1906. Victorian workhouses were usually large-scale institutions with separate accommodation for men, women, and children and provision, albeit frugal and parsimonious, for every aspect of their lives. At Poplar the 3 acre workhouse site included living-quarters, casual ward, laundry, stores, refectory, and hospital. The Poplar guardians were also responsible for the education of their pauper children, with a new school under construction at Shenfield and a newly established farm colony at Laindon in Essex.

Lansbury's evidence to the Davy Inquiry provides some fascinating insights into the *minutiae* of the Victorian poor law system and the extent to which the LGB pursued the charges against the guardians. Nor was this the first investigation. In 1894 the LGB Inspector inquired into accusations against the Poplar workhouse master and ten years later the LGB were back to vet the guardians' application for increased financial powers to meet the large expenditure incurred in the construction of the new pauper school at Shenfield. At this stage the Municipal Alliance brought the charges against the guardians, which provided the evidence for the LGB to inquire into a prima-facie case. Few stones were left unturned. A detailed

---

[42] B. Webb, Diary, 19 Mar. 1906.
[43] For the Municipal Alliance, see George Lansbury's letter in *Justice*, 19 Nov. 1906.

audit of the accounts raised questions, for instance, about the £28. 9s. 9d. spent on the 'Olympia typewriter, duplication and accessories', the cost of journeys by broughams, and the expenditure of £105. 17s. 7d. on second-hand clothing over eleven months up to Lady Day 1905, not to mention £600 spent on a Yorkshire steam-wagon which turned out to be impractical at the Laindon Farm colony. Besides this examination of the books, policy was also dissected in detail—the Poplar Board had paid out relief to the unemployed, ostensibly after receiving a deputation during the depression of 1904. The Davy Inquiry took the view it was a deliberate decision to put political pressure on the government over unemployment.

Lansbury was able to mount a reasonable defence to the various charges. The guardians were not always as profligate as their opponents alleged and had themselves suggested ways of eliminating inefficiency and corruption in the poor law by one central system of contracting and supplying workhouses.[44] Well before the Inquiry Lansbury had publicly explained the true causes for the seemingly large increase in pauperism in Poplar.[45] At the end of the day, Lansbury and Crooks were absolved of any personal corruption or wrongdoing, but Davy concluded that 'the rise and decrease in pauperism were mainly due to the deliberate action of the Guardians; and that the absence of thrift and economy which characterised their general administration was also in a great measure deliberate.'[46] In other words, the policies pursued on the Poplar Board by Lansbury and Crooks, held responsible by Davy even though their group was then in a minority of ten to twenty-four on the board, had overt political aims, which clashed with poor law orthodoxy. Fifteen years later, the Poplar councillors had an even more explicit agenda. In 1906 the results of the inquiry were politically damaging—Crooks resigned and the adverse publicity severely hampered Lansbury's work on labour colonies on the Central (Unemployed) Body.

The Davy Inquiry took place one year after Lansbury started serving on the Royal Commission on the Poor Laws (1905–9), one of the most famous government investigations of the early twentieth century. In a modern study of the Royal Commission, A. M. McBriar has revealed the interplay of ideas and attitudes among the different members of the investigation and their supporters. In particular, the central clash between the main protagonists, Helen and Bernard Bosanquet of the COS versus the Fabian socialists, Beatrice and Sidney Webb, is depicted in terms of the contemporary metaphor of an Edwardian lawn tennis tournament. Their long-standing contest over social policy stretched back to the 1890s.[47]

Chaired by a former Conservative Cabinet minister, Lord George Hamilton, the Royal Commission comprised nine poor law administrators, six representatives of

[44] Report to the President of the Local Government Board on the Poplar Union, by J. S. Davy, *Parliamentary Papers*, civ, 1906 (Accounts and Papers, 40) (Cd. 3240), pp. 379–98.
[45] See Lansbury's letter 'on the legal poor of London' in *The Times*, 29 Dec. 1904.
[46] Report . . . on the Poplar Union, p. 40.
[47] A. M. McBriar, *An Edwardian Mixed Doubles: The Bosanquets versus the Webbs: A Study in British Social Policy, 1890–1929* (1987).

the COS, two political economists, as well as members of the Anglican and Roman Catholic Churches—a wide range of opinion on the 'Condition of England' question. The strong COS representation included Charles Booth; Octavia Hill, the housing reformer; Charles Loch, COS secretary; and four other delegates. Opposed to the COS were Beatrice Webb and George Lansbury who were joined by the Lib–Lab trade unionist, Francis Chandler. Lansbury wrote that he 'received this appointment without any influence being used on my behalf, either by myself or anyone else'. The Labour party welcomed Lansbury's selection, but he was not regarded as an official representative, a revealing insight on his current status within the eyes of the Labour leadership.

At first Hamilton had tried to block Lansbury's appointment, but the forty-six-year-old East London socialist had considerable experience and a growing reputation in poor law circles. During twelve years as a Poplar guardian, he had made an important impression at the annual Poor Law Conference and honed his ideas on policy, principles, and reform. His work as an advocate of labour colonies also made him famous, if somewhat notorious in official quarters.[48]

The history of the Commission has been dominated by the role played by Beatrice Webb, who wanted to thwart the orthodoxy of Sir James Davy and the Local Government Board entrenched in the strict principles of the 1834 Poor Law Amendment Act. The subsequent publication of her diaries revealed how far she had deceived herself about her success in manipulating people and proceedings on the Commission.

In her determination to break up the Victorian poor law, Beatrice Webb regarded George Lansbury as an important ally on the Commission, albeit one who was socially and intellectually inferior. Later, in one of those characteristically patronising sketches of trade union and labour leaders to be found in her diary, she compared Lansbury with the former American Secretary of State, William Jennings Bryan. She noted 'a curious likeness alike in body and mind to W. J. Bryan of USA . . . [L]arge-limbed, debonair, big-mouthed, with a splendidly resonant voice; in face, half handsome, half stupid'. Somewhat grudgingly, she acknowledged both men's 'common good qualities'. 'Overflowing with public spirit and private benevolence—almost ostentatiously so; immaculate in family life, devoted husband, indulgent parent, non-smoker, teetotaller—even the same sort of simple minded religious faith and personal purity', she thought.

Most damning in Beatrice Webb's view were their 'common defects': 'No brains to speak of—certainly no capacity for solving intellectual problems—and a big dosage of personal vanity and passion for applause'. Finally, Lansbury was dismissed as 'hardly a great public personality'—scarcely a sound judgement on one of the most revered and acclaimed Labour figures of the inter-war years.[49]

Lansbury's support was important to Beatrice Webb, but he played a more significant and independent part than that she attributed to him as her subordinate.

---

[48] A. M. McBriar, *An Edwardian Mixed Doubles: The Bosanquets versus the Webbs: A Study in British Social Policy, 1890–1929* (1987), p. 193.

[49] B. Webb, Diary, 11 Oct. 1928, PP; *Beatrice Webb's Diaries, 1924–1932*, ed. M. Cole (1955), pp. 183–4.

His correspondence with her reveals a fair degree of autonomy during the proceedings of the Commission and his differing views on poor law reform. Lansbury made some critical points on the memorandum that Beatrice Webb forwarded to the chairman for the first meeting. Her main aims were not challenged; but her desire to devolve work to expert committees met with Lansbury's disapproval. He was unhesitatingly frank: 'It may be sheer ignorance on my part, but, in my judgement, experts are not always people who arrive at true conclusions.' Lansbury thought little of 'experts', especially those from outside the East End who arrived at Toynbee Hall on the Commercial Road with ready-made solutions for their less fortunate brethren in Whitechapel and beyond.[50]

At the same time, Lansbury confessed to Beatrice Webb his unease with middle-class colleagues that prevented him preparing memoranda for discussion.

It appears to me to be a waste of time to write documents for the Commission to read. I should have tried to make myself understood by the rest of the Commission. Men like [the Revd] Phelps are so very learned and have such an uncommon good opinion of themselves that for a person like me to try to instruct them is not worth the attempt.[51]

Notwithstanding this admission, his own well-defined opinions meant he did not naturally assume the views of fellow commissioners drawn from a different social background. Earlier he had told Beatrice Webb he felt he stood against the rest of the Commission, as he was the only one opposed to the idea of industrial day-schools.[52]

None the less, Lansbury put forward strong views on the causes of unemployment and the working of the Victorian poor law. Among the subjects he wanted investigated was how effective provision for the unemployed had been since the Chamberlain Circular of 1886 which had asked local authorities to implement public works and to co-operate with the poor law bodies in finding appropriate work for the temporary jobless.[53] From the outset he demanded radical outcomes to their inquiry which would take them away from merely 'relieving the destitute'. He wrote: 'Now with regard to the Poor Law side of the inquiry, my position, roughly, is this, namely, that I want to obtain Old Age Pensions for the aged, and that I want the entire removal from the Poor Law of children and the sick.' To these aims, he added the setting-up of separate and free medical provision, that was finally realized with the establishment of the National Health Service forty years later. For Lansbury, education and health were vital priorities that should not be dependent upon income.[54]

Underlying his various proposals was his adamant conviction—expressed on many occasions during this time—that those who had fallen on hard times were unemployed or poor through no failing or moral weakness of their own. 'Therefore

[50] George Lansbury to Beatrice Webb, 15 Feb. 1906, WLGC, vol. 286.
[51] George Lansbury to Beatrice Webb, 23 Apr. 1907, ibid. Revd Lancelot Ridley Phelps was an economist, Fellow of Oriel College, Oxford and member of the COS.
[52] George Lansbury to Beatrice Webb, 23 Oct. 1906, WLGC, vol. 286.
[53] George Lansbury to Beatrice Webb, 7 Feb. 1906, WLGC, sect. II 4d. 8.
[54] George Lansbury to Beatrice Webb, 23 Apr. 1907, WLGC, vol. 286.

I hope we shall get together as much evidence as possible to prove the futility of present methods. We must also demonstrate that unemployment is not caused by the fault of individuals, but is due to conditions over which individuals have no control', he emphasized.[55]

Where he differed markedly from Beatrice Webb was in his advocacy of the use of farm colonies as a workable solution for urban employment. 'In reference to labour colonies, I am aware, of course, that you are opposed to them, but so far, the labour colony which we wish to establish at Hollesley Bay has never been really discussed', he told her.[56] Despite the stern opposition of John Burns at the LGB to social experiments, such as the Hollesley Bay colony, training in agriculture and horticulture—often linked with emigration—was Lansbury's main solution to the problem of those out of work.

In addition, like many in Labour circles, he wanted the direct intervention of the state through the creation of a Ministry of Labour to administer and fund initiatives to solve unemployment:

I would like to see a Central Department, which would be called a Public Works of Labour Department to which should be entrusted the duty of taking charge of all main roads, foreshores, waste lands, Crown lands etc. Parliament should vote a certain sum each year for public works . . . under the control and direction of the Central Department.[57]

On the appointment of possible assistant commissioners, he reminded Beatrice Webb of the importance of the women's voice in poor law matters. 'I certainly should have liked, for London at least, one of our people should have been a woman, if not two. People seem to forget that the Poor Law deals very largely with women and children', he commented.[58] In 1907 Beatrice compiled a detailed memorandum of suggestions for the working of the Commission, including the calling of expert witnesses and topics for inquiry. When some commissioners failed to agree to calling her husband, Sidney Webb, as a witness, both Lansbury and Francis Chandler supported this proposal.

Lansbury brought to the Royal Commission his own analysis of the causes of unemployment and poverty in Britain and how these problems could be tackled, as well as those he derived from his Labour contacts. He achieved his ambition to travel to Germany, Belgium, and Scandinavia on a fact-finding mission for the Commission on European ways of tackling unemployment and poverty. Throughout he remained an important ally, if critical friend, for Beatrice Webb whose support she could depend upon in her various machinations with her fellow commissioners.

As the work of the Royal Commission progressed, Beatrice Webb determined on writing a separate report to advance her proposals for the prevention of poverty and ill-health which she knew would command Lansbury's support. Her *Minority Report* called for the total abolition of the Victorian poor law—rather than any

[55] George Lansbury to Beatrice Webb, 17 Apr. 1907, ibid.
[56] George Lansbury to Beatrice Webb, 23 Apr. 1907, ibid.
[57] George Lansbury to Beatrice Webb, 24 Apr. 1907, ibid.
[58] George Lansbury to Beatrice Webb, 15 Feb. 1906, ibid.

revisions to the existing system—and its replacement by a new government department and special local authorities' committees to deal with children, the sick, and the elderly.

Lansbury's co-operation with Beatrice Webb on the Royal Commission had some important outcomes: she compiled two case-studies of local poor law administration in Poplar and Bradford in her memoranda. The Labour party's proposal for the state to take responsibility for employment—seen later in the Ministry of Labour—also found its way into her famous *Minority Report*, with Lansbury as a co-signatory.[59] Once the *Minority Report* was published, Beatrice and Sidney Webb embarked on a three-year national crusade to secure its implementation.[60] Lansbury played an important part in this campaign, particularly through his links to the Labour movement. 'I think it [the *Minority Report*] will be a text book for years on the subject of the Poor Law & Unemployment', he told Ramsay MacDonald.[61] In September 1910 Lansbury participated in a two-day debate against Harry Quelch, editor of *Justice*, in support of the *Minority Report* at the Holborn town hall.[62] In this spirited contest, Lansbury made the case for replacing the poor law by 'work or maintenance' for the unemployed administered through the new labour exchanges. However, Edgar Lansbury recalled in 1934 that history demonstrated that Quelch had had the better of the argument against his father. The abolition of the guardians destroyed a democratic institution, to which working people had secured increasing representation, and handed control over to Tory-dominated borough and county councils.[63] In the same year, in a Christian appeal to abolish the Victorian poor law, Lansbury 'put his hand to the plough' with an ILP pamphlet, *Smash up the Workhouse*.

In the general election of December 1910 Lansbury was returned to Westminster as the member for Bow and Bromley. The twenty-seven-year-old Clem Attlee, who wrote the candidate's election song that East End children sang with gusto, walked down the Bow Road in triumph to Mile End with a huge placard displaying the figures of Lansbury's majority. As the people's guardian, George Lansbury had successfully confronted the Victorian poor law system and its officialdom head-on. He had become a popular voice in municipal government, widely recognized and revered for his humanity and compassion for the destitute and unemployed. Now, this local representative had a national platform in Parliament and outside Westminster to crusade for the downtrodden and marginalized in society.

[59] George Lansbury to Beatrice Webb, 24 Apr. 1907, PP.

[60] For the national campaign for the *Minority Report*, see McBriar, *An Edwardian Mixed Doubles*, pp. 280–317.

[61] *Labour Leader*, 19 Feb. 1909; George Lansbury to Ramsay MacDonald, 12 Dec. 1908, JRMP, PRO 30/69/1152/165.

[62] For the 'Lansbury v. Quelch Debate' as part of the national campaign, see *Report of the Debate on the Poor Law Minority Report between Geo. Lansbury, LCC, and H. Quelch (Editor of Justice), 20–21 September 1910* [copy in BLPES]. See also E. Lansbury, *George Lansbury*, p. 192.

[63] E. Lansbury, *George Lansbury*, p. 192.

5
Parliamentary Contests, 1900–1910

In his memoirs George Lansbury recalled that as a child he wrote his name in a church prayer book as 'George Lansbury MP' and probably added the name of an East End constituency. Other early memories, besides witnessing the hurly-burly of the political hustings at Greenwich during the 1868 general election, included the popular agitation that engulfed London during the remarkable case of the Tichborne Claimant in the 1870s.[1] The young Lansbury was in the vast and frenzied crowd that tried to gain entry to the court at Westminster where the Tichborne claimant's case was being heard. Some of the great debates on the Eastern Question between Gladstone and Disraeli in the late 1870s, as already noted, also made an enduring impression on the young labourer from the East End who watched spellbound from the Strangers' Gallery of the House of Commons.[2]

This early fascination with the history and tradition associated with the Victorian mother of parliaments remained with George Lansbury throughout his life. In the 1930s, in his seventies, no one was a more enthusiastic guide for young constituents and visitors to the Palace of Westminster or a firmer believer that Parliament was their birthright than the Member for Bow and Bromley. Groups of children he took round Parliament were shown historic features such as the Royal Gallery, Robing Room, and the Woolsack, as well as the site where Charles I was tried in Westminster Hall. But they also walked the floor where the atheist, Charles Bradlaugh, stood resolutely at the bar of the Commons and visited Emily Davison's hiding-place where the suffragette concealed herself in 1911 to avoid being counted on census night.[3]

From 1922 to 1940 George Lansbury was unassailable as the MP for Poplar, Bow, and Bromley, an overwhelmingly working-class area and solidly part of the Labour heartland of East London. After 1918, with an electorate three times its pre-war number, the local party built up a powerful organization for municipal and parliamentary elections. So closely was Lansbury identified with his constituency that his share of the poll in six elections never fell below 61 per cent, even in the 1931 rout

---

[1] Many associations were established in different parts of Britain in connection with the Tichborne case, including eleven committees in the East End, and demonstrations took place regularly in Hyde Park up to the mid-1880s. For an excellent survey, see R. McWilliam, 'Radicalism and Popular Culture: The Tichborne Case and the Policies of Fair Play, 1867–1886' in E. F. Biagini and A. J. Reid (eds.), *Currents of Radicalism: Popular Radicalism, Organised Labour and Party Politics in Britain, 1850–1914* (1995), pp. 44–64.

[2] For his early recollections of Parliament, see Lansbury, *Looking Backwards and Forwards*, pp. 83–92, 128–9, 137–49.

[3] See Lansbury's account of the Tichborne claimant, suffragettes, and other parliamentary reminiscences in *Star*, 27–9 Apr. 1935. Lansbury, *Looking Backwards and Forwards*, pp. 137–49.

that obliterated most of the Labour front bench. Four years later, only weeks after resigning the party leadership, the electors returned the Rt. Hon. George Lansbury to Parliament with a thumping majority of 13,357, 77 per cent of the total votes cast. According to Raymond Postgate, his personal rapport with the voters was such that he need not have stepped outside his front door at 39 Bow Road at election time.[4]

Yet in the pre-war period electioneering was very different. The parliamentary division of Bow and Bromley was not a safe seat for any candidate on the political left. In the ten parliamentary elections between 1885 and 1912 political control changed hands seven times, mainly between the Conservative and Liberal parties. Lansbury contested the seat as a Labour and Socialist candidate on four occasions, in 1900, January and December 1910, and again in 1912. In a straight contest with a Conservative opponent, he was finally elected in December 1910, probably helped by most of the Liberal vote, only to be defeated in the famed women's suffrage by-election of 1912.

In a poor East End constituency like Bow and Bromley, an anomalous voting system based on property qualifications disfranchised all women and probably more than a third of working men. Parliamentary elections were costly affairs in time and money. Working-class candidates required the financial backing of their trade union or the assistance of some private patron to run a campaign. For those entering the House of Commons no salaries were paid by the state to back-bench members until 1911. In addition, at election time there was the added burden of the returning officer's expenses, often a substantial amount, to be shared by each election candidate.

Whether in the SDF, the ILP, or eventually in the Labour party, George Lansbury spent a considerable proportion of his career as a Member of Parliament and in campaigns to be returned to the House of Commons. At Westminster, by any measure, Lansbury was not one of the great parliamentarians to be compared with Disraeli, Gladstone, Lloyd George, or Churchill; but his contribution to parliamentary life was considerable, colourful, and not to be underestimated. What motivated him to pursue a parliamentary career? Jonathan Schneer's view that Lansbury's lack of personal ambition—expressed in an unselfish and democratic commitment—'only to do his bit for the common cause . . . [which] *could* mean campaigning for Parliament and serving in it'[5]—rightly stresses Lansbury's altruism and sincere belief in the parliamentary road to socialism. However, a natural belief in representative democracy and personal service to the community were not necessarily incompatible with a genuine desire, strongly held from Lansbury's earliest days, to tread the parliamentary path. The two attempts at Walworth in 1895, where Lansbury finished bottom of the poll twice, may be construed as propaganda ventures on behalf of the SDF. Nevertheless, to reach Westminster Lansbury had to participate in a further four parliamentary elections over the next fifteen years, with a dedication that strained his spirit and human endurance to the limits. In 1906

---

[4] Postgate, *Lansbury*, p. 220.   [5] Schneer, *George Lansbury*, p. 37.

campaigning at Middlesbrough reduced Lansbury to exhaustion and serious illness on polling day.

After Walworth, Lansbury returned to his own political base in East London, where he was soon adopted by his Federation branch in September 1895 as the prospective parliamentary candidate for Bow and Bromley, one of seven predominantly working-class East End constituencies in Tower Hamlets. It was a sensible and logical move back to the locality where he was already a familiar figure and where his family home was a popular centre of community advice for every resident who knocked on the front door for help.

In March 1896 the death of his father-in-law, Isaac Brine, ended Lansbury's stint of paid work for the SDF and took him back to manage the family sawmill and timber yard full-time until 1914. According to his son Edgar, his father was a popular local employer, if not always very effective at making money. Characteristically, he was always ready to take on 'a variety of characters . . . from the storms and stresses of the outside world': 'a pimply-faced, anaemic looking youth' recommended by the curate; the 'consumptive old fellow with only a few months to live' sent by a fellow guardian.[6] The doyen of labour representatives, George Lansbury was hardly a capitalist employer of sweated labour and, interestingly, was never portrayed as such by his opponents. Indeed, as the expert witness before the Royal Commission on the Aged Poor in 1894 who declared his trade as an unskilled veneer-dryer, Lansbury continued to work, with his sleeves literally rolled up, for many years. Although his East End family business seemingly gave him a degree of financial independence and time for politics, in reality money difficulties constantly beset the family firm, leading to unsuccessful mergers and ultimate bankruptcy.

Lansbury's standing as a mercurial and theatrical East End figure spread quickly beyond Bow and Bromley. In the 1890s his immediate impact on the local Board of Guardians brought official summonses to give evidence to parliamentary inquiries as an expert witness. With growing popularity, there was the possibility that he might capture the parliamentary seat, a prospect not lost on the sitting member for Bow and Bromley, Lansbury's old friend Murray MacDonald, when he represented the constituency from 1892 to 1895.

In 1895 George Lansbury was adopted as the SDF parliamentary candidate for Bow and Bromley, only a few weeks after the general election.[7] He would probably not have expected to go to the polls for some time, since the maximum period between elections was then seven years. However, the unexpected retirement of the Conservative member, Lionel Holland, produced a parliamentary by-election in Bow and Bromley in 1899, at the outbreak of the Boer War. Lansbury was unable to stand on that occasion. Thus, the potentially three-cornered contest became a straight fight between the Conservative candidate, William Guthrie, the eventual victor, and the Liberal candidate, the journalist Harold Spender.[8]

---

[6] E. Lansbury, *George Lansbury*, pp. 123–4.
[7] Undated newscutting [wrongly annotated Sept. 1899, but probably 1895], LP, vol. 1, fo. 320.
[8] *The Times*, 21 Oct. 1899.

There is some evidence that an electoral pact or understanding in 1899 may explain Lansbury's decision not to press on with his candidature at the by-election.[9] At the time the Poplar Labour League, the strongest labour organization in the southern part of Poplar, usually opposed Lansbury in municipal politics and would have delivered a significant part of the working-class vote to the Liberal candidate.[10] Like many socialist candidates in a three-cornered contest, Lansbury realized he was open to the jibe of 'splitting the progressive vote! . . . letting the Tory in!'.[11]

There was significant common ground between Harold Spender and George Lansbury. Both totally opposed the Boer War and took a similar view on social policy from pensions to housing and land-reform. Equally anxious about a three-cornered contest, Spender proposed a pact against the Tory candidate with the probability that later the Liberals would allow Lansbury a free run. 'I would work hand in glove with your fellows to produce a new union in this district. And then . . . if impartial judges thought it just, I would stand aside for you in my time', Spender offered.[12]

The public response of the executive council of the SDF was unequivocal. Statements in the Liberal press that the Social Democrats were aiding Harold Spender were rigorously rejected: 'no Social Democrat has any right whatever under the rules of the organization to support or work for either candidate, Liberal or Tory.'[13]

This was not always the case. In Poplar the Labour movement was divided on electoral strategy. Will Crooks's Poplar Labour League followed the Progressive–Labour alliance line, seen openly on the London County Council where Crooks, Burns, Tillett, and others, including Ramsay MacDonald, co-operated with the Liberals. In Poplar, the League normally contested local elections in alliance with the Liberal Association.

Normally, Lansbury resolutely opposed this Lib–Lab or Progressive policy: 'We modelled ourselves on Will Thorne and his West Ham colleagues as Socialist and Labour candidates', he stated defiantly in his autobiography.[14] However, there were occasions in Bow and Bromley—in 1894, 1896, and 1898—when a broad socialist-trade union-progressive alliance was formed with some success for the vestry elections.[15] Though, of course, these were municipal elections, very different from parliamentary politics.

Why then did Lansbury not contest the 1899 parliamentary by-election? Probably because he remembered he had already polled fewest votes twice in Walworth in previous three-cornered elections. Four years later, he may well have thought that limited resources should be conserved for the main parliamentary battle where there was the probability of no Liberal opposition. Moreover, a necessary and overriding national cause had to be served: a united front on the left in opposition to the

---

[9] *Daily Chronicle*, 20 Oct. 1899.   [10] Ibid. 19 Oct. 1899.
[11] Lansbury gave this explanation for his loss of support in his first parliamentary contest, the Walworth by-election, May 1895. See Lansbury, *Looking Backwards and Forwards*, p. 78.
[12] Harold Spender to George Lansbury, 18 Oct. 1899, LP, vol. 1, fo. 325.
[13] *The Times*, 26 Oct. 1899.   [14] Lansbury, *My Life*, p. 163.
[15] P. Thompson, *Socialists, Liberals and Labour: The Struggle for London, 1885–1914* (1967), p. 129.

strong Tory war feeling in the country. Spender appealed to him: '[B]ut you must admit that the circumstances require grave consideration. This election is virtually being fought on the Transvaal question ... if we face the Govt. with a divided front we shall give an impression to the whole world that they are stronger than they are.'[16]

In 1899 Spender was granted a straight fight but, despite the services of the national Liberal agent, Renwick Seager, and a bevy of Liberal MPs including Lloyd George and Sydney Buxton, was roundly defeated by the Tory, William Guthrie.[17] After the by-election, Spender suggested that Liberal Central Office would not oppose Lansbury at Bow and Bromley in the future. This proposition, he hinted, had the personal blessing of Herbert Gladstone, the new Liberal Chief Whip. Spender added: 'the Liberal Central [Association] would take no steps if they could be convinced that the Trade Unions in the locality were on your side ... If the [Liberal] authorities found that you were backed by the Trade Unions, they might not trouble about the name under which you stood.'[18]

Electoral pacts and party realignments on the political left were very much in the political air, most notably in the calculations of Herbert Gladstone. In 1900 the founding of the LRC established a new party with the financial support of the trade union movement, and the affiliations flowed in after the Taff Vale legal judgment of 1901. In the restoration of his party's finances and the revitalization of its electoral organization in 1903 Gladstone concluded an agreement to give the LRC a clear run in some thirty constituencies at the 1906 general election.[19] Key by-election triumphs at Clitheroe, Woolwich, and Barnard Castle demonstrated the ability of the new LRC to win parliamentary contests in seats where the Liberal party would have difficulty in doing so. It proved a lesson not lost on that party's Chief Whip in striking the secret electoral pact of 1903 with Ramsay MacDonald at the Leicester Isolation Hospital.

In 1900 the name of George Lansbury appeared on the approved list of parliamentary candidates to contest the forthcoming general election as endorsed by the Federation under the auspices of the new LRC. Within months of its formation the new body was faced by its first general election. The LRC was short of money, lacked organization, and was reduced to using Margaret and Ramsay MacDonald's flat at 3 Lincoln's Inn Fields as its London headquarters. In the prevailing circumstances the new party backed the candidates adopted by its affiliated organizations.

On the historic occasion of the foundation conference of the LRC, as noted previously, George Lansbury was not among the original 129 delegates from the various trade unions and the three main socialist groups, the ILP, the Fabian Society, and the SDF. Instead, Harry Quelch and others led the SDF representatives; and the Gas Workers' Union (where Lansbury was a trustee and a member) fielded a delegation

---

[16] Harold Spender to George Lansbury, 18 Oct. 1899, LP, vol. 1, fo. 325.

[17] *Daily Chronicle*, 20–8 Oct. 1899.

[18] Harold Spender to George Lansbury, 14 Nov. 1899, LP, vol. 1, fo. 328.

[19] A. K. Russell, 'Laying the Charges for the Landslide: The Revival of the Liberal Party Organization, 1902–1905', in A. J. A. Morris (ed.), *Edwardian Radicalism, 1900–1914* (1974), pp. 62–74.

of thirteen led by Will Thorne. The absence of the leading London member of the Federation from both delegations—Lansbury was also not present at the SDF annual conference in 1901—suggests he was beginning to move away from the organization and towards a new political home.

Yet what was Lansbury's attitude towards independent labour representation and the successful attempt to found a Labour party in 1900? In fact, there is no exact record of the date when George Lansbury first joined the Labour party, something that, before individual membership was introduced in 1918, would have been through an affiliated organization such as the ILP. Raymond Postgate suggests that George Lansbury gave up the SDF in *c.*1903–4 and then joined the ILP, a time when he was using the designation 'LRC' in local elections. These details are sketchy: when Lansbury was elected to the Poplar Borough Council, where he topped the poll in West Ward in 1903, he was variously described as 'Progressive', 'Socialist', and 'Labour'.[20]

During a time of considerable division in party politics over the Boer War, there were a number of initiatives to bring about a political realignment on the Left. Keir Hardie unsuccessfully appealed to John Morley and then to John Burns to provide such a lead. Where they did not oppose Liberals, the Radical manufacturer and philanthropist, George Cadbury, willingly funded ILP candidates.[21]

In the year 2000 the Labour party celebrated its centenary as the major party on the political left in British politics. In fact, in 1900 there were three other important attempts to establish a new national political party or a similar organization to widen democratic parliamentary representation. The foundation conference of the Scottish Workers' Parliamentary Elections Committee (later the Scottish Workers' Representation Committee) took place in Edinburgh seven weeks before the Memorial Hall gathering that led to the LRC. The Miners' Federation of Great Britain, pioneers of labour representation, expanded its electoral fund to run more coal miners for Parliament, and in London a broad mix of trade unionists and socialists combined to start the relatively short-lived National Democratic League in October 1900.

The prime mover behind the National Democratic League was journalist and publisher, W. M. Thompson. His project in British politics was to reconstruct the political forces on the left based on a democratic programme of constitutional change, akin to the Chartist manifesto over fifty years before.[22] Nearly two months after the establishment of the LRC, on 8 April 1900, George Lansbury appeared on the same platform as the editor of the *Reynolds Newspaper*, to address a crowded meeting in Shoreditch on 'The Electoral Policy of the SDF'. Thompson used this occasion to call for an alliance of socialists and the Radical Party, which could send fifty labour members to Parliament.[23]

---

[20] *East London Advertiser*, 24, 31 Oct., 7 Nov. 1903.
[21] F. Bealey and H. Pelling, *Labour and Politics, 1900–1906: A History of the Labour Representation Committee* (1958), pp. 50–1.
[22] Ibid.   [23] *Reynolds Newspaper*, 15 Apr. 1900.

It was a propitious time for the members of the SDF and all Socialist men . . . to see if they could not come to some agreement with the Radical Party . . . many members in the House were willing to work with any Socialist party, and he particularly named Mr Lloyd George as one willing to co-operate.[24]

Nevertheless, Lansbury, uncomfortable with Thompson's appeal, had no intention of moving in that particular direction in 1900. Instead he demanded: 'Who were the Radicals . . . They had left him alone [at Bow] because they could not find a capitalist rich enough to contest the constituency . . . It was for the Radicals to . . . show that they were ready to support real Socialism before they could expect the co-operation of the Socialists.'[25]

In October 1900 George Lansbury remained a prominent member of the Federation and fought his first parliamentary contest in the 'Khaki Election' at Bow and Bromley under this political flag. It was an extremely difficult time, with the South African War at its height, for a socialist candidate openly opposed to that conflict involving his country, to stand against the sitting member from 1899, the Tory and imperialist, William Guthrie.

Raymond Postgate wrote that the subject of the war was tactfully avoided at Lansbury's adoption meeting, where 'nobody mentioned the War—not the chairman Harry Quelch, nor the distinguished attendance . . . nor even the candidate'.[26] However, this interpretation is mistakenly based on an undated news-cutting (probably dating from September 1899) of Lansbury's address at the Bromley Vestry Hall as the newly adopted candidate. In fact, this occasion was in 1895, four years before the war started.[27] George Lansbury did not ignore the Boer War in his campaign or his election literature, even though he had been threatened on a number of occasions by the hostile, jingoistic crowd months before the election campaign.

In 1899–1902 the South African War caused bitter divisions rarely seen in British domestic politics and society in the twentieth century. The Liberal party was split into three main camps. Anti-war meetings were frequently attacked and broken up by jingoistic crowds. Lloyd George was assaulted after speaking at Bangor in his native Wales and made a fortunate escape with his life after addressing an anti-war meeting in Birmingham town hall.[28] In the East End and elsewhere, the term 'pro-Boer' carried the connotation of being a traitor, especially for a politician with George Lansbury's known views on peace and war. Some alarming and threatening incidents put his pacifism to the test. Crowds attacked him and his family, as well as attempting to disrupt his public meetings.

---

[24] Ibid.; see also *Justice*, 14 Apr. 1900.   [25] *Reynolds Newspaper*, 15 Apr. 1900.

[26] Postgate, *Lansbury*, p. 53.

[27] LP, vol. 1, fo. 320. Internal evidence (e.g. Lansbury's references to 'the third birthday' of the Bow and Bromley Branch of the SDF and 'last winter . . . Mr [J. A. Murray] MacDonald came here . . . as a then member of the House of Commons, with a Liberal party in power') places the meeting in 1895. Postgate was also wrong in implying that the SDF wanted to contest the election on social and economic issues, but was forced to focus on the war by the electorate.

[28] K. O. Morgan, 'Riding the Wave of War Frenzy', *BBC History Magazine* (Dec. 2001), pp. 22–5.

The South African War added the word 'mafficking' to the English language after the news of the famous relief of the siege spread like wildfire in Britain. The celebratory behaviour on the evening of 18 May 1900 when the news arrived, in London, and elsewhere, was unlike the hysteria of the crudely patriotic crowds, which attempted to break up anti-war meetings during the war.[29]

In his memoirs George Lansbury remembered some unruly and life-threatening incidents during the Boer War. On 12 February 1900 H. M. Hyndman was the principal speaker at the Mile End SDF public meeting at the Vestry Hall in Bancroft Road. Posters in the district denounced 'Kruger's Boer Brigands in Mile End . . . Down with Traitors'. A jingoistic crowd invaded the building and the iron railings on the staircase collapsed. As chairman, Lansbury twice summoned the police. The scene was described in *Justice.*

Immediately after Hyndman's arrival a number of the opponents of peace swarmed into the lobby and up the stairs [for a fight] . . . Lansbury, fearing the ballusters would give way, sent for the police, but they declined to come in. Finally . . . the iron ballusters did give way, many of the surging crowd falling with them.

As this account indicated, the attempt failed to break up the anti-war meeting, which continued successfully.[30] Earlier, Lansbury had been present at a large rally in Trafalgar Square, where stones, knives, and other missiles were thrown at the speakers.[31]

On 9 April 1900 Lansbury chaired a 'Stop the War' public meeting in the East End attended by 1,500 people where Hyndman was the principal speaker. The meeting was interrupted by the jingoistic singing of 'Rule, Britannia!' and other disturbances, including the throwing of a bottle of eucalyptus oil, which resulted in Lansbury ordering the ejection of members of the audience. Afterwards J. E. Williams was almost murdered by 'a gang of savages' who followed him to Bishopsgate station.[32]

At Battersea old enmities were temporarily discarded as George Lansbury spoke at anti-war meetings on the same platform as John Burns. The Boer War was the only occasion that Lansbury met Lloyd George before his famous remark in the East End about 'my friend Lansbury', which was to assist Lansbury's chances in the 1910 election.

For his 1900 general election campaign George Lansbury rented 177 Bow Road, which the local SDF also used for meetings for his political work. Without a Liberal candidate, the 1900 general election campaign was a straight fight between George Lansbury and the Tory, William Guthrie, on two main themes—the South African War and social reform. Guthrie's portrait depicted him in military uniform, and his election campaign was full of references to the war and to Mrs Guthrie's nursing experience in South Africa.

---

[29] R. Price, *An Imperial War and the British Working Class: Working Class Attitudes and Reactions to the Boer War* (1972), pp. 132–3.

[30] *Justice*, 17 Feb. 1900.   [31] Lansbury, *My Life*, p. 199.

[32] *Reynolds Newspaper*, 15 Apr. 1900.

In his campaign speeches George Lansbury focused on two themes: opposition to the war on moral grounds and the demand for social reform in Britain. He did not hesitate to mention the conflict, which embroiled his country, though his family were attacked and abused on the streets of Bow and the probability of disruption to his campaign meetings persisted:

You will be told that this election must be fought on the right or wrong of the South African War. I decline altogether to so regard it, and shall . . . keep before you those matters which . . . are of far more importance. At the same time . . . the war in South Africa was an unjust war, got up, like the Jameson Raid, in the interests solely of gold and diamond mine owners and millionaires.[33]

Lansbury also included criticism of Guthrie's remarks about medical services published in *Nineteenth Century*: 'From start to finish it has been grossly mismanaged, and the British soldier, plucky as ever, has been sacrificed over and over again by the carelessness and ignorance of the officers.' The war was also condemned for creating widespread poverty in Britain. He reminded his audience:

you are now feeling the pinch—dear coal, dear bread, dear house rent, . . . everything has gone up except your wage . . . The Government which spent your money and shed the blood of England's sons to gain the votes for the Uitlanders of the Transvaal finally dissolves Parliament . . . when . . . workmen will be robbed of their votes owing to the iniquities of our Registration Laws.[34]

Typical of his campaign was the large indoor meeting, chaired by George Barnes, secretary of the Amalgamated Society of Engineers. Outright denunciation of the war was followed by a demand for a comprehensive programme of social reform: work for the unemployed, slum clearance, better housing, and land nationalization. The Tory government performance since the 1895 election was also examined:

The Conservatives had Old Age Pensions on their programmes . . . Had Mr. Chamberlain done anything (hisses)—oh, don't hiss him, but try and turn Guthrie out (hear, hear) . . . the only solution to the Old Age Pension plan was a graduated income tax (cheers) . . . The present Government said that it would involve a large expenditure, but if it was right to spend 115 millions to deal with the Uitlanders in the Transvaal, surely they might have found the means for dealing with the millions of old people in this country.[35]

Compared to a year before, there was now a considerable degree of unity on the Left among the socialist–Labour–Liberal camps, with support from Will Crooks and other Liberal and Labour figures for Lansbury's candidature. Again, Lansbury was endorsed by Dr John Clifford, the Nonconformist leader, who declared enthusiastically:

You are one of the men I most of all desire to see returned to the next Parliament. Your principles and programme ought to commend the support of all genuine Radicals. I trust every

[33] G. Lansbury, 'Parliamentary Election, 1900: To the Electors of the Bow and Bromley Division of Tower Hamlets', n.d. [*c.* Sept. 1900], LP, vol. 1, fo. 334.
[34] Ibid.
[35] *East End News and London Shipping Chronicle*, 25 Sept. 1900; *East London Advertiser*, 2 Oct. 1900.

Free Churchman and Radical . . . will not only vote for your return but also work for you up to the full limit of their strength.[36]

In the end Guthrie was elected by 4,403 votes to Lansbury's 2,558. It was a creditable performance in his first straight fight, particularly in the atmosphere of war fever.[37]

In 1901, with the Federation's secession from the LRC, George Lansbury decided not to stand for Bow again and, indeed, to leave the Social Democratic Federation for a new political home. His reasons were a mixture of the personal, professional, and political. Politics were affecting his health periodically and his sawmill and timber yard required full-time attention.

In particular, Lansbury evidently believed that the parliamentary future lay with the recently formed LRC. In Bow and Bromley his local Federation branch remained with the LRC after the national body seceded in 1901. The decision to abandon the new party was probably the final straw for Lansbury. Even so, he appeared somewhat reluctant to depart from a party he had served for over ten years. He wrote at the time: 'I don't agree with fighting independently, but, had I time, and were I in good health, and my business not so exacting, I should have a real good try to get the SDF round to my view.'[38]

Nevertheless, when he did move on, the legacy of his busy years in the Federation proved something of a political liability. It was not for some years that the national leadership of the Labour party, particularly Ramsay MacDonald, fully accepted that the former national organizer of the Federation, who had intervened at the Southampton by-election in 1896, was a loyal member of the Labour party.

In the early 1900s Lansbury rediscovered his Christian faith. At the age of forty-five he rejoined the Anglican Church around the same time that he left the SDF after disillusion set in with the anti-religious and anti-women stance prevalent in some quarters of the Federation. While he said little about this troubled time 'of twelve months reading and prayer', it is clear that these two events in his life were linked. 'Why I Returned to Christianity' (1904) was his only public statement on the circumstances in which he regained his faith and sought a new moral basis for his life and public work.[39] This article, an important profession of his born-again life in Christianity, was also published. Three years later it was circulated in the Woolwich LCC election of 1907, where Lansbury was a candidate, to counter opposition rumours that he was an atheist.[40]

For George Lansbury life was essentially a struggle between right and wrong, good and evil. A materialist analysis of the world, which had sustained him for ten years as an agnostic, was now insufficient and inadequate as a philosophy to carry him through life's difficulties and struggles. Only a belief in God and a personal commitment to Christ provided the moral basis for his own redemption and the inspiration to serve his community.

[36] *Daily Chronicle*, 1 Oct. 1900.   [37] *East London Advertiser*, 6 Oct. 1900.
[38] G. Lansbury to H. W. Lee, 23 Feb. 1902, printed in *Socialist* (Edinburgh), May 1905, quoted in Bealey and Pelling, *Labour and Politics*, p. 165 n. 1.
[39] George Lansbury, 'Why I Returned to Christianity', *Clarion*, 29 July 1904.
[40] *Woolwich Pioneer*, 22 Feb. 1907.

Serious sectarian divisions within the socialist movement, seen at first hand, compelled Lansbury to question the basis on which he had previously turned away from a faith of idealism and commitment. He acknowledged that he had 'seen Socialist branches broken up because men and women thought only of their own selfish gratification, and had no regard for the movement at all'; instead, he openly confessed that 'I find my moral basis in the teachings of Christ, and . . . in the Church and its services . . . Christianity helps and sustains me in my hours of trial and trouble, and gives me just the spur I need to work with, and on behalf of others'.

The bishop of Stepney, Cosmo Lang, future archbishop of Canterbury, encouraged George Lansbury to return to the Anglican Church. The rector at Bow church, Manley Power, told Lang of 'a secularist lecturer, by name Lansbury, who seemed to be feeling his way back to the Church. He came to Bow church, very shamefacedly, and sat in the back behind a pillar'. Afterwards at Cosmo Lang's invitation, Lansbury disclosed his renewed faith to a crowded and somewhat noisy meeting at Bow Baths Hall.[41]

Edgar, who now walked the mile or so to church on Sundays with his father, described these years as probably the happiest time for Lansbury and his family. He was at home more often, where he and Bessie conducted their family hymn-singing on Sunday evenings. Lansbury played an active and full role in the religious and social life of Bow church and gave a regular Sunday afternoon bible-class. His stentorian tones also wafted across Hackney Marshes and Wanstead Flats in loyal support of Edgar and his church football team.

For the remainder of his life George Lansbury found help, comfort, and guidance from regular attendance at Bow church. His Christianity once again became the inspiration for his politics, the faith that underpinned his unflagging commitment to socialism and pacifism, as well as the feminist and internationalist causes he would take up. He also played an influential and leading part in the organizations that formed the Christian socialist movement in twentieth-century Britain, especially the Church Socialist League founded in 1906.

In the early years of the twentieth century, Poplar and West Ham became the two strongest socialist-led local Labour parties formed before 1914 in London. During these years, the political allegiance of Bow and Bromley fluctuated constantly, with Liberal victories in 1885, 1892, and 1906, paralleled by Conservative successes in 1886, 1895, 1900, and January 1910. In this respect George Lansbury's eventual general election victory in December 1910 was a significant socialist breakthrough in the politics of Bow and Bromley, and he became the ILP's only MP in London, albeit briefly, as he sacrificed his parliamentary seat in 1912 over the women's suffrage issue.

The origins of the Poplar Labour party can be traced back to the presence of the Labour minority among the local guardians and borough councillors at the turn of the century. Success at parliamentary level was built on the hard-gained advances made in local government by George Lansbury and other largely unsung pioneer

---

[41] J. G. Lockhart, *Cosmo Gordon Lang* (1949), pp. 160–1.

figures in the East End socialist and labour movement at that time. In 1903 the Poplar Trades Council and Labour Representation Committee was formed, to which local trade unions and socialist groups affiliated, largely owing to the endeavours of J. H. Banks of 6 Campbell Road, Bow, a railwayman and former member of the Poplar Labour League. The new local party's membership was based strongly on the SDF in Bow and among the Gasworkers' Union in Bromley. Banks became a stalwart of the new party and Lansbury's future election agent in Bow and Bromley, an unpaid position that cost him his job on the railway.

In 1908 Lansbury reminded Ramsay MacDonald of the importance of this pioneering work of the East End labour movement:

About 5 years ago J. H. Banks from the Poplar Labour League thought we should attempt to bind all the labour forces throughout the Borough . . . and to this end the LRC was formed, which consists of practically every trade union branch in the district, together with the SDF & ILP, forming I believe one of the strongest local Labour Parties in the country. We have a dozen representatives on the Borough Council (of whom I am chairman) forming the most influential section of that Council of 49 members. On the Guardians we have 8 members out of 24, and at the next election we shall probably increase our number, as we did at the last. The bulk of these members come from the Bow and Bromley part of the division, not Poplar.[42]

Yet, in the 1906 general election, George Lansbury capitalized neither on the advances being made by the East End labour movement in municipal politics nor on the recognition his work on unemployment brought him in the East End labour movement. Instead, he chose to stand at Middlesbrough as an independent socialist candidate, his only parliamentary election contest outside London. In a three-cornered contest, which returned the Lib–Lab seamen's leader, Joseph Havelock Wilson, to Parliament, Lansbury finished bottom of the poll, well behind the other two candidates with fewer than 10 per cent of the votes cast.

None the less, despite the dismal result, this parliamentary campaign should not be overlooked. The Middlesbrough election was crucial to George Lansbury's political career: it represented his first contact with the Edwardian women's movement, as well as an important stage in his relations with the Labour party.

In the second half of the nineteenth century, Middlesbrough was the fastest-growing town in England. Following the discovery of rich iron ore deposits in the local Cleveland Hills, the town was transformed from a small village of 150 to the major iron and steel industrial centre of 90,000 in seventy years. By the end of the Victorian period, Middlesbrough, the largest single member constituency in the North East, was normally a Liberal parliamentary stronghold, represented from 1892–1900 by Joseph Havelock Wilson, the able but controversial Lib–Lab trade union leader.

The origins of Lansbury's candidature can be seen in the determination of the local ILP to run a socialist candidate against the much-disliked Wilson. In 1892, in a memorable contest, Wilson had originally shaken the Liberal caucus in Middlesbrough by his remarkable capture of their seat as an independent candidate, in the

---

[42] George Lansbury to Ramsay MacDonald, 28 May 1908, ILP Papers 1908/221.

general election which returned the first two socialists to Parliament, John Burns at Battersea and Keir Hardie at West Ham.

Soon afterwards, Wilson's independent stance evaporated. To those on the political left, especially his fellow member Keir Hardie, he embodied the worst aspects of Lib–Lab politics because of his political accommodation and deals with local employers, and a personal reputation for drink and fondness for a high lifestyle. Wilson was the official Liberal candidate in 1895 and again in 1900, when he lost narrowly by fifty-five votes to the chemical magnate, Sir Samuel Sadler.

There were considerable tensions in local Labour politics in Middlesbrough, arising from the divisions between the socialist ILP and the trade union movement which still retained strong residual links with organized Liberalism. The moderate trades council backed Wilson, who after 1900 was frequently seen on Liberal platforms and actively opposed the LRC in the North East. He defiantly refused to sign the LRC constitution, but as a Labour leader enjoyed considerable support from local unionists in his efforts to win back the parliamentary seat.

There were two local ILP branches in Middlesbrough and South Bank. The possibility of running a socialist candidate was considered as early as 1903, when Ramsay MacDonald was approached without success.[43] From this time onwards, a small circle of wealthy middle-class socialists drawn from the Coates and Hansen families dominated ILP politics. The driving force behind the local branch was the important figure of Marion Coates Hansen, a passionate, but largely forgotten, feminist who rarely receives a mention in histories of the women's movement. She and her husband, Frederick Hansen; her brother, Charles Coates, and his wife, Alice Schofield Coates—imprisoned in Holloway for her suffrage activities at one point—were all known in the politics of the local ILP as the 'Linthorpe Gang'.[44] The finance and organizational flair behind the local branch came from these left-wing activists, who normally held the posts of branch secretary and treasurer, as well as regular membership of the executive committee.[45] But their influence over the branch, and at times their attitudes, were resented and attracted constant criticism from socialist opponents, especially working-class trade unionists.[46]

In 1906 strong complaints were voiced at branch meetings about Marion Coates Hansen's conflict of interest between her socialism and feminism, after she supported Christabel Pankhurst campaigning against the Labour candidate at the

---

[43] Charles Coates to Ramsay MacDonald, 16 Apr. 1903, JRMP, PRO 30/69/1147.

[44] R. Lewis, 'The Evolution of a Political Culture: Middlesbrough, 1850–1950', in A. J. Pollard (ed.), *Middlesbrough: Town and Community, 1830–1950* (1996), pp. 118–19.

[45] At the 1906 AGM, with 45 members present, Marion and Frederick Coates Hansen were elected unopposed, as organizing secretary and treasurer respectively; Charles Coates topped the poll for the seven-member branch committee. Marion was among those nominated, with Keir Hardie, George Lansbury, Emmeline Pankhurst, and Philip Snowden, for the ILP NAC. Middlesbrough ILP, AGM minutes, 29 Jan. 1906.

[46] Again, in April 1909, Marion Coates Hansen attempted without success to raise the question of whether or not she was 'a fit and proper person to continue as secretary', following remarks about her (e.g. 'plutocrat'; certain members doing things for 'self aggrandisement . . . and the secretary . . . bossing the Branch'). Ibid. 8 Apr. 1909.

Cockermouth by-election. In Middlesbrough, it resulted in Marion Coates Hansen's temperamental though temporary resignation, until she was persuaded to resume as branch secretary.[47]

In the Women's Social and Political Union (WSPU), Marion Coates Hansen was a close associate of Emmeline and Christabel Pankhurst. However, at times conflicts of loyalties tested her hot temper. Her dedication to feminism was matched by her ardent socialism: as she later put it succinctly: 'I am a keen suffragist but I am a keener socialist (that is why I am a keen suffragist).'[48] In 1907 tensions reached bursting point over the autocracy of the Pankhurst leadership. Marion Coates Hansen was one of the small cabal led by Charlotte Despard that broke away to set up the rival and long-standing Women's Freedom League (WFL).[49]

Marion Coates Hansen was the prime mover in securing George Lansbury to contest Middlesbrough as an independent socialist candidate through her connection with Mary and Joseph Fels for whom she had worked as a nanny many years before in the United States. Her brother, Walter Coates, was Fels's business associate and virtually an adopted son. All were bound together by an admiration for the American poet, Walt Whitman, which had first taken Marion Coates Hansen to Philadelphia.[50]

Raymond Postgate said nothing about Lansbury's connection with the Coates family but implied that Lansbury felt compelled to go to Middlesbrough in 1906 to fight Wilson, rather than stay in his native Bow and Bromley. However, Lansbury was committed to Middlesbrough well before the general election in January 1906. His main difficulty, which he never overcame, was the failure to secure official support from the Labour leadership in London.

In 1906 the lack of an official endorsement by the Labour Representation Committee was probably an important factor in his poor showing at the polls. Ostensibly, the reason provided was a technicality in the official rule-book—that he had been nominated by the local LRC, then an unaffiliated body. The rules permitted the affiliation of the local party, if it could be demonstrated the Middlesbrough Trades Council did not cover the whole of the constituency.[51] But the next meeting of the National Executive Committee (NEC) to consider the matter was after the general election. Professor Purdue has judged that MacDonald and the NEC were sympathetic to Lansbury and that 'it was a lack of time rather than anything else which prevented Lansbury running as an official LRC candidate'.[52] Three weeks before national polling started on 12 January MacDonald informed Lansbury that: '[T]his application has come so late it does not give us time to enquire and settle before the election whether the position in Middlesbrough enables the

[47] G. E. F. Hansen to George Lansbury, 14 Oct. 1906, LP, vol. 2, fos. 290–1.

[48] Marion Coates Hansen to George Lansbury, 27 Nov. 1912, ibid. vol. 6, fo. 242.

[49] WFL minutes, 1 Feb. 1908, WFL; A. Linklater, *An Unhusbanded Life: Charlotte Despard: Suffragette, Socialist and Sinn Feiner* (1980), pp. 117–20.

[50] Dudden, *Joseph Fels*, pp. 34–45.

[51] Ramsay MacDonald to Marion Coates Hansen, 20, 21, 28 Nov. 1905, LPLF, 27, 184–5, 187.

[52] A. W. Purdue, 'George Lansbury and the Middlesbrough Election of 1906', *International Review of Social History*, 18 (1973), p. 343.

Middlesbrough LRC to come under that rule. Until that technical difficulty is out of the way, my committee is debarred from taking any action.'[53]

It is difficult to believe that this was the case and that the real reason did not lie in the conflicted politics of the North East, where an LRC decision to oppose even a shady and dubious character like Joseph Havelock Wilson could have brought Liberal party retaliation in 1906. Wilson was a substantial local figure and the former MP with local trades council support. His candidature appealed directly to the coalition of business radicalism, nonconformity, and organized labour that comprised Middlesbrough Liberalism.

Indeed, Ramsay MacDonald and his committee had known about Lansbury's interest in Middlesbrough for many months and had been kept in touch with developments in the town by Marion Coates Hansen and by Lansbury himself.[54] During the summer of 1905 he wrote to MacDonald to advance his name as the next candidate for Middlesbrough. He was ebullient after a barnstorming eight days in the town spreading the socialist message at crowded and enthusiastic meetings:

... They are quite apart from the Coates family a really splendid lot of men and women & if a candidate is not run will be cruelly cast down ... I had made up my mind never to fight a three cornered fight & *not* to join the SLP or the SDF again. There am I a member of the ILP talking of fighting a 3 cornered fight where I don't think I will win at any rate the first time. I can only explain it by saying the whole spirit of the Middlesboro people appeals to me & I feel I would like to be their man carrying their flag. If it means only a 100 votes they are a branch of the ILP which will I am certain make its mark.[55]

Lansbury was formally adopted on 30 September 1905, after further visits to Middlesbrough where he spoke on unemployment and attracted interest as a likely candidate.[56] In July, Marion Coates Hansen also contacted Ramsay MacDonald to point out the favourable circumstances for a labour candidature and the opportunity to be rid of Wilson. Also, there was a crucial guarantee—that Joseph Fels would meet the cost of the campaign.[57] Once more George Lansbury wrote to pledge loyalty to the party: 'I shall not attempt to do anything either the NAC or LRC disapprove. I am, however, certain Wilson is quite past praying for as far as the ILP or LRC is concerned.'[58] But the official endorsement never came and was conveniently lost in the bureaucracy of the rules and regulations of affiliated organizations. MacDonald made one or two soothing noises to both candidate and his agent, but his correspondence with Frank Rose, who stood at nearby Stockton in the labour cause in 1906, is more revealing in showing MacDonald's concern about the local political situation rather than the niceties of the rule-book.

---

[53] Ramsay MacDonald to George Lansbury, 23 Dec. 1905, LPLF, LRC, 28/234.

[54] NEC, minutes, 5 Oct. 1905.

[55] George Lansbury to Ramsay MacDonald, 24 Aug. 1905, JRMP, PRO 30/69/1149.

[56] *North Eastern Daily Gazette*, 2 Oct. 1905; Marion Coates Hansen to Ramsay MacDonald, 1 Oct. 1905, LPLF, LRC 26/115. For MacDonald's disappointing reply, see Ramsay MacDonald to Marion Coates Hansen, 7 Oct. 1905, ibid. LRC 26/116.

[57] Marion Coates Hansen to George Lansbury, 4 July 1905, LPLF, LRC 24/185.

[58] George Lansbury to Ramsay MacDonald, 6 July 1905, ibid. LRC 24/259.

On 18 December 1905 MacDonald penned Rose one letter—about how to handle press enquiries about the official status of Lansbury's candidature—only to follow it up immediately with a more circumspect reply for probable publication. What he told Rose was that the LRC was in no way responsible for Lansbury's candidature, which was a local initiative. The next day he changed tack to emphasize the equal division on the Middlesbrough Trades Council over backing Wilson or Lansbury. His committee had 'decided to take no part in the Middlesbrough contest but to allow the two sides to fight the matter out'. He ended with an instruction: 'the only official statement you can make me responsible for . . . so far as the contest is concerned [is] we are quite out of it and nobody responsible for you is responsible for Lansbury.'[59]

In these circumstances George Lansbury fought his fourth parliamentary election on unfamiliar territory and with the political cards stacked against him. Middlesbrough was over 200 miles away from his political base in East London and at the very start of the campaign Lansbury was absent. This disadvantage was increased by the demoralizing failure to secure official endorsement from the Labour leadership.[60] Marion Coates Hansen was furious with MacDonald, particularly once the National Administrative Council (NAC) of the ILP refused to endorse her candidate after an initially warm response.[61] Anger screamed out from every line: 'I told Hardie that we could *not* afford a refusal. We could get along all right *without* applying but a refusal was impossible. I think some of us had better leave the labour movement . . .' Five days later, she made this crucial point once more: 'All we wanted was *not* to be refused endorsement and considering the nearness of the election that is all we have a *chance* to expect. I say "chance" advisedly.'[62]

Despite this formidable set-back, George Lansbury challenged Havelock Wilson at Middlesbrough, though only Keir Hardie and Frank Smith journeyed to the town to support the candidate and the dedicated band of local socialists and one or two sympathetic clergy who supported him.[63] Yet in Marion Coates Hansen, Lansbury had a first-rate and committed local election agent on whom he could rely: tireless, fearless, and utterly determined to promote his candidature. Moreover, she displayed the essential quality of any agent in those circumstances—to maintain optimism in all situations, whatever the daunting difficulties. As a feminist, she was also articulate and well versed in the barriers women encountered in the male domain of parliamentary politics. Her frustrated anger at the injustices faced by women in the separate sphere of Edwardian politics and society is a constant theme in her correspondence with her candidate. An early glimpse can be seen in her decision not to allow any legal impediment to bar her as Lansbury's election agent: 'Will

[59] Ramsay MacDonald to Frank Rose, 18, 19 Dec. 1905, ibid. LRC 28/259; 261.

[60] Ramsay MacDonald to Marion Coates Hansen, 5 Dec. 1905, ibid. LRC, 28/246. See also 7 Dec. 1905, ibid. LRC 28/249.

[61] ILP NAC, minutes, 18 Dec. 1905. For the NAC's initially warm response to Lansbury's candidature, see ILP, minutes, 7, 8 July; 2, 3 Oct. 1905.

[62] Marion Coates Hansen to Ramsay MacDonald, 22, 27 Dec. 1905, ibid. LRC 28/252–3, 255.

[63] For his Christian Socialist support at Middlesbrough, see M. Gobat, *T. C. Gobat: His Life, Work, and Teaching* (1938), pp. 42–4.

there be any legal objection to my acting as your agent? You must not forget that I am not even "a person" in the eyes of the law as far as elections etc are concerned. You might find that out, for I shall be responsible for lots of things you know full well.'[64]

Marion Coates Hansen did not neglect any aspect of Lansbury's parliamentary campaign: election finance, committee rooms, speakers, and the production of six issues of the *Middlesbrough Election News* to carry the campaign message to the electors received her meticulous attention. An election fund was opened with Frederick as treasurer, though the bulk of the campaign money came, as promised, from Joseph Fels and Walter Coates. Lansbury was kept fully up to date on the activities of the rival candidates, especially the loathed Wilson.[65]

In 1906 Marion Coates Hansen was primarily responsible for the inclusion of 'Votes for Women' as part of Lansbury's election manifesto—alongside Work for All, Irish Home Rule, Religious Freedom, Old Age Pensions, Trade Union Rights.[66] This manifesto is probably another reason why Lansbury finished bottom of the poll. His programme, including women's enfranchisement, was too advanced in 1906 for the predominantly working-class, all-male electorate used to a staple diet of northern Liberalism and moderate Labour politics.

The appearance of Keir Hardie during Lansbury's campaign brought Lloyd George to Middlesbrough in hearty support of Havelock Wilson. Lansbury failed to win over the sizeable Irish Catholic vote in the town and the influential Welsh Nonconformists were equally unimpressed with an Anglican socialist's support for the provisions of the Tory Education Act of 1902. Lansbury brought his usual fervour and energy to a hapless campaign, but at the cost of his exhaustion. On polling day he was very ill with a serious bout of pleurisy in the Coates's house in the leafy suburb of Linthorpe. He was therefore not present to hear that his share of the poll was less than 9 per cent—only 1,484 votes. Wilson was returned to Parliament with 9,227 votes (52.6 per cent) and Samuel Sadler had taken second place with 6,846 votes (39.0 per cent).

In the 1906 Liberal landslide, Labour's election success with a group of twenty-nine MPs returned depended in part on the Lib–Lab pact of 1903, as well as the association of the party with Free Trade and the surging radical tide that had swept the Liberals back to Westminster. Characteristically, the socialist George Lansbury did not match the profile of the trade unionists and moderate Labour men who now largely composed the new ranks of the newly returned parliamentary Labour party.[67] His lack of success at Middlesbrough was unsurprising, and not only because he fought unendorsed and on an advanced manifesto. In January 1910 the official Labour candidate, Pat Walls, a local trade union leader of Irish extraction, who had the trades council's support, still finished in third place, over 4,000 votes

---

[64] Marion Coates Hansen to George Lansbury, 7 Dec. 1905, LP, vol. 2, fo. 154.

[65] Marion Coates Hansen to George Lansbury, 7, 8, 24 Dec., also n.d. [Dec.] 1905, ibid. vol. 2, fos. 150–1, 154–9, 161–2, 175; 'George Lansbury Middlesbrough Election 1906', ibid. fo. 203.

[66] Marion Coates Hansen to George Lansbury, 8 Dec. 1905, ibid. vol. 2, fo. 162.

[67] D. Martin, 'Ideology and Composition', in K. D. Brown (ed.), *The First Labour Party, 1906–1914* (1985), ch. 2.

behind the second candidate, while in December 1910 the Labour party did not contest Middlesbrough at all.

There was one other important legacy from his contest at Middlesbrough—his commitment to women's rights. Lansbury told Marion Coates Hansen:

Now you must take some responsibility for having educated me on the women's question. You know that when I came to Middlesbrough, I was an adult suffragist, and put it just as part of my propaganda. I have learned during the seven years that have passed to understand it in another sense altogether.

Women's enfranchisement was now firmly on his political programme, and to such an extent that, by the time he entered Parliament after the December 1910 general election, gender was to replace social class at the head of his list of concerns and preoccupations.[68]

After his appointment to the Royal Commission and his Middlesbrough contest, Lansbury received regular invitations to fight constituencies in different parts of the country. In early 1907 he was sounded out about the East Birmingham seat, where he was seen as one of the few Labour figures with 'a chance of breaking the "Joe" [Chamberlain] influence'. [69]

At this time, C. H. Grinling, a leading light of the Woolwich Labour Party and fellow socialist on the CUB enticed George Lansbury to Woolwich, where Will Crooks was the Labour MP, to contest the LCC election.[70] There, in a constituency dominated by the Woolwich Arsenal, the main government armaments works, the pacifist George Lansbury put up his usual sterling performance, including a direct appeal to the new women voters, only to be defeated once more. His campaign workers blamed the fact that polling day fell on Saturday 2 March. It meant traditional Labour supporters were more interested in watching their local team, Woolwich Arsenal, battle against Sheffield United than in voting for the Labour candidate. After his defeat George Lansbury was told: '. . . it was very disheartening for some of us who were flitting about on our bikes, like paper men in a gale wind, to get the favourable to the poll, for the reply was oft repeated, "ees gan ter football match" and that over, "now ees having ees tee"' (*sic*).[71] A few days later, Hardie wrote to explain that 'some sinister [had] intervened' to thwart an electoral arrangement with the Progressive Party and asked Lansbury to press Crooks to form a distinct Labour group on the Council.[72]

Despite a political friendship with Keir Hardie, George Lansbury needed to rebuild his fences with the Labour leadership, even though at the time of his appointment to the Royal Commission on the Poor Law, he was counted as a friend of labour. In particular, Lansbury required official party endorsement and financial

[68] George Lansbury to Mrs Frederick [Marion] Hansen, 31 Oct. 1912, LP, vol. 28, fo. 80.
[69] Revd James Atterley to George Lansbury, 4 Mar. 1907, ibid. vol. 3, fo. 44.
[70] C. H. Grinling to George Lansbury, 2 Jan. 1907, ibid. vol. 3, fo. 25.
[71] Septimus Davison to George Lansbury, 3 Mar. 1907, ibid. vol. 3, fos. 38–9, quoted in E. Shepherd, 'The Foundation and Early Social History of Woolwich Arsenal Football Club, 1886–1913', B.A. diss. (Salford, 1999), p. 18.
[72] Keir Hardie to George Lansbury, 7 Mar. 1907, LP, vol. 3, fos. 49–50.

support, if he was to win a parliamentary election. Disappointed that the NEC had not endorsed him at Middlesbrough, he went to considerable lengths to demonstrate his loyalty to the Labour party, both in the past and for the future. Most likely he was aware of the impact on the Labour party of the controversial and mercurial Victor Grayson following his dramatic Colne Valley by-election victory as a socialist candidate independent of the central party organization.[73] Lansbury promised MacDonald utter loyalty, if elected, and in no uncertain terms—particularly when his eventual conduct in Parliament is remembered:

Firstly, I want to be a loyal member of the Labour Party if I am returned to the House of Commons. Secondly, I want to extend its influence as far as I can wherever possible. I have given proof of this by the many scores of lectures that I have delivered up and down the country advocating its cause. I also stood at Middlesbrough as a Labour candidate and was prepared to stand anywhere else in the same manner. I also really need the yearly allowance that the Party would grant to any successful candidate. And therefore it must be dismissed altogether from the mind of your Committee that personally I want to stand independently of it.[74]

None the less, without national Labour party endorsement, Lansbury was privately despondent about his political prospects at Bow and Bromley, where he had been adopted nearly two years before.[75] He told MacDonald firmly 'that if the seat is to be fought effectively while I am alive I am the person to do it', and that he had therefore turned down offers of constituencies in Paisley, Govan, Darlington, East Birmingham, and East Northamptonshire to put his services at the disposal of Bow and Bromley.[76] Both Lansbury and his friend Joe Banks, who was to be his election agent, went to considerable lengths to explain the local political situation to the Labour leadership and to persuade them 'that there is no question at all of us down here wanting to fight the Labour party'.[77]

In September 1909 Lansbury reviewed his political prospects in Bow and Bromley, where he felt he could win, if the local Social Democratic Party backed him—otherwise he would lose heavily. He told Hardie: 'If I am to go on here it must be as a candidate of the National Labour Party with to say the least a kind of armed neutrality on the part of the SDP.'[78]

More encouraging news came from his Fabian friend, R. C. K. Ensor, who reassured Lansbury that he should press on to Westminster. His electoral chances as a parliamentary candidate in Bow and Bromley were promising, whatever the state of local socialist politics, and to try elsewhere would be a grave mistake. Ensor warned Lansbury: 'It is late to fit you in any other promising place; and after all the work done and expectations roused in B. & B., your retirement (which wd. pretty

---

[73] D. Clark, *Victor Grayson: Labour's Lost Leader* (1985), pp. 25–44.

[74] George Lansbury to Ramsay MacDonald, 28 May 1908, ILP Papers 1908/221.

[75] *The Times*, 16 Nov. 1907.

[76] George Lansbury to Ramsay MacDonald, 29 May 1908, ILP Papers 1908/221.

[77] J. H. Banks to Keir Hardie, 11 Aug. 1909, ibid. 1909/294; George Lansbury to Ramsay MacDonald, 28 May 1908, ibid. 1908/221.

[78] George Lansbury to Keir Hardie, 5 Sept. 1909, ibid. 1909/349.

well ruin the B.&B. movement) wd. look bad against you everywhere'. He remained optimistic that local difficulties with the SDP could be overcome with a national endorsement, and if outside help was brought in.[79]

In the event, in 1910, George Lansbury contested Bow and Bromley twice with national Labour party endorsement.[80] The decisive factor was not so much the attitude of those local socialists in a party he had left a few years before. In January 1910 he did well and pushed the Liberal candidate into third place in Bow and Bromley. In December 1910 Lansbury's electoral opportunity of a straight fight against Conservative opposition, and the possibility of an eventual victory, hinged on the local Liberal Association and the Liberal voters of Bow and Bromley. Surprisingly, they were to be influenced by some public remarks by the Liberal Chancellor of the Exchequer during a campaign visit to Lansbury's East End.

[79] R. C. K. Ensor to George Lansbury, 8 Sept. 1909, LP, vol. 3, fos. 247–8.
[80] For his official endorsement, see NEC, minutes, 8 Oct., 2 Dec. 1909.

6

At Westminster, 1911–1912

In 1911 George Lansbury entered Parliament as the member for Bow and Bromley during the political crisis in the Edwardian state caused by a series of major domestic conflicts in the immediate pre-war years. The Liberal government faced widespread unrest in the trade union and labour movement, with major large-scale strikes and disturbances, and a serious threat of civil war over the crisis in Ulster. From 1909 the rejection at Westminster of the 'People's Budget' produced a constitutional impasse in the House of Lords over the passage of the Parliament Bill. Outside Parliament, the WSPU, led by Emmeline and Christabel Pankhurst, escalated the militant women's campaign for the parliamentary franchise by the use of civil disobedience and arson.

Thirty years later, during the years of the inter-war Depression and the rise of international fascism, George Dangerfield writing in the USA produced a memorable account of the politics and society of this bygone era in Britain, which he entitled *The Strange Death of Liberal England* (1935). Dangerfield concluded that the series of conflicts had torn the social and political fabric of the country apart. In 1951 Postgate agreed with this verdict in describing Lansbury's early years as a Member of Parliament. He believed that in deliberately attempting to out-manoeuvre these crises and conflicts, the Liberal leadership inflicted a death wound on its own party between 1910–14. Since then, Dangerfield's thesis of an 'Edwardian Crisis', which expanded the French historian Elie Halevy's interpretation of this subject, has been seriously questioned; but his book remains a vivid source for examining politics and society in pre-war Britain.[1]

In the December 1910 general election George Lansbury had been returned to Parliament at his sixth attempt. He had won in a straight fight against a young Unionist candidate, who had earlier lost the Wolverhampton by-election of 1908 by only eight votes, L. S. Amery—a future Conservative Cabinet minister. At Bow and Bromley in the January 1910 general election Lansbury, with a popular campaign on 'Peers and Plutocrats, Pauperism and Poverty', had polled the highest Labour vote in the country in a three-cornered contest against Liberal opposition that relegated the former Liberal MP Stopford Brooke to bottom place. Beatrice Webb told Lansbury 'if you stick to it you will get in next time . . . work up your electorates and appeal to each section separately, with Nonconformist backing'.[2] As the year progressed, the political tide was beginning to turn in Lansbury's favour. A few

---

[1] Postgate, *Lansbury*, p. 109. E. Halevy, *The Rule of Democracy, 1905–1914* (revised edn., 1952). For a recent account, see D. Powell, *The Edwardian Crisis: Britain, 1901–1914* (1996).

[2] Beatrice Webb to George Lansbury, n.d. [Jan. 1910], PP, Section A part 1.K/L.

weeks later, at Bow and Bromley with the support of the Gasworkers' Union and the Fabian Society, he stood as a socialist in the London County Council of March 1910 and finished at the head of the poll with 4,002 votes.[3] At County Hall he formed an independent Labour bench with R. C. K. Ensor and Frank Smith.[4]

With a Conservative parliamentary majority of 740 at Bow and Bromley, covert negotiations mainly involving Beatrice and Sidney Webb took place in the intervening time before the general election in December.[5] Their endeavours assisted in securing a public endorsement of Lansbury by Dr John Clifford whose influence with local Nonconformist voters had helped to return the preacher Stopford Brooke in the Liberal cause in the previous election.[6]

Nevertheless, the intervention of another more public figure was regarded as the decisive factor that turned the scales in Lansbury's favour and produced a winning outcome in the December 1910 general election. On 21 November Lloyd George addressed a meeting of 5,000 electors in the Paragon Music Hall in the Mile End Road to open the Liberal campaign in Tower Hamlets. He gave a vintage performance for an hour and a half, including a trenchant attack on the House of Lords full of familiar gibes—'An aristocracy is like cheese; the older it is the higher it becomes'. However, it was Lloyd George's unexpected closing remarks that echoed around the East End for the rest of the campaign as he gave this unsolicited public endorsement for a socialist opponent: 'we want to see that Mr Lansbury gets in. (Cheers). *I hope he will not be opposed by the party to which I belong* . . . I say he is a true friend of the people and I for one should like to see him in.'[7]

Despite some local muttering, the Bow and Bromley Liberal Association did not put up a candidate at the general election. George Lansbury had a winning margin of 863 votes (11.2 per cent) against his Conservative opponent and found the parliamentary way clear to Westminster.[8] However, it was widely remembered that he got there with the aid of Liberal votes—as *Reynold's Newspaper* put it: 'Mr. Lansbury is fortunate to have the endorsement which the Chancellor of the Exchequer, in his speech at Mile End, gave to his candidature.'[9] In Parliament Lansbury, still battling for the implementation of the Minority Report of the Royal Commission, was to discover that Lloyd George had a different welfare agenda to implement in 1911 and one that the new Member for Bow and Bromley was not prepared to support.

[3] *East London Observer*, 5 Mar. 1910.   [4] *East End News and Shipping Chronicle*, 8 Mar. 1910.
[5] Sidney Webb to Beatrice Webb, 1 Dec. 1910, PP, quoted in *The Letters of Sidney and Beatrice Webb*, ii, ed. N. Mackenzie (1978), pp. 362–3.
[6] N. Blewett, *The Peers, The Parties and The People: The General Elections of 1910* (1972), pp. 259–60; See also, Bessie Lansbury's appeal to 'the Electors and Non-Electors of Bow and Bromley' to 'vote solidly for my husband'. In a postscript she added: 'I've been taking care of my daughter who, as you know, has been seriously ill. We are coming home, and hope to help just a little in the final rush to victory.' Election leaflet, 3 Dec. 1910, LP, vol. 4, fo. 72.
[7] *The Times*, 22 Nov. 1910 (emph. added).
[8] For George Lansbury's campaign, see *East London Observer*, 26 Nov.; 3, 10 Dec. 1910. After Lansbury's victory, among the flood of congratulations, Eleanor Coates wrote; 'I let my voice be heard very decidedly last night in the theatre when the result was shown on the screen between the acts'. Eleanor Coates to Bessie Lansbury, 7 Dec. 1910, LP, vol. 4, fo. 95.
[9] *Reynold's Newspaper*, 27 Nov. 1910.

In 1928, as chairman of the annual labour party conference, George Lansbury declared that from the first moment he stepped into Parliament in 1911 as a new backbencher he was in hot water with his party. In his memoirs he recalled that he had been unable to 'settle down as an ordinary rank and filer' and that he had taken his own line on most questions of policy:

Because of my indignation and my belief in woman suffrage I became one of their champions in the House of Commons . . . There were also a number of Labour disputes: the big mining dispute in the Rhondda Valley . . . a big dock strike in the East End . . . I opposed the National and Unemployment Insurance Bills.'[10]

By the 1910–14 Parliament the Liberal government no longer held the imposing majority it had won in the landslide election victory of 1906. The December 1910 general election left the Irish Nationalists (84 MPs) and Labour (42 MPs) holding the balance of power between the Liberal government (272 MPs) and the Conservative opposition (272 MPs). The Liberal Prime Minister, H. H. Asquith, was dependent upon Irish Nationalist and Labour votes in the House of Commons to secure majorities for his legislative programme, including the Parliament Bill, Irish Home Rule, Welsh Disestablishment, and other measures. To the disquiet of its left wing, the Parliamentary Labour Party (PLP) had only occasionally opposed the government, even when the Liberal administration was secure behind its massive majority between 1906 and 1910. After the two parliamentary campaigns in 1910 the Labour leadership feared another difficult and costly general election, if the Liberal Government was defeated and turned out. Thus, after 1910, instead of opposition at Westminster to exploit the balance of power, MacDonald instead bartered propping up the Liberal government in return for the introduction of Payment of Members and some measure of trade union reform.

Nevertheless, MacDonald's concordat with the Liberal administration proved increasingly unpopular with those ardent members of the PLP who advocated socialism rather than subservience to Liberalism at Westminster.[11] In the years after the Labour triumph at the 1906 general election, there was considerable disappointment over MacDonald's cosy relationship with the Liberal government and the tame performance of the twenty-nine Labour MPs returned to Westminster. The Gladstone–MacDonald pact of 1903 remained secret: many in the Labour party, however, sensed its existence when the PLP failed to promote socialism and lacked an independent stance in the House of Commons. In particular, Labour disquiet was symbolized by a series of challenges from the Left of the party. In 1907 a young maverick socialist, Victor Grayson, won the legendary Colne Valley by-election without official Labour support. Until his defeat three years later Grayson provided an independent and controversial presence at Westminster, a role inherited in many respects by George Lansbury when he joined the Labour ranks there. In 1908

---

[10] Lansbury, *My Life*, pp. 115–16.
[11] R. I. McKibbin, 'James Ramsay MacDonald and the Problem of the Independence of the Labour Party, 1910–1914', *Journal of Modern History*, 42 (1970), pp. 216–35.

Ben Tillett echoed the discontent on the left with a bitter polemic entitled *Is the P.L.P. a Failure?*[12]

Two years later, from within the heart of the Independent Labour Party, where MacDonald, Hardie, Glasier, and Snowden dominated proceedings, came another challenge. This altercation embroiled George Lansbury, an emerging force within the ILP and elected to its NAC in the previous year. Four activists on the NAC, Leonard Hall, J. M. MacLachan, J. H. Belcher, and C. T. Douthwaite published *Let Us Reform the Labour Party* (1910), a pamphlet commonly known as the 'Green Manifesto' from the colour of its cover. It was critical of the PLP and called for a more forthright socialist programme. At the annual conference in 1910 Lansbury had moved the NAC resolution on arms limitation.[13] A year later, when the ILP assembled at Birmingham, as a newly elected MP he was chosen to explain the NAC case against the *Green Manifesto*, which had been circulated first among the ILP branches. Lansbury stated that the NAC 'could not run an Executive Committee with a second committee inside it taking distinct action.'[14] In 1912 Lansbury was to find himself in a very similar position to that of the authors of the *Green Manifesto* in his policy dispute with the Labour leadership on women's enfranchisement.

None the less, at Birmingham in his second contribution to the proceedings Lansbury took issue with MacDonald over the Fred Jowett proposal that the PLP vote on every parliamentary question on the basis of its specific merits. According to Fenner Brockway, the editor of the *Labour Leader*, Lansbury's conference speech 'was a burning oration. It stirred the Conference profoundly', as he took the opportunity to protest against the compromising policy of the PLP under MacDonald's leadership. Lansbury had only been in the Commons a few weeks but he argued passionately that 'if they wanted to see some great steps towards Socialism, they must put the fear of their votes into the hearts of the Government whips'. He added: 'I am in the House of Commons with the picture before me of those men and women, who night after night, toiled in the slums of Bow and Bromley to send me there . . . they thought that I was different from the Liberals and the Tories . . .'[15]

George Lansbury had only been at Westminster a short while, but this conference speech marked his emergence as the rising star in the ILP. Keir Hardie warmly welcomed his presence in the House and saw Lansbury as an asset to the PLP. He told Bruce Glasier that 'Lansbury promises to be a most valuable member. He has a fine manner & presence and is in grim earnest'.[16] However, between MacDonald and Lansbury there was an ideological divide in their respective attitudes to Labour politics and socialism. MacDonald's revisionist approach and his close association with New Liberalism contrasted sharply with Lansbury's revolutionary socialism that brooked no compromise with capitalism. As a result, after 1910 Lansbury

[12] J. Schneer, *Ben Tillett: Portrait of a Labour Leader* (1982), pp. 133–6.
[13] ILP, *Report of the Eighteenth Annual Conference, Memorial Hall, London, 28 and 29 March 1910*.
[14] *Labour Leader*, 21 Apr. 1911. [15] Ibid.
[16] Keir Hardie to John Bruce Glasier, 8 Feb. 1911, J. B. Glasier Papers.

remained the most active and fiercest critic among those opposed to MacDonald's cautious leadership in Parliament.[17]

During the parliamentary sessions of 1911 and 1912 Lansbury was constantly at odds with the Labour leadership over the National Insurance Bill and the question of women's enfranchisement. Moreover, on these two crucial issues his outspokenness exposed divisions within the parliamentary party. More disastrously, in 1912, his fervent commitment to the women's cause brought about his own suspension from the House of Commons and eventually took him out of parliamentary politics at Westminster for ten years.

For the new MP for Bow and Bromley himself, his response to the parliamentary situation constituted a political and moral dilemma: that of the conscience of the individual against loyalty to the party machine. As Lansbury put it: 'At any rate I am going to refuse to vote according to the bidding of those who look at politics more or less from the Liberal standpoint. It is an intolerable position, and I for one could not stand for it for 48 hours.'

He saw his role as an independent on the left, unfettered by decisions of the caucus, party organization, and matters of internal discipline:

It is no use separating from the Labour Party; we must make the best use of it we can. We socialist members must form an advanced wing to speed things on as rapidly as possible . . . Unless we are allowed the same freedom, the presence of Socialists in the House is of very little value. It will mean that the Labour Party, instead of advancing towards Socialism, will drift back towards Liberalism, and I am not going there.[18]

In 1911–12, as an East End MP, George Lansbury was typical of a small group of prominent Labour figures that included Will Crooks (Woolwich), Will Thorne (West Ham), and Jack Jones (Silvertown), each closely identified with their constituency. All drew their power and personal popularity from being representatives of their people: they lived in their local communities and spoke with a valuable knowledge drawn from working-class life and a practical experience of working conditions. Local residents instantly recognized the Labour and Socialist member for Bow and Bromley as the gregarious politician who lived at 39 Bow Road, where his family home also served as his parliamentary 'surgery' and local advice centre. George Lansbury was symbolic of a new tradition in parliamentary politics, whereby elected Labour members were the direct representatives of the social class that sent them to Westminster.

Unsurprisingly, Lansbury found that he had little in common with the vast majority of those who sat beside him in the Commons, whom he associated with the rise of plutocracy in Edwardian Britain. Instead, Lansbury campaigned on poverty, unemployment, and working-class conditions, the major concerns of the majority of his constituents in Bow and Bromley. There were constant initiatives to reform

---

[17] See further D. Tanner, 'Ideological Debate in Edwardian Politics', in E. Biagini and A. J. Reid (eds.), *Currents of Radicalism: Popular radicalism, Organized Labour and Party Politics in Britain, 1850–1914* (1991), ch. 12.

[18] *Labour Leader*, 24 Mar. 1911.

the Poor Law. Lansbury questioned the waste of state expenditure on the corona-tion of George V and its effects on a poor constituency. He also attempted to intro-duce a private member's bill to provide workers with paid holidays.

Elected with the support of the Poplar Trades and Labour Representation Com-mittee, George Lansbury was sponsored as a Labour and Socialist MP by the ILP. He joined the ranks of the PLP, composed mainly of moderate trade unionists. At Westminster Lansbury saw himself therefore outside the mainstream of the PLP, as his ultimate purpose was to secure socialism rather than the short term social reforms envisaged by the majority of his party.

George Lansbury's early years in Parliament also coincided with his membership of the Church Socialist League, founded in 1906 by Anglican clergymen who envisaged a reconstruction of society on socialist lines as an extension of God's kingdom on earth.[19] Lansbury, who became chairman of the League in 1912, was one of its few lead-ing lay people and active in its London branch.[20] The Church Socialist League gave him considerable support during his elections and individual clergy were prominent on his election platforms.[21] As a dedicated Christian Socialist, his mission was to preach the religion of socialism with the energy and conviction of a religious convert.[22]

In 1911, on entering the House of Commons, Lansbury was straightaway in con-flict with an old foe, John Burns. The President of the LGB was well remembered for launching the Davy Inquiry into the conduct of Poplar guardians, as well as for his hostility that ended their Hollesley Bay experiment. Burns was also an implacable opponent of the *Minority Report* of the Poor Law Commission that Lansbury had campaigned for so vigorously, prior to entering Parliament. On 8 February 1911 the new Member for Bow and Bromley's first parliamentary action was to question Burns on the number of registered unemployed in London during the previous six months. His next act was to demand an inquiry into a riot at the Belmont work-house in Fulham.

---

[19] For the Church Socialist League, see I. Goodfellow, 'The Church Socialist League, 1906–1923: Origins, Development and Disintegration', Ph.D. thesis (Durham, 1983).

[20] See G. Lansbury, 'What is Christianity?', *The Optimist*, 6 (1912); G. C. Binyon, *The Christian Socialist Movement in England* (1931), p. 190.

[21] 'The Bow and Bromley Election', *Church Socialist Quarterly*, 6 (1911), pp. 1–3. At the Bow and Brom-ley Public Hall, during the Jan. 1910 campaign, the Revd Drew Roberts claimed that 'he was converted to socialism by Mr. Lansbury'. *East London Observer*, 15 Jan. 1910.

[22] Lansbury was one of the most prominent lay members of the League, which rejected a resolution in 1909 to affiliate to the Labour party. The ideas of guild socialism and syndicalism for a while had con-siderable influence with some League members. During the First World War, when the League had a closer association with the Church of England, Lansbury was appointed in 1916 to the Central Council of National Mission of Repentance and Hope. He was also, with R. H. Tawney, a member of the Arch-bishop of Canterbury's Enquiry into Christianity and Industrial Problems and a signatory to its 1918 Report. However, his failure to move the 'official' Church towards socialism resulted in the publication of his influential, *Your Part in Poverty*. I. Goodfellow, 'The Church Socialist League', in J. Bellamy and J. Saville, with D. Martin (eds.), *Dictionary of Labour History*, viii (1987), pp. 167–73; G. Lansbury, *My Faith and Hope in View of the National Mission* (n.d.), p. 12; *My Life*, pp. 220–2; his contribution to G. Haw (ed.), *Christianity and the Working Classes* (1906), pp. 163–80. Lansbury was also connected with the Christian Socialist, Conrad le Despenser Roden Noel, radical vicar of Thaxted for thirty years, who formed the Catholic Crusade in 1918. R. Groves, *Conrad Noel and the Thaxted Movement* (1968), pp. 43, 83, 111–12, 114, 180, 246, 317–18.

Two days later, in the debate on the Address, Lansbury made his maiden speech on 'state provision of work or maintenance', a major theme of labour politics that he had campaigned on in previous years, which also turned into a polemic against the President of the LGB. That day Lansbury's address, lasting forty-five minutes, was full of the passionate crusading and irreverent disregard for parliamentary sensibilities that were to endear him to his supporters and infuriate his opponents whenever he spoke in the future. He used the occasion to taunt Burns about an earlier time when his socialist heart had sought social justice: 'I have in mind a speech made some years ago in which a gentleman said he had a vision of hungry children and homeless men, of women driven to prostitution and shame because of want of employment . . . it was that which had driven him into revolt against society . . . '[23]

In making his case Lansbury referred directly to his own experience in his East End constituency: 'I live within a stone's throw of the docks, and I have also to administer the poor law in the district affected.' When challenged about 'loafers', he responded in a theatrical style that was also to become familiar in the years to come at Westminster. He told the House of Commons:

I think I ought to say here what I said outside, that when I deal with loafers I will deal with those who canter around Rotten Row for want of any other exercise to obtain an appetite for their meals. If ever the democracy of this country deals with loafers, they will deal with them at both ends of the social scale.[24]

During this time in Parliament, Lansbury penned a weekly article in *Forward* that provides some insight into his progress as a new member. He noted that the President of the LGB 'has simply been pelted . . . from all quarters in reference to his proposed new circular on the poor law administration'. Lansbury also exposed the failure of the LGB to take action to deal with the severe epidemic of measles, and the death rate of 200 children a week in the poorer areas of London. On this failure he castigated Burns at length:

Fancy it being possible that the leader of the Dock Strike, the champion of the Unemployed, the man who knows the social conditions of the people, could calmly tell us today that these matters are going to receive his consideration, and has been in office five solid years, controlling the very department whose business it is to deal with these matters.[25]

By convention, parliamentary debuts are brief and non-controversial affairs. However, Lansbury's maiden speech was more reminiscent of the parliamentary outbursts of the mercurial and controversial Victor Grayson during his brief sojourn at Westminster. In Bow and Bromley the *East London Observer* gave Lansbury's parliamentary debut scant praise and quoted one of the experienced critics in the Commons' press gallery on the new member's antics: 'Mr Lansbury's style is that of the street corner—long gushing sentences, in which even the full-stops are over-run; a panting, breathless chase for some elusive truth . . .'[26]

On 8 December 1910 Revd D. Hayes, pastor and superintendent of Berger Hall in

[23] *Hansard*, 10 Feb. 1911, col. 640.   [24] Ibid. col. 641.
[25] *Forward*, 15 Apr. 1911.   [26] *East London Observer*, 18 Feb. 1911.

East Bromley, had warmly congratulated George Lansbury on his election victory, but advised him on keeping the sympathy of Liberals who had voted for him: 'don't lose sight of the fact that you represent considerable Liberal interests . . . emphasise Labour representation rather than social reform and you will build an unshakeable foundation.'[27] However, Lansbury's stance on the National Insurance Bill, more than any other issue during his time in Parliament in 1911–12, identified him as the rebel back-bench MP whose dissent antagonized the leadership of the Liberal–Labour progressive coalition at Westminster.

On 6 February the King's Speech included the National Insurance Bill, the first example of government intervention in the lives of able-bodied employed workers in this country. Lloyd George's major measure of unemployment and health insurance, with some British modifications, was based on the German insurance scheme he had studied on his visit to Germany in 1908. In Part I of the scheme, unemployment insurance covered 2.25 million workers in various trades with a weekly benefit for a maximum of fifteen weeks per annum. Part II provided health insurance for all regularly employed adults with incomes below £160 per annum to provide sickness benefit for twenty-six weeks (and then disability benefit), as well as medical treatment and maternity benefit for wives.[28]

The announcement of the new bill received a broad welcome by the Labour party and on 4 May Ramsay MacDonald and George Barnes cautiously supported the new measure during its first reading in Parliament. MacDonald believed the bill was popular in the country and he pledged Labour support in return for a Liberal promise concerning the payment of MPs.

George Lansbury, too, voiced a guarded approval on National Insurance at first. He had not studied the measure, though he was aware of certain inadequacies in terms of the very poor and women. His first comments were that 'the payments by workpeople are too high. No one earning less than 25*s.* a week—certainly no married man—should be asked to contribute anything. I should like to see the scale of payments to women the same as to men . . . women are often paid one-half the wage of men, not because they are less efficient, but simply because they are women.'[29]

Moreover, Lansbury did not want attention diverted from the minimum wage and limitation on the working week. He insisted that 'the ILP must still keep its ideal in front of it, remembering that every penny . . . will, in the last resort, come from Labour . . . whilst accepting this bill . . . we must go forward with our agitation for a minimum wage and minimum working week.'[30]

The unemployment insurance in Part I of the new bill was largely uncontroversial and in consequence its twenty-three clauses passed through the committee stage in the House of Commons in a record number of six sittings. However, by 24 May the Labour party became openly divided on the contributory health proposals. From this point George Lansbury played a key role in leading the opposition to the measure at Westminster and outside Parliament.

[27] Revd D. Hayes to George Lansbury, 8 Dec. 1910, LP, vol. 4, fo. 107.
[28] C. Wrigley, *Lloyd George* (1992), pp. 50–4.
[29] *Labour Leader*, 12 May 1911.   [30] Ibid.

During its different stages through the Commons, this measure was the subject of long debates and indicative of the Labour party's attitude to welfare in the pre-war period. At Westminster, the Labour leadership supported the Liberal government over the social insurance for two good reasons. A majority of trade union members gave conditional support to the welfare benefits. Moreover, the government approved many of their unions and friendly societies as official agencies and offered a large number of union officials lucrative positions in the state bureaucracy to administer the new scheme. Lansbury, who kept Beatrice Webb in touch with the detailed progress of the National Insurance Bill, told her: 'of course the vested interests have been squared—insurance companies, friendly societies . . . in fact he [Lloyd George] is ready to pledge anything so that he gets his bill.'[31]

In Parliament, Lansbury led a small group of Labour MPs, including Philip Snowden, Will Thorne, and James O'Grady, who vehemently opposed the contributory principle in the National Insurance proposals and campaigned unsuccessfully for a non-contributory scheme and the state provision of a national health service.[32] Lansbury articulated a general concern among working people that the measure provided only a limited and inadequate provision. In particular, National Insurance was regarded as a poll tax on the poorest and least favoured in society. Non-unionists were compelled to insure through the Post Office as casual workers.

After the special joint conference of the Labour party, TUC, and the General Federation of Trade Unions, which declared in favour of the contributory principle, Lansbury openly opposed his party leader: 'I heard his speech on the latter question [opposing the exemption of underpaid workers from payment] with sheer amazement . . . we shall not be able to get a non-contributory scheme, but let our minimum demand be that every expectant mother shall have the maternity benefit she needs . . .'[33]

George Lansbury believed the contributory scheme would create an expensive bureaucracy and would not solve poverty and destitution. Instead, he argued that money raised by this scheme should be spent on prevention rather than treatment. At Westminster he was indefatigable in attempting to amend the bill in detail during the laborious passage through the Commons. On 5 July 1911 Lansbury seconded a motion that the bill be divided into two parts, with the unemployment section being taken first, which gave him the opportunity to remind the House that the bulk of women and children were excluded from the measure. During the committee stage, he unsuccessfully moved several amendments: to exempt low-paid workers from contributions; to limit their part-time casual workers' contributions pro rata to the fraction of the week employed; to include women and children in medical provision.

On 10 July Lansbury unsuccessfully proposed an amendment concerning contributions of the very poor (which he later raised at the third reading), as he feared

[31] George Lansbury to Beatrice Webb, 1 Nov. 1911, PP.
[32] *Labour Leader*, 14 July 1911.   [33] Ibid. 30 June 1911.

compulsory contributions from employers would lead to more unemployment. On the fifth day in committee, his amendment to include the wives and children (under sixteen) of insured people was also defeated. A similar fate awaited his next amendment concerning single women. During the committee stage George Lansbury also unsuccessfully moved an amendment to remove the liability for payment of the full contribution by workers in part-time employment:

It will be a tax on the bricklayer's labourer in London, who may get $6\frac{1}{2}d$. stopped off half a day's work. It will be an awful tax on the dock labourer, whose $4d$. will be stopped off probably one day's work in the week. There is no comparison at all between this and stopping the contribution from the wages of the skilled workmen or some person who may be getting $30s$. or £3 a week.[34]

Different tactics were employed as Lansbury spoke first as a trade union member and then as the former royal commissioner with direct experience of East End conditions. On 6 July he declared: 'I happen to be a trustee of the biggest unskilled union in the country, and I have been asked specifically to oppose a contributory scheme'.[35] Earlier he tried a different tack:

here, again, I invite Members of this House to consider the Poor Law Commission . . . and they will find that the children who are orphans, sometimes without fathers, and sometimes without mothers also, are the children who grow up and form the large mass of men and women who are physically unfit in the community.[36]

Outside Parliament he appealed directly to the ILP 'to take such action in their branches as will make clear to the Labour party in the House of Commons the need for wringing great and important concessions from the Government'.[37] Throughout the passage of the National Insurance Bill through Parliament Lansbury carried on a country-wide crusade to amend the measure. At St Helens he addressed a large and enthusiastic audience in the Palatine Ring where he attacked the bill as a reactionary measure.[38] At a large trade union and labour demonstration in Victoria Park, on the same platform as Ben Tillett, Marion Phillips, Harry Quelch, and others, Lansbury again attacked the bill on the grounds that it did not prevent poverty and excluded millions of working-class wives from any welfare benefits. In his opposition to the National Insurance Bill, Lansbury arranged a series of meetings to explain his position and to hear the views of his constituents. There were two main objections. The measure was a poll tax of between $15s$. and £3 per week, particularly affecting the very poor. Poverty, destitution, and sickness should be prevented, not insured against. Particular attention was given to the effect on the very poor. In Parliament he argued that 'one of the worst features of the bill is the treatment proposed to be meted out to the poorest and the weakest . . . to women as compared to men . . . to labourers as compared to artisans and to those who are too poor or weak to be admitted as members of "approved societies".'

Lansbury's attitude to the National Insurance Bill brought him into direct

[34] *Hansard*, 10 July 1911, col. 105.   [35] Ibid. 6 July 1911, col. 1426.   [36] Ibid. cols. 1419–20.
[37] *Labour Leader*, 2 June 1911.   [38] Ibid. 7 July 1911.

conflict, not only with the leader of his party but also with David Lloyd George, the main architect of the measure. Ironically, Lloyd George's support in December 1910 at Limehouse for 'his friend George Lansbury', had been an important factor in persuading Bow Liberals to vote for the socialist candidate. However, this did nothing to influence Lansbury in his defence of the very poor as he opposed the Chancellor's bill:

I hear sometimes in the House—and the Chancellor of the Exchequer in one of his speeches said, that he wanted to get at the casual [workers] . . . to find out the people who would not work . . . I have lived most of my life amongst these men, and they are as industrious a class as any in the whole community. Many of them are men who have walked mile after mile for the purpose of getting work . . .[39]

On 6 December 1911, during the third reading, George Lansbury led a parliamentary revolt of three socialists—Lansbury, Jowett, and Snowden—as well as the trade unionists O'Grady and Thorne, in a final assault against the measure.[40] MacDonald and the great bulk of the PLP stiffened their support for the measure, after the chief whip, the Master of Elibank, complained about the insubordination of the Labour left. Quoting from Seebohm Rowntree's survey of poverty in York, that a family of two adults and three children required an income of 21s. 8d. per week to maintain 'mere physical efficiency', George Lansbury denounced the contributory principle in the health and unemployment provisions as a poll tax levied upon those of low income who simply could not afford it. As an East End MP, he had no problem in providing the Commons with adequate first-hand evidence on this point:

After spending on absolutely necessary food and clothing and rent there is exactly 1s. 6d. left for every other emergency of life . . . we who are going to vote against this Bill are doing so in order to register our vote against the idea that Parliament ought to compel people living on this kind of wage to pay money and so stint their physical efficiency.

Once more Lansbury drew on his recent experience on the Royal Commission on the Poor Laws to pour scorn on proposals that failed to tackle the cause of unemployment:

I believe unemployment is caused by, and is inherent in the social system . . . It cannot be got rid of until you get rid of the profit system . . . this House, instead of having sat down to consider the problem from the point of view of prevention, has allowed itself merely to be chloroformed into this idea of insurance.

Characteristically, Lansbury made nonsense of the universal myth that state benefits demoralized the recipients:

think of the advantages everybody gets from education without paying for it. Does one's independence suffer because he pays nothing out of his pocket for education? Is his moral fibre injured? . . . I have seen them in their carriages and motor cars in Rotten Row, and I have not noticed their self-respect has been injured because they are having a free education . . .[41]

[39] *Hansard*, 7 July 1911, cols. 1419–20.
[40] H. A. Clegg, *A History of British Trade Unions since 1889*, ii, *1911–1933* (1985), pp. 219–20.
[41] *Hansard*, 6 Dec. 1911, col. 1491.

Despite some redoubtable efforts in Parliament and campaigning in the country, George Lansbury failed to prevent the passage of the National Insurance Bill. In a final declaration he revealed that his opposition was one of principle and conscience. Within less than a year, Lansbury was to surrender his parliamentary seat on an even greater question of principle. His opposition to national insurance, in defence of his working-class constituents as an East End MP, was an important milestone on the route to that resignation.

During 1911 the National Insurance Bill was the dominant measure engaging the new Member's attention. However, George Lansbury entered the House of Commons after the December 1910 general election at the height of the constitutional crisis created by the long-standing conflict between the Commons and the Lords. Asquith and Lloyd George had declared that the issue of the Lords was to be settled in the new Parliament. The Finance Bill finally went through the Lords in April 1911. The Parliament Act was then introduced to weaken the delaying powers of the Upper House by the use of the suspensory veto but Lansbury, suspicious of the government's intentions, declared:

It appears to me that the Parliament Act is being passed for the sole purpose . . . Irish Home Rule, and Welsh Disestablishment . . . if there is to be a Second Chamber elected in such a manner that only rich men can secure seats, it will be a greater barrier to social progress than the present House of Lords.[42]

On 3 May 1911, during the committee stage of the Parliament Bill, Lansbury proposed that Home Rule for Ireland was inevitable and called for a Federation of the British Empire:

I am a Federationist of the Empire. I believe that time has long gone by for all parts of the empire into one solid whole . . . In my opinion we should have a really Imperial Parliament, representative of the whole Empire to deal with matters connected with the whole Empire. I said that to my constituents down among the poorest people in the Metropolis. They understood it, believed it, and supported it . . .[43]

The appearance of the Women's Enfranchisement Bill at this time provided the Member for Bow and Bromley with an early opportunity to support at Westminster the women's cause that he was to take up throughout 1911 and 1912 until his dramatic resignation. During the second reading he intervened decisively to counter traditional arguments used to deny women the parliamentary vote. Instead, Lansbury emphasized the valuable contributions made by Beatrice Webb and Helen Bosanquet on the Royal Commission on the Poor Law, Susan Lawrence's work on the LCC, as well as the positive outcome of granting the vote to women in various parts of Australia and the United States.

Typically, Lansbury's most powerful argument concerned the valuable contribution made to their communities by working women in paid employment as well as at home: 'In the East End of London, and in every industrial centre, the bulk of women

[42] Ibid. 3 May 1911, cols. 497–501.   [43] Ibid. 3 May 1911, col. 500.

who will get the vote will be working women . . . You have no right to make laws to govern them without giving them a vote . . . That is an argument always applied to men.'[44]

George Lansbury's first spell in Parliament coincided with 'the Workers' Rebellion', the period of 'labour unrest' of 1911–14, characterized by waves of strikes and the appearance of a new philosophy of extra-parliamentary action—'Syndicalism', which had some influence on certain trade unionists. Essentially, syndicalists advocated using the industrial strength of organized workers, instead of parliamentary methods, to secure workers' control and the re-organization of society. During these years, many bitter industrial disputes broke out, principally affecting coal-miners, seamen, railwaymen, cotton-weavers, dockers and carters, cab-drivers, tube- and metal-workers, and transport workers, though only a few could be attributed directly to syndicalist influence.[45]

In Parliament and outside it, Lansbury was closely identified with this period of severe industrial conflicts, many taking place on a regional or national scale. As an East End MP with many dock-workers as constituents or near-neighbours, Lansbury gave considerable support at the time of the Dock and Transport Federation Strikes during the summers of 1911 and 1912 which involved over 100,000 workers. In particular, Lansbury and other Labour MPs frequently raised the issue of the use of police and armed troops during these embittered conflicts.[46] In August 1911, for example, there was a typical clash in Parliament between Lansbury and the Home Secretary, Winston Churchill, on the question of the employment of the military in labour disputes. Lansbury used the occasion to draw a comparison between the action of the members of the Liberal government and that of their predecessors during the Michelstown Debate when they were in opposition in 1887: 'I would like to point out . . . that everything that has been said from the Front bench in defence of the employment of soldiers, has been said against their own party at the time the present leader of the Opposition was Chief Secretary for Ireland.'[47]

As will become clear, during the period of labour unrest, Ben Tillett approached George Lansbury at Westminster to secure his support for the relaunching of the *Daily Herald*, which first reappeared in April 1912. Under Lansbury's influence and his eventual editorship, the new labour daily became directly involved at every turn in the workers' cause with Lansbury providing an early article in 1912 on the 'Labour Unrest'.[48] The paper fostered a rebel culture in Edwardian labour politics and its columns were generously available to socialists, syndicalists, suffragists, and strikers—all voices of dissent that Lansbury represented at Westminster and elsewhere.

After only six weeks in Parliament, George Lansbury had already formed his first impressions and was ready to voice his criticisms in public. According to the new

[44] *Hansard*, 5 May 1911, cols. 763–73.

[45] For different views of syndicalist influence on 'Labour Unrest', 1910–14, see H. Pelling, *Popular Politics and Society in Late Victorian Britain* (1968), ch. 9; B. Holton, *British Syndicalism, 1900–1914* (1976), esp. ch. 9. For Lansbury and the *Daily Herald*'s connections with syndicalism, see ibid. pp. 180–6.

[46] For this period, see H. Pelling, *Popular Politics and Society in Late Victorian Britain* (1968), ch. 9; for a local study: E. Frow and R. Frow, *The General Strike in Salford in 1911* (1990).

[47] *Hansard*, 22 Aug. 1911, cols. 2364–5.   [48] *Daily Herald*, 20 May 1912.

Member, the House of Commons was 'the most delightful club in the world', but full of complacent and satisfied parliamentarians. He felt the procedures of the House, especially the all-night sittings, were worthy of a lunatic asylum.

In particular, as we have seen, Lansbury was disenchanted with the Labour leadership's support of the Liberal government which, compared to the Irish party and other members, had achieved little by way of legislation or pledges. He admitted to Fenner Brockway:

we have no pledge in relation to the Osborne Judgment, the Right to Work, the Poor Law, or any of those questions . . . The Irish Party have a pledge on Home Rule . . . the Welsh Party have an assurance that Church Disestablishment is to be introduced . . . and the Scotch members are promised a Land Bill. Heaven knows what England and the Labour Party are to have![49]

On the crucial issue of endangering the Liberal government, Lansbury was equally blunt:

I have given no pledge to that effect. Some members say that since we are in favour of the limitation of the Veto and the Government has put it down, we must see it through. But there is a great danger that if the Government once imagine in the Labour party they may count on 42 safe votes, under all conditions and circumstances, they will see us to Heaven or Hades before they will trouble about the unemployed, the destitute and the women's question. I am not content that the next two or three years should be devoted to Constitutional Reform, plus Welsh Disestablishment. The condition-of-the-people question is of greater importance than any other reform.[50]

The growth of syndicalism with which George Lansbury was closely associated, and the belief in direct action by the industrial working class rather than the parliamentary route to socialism coincided with a loss of faith in parliamentarianism which also prompted a reaction against the growth of state power—most notably expressed at this time in Hilaire Belloc's *The Servile State*, a forthright condemnation of National Insurance and other Liberal social reforms. From 1913, as editor of the *Daily Herald*, Lansbury developed many of these notions in his newspaper, which was to become the radical rallying-point for all those dissenting groups in British politics outside Parliament.

In April 1911 George Lansbury had told the delegates assembled at the ILP Conference at Birmingham that he knew 'the general view of himself was that he was a good-hearted sort of a person, *but without any brain.*'[51] In fact, this was a popular misconception of George Lansbury, predominantly a politician of great passion, honesty, and moral fervour. Of course, he does not belong to the ranks of such twentieth-century Labour intellectuals and planners as G. D. H. Cole, R. H. Tawney, Harold Laski, and others—though, significantly, many of them became Lansbury's close associates. But Lansbury did not lack the facility to generate ideas or work out theories. And this early period in Parliament provides some evidence to

---

[49] *Labour Leader*, 24 Mar. 1911.   [50] Ibid.
[51] *Labour Leader*, 21 Apr. 1912 (emph. added).

this effect. In 1911 and 1912 Lansbury used Belloc's journals to advance his ideas on constitutional reform. He advocated the use of the Referendum ('on all questions affecting people's lives'), the Initiative ('to enable people to initiate legislation themselves'), and the Recall (or Re-Selection of MPs) to increase the accountability of Parliament, the Executive, and MPs.[52]

In May 1912 Lansbury explained his belief in socialism as the only way to rebuild the social and economic condition of Britain based on the power of the people:

So the socialism which I am doing my best to get people to accept is the theory of life ... that human beings are entitled to the fullest opportunity of mental and moral development that is possible; that the object of civilisation should be not merely to increase riches, learning, and culture for the few, but the raising of the whole of society.[53]

His first experience of Parliament and the party system had changed his views on how this could be achieved. No longer did he believe in the power of the state:

A few years ago I should have sworn by a Socialist state dominated and organised by officials ... however, my mind has undergone a great change. I no longer want a bureaucratic State, even if the bureaucrats are elected by direct suffrage of the people. Labour Exchanges, Boards of Arbitration, Insurance Acts, have sickened me of the whole paraphernalia of State officials.[54]

Nevertheless, George Lansbury never completely lost his faith in Parliament as an institution. While proclaiming the need for root-and-branch reform of Parliament, he declared: 'And my object in remaining in Parliament is to endeavour to make all those whom I can influence in that House feel that Parliament should be representative of all women and men.'[55]

At the close of the 1911 session Lansbury gave his view of the Westminster scene. He declared the Parliament Act and the National Insurance Act two of the most controversial measures passed during the session, as were the Coal Mines Bill and the Shops Bill. He also pointed out the absence of specific legislation on the Right to Work, necessitous children, and the Osborne Judgment. He concluded that the Labour party had 'been led at the heels of the Liberals almost entirely through the session'. He therefore advocated that:

By some means we must bring Parliament into line with working class needs ... Unless Parliament stands for these things it is no earthly use to the workers at all, and this can only be obtained by Parliament controlling in a democratic sense all the great monopolies of production, exchange, and transport—at present in private hands.[56]

During 1912 George Lansbury contributed a regular column to the feminist journal, *The Link*. In his first article in January he reported on the passage of the

---

[52] For Lansbury's articles on constitutional reform, see 'Parliament', *The Eye-Witness*, 23 November 1911; and, 'Is Parliament Useless?', *The New Witness*, 19 Dec. 1912.
[53] *Labour Leader*, 12 May 1912.   [54] Ibid.
[55] The article must have been written before Lansbury's resignation in Oct. 1912. *The New Witness*, 19 Dec. 1912.
[56] *The Link*, Jan. 1912.

measures concerning the House of Lords, coal mines, and shops, but his general conclusion was that 'the first need of the workers is more wages and less work'. The following month George Lansbury dealt with two issues: women's suffrage and the sovereignty of Parliament. He was in favour of settling the first issue by a national referendum of women as well as men. On Parliament he was strongly anti-party in his views and advocated that Committees of the Whole House should be used to control the main offices of state. He declared that: 'We shall never get true voting in the House of Commons until we are free from the domination of Party government. The more I think about my twelve months in the House the more I realise what a tiny amount of influence we private members have . . .'[57]

Also in 1912, Lansbury became particularly active in a number of parliamentary episodes and extra-parliamentary causes which combined the different groups on the left of British politics with the organized trade union and labour movements, as well as those battling in the women's cause. On 25 March 1912 George Lansbury, the Liberal MP, Josiah Wedgwood, and others formed the Free Speech Defence Committee (FSDC) as part of a national campaign on behalf of the eight syndicalists and socialists prosecuted by the government in what was known as the 'Don't Shoot' agitation. The affair arose out of the increasing use by the government of the troops in bitter industrial disputes that led to the deaths of strikers fired on by soldiers in Liverpool, Llanelli, and Tonypandy. There was a history of the use of military force by Liberal governments in industrial disputes that went back to earlier occasions when strikers were shot dead during the notorious Belfast Strike of 1907 and the 'Featherstone Massacre' during the 1893 'Coal War'.

In August 1911 George Lansbury had joined Ben Tillett, Fred Knee, and other campaigners at the Trafalgar Square meeting organized by the Social Democratic Party (SDP), at which a leaflet 'A Word to My Fellow Workers' was circulated to denounce the use of the military in industrial disputes. The matter came to a head after the syndicalist, Fred Bowyer, composed 'An Open Letter to British Soldiers', a direct appeal to troops not to fire on unarmed fellow citizens during disputes and disturbances in Britain. In the first few lines he stated the main theme of pacifism and community, the common bond of class and family between workers and soldiers:

Men! Comrades! Brothers!
You are Workingmen's Sons
When we go on Strike to better our lot, which is the lot also of Your Fathers, Mothers,
   Brothers, and Sisters, you are called upon by your officers to MURDER US . . .
'Thou shalt not kill', says the Book.
Don't forget that!
It does not say, 'unless you have a uniform on.'

Jim Larkin's *Irish Worker* published the 'Open Letter' which was distributed as a leaflet during the 1911 Liverpool Dock Strike.

---

[57] Ibid. Feb. 1912.

At first the Liberal government declined to take action, but in early 1912 it commenced on a number of prosecutions that, in response, provoked a national crusade in defence of civil liberties. On 25 February 1912, Fred Crowsley, an ILP railwayman, was arrested after he distributed hundreds of copies of the 'Open Letter' in leaflet form outside Hounslow Barracks and Aldershot Army Camp. His arrest went mainly unnoticed, except that on 28 February 1912 George Lansbury and Josiah Wedgwood asked questions in Parliament and attempted to move the adjournment of the House. Instead of prosecuting the printers of Crowsley's leaflet (the National Labour Press, or the ILP), the attorney general, Sir Rufus Isaacs, proceeded against others.

Nelson King, Thomas Mayfield, and James Morley were three members of the Ilkeston branch of the British Socialist Party (BSP) and responsible for the February 1912 issue of *Dawn* that urged workers to arm against police and soldiers. As a consequence, in March 1912 they were arrested, charged with conspiracy and incitement to murder and disorder, and then committed for trial at Derby Assizes in June 1912. Guy Bowman, journalist and publisher of the *Syndicalist*, and Benjamin and Charles Buck, printers of the *Syndicalist*, were also charged with incitement to mutiny and tried at the Old Bailey on 22 March 1912. Finally, on 19 March 1912, Tom Mann was arrested for repeating the 'Don't Shoot' appeal and sent for trial at Manchester Assizes in May 1912. Mann was sentenced to six month's imprisonment in Strangeways Prison, a sentence that brought a storm of protest in Parliament and in the country.

What particularly incensed George Lansbury and others who protested over the 'Don't Shoot' prosecutions was the Liberal government's blatant double standard in prosecuting syndicalists and suffragists, as well as using armed soldiers against strikers. However, no action was taken against the Ulster leader, Sir Edward Carson MP, who, despite public proclamations of sedition, remained at liberty. From April 1912 until the outbreak of the First World War, the Ulster crisis brought the province to the brink of civil war and was the most serious of the domestic crises that threatened the political stability of Edwardian Britain. Backed by Bonar Law and the Conservative opposition, Carson on several occasions openly defied the Liberal Government over Irish Home Rule and had nearly 100,000 Ulster Volunteers armed and drilling to support a provisional government in Ulster, for when the Irish Home Rule measure became law. Lansbury protested in the House of Commons: 'If you were right in prosecuting Bowman and the Bucks, you ought also to prosecute the right Hon. Gentleman, the Member for Dublin University [Sir Edward Carson] and his colleagues behind him.'[58]

Nor was this the only time Lansbury and other Labour members raised this grievance. The different treatment meted out to Carson in the Ulster crisis was a constant theme in Labour politics well into the 1920s.[59] After the formation of the FSDC Lansbury raised the 'Don't Shoot Prosecutions' in the House of Commons with

---

[58] *Hansard*, 25 Mar. 1912, cols. 84–5.
[59] M. Shefftz, 'The Impact of the Ulster Crisis (1912–1914) on the British Labour Party', *Albion*, 5 (1973), pp. 169–83.

parliamentary questions to the Home Secretary, Attorney General, and other ministers after Crowsley's arrest. Lansbury's article in the *Clarion* reported on the country-wide agitation that in due course produced a gradual climb-down on the part of the government: 'the using of armed force against unarmed men and women, the bringing of soldiers to fire on strikers . . . is wicked and atrocious work, and . . . no soldiers ought to be recruited for any such purchase . . .'[60]

On 20 March 1912 the suffragette Mary Gawthorpe wrote to warn Lansbury that there were ominous links between the issue of free speech and the women's question. She warned that unless working men were constantly vigilant about every denial of democratic rights, they could lose those fundamental liberties they currently enjoyed.

With the trial of Bowman and the Buck brothers in London on 22 March 1912, Wedgwood and Lansbury raised this matter in a full-scale debate on the same day. In May 1912 Lansbury moved the adjournment of the House concerning the gaol sentence passed on Tom Mann but without success, as only thirty members supported Lansbury's initiative.[61] A wide-ranging session took place in the Commons on 22 May. With Crowsley's trial pending, Lansbury was one of the speakers at a large rally on 9 June at Trafalgar Square.

Wedgwood's links with Lansbury originated in their common interest in the Single Tax agitation but were to extend to many other questions in the forthcoming months and years. Wedgwood later recalled that 'We went to Bow to see George Lansbury—Fels, Ingersoll and I. "Here we are", said Robert Ingersoll, "the three best advertised men in the world, on a bus-top in the East End, going down to a slum to persuade a Socialist to destroy us . . .".'

In fact, their association led to an informal progressive alliance, which came together in 1912, particularly over the National Insurance Bill and the 'Don't Shoot protest'. Thirty years later Wedgwood recalled the mood in 1912:

all were going mad; even trade unions and politicians. The sympathetic strike was invented to curse the Parliamentary Labour Party . . . Syndicalism came over the air from France to breed with Will Dyson's cartoons in the [*Daily*] *Herald*, or with G.K.C [Chesterton's] medieval guilds. The Suffragettes screamed at all our meetings. George Lansbury shook his fist in the Prime Minister's face; resigned his seat, and went down and out at Bow . . .[62]

Another major episode in which George Lansbury was involved during his first years in Parliament was the celebrated Marconi scandal that lasted eighteen months. During the 1910–14 Parliament this scandal brought cabinet ministers close to resignation and even the possibility of the collapse of the Liberal government and a general election. The main events lasted from the summer of 1912 into 1913. The Liberal Postmaster General, Herbert Samuel, signed an unfavourable government contract with the British Marconi Company to build an international network of wireless telegraphy stations throughout the empire. The Managing

[60] *Clarion*, 29 Mar. 1912.   [61] *Eye Witness*, 28 Mar., 16 May 1912.
[62] J. C. Wedgwood, *Memoirs of a Fighting Life* (1941), pp. 66–7, 78–9, 82–3.

Director of the company was Geoffrey Isaacs, brother of Rufus Isaacs, the Attorney-General, who had allegedly influenced Samuel's decision. Rumours of corruption and financial impropriety embroiled four Cabinet ministers: Samuel, Isaacs, the Chancellor of the Exchequer, David Lloyd George, and Alexander Murray, the Master of Elibank. Not only had the government favoured the English Marconi Company to the detriment of other rival firms, but the cabinet ministers were also accused of using insider information to deal in the shares of the company at a favourable price and to their financial benefit.

When Parliament reassembled after the summer recess of 1912, an important debate took place on 11 October 1912 in the Commons on a motion to appoint a Select Committee to investigate, which provided the opportunity to ventilate the accusations of ministerial corruption and gambling in shares.

In a packed and attentive House of Commons, the debate revolved around two issues: criticism of the Marconi contract and the rumours concerning gambling in shares and ministerial corruption which had circulated extensively during the summer outside Parliament and in the press. After speeches by Sir Henry Norman, Major Archer-Shee, Lord Robert Cecil, and others, Lansbury intervened to tell the House that he had put down a motion to refer the contract to a Select Committee, but now understood that the government wanted reasons for establishing it. His next comment stirred the House and brought the Chancellor of the Exchequer and the Attorney-General into the debate:

> considerable sums of money have been made out of the sale of these shares, and ... they have been made by people who had information in connection with this matter previous to other people ... Whether that is so or not, the fact remains, he the Hon. Baronet, the Member for the City stated, that considerable sums of money have been made on the Stock Exchange through this agreement ... I hope there will be no kind of shrinking on the Committee with regard to this matter.
>
> The CHANCELLOR of the EXCHEQUER (Mr Lloyd George): I hope, too, there will be no shrinking on the part of those who make the allegations.
>
> MR LANSBURY: The irritation expressed on the Treasury Bench this afternoon when people are making speeches is, I think, not a very nice sign at all. I am entitled to say what other Hon. Members have said this afternoon without interruption, that there have been very grave rumours all over the City that people have made money out of this business who ought not to have made money out of it. I am entitled to say that without interruption.
>
> MR LLOYD GEORGE made a remark, which was inaudible.
>
> MR LANSBURY: I do not think you are. I never mentioned the Right Hon. Gentleman. Why he should be so eager to rise in his place and speak as he has done so I do not know.

MR LLOYD GEORGE: The Hon. Member said something about the Government and he has talked about 'rumours'. I want to know what these rumours are. If the Hon. Gentleman has any charge to make against the Government as a whole, or against individual Members of it, I think it ought to be stated openly. The reason why the Government wanted a frank discussion before going to Committee was because we wanted to bring here these rumours, these sinister rumours, that have been passed from one foul lip to another behind the backs of the House.

MR LANSBURY: Of course that is a very easy thing to get up and say to me. Why was it not said to other Hon. Gentlemen?

MR LLOYD G: Because nobody said it.[63]

The increasingly acrimonious exchange continued between Lloyd George and Lansbury until the Attorney-General, Sir Rufus Isaacs, intervened. He rose to state that he had 'no more to do with that contract than any Hon. Member who is sitting upon the opposite side of the House or my Hon. Friend the Member for Bow and Bromley'.

Lansbury later wrote that he had a considerable amount of information on these transactions but was unable to use it, as it was anonymous. The next day, the *Daily News* described him as 'the only man in the House of Commons with a mind bad enough to think such evil of honourable men as to suggest that any of them had made money out of dealings in Marconi shares'. In his autobiography Lansbury gave a different verdict: 'we can trace a definite lowering in the standard demanded of Members of Parliament since these transactions.'[64]

By 1912 George Lansbury had become closely identified with the women's suffrage campaign which had reached its height with the militant activities of the WSPU directed by Emmeline and Christabel Pankhurst.[65] The new name 'suffragette' (which had been coined in 1906 by Lord Northcliffe's *Daily Mail*) was synonymous with demonstrations, heckling at politicians' meetings, and the imprisonment of the Pankhursts and their supporters. Now, as far as the authorities were concerned, events had taken a more sinister and serious turn. Window-breaking, arson, and attacks on property led to the prosecution and imprisonment of greater numbers of suffragettes; many then used the tactic of the hunger and thirst strike in prison.[66]

In Parliament the treatment of suffragette prisoners was raised frequently—especially the horrific practice of forcible feeding while on hunger strike in prison. Suffragettes in Holloway Prison kept Lansbury informed about their conditions in custody and on at least one occasion smuggled out a letter to the East End MP about

---

[63] *Hansard*, 11 Oct. 1912, cols. 712–14.   [64] Lansbury, *My Life*, pp. 119–20.
[65] For more on the women's suffrage movement, see below, Ch. 7.
[66] S. S. Holton, 'Manliness and Militancy: The Political Protest of Male Suffragists and the Gendering of the "Suffragette" Identity', in A. V. John and C. Eustance (eds.), *The Men's Share? Masculinities, Male Support and Women's Suffrage in Britain, 1890–1920* (1997), pp. 110–34; S. S. Holton, *Suffrage Days: Stories from the Women's Suffrage Movement* (1996), pp. 3, 144, 166–7, 172–3, 240–1, 243–4.

their treatment.[67] In the House of Commons George Lansbury and Keir Hardie took up the women's cause which was to lead to Lansbury's memorable confrontation with Asquith. On 25 June 1912, at Question Time, Hardie raised the case of Emily Wilding Davison, one of the suffragettes being forcibly fed in Holloway Prison. During her imprisonment she had been injured, allegedly in a suicide attempt. The Irish MP, Tim Healy followed by asking for the early release of certain prisoners—'a slight concession', adding, 'why keep up this needless torture?'.

What followed was one of the most famous encounters in the House of Commons of the early twentieth century. The Prime Minister replied 'I must point out that there is not a single one of those women but could come out of prison.' Immediately, Lansbury intervened to bellow: 'You know they cannot (Hon. Members: "Order, Order"). It is perfectly disgraceful that the Prime Minister of England should make such a statement.'

The Times described the next few turbulent minutes as 'a disorderly scene' and 'an exciting incident, which, happily was discreditable to only one member'.[68] *Reynolds Newspaper* made even more of it: 'One of the most sensational scenes witnessed in the House of Commons during recent years.'[69]

Lansbury rushed from his customary seat close to the Bar, advanced up the gangway and half-way down the Treasury bench and stood in front of Asquith 'in the most threatening vehement manner with the House in uproar'. White and shaking with rage, Lansbury addressed Asquith to his face:

You are beneath contempt: ('Order, order') You call yourselves gentlemen and you forcibly feed and murder women in this fashion! You ought to be driven out of office. (Interruption) It is perfectly disgraceful. Talk about protesting! ('Order' and interruption.) It is the most disgraceful thing that ever happened in the history of England! ('Order, order', and interruption) You will go down in history as the man who tortured innocent women. ('Order, order.') That is what you will go down in history as.

Returning to his place below the gangway, Mr Lansbury then addressed Mr Speaker, including a comparison of the treatment of the suffragette prisoners with the government's handling of the events in Ireland:

I have had my say, Mr Speaker. (Hon. Members, 'Sit down,' 'Order, order', and interruption). It is disgraceful that the Prime Minister of this country should tell women in prison on principle that they can walk out. (Hon Members: 'Order, order'.) He knows perfectly well they cannot walk out. The Hon. Member for Cork (Mr William O'Brien) knew he could walk out of prison, but he did not, and the Liberal party, for the sake of votes, defended William O'Brien when he refused to wear the prison clothes. (Hon. Members: 'Order, order.')

At this point, amid further interruptions and cries of 'order', 'order', the Speaker asked the Honourable Member for Bow and Bromley to leave the House in consequence of his grossly disorderly conduct.

Lansbury retorted that he was not leaving the chamber,

---

[67] Vern Wentworth to George Lansbury, 23 Apr. 1912, LP, vol. 6, fos. 32–3.
[68] *The Times*, 26 June 1912.   [69] *Reynolds Newspaper*, 30 June 1912.

while this contemptible thing is being done (Hon. Members: 'Withdraw', and 'Order, order') murdering, torturing, and driving women mad, and telling them they can walkout . . . You may talk about principle and fight in Ulster. You ought to be driven out of public life. You do not know what principle is. You should honour them standing up for their woman-hood. I say for the Prime Minister to say they could walk out is beneath contempt . . .[70]

George Lansbury's refusal to accede to the authority of the Chair brought more exchanges with the Speaker, until Will Crooks persuaded the member for Bow and Bromley to leave the House.[71] According to Postgate, an ILP colleague, Harry Dubery, concerned that Lansbury looked so ill, took him to the under-ground station and also wanted to accompany him home 'fearing his friend was on the edge of a breakdown'.[72] In fact, after withdrawing from the chamber, Lansbury met two constituents waiting in the parliamentary lobby and took them to the Members' tea-room. There, eventually, the Deputy Serjeant-at-Arms persuaded him to leave 'the House and its precincts' to comply with the order of the Speaker.[73]

The dramatic clash between the MP for Bow and Bromley and the Prime Minis-ter did not end there, as the events in Parliament received widespread coverage in the press. The headline in *Reynolds Newspaper* stated bluntly 'MP Suspended', though the Speaker had only asked Lansbury to withdraw from the Commons for the rest of the day. The tense spectacle of 25 June 1912 at Westminster brought an immediate and astonishing response. Letters and telegrams congratulating Lans-bury on his defiant parliamentary stance flowed in from different parts of the coun-try and from abroad. Moreover, this deluge included messages of support and encouragement from opponents across the political spectrum. The Liberal govern-ment's forcible feeding of imprisoned suffragettes had outraged many who wrote to Lansbury. A Somerset magistrate told him that he was 'not a believer in window smashing' but thanked him for his 'splendid championship of the right which every woman has to have her person protected from the hideous torture & degradation of forcible feeding'.[74]

Typical of those who wrote was Louisa Thomas-Price: 'For years I worked and spoke for the Women's Liberal Federation. Never again! When I get my vote, it will be used for the Independent Labour party . . . to thank you from the bottom of my heart for the magnificent protest . . .'[75] Marianne Dale exclaimed: 'I only wish you *had* hit Asquith !!!' 'As an East-End working-woman I thank you from my heart', Ellen Spencer declared. The *Daily Herald* celebrated: 'Thank God for Lansbury.' And there were many, many more expressions of gratitude, praise, and thanks-giving.[76] Literally overnight, the Member for Bow and Bromley had become the champion of the women's movement in Britain.

---

[70] *Hansard*, 25 June 1912, cols. 217–18; *Daily Chronicle*, 26 June 1912.
[71] Ibid. [72] Quoted in Postgate, *Lansbury*, pp. 125–6. [73] *Daily Chronicle*, 29 June 1912.
[74] W. P. Brown to George Lansbury, 27 June 1912, LP, vol. 6, fo. 13.
[75] Louisa Thomson-Price to George Lansbury, 27 June 1912, LP, vol. 6, fo. 42.
[76] Postgate, *Lansbury*, p. 125.

One letter, as Postgate noted, was particularly unexpected. Ramsay MacDonald wrote in the following terms:

I wanted a word with you, for one thing to tell you how deeply obliged I am to you for taking my advice [to leave the House] . . . As you know, I am not made as you are and—probably it is a great weakness—I always regret scenes. I would run to the wilderness to avoid them. But you stood manfully up, and if I thought you were right, I would offer you the most unqualified praise. But, my dear man, are you sure you are right? Is all this going to enfranchise women . . .'[77]

Postgate, however, did not publish Lansbury's reply which was in similar general conciliatory terms: 'Many many thanks it was more than good of you to write, yes we are different—I suppose each have our bit of work to do. I often feel like being a coward and just running away, it is the poor devils who believe and trust in me down here that keeps me going, I should just clear out . . .'[78]

As their correspondence revealed, despite its seeming civility, there was considerable political distance between MacDonald and Lansbury. The day after Lansbury's protest in the House of Commons, MacDonald penned an extraordinary letter to the press about 'the events of the past week [that] have put almost insuperable difficulties' in achieving votes for women. In a scathing attack on the militancy of WSPU, MacDonald denied any heroism by hunger strikers. 'The whole of this tomfoolery is the creation of women who are in a position to throw into collecting plates handed round in the Albert Hall, £10,000 at a minute's notice', he declared.[79] Two days later, Sylvia Pankhurst answered his tirade in a reply that praised Lansbury's chivalry in championing women who were not represented at Westminster.[80]

Nevertheless, George Lansbury realized he still had considerable work to do in the various causes he so passionately supported. In a few years he had come a long way in feminist politics since Marion Coates Hansen chided him about taking his family on holiday instead of attending a women's rally in Trafalgar Square. Later in 1912 he was to surrender his seat by resigning from Parliament to force a by-election on behalf of one of those causes. No one in October 1912 could then accuse him of 'just running away or clearing out'.

---

[77] Quoted in Postgate, *Lansbury*, pp. 125–6.
[78] George Lansbury to Ramsay MacDonald, 26 June 1912, JRMP, PRO 30/69/1156.
[79] *Daily Chronicle*, 27 June 1912.   [80] Ibid. 29 June 1912.

7

By-Election and Prison, 1912–1913

On 11 November 1912 *The Times* reported that two days previously George Lansbury MP had crossed the English Channel to Boulogne with the suffragette leader, Emmeline Pankhurst, to confer with her daughter, Christabel, hiding from the English police at the Parisian Hôtel Cité Bergère as 'Miss Amy Richards'.[1] A few days later, Lansbury dramatically resigned his parliamentary seat to force a by-election at Bow and Bromley over 'Votes for Women'. According to Raymond Postgate, the Pankhursts, who led the militant WSPU, had persuaded the Labour MP and champion of the East End working class that by taking this course of action he would strike a brilliant publicity coup for the women's cause.[2]

The Bow and Bromley by-election attracted national attention as suffrage and anti-suffrage societies poured into the poor East End constituency. A French company, Pathé Frérès Cinema Ltd., captured the two parliamentary candidates—with Lansbury shown with a group of schoolchildren—on film that, remarkably, still survives.[3] In a straight fight George Lansbury lost by 751 votes to the Conservative and Unionist (CU) candidate—the anti-suffragist, Reginald Blair—and was out of Parliament for ten years.

His resignation was an extraordinary decision, especially as he had only been at Westminster for less than two years. Why did George Lansbury decide to cause a by-election at Bow and Bromley by relinquishing his parliamentary seat? In his autobiography in 1928 there is only a brief statement that he left the House of Commons in October 1912 following a serious disagreement with the Labour party over the subject of the women's franchise:

The Government had declared its intention of bringing in what would to all intents and purposes have been a Manhood Suffrage Bill. I proposed that the Party should move an amendment to that bill and vote against it unless women were included. *It was a question on which I felt it impossible to compromise.* I consulted my friends at Bow and they supported me in my point of view and also took the view that I was responsible to them and not to the Party in the House of Commons.[4]

In other words, George Lansbury had reached a position in his thinking on the women's question that left him only one course of action. Moreover, according to his idea of party democracy, Lansbury was accountable to his local constituency who had sent him to Westminster as their representative—although there is some

---

[1] *The Times*, 31 Oct. 1912. [2] Postgate, *Lansbury*, p. 127.
[3] *London: The Suffragette Election* (1912), BFI Films, National Film and Television Archive.
[4] Lansbury, *My Life*, pp. 120–1 (emph. added).

doubt about when exactly he announced his intentions to the local party. After the by-election, a broader question was raised by the defeated candidate—that of an individual's conscience versus loyalty to a political party and its policy decisions.

In 1951 Postgate brought a different perspective to the events of 1912. He portrayed George Lansbury as a 'Victorian father of a family [who] believed, with all his mind, in sex equality; with all his emotions he believed that women were weaker vessels who needed protection'. Postgate was clearly unhappy about his father-in-law's participation in the women's movement, which he described as a 'complete obsession for a short while'. In his view, Lansbury's failure to consult the ILP about his resignation and, indeed, his own supporters in the Poplar Labour Representation Committee was the result of overwork and overtiredness.[5]

However, in October 1912, George Lansbury did not decide in haste to apply for the Chiltern Hundreds. The strains and stresses of the private member's life at Westminster alone are not an adequate explanation for his course of action. For George Lansbury, the question of the parliamentary franchise for women was a deeply moral issue, which surpassed all others, and one that he had anguished over for some time. By 1912 the member for Bow and Bromley put gender above social class as a principle on which there could be no compromise.

From his early life, George Lansbury showed a growing awareness of the inequalities between men and women, as well as between rich and poor. In the pre-war period, with Keir Hardie, he was one of a small number of men in public life, mainly politicians, journalists, and writers on the political left, who were sympathetic and active in the women's cause. George Lansbury differed from most of this group in that he viewed the franchise question through the perspective of working-class women, based on an experience of living in the East End for forty years. His insight and sensitivity is revealed in these observations he made in 1913:

I knew how hard the working woman's life was, spent in unending labour, cooped up in a little brick house in an interminable street of similar brick houses. I saw too that if the boy went out to work he could have his evenings to himself for play or study, but the girls, however hard their work, must always work in the house and wait on the men and boys. This always seemed to me grossly unfair.[6]

George Lansbury freely acknowledged the important influence spirited women, as well as certain influential men, played in the development of his own political thinking. From his earliest years, when his shrewd Welsh grandmother introduced him to the *Reynolds Newspaper* and his young mother took him to the election hustings at Blackheath at the age of nine, there were a number of other important milestones on the road to 1912.

In 1906 Lansbury became directly involved with the organized Edwardian women's movement, but his political awareness had been sharpened nearly twenty years earlier by Annie Besant and the Match Girls' Strike, and again during his stewardship of Jane Cobden's campaign for the LCC. As a poor law guardian from the

[5] Postgate, *Lansbury*, pp. 119, 126–7.   [6] *Votes for Women*, 25 Apr. 1913.

early 1890s, Lansbury continued to battle alongside Lena Wilson and others for women and their families. He told Fenner Brockway, fellow socialist and journalist: 'in one of the very poor districts of Bow a woman came to the door . . . She asked me with an oath what was the good of a vote for her and her unemployed husband, when every scrap of clothing had been pawned . . .?'[7]

When the unemployment question once more brought the position of impoverished women and their families to Lansbury's attention, as we have seen, he involved the working women of East London directly in political lobbying at the time. Large-scale marches of women from different parts of the capital to Westminster were arranged by Lansbury and others in an endeavour to influence the Prime Minister and members of the government. The banner of the Poplar contingent read: 'Women demand the right to vote in order to work out their social salvation.'[8] Lansbury likened this pioneering event, consisting at first of 1,000 women, to the eighteenth-century women's demonstration in Versailles against Louis XVI during the French Revolution. It was a form of popular agitation George Lansbury repeated on two further occasions during those years.[9]

Two years later George Lansbury had contested Middlesbrough in the 1906 general election where, as we have seen, his local agent, Marion Coates Hansen, prompted him to include 'votes for women' in his election manifesto. It was more than a gesture on Lansbury's part. The campaign proved a watershed in his relations with the Edwardian women's movement. After his defeat, Marion Coates Hansen maintained a long and influential association with George Lansbury and members of his family. She befriended Bessie Lansbury and was constantly worried about Bessie coping with the large Bow household. She also pressed her to leave her children behind and take a holiday at her Middlesbrough home. 'It seems to me your soul has cultivated a habit of work,' she wrote to Bessie.[10]

Marion Coates Hansen was a prime example that 'the power of the pen is mightier than the sword'. Lansbury described her as 'a very slightly built woman: her frail body possesses an iron will and a courageous spirit. The freedom for which she strove was one which would emancipate body, soul and spirit.' During these years, not only did she consult Lansbury—as she stood for the Middlesbrough Board of Guardians—but offered her advice on current political questions. Probably more than anyone else, Marion Coates Hansen kept the inequalities suffered by women in Edwardian society uppermost in Lansbury's mind.

Her correspondence reveals some of the powerful arguments that she used to bring Lansbury directly into the women's movement, then entering a new phase with the founding of the WSPU in 1903 and the adoption of militant tactics from 1905. Marion Coates Hansen was always frank and fearless in speaking her mind:

I'm not always satisfied with you men. And I'm as old as any of you—and have a right to stand as judge once in a while. My sex has been judged unheard and undefended for

---

[7] *Christian Commonwealth*, 12 Jan. 1910.   [8] *Star*, 6 Nov. 1905.
[9] Lansbury, *Looking Backwards and Forwards*, pp. 101–9.
[10] Marion Coates Hansen to Bessie Lansbury, 10 June 1906, LP, vol. 5, fo. 258.

centuries. Those centuries of experience and injustice made some of us very very old—for we can live them all over again in *one life*.[11]

In the same letter she condemned the White Slave Trade in young Edwardian girls in graphic terms:

I spent Tuesday with a young girl whose life has been torn and soiled . . . if something is not done Walt Whitman's poem 'In the City Deadhouse' may apply to her. What is your 'unemployed' compared with such a ghastly horrible tragedy! . . . Who has the power to change it all? . . . the male culprit is still at large. He is free to continue his baseness, and forsooth—to choose *my* rulers-governors-legislators![12]

George Lansbury readily acknowledged that she was the seminal influence that swayed his political views at this time, but he added 'Mrs Coates Hansen did not have to argue with me the rights of women's demands. I needed no conversion on that subject. My mind had been made up when I was quite young.'[13]

In the Edwardian period, the campaign for the parliamentary vote dominated women's politics and was waged by a wide spectrum of suffrage bodies and individuals. Traditionally, the two main wings of the organized movement, the National Union of Women's Suffrage Societies (NUWSS, 1897) and the Women's Social and Political Union (WSPU, 1903), have been depicted as traditionally in opposition to each other over objectives and strategy. However, recent research has modified this conventional picture of a precise division between the 'constitutional' versus the 'militant' wings, as well as revealing the differences *within* various groups in suffrage history.[14]

The NUWSS, a confederation of London and provincial suffrage societies, was the largest women's body with a membership of around 54,000 by 1914. Under the leadership of Millicent Garrett Fawcett, the constitutional NUWSS declared itself law-abiding and non-party to attract women from the different political parties, although there was probably a preponderance of Liberal women in its ranks. These 'non militants' had relied on conventional political lobbying, including the promotion of private Members' bills, as well as three Conciliation bills with cross-party support in 1910–12, to secure the passage of a women's franchise measure through Parliament. However, by the time of the Bow and Bromley by-election, the NUWSS had changed its policy, following the defeat of the Third Conciliation Bill in March 1912. Katherine Courtney and Catherine Marshall of the NUWSS and Arthur Henderson, the Labour party secretary, had negotiated a delicate electoral concordat on behalf of their organizations to raise an Election Fighting Fund (EFF) to support official Labour candidates at by-elections contested by anti-suffragist opponents.[15] The Fund did not apply to the Bow and Bromley contest,

[11]   Marion Coates Hansen to George Lansbury, 24 May 1906, ibid. fo. 254.   [12]   Ibid.
[13]   Lansbury, *Looking Backwards and Forwards*, pp. 94–5.
[14]   See J. Purvis and S. S. Holton, *Votes For Women* (2000), pp. 1–12; M. Pugh, *The March of Women: A Revisionist Analysis of the Campaign for Women's Suffrage, 1866–1914* (Oxford, 2000), ch. 8.
[15]   S. S. Holton, *Feminism and Democracy: Women's Suffrage and Reform Politics in Britain, 1900–1918* (1986), ch. 4; Wrigley, *Arthur Henderson*, p. 62.

although Catherine Marshall and other NUWSS members were active campaigners in the constituency.[16]

During the pre-war period George Lansbury was not identified with the NUWSS, though he shared political platforms with those promoting votes for women as part of an adult suffrage measure.[17] Instead, in 1906 a donation of £2 signified Bessie's membership of the WSPU. George Lansbury had sent it, although membership was not open to men. After forty years of unsuccessful campaigns by constitutional methods, the WSPU represented a new strategy of direct action to secure the franchise for women. Emmeline Pethick Lawrence, one of the WSPU leading lights with her husband Frederick, until expelled by the Pankhursts in 1912, thanked George Lansbury for his contribution: 'You can help immensely. Come tomorrow here. Endless clerical work—we have sent round thousands of resolutions & letters. There are still thousands to send—the whole country is going to be roused.'[18]

At this crucial point, when Lansbury was faced with the rigours of an official Davy Inquiry into the Poplar Board of Guardians, Marion Coates Hansen pressed him to answer Emmeline Pethick Lawrence's appeal:

But do call . . . You are suffering I know and that should make you ever so much more sympathetic to us. We get howled at by far more people than the questioners and witnesses appearing in the Poplar Guardians affair. We've waited for centuries and are still 'beyond the pale'. Do offer to speak for them. They've already had meetings in Bow. Nearly *all* the Labour MPs are refusing to speak for us . . .[19]

What the WSPU brought to women's politics was a new militancy in the campaign to win the vote in distinct contrast to the traditional parliamentary lobbying methods employed by the NUWSS. But it also included a sex war that challenged male politicians and confronted those that denied women the vote and equal citizenship. Militancy took varying forms: passive resistance, civil disobedience, and eventually criminal acts. In 1892 Lansbury had joined the Women's Franchise League Lobby against Sir Albert Rollit's conservative suffrage bill. A decade later, suffragette attacks on politicians, window breaking, and incendiarism outraged Edwardian public opinion. Historians differ on whether militancy secured the WSPU indispensable publicity, compared to widespread industrial unrest in Britain and the deepening ulster crisis, or provoked government intransigence and police violence. However, this was the women's cause that George Lansbury took up, and the campaigning methods of the WSPU that he defended in Parliament and outside. A few weeks before he resigned he wrote to the *Manchester Guardian* about the protests against militancy: 'there must be some serious cause which is leading

---

[16] Catherine Marshall to Josiah Wedgwood, 21 Nov. 1912; 'Bow and Bromley' [Catherine Marshall's handwritten campaign notes], Catherine Marshall Papers, D/Mar/3/53.

[17] See *The Worker*, Jan. 1912, for Lansbury's presence (28 Jan. 1912) at 'A Mass Meeting in support of votes for All Men & Women Next Session'.

[18] Emmeline Pethick Lawrence to George Lansbury, 25 June 1912, with receipt, LP, vol. 2, fos. 260–1.

[19] Marion Coates Hansen to George Lansbury, 26 June 1912, LP, vol. 2, fo. 262.

well-educated women to take the very drastic steps . . . to call public attention to their grievances.'[20]

Advocates of women's enfranchisement also differed between those—'adult suffragists'—who saw votes for women as part of overall democratic reform embracing both men and women and those—'equal suffragists'—who demanded votes for women immediately on the same, albeit limited, basis as men. In reality, the cross-currents in the women's movement meant that there was often co-operation between these different groupings, particularly at branch level, as well as changes in strategies and tactics by individuals and bodies engaged in the women's struggle in the pre-war years.

George Lansbury's own position changed more than once, although the principal shift was the direct result of Marion Coates Hansen's influence. By the 1890s, as we have seen, Lansbury believed firmly in women's enfranchisement as a final phase of parliamentary democracy, though, at that time, the official position of the SDF was that the women's question was a matter of individual conscience. However, the SDF included some powerful feminists, such as Dora Montefiore, who later established the 'spin-off' Adult Suffrage organization. In 1912 Lansbury reminded Marion Coates Hansen of her significant contribution in his move to an equal suffrage position, the main objective of the WSPU:

Now you must take some responsibility for having educated me on the women's question. You know that when I came to Middlesbrough, I was an adult suffragist, and put it just as one part of my propaganda. I have learned during the seven years that have passed to understand it in another sense altogether. You continually appeal to me about Bessie. It is because of Bessie and millions like her that I have come to understand all that is meant by citizenship, comradeship and a real place in life.[21]

The Labour party and the women's movement appeared natural allies in Edwardian politics, but the rival merits of socialism and feminism led to a powerful contemporary discourse and caused tensions between members of the party and those who supported the women's cause. The Pankhurst family had strong roots in the ILP in the North of England. Emmeline Pankhurst and her three daughters, Adela, Christabel, and Sylvia, had founded the WSPU in their Manchester home to foster the links of ILP women with the Labour party and trade unions. However, in 1906, the year in which the organization's headquarters moved to London, Christabel Pankhurst, now chief organizer of the WSPU, announced a new policy of independence from all male-dominated political parties.[22]

At the Cockermouth by-election of 1906 Christabel Pankhurst campaigned for the women's cause on a non-party basis and not, as expected, for the Labour candidate, Robert Smillie. The miners' leader, although a sympathizer with the women's cause, finished bottom of the poll.[23] Marion Coates Hansen joined Christabel

[20] Quoted in *Votes For Women*, 2 Aug. 1912; for Lansbury and the Women's Franchise, see Holton, *Suffrage Days*, pp. 84–6.

[21] George Lansbury to Marion Coates Hansen, 31 Oct. 1912, LP, vol. 28, fo. 80.

[22] For a generally hostile view of Christabel Pankhurst, see D. Mitchell, *Queen Christabel: A Biography of Christabel Pankhurst* (1977), pp. 82–5.

[23] For the Cockermouth by-election, see *Cockermouth Free Press*, 13 July, 10 Aug. 1906; *Carlisle Express*

Pankhurst and Teresa Billington Greig at the by-election campaign, but the new WSPU stance caused her grave personal doubts. It also brought severe criticism from her ILP colleagues in Middlesbrough, who accused her of divided loyalties.

All in all, this disengagement from the Labour party contributed to the first of a number of splits in the WSPU. In 1907 Marion Coates Hansen joined Charlotte Despard and those critical of the autocratic leadership of the Pankhurst circle and the lack of a democratic constitution to form the WFL. Though organized on non-party lines, ILP members were well represented in the leadership and ranks of the new body. Dorothy Lansbury joined the WFL as well as the moderate Women's Labour League (WLL), formed a year earlier.

However, George Lansbury continued to give unflagging support to the WSPU, particularly after his friendship with Keir Hardie brought him into contact with Sylvia Pankhurst. She saw the future of the women's movement differently from her mother and sister and chose to campaign with working women of East London. Hardie and Lansbury were two champions of the women's question whose personalities and political sympathies for the feminist cause allowed them to work side by side with powerful campaigners such as the Pankhursts, Marion Coates Hansen, and others who challenged patriarchy in Edwardian politics and society.[24] In 1912 there was no greater symbol of male power to confront on the women's question than the imperial Parliament at Westminster.

In 1911 Lansbury had rebelled against his party's support for the Liberal government and, as we have seen, with other Labour MPs campaigned strongly against the National Insurance Bill. In 1912 matters finally came to a head over the issue of women's suffrage. He told Marion Coates Hansen:

Ever since I have been in the House I have been more or less at loggerheads with them, and they with me. Hardly a meeting of the [Labour] party has taken place without my being reproached that I was a member of the party . . . and that I continually when beaten on a vote, refused to abide by the decisions of the majority . . . Now this year things have been going from bad to worse.[25]

By this stage George Lansbury was unshakeable in his belief that women's rights took precedence over all other political questions, including Irish Home Rule and Trade Union Reform. He confided to Marion Coates Hansen his intentions to raise the women's question above all others: 'I have made up my mind that the franchise question is of paramount importance, and, at whatever cost, I am going to fight it through.'[26]

After an attempt to introduce his own private member's bill had been ruled out by the Speaker of the House of Commons, Lansbury retained little faith in the Labour party to secure votes for women, even though it was the only party with a

and Examiner, 28 July 1906; and for a brief reference to 'Mrs Marion C. Hunsen (*sic*)', *West Cumberland Times*, 21 July 1906.

[24] M. Pugh, 'Labour and Women's Suffrage', in K. D. Brown (ed.), *The First Labour Party, 1906–1914* (1985), pp. 236–7.

[25] Lansbury to Marion Coates Hansen, 31 Oct. 1912, LP, vol. 28, fo. 87.

[26] George Lansbury to Marion Coates Hansen, 31 Oct. 1912, ibid. fo. 80.

formal commitment. The official stance of the Labour party was to support adult suffrage reform, which advocates of women's enfranchisement dismissed as a distant prospect and therefore no more than a delaying tactic. After the death of his wife Margaret, a keen suffragist and member of the WLL, Ramsay MacDonald appeared lukewarm on the issue of votes for women and in 1912 publicly hostile to the militancy of the WSPU.[27]

After campaigning at Westminster, and following his challenge to Asquith and his suspension by the Speaker, Lansbury continued to ask parliamentary questions on his return about the arrest and imprisonment of suffragettes and hunger strikers. Finally, he took matters into his own hands. He canvassed local Labour parties directly on a policy of total opposition to every government measure until a franchise bill for women was introduced. The *Labour Leader* was scathing about the circular Lansbury distributed among the constituency parties: 'Mr Lansbury has taken it upon himself the task of directing from outside the policy of the party on the question of women's enfranchisement.'[28]

George Lansbury's last action in the House of Commons before his resignation was to support Philip Snowden's unsuccessful amendment to give Irish women votes in the Government of Ireland Bill.[29] However, Snowden and Lansbury received little official Labour support. Lansbury was by now thoroughly disenchanted with a Labour leadership that gave priority to supporting the Liberal government rather than promoting socialism. As far as he was concerned, Lansbury had reached the end of his parliamentary road. The National Insurance Act, the 'Don't Shoot' prosecutions and gaol sentences, the lack of action over Carson and the Ulster Unionists, were all allied to the cause of women's rights in causing his resignation—and without consulting party officials.[30] However, he did consult Marion Coates Hansen, who appealed to him without success to stay his hand and fight his corner within the Labour party:

The very fact that you are told that your 'business is to get out of the Party' appears to me to be the supreme reason for your staying in *at least until after the next Labour Party conference and until after the next ILP Conference*. If the Labour Party is to become a wing of the Liberal Party . . . the question ought to be brought before the Labour Party's own conference . . . you appear to me to have a genius for presenting a case faithfully and yet with depth and intensity . . . I still say—wait, wait, wait—and fight, fight, fight. There *isn't* room for a fourth party in England. There *is* room for the saving of a third party.[31]

It was sound advice from an ardent feminist. But Lansbury, flushed with rage over the attitude of the Liberal government, ignored it. George Lansbury's action in contacting constituency parties brought him into direct confrontation with the Labour leadership, particularly the party secretary, Arthur Henderson, who had been endeavouring to tighten up discipline within the parliamentary party. Naturally, the NEC disapproved heartily of George Lansbury's resignation, which flew

---

[27] D. Marquand, *Ramsay MacDonald* (1977), pp. 148–9.
[28] *Labour Leader*, 17 Oct. 1912.   [29] *Hansard*, 5 Nov. 1912, cols. 1103–7.
[30] *Labour Leader*, 5 Dec. 1912.   [31] Marion Coates Hansen, 3 Nov. 1912, LP, vol. 6, fo. 163–5.

in the face of party discipline once more. However, Lansbury had been an official party candidate in 1910 and one of those endorsed and financed by the ILP. The party leadership therefore had to consider what line to take if Lansbury ran again as a Labour candidate at Bow and Bromley. Two weeks before the by-election, an emergency NEC sub-committee, including the party secretary, Arthur Henderson, met at the House of Commons to consider the situation and subsequently inter-viewed the rebel member about his future position. Asked if he intended to accept the party whip, if re-elected, Lansbury's indefinite reply turned on 'whether the Labour Party was prepared to make his policy on Women's Suffrage the policy of the Party'. In the end, Ramsay MacDonald signed the official minute that resolved not to support Lansbury. The next day, the NEC heard that the ILP had also with-held their official support and considered the Bow and Bromley Labour Party to be in breach of the Labour party and the ILP constitutions. In the circumstances, the NEC took a similar line and also accepted no responsibility for George Lansbury's candidature.[32]

In 1912 the Bow and Bromley by-election was held in somewhat unusual circum-stances and not only because George Lansbury wanted to test the single issue of women's suffrage. As the local Liberal association declined to put up an official can-didate, the constituency was contested by two candidates, both opponents of the Liberal government.

The fifty-three-year-old George Lansbury (Women's Suffrage and Socialist) found himself without official party support and opposed by Reginald Blair (Con-servative and Unionist), a thirty-year-old wealthy Scottish accountant from Har-row. Among the Labour ranks, Lansbury could rely only on some individual sympathizers and the loyalty of his local party, who rallied round their embattled candidate. Poplar councillor and guardian, J. ('Joe') H. Banks, once more organized the election campaign, assisted by Edgar Lansbury as treasurer. In addition, a small number of Labour and Liberal MPs and other figures journeyed to the East End to provide moral and political support.[33] Of those who participated in the Bow and Bromley campaign, Keir Hardie and Philip Snowden openly defied the Labour leadership. At the time Josiah Wedgwood, who later joined the Labour party and served in the first Labour government, was Lansbury's associate in the 'Don't Shoot' agitation and typical of a few Liberal MPs who supported the Labour rebel. Another supporter was the journalist, Henry Noel Brailsford, who had resigned earlier from the *Daily News* in protest over forcible feeding, and in 1912 was instru-mental, with Arthur Henderson, in negotiating the Labour party electoral alliance with the NUWSS.

In Bow, Bessie Lansbury emerged from her relative obscurity to make a special election appeal on behalf of her husband: 'I have felt for many years the very great

---

[32] NEC, *Minutes of the Emergency Sub-Committee*, 13 Nov. 1912; *Minutes*, 14 Nov. 1912; see also Wrigley, *Arthur Henderson* (1990), pp. 61–3.

[33] For the election campaign, see *Votes for Women*, 22, 29 Nov. 1912; *Daily Citizen*; *Daily Herald*; *Manchester Guardian*; *Daily Telegraph*, 12–29 Nov. 1912; *The Suffragette*, 15, 22, 29 Nov. 1912; *East London Observer*; *East London Advertiser*; *Eastern Post*, 16, 23, 30 Nov. 1912.

need for women on all our public bodies and therefore feel glad indeed to support him in our great movement for VOTES FOR WOMEN.'[34]

George Lansbury's election address underlined the primacy of the women's question, especially in relation to working-class women. Lansbury told his electors: 'I want to go back to St. Stephen's with a mandate from the men of Bow and Bromley to put this question of Votes for Women in the very foremost rank of social reform.' However, it was the election manifesto of an independent and principled Labour candidate that opened with an honest account of his opposition to the National Insurance Bill and made explicit his fundamental disagreement with the party leadership. In the circumstances, a more circumspect document might have served George Lansbury better in the by-election.

In the run-up to polling day, the Bow Road became a hive of election activity. George Lansbury's election headquarters were at number 150, on the same thorough-fare as those of the WSPU, the NUWSS, the Votes for Women Fellowship, and the Men's Political Union for Women's Emancipation. Located even nearer at number 151 Bow Road were the principal Unionist committee rooms and the National League for Opposing Woman Suffrage a few doors away at number 142.

In effect, there were several campaigns in progress, waged by feminist organiza-tions, besides those of the two main parties. According to the *Suffragette*, women selling in the Roman Road market took it in turns to go in relays to hear the femi-nist speakers. *The Daily Telegraph* reported:

The purple, green and white of the Women's Social and Political Union and the green, yellow and white of the Women's Freedom League are to be seen floating from motor-cars and vans all over Bow and Bromley; and there were no fewer than three indoor meetings addressed by Mrs Pankhurst yesterday . . . [one meeting was] composed almost entirely of women, many of them carrying babies.[35]

Probably the outstanding contribution to the campaign was the performance of the charismatic Emmeline Pankhurst, who spoke throughout the constituency. Once more, she turned out to attempt to return George Lansbury to Parliament. Five months before, Lansbury had reminded a large suffragist audience at the Savoy Theatre of her earlier efforts that had first ensured his support for the women's cause:

I was fighting a very forlorn kind of fight in Walworth in days when it was not as easy to fight three-cornered fights as it is now. Two of the people who came up to help me and who worked like Trojans were Mrs. Pankhurst and her husband. They took me by the hand, a man comparatively unknown, almost unknown in the country, and made me feel I was really in a big movement![36]

At the Savoy Theatre, George Lansbury had remarked on the courage needed 'for a woman to go out with a hammer, thinking about it for nights probably, and break a window, knowing . . . she is going to jail to be forcibly fed'. In 1912 at Bow Baths

[34] *Votes for Women*, 22 Nov. 1912.   [35] *Daily Telegraph*, 22 Nov. 1912.
[36] *Votes For Women*, 5 July 1912.

Hall, Emmeline Pankhurst defended the WSPU window-smashing campaign: 'At the end of nearly fifty years [of constitutional lobbying] . . . they had to adopt militant methods . . .' She also wondered whether men would have been as patient for fifty years.[37] By contrast, Millicent Fawcett, President of the National Union of Women's Suffrage Societies, campaigned simply 'as the widow of Henry Fawcett who represented the Borough of Hackney for nine years . . . to vindicate the independence of another East End constituency by returning Mr Lansbury to parliament.'[38]

Surprisingly, the official Labour party newspaper, the *Daily Citizen* gave the election considerable attention and photographed Lansbury as he campaigned in the constituency. During the day, Lansbury visited local factories and workshops and held at least three main meetings each evening in halls and schools. In the streets children sang election songs, always a common feature of a George Lansbury campaign. In *The Worker*, Poplar Trades Council and Labour Representation Committee's newspaper, Lansbury wrote: 'it is all to do with your mothers and your sisters . . . we want that they shall have the vote . . . much nicer homes, much better food and better home life for you all.'[39]

In 1912 George Lansbury had helped relaunch the *Daily Herald* and his by-election contest now became one of its early campaigns. The new Labour daily had greeted the possibility of his resignation with no surprise: 'Mr Lansbury certainly is contemplating resigning, but it is from the Labour Party and not from Parliament that he contemplates resignation.'[40]

During the by-election the readers of the *Daily Herald* received detailed and stirring coverage of George Lansbury's campaign, and one that portrayed him as the local hero and a son of East London:

What you have to remember is that the man for whom you are working is not unknown among the people he has represented in Parliament for the past two years, and upon other bodies for many years. The children . . . the women and men know George Lansbury as a comrade and a neighbour. They know his life—but, more important still, he knows theirs.[41]

Probably Lansbury's main difficulty was to explain to his electors why he had surrendered the parliamentary seat he had worked so hard to win only two years before. At St Gabriel's School in Morris Road, he made it clear that, as a socialist, 'matters had arrived at a point in the history of women's suffrage which necessitated that it should be settled'. Why did he believe that women should have votes? 'Because they were human beings, the same as men.'[42]

At the Poplar and Bromley Tabernacle, Lansbury argued the case for equal suffrage—that 'to give the vote to some men and not give it to women was the greatest possible insult . . . (Hear, hear.)'[43] The anti-suffragist Reginald Blair's campaign started with a public endorsement from the CU party leader, Andrew Bonar Law.

---

[37] *East London Observer*, 23 Nov. 1912.   [38] *Eastern Post and City Chronicle*, 23 Nov. 1912.
[39] Copies of *The Worker*, Oct., Nov. 1912 are in THLLH&A.   [40] *Daily Herald*, 30 Oct. 1912.
[41] Ibid. 13 Nov. 1912. For George Lansbury's campaign, see also ibid. 12–27 Nov. 1912.
[42] *East End News*, 22 Nov. 1912.   [43] *East London Observer*, 23 Nov. 1912.

His chief supporters included the Conservative Women's Primrose League and the National League for Opposing Women's Suffrage. Both bodies hammered out a similar message, proclaimed on election posters throughout the constituency: 'WOMEN DO NOT WANT VOTES' and 'BLAIR IS FOR GOVERNMENT BY MEN, LANSBURY BY WOMEN.'

At a packed meeting at St Stephen's Hall in Saxon Road, Blair opposed National Insurance and the payment of MPs, a measure of political reform already passed. Though opposed to women's enfranchisement, Blair refused to campaign only on this specific question:

He stood for the restoration of the British Constitution—(cheers) the Union between Great Britain and Ireland—(cheers) . . . the integrity of the Church of England in Wales (renewed cheers) . . . the efficiency of our national defences . . . for a land . . . and last, but not least, he stood for the policy of Tariff Reform.[44]

On the Saturday before polling, a large-scale rally was arranged for George Lansbury at Bow Baths in Roman Road. *The Times* reported: 'Every train, tram car and motor omnibus on Saturday afternoon brought fresh reserves of feminine canvassers and bill-distributors. There seemed to be thousands of suffragist volunteers in the division, and the pavements were white with their discarded gifts.'[45]

On the eve of polling day, the various suffrage societies combined outside Bow church for a last spectacular torchlight gathering. The procession set off around the constituency with swinging coloured lanterns and banners, preceded by a brass band playing the Marseillaise. The next day Christabel Pankhurst wrote from Paris: 'Best wishes from an absent friend to Mrs Lansbury and yourself for success . . . Whatever the result the fight has been gloriously worthwhile and has done untold good.'[46]

On polling day, 26 November 1912, the weather was wild and blustery, with the rain teeming down in wind-driven torrents by the evening. Suffrage women remained at every polling booth, sometimes without cloaks and umbrellas, drenched to the skin, until voting picked up as factories closed. Little rowdyism was reported, except for a broken window at Cllr. Bassett's shop at 250 Roman Road and mud-slinging at campaign vehicles. Tracing those electors who had moved out of the constituency and getting their voters to the poll were important matters for the campaign organizers. The energetic Catherine Marshall had warned Josiah Wedgwood about potential transport problems: 'Are they well organised as regards the management of polling day? Lady De La Warr will be responsible for providing three motor cars, but would rather they took their orders from us than from Mr Lansbury's com. [committee] room'.[47]

At the Blair camp there were ninety motors at his disposal. However, owing to a fatal dispute between the WSPU and the local Labour party, suffragette cars were not made available to convey Lansbury voters to the polls until Mrs Pankhurst's very belated intervention.

[44] *East London Observer*, 23 Nov. 1912.   [45] *The Times*, 25 Nov. 1912.
[46] Christabel Pankhurst to George Lansbury, 24 Nov. 1912, LP, vol. 6.
[47] Catherine Marshall to Josiah Wedgwood, 21 Nov. 1912, Marshall Papers D/Mar/3/53.

The remarkable and bizarre feature of the Bow and Bromley contest, which has never been mentioned in any modern accounts of the by-election, was the existence of three women voters on the parliamentary register, though only one was in the constituency on polling day. Despite a personal visit from Mrs Pankhurst to change her mind, she declined the offer of a suffragette vehicle. During the afternoon, this sole woman voter, Unity Dawkins of 135 Campbell Road—described as 'the widow of a strong Unionist worker'—travelled defiantly to Bromley town hall in a Tory car, festooned with a large blue card of Mr Blair, to cast her parliamentary vote for the anti-suffragist candidate.[48]

Just before ten o'clock in the evening the returning officer, J. Kynaston Metcalfe, declared the result inside Bromley town hall:

Mr Reginald Blair (Unionist)	4,042
Mr George Lansbury (Socialist and Suffragist)	3,291
Unionist Majority	751[49]

While a deeply disappointed George Lansbury addressed his supporters near the famous local obelisk in Devons Road, the blue lights and rockets went off at the Bow and Bromley Conservative Club to greet the result. A triumphant Reginald Blair declared 'I have stood for the principles of the Unionist party'.[50]

The next day *The Times* believed the result 'renders impossible any pretence that women's suffrage has been approved by a constituency'.[51] Locally, George Lansbury was heavily criticized by the *Eastern Post and Chronicle* for causing the by-election on a subject 'that had been brought before the public by means of violence, arson and outrage'.[52]

On the same day the Labour party issued a statement—purposely withheld in order not to prejudice Lansbury's election chances. It denied he was 'the victim of a

[48] Only the *Daily Mail* named the two women who did not vote, as Vincent Gerrard ('in a convent') and Augustine O'Bryen ('removed to Scotland'). The electoral registration officer may have mistaken their unusual first names for male householders. *Daily Mail*, 23, 27 Nov. 1912; see also *Eastern Post and City Chronicle*, 30 Nov. 1912; *Daily Telegraph*, 27 Nov. 1912.

[49]

Table to compare the General Election result with that of the 1912 by-election

Year of election	Number of electors	Turn-out (%)	Candidate	Party	Votes	Majority
1912	10,863	67.5	R. Blair	Con.	4,042	
			G. Lansbury	Ind. Lab.	3,291	
						751 (10.2%) Unionist
1910 (Dec.)	10,330	75.2	G. Lansbury	Soc.	4,315	
			L. M. S. Amery	Lib. Union	3,452	
					863	863 (11.2)% Socialist

[50] *Daily Telegraph*, 27 Nov. 1912.   [51] *The Times*, 27 Nov. 1912.
[52] *Eastern Post and Chronicle*, 30 Nov. 1912.

caucus' that had coerced him and caused him 'to sever his connection with the party and resign his seat'. What followed was an acrimonious public debate conducted mainly in the columns of the *Labour Leader* and the *Daily Herald* between the Labour leadership and the Lansbury camp over the respective merits of loyalty to party policy and freedom of conscience to follow a different course of action. The women's question had revealed that the two sides remained poles apart over party policy and discipline. The Labour leadership could not countenance an independent stance—especially one in alliance with the WSPU. George Lansbury immovably opposed their support for a capitalist Liberal government.[53] It was left to Philip Snowden in the *Christian Commonwealth* to weigh the various arguments and to deplore 'Mr Lansbury's loss from Parliament . . . most of all because of his individuality and independence'.[54]

A distraught Marion Coates Hansen described Lansbury's defeat—which meant that the ILP no longer had a London MP—as a double catastrophe for the women's cause and for those campaigning to establish socialism within the Labour movement. She was irreconcilable and poured out her grief: 'You risked the weapon the Lord granted to you to hold for a spell, and you lost . . . A more unhappy time I have never lived through . . .'[55] Ben Tillett wrote, 'I felt for you and the courage and the splendid quality of your fight', adding, 'I think the womenfolk are splendid. It is good to know that women like this live—if only for the sake of the race.'[56]

In her memoirs, Sylvia Pankhurst, who had become more distant from her mother and sister, told a sorry story of friction between the local Labour party and wealthy feminists whose invasion of the constituency upset a largely proletarian and male electorate. As she put it, a young ally of Christabel Pankhurst, Grace Roe, inexperienced and unsympathetic to Labour, had been dispatched to Bow and Bromley from the Lincoln's Inn headquarters to run the WSPU election campaign instead of Sylvia. There had been little co-operation between her and Lansbury's agent, Joe Banks, who apparently disliked the suffragettes.[57]

One of 'GL's' workers complained: 'You cannot rely on all . . . of the women's organisations . . . when some of their canvassers go round saying that they do not agree with your socialism.'[58] Labour MP, Will Thorne, who had also helped Lansbury's campaign, observed sympathetically that he was 'firmly convinced that no constituency would be won on "Votes for Women". I do not think that my majority of over 4,000 could win on a question of that kind.'[59]

After his defeat, Lansbury himself explained his resignation in terms of his differences with the Labour leadership on women's enfranchisement, as well their subservience to the Liberal party. He had fought the by-election, 'not for votes for

---

[53] *Labour Leader*, 28 Nov. 1912; *Daily Herald*, 27 Nov. 1912.
[54] *Christian Commonwealth*, 4 Dec. 1912.
[55] Marion Coates Hansen to George Lansbury, 27 Nov. 1912, LP, vol. 6, fo. 242.
[56] Ben Tillett to George Lansbury, 9 May 1913, LP, vol. 7, fo. 35.
[57] E. S. Pankhurst, *The Suffragette Movement: An Intimate Account of Persons and Ideals* (1977), pp. 424–6.
[58] Sanders Jacobs to George Lansbury, 27 Nov. 1912, LP, vol. 6, fo. 245.
[59] Will Thorne to George Lansbury, 27 Nov. 1912, ibid. vol. 28, fo. 85.

Fine Ladies, but votes for all men and all women'. But his outstanding reason was that he 'wanted the men who had elected me to say that they endorsed my belief that all men and all women should have full rights of citizenship.'[60] Many years later, George Lansbury believed firmly that some constituents still refused to vote for him, as they felt let down by their Labour MP. His famous subsequent principle, 'Never Resign!', suggests he recognized his miscalculation in 1912. Bow and Bromley was not a safe seat for any Labour candidate at that time.[61]

In the December 1910 election Lloyd George's public declaration for 'my friend, George Lansbury' probably meant Liberals voted for 'G. L.'. Two years later, the *Morning Post* reported an absence of Liberal posters in Bow and Bromley: 'Silent windows . . . all mean abstentions tomorrow'—an uncanny augury of Lansbury's defeat.[62] Not until normal party politics resumed after the First World War, with an increased working-class electorate, did the popular George Lansbury become unassailable, representing Bow and Bromley from 1922–40.

However, the loss of his parliamentary seat did not diminish George Lansbury's commitment to the women's cause or that of his family. In Bow Road, the Lansburys were a well-known family and their socialism earned them a reputation as a highly political household. As they grew up, all of Bessie and George's children became engaged in some aspect of local politics. George Lansbury later recalled that in 1913 six members of his family were in prison or narrowly escaped going there.

In these pre-war years no single issue demonstrated the family's burning political commitment more than the women's franchise question. Marsland Gander, from an almost equally large Conservative and imperialist family nearby in Bow, recalled his sister Evelyn's friendly pram-pushing expeditions to Victoria Park with Daisy Lansbury. About Daisy's father he remembered:

George Lansbury was something so dreadful that we hardly dared mention the word above a whisper—he was a socialist. Moreover, and this was so appalling that it was kept as a secret from the youngest children, he HAD BEEN IN PRISON. This was not all. He was supporting women's suffrage and it was believed that his daughters were mixed up with this infamous movement led by dangerous and fanatical viragoes. Even then, however, I think I could distinguish between imprisonment for a political as distinct from a criminal offence.[63]

George Lansbury suffered imprisonment twice for his political beliefs—in 1913 and 1921—and on the first occasion it was in connection with the suffragette movement. In his autobiography Lansbury outlined the fate of his family, as far as prison was concerned in 1913:

My eldest daughter, Annie, served a month in Holloway, and my eldest son, William, two months in Pentonville. My next son, Edgar came into conflict with the authorities owing to a disturbance at a public meeting, and escaped with a caution. My daughter, Daisy, who is

[60] *New Witness*, 5 Dec. 1912.

[61] For George Lansbury's resignation of the Labour Party leadership in 1935, see J. Shepherd, 'George Lansbury, Ernest Bevin and the Labour Leadership Crisis of 1935', in C. Wrigley and J. Shepherd (eds.), *On the Move: Essays in Labour and Transport History Presented to Philip Bagwell* (1991), pp. 204–30.

[62] *Morning Post*, 25 Nov. 1912.   [63] M. Gander, *After These Many Quests* (1949), pp. 20–1.

now the wife of Raymond Postgate, was arrested disguised as Sylvia Pankhurst. But she had done nothing wrong but dress herself in the clothes she chose to wear, which was hardly an offence, even if she had deceived the very *elite* of the CID. She was allowed to go free.[64]

However, while all members of the family enthusiastically and loyally supported Lansbury on his courageous stand after he resigned from Parliament, there were clearly divergent views within the Lansbury household on the question of 'votes for women'. On this issue, Edgar believed that his father had 'burned his boats by resigning his seat'. He also thought that the Pankhursts 'must have looked askance at our household and wondered what sort of suffragist father . . . kept his wife "in subjection" by having such a large family; and what sort of woman suffragist mother was to allow her husband to get away with all the glory. They never understood'.

According to Edgar, his mother in 1912 may have been secluded in a separate sphere of the home—apparently her choice—but she remained a staunch socialist and an uncompromising internationalist. No member of the family was a keener champion of the Soviet régime in the early 1930s. However, Bessie's socialist faith did not extend to enthusiastic support for the well-heeled feminists of the WSPU and their demand for the immediate granting of equal suffrage. In Edgar Lansbury's words: '[I]n a way, she resented their coming into Bow and sidetracking the enthusiasm of the growing movement for Socialism into an agitation for "votes for women" which in her view was always a subsidiary issue . . .'[65]

After the WSPU headquarters were relocated in London, Christabel Pankhurst preferred to recruit members from moneyed middle-class and upper-class women. Sylvia Pankhurst instead opened WSPU shops in East London. At number 198 Bow Road she renovated a disused baker's shop (opposite St Mary's parish church standing in the middle of the road), with help from George Lansbury and his sons Edgar and William, who also supplied timber from their sawmill business.[66]

The Lansbury family had a strong association with Sylvia Pankhurst for a number of years, particularly after she began her East End campaign for working women. Sylvia Pankhurst decided to start her campaign in East London where there was a strong tradition of women's political and suffrage activity.[67] Outside sympathizers had been attracted to the cause of working men and women, as we have seen, notably Annie Besant during the famous Match Girls' Strike in 1888 at the Bryant and May factory in Fairfield Road and Eleanor Marx who assisted the Gasworkers' Union. From as early as January 1887, working women in East London had campaigned for the vote in nearby Stratford.

    [64] Lansbury, *Looking Backwards and Forwards*, pp. 110–11.
    [65] E. Lansbury, *George Lansbury*, pp. 140–1.
    [66] R. Taylor, *In Letters of Gold: The Story of Sylvia Pankhurst and the East London Federation of the Suffragettes in Bow* (1993), p. 6.
    [67] For Sylvia Pankhurst's East End campaign, see *Suffragette*, 18 Oct. 1912; E. S. Pankhurst, *The Suffragette Movement*, pp. 416–37. See also D. B. Montefiore, *From a Victorian to a Modern* (1927), pp. 50–1. Dora Montefiore recalls that the London Committee of the WSPU had been active in East London for several months before the arrival of Sylvia Pankhurst. See also B. Winslow, *Sylvia Pankhurst: Sexual Politics and Political Activism* (1996), pp. 27–39.

Sylvia Pankhurst had participated in George Lansbury's by-election contest, but it was after this campaign that members of the Lansbury family became closely identified with her East London Federation of the Suffragettes (ELFS), established on 27 May 1913. Some weeks earlier, Sylvia Pankhurst had been convicted at Thames Police Court of window-breaking at Bow. At the same time Daisy Lansbury was discharged by the magistrate, Mr Leycester, who accepted her denial of assaulting a policeman, though the same magistrate imprisoned Annie and William Lansbury, along with Sylvia Pankhurst and other suffragettes, for window-breaking.

William Lansbury, who had broken a window of Bromley Public Hall, declared that he was 'a native of Bow . . . I did it because of the terrible and hideous state of the women and children that go by there . . . I see enough miserable women in one day to make me go and break 50,000 windows.'[68]

The Lansbury family was among those who rallied around Sylvia Pankhurst to support her public demonstrations and supported her recruitment of a 'People's Army' for her protection against the authorities. Jessie Lansbury, William's wife, at seventeen had become the secretary of the Bow and Bromley branch of the ELFS, and other members of the family joined her in Sylvia Pankhurst's community and political work.

In the twelve months from June 1913, Sylvia Pankhurst was imprisoned ten times, and each time undertook a hunger and thirst strike. On each occasion she was released temporarily under the infamous 'Cat and Mouse Act' until she regained her health. In one of a number of memorable escapades in the streets of Bow, Daisy Lansbury, disguised as Sylvia Pankhurst, with her brothers Edgar and William, assisted the suffragette campaigner to evade capture by the police. In the end, George Lansbury appealed directly to the King that Sylvia Pankhurst 'is now lying in Holloway on hunger strike, and slowly but surely is being starved to death'. Lansbury also pointed out that he had committed a similar offence, but had never been rearrested after his early release.[69]

On 10 April 1913 George Lansbury had been one of the main speakers at the WSPU rally at the Albert Hall held after the conviction and imprisonment of Emmeline Pankhurst. Lansbury made an impassioned speech in defence of suffragette militancy. He was critical of London MPs for their profound lack of support for women's suffrage and appealed for men to support the women's cause:

Therefore I ask all of us here to stand shoulder to shoulder with the militant women: hold them up in the fight they are waging: let them burn and destroy property and do anything they will, and for every leader that is taken away, let a dozen step forward in her place . . . You take their word for it that every window which is broken, every golf course which is attacked and every racing stand which is burned down worries them a million times more . . .[70]

Five days later, a summons was granted against George Lansbury. Under an obsolete statute of Edward III (1 Edw III, c. 16), originally designed to deal with

---

[68] *Daily Herald*, 19 Feb. 1913. See Winslow, *Sylvia Pankhurst*, pp. 42–4.
[69] George Lansbury to George V, 11 June 1914, PRO, HO 144/1264/237169.
[70] 'Report of Inspector Edward Parker', 11 Aug. 1913, PRO, HO 144/1264/237169, 184061.

the disturbed times of the Hundred Years War, it stated that he was allegedly 'a disturber of the peace and an inciter of others to commit divers crimes and misdemeanours'.

According to Postgate, Lansbury 'was sentenced to be bound over to serve six months; he refused to be bound over, and was taken to Pentonville Prison, and went on hunger and thirst strike'.[71] In fact, Postgate somewhat truncated the legal process that confined Lansbury in Pentonville. In 1913, George Lansbury appeared before the police magistrate at Bow Street Magistrates Court. He faced three months in prison unless he entered into his own recognizance for his future good behaviour for twelve months by finding two sureties of £500 each.

At the High Court on 28 July, in a special case (*Lansbury* v. *Riley*) of the Divisional Court of the King's Bench, Justices Bray, Avory, and Lash decided unanimously that the jurisdiction of the Magistrates' Court had been properly exercised and dismissed George Lansbury's appeal. Two days later, Lansbury appeared once more at Bow Street Magistrates' Court, where he told the stipendiary, Sir John Dickinson, he was unable to find the required sureties of £1,000 and was accordingly ordered to be imprisoned for three months.

George Lansbury had committed no crime and had no criminal conviction or outstanding charge against him. The total figure of £1,000 (probably around £100,000 in present-day values) was an incredible sum then, and the magistrate must have known that a working-class politician would be placed in considerable difficulty to find sureties on such a scale. However, the courts that year had already imprisoned his young son and daughter for two months and for one month with hard labour, respectively, for a first offence of window-breaking.[72]

In Pentonville, prisoner number 237,169 went on an immediate hunger and thirst strike. He also commented on his predicament. He used the columns of the *Daily Herald to* accuse the Liberal Government of complicity in his imprisonment, as he was 'the most unsparing critic in regard to their transactions in the Marconi gamble, and in that fraudulent imposture, the nine pence for four pence Insurance Act'. Not only that: he had committed no offence and again drew parallels with the Ulster situation:

Therefore, I go to prison as a definite protest against differentiation of treatment as between myself, Mr Bonar Law, the Duke of Abercorn and Sir Edward Carson. These three men have not only cited, but have caused riots and loss of life in Ulster. At this moment they are seditiously inciting officers of the British Army to turn traitor to King and Parliament.[73]

There was a considerable reaction to Lansbury's term of imprisonment among his supporters and a wave of protests swept East London and elsewhere. Meetings were held at Devon Road, Bow addressed by Josiah Wedgwood and Henry D. Harben. Harry Gosling spoke at a large rally outside the East India Dock gates, a traditional

---

[71] Postgate, *Lansbury*, pp. 130–1.
[72] Today, in a magistrates court, a defendant can agree to a bind-over to keep the peace for a specified time (which is not a conviction) for a far smaller surety, e.g. £100.
[73] *Daily Herald*, 31 July 1913.

gathering-place. The *Daily Herald* received scores of resolutions demanding Lansbury's release from labour organizations and trade unions throughout the country. Included in this number were those sent by the Paddington British Socialist Party (BSP), the Poplar Men's Federation for Women's Suffrage, and even one from the Caister Holiday Camp. The Poplar Trades Council and Labour Representation Committee arranged marches to demonstrate outside Pentonville Prison until Lansbury's release.

Margaret McMillan wrote to Bessie Lansbury: 'Long live George Lansbury. May God keep him. Gaols are better than Churches today.'[74] In offering financial support for the already financially embattled *Daily Herald*, Henry D. Harben commented that 'if you have to do 3 months, it will only endear you to thousands of people.'[75] On this occasion Marion Coates Hansen wrote approvingly:

All the same you have done a big thing for us. It looms especially big, because you really have *not* committed any crime whatever—even a small crime such as breaking a window. It is absolutely shameless to give you 'three months' and shows how far in the dark ages we still are, especially in matters concerning the welfare of women.[76]

George Lansbury's imprisonment was compared to the martyrdom of forty-one-year-old Emily Wilding Davison, who had been force-fed almost fifty times in prison. On Derby Day, 4 June 1913, at Epsom, she was seriously injured, after dramatically dashing out in front of the king's horse, Anmer, at Tattenham corner, and died four days later.[77] In the period between his arrest and eventual imprisonment, Margaret McMillan comforted George Lansbury: 'You and your dear wife are fighting a good fight: Miss Davison (gallant heart) will die, I think. What a struggle. What a victory the life of the brave is. *She* won the Derby. She sacrificed the Race-Course. She won the race.'[78] In the *Daily Herald* Lansbury called on its readers and the *Daily Herald* League supporters to turn out for Emily Wilding Davison's funeral procession.[79]

At Westminster Tim Healey and Josiah Wedgwood raised questions about Lansbury's imprisonment and pressed for his release. Wedgwood attempted without success to move the adjournment of the Commons. From Bow, Annie Banks, wife of Lansbury's election agent, wrote direct to the Home Secretary: 'He can never be classed as one of this sort [a criminal], for he is so highly respected wherever he goes, not only in Bow and Bromley but in other parts as well . . .'[80]

---

[74] Margaret McMillan to Bessie Lansbury, 31 July 1913, LP, vol. 7, fos. 76–7.

[75] Henry D. Harben to George Lansbury, 6 May 1913, ibid. fo. 33. For Henry D. Harben, see Brian Harrison, *Prudent Revolutionaries: Portraits of British Feminists between the Wars* (Oxford, 1987), ch. 8.

[76] Marion Coates Hansen to George Lansbury, 5 Aug. 1913, ibid. fos. 107–8.

[77] Emily Wilding Davison's personal effects included the return part of her train ticket to Victoria Station, suggesting she did not contemplate 'suicidal martyrdom' that day.

[78] Margaret McMillan to George Lansbury, 7 June 1913, ibid. fos. 53–5. There is remarkable footage of Emily Wilding Davison's fatal dash onto the racecourse on Derby Day, shown on British Pathé News, 'Rise Up Women!. The Suffragette Campaign in London' (Museum of London, 1992), PAL VHS. See also A. Morley with L. Stanley, *The Life and Death of Emily Wilding Davison* (1988).

[79] Undated newscutting [probably *Daily Herald*, 7 June 1913], ibid. fo. 55.

[80] Mrs J. H. Barker to Reginald McKenna, 2 Aug. 1913, ibid. fo. 92.

This episode in Lansbury's life also demonstrates his political adroitness in stage-managing popular protest in the East End. Two coaches took Lansbury and his enthusiastic supporters to Bow Street, in the heart of the West End, when he surrendered to the police court on 30 July. During his imprisonment thousands demonstrated, with musical accompaniment from the local band, outside Pentonville Prison. The Borough of Poplar Trades Council and Labour Representation League published a special edition of *The Worker* with an article by George Lansbury on the circumstances of his imprisonment. Special attention was given to the imprisonment twelve months before of Tom Mann, Guy Bowman, and Fred Crossley for 'merely asking soldiers not to shoot'. By comparison, Lansbury identified CU politicians such as Bonar Law, F. E. Smith, and Sir Edward Carson, who 'arm men in Ulster, spread sedition in the British army and collect names of officers prepared to break the oath of allegiance'.

On 2 August 1913 George Lansbury was released by order of the Secretary of State, Reginald McKenna, under the Prisoners (Temporary Discharge for Ill-Health) Act, 1913, though probably not as a result of the hue and cry throughout the country. The infamous 'Cat and Mouse' Act, as it was known, was used to provide temporary and conditional release for suffragette prisoners ill from forcible feeding who, on recovery, were then rearrested by the police and returned to gaol. In Lansbury's case, the regular medical reports reveal why he was suddenly released after only four days.

On Wednesday 31 July the prison doctor noted: 'I think he may be able to stand five or six days without food and possibly without drink without serious risk but not longer', but on the next day advised Lansbury's release 'on Sunday or early on Monday', owing to his heart condition. Included in the official report was a medical history indicating Lansbury had a heart condition: 'The prisoner has suffered from palpitations and cardiac pain, I understand, for years and in view of his cardiac condition.' By Friday, Lansbury had been admitted to hospital and a telephone report from the medical officer at 5.15 p.m. noted that the prisoner 'has a bad heart and is subject to attacks of cardiac failure. Ten years ago his life policy premium was raised above the ordinary rate on this account'—and asked for authority to release him. A further telephone report at 11.20 a.m. the next morning recommended Lansbury's release and it was duly authorized that day.

Alice MacDonald, wife of J. A. Murray MacDonald, wrote to Bessie Lansbury to express delight at his release. She was highly critical of Lansbury's association with the militancy of WSPU: 'I have often felt of late I should write to him and tell him what I thought of militant methods *as I had some little share in helping to interest him in Women's Suffrage in the old days . . .*'[81]

Fifteen years later, in his autobiography, George Lansbury recollected some of the details of his time in Pentonville Prison. He remembered that he was summonsed under a specific clause of the medieval statute as a 'wanderer, a beggar, and a pillar from across the seas' but stated incorrectly that he 'was given the chance

---

[81] Alice MacDonald to Bessie Lansbury, 4 Aug. 1913, ibid. fos. 101–2 (emph. added).

of being bound over or *serving six months' imprisonment*. George Lansbury was physically weak on entering Pentonville, as he had undertaken a preparatory hunger strike. Inside, he discovered a prison régime designed to dehumanize the inmates. He debated theology briefly with a young chaplain. He also recuperated on a lawn in the prison yard among 'the tombs of many noted murderers'.[82]

Finally, the most interesting part of Lansbury's account is his admission that, in campaigning throughout the country on behalf of women's suffrage, he 'nearly overstepped the line between legal and illegal speeches, and *finally did so at a great demonstration in the Albert hall held on 10th April, 1913*'.

George Lansbury was released on licence until 11 August 1913. According to the *Daily Herald*, 10,000 of his constituents marched to Joseph Fels's house in Cornwall Terrace, Regent's Park, where Lansbury was taken to recuperate after his release. Among those in the procession 'Dockers, Poplar Trades Council, Gasworkers, Herald League, and many Trades Unions were noted on the banners'.[83]

However, George Lansbury was never rearrested. This fact led to accusations of gender bias by the Liberal government in the treatment of WSPU prisoners.[84] Many years later, Lansbury jested that to confess that he had never completed his term of imprisonment might lead to his rearrest. After his release, his licence was put up for sale to the highest bidder for the benefit of the *Daily Herald* Fund.[85]

Clearly, different members of the Lansbury family participated actively in the women's movement, especially in the assistance given to Sylvia Pankhurst and her ELFS. However, these imprisonments in 1913 revealed tensions within the Lansbury family.

On 21 June 1913, Joseph Fels wrote to Bessie Lansbury to complain about a critical article on suffragette militancy forwarded to him by 'one of your relatives'. He added bluntly: 'It is a pity any relative of yours should be so foolish as to condemn a thing without taking the trouble to understand what she is condemning.'[86] A member of the WFL and the WLL, Dorothy Lansbury disagreed with the militant and violent activities of the WSPU. Earlier in 1913 she wrote to her brother William, serving two months in prison, to suggest that his illegal window-breaking could have been employed for a higher cause of improving the condition of the workers than votes for women.[87]

After the loss of his parliamentary seat, George Lansbury embarked on a new career in journalism by assuming the editorship of the *Daily Herald*. Before taking

---

[82] Lansbury, *My Life*, pp. 121–4 (emph. added).
[83] *Daily Herald*, 4 Aug. 1913 (emph. added).
[84] 'Why is Lansbury still at large, when [he] is out on licence under the exact conditions and same sentence as Sylvia Pankhurst who was [re-]arrested last Tuesday at Poplar Town Hall and is still in Holloway undergoing the terrible torture of a Hunger and Thirst Strike, does not this show there is a law for man very different to that which is administered to women'. Blanche Pagesmith to Reginald McKenna, 21 Oct. 1913, PRO, HO 144/1264/237169, 184061.
[85] Ibid.
[86] '[O]ne of your relatives' was an unnamed reference to Dorothy Lansbury, who had gone to Philadelphia in 1912 to marry Ernest Thurtle. Joseph Fels to Bessie Lansbury, 21 June, 1913, LP, vol. 7, fos. 62–3.
[87] Dorothy and Ernest Thurtle to William Lansbury, 2 Feb. 1913. Esme Whiskin Papers.

up the post, however, he and Bessie accepted an invitation from the Felses to visit the United States, sailing with the American couple to New York on the liner *Kaiser Wilhelm II* towards the end of 1913.

As a British socialist, Lansbury's presence in America attracted considerable interest and he was in demand for interviews and lectures virtually every night. Women's suffrage, Ulster, and unemployment were among the main topics, as well as his endeavours with Joseph Fels to promote the single tax to American business-men. Lansbury was a popular speaker at church congregations and the guest of the New York Luncheon Club. By Christmas, on their busy itinerary the couple had arrived in Philadelphia and visited the huge Fels naptha-soap works. While Bessie remained behind, Lansbury went on to Cleveland, Chicago, and Cincinatti for more visits to industrial works, speeches to groups of socialists, and an opportunity to study the American newspaper industry at first hand.

Returning to New York, their newly married daughter Dorothy joined her par-ents with her husband, Ernest Thurtle. Harvard and Yale Universities were the next stops in a schedule that also included a tour of a modern sawmill. It was a hectic itin-erary that reflected Lansbury's interests in politics, business, and journalism. In 1936 he was to undertake an even more demanding tour of the United States in the cause of pacifism and world peace.

For the last part of their stay, Bessie and George Lansbury went on to Canada to see relatives who had emigrated from Britain. In Ottawa, where Lansbury accepted more lecture invitations, they visited the Canadian Parliament. Finally back in England, Bessie and George found the younger members of their family waiting to meet them at Tilbury. Lansbury recalled their greeting: 'We are all grown up. We are children no longer.'[88]

After their American trip, Lansbury straightaway took up his editorship of the *Daily Herald*, opening the columns of his paper to a range of rebel and dissenting groups from the syndicalists to the suffragettes. However, although Lansbury was prepared to work with Christabel Pankhurst to forge a socialist–suffragist alliance on the British Left, he was thwarted by the Pankhurst policy of opposition to male politics. Christabel Pankhurst rejected the notion of any association of the WPSU with the *Daily Herald* League, which she described as a class-based movement. She told Harben, who had travelled to Paris as an intermediary, that women needed to gain experience of standing and acting alone. For Christabel Pankhurst, what bound women—of all social backgrounds—together was womanhood.[89] By 1914 the door was finally closed. An irreconcilable rift had developed within the Pankhurst family. Sylvia Pankhurst's association with Lansbury and the labour movement in East London infuriated her sister, Christabel, who regarded this connection with socialism as a threat to her franchise campaign. In particular, she was angry about Sylvia's presence with George Lansbury and James Connolly, on the platform at a mass rally, attended by ten thousand, at the Albert Hall in

---

[88] Lansbury, *My Life*, pp. 102–9.
[89] Christabel Pankhurst to H. D. Harben, 7 Aug. 1913, Harben Papers, BL Add. MS 58,226, fos. 34–6.

November 1913. This gathering had been organized by the *Daily Herald* League to support the transport workers in the Dublin Lock-Out and to protest against the imprisonment of their leader, Jim Larkin. Finally, Christabel Pankhurst summoned her sister to Paris and, in the presence of the upset Emmeline, effectively expelled Sylvia and her ELFS from the WSPU.[90] Her action confirmed the split between the two organizations which had been visible for some time. By resigning his parliamentary seat and by his willingness to go to prison, George Lansbury—supported steadfastly by members of his family—had shown his overriding commitment to the women's movement and, in particular, to the militant politics of the WSPU. The Lansbury family continued to support the ELFS. 'Deeds not words'—the WSPU slogan, which Lansbury signed in copies of *My Life* in 1928, the year when all women finally gained the vote in Britain—remained the order of the day.

[90] M. Davis, *Sylvia Pankhurst: A Life in Radical Politics* (1999), pp. 41–2. For a recent account of the politics of the Pankhurst family, see M. Pugh, *The Pankhursts* (2001).

8
Daily Herald, 1911–1914

On 14 April 1912 at 10.25 p.m. New York time, the 46,382 ton flagship of the White Star line on her maiden voyage from Southampton to New York collided with an iceberg in mid-Atlantic at or near latitude 41 46., longitude 50 14., North Atlantic Ocean, and early on the following morning foundered with the loss of over 1,300 passengers and crew. The sinking of RMS *Titanic*, one of the greatest maritime disasters of the twentieth century, occurred on the very day that a new *Daily Herald* was published in Britain. The tragedy gave the fledgling Labour daily—the newspaper with which George Lansbury, now out of Parliament, was to be associated for the next thirteen years—its first major story and crusade.[1] As the various *Titanic* inquiries revealed the full horror of the disaster, the *Daily Herald* exposed the class-based nature of the death toll with damning headlines that indicted Mr Bruce Ismay and his steam ship company—'Women and Children Last!', 'Profits first—Passengers Afterwards', 'Thirty Per cent. For Shareholders And 53 Steerage Children Drowned'.[2] Of those who perished in the icy Atlantic Ocean, a disproportionate number of steerage passengers had lost their lives in the catastrophe compared to those who enjoyed the luxuries of the first- and second-class decks of the 'unsinkable' Leviathan.

As a populist newspaper on the left of British politics, the *Daily Herald* survived periodic financial crises from 1912 until its demise and replacement by the *Sun* in 1964. During its lifetime as Huw Richards has shown, the newspaper had three 'incarnations' in fifty-two years. After ten years, only a negotiated take-over in 1922, by the Labour party and the TUC, could keep the *Daily Herald* alive as a mass circulation daily and the official voice of the labour movement. From 1930 Odhams Press published the paper in commercial partnership with the TUC but, after the Second World War, in a competitive newspaper world the left-of-centre daily suffered inexorable decline and eventually closed.[3]

From 1912 to 1925 George Lansbury was closely identified with the famous pioneering phase in the *Daily Herald*'s history, first as the proprietor, then as editor from 1913, and subsequently as the paper's general manager. In these years the newspaper gained its fearsome reputation as a fiery and independent daily with clear-cut political objectives to champion working-class interests. George Lansbury made its columns available to a host of radical and dissenting voices that challenged the establishment in Edwardian politics. Press baron and proprietor of the *Daily Mail*, Lord Northcliffe, labelled Lansbury's paper 'The Miracle of Fleet Street', when

---

[1] *Daily Herald*, 16 Apr. 1912.   [2] Ibid. 26 Apr. 1912.   [3] See Richards, *The Bloody Circus*.

the *Daily Herald,* restored to daily publication after the Great War, survived a price increase to 2*d.* while its main competitors sold at 1*d.* During the First World War, as a pacifist weekly, the *Daily Herald* had scared the authorities by attacking profiteering, championing conscientious objectors, and celebrating the Bolshevik Revolution. After 1919 the paper boldly supported direct action by the labour movement in Britain, including the Poplar Rates Rebellion that resulted in the imprisonment of its editor, members of his family, and other Poplar councillors in 1921.

Raymond Postgate worked closely with George Lansbury on the *Daily Herald* and afterwards on *Lansbury's Labour Weekly* during 1925–7. He considered his father-in-law one of the three great editors of the early twentieth century—alongside C. P. Scott of the Liberal *Manchester Guardian* and J. L. Garvin of the Conservative *Observer.* All three men possessed the essential expertise of journalism: practical knowledge, news sense, team skills, accompanied by charisma and a deep conviction about everything that they did.[4] A future Labour party leader and celebrated journalist, who worked with George Lansbury on the *Tribune* in the late 1930s, endorsed this view of the *Daily Herald's* editor-proprietor. According to Michael Foot, during these years his predecessor played a vital role in the Labour movement that has seldom been fully recognized:

Considering George Lansbury wasn't trained as a journalist, his was a remarkable achievement. He was one of the great editors of the twentieth century and under his control the *Daily Herald* . . . just before the First World War and after had its greatest time. The people he assembled to write for it were really extraordinary—a wonderful paper . . . the *Daily Herald* made a magnificent contribution to journalism, socialism and the building of the Labour Party and that period owes more to George Lansbury than anyone else.[5]

Lansbury had no intention of managing or editing a newspaper in 1912. In the end, the persuasive Ben Tillett, hero of the London Dock Strike of 1889 and secretary of the Dockers' Union, was responsible for securing the services of the popular Member for Bow and Bromley.[6] Over a memorable cup of tea in the House of Commons, Lansbury agreed to join a committee of mainly London trade unionists. Chaired by David Walls of the Association of Correctors of the Press, they were reviving the *Daily Herald* as a successor to the temporary news-sheet published by the compositors in Fleet Street during the London printers' strike of 1911.

The London Society of Compositors, enthusiastic advocates of a new daily paper, had created the original *Daily Herald* as an independent voice against a hostile capitalist press during their dispute over the forty-eight hour week.[7] The strike organ— a four-sheet newspaper priced at $\frac{1}{2}d.$—started life on 25 January 1911 and featured one of William Morris's socialist poems. It was not strictly a daily and appeared only on 'Tuesday, Wednesday, Thursday and Friday at 12 noon'.[8] With an initial print

[4] Postgate, *Lansbury*, pp. 134–5.
[5] Interview with Michael Foot at Westminster, 7 Aug. 1991.
[6] For Tillett, see Schneer, *Ben Tillett.*
[7] T. E. Naylor, 'Life-Story of the *"Daily Herald"*: A Drama of Newspaper Production', *Daily Herald*, 15 Apr. 1913.
[8] Kenney, *Westering* (1939), p. 172.

run of 13,000, the paper eventually achieved sales of 27,000 and broadened into a labour daily that also added football, cycling, and gardening to its political coverage. After the industrial dispute ended, the newspaper survived until 28 April 1911. However, appeals during the remainder of the year to start it again as a permanent Labour daily eventually proved successful.[9]

On 15 April 1912 Lansbury took some of the younger members of his family on a long tram ride around East London to see the posters advertising the start of Labour's new daily paper.[10] Ben Tillett and his associates planned to run 'a Labour organ . . . conducted on the broadest and most democratic lines'. They envisaged an 80,000 daily sale with £7,500 advertising income per annum and accordingly appealed for £10,000 in start-up capital, later adjusted to £5,000 in 5 shilling shares.[11] In this new venture for organized Labour and ordinary people, George Lansbury was their valued asset—a socialist politician with a natural flair for publicity and important political connections, as well as valuable business experience running one of the largest sawmills and timber yards in the country. During the precarious early existence of the paper, Lansbury raised the funds that meant the difference between survival and closing. His inspiration at the helm of the paper kept the *Daily Herald* alive and laid the foundations for its remarkable success in the first half of the twentieth century.

At first, however, George Lansbury was a somewhat hesitant recruit. Although he saw the advantages of a daily newspaper that represented the labour movement in Britain, even he doubted the wisdom of a project plainly lacking adequate start-up capital. He later confessed: 'My faith is said to be great; often I have been told my optimism is marvellous. This may or may not be so; but this proposal to start a national Labour daily with a capital of £300 knocked all optimism and faith out of me, and left me speechless.'[12] In 1913 the *New Statesman* started as a weekly publication with £5,000 and that figure was considered totally inadequate.

During these years important changes occurred in the British national press. Between 1890 and 1914 thirteen new dailies were launched in London, including three papers that achieved mass sales circulation: *Daily Express* (1900), *Daily Mail* (1900), and *Daily Mirror* (1906). In London alone there were six evening newspapers. On the political left there were around 150 titles at this time—mostly local and short-lived ventures, though Robert Blatchford's *Clarion* and Keir Hardie's *Labour Leader*—both weekly productions—were among the exceptions.

To start a new daily paper in competition with the mighty organs of the capitalist press, and one that would give the Labour movement an independent voice, was a risky and uncertain commercial venture. Earlier signs were not promising in an age littered with short-lived initiatives and outright publishing failures. Keir Hardie and others regularly aired the subject at Independent Labour party and TUC conferences. By 1907 the TUC had agreed to start a labour newspaper and held a special

[9] Richards, *The Bloody Circus*, p. 13.
[10] G. Lansbury, *The Miracle of Fleet Street: The Story of the Daily Herald* (n.d. [1925]), pp. 9–11.
[11] Ibid. p. 13.   [12] Ibid. p. 10.

conference during the following year. In fact, in 1912 there were *two* national daily labour papers. The first was the *Daily Herald*, published as an independent venture; six months later, the rival *Daily Citizen* appeared.

In 1912 with the formation of a new company, Labour Newspapers Limited, preparations went ahead to bring out the projected *Daily Citizen* as the official newspaper of the Labour party. A young Cambridge history graduate and already a member of the Fabian Society Executive Committee, Clifford Allen (later Lord Allen of Hurtwood), became secretary and eventually general manager of the newspaper. From the autumn of 1911, he had played a central role in arranging publicity and attracting the necessary trade union backing to start the paper. However, according to Allen's biographer, who in 1963 attributed the longevity of George Lansbury's newspaper to his 'journalistic flair', the *Daily Herald* was perceived as a threat to the *Daily Citizen*, rather than the reverse. The socialist and pacifist Allen even told Ramsay MacDonald to advertise the prospectus of the *Daily Citizen* in the London press on its rival's launch day. Once the *Daily Herald* appeared, plans to produce the *Daily Citizen* gained momentum. In the summer of 1912 offices were established in Fleet Street and in Manchester. Six thousand circulation committees were formed throughout the Labour and trade union movement. Publicity for the launch on 8 October 1912 included the floating of a hot-air balloon above St Paul's.[13]

The publication of the *Daily Citizen* as a progressive labour daily, rather than a specific socialist paper, reflected the influence of Ramsay MacDonald. He became chairman of the first board of directors which included prominent ILP figures, such as J. Bruce Glasier and, among the trade union leaders, Arthur Henderson, Secretary of the Labour party. As Bob Holton has pointed out, the *Daily Citizen* sought respectability and opened with testimonials from several non-Labour figures, including the editor of the Liberal *Daily Chronicle*, the Lord Provost of Glasgow, and Lord Northcliffe:

In practice the presentation of representative 'voices' in the paper was severely restricted to orthodox opinion centred on Labour Party pragmatism . . . Editorial initiative was narrowly based and came from above. It was geared to the incorporation of Labour unrest into conciliatory forms of protest and pressure, harmonising relations between labour and capital, and redirecting energies towards the Parliamentary area.[14]

The *Daily Citizen*, with all the resources of the Labour party behind it, had a more promising start than the *Daily Herald* and was launched with £85,000 of its projected £150,000 start-up capital. However, it lacked the fire and vitality of its rival, as can be seen in the comments made by one of the first *Daily Herald* editors on the mediocre prototype he had been sent: 'It simply could not be true. This attempt was too poor to be believed . . .'[15]

---

[13] A. Marwick, *Clifford Allen: The Open Conspirator* (1964), pp. 15–16. See also M. Gilbert, *Plough My Own Furrow: The Story of Lord Allen of Hurtwood as Told through His Writings and Correspondence* (1965), p. 4.

[14] R. J. Holton, 'Daily Herald v. Daily Citizen, 1912–1915', *International Review of Social History*, 19 (1974), pp. 360–1.

[15] Kenney, *Westering*, p. 190.

Surprisingly, MacDonald's official biographer, David Marquand, said nothing about his subject's involvement with the new Labour paper, though the rivalry of the two dailies between 1912 and 1915 paralleled the two irreconcilable strands within the pre-war labour movement. The *Daily Citizen* advocated parliamentarianism and was the official creation and creature of the Labour party in alliance with the trade union movement. But it was staffed by Fleet Street journalists, mainly non-Labour activists, excluded racing news and betting tips until 1913 and lasted only three years.

As an independent venture by individual socialists and trade unionists the *Daily Herald* lacked its rival's planning and money, but it became the pivotal point and inspiration of a rebel milieu that promoted and supported extra-parliamentary activity. In Edwardian Britain the *Daily Citizen* and the *Daily Herald*, with their fundamental ideological differences and perspectives, provided an important reflection of the differing political philosophies of MacDonald and Lansbury within the socialist and labour movement.

George Lansbury drew upon a limited background in journalism in running the *Daily Herald*. Thirty years before, he had helped publish the radical *Coming Times*, that circulated in the Bow district and to which he contributed under the *nom de plume* of 'John Blunt'. Before this venture, he was involved only in a news-sheet in connection with the Whitechapel Church Young Men's Society, and in helping to sell the *Link*, the paper established by Annie Besant and W. T. Stead during the Match Girls' Strike in 1888. Later, he was associated with the *Bow and Bromley Worker*, produced locally by Social Democrats.

Lansbury had, however, undertaken some writing in connection with his socialist politics. Before the introduction of parliamentary salaries many Labour and Irish Nationalist MPs supplemented their income through journalism and authorship.[16] Lansbury wrote articles for the *Clarion* and the *Labour Leader*, as well as occasionally for other weekly journals. On entering Parliament he contributed regularly to the Glasgow left-wing *Forward* and to the feminist *Link*.

In 1925 George Lansbury published a short history of the *Daily Herald*, which is a main source for the early years, including stories about the loyal readers and staff whose heroic efforts kept the newspaper from insolvency. In fact, the paper soon produced its own historians, as well as other writers who recorded their memories of George Lansbury in his *Daily Herald* days in their autobiographies.[17] Exactly one year to the day that it was first sold on the streets of Britain, T. E. Naylor compiled a two-page chronicle of its hectic and dramatic early days. He recalled vividly one crisis meeting, held ironically in Parliament by *Daily Herald* staff, to save their irreverent newspaper:

More than one memorable meeting took place in the House of Commons . . . [I]t was a grim struggle with death. Sitting there were Lansbury, Tillett, Newland, Evans, Gordon, Bexley

---

[16] Ibid. pp. 9–11.
[17] For examples, see Kenney, *Westering*; F. Meynell, *My Lives* (1971); G. Slocombe, *The Tumult and the Shouting* (1935).

and myself. Haywood, our business manager, had exhausted all possibilities: there would be no *Herald* that night until so much was forthcoming . . . [M]ust we die? Even were enough money scraped together . . . what of the next day and the day after that? . . . The proceedings were somewhat prolonged . . . to enable first one then the other to seek an interview with or ring up some friend . . . [B]ut all to no purpose . . . During one of the intervals . . . Tillett could not be restrained. House of Commons be damned. Up went the window, and across the water [the River Thames] went a full throated shout from Ben [to a crew of jolly watermen], answered with equal warmth . . . It might be our death cry—no matter: 'Three cheers for the *Daily Herald*'.

Late that night I made my way from St Bride Street to the *Herald* offices—to meet, as I thought, the disappointment and resentment of the staff. But no—marvel of marvels—they were all busy as bees . . . at the twelfth hour the Goddess of Fortune had again turned her smiling face towards us, and saved us—for our sins.[18]

Naylor's early account can be supplemented by some unpublished notes, based on a detailed analysis of the editions of the newspaper up to 1923. These were assembled by Raymond Postgate, foreign sub-editor, probably to write a history of the paper that he never completed.[19]

The business history of the *Daily Herald* is a remarkable tale of a hand-to-mouth existence, as all concerned coped with difficulties over paper supplies, massive bank overdrafts, and a lack of commercial advertising. Postgate identified three major financial crises in the first year alone that threatened to end production in June, August, and October 1912.

In these circumstances, the *Daily Herald* needed individuals and organizations to provide the necessary funding to maintain it in existence. Some of the associated stories also merit a brief retelling to illustrate the pioneering and missionary spirit that stamped the paper's early history. On 26 October 1912 Lansbury paid tribute in an editorial to the army of unknown readers who gave their savings—in some cases pawned their jewels—to keep the paper alive. A socialist parson and his wife brought in £150 at one critical moment. On another occasion, after it was decided to cease production, Lansbury left Fleet Street to address political meetings in the North. The next morning he discovered that the paper was still alive and on sale in Hanley and Crewe. On another occasion when the bailiffs entered the premises at St Bride Street, George Lansbury, Ben Tillett, and Robert Williams, Secretary of the Transport Workers' Federation blocked the doorway until help arrived. Lansbury also acknowledged the goodwill and munificent cash credit given by Mr Drew, Manager of Victoria House, the paper's publishing house, and his principal, Sir F. Newnes, as well as the paper merchants, Bowater and Co.

Besides the financial lifeline thrown by its rank-and-file readers on numerous occasions, major sums of finance for the newspaper came from a group of wealthy political sympathizers attracted by the passionate and sincere commitment to

---

[18] *Daily Herald*, 15 Apr. 1913.
[19] R[aymond] P[ostgate], '*Daily Herald*: Analysis', G. D. H. Cole Papers, GDHC/G5/9/1/1–2; G5/2/1–3; G5/9/3/1–33; G5/4/1–52. I am grateful to Dr Huw Richards for bringing this material to my attention.

radical and feminist causes of its most famous figure. It was characteristic of George Lansbury's remarkable natural talent both to inspire people and to be held in genuine affection and reverence by so many. Remarkably in political life, Lansbury was a public figure totally free from any hint of personal corruption, scandal, or impropriety. Nor did he accumulate personal wealth or conspicuous possessions. Probably during his lifetime some £300,000—around £3 million or more in modern values—passed through his hands to various worthy causes, and nothing was trousered by him. However, as we shall see, the *Daily Herald* was not free from political scandal immediately after the First World War when, as editor, Lansbury was accused of receiving first 'Chinese bonds' and then Bolshevik funds—concealed in a box of chocolates—to bolster his ailing paper.

In the pre-war period those bankrolling the *Daily Herald* included George Lansbury's American philanthropist friend, Joseph Fels, who had sponsored his parliamentary election campaigns, and a number of wealthy feminists who appreciated the courageous support and sacrifices made by the Lansbury family on behalf of the suffragette movement. One such monied ally of the newspaper was a suffragist, theosophist, and friend of Annie Besant with socialist sympathies, Muriel Countess De La Warr. In turn, she acted as the go-between for an American millionairess, Mary Dodge, who remained a secret backer of the newspaper.[20]

Others included the Revd Harold Jocelyn Buxton of Thaxted, where Lansbury had Christian socialist connections, who wrote to him: 'I am determined to do my utmost to keep the *Herald* going and to back your splendid efforts.' He matched this sentiment with £600 as part of a pledge of £1,000.[21] During this time of financial plight and organizational difficulties, a crucial part was also played by the Fabian, H. D. Harben, heir to the Prudential Insurance Company empire, who Lady De La Warr introduced to Lansbury.

Henry Harben was an Old Etonian, Oxford graduate, and Fabian Society barrister. His wealth made him an important and active intermediary in the different currents of pre-war radical and women's politics. As the Fabian liaison officer with the Inter-University Socialist Federation, founded by Clifford Allen in 1912, he endeavoured to halt the wrangling over the admission of Liberals that bedevilled its beginning. He was Chairman of the 1912 Fabian Committee of Enquiry—its findings were published as a book, *The Rural Problem* (1913). A director and shareholder on the *Daily Citizen*, Harben endeavoured to influence Ramsay MacDonald after concerned Fabian women lobbied him about editorial policy on suffrage issues.[22] As a matter of principle, Harben made a personal protest over the Liberals' refusal to enfranchise women by deliberately abandoning an opportunity to become a Liberal MP.[23]

In 1913 Harben joined the Board of the *Daily Herald* and became Lansbury's main assistant in reorganizing the paper's finances. Lansbury recalled that at one meeting

[20] Meynell, *My Lives*, pp. 72–4; 78–9; Lansbury, *The Miracle of Fleet Street*, p. 13.
[21] Rt. Revd Harold Jocelyn Buxton to George Lansbury, 27 May 1913, LP, vol. 7, fos. 50–1.
[22] P. Pugh, *Educate, Agitate, Organize: 100 years of Fabian Socialism* (1984), pp. 104, 113.
[23] Mitchell, *Queen Christabel*, p. 231; M. Cole, *The Story of Fabian Socialism* (1961), p. 150.

on 13 February 1913 at the Memorial Hall, Farringdon Street, nearly £12,000 was raised as a result of Harben's singular efforts. To quell press speculation rife after the First World War that there was some sinister influence and control exerted over the newspaper's policy by foreign money, Lansbury reprinted Harben's letter to *John Bull* stating bluntly that 'from December, 1912, till September, 1914, the whole of the money which was required, week by week, for the financing of the *Daily Herald* was furnished by myself from money subscribed, either by me or through me by my personal friends'.[24]

Harben personally underwrote the newspaper for six months to provide financial stability and staff contracts. He successfully defused two dangerous libel cases that threatened the *Daily Herald* and those associated with it. J. H. Thomas's lawsuit was deftly settled out of court with an apology and the sum of £800. In July 1914 the biscuit and cake manufacturers, W. and R. Jacobs, whose factory had been involved in the Dublin Lock-Out of 1913, brought a libel action in the King's Bench of High Court against George Lansbury, Will Dyson, and the printers and proprietors of the newspaper. On 9 February the *Daily Herald* had published one of Dyson's acerbic and wounding cartoons, accompanied by twelve verses, depicting a starving and abused girl which impugned the humanity of Messrs Jacobs. Harben resolved the matter by a full and frank apology, publication of the court proceedings in the paper, and only £250 costs, thereby avoiding punitive damages against the defendants.[25] Harben, who was also a director of the *New Statesman*, played a key role in the decision not to amalgamate the *Daily Herald* with the rival *Daily Citizen*, and thereby subject it to direct trade union control. He remained most active in the *Daily Herald* League movement, established in 1912, and was an important figure in the abortive negotiations with Christabel Pankhurst over the possibility of a suffrage–*Herald* League alliance.[26]

In addition to parlous finances and a lack of commercial advertising, the *Daily Herald* also suffered from a succession of editors and proprietors at first. The paper initially lacked an overall editor and was produced by a committee. At one point Ben Tillett even considered the appointment of the bizarre Frank Harris, described as 'a gallant if indiscreet adventurer always with his great bristling black moustachios', who earned a reputation for his 'shoulder-rubbing acquaintance with earls and millionaires, artists and stockbrokers, chorus girls and blackmailers'.[27]

However, in early June 1912, George Lansbury intervened to appoint the labour editor, Rowland Kenney, as the *Daily Herald*'s editor. Kenney was the brother of the well-known suffragette, Annie Kenney, had experienced life as a tramp, navvy, and sailor. He was preferred to the Irish journalist and *Daily Herald* stalwart, W. P. Ryan, described as one 'whose body was nourished on Fleet Street printers ink',

---

[24] Lansbury, *Miracle of Fleet Street*, pp. 15–16. Harben also funded Sylvia Pankhurst's suffrage activities. See Sylvia Pankhurst to H. D. Harben, 20 Mar., n.d. [probably Aug.] 1913, Harben Papers, BL, Add. MS 58,226, fos. 18, 21.

[25] *East End News and Shipping Chronicle*, 31 July 1914.

[26] For the *Daily Herald* League Movement, see below pp. 148–9.

[27] Slocombe, *The Tumult and the Shouting*, p. 30.

who played an important part in the links between the newspaper and the Irish Labour movement.

At the time, Kenney, a freelance who had written for the *Labour Leader*, *New Age*, and *English Review* wrote virtually all the editorials that, in effect, decided the policy of the *Daily Herald*. He recalled that his policy 'was one of no compromise with the enemy—the "capitalist" '.[28]

At this time the *Daily Herald* was in one of its recurrent crises with daily sales ranging from 60,000 to 140,000. George Lansbury was chairman of the board of directors that converted the Daily Herald Printing and Publishing Society, Limited, which had been formed in April 1912, into a limited company and appealed for a capital sum of £50,000 by offering 800,000 preference shares and 200,000 ordinary shares for sale. At the same time the wealthy and resourceful proprietor of the *New Eye*, Charles Granville, joined the paper as Managing Director to inject new money.[29] Granville's tenure was very brief, but he left behind two important legacies. He appointed Charles Lapworth—an advocate of syndicalism and industrial unionism—to replace Kenney as editor-in-chief and then secured the services of the brilliant Australian cartoonist, Will Dyson. However, Granville's company soon collapsed. He left the paper and was later convicted of fraudulent conversion and bigamy.

From this point George Lansbury took over the direction of the *Daily Herald* with a new group of directors and called the company 'The Limit', a parody of Lloyd George's parliamentary comments about the newspaper. He appointed Francis Meynell—only twenty-two—as the paper's business manager, though Meynell later claimed he largely followed Lansbury's directions. In 1913 Lansbury had bought the title and copyright of the paper from the Official Receiver for £100 and most of the shares were in his name.[30] After the First World War a secret Metropolitan Police investigation into the finances of the *Daily Herald* revealed the names of fifteen shareholders. George Lansbury still had a substantial holding of 6,248 shares—the same number as five others. There had also been a considerable infusion of capital as a result of Lansbury's association with the India Home Rule Movement. This link was represented in the shareholding of Annie Besant, George Arundale, C. Jinarajodasa, and Annie Besant's solicitor, the future Labour MP and close friend of Lansbury, David Graham Pole.[31]

The *Daily Herald* owed a great deal of its reputation in the period 1912–25 to a galaxy of talented journalists and writers—not all of them socialists—brought to the paper as regular staffers or occasional contributors by Charles Lapworth and George Lansbury. A number of these mainly middle-class intellectuals later became known as 'Lansbury's Lambs', their journalism famed for its sparkling literary discourse and political debate. In the pre-war years the economist and historian, G. D. H. Cole, later Chichele professor of social and political theory at Oxford, and

[28] Kenney, *Westering*, pp. 172–86.   [29] *Daily Herald*, 13 Sept. 1912.
[30] Meynell, *My Lives*, p. 79.
[31] Metropolitan Police CID Report: Subject: Mrs Besant and G. S. Arundale, 2 Feb. 1918; Basil Thompson to [Edwin] Montague, 25 May 1918, PRO, FO 395/245/41703.

William Mellor, a founding member of the Communist Party of Great Britain and the newspaper's future deputy editor and editor, wrote regularly on industrial matters. Both were products of Oxford University and fervent advocates of the theory of guild socialism.[32]

Others included the long-serving Norman Ewer, who arranged subsidies from the Liberal MP, Baron de Forest, and two fearless critics of the bureaucratic state and proponents of an alternative distributivism: the Catholic apologist, children's writer, and former Liberal MP, Hilaire Belloc, and the provocative journalist and poet, G. K. Chesterton. Rebecca West joined the paper for two weeks as its women's editor. Contributions also appeared by the humourist, Langdon Everard, and from three celebrated *literati*, H. G. Wells, George Bernard Shaw, and the young Osbert Sitwell. Barbara and Gerald Gould formed a husband-and-wife team working on the newspaper before and after the First World War. They started by sacrificing their holiday money of £50 as a contribution towards the paper's parlous finances. The poet and former academic, Gerald Gould, joined the *Daily Herald* editorial staff in 1913 and later journeyed with Lansbury to the Western Front and the French hospitals. Barbara Gould, a future publicity manager on the *Daily Herald* and Labour MP, had been imprisoned as a suffragette in 1912 and spent time in exile abroad. She was another contact through Lansbury's association with the WSPU and later became the first secretary of the United Suffragists, which Lansbury also joined.[33]

In particular, the rebel paper is remembered for the awesome work of the Australian cartoonist Will Dyson. A world-wide reputation, gained primarily on the *Daily Herald*, undoubtedly placed Dyson in a pantheon of outstanding cartoonists and caricaturists, alongside eminent predecessors of the eighteenth and nineteenth centuries, James Gillray and Honoré Daumier. His cartoons achieved such immediate and stunning success that they were subsequently published separately in book form by the newspaper. Dyson was also politically active in speaking at *Daily Herald* rallies and mass meetings.

Of all the paper's contributors, Will Dyson was the highest paid, at £5 per week, and soon earned a princely contract of £1,000 or more per annum after other newspaper proprietors, including the American tycoon William Hearst, eagerly sought his services. On the *Daily Herald*, Will Dyson enjoyed unrestricted freedom to produce full-page cartoons—featuring, for the first time in Britain, workers as young and victorious, pitted against 'Fat', an obese cigar-smoking businessman—a trenchant symbol of evil and rapacious capitalism. Dyson's sensational cartooning

---

[32] Guild Socialism was a left-wing philosophy of industrial democracy—to be achieved through workers' control rather than parliamentary means. These ideas were put forward in A. R. Orage's *New Age* and taken up by G. D. H. Cole. Like syndicalism, guild socialism offered an alternative vision of society to the state socialism roundly criticized by Hilaire Belloc in *The Servile State*. In *Your Part in Poverty* (1917), Lansbury gave his support to the National Guilds League, formed two years before. However, League membership never exceeded 1,000 members and guild socialism faded after the First World War. Lansbury, *Your Part in Poverty*, pp. 113–15. See also M. Cole, *The Life of G. D. H. Cole* (1971).

[33] For the Goulds, see J. M. Bellamy and J. Saville (eds.), *Dictionary of Labour Biography*, vii (1984), pp. 91–6, 96–8.

challenged and mocked the old guard in contemporary politics. He exposed the inequality and injustice in Edwardian Britain that Lansbury battled against in Parliament and on public platforms. Even so, the Christian socialist Lansbury was unhappy that the *Daily Herald* under Charles Lapworth's editorship often went too far in personally denigrating political opponents and depicting them as evil and devilish. As a result, Will Dyson did not always see eye to eye with George Lansbury, especially after a casting vote from Lansbury ousted his mentor, Lapworth, from the editor's chair towards the end of 1913.[34]

Henry D. Harben is the source for another interesting revelation about the important change of editorship from Charles Lapworth to George Lansbury at the end of 1913. Lapworth's improvements to the paper had been achieved at some cost. Difficulties between the editor and his chairman came to a head on 28 September 1912. Lapworth devoted part of the paper's editorial to a venomous attack on the Labour MP, Philip Snowden, who had denounced strikes as inconsistent with the principles of socialism in a recently published book, *The Living Wage*. George Lansbury penned an immediate protest to his own newspaper: 'I wish to enter my strongest protest against your attack on Philip Snowden. It was unworthy any journal devoted to Labour [*sic*]. If we cannot disagree without charging each other with all manner of sordid meanness, then there is no hope for the Labour movement.'[35]

Lapworth's public response—to defend the fundamental right to withdraw labour by citing the failure of Labour MPs to assist the striking navvies at the Rosyth naval base—did little to repair damaged relations on the *Daily Herald*.[36] In the circumstances, Henry Harben's choice as Charles Lapworth's successor was Rebecca West, a nineteen-year-old suffragette whose experience included promising stints on the *Freewoman* and the *Clarion*. Adding that his proposal was warmly received at the time, Harben later explained his views on this change of editorship: 'the Editorship is a special job, needing special qualifications; that we should have someone young and with a racy and pungent pen. So I suggested Rebecca West as a revolutionary idea . . . there had never been a lady Editor of a Daily Paper before.'

However, the gifted Rebecca West was involved in a secret relationship with the Fabian novelist, H. G. Wells. She confided that she was expecting a baby in six months' time and declined the offer.[37] George Lansbury himself therefore took over the editorship, though he did not exercise day-to-day control until early 1914 after his return from his visit to the USA.

One extraordinary innovation associated with the pioneering years of the newspaper was the creation of a network of *Daily Herald* Leagues throughout the country that became the focus for the paper's various political crusades. On

---

[34] For Will Dyson, see R. McMullin, *Will Dyson: Cartoonist, Etcher and Australia's Finest War Artist* (1984).

[35] *Daily Herald*, 28 Sept., 2 Oct. 1912.   [36] Ibid. 4 Oct. 1912.

[37] In 1948 Henry Harben wrote a confidential memorandum on his involvement with the *Daily Herald*, which Raymond Postgate probably did not use in his biography. See LP, vol. 28, b, ii, fos. 2–4. For the relationship between Rebecca West and H. G. Wells, see G. N. Ray, *H. G. Wells and Rebecca West* (London, 1975).

14 November 1912 the *Daily Herald* League was established in London with the objective of building a complex of four to five hundred centres throughout the country each with 150 members. The scheme was designed to raise £50,000 to support the newspaper by each League supporter contributing 3*d.* per week for a year. At the Hall of the London Society of Compositors in St Bride Street in London, George Lansbury—supported by Ben Tillett, Victor Grayson, Dora Montefiore, Charles Lapworth, the editor, and other *Daily Herald* staff—outlined to a gathering of several hundred *Daily Herald* supporters plans for the formation of a *Herald* League.[38]

However, the League's role also developed beyond important fundraising and publicity for the newspaper. Social and recreational activities in towns and cities provided fellowship and a sense of a co-operative community for *Daily Herald* readers and mobilized them in crucial political activity. The role of the *Herald* Leagues can be clearly observed in the great rallies at the Albert Hall to support Jim Larkin and his Dublin workers and in the *Daily Herald*'s campaigns for independent socialist candidates at by-elections. A spectacular success was achieved when Heraldites turned out *en masse* on the East London streets to help Sylvia Pankhurst evade the police. One of the most active and independent branches was the North London *Herald* League, founded in 1913, which later played an important part in the anti-war agitation and the 'Hands off Russia' campaign in 1920.[39]

In the second issue of the *Daily Herald* George Lansbury had explained the policy of 'scope for all': a non-aligned and independent stance, with editorial policy free from trade union and Labour party control: 'In the *Daily Herald*, Trade Unionists, Socialists of every creed and kin, Parliamentary and anti-Parliamentary, Syndicalist and non-Syndicalist, will have room and scope to state their ideas in their own way. No committee and no editor will edit the people's opinions . . .'[40]

As we have seen, this unambiguous policy of political independence made the *Daily Herald* a prominent forum for radical dissent in Edwardian Britain. From the outset the paper's columns were open to a wide range of dissident opinions. Syndicalism, Christian socialism, feminism, guild socialism, and distributivism were all represented and supported by the paper. Moreover, there was considerable cross-fertilization among these different groupings in the creation of a rebel atmosphere surrounding the *Daily Herald*. The presence of two TUC representatives, C. W. Bowerman MP, Secretary of the Parliamentary Committee, and William Matkin, General Secretary of the Carpenters and Joiners, on the management committee did not alter the anti-establishment and often anti-Labour party stance of the *Daily Herald*.

The *Daily Herald* was established during the turbulent period of labour unrest in the years immediately before the First World War. As Raymond Postgate pointed out, the history of the paper at this time is very much the industrial history of Britain. The *Daily Herald* was not only constantly full of reports and accounts of

---

[38] *Daily Herald*, 15 Nov. 1912.
[39] For an account of the North London *Herald* League, see K. Weller, *Don't Be a Soldier! The Radical Anti-War Movement in North London, 1914–1918* (1985), esp. chs. 6–10.
[40] *Daily Herald*, 16 Apr. 1912.

strikes and lock-outs, but provided active leadership for the organized trade union and labour movement at a time of growing disillusion among the rank and file. As George Lansbury observed, his newspaper was the successor of a strike-sheet—to which Ben Tillett added that 'The *Daily Herald* is the expression of an entirely revolutionary phase of British Labour'. In the second issue of the newspaper, an electrician's strike at the Earl's Court Exhibition—addressed by Tom Mann—became the first of the many industrial disputes both small- and large-scale that the newspaper solidly supported, often in the face of trade union leaders' official directives.[41] In 1912 typical headlines carried by the Labour daily newspaper on its front page included: 'TRANSPORT WORKERS' TREMENDOUS FIGHT' (with photographs of 'LEADERS OF THE MEN', Harry Gosling and Ben Tillett); 'A HUNDRED THOUSAND. Huge Demonstration of Strikers in Hyde Park. EIGHT MILES ROUTE'; and 'ON THE BRINK. Another National Railway Strike Imminent'.[42]

The ambience of Edwardian labour politics that the *Daily Herald* reported, and helped to create, was captured admirably sixty years later by the Fabian socialist and Labour historian, Dame Margaret Cole:

One has to think oneself back into the social conditions of that time—the disappointments of liberal politics, the slowly rising and little-understood cost of living pressing so heavily upon low wages and provoking the great strikes in the mines and the docks, in shipping and on the railways—above all in the Dublin Lock-Out of 1913, when Jim Larkin deployed the battalions of his Irish Transport Workers in and out of the factories like a general fighting a guerrilla battle. One has to see again the American tourists sitting sadly on their Saratoga trunks on the quayside when all the Liverpool transport had stopped, the grey cruiser *Antrim* lying in the Mersey keeping watch on the strike-bound city, and Ben Tillett on Tower Hill crying to heaven to 'strike Lord Devonport dead!'; the railway workers, after partial victory in their national strike, reorganising themselves in the 'new model' National Union of Railwaymen and joining with the miners and the transport workers in a magnificent-looking Triple Alliance whose purpose was so to organise the industrial policy of the three great groups as to make concerted action against the employers a real possibility.[43]

The extensive strike wave—particularly among miners, dockers, and transport workers in 1910–13—that characterized the period of labour unrest was the subject of considerable attention and enquiry by government, Parliament, and the press. In an early issue of the *Daily Herald*, George Lansbury added his voice to identify incessant mass poverty and an inequitable distribution of wealth as the root causes of the widespread agitation:

For, after all, what are the facts of the case? In the *Fabian Essays*, twenty years ago, and later on, in Chiozza Money's book on 'Riches and Poverty', it has quite clearly been demonstrated that at least two-thirds of all the workers' produce is robbed from them in the shape of rent, profit, and interest. This is the cause of their poverty—not bad trade—not the laziness of the working classes; but they are in their present plight solely because those things which they produce are taken from them by a system of legalised robbery.[44]

[41] Lansbury, *Miracle of Fleet Street*, p. 4; *Daily Herald*, 16 Apr. 1912.
[42] *Daily Herald*, 24 May, 24 and 26 June 1912.   [43] Cole, *The Life of G. D. H. Cole*, pp. 57–8.
[44] *Daily Herald*, 20 May 1912.

George Lansbury's writings in the *Daily Herald* provide an insight into the important development of his political thinking at this time. He argued that only 'an entire change in the industrial system' would remedy inequality in class and gender, between rich and poor, men and women. George Lansbury was adamant that workers must be their own saviours. He rejected Fabian bureaucratic schemes of socialist education and social reform: 'We of the *Daily Herald* . . . must point out that reform or revolution, imposed or bestowed from above, is of little use in the true development of democracy.'[45] As he revealed elsewhere, his socialist message no longer had any truck with statism.[46]

Two disputes stand out in the history of the *Daily Herald*: the legendary Dublin Strike of 1913 and London Builders Lock-Out of 1914. From late 1913 to mid-1914 the industrial struggles of James Larkin and the Irish Labour movement became a major issue for the *Daily Herald* as the newspaper became deeply involved with the plight of the locked-out Dublin workers and their families. As the *Daily Herald* campaigned tirelessly, the network of *Herald* Leagues in Britain arranged fund-raising meetings and shipped food and clothing to Dublin.

By 1913 the charismatic Jim Larkin, founder of the Irish Transport and General Workers' Union (ITGWU), had organized most of the Dublin workers within his organization and was locked in a deadly struggle with the autocratic William Murphy, leader of the Dublin employers determined to crush unionism in the city. The Dublin Lock-Out of 1913 began on 29 August when 400 Dublin employers locked out all employees, who were members of the Transport Workers' Union, with the demand that every labourer should sign an agreement either to resign union membership or never to join one. The result was one of the most bitter and violent industrial disputes in pre-First World War Britain. With employers in other trades taking similar action, by 22 September about 25,000 men were affected and even larger numbers thereafter.

By any social calculations, Dublin had the worst employment, housing, and living conditions in Edwardian Britain. To goad the British trade union movement into action, the *Daily Herald* publicized the endemic poverty, ill-health, and destitution in Dublin. The newspaper cited wage rates of only 12–17 shillings per week; 21,000 crowded one-room tenements, and the highest death-rate among families in any European city.

George Lansbury had a long-standing sympathy for Irish nationalism and the political struggles of the Irish labour movement stretching back to his schooldays, when he first heard of the Fenians and wrote an erudite essay, full of empathy and compassion, on Irish Home Rule.[47] What the *Daily Herald*'s campaign for the Dublin workers reveals are the links between industrialism and suffragism that characterized the lock-out. Women in Ireland and in Britain, such as Delia Larkin, Dora Montefiore, and Hannah Sheehy Skeffington played a key role in the struggle. The *Daily Herald* publicized their work, particularly at Liberty Hall, the former

---

[45] Ibid. 15 Apr. 1913.   [46] *Labour Leader*, 17 May 1912.
[47] This early and remarkable scholastic effort—in the hand of Bessie Brine (Lansbury)—has survived, with his teachers' comments: see G. Lansbury, 'Home Rule for Ireland' (n.d.), LP, vol. 28, fos. 1–8.

Northumberland Hotel converted as a strike headquarters, as well as carrying Jim Larkin's direct appeal to the British trade union movement.[48]

George Lansbury crossed the Irish Sea on more than one occasion to address the Dublin workers, who had organized a *Herald* League in the city, and the Irish Women's Franchise League.[49] The pacifists and feminists, Hannah and Francis Sheehy Skeffington—the latter an original *Daily Herald* shareholder and its Irish correspondent, who was murdered in the 1916 Easter Rising—were close associates of Lansbury as he endeavoured to raise awareness of conditions in Ireland. What united those involved in the Irish struggle and the *Herald* League movement was a common belief expressed in the Gaelic ideal of *Cumannacht*—the vision of building a new social order based on 'a co-operative commonwealth'.[50]

In October 1913 at the Memorial Hall in London, the *Daily Herald* held the first of its mass meetings to support the Dublin workers by collecting £200 and arranging to send shiploads of food funded by public subscriptions. The newspaper called for a twenty-four-hour general strike. While the TUC debated the police brutality on 'Bloody Sunday' in Dublin and dispatched a deputation to investigate events in the city without success, the *Daily Herald* opened its campaign by hiring the Albert Hall in London. Normally used for musical and similar functions, this venue became the centre for many of the *Daily Herald* mass meetings for socialism, women's suffrage, and the Russian Revolution organized during 1913–20 with George Lansbury and other prominent figures in the British and Irish Labour Movements on the platform.

Delia Larkin addressed the first Albert Hall rally on 1 November 1913, supported by Lansbury, James Connolly, George Bernard Shaw, Sylvia Pankhurst, Charlotte Despard, and Ben Tillett, to protest at the arrest and imprisonment of her brother Jim. Lansbury wrote later: '[I]t is impossible to describe the red-hot enthusiasm which prevailed throughout the meeting, which was more like a religious revival than anything else.' By 14 November 1913, following mounting public pressure and poor by-election results, the Liberal government freed Jim Larkin unconditionally after seventeen days of imprisonment.[51]

Larkin then conducted a 'Fiery Cross' campaign which was arranged by local *Daily Herald* Leagues across mainland Britain to mobilize the labour movement in support of the Dublin workers. On 17 November a crowd of 25,000 turned out at Manchester to hear Larkin and other speakers—a scene that was repeated throughout the country. Two days later there was another packed rally at the Albert Hall to hear Larkin when 300 medical and university students tried to break up the meeting. In a memorable confrontation between the intruders and Larkin supporters—taxi-drivers and East Enders—Edgar Lansbury and his friends

[48] For examples of strike activity, see *Daily Herald*, 28 Nov., 24 Dec. 1913; for Larkin's appeal, ibid. 22 Nov. 1913.

[49] Lansbury, *My Life*, pp. 66–9.

[50] For the Gaelic concept of *Cumannacht*, see K. Harding, 'The "Co-Operative Commonwealth": Ireland, Larkin, and the *Daily Herald*', in S. Yeo (ed.), *New Views of Co-Operation* (1988), ch. 6.

[51] For Larkin, see E. Larkin, *James Larkin: Irish Labour Leader, 1876–1947* (1965).

dropped down dramatically from the top galleries of the Albert Hall from one tier to the next to join the fray.

Other examples of important assistance given by the *Herald* League members included an imaginative holiday scheme arranged by Dora Montefiore, and supported by Emmeline Pethick Lawrence and Charlotte Despard, to evacuate children of those in the Dublin lock-out to stay with families in mainland Britain. Practical help arrived in the form of clothing and funding for fares, as well as homes for the children and their mothers.[52] The *Daily Herald* continued to support Jim Larkin, despite the bitter recriminations that broke out between the Irish labour leader and certain British trade unionists. However, it was Ben Tillett, a member of the *Daily Herald* group, who, in one of those unpredictable changes of behaviour that marked his political career, at the special conference of the TUC—called to discuss the Dublin dispute on 9 December 1913—moved the resolution condemning Larkin's attacks. Hopes of official support and sympathetic strike action for the Dublin dispute were destroyed. In 1914 as the bitter Dublin lock-out moved towards a final collapse, the Irish workers' Dramatic Society undertook a fund-raising tour with the *Herald* League in the vanguard of those organizations and individuals assisting with the arrangements.[53]

The London Builders' Lock-Out, which started on 24 January 1914, had echoes of the great conflicts in the building industry of 1834, 1859, and 1872 and was inspired by the victory gained by William Murphy and his employers in the Dublin dispute of 1913. Following a strike at the Pearl Insurance construction site in Holborn, the London Master Builders' Association locked out around 40,000 operatives until they had signed an agreement to work with non-unionists instead. As the dispute progressed, the *Daily Citizen* and the *Daily Herald* took up different positions as divisions appeared between the union leadership and the rank and file. The *Daily Citizen* recommended that the men accept the terms drawn up by the National Conciliation Board, whereas the *Daily Herald* solidly backed the operatives who voted 23,481–2,021 against accepting the terms. In a complicated dispute, where the master builders threatened to turn the London dispute into a national lock-out, the *Daily Herald* organized another Albert Hall mass rally and continued to support the various groups of workers comprising the different trades in the building industry. Finally, the solidarity of those locked out was broken by the stonemasons' desertion and unilateral settlement with the master builders depicted in the *Daily Herald* headline: 'NO OTHER UNION DARE FOLLOW THE MASONS AND TURN TRAITOR'.[54]

From its first issue the *Daily Herald* was closely identified with the suffragette movement, when its front page carried a report of the Hyde Park demonstration addressed by Sylvia Pankhurst to protest against forcible feeding of imprisoned suffragettes.[55] As we know, the women's cause was the issue that George Lansbury placed above all others in Edwardian labour politics. In 1912 the *Daily Herald*

[52] C. D. Greaves, *The Life and Times of James Connolly* (1986), pp. 319–21.
[53] Schneer, *Ben Tillett*, pp. 166–71; E. Larkin, *James Larkin*, pp. 145–58.
[54] For the London Builders' Dispute, see R. W. Postgate, *The Builders' History* (1923), pp. 414–22.
[55] *Daily Herald*, 15 Apr. 1912.

naturally publicized and applauded his crusades on the women's question from his suspension by the Speaker from the House of Commons after his famous altercation with Asquith to his dramatic resignation from Parliament. Later in the year, the newspaper campaigned side by side with George Lansbury in the Bow and Bromley by-election, which, as previously noted, brought the benefit of suffragist money when the defeated candidate turned his full attention to running the newspaper.

However, there were other costs to be counted. The aftermath of George Lansbury's loss of his Labour seat in the Bow and Bromley by-election surfaced in some ugly scenes at the annual party conferences in 1913. At the ILP conference in Manchester, where George Lansbury and Marion Coates Hansen attempted unsuccessfully to amend the annual report, Miss Barclay (Poplar) expressed the general anger of the delegates against Lansbury's support for the WSPU: 'Mr Lansbury's action had put the clock back and had made the Labour party work in Poplar.'[56] Marion Coates Hansen wrote to the *Manchester Guardian* to complain indignantly about the heavy-handed treatment of feminists by Labour party stewards on the eve of the conference.[57] At this time, however, some support for Lansbury and the *Daily Herald* came from Fabian circles. Beatrice Webb, commenting on the treatment of her former associate on the Poor Law Commission, observed that the Labour party in 1913 denied George Lansbury admission as a delegate from Poplar and banned the *Daily Herald*'s placards at the uncomfortable Prince's Hall conference-centre in Lambeth.[58]

The history of the Edwardian women's suffrage movement has attracted considerable attention from participants and historians alike. Those who played a prominent part in the militant struggle in the pre-First World War period were the first to write about the movement which had its own women's press. In this respect, the Pankhurst women have been roundly criticized by male historians and some feminists for their version of the suffragette movement, which portrayed the WSPU as the dominant body at the expense of the many other suffrage societies and glorified their own part in the women's struggle. A typical example is Sylvia Pankhurst's monumental account published in 1931 with a frontispiece of Emmeline Pankhurst, which has been criticized as a biased attempt to depict the author's mother and herself as the central key protagonists in the women's struggle for the vote.[59] Christabel Pankhurst's authoritarian style of leadership—exercised in the main from safe exile in Paris—which caused so many rifts and expulsions from the WSPU has received similar hostile treatment, even to the ludicrous extreme of comparison with the Baader-Meinhof terrorists.[60]

An examination of the *Daily Herald* during 1912 to mid-1914 and of the role of its Christian socialist editor's consistent support for the WSPU, despite the divisions that undoubtedly developed, casts a different light on the Pankhursts and their leadership of the militant women's movement. In 1912 the *Daily Herald* covered the annual conference of the Independent Labour Party where George Lansbury

[56] *East End News and Shipping Chronicle*, 28 Mar. 1912.
[57] *Manchester Guardian*, 24 Mar. 1913.   [58] *Fabian News*, 24 no. 4, Mar. 1913.
[59] Pankhurst, *The Suffragette Movement*.   [60] Mitchell, *Queen Christabel*, esp. ch. 18.

appealed for Labour supporters 'to judge the militant Suffragists in the perspective of the righteous rebellion of the workers against their own class-imposed injustice'. Lansbury underlined his conference speech with a special message for the readers of the *Daily Herald*: 'Never were the two great movements for the emancipation of women and the emancipation of Labour closer than they are today. Ibsen said long ago that if these two causes ever united they would revolutionize the world.'[61]

Moreover, in reporting the women's movement the *Daily Herald* did not restrict its coverage exclusively to the activities of the most militant women's society. In October 1912, in an interview with Mrs Pankhurst, the newspaper explained the WSPU strategy of war on the Labour party but also featured the election policy of the NUWSS, as well as a newly published pamphlet by the Women's Freedom League.[62] The paper was full of advertisements and details of meetings and conferences for the whole spectrum of the women's movement.

However, in the *Daily Herald* the militants formed the subject of many of Will Dyson's memorable cartoons, such as the death of Emily Wilding Davison at the Derby, with their savage commentary on the attitude of the government and the treatment of gaoled suffragettes by the prison authorities. In his history of the *Daily Herald*, George Lansbury mainly recounted the unwavering public support the newspaper gave in the pre-war period to the militancy of the women's movement, largely through the activities of the *Herald* League. As Lansbury acknowledged: 'militancy was the result of conditions which ought to be removed . . . when mansions were being burnt down, letters in pillar boxes being destroyed, or politicians annoyed, the answer the paper gave to all complaints was "Give the women the vote, and so remove the causes which produce this wrong-doing".'[63]

Among the episodes Lansbury described were those in which *Herald* League members organized meetings and gave crucial help to suffragettes in conflict with the authorities as a result of legal and illegal activities. Members of the Lansbury family were active in aiding Sylvia Pankhurst avoid the police so that she could address public meetings in the East End. The imprisonment of Annie and William Lansbury for window-breaking was roundly condemned by the newspaper, which featured the editor's articles from gaol during his first famous imprisonment in 1913.

Other episodes which demonstrate how far the *Daily Herald*'s editor was committed to the militant women's cause received extensive coverage in the women's press. In June 1914, after negotiations between George Lansbury and Percy Illingworth, the Liberal chief whip, Asquith agreed for the first time to receive a deputation from the ELFS. Sylvia Pankhurst had carried her protest in the form of an indefinite hunger and thirst strike to the steps of Parliament. She had been driven directly to Westminster on her release from her ninth term of imprisonment. The deputation consisted of six working-class women from the East End: Julia Scurr (later one of the imprisoned Poplar councillors), Elsie Watkins, Mrs Parsons, Jessie Payne, Mrs Savoy, and Mrs Bird. George Lansbury was also at 10 Downing Street for

---

[61] *Daily Herald*, 27 May 1912.   [62] Ibid. 19 Oct. 1912.
[63] Lansbury, *Miracle of Fleet Street*, p. 75.

this noteworthy meeting—apparently, more to reassure the apprehensive and stubborn Asquith than from any need to assist the delegation.

On another occasion George Lansbury and Sylvia Pankhurst negotiated with David Lloyd George at one of his famous breakfast-table conferences, previously criticized by the *Daily Herald*, about further parliamentary initiatives to secure women's enfranchisement. Of the two different versions of this encounter, Lansbury recalled that Lloyd George promised that, with Sir Edward Grey and Sir John Simon, he would refuse to join any government after the next election, unless agreement had been reached on women's suffrage. However, Sylvia Pankhurst, who as we shall see, often slighted George Lansbury in her various memoirs, published a fuller and probably more accurate account. She claimed that Lloyd George wanted the immediate cessation of militancy in return for promised guarantees of his sponsorship of an amendment on votes for women's enfranchisement and a private member's bill with his public support. He also promised to resign, if defeated over votes for women.[64]

On 30 April 1913 the police had raided the London headquarters of the WSPU in Kingsway in an attempt to prevent the publication of the *Suffragette*, its official paper. However, an eight-page edition of the proscribed newspaper rolled off the presses at Victoria House Printing Company where the *Daily Herald* was published. On 2 May the *Daily Herald* triumphantly carried an impression of the *Suffragette* front page with the headline 'Raided' and announced gleefully the successful dispatch of the banned *Suffragette*:

All day yesterday Suffragists were calling at the *Daily Herald* office, carrying off large bundles in taxicabs, and serving them out to women on the various news pitches, and, needless to say, they sold like hot cakes . . .

One page is devoted to 'A Record of Fact', consisting entirely of reports concerning attacks on property, ascribed, rightly or wrongly to the militant women. An article by the redoubtable Christabel, 'What Militancy Means' occupies another page, whilst comprehensive reports of the recent prosecutions, of the raid, and of the debate on the Cat and Mouse Bill are also given.[65]

Such expressed co-operation between the two movements soon ran into the buffers. In 1913 Christabel Pankhurst was alarmed by the news that the *Daily Herald* might promote some pact between the women's movement and the labour movement that would threaten the independence of the WSPU. Her policy was to achieve women's emancipation by destroying male domination in Edwardian politics. This strategy meant building a new and forceful women's movement that was not constrained, subordinated, and oppressed by traditional male power.

With these views Christabel Pankhurst firmly rejected any form of alliance of militant feminism with male politics. She told Henry Harben who had travelled to Paris to negotiate the possibility of an alliance:

[64] The surviving correspondence largely supports Sylvia Pankhurst's version. See Sylvia Pankhurst to David Lloyd George, 21 July 1914, Lloyd George Papers, C/11/174; also Pankhurst, *The Suffragette Movement*, pp. 581–2; Lansbury, *My Life*, p. 127.

[65] *Daily Herald*, 2 May 1913.

Between the WSPU and the *Daily Herald* League or Movement there can be no connection. Ours is a Woman's Movement and the *Herald* League is primarily a Man's Movement, or at any rate a mixed Movement.

The great need of this time is for women to learn to stand and to act alone . . . the point of view of men and women is so different. No men, even the best men, ever view the Suffrage question from quite the same standpoint . . . the *Herald* League tends to be a class movement. Ours is not a class movement at all. We let in everybody—the highest and the lowest, the richest and the poorest. *The bond is womanhood.*[66]

From Paris, Christabel Pankhurst declared her outright opposition to any suspension of militancy, thereby smashing the possibility of any such pact. Henry Harben had told her of the Sylvia Pankhurst–Lloyd George interview and that Lansbury was 'jubilant at Lloyd George's offer'. Her implacable stance brought forth Lansbury's only public criticism of the women's movement—a stern rebuke to the exiled leader—in a career in which he otherwise gave his undivided support to the militant women's movement: 'I always found fanatical women as difficult to deal with as fanatical men; they always seem to me to want the best, not merely of two, but of all, worlds.'[67]

When Sylvia Pankhurst appeared on the same *Herald* League platform as George Lansbury at the Albert Hall—in support of Jim Larkin and the Dublin workers—Christabel finally expelled her sister from the WSPU. During these years George Lansbury's association with the suffragette movement brought one other important contact, who also briefly joined the *Daily Herald*. Harold Laski, the brilliant Marxist intellectual and later Professor of Political Science at the London School of Economics, worked on the newspaper during the pre-war period as a young man. He met George Lansbury as an Oxford undergraduate through his wife Frida's connection with suffragism—she was also a friend of Dorothy Lansbury. Laski was active in the Oxford branch of the Men's Political Union for Women's Suffrage with G. D. H. Cole and Lansbury was one of the invited speakers.

Frida and Harold Laski supported Sylvia Pankhurst after her rift with her sister, Christabel, in 1914. On his graduation from Oxford in the summer of 1914, Lansbury offered him temporary employment on the newspaper and Lady De La Warr loaned Frida and Harold Laski the use of a house outside London. Laski reviewed books for the newspaper and was responsible for several editorials during the summer of 1914, including those covering the advent of the First World War.[68]

On the 28 June 1914 'the infamous shot that rang around the world' and assassinated Archduke Franz Ferdinand at Sarajevo at first received limited coverage in the newspaper. Soon the *Daily Herald* was warning about the approach of the war that would affect drastically the fortunes of so many, including the labour newspaper and its pacifist editor.

---

[66] Christabel Pankhurst to Henry Harben, 7 Aug. 1913, Harben Papers, BL, Add. MS 58,226, fos. 34–6.
[67] Lansbury, *My Life*, pp. 127–8.
[68] I. Kramnick and B. Sheerman, *Harold Laski: A Life on the Left* (1993), pp. 61–70; G. Eastwood, *Harold Laski* (1977), pp. 9–10.

9
The Great War Years, 1914–1919

On 5 August 1914 the *Daily Herald* carried a short and utterly bleak headline on its front page: 'ENGLAND AND GERMANY AT WAR'. Underneath it was the official government statement: 'His Majesty's Ambassador to Berlin has received his passports, and His Majesty's Government declared to the German Government that a state of war exists between Great Britain and Germany as from 11 p.m. on August 4th'.[1]

George Lansbury later remarked that the outbreak of war was 'like a bolt from the blue'. Like many of the leading socialists in Europe, events in August 1914 took him by surprise. He shared the views of many in Britain and elsewhere who, after a relatively peaceful century virtually free from international conflict, were unaware of the nature of total war. At first the *Daily Herald* had treated the assassination of the Archduke Franz-Ferdinand, heir to the Austrian throne, and his wife on 28 June 1914 as another news story. Unsurprisingly, there was little comprehension of the scale of the conflict to come during the following days.

On 27 July the *Daily Herald* declared the 'Angel of Death Beats His Wings', about the local crisis between Austria and Serbia, but not until four days later did the Labour daily realize that Britain might be involved in the European conflict.[2] The paper then urged workers to 'stop the war' and to attend the rally in Trafalgar Square 'in thousands'. The front-page headline displayed the rallying cry of 'Workers Must Stop the War! The Greatest Crime of the Century. Next Sunday's Great Protest. Rally in Thousands to Trafalgar Square'.[3] On 3 August the *Daily Herald* staffer, John Scurr, later Poplar councillor and Labour MP, blamed the possibility of a European War on 'the blundering diplomacy of our rulers during the last generation'.[4] The following day the newspaper carried a full-page advertisement 'Keep your country out of War!'[5]

Raymond Postgate judged the *Daily Herald* to be probably 'the most powerful and incomparably the widest-circulated "anti-war" journal in the country'. The next few years made George Lansbury a Labour figure of national standing and influence. In particular, Lansbury's role as the editor of the *Daily Herald* transformed him from a well-known and honourable local politician to 'one of the best loved men in the world'. In 1951, when Postgate published the biography of his father-in-law, the *Daily Herald* was still alive as the only Labour daily. It owed its loyal readership, and much of its commercial existence, to Lansbury's contribution in establishing it over thirty years before. An important and crucial part had been

---

[1] *Daily Herald*, 5 Aug. 1914.   [2] Ibid. 27 July 1914.   [3] Ibid. 31 July 1914.
[4] Ibid. 3 Aug. 1914.   [5] Ibid. 4 Aug. 1914.

the Lansbury hand on the tiller that steered the paper through the turmoil of the First World War.[6]

As editor of the *Herald*, Lansbury kept alive the principles of socialism and religion through his weekly Saturday column in the paper that at times had almost the tone of a sermon. He later observed: 'My correspondence during the War years and since convinces me that much more than many churches or clergy, the *Herald* helped people to preserve their faith in religion.'

The horrors of the Great War confirmed his righteousness of his Christian pacifism—the inspiration for his socialism and humanity that underpinned his many crusades during these years and beyond. In a letter to Revd 'Dick' Sheppard, who in 1916 had yet to convert to pacifism, Lansbury made this clear declaration of his Christian faith and the reasons for his ardent support for pacifism:

It seems to me that in the present circumstances humanity is not sufficiently developed for us to trust ourselves unarmed before all nations, yet it seems to me that this is the only ideal Christ would have put before the world. I cannot believe that war does anything else but debase and demoralise mankind.[7]

Nevertheless, in August 1914 the outbreak of hostilities changed the attitude of the majority of socialists in most of the belligerent countries away from the question of peace and towards war. Seven years before, at the Stuttgart Congress of the International Socialist Movement, the member parties had pledged themselves to prevent war by all possible means or to use any international conflict to promote revolution. Nevertheless, in 1914 the majority of those on the left in Germany, France, Austria–Hungary, and Great Britain took a 'pro-war' line and supported their government's action in entering the war.[8] In August 1914 vast cheering crowds in the main capitals of Europe greeted the declarations of war. In East London, as elsewhere, men volunteered enthusiastically for military service. Lansbury later recalled that the spirit of internationalism of the past twenty-five years had been swept away by the widespread enthusiasm for the war and the popular belief, engendered by the mass press, that the independence of Belgium was at stake in the face of German militarism.[9]

At first, the British Labour movement had been briefly united in opposition to the conflict in Europe.[10] The *Daily Herald* added its voice against British involvement, denouncing the pending conflict as the instrument of international financiers and capitalists:

we make an appeal to every section of the working-class movement to come together in the [Trafalgar] Square ... to show the whole world that here in London there is a great party who

---

[6] Postgate, *Lansbury*.

[7] George Lansbury to Revd H. R. L. ('Dick') Sheppard, 18 Dec. 1916, Sheppard Papers, fo. 245. In 1928 he made the remarkably candid revelation that, if he had been of military age during the Great War, he would have volunteered for '*some dangerous non-combatant work*' in similar fashion to the ninth Earl De La Warr, who left Eton at 16 to enlist in the Royal Naval Reserve and served on a mine-sweeper: Lansbury, *My Life*, p. 205 (emph. added). For De La Warr, see A. Fairley, *Bucking the Trend: The Life and Times of the Ninth Earl De La Warr* (Bexhill on Sea, 2001), p. 27.

[8] D. Sassoon, *One Hundred Years of Socialism: The West European Left in the Twentieth Century* (1994), pp. 27–31.

[9] *Lansbury's Labour Weekly*, 7 Mar. 1925.   [10] Lansbury, *My Life*, pp. 203–4.

believe in peace and brotherhood, and will have no part in war between themselves or against any other nation . . .[11]

The *Daily Herald* League organized the Trafalgar Square rally, though Keir Hardie accused George Lansbury of using the occasion to benefit his newspaper. In turn Lansbury protested: 'It is absolutely untrue I wanted anything for the paper or myself and the accusation is unworthy of you.' With Hardie, the Labour party and socialist movement took over the demonstration to provide a broad spectrum in opposition to the war.[12]

On Sunday 2 August, 20,000 people gathered in the pouring rain, including a group of 5,000 socialists and trade unionists who had marched to Trafalgar Square from the East End. Keir Hardie and Henry Hyndman joined George Lansbury on the platform to chair the demonstration. Among the other speakers were Robert Cunninghame Graham, Arthur Henderson, Ben Tillett, Will Thorne, and Margaret Bondfield, some of whom were soon to back Britain's entry into the war. Lansbury opened with a tribute to the assassinated French socialist leader, Jean Jaurès. He then concentrated on the European situation, calling on the Labour movement to take direct action to prevent British participation in a European war. Lansbury told those gathered:

We are meeting at a serious and critical time . . . because statesmen and diplomatists had grossly mismanaged our affairs . . . It will be to the indelible dishonour of Great Britain to back up the autocracy of Russia . . . Let the Great Triple Alliance, the Miners, Transport Workers and Railwaymen, refuse to produce coal, run trains or transport materials. Already the South Wales miners have refused to mine coal during their holidays [Loud cheers].[13]

That weekend, the Bank Holiday was extended to three days, during which time the Bank of England and the Stock Exchange closed for business and London was crowded with tourists and visitors. Beatrice Webb, who with Sidney had passed through the demonstration on their way to the National Liberal Club in Whitehall, added a dismissive note in her diary:

We sauntered through the crowd to Trafalgar Square, where Labour, socialist and pacifist demonstrators, with a few trade union flags, were gesticulating from the steps of the monument to a mixed crowd of admirers, hooligan warmongers and merely curious holiday-makers. It was an undignified and futile exhibition, this singing of the 'Red Flag' and passing of well-worn radical resolutions in favour of universal peace.[14]

However, within a few days, German troops had invaded neutral Belgium and the Labour movement unity displayed on the plinth of Trafalgar Square was shattered. What Beatrice Webb had witnessed in Trafalgar Square was the last attempt of the international socialist movement to prevent the outbreak of hostilities by

---

[11] *Daily Herald*, 1 Aug. 1914.
[12] Lansbury to Hardie, n.d. [probably 31 July 1914], Francis Johnson Correspondence, ILP Collection, 1914/279.
[13] *Daily Herald*, 3 Aug. 1914.
[14] B. Webb, Diary, 2 Aug. 1914, PP. See also *The Diary of Beatrice Webb*, iii, N. Mackenzie and J. Mackenzie (eds.) (1984), pp. 212–13.

organized action, such as a general strike against war. With the violation of Belgian neutrality providing a popularly supported pretext for the Asquith government to take Britain and the British Empire into the war, George Lansbury and his *Daily Herald* became part of the minority that formed the anti-war movement in the country.

At the end of August 1914, the National Executive Committee of the British Labour Party agreed unanimously to support an electoral truce and by a seven to four vote that the party's whips join the government's recruitment campaign. Though previously an opponent of the Boer War, Will Crooks became the first Labour politician to declare for war and led the singing of the National Anthem in Parliament. He soon appeared on recruitment platforms throughout the country. On 7 August, Ramsay MacDonald resigned the leadership of the PLP. He joined left-wing intellectuals and radical Liberals, suspicious of British secret diplomacy, to establish the Union of Democratic Control (UDC), one of the organizations associated with the British anti-war and peace movement.[15] However, the *Daily Citizen* remained firmly patriotic, which precipitated the resignation of Clifford Allen who became a founding member of the No Conscription Fellowship (NCF).[16] At Westminster, MacDonald's replacement was Arthur Henderson, the main Labour politician to back the war. In 1915 he became President of the Board of Education when Asquith formed his Coalition government.[17]

By early September 1914 George Lansbury and the directors of the *Daily Herald*, faced with a falling circulation and the rationing of newsprint, took a crucial decision that ensured their commercial survival among the Fleet Street organs that dispensed daily war news. From 6 September, and for the duration of the war, the *Daily Herald* became a weekly publication, the *Herald*, with a price rise from $\frac{1}{2}d$. to $1d$. Even so, the entire staff was temporarily on notice of dismissal.[18] As editor, Lansbury announced 'A Call to Arms' to the members of the *Herald* League, which remained strong in London and elsewhere: 'Nothing else than war could have caused our present stoppage . . . when we resume our daily publication . . . we shall have a great public ready to respond to our call.'

Under George Lansbury's editorship, the *Herald* survived the war and re-emerged as a Labour daily in 1919. The *Daily Citizen*, however, unlike its rival, carried accounts of conflict from the Western Front and limped on after an adverse legal decision affected funding until closure in 1915.[19]

It is the view of the *Daily Herald*'s historian that the change to a weekly format benefited the paper financially and editorially.[20] Nevertheless, the Great War brought George Lansbury and his newspaper new crusades to wage—against war profiteering, government bureaucracy, and military conscription—as well as the cause of peace and reconstruction. The *Herald* was also at the centre of British support for the Russian Revolution and contributed to the debates about the changes

---

[15] A. Morgan, *J. Ramsay MacDonald* (Manchester, 1987), pp. 59–62.
[16] Marwick, *Clifford Allen*, pp. 22–3.   [17] Wrigley, *Arthur Henderson*, pp. 70–1.
[18] Richards, *The Bloody Circus*, pp. 21–3.   [19] Holton, '*Daily Herald* v. *Daily Citizen*', pp. 371–4.
[20] Richards, *The Bloody Circus*, pp. 22–3.

in the Labour party. A few years after the Great War, George Lansbury gave his verdict, 'Financially it was our easiest time. We were very successful as a weekly, and ... the losses were manageable ... so when the Armistice was declared we at once set our plans afoot for restarting as a daily.'[21]

One successful appeal for financial help with the struggling newspaper during the war years was to a solicitor and future Labour MP, David Graham Pole. Though at the time he was a Conservative in politics and a freemason, he became a close friend and political ally of George Lansbury for the next twenty-five years. Major Pole, who was wounded at the battle of Loos and invalided out, served in France with the Northumberland Fusiliers whose battalion of miners also swayed his politics. He later recalled his part in keeping the newspaper's presses rolling during the war years:

I saw a great deal of George Lansbury who was then running the weekly *Herald*. To add to his troubles it was not long before the Victoria House Printing Company, which printed the *Herald*, refused to continue with it. The printing had to be done in Manchester which was a most unsatisfactory arrangement. However, as the Victoria Printing House Company was itself not in a very good financial state we got together the money and I arranged with the chairman, Sir Frank Newnes, that I would buy all the shares in the Company at sixpence a share—if I could have every share transferred to me or to my nominees. In this way I became Chairman of the Victoria House Printing company and immediately brought back the printing from Manchester to London.[22]

During the war years and beyond, Pole was also associated with George Lansbury's strong stand against British imperialism. Both were active in the British Auxiliary section of the Home Rule for India League, established by Annie Besant in India in 1916 to secure self-government for India within the British Commonwealth.[23] In 1907 Pole had joined the Theosophical Society and before the war twice visited India with Annie Besant, eventually becoming her solicitor. In the inter-war years Lansbury and Pole worked closely together as Labour MPs, particularly in relation to British imperialism and India.[24]

At the start of the Great War, some old animosities were laid aside. The editor of the *Daily Herald* warmly acknowledged the action of John Burns, John Morley, and Charles Trevelyan, the only members of the Liberal government to resign office in protest against British involvement, as well as that of Ramsay MacDonald who gave up the Labour party leadership.

By 1918 John Burns had voted against conscription. Lansbury even put forward his name as Prime Minister as an alternative to Lloyd George, dismissed contemptuously by Lansbury as 'a country solicitor [who] accidentally came into

---

[21] Lansbury, *Miracle of Fleet Street*, p. 16.

[22] D. G. Pole, *War Letters and Autobiography* (Chelmsford, 1961), p. 177.

[23] See e.g. George Lansbury's appeal (with Charlotte Despard) against the banning order of the Governor of Madras, Lord Pentland, against officials of the League, in 'Home Rule For India (British Auxiliary)', circular (n.d.); see also D. Graham Pole *et al.* to Secretaries of Trades Unions & other Labour organisations, 12 June 1923, copies in The Theosophical Society Archives, Adyar, India.

[24] Pole, *War Letters and Autobiography*. I am very grateful to Prof. Chris Wrigley for bringing the Pole Papers to my attention.

prominence by assisting others to break the law in a country churchyard'.[25] Lansbury later wrote to Trevelyan, 'I agree we must unite in spirit & not on cut and dried formulae . . . I haven't anything to propose only I like to meet with those whose faith is mine too . . . & these dark gloomy days makes us all need the strength that comes from fellowship.' [26]

In 1914 suffragette militancy ended as Emmeline and Christabel Pankhurst famously backed the national military recruitment drive. In the same editorial, therefore, before he put down his pen about those leaving office, Lansbury could not deny himself an ironic comment about his competitors' coverage of the suffragette issue:

> It is truly astonishing. Perhaps no more absurd volte face has ever been executed by the English Press. Ten days ago the women were not to be given political freedom because they were militant. Today they are covered with glory because they spare no effort to second the militancy of men.[27]

Though a halt had been called to militancy, women's enfranchisement did not disappear altogether during the years of the Great War. Lansbury assisted Sylvia Pankhurst's endeavours to keep women's suffrage as an important issue at the front of domestic politics. In 1914 Bessie and George Lansbury became vice-presidents of the United Suffragists (US), a new breakaway organization from the WSPU that brought together both men and women of different persuasions from various suffrage groups. George Lansbury became a popular speaker in the US campaign for franchise reform. Among the other leading figures were Gerald Gould, H. W. Nevinson, Evelyn Sharp, Julia Scurr, and Agnes Harben, as well as Emmeline and Frederick Pethick-Lawrence, who donated their paper, *Votes for Women*, to the organization.[28]

When, in 1916, a Speaker's Conference was convened at Westminster, George Lansbury was one of the labour and socialist leaders to collaborate with democratic suffragists in establishing the National Council for Adult Suffrage. Sylvia Pankhurst withdrew from the National Council determined to secure complete adult suffrage, whereas Lansbury accepted the Speaker's Conference recommendation to enfranchise around 6 million women, while continuing to press for parliamentary votes for women industrial workers, and war widows.[29] The years 1917–18 saw the start of a split between Sylvia Pankhurst and George Lansbury over women's suffrage, and over their differing views on the parliamentary road to socialism.

After the outbreak of the war, other important changes on the *Daily Herald* included the departure of regular contributors, such as G. K. Chesterton, who after an initial debate about peace and war with Lansbury, no longer supported the

---

[25] *Herald*, 5 June 1918.
[26] George Lansbury to Charles Trevelyan, 2 Oct. 1914, Trevelyan Papers, CPT 73.
[27] *Daily Herald*, 11 Aug. 1914.
[28] K. Cowan, 'A Party between Revolution and Peaceful Persuasion: A Fresh Look at the United Suffragettes', in M. Joannou and J. Purvis (eds.), *The Women's Suffrage Movement: New Feminist Perspectives* (1998).
[29] Holton, *Feminism and Democracy*, pp. 146–9.

paper's stance, and Ben Tillett, who eventually became prominent with others in the 'pro-war' Labour movement. However, when Will Dyson left the *Herald* in early 1916, the paper suffered its greatest loss. At first the Australian cartoonist displayed his usual venom and penetrating technique in a series of savage caricatures of armament manufacturers and arms dealers. In 1915 he turned his attention to assisting the *Herald* fight 'the vicious conscriptionist campaign'. However, his fierce nationalism gradually distanced him from Lansbury's avowed pacifism, as others such as even Lord Northcliffe, who found space in his *Daily Mail* for Dyson, welcomed the anti-Prussian militarism in his work. Dyson complained publicly to Lansbury about a pacifist caption the editor had used with one of his cartoons. In 1916, after joining the *Daily Sketch* for a while, Lieut. Dyson was, by the end of the year, at the Western Front as a non-combatant war artist.[30]

The stalwarts on the *Herald* now included the pacifist John Scurr, also associated with George Lansbury in the British Auxiliary of the India Home Rule League. Other important staff members were Lansbury's associate editor, Gerald Gould; the long-serving diplomatic editor, W. N. Ewer; H. N. Brailsford, the former *Daily News* journalist; the feminist, Evelyn Sharp, and the two advocates of Guild Socialism, G. D. H. Cole and William Mellor.[31]

According to Raymond Postgate, the initial attitude of the *Herald* was to support Britain's involvement in the war, as the paper 'like nearly all the rest of Britain, assumed at first that nothing else could have been done but to declare war and to fight to the end'.[32] However, under George Lansbury's leadership the *Herald* was transformed into a pacifist weekly, symbolized at first in Francis Meynell's powerful article 'The War's a Crime' at the end of 1914.[33]

George Lansbury combined being a national politician, through his position as editor of the *Daily Herald* with a regular Saturday column, with remaining an important local politician in East London. When at the end of 1918 normal politics returned after the wartime electoral truce, his Conservative opponents in the general election campaign attacked him as much for his role in municipal politics as for his well-known pacifism.[34]

George Lansbury also used his position as editor to condemn the violence that occurred in East London against shops owned by Germans or any property with a foreign association. There were riots in London in August 1914, October 1914, May 1915, June 1916, and July 1917. The first incidents occurred on 6 August 1914 in Old Ford Road where a baker's shop was looted, followed by further outbreaks of violence in Poplar later in the month. The most serious disturbances against alien communities were in May 1915—shortly after the sinking of the *Lusitania*—and were among the most widespread riots in the twentieth century stretching from Liverpool to the Midlands, South Wales, and London.[35]

George Lansbury roundly denounced the anti-German violence in Britain—in

---

[30] For more on Dyson's departure from the *Herald*, see McMullen, *Will Dyson*, pp. 107–25.
[31] *Herald*, 18 Sept. 1914.   [32] Postgate, *Lansbury*, pp. 152–3.   [33] *Herald*, 19 Dec. 1914.
[34] J. Bush, *Behind the Lines: East End Labour, 1914–1919* (1984), p. 222.
[35] P. Panayi, 'Anti-German Riots in London 1914–1918', *German History*, 7 (1989), pp. 184–203.

his view 'worked up in good measure by the Press, against Germans naturalised and unnaturalised in our midst'. He reminded his readers that:

the shops wrecked in East London were owned by men and women whose families have lived for generations there. One of the men is a leader of the Liberal Party in the burgh of Poplar; another is a leading member of the Borough council, backed and supported by the Borough of Poplar Municipal Alliance . . .[36]

In his native Bow, despite his personal popularity, George Lansbury had his critics—including one from a surprising quarter—Sylvia Pankhurst. On the declaration of war, Sylvia Pankhurst hurried back from Dublin to East London where her ELFS continued to work for adult suffrage. In 1932 she published a highly personalized narrative of her anti-war work among the people of East London in wartime Britain.[37] Her study of the domestic front also chronicled the valiant attempts she made to combat the appalling poverty in the East End by lobbying the national government about war profiteering and establishing community projects—a cost-price restaurant, day nursery, clinic, and toy factory. By February 1917 the ELFS had been transformed from a women's suffrage organization in the East End into the Workers' Suffrage Federation with thirty branches in London, South Wales, and Scotland. This development reflected a changing and broader role in the provision of local welfare services and the campaign for political democracy. After the Russian Revolution, Sylvia Pankhurst's anti-war and revolutionary socialist views shifted away from parliamentary politics. Her renamed Workers' Socialist Federation became actively involved in international and revolutionary politics with branches in England and Scotland.[38]

In her description of the domestic front, Sylvia Pankhurst included some less sympathetic glimpses of George Lansbury and depicted him as an authoritarian patriarch of Bow. She recalled the episode of Lansbury scolding a tearful woman who had a reputation for drunkenness and had applied to the Bow West War Relief Committee for food coupons.[39] Despite the help given by the Lansbury family to her ELFS, Sylvia Pankhurst's references to her political ally in the pre-war period as well as the war years were mainly critical. On her first visit to the Lansbury family home in St Stephen's Road she noted that Lansbury's pride in introducing his son did not extend to Edgar's many sisters. George Lansbury's behaviour at the time of the Bow and Bromley by-election was also censured as, in Sylvia's view, he had followed 'the policy of Christabel Pankhurst' in urging the Labour party to oppose every parliamentary measure until women's enfranchisement was introduced. However, these observations were made over a decade later and it is doubtful if Sylvia Pankhurst articulated them at the time.[40]

Instead, in Bow and Bromley the Lansbury family remained active supporters of the various causes associated with Sylvia Pankhurst and her ELFS.[41] In February

[36] *Herald*, 15 May 1915.
[37] E. S. Pankhurst, *The Home Front: A Mirror to Life in England during the First World War* (1987).
[38] B. Winslow, *Sylvia Pankhurst*, ch. 5.
[39] *Woman's Dreadnought*, 5, 26 Sept. 1914.   [40] Pankhurst, *The Suffragette Movement*, p. 198.
[41] For Sylvia Pankhurst's campaigns in the East End, see also Winslow, *Sylvia Pankhurst*, ch. 4.

1915 the establishment of a League of Rights for Soldiers' and Sailors' Wives and Relatives to empower East End women and their families to protect and defend working-class living standards was one result of this political alliance. The new organization, with Lansbury and Joe Banks as prominent office-holders, fought valiantly for various pensions and allowances denied to the dependants of armed forces personnel by the bungling of a hard-hearted state bureaucracy. Sylvia Pankhurst used Lansbury's political connections in an attempt to secure the support of the trade union and labour movement.

Yet again, Sylvia's account of her work for the League of Rights based at 400 Old Ford Road contains some swingeing comments on George Lansbury's token participation in the new organization and his implied neglect of his wife. Sylvia noted dismissively: 'Lansbury protested that he could not give his time to these small gatherings. Where real spade-work was being accomplished . . . he was too much occupied and merely gave his name . . . [H]appily in after years Lansbury was pleased to recall his association with the League of Rights.'

Prominent in the distress work at this time was Minnie Lansbury (*née* Glassman) who, on Sylvia's invitation, gave up her East End teaching post to become the honorary secretary of the ELFS. Sylvia had also suggested Bessie Lansbury as 'honorary secretary' of the League of Rights and later commented scathingly on Bessie's domestic situation:

It was no surprise that Mrs Lansbury never signed a letter or attended a committee; no one expected that she would. If ever she had taken any active part in the Labour movement it was before I went to the East End. In my knowledge of her she was far too much overwhelmed, depressed by her housework, her excessively large family. And the long-standing varicose ulcers, from which so many working mothers suffered a martyrdom, to the disgrace of our so-called civilised standards. Indeed she was one of the sort of women who made women of my sort suffragettes; hers to stint, suffer, and work in silence, enduring all the hardships of participation in pioneer causes, without the breath of the exhilaration.[42]

There was a considerable grain of truth in Sylvia Pankhurst's caustic comments on the Lansbury household, though her scorn was being heaped directly on Bessie's husband whose politics left little time, in the suffragette leader's view, for sharing the burden of domestic duties.

George Lansbury used his regular Saturday column in the *Herald* to campaign for the dependants of soldiers and sailors and highlighted the Asquith government's failure to deal with war profiteering. Lansbury campaigned tirelessly over the bureaucratic administration of the Prince of Wales's Relief Fund concerning the inadequate relief payment scales. He called on members of the *Herald* League to lobby Parliament:

let us all set to write, and by agitation secure . . . full and adequate maintenance for wives and children of all the soldiers and sailors at the front, and of those who are killed or disabled, and for all able-bodied men and women unable to get employment . . . and for children and young people under 19 training and maintenance . . .[43]

[42] Pankhurst, *The Home Front*, p. 131.   [43] Ibid. 31 Oct. 1914. See also *Herald*, 7, 14, 28 Nov. 1914.

As 1914 closed, Lansbury turned his campaign into a direct attack on the Labour leadership's neglect of the victims of war at home:

this question of provision for soldiers, sailors and their dependants is a test one for the whole Labour and Socialist Movement... If organised labour falters in this... by those leaders from their own class ... the country will once more learn that independent champions of labour are only weak tools useful to bolster up the governing and possessing classes.[44]

He also opened the columns of the *Herald* directly to Sylvia Pankhurst for her home front campaign. Lansbury reminded 'the powers that be at Whitehall [that they] reckoned without Sylvia Pankhurst and the women of the East End', who led a successful deputation to the President of the Local Government Board to stop reductions in relief. She then contributed her own defence of her actions ending with an appeal for the parliamentary vote for women.[45]

In early 1915, at the time when there were no accredited war correspondents to the Western Front, George Lansbury visited France for eight days with Gerald Gould and sent back four reports for publication in the *Herald*.[46] On the outbreak of hostilities in August 1914, British war correspondents had been banned from the Western Front war zone by the Secretary of State for War, Lord Kitchener. Instead, the official Press Bureau, established by the War Office to disseminate information to the press, censored reports for publication in Britain.

During the First World War, as a result of these official restrictions on reporting the war, the population at home at first had little knowledge of conditions on the battlefields of the Western Front. Between May 1915 and April 1917 war correspondents were granted some controlled access. However, not until the period April 1917 to the armistice of 1918 were war correspondents accepted by the authorities and used by the British Army for propaganda purposes.[47]

George Lansbury encountered the tentacles of official secrecy first over the difficulty of obtaining a passport and then through the frequent and thorough searches he was subjected to at Victoria, Folkestone, Dieppe, and Paris. In France he visited the British hospital at the Hôtel Majestic in Paris, plus a number of French hospitals, toured the ruined town of Senlis and continued on to Compiègne. He also interviewed the leaders of the General Federation of Trades and met British residents in France, as well as East End dockers and stevedores serving in the British army. He was able to travel around relatively freely because Henry Harben, in France in charge of hospital administration, arranged military passes. However, while Lansbury's reports give some indication of the horrors of war from his details of the wounded he encountered and the wholesale destruction he saw, he was turned back as soon as he was close to any fighting.

From Christmas 1915, Lansbury's campaigning also took him at different times to 'Red Clydeside', where the shop steward's movement organized by Arthur

---

[44] Ibid. 5 Dec. 1914.   [45] Ibid. 28 Nov., 19 Dec. 1914.
[46] Ibid. 16, 23, 30 Jan. and 6 Feb. 1915.
[47] M. J. Farrar, *News from the Front: War Correspondents on the Western Front, 1914–1918* (1990), pp. ix–x, 4–6.

MacManus, Willie Gallacher, David Kirkwood, and others used the *Herald* League office in Glasgow as a base. The myth or reality of 'Red Clydeside'—and its origins and influence—are a subject of considerable recent debate.[48] However, Lansbury attributed the industrial unrest on Clydeside directly to war profiteering: 'Men knew the directors, shareholders, owners of munition works, shipyards and great iron and steel works were making money hand over fist . . . I asked to be allowed to bring the capitalist pressmen along . . . and within a few hours the men's case was more or less correctly reported in the Press.'

It was also a campaign that George Lansbury took directly to Whitehall, to be told that 'I was treading on dangerous ground, that if I was not careful I should find myself in prison'.[49]

Lansbury returned to Scotland in an attempt to intervene against the deportation of David Kirkwood, Arthur MacManus, and other shop stewards. His endeavours were risky, for they might have resulted in a ban on the *Herald*, as the Glasgow-based paper, *Forward*, the *Worker*, and the *Socialist* had been suppressed by the authorities.

One remarkable example of George Lansbury's selflessness was his subsequent lobbying on behalf of the imprisoned Scottish Marxist, John Maclean, who was serving a five-year prison sentence for sedition. On the eve of major surgery, Lansbury wrote directly from his nursing home to Lloyd George to offer to stand bail so that Maclean could be released into Lansbury's charge. On Maclean's release, while he was still recovering from his gall-bladder operation, Lansbury was actively involved in arranging a period of convalescence for Maclean in the south of England.[50]

While the *Daily Herald* had made its popular reputation for its solid support for strikers in every type of dispute before the Great War, industrial news largely disappeared from the weekly *Herald*. Except for the South Wales miners' defiance of the Munition Acts the paper's industrial columns were mainly replaced by the cause of pacifism and war resistance. In an interview in 1915, he revealed that, as well as the War, the futility of ruthless industrial strife—seen in the Colorado mining dispute and other conflicts in Britain—had deepened his pacifism. 'All my life I have been more or less a pacifist but never an out and out pacifist until now,' Lansbury admitted. 'We can only overcome evil by good . . . After all the greatest force in the world is the force exerted by Christ, passive resistance to all wrong doing.'[51]

As editor of the *Herald*, George Lansbury was an active propagandist for the new peace groups that were established during the First World War. His longest association was with the Fellowship of Reconciliation formed at a conference held in the Arts Theatre in Cambridge during the last four days of December 1914. Lansbury was one of 130 delegates who gathered to discuss the issues of Christianity and war

---

[48] For 'Red Clydeside', see I. McLean, *The Legend of Red Clydeside* (Edinburgh, 1983).
[49] Lansbury, *My Life*, pp. 206–7. For the state and industrial relations during the war, see C. Wrigley, *Lloyd George and the British Labour Movement: Peace and War* (1976).
[50] George Lansbury to Mrs Maclean, 3 July 1917, Emrys Hughes Papers, Acc. 4251, Box 1, File 2.
[51] *Christian Commonwealth*, 11 Aug. 1915.

to found a predominantly Nonconformist and Quaker organization based on Christian principles. The Cambridge conference adopted a five-point statement in defining Christian pacifism based on the first principle of love, as revealed and interpreted in the life and death of Jesus Christ, 'the only power by which evil can be overcome, and the only sufficient basis of human society'. Lansbury later recollected that: 'We were rather nebulous in our conclusions and did not, as an organised body, do very much against the war . . . We talked a lot about Christian witness, but few among us were willing to say war was murder.'[52]

George Lansbury remained with the Fellowship, under whose auspices he undertook his peace journeys to the USA and European countries in the late 1930s. During the Great War, the most active anti-war organization with which George Lansbury was associated was the NCF started in 1914 by Fenner Brockway to oppose any possibility of conscription. By early 1916 when conscription was introduced there were probably around 15,000 members pledged to 'refuse for conscientious reasons to bear arms'.[53] Curiously, despite George Lansbury's unfailing work on behalf of conscientious objectors, famous and unknown, this pacifist body is not mentioned by name in Lansbury's autobiography. Two anti-conscription meetings, both greeted by a hostile public reception, which he attended in the Memorial Hall and the gathering in the South Place Chapel, where he 'came in for a little danger', receive brief references.[54]

Lansbury was also present at the first national convention of the NCF at the Memorial Hall when the president, Clifford Allen, pledged that members would resist any Military Service Bill and were willing to suffer 'the penalties that the State may inflict—yes, even death itself—rather than go back upon our conviction'.[55]

In 1916 Lansbury also spoke at the second NCF national convention held close to Easter. It is worth recalling in some detail a speech, full of religious imagery, that went beyond a Christian condemnation of the militarism of the Great War to a greater fight for a socialist future in Britain:

I wish I were years younger so that I might stand along with you in this fight, because I believe you are doing ever so much more than standing out against the war . . . You are fighting against the horrors of peace as well as the horrors of war (Great applause). We none of us can be content with the world as it was before August 1914. If the world is to be builded (*sic*) anew, it must be builded in brotherhood and comradeship . . . I feel that we older men and women should stand by you. We believe that you are standing in line with that man who was God and who in Gethsemane stood alone and who, forsaken by everyone, even then loved his enemies. There must be no hatred in us. There is something that follows Gethsemane, and that is Easter—the resurrection of this old world from the damnable conditions of today (Applause). If you go to prison, we will go with you. We will try to make you realise that the

---

[52] Lansbury, *My Life*, p. 211.

[53] J. Rae, *Conscience and Politics: The British Government and the Conscientious Objector to Military Service, 1916–1919* (1970), pp. 11–12. For the NCF, see also T. C. Kennedy, *The Hound of Conscience: A History of the No-Conscription Fellowship, 1914–1919* (1918).

[54] Lansbury, *My Life*, pp. 209–10.

[55] F. L. Carsten, *War against War: British and German Radical Movements in the First World War* (1982), pp. 66–7.

thing to do in prison is not to think of failure but of victory, the victory that you are winning by your witness to the right and true . . . (Great applause).[56]

Among George Lansbury's surviving correspondence from 1917 was a letter asking him to enquire about prisoner 3267 Henry Williams, an eighteen-year-old conscientious objector serving twelve months in Wormwood Scrubs:

Kindly allow my wife & myself to thank you from the bottom of our hearts for the great service you are rendering to the COs at Wormwood Scrubs & elsewhere. We read with joy and delight in the *Herald* . . . of those boys who are imprisoned for refusing to commit a crime . . .[57]

This moving request illustrates one of the most important crusades that George Lansbury undertook, not only to oppose the demand for introduction of conscription, but also on behalf of conscientious objectors tried and imprisoned by the state during the Great War. From August 1914 until 1916 the British army consisted of volunteers who had answered the national recruitment campaign symbolized by one of the most celebrated posters of all time. It depicted the face of a demonstrative Lord Kitchener who demanded 'Britons Kitchener wants YOU. Join your Country's army! God save the King.' Though 500,000 volunteered in the first wave, the relentless slaughter on the Western Front in 1914 and 1915 severely depleted the Kitchener armies. During this time, 512,520 British soldiers were killed.

The pressure from the press, military, and politicians for the introduction of conscription increased, though at first a precise figure was not available for the numbers that could be conscripted. During 1915–16 the *Herald* campaigned vigorously against the different phases in the course of 1915 which led inevitably to the introduction of conscription. In 1915 the Local Government Board had compiled a National Register of over 2,179,231 single men aged between eighteen and forty who had not enlisted in the armed forces. Under the 'Derby Scheme', named after the government's Director of Recruitment and by which men were invited to attest, only 1,150,000 single men and a similar percentage figure for married men put their names forward. On 8 January 1916, as the Military Service Bill went before Parliament, the *Herald*'s main headline '5,000,000 VOLUNTEERS KILL CONSCRIPTION' was a last ditch attempt by Lansbury to stop the Labour party's endorsement of military conscription.[58] It was followed by the demand that Arthur Henderson, George Roberts, and William Brace should not remain in the Coalition government.

In 1916 conscription in Britain was finally introduced in two stages. Under the first Military Service Bill of 5 January 1916, all single men between the ages of eighteen and forty-one were deemed liable for service in the armed forces and to be called up by age groups. The adoption of conscription by the Liberal government in 1916 brought pacifism into conflict with the British state as large numbers of men applied for exemption under the system of military service tribunals.

In the Great War, conscientious objection in Britain was defined as either a political objection to all wars or to certain ones, which at first caused variations in

---

[56] *Labour Leader*, 13 Apr. 1916.
[57] P. B. Williams and L. A. Williams to George Lansbury, 12 April 1917, LP, vol. 7, fo. 309.
[58] *Herald*, 8 Jan. 1916.

interpretation. Exemption from military (in other words, combatant) service on religious grounds was generally accepted, even by some Conservative politicians and advocates of conscription among the military. Some absolute pacifists, such as the Catholic Socialist Francis Meynell, who continued to work on the *Herald* with Lansbury, were exempted primarily on religious grounds though he clearly held a political objection to conscription. However, in practice local tribunals determined the outcome of those who claimed conscientious objection on other grounds.

In general, socialists accepted the use of military force to overthrow capitalism, but opposed wars caused by capitalism. Resistance to war could therefore include the evasion of conscription. Socialist pacifism, a profound conviction based on the socialist brotherhood, deemed war was morally incompatible with this conception of the socialist faith.

In particular, the Christian pacifism of such men as Revd Reginald Sorenson, Dr Alfred Salter, and George Lansbury were examples of socialist and pacifist beliefs derived from Christianity. Two of the most famous conscientious objectors were Fenner Brockway and Clifford Allen—both members of the ILP—whose objections to war were based firmly on socialist principles.

In 1916 George Lansbury was present at the London Appeal tribunal (City section), when Clifford Allen appealed against the decision of the local Battersea Tribunal ordering him to undertake non-combatant service on the grounds of conscience. During the hearing of another appeal by a socialist, Lansbury exclaimed, 'Shame on you Rothschild. Herbert Samuel said that a moral objection is as good as a religious objection. You ought to be ashamed of yourself.'[59]

In happier times, George Lansbury later shared a political platform with Philip William Bagwell, a newsagent in the Isle of Wight who went before the military service tribunal at Ventnor. Influenced by the new theology of the Revd R. J. Campbell and the political doctrines of the Independent Labour Party, he refused both to attest for military service and to enlist in the armed forces, as he believed that all war was contrary to the teachings of Jesus Christ. He was imprisoned for twenty-seven months and after the Great War was elected to his local council on which he served for twenty-four years. At the end of the war the *Herald* had drafted a petition on behalf of the NCF to press for the immediate release of the conscientious objectors. The petition circulated in the Isle of Wight, as in other parts of Britain. On 4 March 1919 George Lansbury and Gerald Gould presented the petition of 130,000 signatures to Edward Shortt in his room at Westminster. Five years later George Lansbury received the support of Philip Bagwell and his wife Nell, when they shared the platform at a packed meeting in the Ventnor town hall on 29 September 1924.[60]

At this time the tribulations of the conscientious objectors came even closer to the Lansbury home. In 1917 Edgar Lansbury appealed successfully to the Poplar Military Tribunal against an earlier decision, by the casting vote of the chairman, to

---

[59] *The Times*, 11 Apr. 1916.
[60] P. S. Bagwell and J. Lawley, *From Prison Cell to Council Chamber: The Life of Philip William Bagwell, 1885–1958* (1994), especially ch. 16.

deny his claim for exemption from military service. He gave his full name, address, and occupation as 'Edgar Isaac Lansbury, 25 Mornington Road, Bow, Timber Merchant and Three Ply Manufacturer', and included a letter from his father. Edgar's case illustrates the difficulties encountered by applicants with the system of local tribunals:

I am a member of the Poplar Borough Council and an active member in the Socialist and Political Labour Movement of Poplar and East London. This brings me into conflict with my colleagues on the Borough Council. The Tribunal was composed of a majority of my opponents whom I consider to be not the best qualified people to consider my application. Without the Chairman's vote, the voting on the qu[estion] of work of national importance was 4 to 4.[61]

According to A. J. P. Taylor, the modern world started in 1917 with the emergence of the two global powers—Russia and the United States. In Russia the Bolsheviks seized power in the October Revolution and the United States of America entered the First World War. However, the first Russian Revolution in February 1917, ending the tyranny of the Tsarist régime, had a greater impact of world-wide significance. For George Lansbury the ending of Russian autocracy was the single biggest event of the First World War, with immense consequence for the British Labour and socialist movement. In his words 'it was the dawn of a new age', though he made clear he 'cared not whose revolution it was whether Menshevik or Bolshevik for it was enough that the Tsardom had fallen'.

In the *Herald,* Lansbury related the deposing of Nicholas II to the Easter 1916 uprising in Ireland and the implications for British imperialist rule elsewhere:

For more than seven centuries Britain has attempted to rule Ireland against the will of the Irish people . . . the same is true of India. That great nation of 350 millions of human souls is awakening as Russia awakened . . . the British people . . . must understand that our approval of revolution in Russia makes it unthinkable that we should perpetrate the domination of India by Europeans.[62]

The *Herald* printed the 'Russian Charter of Freedom' promised by the new régime in Russia—which included universal suffrage and the freedoms of speech, of association and to strike—to press the British government to lift similar restrictions in Britain and grant universal suffrage. Finally, Lansbury called for an international effort with French, Italian, Belgian, and Russian socialists to end the war by a negotiated peace. It was a rallying cry with a historic ring:

These are the days when from the house tops we should all cry aloud: 'Workers of all countries unite. You have nothing to lose but your chains. You have a world to gain'. Yes, unite, not to dominate, but to co-operate in the bonds of love and friendship, comradeship and brotherhood.[63]

In Britain, the Russian Revolution inspired a round of celebratory meetings and

---

[61] 'Notice of Appeal', 13 Sept. 1917, LP, vol. 7, fo. 369. See also George Lansbury to Wait Sewell, n.d., ibid. vol. 8, fo. 3.
[62] *Herald*, 24 Mar. 1916.   [63] Ibid.

rallies organized by different groups on the political left. In the East End over 7,000 were present at the Great Assembly Hall in Mile End for a meeting arranged by the Committee of Delegates of Russian socialist groups to London. On 31 March the *Herald* organized a mass rally chaired by George Lansbury in the Albert Hall. One of the 10,000 present tried to convey the emotion of the occasion, which was almost beyond the power of pen and paper. E. Philippa McDougall later described the occasion:

that which must have inspired every individual present was . . . the intense, passionate feeling for liberty, for peace, which prevailed in that splendid gathering. It seemed as though a torrent of emotion, pent up, perhaps, since the fateful day of August 1914, was loosed from the soul of each individual, and the collective result was to give the assembly a life force more glorious than anything which could have been said or sung.[64]

The most remarkable event inspired by the Russian Revolution in Britain was the Leeds Convention of 3 June 1917, attended by 1,150 delegates from trade unions, trades councils, local Labour parties, women's groups, and peace groups. This broad spectrum of the political left, comprising revolutionary shop stewards, pacifists, feminists, and pro-war Labourites and socialists, was chaired by Robert Smillie. Those present included Ramsay MacDonald, Dora Montefiore, Tom Mann, Philip Snowden, Ben Tillett, Bertrand Russell, Sylvia Pankhurst, Ernie Bevin, Charlotte Despard, Robert Williams, and W. C. Anderson MP.

Messages were read out from two prominent figures absent from the Convention—Clifford Allen and George Lansbury. Allen wrote:

Three hours ago I received my third sentence of hard labour here . . . (Shame) . . . convey to the Leeds Convention the greetings of 1,000 Conscientious Objectors . . . I thrilled with delight when within the prison it was whispered that the Russian Democracy had at last triumphed . . . I go back to prison tomorrow for two years with renewed courage . . .[65]

Though the *Herald* League had helped to bring about the Leeds Convention, George Lansbury was missing, sadly sidelined in hospital after an emergency gall bladder operation.[66] His message, which conveyed his disappointment at his enforced absence, congratulated those assembled in Leeds:

You are taking part in a world-wide movement . . . The Russian revolutionists have not just an academic belief in their principles. They are determined to put them into action. They *are* putting them into action. *It is the uprising of the proletariat.* How shall we answer? *We*, too must prove that when we talk of Liberty, Equality, Fraternity, we mean exactly what we say. Not liberty for just a few . . . but liberty, equality, fraternity the *world over* . . .[67]

Although Lansbury was not present, Edgar attended the historic event, travelling

---

[64] The *Herald* Office, *Russia Free! Ten Speeches Delivered at the Royal Albert Hall London on 31 March 1917* (1917).

[65] Quoted in *British Labour and the Russian Revolution: The Leeds Convention: A Report from the Daily Herald, with an Introduction by Ken Coates* (n.d.), p. 20.

[66] S. White, 'Soviets in Britain: The Leeds Convention of 1917', *International Review of Social History*, 19 (1974), pp. 165–93.

[67] *The Call*, June 1917.

with Bertrand Russell and others, according to Lady Constance Malleson.[68] The East End Labour movement was also well represented. George Lansbury's comrades, Charlie Sumner, Robert Palmer, Sam March, and Joe Banks, wrote warmly from Leeds Station, immediately after the conference, to tell Lansbury that the only opposition came from Ernie Bevin, Captain Tupper (of the Seamen's Union), and Ben Tillett, who had left early. Otherwise the Convention 'was a great success. All the resolutions were carried practically unanimously. The conference was one of the greatest we have ever attended. Your letter was received with great enthusiasm'.[69]

At the Convention, Ramsay MacDonald had moved the first resolution of congratulations to the Russian people and the fourth resolution had called for the formation of Soviet-style Councils of Workmen and Soldiers' Delegates throughout Britain.[70] The main outcome of the Leeds Convention in June 1917 was the attempt in different parts of the country to organize these local councils.

In London this movement revealed the degree of hostility to anti-war and pacifist groups from their political opponents. On Saturday, 28 July 1917 the conference called at the Brotherhood Church, Southgate Road, in Hackney was broken up and the church wrecked by a violent, jingoistic crowd led by soldiers, singing 'Rule Britannia'. Similar scenes took place in Swansea and in Newcastle, where a peace meeting addressed by Charlotte Despard was temporarily disrupted. At the Brotherhood church, which was an established centre of the anti-war movement in North-East London, George Lansbury noted the display of pacifism by the audience quietly awaiting the peace meeting in the school room attached to the main church, commenting 'this exhibition of pacifism just nonplussed the invaders, who not being attacked, were quite unable to decide their course of action'. He added: 'For all I have read and heard about last Saturday, I am stronger than ever in my conviction that force and violence lead nowhere at all . . .'[71]

One important outcome of the Bolshevik Revolution was that on 11 May 1918 Trotsky published the secret treaties that the Tsar had made with the Allies. George Lansbury told the story again in his history of the *Daily Herald*. While the details of these treaties became public knowledge in France, Germany, America, and elsewhere, in Britain only the *Manchester Guardian* and the *Herald* published them, to the consternation of Downing Street and Whitehall. In 1923, demanding that the Government publish the treaties in their entirety, Lansbury told the House of Commons how at the time of publication he feared he would be 'hauled off to prison', adding that, 'All of us who had a hand in publishing them in this country were all the time under the threat of going to prison for doing so'.[72]

The shocking revelations of these secret treaties spelt out the unprincipled diplomacy of the First World War fought by the Allied Powers, not for the independence

[68] C. Malleson, *After Ten Years: A Personal Record* (1931), p. 13.
[69] Charlie Sumner, Robert Palmer, Sam March, and Joe Banks to George Lansbury, 3 June 1917, LP, vol. 7, fo. 330.
[70] R. Miliband, *Parliamentary Socialism: A Study in the Politics of Labour*, 2nd edn. (1972), pp. 54–5.
[71] *Herald*, 4 Aug. 1917.   [72] *Hansard*, 20 Mar. 1923, col. 2459.

of Belgium but in order to carve up European territory and for economic resources. As an ardent pacifist in the 1930s, George Lansbury made it his unrelenting mission to seek the resolution of the economic rivalries of the Great Powers that threatened another international conflagration.

The First World War had a major impact on domestic British politics and brought about fundamental changes to the party system with the decline of Liberalism and the rise of Labour. By the early 1920s, with the end of Coalition politics, the Labour party had replaced the Liberal party as the main opposition party in Parliament and took office in 1924. During the Great War the transition from a peacetime to a war-time economy strengthened the position of the trade union movement, whose support was essential for the successful prosecution of the war and was to the benefit of the Labour party. While the wider Labour movement, as we have seen, had split over its attitude towards British involvement in the war, the majority had supported the war effort. Labour leaders took office in the Asquith Coalition government in April 1915 and the Lloyd George Coalition government in December 1916, with Arthur Henderson joining a small War Cabinet.

However, by 1917 there was a general disillusion with the war in many quarters of British society and a growing desire for peace and a better world. At this time—with the anticipation of an increased electorate under the Representation of the People Act of 1918—Labour modernized its party organization with a structure of new local Labour parties and a mass individual membership. In 1918 the Labour party conference also adopted a new constitution that included the Clause Four commitment to public ownership. Arthur Henderson had resigned in August 1917 as leader of the Labour party in the House of Commons and from the War Cabinet to devote himself to bringing about these important changes to prepare the Labour party for a future of political power.[73]

During this period George Lansbury had been out of Parliament since his defeat at the Bow and Bromley by-election of 1912 and out of favour with the Labour party leadership. He did not attend the annual party conference in 1914, nor the next two conferences in 1916 and 1917. However, Lansbury was not on the sidelines. As editor of the *Herald*, he remained an active propagandist at the centre of a world of dissent that made him a tribune of the left in Britain, particularly in the post-war years. George Lansbury now commanded large audiences, as demonstrated by the successful Albert Hall rallies held from 1917. In its campaign for peace, the *Herald* had also lobbied hard and consistently in Labour and socialist circles that Britain should send delegates to the International Congress at Stockholm, only to be thwarted by the government ban on passports. The latter years of the Great War, an important and influential time in Labour politics, were also a period of growing *rapprochement* between George Lansbury and the Labour party.

In January 1918 at the Manchester Conference, where the party delegates discussed a new constitution drafted by Arthur Henderson and Sidney Webb to establish a new national party with a mass membership, Lansbury returned to the party

---

[73] Wrigley, *Arthur Henderson*, pp. 120–1.

conference to play his part in the new changes to the party organization. As the delegate for the Poplar Trades Council and Labour Representation Committee, at a
crucial moment in the debate, as the proposal for the new Constitution swung in
the balance, Lansbury 'seized the moment' by successfully moving an amendment
that the referral back should be for one month only.[74]

There was one other important contribution from George Lansbury at the 1918
Labour party conference. Divisions among the delegates on the issue of those
Labour members associated with the British Workers' League, possibly contesting
seats against official Labour parliamentary candidates, brought a passionate appeal
for party unity from the prospective parliamentary candidate for Poplar, Bow, and
Bromley. Lansbury reminded his fellow delegates that he was in a similar predicament with the Party in 1912:

Against his own feelings he went out and had been in the wilderness for some years. This big
Labour movement had brought him back to this conference because in his soul he believed
that unless they stuck together during the next few years it would be bad for the Movement
they all loved and had done so much for . . . the Movement just now needed every man and
woman to build up what the war has pulled down. He had come back because he felt that in
the few more years he had to live he must do everything in his power to unite, not divide.[75]

After the conference in January 1918, George Lansbury continued to play an
increasingly important part in Labour party politics, since his position as editor of
the *Herald* made him a prominent, powerful, and revered figure in Labour circles.
On 17 May 1917 George Lansbury, the embodiment of grassroots democracy, was
the popular choice to lay the foundation-stone for the new strike school—which
remains to this day—in the remote Norfolk village of Burston, the scene of the
remarkable and lengthy Burston School Strike. Burston first achieved national
prominence in 1914 after two popular socialist schoolteachers, Kitty and Tom Higdon, who had assisted local farm labourers in winning the parish council elections,
were dismissed. Their victimization provoked the strike by the schoolchildren who
were then taught by the Higdons on the village green and in a local carpenter's shop.
During the next three years George Lansbury, Tom Mann, Keir Hardie, and Philip
Snowden were among the many Labour leaders who took the train from London to
address open-air rallies on the village green. George Lansbury championed the
Burston Rebellion in the *Herald* and became President of the national committee
that raised funds.[76]

George Lansbury had not lost his touch for the theatrical in politics during the
years of the Great War. On 20 November 1917 the *Herald* had published one of the
most famous *exposés* of the First World War, when George Lansbury sent Francis
Meynell and an unnamed woman companion to dine at the prestigious Ritz Hotel
in the opulent West End. 'How They Starve At the Ritz'—a full one-page report

[74] *Labour Leader*, 31 Jan. 1918.   [75] Labour Party, *Annual Conference Report*, June 1918.
[76] T. G. Higdon, *The Burston Rebellion* (1984), p. 84; R. Groves, *Sharpen the Sickle: The History of the
Farm Workers' Union* (1981), pp. 151–9; Bertram Edwards, *The Burston School Strike* (1974), pp. 125, 126,
129–31, 142, 148–9.

complete with the printed *Carte du Jour* menu—was followed one month later by a sequel—'Still Starving at the Ritz'. Both reports revealed the patriotic rich enjoying conspicuous consumption while the nation's food supplies were threatened by unrestricted submarine warfare, and may well have played some part in the introduction of rationing.

In April 1918 he was present at a series of meetings hosted by Sidney and Beatrice Webb at 41 Grosvenor Road to discuss Labour policy with Arthur Henderson. Beatrice Webb noted in her diary that at least Henderson in the Labour leadership was prepared to consider the possibility of the inclusion of George Lansbury in a future government:

The main question raised was what should Labour do if the Lloyd George combination collapsed over Ireland or over the ill success of the war. Henderson put forward the view that if Asquith were asked to form a government and . . . could not do so without the participation of the Labour Party . . . he [Henderson] would ask the Liberal leaders to support and accept the war aims of the Labour Party and give a guarantee of good faith by offering a sufficient number of places to the Labour Party . . . He intimated that the leaders not in Parliament would have to be taken in—Webb and Lansbury, he suggested half jocularly. [J. H.] Thomas supported him.[77]

Lansbury responded that he would back any initiative to end the war and would judge any Liberal offer 'exclusively from that standpoint'.[78] What George Lansbury felt about the changes in the Labour party and socialism can be found in his 126-page book *Your Part in Poverty*, published as part of a series by the *Herald*. According to Postgate, 'it probably turned more people away from selfish preoccupations into working for Socialism than anything else he wrote'.[79] Lansbury's message was a simple statement of the Christian socialist principles he followed in his public and private lives:

Therefore, those who are convinced the present methods of money-making are wrong are called upon to live in the simplest manner, and to devote every hour of leisure and every penny of money they can spare to assisting the workers in their task of organising the transformation of the present social order from competition to co-operation.[80]

In 1918, as the general election approached, the *Herald* launched its campaign to raise £100,000 for Labour party funds, as well as opening its columns to MacDonald, Henderson, and other Labour figures. One particular episode in November 1918 illustrates Lansbury's position within the Labour ranks at this time. After the

---

[77] B. Webb, Diary, 25 Apr. 1918, PP. See also *Diary of Beatrice Webb*, iii, ed. Mackenzie and Mackenzie, pp. 306–7.

[78] Ibid. [79] Postgate, *Lansbury*, pp. 181–2.

[80] G. Lansbury, *Your Part in Poverty* (1917), pp. 106–7. *Your Part in Poverty* was a seminal work in the life of one self-educated Welsh socialist, Gordon MacDonald (1888–1966), who started twenty years of pit work at 13. He became Labour MP for Ince and Governor of Newfoundland. As Lord MacDonald of Gwaenysgor, he was Paymaster-General in the post-war Attlee Government. In Feb. 2000 in addressing Cambridge Labour Party's Centennial Conference, Eryl McNally MEP, Gordon MacDonald's granddaughter, quoted the formative passages her grandfather had underlined in his copy of Lansbury's book over eighty years before. I am grateful to Eryl McNally MEP for this information.

Labour party left the Lloyd George coalition government, Lansbury defended William Adamson, the acting leader, at a stormy meeting at the Albert Hall.

The Poplar Trades Council and Labour Representation Committee had adopted George Lansbury as their parliamentary candidate for Bow and Bromley as early as October 1916 and also decided to re-affiliate to the national Labour party in the following year. Lloyd George seized the opportunity afforded by the end of the war in November 1918 to call the snap 'Coupon Election' of 14 December 1918.

At Poplar, Bow, and Bromley George Lansbury fought an enthusiastic campaign which, combined with his personal popularity, his opponents feared might bring him victory; in fact, he was unsuccessful in the expanded constituency by only a few hundred votes. His Conservative opponent in the 1912 by-election, Reginald Blair, retained the seat with 8,190 votes with Lansbury gaining 7,248 votes to push the Liberal candidate, Mark Dalton, into third place with only 988 votes. Lansbury put up a creditable performance in an election in which many of the main Labour figures, including Ramsay MacDonald, Arthur Henderson, and Philip Snowden were defeated heavily. George Lansbury commented:

Our faith in democracy is not at all shaken . . . a great number of voters went to the poll with nothing clear in their heads except some nonsense about hanging the Kaiser and making the Germans pay. . . it is equally true that a great number went to the poll with a perfectly clear idea in their heads of social reconstruction . . . The future is inevitably ours.[81]

Ten years later, he reflected in his autobiography on the causes of the Great War which, in part, he attributed to the secret diplomacy of politicians and monarchs. He believed that 'more wisdom and understanding among the masses' was required. During these war years, as a leading pacifist, Lansbury had done his best, particularly through his weekly *Herald*, to keep people's faith alive in the principles of socialism, democracy, and religion.

The impact of total war had produced important changes in British society, including to the political party system—with the decisive split in the Liberal party and the rise of Labour. Before the Great War, George Lansbury had established a considerable reputation in municipal politics. In the inter-war years, he was to become a major figure in national politics, particularly as the *Herald* was published once more in 1919 as the daily paper for the Labour left.

---

[81] *Herald*, 4 Jan. 1919.

10

Direct Action, 1919–1920

In the post-war era, as editor of the *Daily Herald*, Lansbury became the established tribune of the political left in Britain. This independent Labour paper—a platform for his views of Christian socialism, pacifism, and passive resistance—was closely identified with the waves of working-class militancy and social disturbance that occurred, as well as its wide-ranging coverage of events in other parts of the world.

Despite a short-lived post-war boom that ended in the summer of 1920, there was unrest in the armed forces. Police strikes in London in August 1918, and during 1919, spread to Liverpool and the provinces. Additionally, there was industrial strife in the mining, transport, and rail industries. Troops were moved to the coalfields and urban areas of potential conflict. Nineteen battalions and six tanks were deployed in Glasgow. At times the authorities considered that this challenge to the British state brought the country close to political revolution. Of greater concern to the Prime Minister, Lloyd George, was the industrial scene that experienced more strikes in 1918–21 than at any other time. Most powerfully, the re-emergence of the Triple Alliance of the miners, railwaymen, and transport workers, formed initially before the First World War, threatened the possibility of a general strike.[1]

Postgate later recalled that during this period of 'direct action' and industrial conflict the *Daily Herald* under George Lansbury's editorship had a far greater influence than anything he had published before. A special relationship existed between the paper's readership and its editor and staff. In September 1919 the *Daily Herald* printed special editions in Manchester and Glasgow at considerable expense and was the only Fleet Street paper to support the railwaymen in their national strike.[2] In its promotion of 'direct action', the *Daily Herald* backed the Triple Alliance enthusiastically until its demise on 15 April 1921. 'Black Friday' produced the paper's lament on the failure of the railwaymen and the transport workers to support the miners:

Yesterday was the heaviest defeat that has befallen the Labour Movement within the memory of man. It is no use trying to minimise it. It is no use pretending that it is other than it is. We on this paper have said throughout that if the organised workers stood together they would win. They have not stood together and they have reaped the reward.[3]

---

[1] For an outstanding analysis of the British government's handling of post-war industrial unrest, see C. Wrigley, *Lloyd George and the Challenge of Labour: The Post-War Coalition, 1918–1922* (Hemel Hempstead, 1990). For the Triple Alliance, see P. Bagwell, 'The Triple Industrial Alliance 1913–1922', in A. Briggs and J. Saville (eds.), *Essays in Labour History, 1886–1923* (1971), pp. 96–128.
[2] Postgate, *Lansbury*, p. 197.   [3] *Daily Herald*, 16 Apr. 1921.

Nevertheless, even before 'Black Friday' not all the paper's activities were successful or, indeed, politically adroit. After the *Daily Herald* reported enthusiastic mass meetings of the police officers' union, some attended by its editor, the lightning police dispute in London, Liverpool, and Birmingham collapsed in disaster, and with victimization of individual strikers. Many of the 1,083 London policemen who were not reinstated were Poplar men. 'The least admirable chapter in the long and gallant story of the *Daily Herald*' was the verdict of police historians.[4]

In the following year, the *Daily Herald* carried a front-page story under the headline, 'Black Scourge in Europe: Sexual Horror Let Loose by France on the Rhine', written by E. D. Morel, secretary of the Union of Democratic Control, founder of the Congo Reform Association and later Labour MP. The article highlighted the French government's use of Black Moroccan troops in the occupation on the Rhine with lurid descriptions in prejudiced and racist language of rape, assault, and the spreading of disease. Morel's article was reprinted as a pamphlet and taken up by the left-wing press in this country and abroad. His sensationalized account was part of an international propaganda war that employed race as a weapon in international diplomacy.[5]

Claude McKay, a young Jamaican socialist poet and novelist, resident in London in 1919–21, complained directly to Lansbury about Morel's racist article. McKay's letter was eventually published in Sylvia Pankhurst's *Workers' Dreadnought*, after Lansbury claimed it was too long for the *Daily Herald*. McKay was then employed as a reporter by Sylvia Pankhurst, which resulted in his allegation—which she declined to publish in the *Worker's Dreadnought*—that scab labour was employed at the Lansbury family sawmill during an industrial dispute.[6]

Morel's offensive and racist article is a mystery in relation to Lansbury's editorship and has not been discussed by his biographers or the historian of the *Daily Herald*. However, Lansbury's policy was one of 'no censorship', and he often gave space to those he disagreed with. His anti-imperialism and commitment to nationalist causes in Ireland, India, and Egypt, particularly at this time, testifies that he was no racist. Bal Gangadhar Tilak was one of three prominent Indian nationalists to make contact with the British left, visiting the Labour party conference and the TUC during his visit to Britain in 1918–19 where he received active support from Lansbury and publication of his articles in the *Daily Herald*. Lansbury was a valuable political contact for Indian nationalists in bringing to British public attention their demand for Home Rule.[7]

[4] G. W. Reynolds and T. Judge, *The Night the Police Went on Strike* (1968), pp. 137, 149–50. See also A. V. Sellwood, *Police Strike, 1919* (1978), *passim*.

[5] *Daily Herald*, 10 Apr. 1920. See also E. D. Morel, 'The Employment of Black Troops', *Nation*, 27 Mar. 1920, p. 893; K. L. Nelson, 'The "Black Horror on the Rhine": Race as a Factor in Post-War I Diplomacy', *Journal of Modern History*, 42 (1970), pp. 606–27.

[6] For more on this episode, see R. C. Rheiners, 'Racialism on the Left: E. D. Morel and the "Black Horror on the Rhine"' *International Review of Social History*, 13 (1968), pp. 1–28.

[7] D. V. Tahmankar, *Lokamanya Tilak: Father of Indian Unrest and Maker of Modern India* (1956), pp. 281–3.

On 31 March 1919, as George Lansbury had always promised, after four-and-a-half years as a weekly, the *Daily Herald* had returned to a daily format. The relaunch was achieved with trade union financial support. Initially, sales were 200,000— rising to 400,000 during the 1919 national rail strike, as the paper spent £14,000 on ensuring its distribution throughout Britain during the dispute.

As Huw Richards has demonstrated, in addition to its coverage of domestic politics, the post-war *Daily Herald* had a stronger international outlook than in its earlier years.[8] Once more George Lansbury possessed a talented team of writers and loyal staff to produce the newspaper. Raymond Postgate, Oxford graduate, conscientious objector and close friend of the Marxist theorist, Rajane Palme Dutt, got his job on the paper as the foreign sub-editor—'he married the boss's daughter, Daisy'.[9] He was among the mainly middle-class revolutionaries on the *Daily Herald* staff who joined, or were associated with, the British Communist Party, founded in 1920.[10] Postgate later emphasized the influence of associate editor Gerald Gould— 'a minor poet, most of whose verse is now forgotten'—who was responsible for securing many of 'the young writers of his day', including Siegfried Sassoon ('Literary Notes'), Havelock Ellis ('reviewed books on sex'), Israel Zangwill, H. W. Nevinson, and Alec Waugh. Among the frequent contributors were Rebecca West, Aldous Huxley, Robert Graves, Walter de la Mare, and Osbert Sitwell.[11]

Besides these literary figures, from 1917 the eminent Labour journalist, H. N. Brailsford, was the most important of the *Daily Herald* correspondents reporting foreign news. His distinguished career also embraced the *Nation*, the *Manchester Guardian*, the *New Statesman*, and *Reynolds*. On the *Daily Herald*, he became a staunch opponent of British imperialism, the First World War, and the Versailles Treaty. As a committed suffragist, Brailsford had resigned as the principal leader-writer of the *Daily News* in 1909 over the forcible feeding of imprisoned suffragettes. In 1919 Brailsford undertook an extensive three-month tour of Central Europe, producing fourteen articles on the political situation in different European countries.[12]

Nevertheless, despite these developments in staffing and news coverage, George Lansbury claimed that the post-war *Daily Herald*, in certain respects, was more moderate in policy and tone, with fewer attacks on the official Labour leadership, than in the days preceding August 1914. As he declared: 'the Movement during the war had been very largely divided as to the support of the Government during the stormy years from 1914 to 1918, and it was felt that if both sides sat down and indulged in recriminations, only the possessing classes would triumph'.[13] While the *Daily Herald* contributed to the party debates on 'direct action' versus the

---

[8] Richards, *The Bloody Circus*, pp. 24–5. For the 1919 Railway Strike, see P. S. Bagwell, *The Railwaymen: The History of the National Union of Railwaymen* (1963), ch. 15.

[9] R. Postgate, 'A Socialist Remembers, 1', *New Statesman*, 9 Apr. 1971, p. 495.

[10] Ibid.; J. Postgate and M. Postgate, *A Stomach for Dissent: The Life of Raymond Postgate, 1896–1971* (Keele, 1994), p. 107.

[11] Postgate, *Lansbury*, pp. 186–7.

[12] For H. N. Brailsford, see F. M. Leventhal, *The Last Dissenter: H. N. Brailsford and His World* (1985).

[13] Lansbury, *Miracle of Fleet Street*, pp. 66–7.

parliamentary path, Lansbury spoke regularly at the post-war annual party conferences and normally topped the poll in elections for the National Executive Committee from 1920 onwards.

After the armistice in 1918, George Lansbury became more involved in international affairs. At the 1920 party conference he tried unsuccessfully to win Labour
delegates over to helping construct the new International.[14] In 1919 he had been one
of the many journalists who reported the peace conference from Paris. Lansbury
roundly condemned the punitive measures towards defeated Germany advocated
by the allied negotiators that he believed had lost the opportunity for a lasting
peace.[15] The *Daily Herald* carried probably the most famous and almost clairvoyant
Will Dyson cartoon called the 'Class of 1940'—the depiction of Lloyd George,
Clemenceau, and their acolytes with a child in the corner accompanied by the caption, 'Curious, I seem to hear a child crying.'[16] Lansbury's attendance in Paris also
afforded him the opportunity later to participate at the first post-war meeting of the
Second International held in Berne.[17]

Like many British Radicals, Lansbury pinned his hopes on the diplomacy of the
American President, Woodrow Wilson, as the best prospect for a 'peace without
victory'. Lansbury was now an important figure on the British political left and his
prominence as the editor of the *Daily Herald* and continued links with Mary Fels
(Joseph Fels had died in 1914) opened important doors in American politics. On
more than one occasion, Lansbury met Col. House, Woodrow Wilson's closest
adviser in foreign affairs who helped draft the Versailles Treaty and the covenant of
the League of Nations. Eventually the British Labour leader—as he was described to
Wilson—gained an interview with the American President on his return to European diplomacy. At Lansbury's direction the *Daily Herald* put its full weight behind
Wilson's 'Fourteen Points' peace proposals.[18] Lansbury wrote to him:

Your manifesto has given us all great hope; we have been watching the proceedings at Paris
with a great deal of anxiety this last three months. Rumours and reports of every sort and
kind are floating here—one day France is to occupy the Rhine valley, another day, Britain,
France and America are to form a new kind of Triple Alliance. But your manifesto seems to
all of us to blow these things sky-high into thin air and we are all trusting that at long last all
the Allied statesmen will come into line and join with you in creating the only sort of peace
which can be lasting.[19]

To ensure official Labour endorsement, Lansbury arranged for Arthur Henderson and others to wire Wilson, Clemenceau, and Lloyd George on the American
President's 'magnificent declaration for peace based on the fourteen points'.[20]

---

[14] Labour Party, *Report of the Twentieth Annual Conference* (1920).
[15] *Herald*, 25 Jan., 1, 15, 22 Feb., 1 Mar. 1919.
[16] Richards, *The Bloody Circus*, p. 24; McMullen, *Will Dyson*, pp. 210–12.
[17] *Daily Herald*, 15 Feb. 1919; Lansbury, *My Life*, pp. 217–21.   [18] *Daily Herald*, 26 Apr. 1919.
[19] George Lansbury to Woodrow Wilson, 11 Feb. 1919; Woodrow Wilson to George Lansbury, 14 Feb.
1919: cited in *The Papers of Woodrow Wilson*, ed. A. S. Link *et al.* (1988), pp. 87, 187.
[20] George Lansbury to Woodrow Wilson, 24 Apr. 1919; Woodrow Wilson to George Lansbury 1 May
1919, cited in *Papers of Woodrow Wilson*, ed. Link, pp. 93, 317.

However, only bitter disappointment lay ahead: Wilson's compromising stance during the peace-making and the punitive nature of the Versailles Treaty. Nearly ten years later, Lansbury devoted several pages in his autobiography to a denunciation of the failure of Lloyd George, Clemenceau, Wilson, and Orlando in Paris. He was clearly unable to contain his anger:

I came away from Germany and France more than ever convinced that the great men of our day were very puny, small-minded persons, that the few who possessed slightly more brain power and idealism than others lacked the moral courage to speak their minds and stand four square for what they believe.[21]

After the Versailles Treaty, George Lansbury's attention turned once more to Russia. Since 1917 Lansbury had attempted to counter the hostile attitude of the British government and press barons towards the revolutionary régime. In particular, as editor of the *Daily Herald*, he crusaded constantly against British armed intervention in Russia. As he put it: 'we took only one line—the Russian people should be left free to work out their own salvation'. After the Treaty of Brest Litovsk (March 1918), by which Russia made a separate peace with Germany that took her out of the First World War, Lansbury's paper was heavily criticized for its support of the Soviet government and promotion of Bolshevism in Britain.[22]

In early 1920, after British forces had been withdrawn from Murmansk and Archangel and the 'Reds v Whites' civil war appeared to be ending, George Lansbury decided to visit Russia. His nine-week tour was the first of two visits in the course of six years. In 1920 Lansbury was granted his British passport to visit Scandinavia to seek supplies of newsprint for his paper. He then crossed the Baltic to Finland, crossing into Russia at a time when there were no official diplomatic and commercial relations with Britain. He was so enthusiastic to observe a socialist government at work that he noted the time he first entered the country—at 4.50 p.m. on the afternoon of Thursday, 5 February 1920. Not surprisingly, Lansbury's Russian journey became well publicized, as he was the first newspaperman to broadcast from that country after the Russian Revolution.

Lansbury's activities were also monitored by the agents of Sir Basil Thomson, the Head of British Intelligence, and his messages telegraphed back to Britain were intercepted. Moreover, the authorities instructed the Marconi Wireless Telegraph Company that 'all telegrams handed in for transmission to Russia should be refused as communication with Soviet Russia is not permitted'. This led to Gerald Gould, in charge of the *Daily Herald* during Lansbury's absence, accusing the government of tampering with the communications. Also included in the official surveillance reports sent back to Britain were the texts of two Lansbury speeches delivered in Finland, as well as a translation of an article about his Russian experience published in *Politiken*.[23]

---

[21] Lansbury, *My Life*, pp. 211–20; see also *Daily Herald*, 8 May 1919.
[22] Lansbury, *Miracle of Fleet Street*, pp. 118–21.
[23] 'Message from *Daily Herald* to Lansbury, Moscow' file; Lord Acton to Lord Curzon, 4 Feb. 1920; 'Speech made by Mr. George Lansbury at a dinner given by Mrs Vuolijoki on Feb. 1, 1920'; 'Speech

George Lansbury was censured then, and in more recent times, as a Bolshevik fellow traveller who naïvely, and willingly, accepted what was shown and what he saw in Russia. He was impressed by the improvements in education and the Soviet treatment of women, as well as being prepared to excuse any shortcomings as the result of the war or the enemy blockade, rather than the nature of the régime.[24] He sent back reports on Soviet factories, co-operatives, labour organizations, the state of the churches, and other aspects of Soviet life.[25] Within weeks of his return, Lansbury had published a full account of his experiences in Russia.[26] As in the case of others who travelled to that country, he met a number of the leading Bolsheviks including, on his sixty-first birthday, the fifty-year-old Lenin. Though the Christian Socialist and atheist revolutionary disagreed over religion, pacifism, and politics, Lansbury was clearly impressed by Lenin's revolutionary vision and the simple lifestyle he led in the Kremlin. Lansbury judged him:

symbolic of a new spirit. He is in very deed a father of his people—a father who toils for them, thinks for them, acts for them, suffers with them, and is ready to stand in danger or in safety struggling on their behalf. Tens of thousands of men and women love him and would die for him because he is their comrade, their champion in the cause of social and economic freedom.[27]

In Russia, Lansbury and Lenin had differed as to how political change could be achieved in society. Lenin rejected Lansbury's pacifism and the possibility that capitalism could be peacefully replaced by socialism. On his return to Britain, Lansbury addressed a large rally at the Albert Hall on 22 March 1919 on the political situation in Russia and read out a message from Lenin:

If you can bring about peaceful revolution in England, no one will be better pleased than we in Russia. Keep in your trade union movement. Don't divide until you have to divide. Don't become disintegrated by premature strikes or premature upheavals. Keep together till you are homogenous and do not be led into resorting to violence.[28]

At this packed gathering George Lansbury denied that the *Daily Herald* was financed by money from abroad—a public rebuttal of incessant rumours that circulated in Britain about the sinister influence of foreign funding in the affairs of the Labour daily. Such stories surrounding George Lansbury and the *Daily Herald* illustrate the hysteria and anti-Communist propaganda that existed in governing circles following the Russian Revolution. As George Lansbury later put it: '[M]any

---

Delivered By Mr Lansbury To the Social Democratic Faction of the Finnish Diet Feb. 2, 1920'; 'Translation of article by Mr George Lansbury of Mar. 11, 1920 published in the "Politiken" of Mar. 13, 1920', PRO, FO 371/4045/41703.

[24] For a recent critical view of Lansbury's tour of Russia, see F. M. Leventhal, 'Seeing the Future: British Left-Wing Travellers to the Soviet Union, 1919–32', in J. M. W. Bean (ed.), *The Political Culture of Modern Britain: Studies in Memory of Stephen Koss* (1987), pp. 212–13.

[25] For examples of Lansbury's reports from Russia, see *Daily Herald*, 10, 16, 17, 19, 21, 23, 24 Feb., 3, 8, 10 Mar. 1920.

[26] G. Lansbury, *What I Saw in Russia* (1920).   [27] Ibid. p. 28.

[28] 'George Lansbury at the Royal Albert Hall on Sunday, Mar. 21st on his return from Soviet Russia', copy of programme with Catherine Marshall's notes, Catherine Marshall Papers.

a true and many an untrue story has been told about the *Daily Herald* and its relationship with Russia and the Bolsheviks.'[29]

The Polish–Russian War now took centre-stage in the next weeks and months in the 'Hands off Russia' campaign. In May 1920, in one of the most famous incidents of 'direct action' in British history, East End dockers refused to load the SS *Jolly George* bound for Poland with war munitions.[30] By August, when the Russian armies had almost reached Warsaw, and the possibility of British armed intervention on the side of Poland seemed highly likely, the *Daily Herald* brought out a special Sunday issue. Its streamer headline exclaimed: 'NOT A MAN, NOT A GUN, NOT A SOU'.[31] A joint meeting of the PLP, the NEC, and the TUC formed a national Council of Action to take any necessary steps—including a general strike—to prevent another war. George Lansbury became a central figure on the Council of Action composed of a remarkable cross-section of the political spectrum in Britain. The influence of the *Daily Herald*, which encouraged the formation of hundreds of local councils of action in Britain, was now at its zenith under his editorship. In East London the 'Hands off Russia' campaign brought together different groups on the political left, including Sylvia Pankhurst's Workers' Socialist Federation, an important force later in the Poplar Rates Dispute.[32] In a rallying call for socialist unity, Lansbury declared:

> In some cases it may be we shall discover that it is best to use the present organizations or elect a committee from these. In any case, we have local and central Labour Parties and trade councils, together with the ILP and the new Communist Party, who must take the lead. We must make our local committees as inclusive as possible. All who are not against us are with us in this matter, and we need the assistance of every man and woman of goodwill who sincerely desires the same ends as ourselves.[33]

As Postgate claimed, even at three times the *Daily Herald*'s creditable circulation figure of 329,869, the *Daily Mail* 'could not have brought out a single brickworks on strike, nor altered a by-election in one industrial town'.[34]

By 10 August the *Daily Herald*'s militant role in the 'Hands off Russia' campaign had compelled Lloyd George to back down and declare that Britain was not going to war. However, it was not the first time that the Labour newspaper had attracted the attention of the British authorities for its political campaigning. For some time it had been the subject of intelligence surveillance, as the Lloyd George coalition government monitored radical movements in the wake of the Russian Revolution. With political instability in Europe, the British authorities attempted to stop the *Daily Herald* reaching British troops in Germany. On 13 May 1919 the War Office had sent a secret circular to British commanding officers—asking about any

---

[29] Lansbury, *Miracle of Fleet Street*, p. 109.
[30] *Daily Herald*, 11 May 1920. For the 'Hands off Russia' Campaign, see S. White, 'Labour's Council of Action, 1920', *Journal of Contemporary History*, 9 (1974), pp. 99–122; L. J. MacFarlane, 'Hands off Russia: British Labour and the Russo-Polish War, 1920', *Past and Present*, 38 (1967), pp. 126–52.
[31] *Daily Herald*, 8 Aug. 1920.
[32] J. Klugman, *History of the Communist Party of Great Britain*, i, *1919–1924* (1961), p. 79.
[33] *The Times*, 16 Aug. 1920.   [34] Postgate, *Lansbury*, pp. 209–10.

incipient trade unionism and the likely mood of their troops if used to break strikes
or ordered to fight in Russia—which, remarkably, came into Lansbury's possession. To the government's annoyance, he published it and a few weeks later
reprinted another leaked official memorandum that ordered the seizure and
burning of bundles of the *Daily Herald* at European railheads. On this occasion,
Osbert Sitwell penned the *Daily Herald*'s response in a free-verse leader of 126 lines,
beginning:

> The *Daily Herald*
> Is Unkind.
> It has been horrid
> About my nice new war.
> I shall burn the *Daily Herald*.[35]

The *Daily Herald* leader made a direct attack on the Secretary of State for War
and Air, Winston Churchill. Churchill was closely associated with Lloyd George in
the allied intervention in the Russian Civil War that attempted to overthrow the
new régime. As David Stafford has written, the *Daily Herald* had been a consistent
thorn in Churchill's side before and during the First World War. It had attacked his
use of the military in industrial disputes, the Dardanelles Expedition, and his
truculent anti-Bolshevism. In 1919, in an article entitled 'Plots against Labour, War
Office organises wide secret service', the left-wing newspaper added further condemnation, citing the Minister for War and Air's counter-espionage within the
British labour movement.[36]

In these post-war years the *Daily Herald* had also been a chief supporter of the
Soldiers', Sailors' and Airmen's Union (SSAU), a recently formed organization of
army veterans and servicemen, considered by British intelligence as a likely source
of subversion during any unrest in the armed forces. From early 1919, the SSAU
endeavoured to recruit returning soldiers for the Labour cause at the expense of
rival groups, such as the National Federation of Discharged and Demobilised
Sailors and Soldiers and the Comrades of the Great War, from which the 'non-
political British Legion' eventually emerged. The radical SSAU campaigned for
union recognition in the armed forces, increased pensions, and no use of troops in
strike-breaking. With the direct help of the *Daily Herald*, which published the
'Army form B 2512A', the SSAU pressed on 11 May 1919 for demobilization of those
serving soldiers who had signed the form and attested their willingness to serve
under the 1915 Derby scheme.[37] This kind of political activity confirmed suspicions
in governing circles that the *Daily Herald* was a subversive paper and, in particular,
earned George Lansbury the bitter enmity of Winston Churchill.[38]

---

[35] Lansbury, *Miracle of Fleet Street*, pp. 123–6.

[36] D. Stafford, *Churchill and the Secret Service* (1997), pp. 90–8.

[37] S. R. Ward, 'Intelligence Surveillance of British Ex-Servicemen, 1918–1920', *Historical Journal*, 16
(1973), pp. 179–88; D. Englander, 'Troops and Trade Unions, 1919', *History Today* (1987), pp. 8–13.

[38] The *Daily Herald* consistently reported the troubled political situation in Ireland, including the rise
of the 'Black and Tans' and the hunger strike that resulted in the death of the Lord Mayor of Cork in
Brixton Prison. For the MacSwiney case, see *Daily Herald*, 23 Aug., 20, 26, 29 Oct. 1920.

By 1920, Lansbury's public sympathies and public association with the new Bolshevik régime provided Churchill with a political opening to strike back, when Lansbury was accused of sedition among British troops in Russia. Churchill specifically instructed M.I.5 to gather information about his activities that would publicly discredit him. 'My object is to secure in one document the complete statement of the case against Mr. Lansbury' was Churchill's note at the end of the official file.[39]

This was not the only attempt to compromise Lansbury through his Russian connections. On 19 August 1920 various British newspapers, but not the *Daily Herald*, received from the British government the details of eight intercepted telegrams between Tchitcherin and Litvinov concerning the feasibility of a subsidy to save the ailing socialist newspaper. Lansbury had journeyed to Scandinavia and then on to Russia for credit facilities to obtain desperately needed supplies of newsprint. Despite the government's published version of events, the editor of the *Daily Herald* wanted a commercial arrangement with Soviet Russia rather than political connections and finance.

On 20 August Lansbury replied to the allegations of foreign dealings by publishing a full list of the paper's directors and debenture holders. It was part of a famous rebuttal—contained under the headline: 'NOT A BOND, NOT A FRANC, NOT A ROUBLE'—accompanied by Lansbury's firm denial: 'We have received no Bolshevist money, no Bolshevist paper, no Chinese bonds.'[40]

Yet, unknown to Lansbury, the youngest *Daily Herald* director, Francis Meynell, had been smuggling Russian money into Britain—at the time of the Krassin–Kameneff trade delegation to this country.[41] Meynell's most celebrated clandestine enterprise took the form of hidden Russian jewels posted back to Britain to the philosopher, Cyril Joad, in a box of chocolate creams. A few months later, in his own newspaper, an unabashed Meynell revealed how he had tricked Thomson and the British Secret Service over the chocolate diamonds and eventually gorged himself in retrieving them.[42] However, these machinations not only brought Meynell's resignation as a director, but also directly implicated the editor's own family in the affair. In London the police interviewed Edgar Lansbury after he had used connections in the jewellery trade to convert the smuggled diamonds and pearls into £75,000—in the form of a British War Loan. The money was offered to the *Daily Herald* to help it survive as a penny paper, only to be rejected after his father publicly consulted the readership.[43] On its front page the *Daily Herald* asked the question: 'Shall we accept £75,000 of Russian money?'[44] The whole business—with *The Times* fulminating about 'Bolshevist Gold'—was regarded as a body-blow to the prospects of the Labour party.[45] A chastened George Lansbury later

---

[39] 'P.S. to S of S; Secretary DMI, minutes 19, 21 & 24, 31 July 1920 & 5 Aug. 1920', PRO, WO 32/5719/53317.

[40] *The Times*, 20 Aug. 1920.   [41] Ibid. 16 Sept. 1920.

[42] *Communist*, 12 Feb. 1921. See also C. Andrew, *Secret Service: The Making of the British Intelligence Service* (1992), pp. 378–9.

[43] Lansbury, *Miracle of Fleet Street*, pp. 149–50.   [44] *Daily Herald*, 10 Sept. 1920.

[45] *The Times*, 11 Sept. 1920.

admitted to Beatrice Webb his ignorance of the secret dealing and his distress at Edgar's involvement.[46]

As we have seen, there were also public allegations that George Lansbury had endeavoured to incite British troops to mutiny during his stay in Russia. These were based on military intelligence from British officers about the meetings with British prisoners of war in Moscow but, on investigation, the evidence was very uncertain. Instead, M.I.5 thought about leaking material to one or two popular newspapers, if Lansbury could not be prosecuted.[47] On his return to Britain, Lansbury had denied the allegations but was challenged to a public debate about what had happened in Russia.[48] An old enemy, Horatio Bottomley MP, campaigned in his paper, *John Bull*, for Lansbury to be dispatched to the Tower of London over his Russian activities and asked questions in Parliament without success.[49] In 1920 no government action was taken to prosecute the mayor of Poplar, who had been released temporarily from official duties in East London to visit Russia. Instead, in 1921, George Lansbury found himself in prison once again—this time as a result of municipal politics in East London.

[46] B. Webb, Diary, 17 Sept., 5 Oct. 1920, PP. See also *Diary of Beatrice Webb*, iii, ed. Mackenzie and Mackenzie, pp. 367–8.

[47] Maj. Ball to DMI, minute 26, 23 Aug. 1920, PRO, WO 32/5719/53317.

[48] For George Lansbury's letter, see *The Times*, 26 May 1920. See also ibid. 17, 27 May, 1, 14 June, 3 July 1920.

[49] *John Bull*, 14, 28 Aug., 4, 11, 18 Sept. 1920; 'Parliamentary Question: Mr Bottomley', 30 Oct.; 3 Dec. 1920, PRO, FO 371/5445/14086.

11
'Poplarism', 1921–1928

On 29 July 1921, preceded by a drum-and-fife band, George Lansbury and twenty-nine Labour councillors—including Charlie Sumner, the deputy mayor, with mace-bearer—headed a procession of over two thousand supporters the five miles from Poplar town hall to the Law Courts. Among the various banners, carried to explain their case to thousands of spectators lining the route, the largest one on that historic march proclaimed proudly and in defiance: 'POPLAR BOROUGH COUNCIL, MARCHING TO THE HIGH COURT, AND POSSIBLY TO PRISON, TO SECURE THE EQUALISATION OF RATES FOR POOR BOROUGHS'.[1]

It was a splendid and dramatic piece of street theatre, typical of the many public scenes orchestrated in subsequent weeks that heralded the famous Poplar Rates Rebellion of 1921. George Lansbury and his fellow Poplar councillors—including Edgar and Minnie Lansbury—willingly spent six weeks in prison to defend their East End community. As part of 'The Long March of Labour', Poplar's elected representatives journeyed more than five miles that day, as their cause, an expression of popular direct action of the post-First World War years, became etched deeply in the collective memory of the Labour movement.

As the symbol of local democracy in defiance of central authority, the memory of the events of 1921 can still touch a proletarian chord today when local councils and Whitehall are in conflict. The term 'Poplarism' itself—defined since 1921 as the policy of giving out-relief on a generous or extravagant scale by the Board of Guardians—rapidly entered the political vocabulary in Britain. Some early examples of its use illustrate the fame or notoriety accorded to the Poplar councillors' action in different quarters. In 1922 the *Glasgow Herald* declared that 'the hard-headed workers of Yorkshire . . . have learned the lesson of Poplarism'. In 1928 the *Daily Telegraph* complained of 'Those . . . will demand increased subsidies, allowances and "Poplarised" social services, to be paid out of the proceeds of very high taxation'. By 1931 *The Times* could remark that 'the chief issue of the election is whether or not the policy of "Poplarism" advocated by the Labour-Socialist party is to be applied to London government'.[2]

Though no longer mayor of Poplar (having served his mayoralty in 1919–20), George Lansbury is always remembered as the chief advocate of 'Poplarism' and this reputation remained with him for the rest of his political life and beyond. Half

---

[1] *Daily Herald*, 30 July 1921. Sam March, the mayor, who was unwell, journeyed to the High Court by taxi. I am grateful to Chris Sumner for informing me that his grandfather led the historic march from the East India Dock Road.

[2] *The Shorter Oxford English Dictionary* provides these examples of 'Poplarism' in the English language.

a century later, Harold Wilson, one of his successors as Labour party leader, recalled how the seventy-year-old Lansbury was offered the one Cabinet post in the second Labour government of 1929–31 where it was considered he could do the least damage: 'It was all done by agreement, [Philip] Snowden recording that, as George Lansbury had to be found a job, despite his "Poplarist" reputation, it was he who suggested Lansbury for the Office of Works.'[3]

The specific origins of the East London councillors' defiance of central authority can be traced back to the early 1890s when George Lansbury and his fellow Labour and Socialist guardians—though in a minority—paid out generous poor law provision. As we have seen, their assault on the Victorian poor law eventually earned the stern disapproval of John Burns and his LGB officials. However, it is the dramatic events of 1921 that have entered and remained in the folklore of Labour history.

In British political and labour history, the Poplar Rates Rebellion was part of a plebeian and democratic tradition of extra-parliamentary radical protest which had continued from the eighteenth and nineteenth centuries. It represented an example of 'direct action' that was evident in Britain in the waves of working-class militancy and social unrest in the immediate post-First World War period as Britain returned to an uneasy peace in 1919 after four years of international conflict. 'Poplarism' has taken its place alongside earlier heroic episodes, such as the Tolpuddle Martyrs, the Newport Chartist Uprising, the London Dock Strike, 'the Revolt on the Clyde', and the 'Hands off Russia!' campaign.[4] The period 1919–21 was one of considerable political and industrial turbulence, when two subjects—'direct action' and Bolshevik Russia—dominated the columns of the *Daily Herald* and brought George Lansbury and his left-wing journal to the continued attention of the authorities.

In November 1919, in the local council elections, the Labour party had swept to power throughout East London and elsewhere, gaining control of twelve out of the twenty-eight metropolitan borough councils. In Poplar, there was a remarkable result: thirty-nine out of the forty-two Labour candidates were returned in the borough council election. In nearby Stepney forty of the sixty Labour candidates were successful and twenty-four of the twenty-eight in Bethnal Green. These victories were not confined to London. There were also significant increases in the number of Labour councillors in different parts of Britain. Labour gained control in the counties of Durham, Monmouthshire, and Glamorgan, and in the City of Bradford.[5] Since the 1918 general election and the Westminster victory of the Lloyd George coalition there had been a remarkable transformation in Labour fortunes. A year later, 'Labour Knocks 'Em In The Old Kent Road' was the *Daily Herald* headline that trumpeted the transfer of power in many town halls in the capital. In

  [3] H. Wilson, *Governance of Britain* (1976), p. 29.
  [4] For more on 'direct action', see R. Benewick and T. Smith (eds.), *Direct Action and Democratic Politics* (1972).
  [5] L. Baston, 'Labour Local Government, 1900–1999', in B. Brivati and R. Heffernan (eds.), *The Labour Party: A Centenary History* (2000), pp. 451–2.

glowing terms, the secretary of the London Labour Party, Herbert Morrison, thanked the *Daily Herald* for its sterling contribution to the Labour victory:

London Labour has achieved stupendous successes . . . [T]his election has proved the enormous value of a Labour daily newspaper in political organisation no less than in the industrial crises which faced organised Labour from time to time. We were able, through your columns, to record daily the progress of the fight, and mobilise the support of the great army of DAILY HERALD readers in London. The DAILY HERALD has helped us magnificently in this great struggle, and has contributed materially to the fine result.[6]

In East London, George Lansbury became the first mayor of the Labour-controlled Metropolitan Borough of Poplar. In a characteristic break with mayoral tradition, on 10 November 1919 at the age of sixty he took office 'without robes, mace or cocked hat'. This was more than a symbolic gesture—Labour's hold on Poplar town hall now meant real political change. George Lansbury made this point clearly and publicly: 'Labour councillors must be different from those we have displaced or why displace them? Our policy is that quite revolutionary one of using *all* the powers Parliament has given us in order to serve the commonweal.'[7]

George Lansbury also did not hide the implications of Labour rule in local government in Poplar. He readily admitted that Labour administration would require higher rates as the policy intended to provide welfare benefits for the unemployed and the sick. He acknowledged: '[t]his will cost money. We have never disputed the fact, and it is no reason for hesitancy . . .'[8]

Critics of Poplarism soon abounded in the London capitalist press which, in the course of the coming weeks and months, was to use terms such as 'Poplar Finance', 'Poplar Methods', as well as the sound-bite 'Poplarism' to denote municipal extravagance by local social administrators. As the Borough Council carried out its policies, George Lansbury also faced opposition to 'the kind of Poplar method of administration' from the official Labour leadership, concerned that the growth of expenditure would damage Labour's prospects of taking office as a party 'fit to govern'.

In 1925 local schoolmaster Charles Key, deputy mayor in 1921, published his account of the Poplar Rates Rebellion, which provided an opportunity to chronicle the work completed in East London during six years of socialist local government. In 1919 Poplar faced acute social problems: overcrowded and unsanitary housing, numerous slum areas, poor social services and amenities, as well as the scourge of unemployment, casual working, and destitution. The plight of post-war Poplar inherited by the incoming Labour régime was easily illustrated. The average rate of infant mortality remained high: the figure of 124 per thousand births had been recorded in the pre-war period. In 1919 the only municipal amenities for washing clothes had been forty washing-stalls at Roman Road and East India Dock Road. As Lansbury and his fellow councillors pointed out, the only class in Poplar was the working class. Poplar employers, shopkeepers, and even some clergy mostly lived outside the borough.

---

[6] *Daily Herald*, 4 Nov. 1919.   [7] Ibid. 13 Dec. 1919.   [8] Ibid.

By the time of the Poplar Rates Rebellion, the Labour Council could claim that substantial inroads had been made into the various urban and social problems it had inherited. As mayor, Lansbury represented Poplar at a conference of local authorities of Greater London held in the Council Chamber of the Guildhall on milk and coal supplies. With Clem Attlee, mayor of Stepney, he later led a large deputation to see the Prime Minister at Downing Street to raise the issue.[9] In Poplar an active public health programme of improved local services brought about a reduction of the infant mortality rate to 60 in a thousand (by 1923). To launch the municipal house-building programme, on 13 January 1920, a jovial George Lansbury, spade in hand, cut the first turf on the Chapel House Street estate of 120 properties—'a garden city' in the making on the Isle of Dogs.[10]

Few municipal stones were left unturned: baths and wash-house facilities were greatly expanded, the borough library service extended and necessary improvements to the local Electricity Undertaking carried out. Progress was also made on other parts of the council's programme—unemployment relief works, street repairs, and better refuse disposal.[11] A host of environmental improvements initiated during Lansbury's mayoralty, including socials at the town hall and extensive tree-planting around urban Poplar, were long remembered by the residents.[12] However, the Labour councillors had a greater enterprise in mind. They intended to use their municipal powers to extend their remit beyond a more efficient delivery of local services to influence and control the local economy, employment, and wages.

In this sphere of municipal policy, one set of Labour measures caused particular public controversy before the famous rate dispute arose. In 1920, after negotiations with local trade unions, the Borough Council introduced its £4 minimum wage for municipal employees whose pre-war wage had been 30 shillings a week. As a significant part of the package, equal pay was given to women doing similar work. The result was that the male employees such as dustmen, road-sweepers, and sewerage workers gained a 25 per cent rise. Women workers, including seven lavatory attendants and twenty-six bath and wash-house attendants, received an increase of nearly 70 per cent. Moreover, the treatment of its council workers had first stirred up a civic rumpus when the vehicle workers' 4 shilling war bonus had been extended to all other employees who joined a trade union.[13]

What was happening in Poplar was more than the local council acting merely as an arm of central government. Once in power, new Labour authorities in the post-First World War years tried new approaches to extending and delivering municipal services. In Poplar achieving fundamental change was what Lansbury and his socialist colleagues had firmly in mind. The Labour Borough Council believed it

---

[9] Metropolitan Borough of Poplar, 'Deputation to the Prime Minister of Local Authorities of Greater London on the Question of the Supply, Price and Distribution of Milk and of Coal', copy in LP, vol. 8, fos. 87–92.

[10] R. Taylor and C. Lloyd, *Britain in Old Photographs: Stepney, Bethnal Green and Poplar* (1995), p. 152.

[11] C. W. Key, *Red Poplar: Six Years of Socialist Rule* (1925), *passim*.

[12] J. Blake, *Memories of Old Poplar* (1977), p. 38.   [13] Branson, *Poplarism*, pp. 21–2.

could directly influence local wages and conditions by the policies it pursued as an important municipal employer of labour. By extending Labour's role in local government, the outcome was a challenge to a minimalist central government and the gradualist philosophy of the national Labour leadership. As George Lansbury explained:

It will be argued that to adopt any such programme will make municipal workers a privileged class. This is so, but it is much too late to complain about this, because long years ago the Labour Movement decided that whenever it got into power the conditions of municipal labour should be such as to attract the best people, and to set an example to other employers. There can be no possible doubt about the effect of this policy. Every step forward taken by organised Labour in its fight for better conditions has been preceded by a struggle, and in many places a victory, for a higher standard of work and wages under municipal and other authorities.[14]

Lansbury made clear that this policy of high wages was not the distribution of municipal largesse but required the very best contractual work in return. As he put it: 'Our motto should be: "No rights or privileges without duties".'[15] Despite the mounting public criticism and allegations of municipal extravagance, according to George Lansbury, there would be no 'dependency culture' in Poplar in the 1920s.

Moreover, 'Red Poplar' with a high percentage of casual workers, especially among the dockers and transport workers, soon faced the problem of mass unemployment as the post-war boom turned into a serious depression in the mid-1920s. Although mass unemployment was a national problem, created by world economic conditions, each borough was considered responsible for maintaining its own destitute and unemployed. In 1921 the national figure of registered unemployed reached 1 million. In Poplar 15,574 persons were unemployed. This was out of a population of 160,000 men, women, and children, of whom a quarter lived below the official poverty-line. According to George Lansbury, in coping with increased numbers of unemployed, 'work or full maintenance' was the central tenet of Labour policy, with a central role for boards of guardians using outdoor relief. He argued passionately that those out of work under capitalism had a right to demand 'full and adequate maintenance'. In an attempt to mobilize the unemployed in a national campaign, he wrote:

there is no more disgrace in a working man getting a £1 a week from a board of guardians than from a Labour Exchange. Lord George Hamilton and Lord Henry Chaplin have received a good many out-of-work doles of about £20 a week and no one thinks them anything but highly moral and respectable people.[16]

A few days before Christmas 1920, in his 'Go to the Guardians' campaign to highlight recalcitrant local guardians, Lansbury strongly advised those out of work: 'Where Boards of Guardians refuse outside assistance all single men and married men should go into the workhouse.'[17]

---

[14] *Daily Herald*, 13 Dec. 1919.   [15] Ibid. *loc. cit.*
[16] Ibid. 4 Dec. 1920.   [17] Ibid. 18 Dec. 1920.

The main political objective of George Lansbury and his fellow Labour council-lors was to wage class war on the lack of equity in the unreformed rating system in London where the greater burden fell on the poorer boroughs of the East End. There was a considerable difference between the wealthier boroughs in West Lon-don and the poorer ones in East London. In 1921 a 1d. rate in Westminster raised £29,000, but only £3,200 in Poplar. A similar comparison revealed that in West-minster the rates were 11s. 2d. in the pound, whereas Poplar ratepayers paid 22s. 10d. in the pound. The Poplar Borough Council was also required to raise its contribu-tion, known as 'precepts', that were due to the various central authorities, namely: the London County Council, the Metropolitan Asylums Board, the Metropolitan Water Board, and the Metropolitan Police. Equalization of the rates across the twenty-eight boroughs of the County of London was therefore a long-standing demand by the Labour movement.

On 22 March the Council, faced with an increased bill of 28 per cent that required a rate of 27s. 3d. in the pound, passed the following resolution: 'That the precepts for the London County Council, the Metropolitan Police, the Metropol-itan Water Board be deleted, and that the estimates as amended be referred to the Valuation and Rating Committee to ascertain the rate in the pound necessary to be levied.'

On 31 March Poplar Council therefore decided to levy a rate of 4s. 4d. in the pound for only the quarter-year for the purposes of the Borough Council and the Poplar Board of Guardians. What this meant was that the Council refused to levy the precept rates for the LCC, the LCC Asylums Board, the Metropolitan Water Board, and the Metropolitan Police. This action was adopted after the failure dur-ing the previous fifteen months to secure the equalization of the rates in London by direct appeals to Parliament and to the central government.

Thus, by refusing to raise these precepts, the Poplar Borough Council deliber-ately provoked the legal action by those central bodies that led to the High Court proceedings and the eventual imprisonment of the thirty councillors for contempt of court. What was the origin of this illegal strategy, once constitutional routes had been exhausted? In the debates on 'direct action' two years before, the pacifist George Lansbury had laid down his right to withhold labour as a protest:

Shall we meet force by force? Speaking for myself, I say no. Let us meet it by the power before which all tyrants tremble—passive resistance, the General Strike.

The Poplar Rate Rebellion was an attempt to put the principles of passive resis-tance to work in municipal politics in defence of an embattled local community.[18] From the outset, the Poplar councillors realized they could not win a legal battle. On 20 June the High Court decided that a writ of *mandamus* should be issued following an application from the LCC to enforce payment.

On 29 July, under the front-page headline 'RATE DRAMA IN HIGH COURT TODAY', the *Daily Herald* reported that: 'Today at 10 a.m. in the High Court of Justice the

---

[18] Ibid. 28 June 1919.

members of the Labour Council of Poplar will appear before His Majesty's judge to show cause why their persons should not be attached . . . officially they are charged with failing to pay the precepts of the London County Council'.

After the failure of an appeal, held in a special sitting after Lansbury had pressed the matter, the members of the Council had been summoned on 29 July 1921 to answer the writ of *mandamus* at the High Court. Writs of attachment were then ordered which on 1 September led to the arrests of the mayor and four councillors, with further arrests on succeeding days.[19]

Since 1921 the 'Poplar Story' itself has attracted the interest of historians, politicians, journalists, and playwrights and has inspired a number of accounts, contemporary and modern, about the Labour councillors, their direct challenge to central government and popular reaction among the residents of the East End.[20] During the confrontation between the Poplar Borough Council and the authorities, George Lansbury and his fellow councillors mobilized popular support on the streets of East London, similar to the scenes witnessed during the escapades of Sylvia Pankhurst and the ELFS. In 1921 the action of the Poplar councillors brought cinematic film cameras to the East End streets and, as noted, provided the *Daily Herald* with one of its most famous campaigns in the early 1920s.

Thirty years later, on the eleventh anniversary of her father's death, Annie Lansbury recounted the 'Poplar Story', and the dramatic scenes during the arrest of the councillors, in understandably heroic terms:

September 1 was the date fixed for arresting the councillors. At five in the afternoon the mayor and four other councillors were arrested.

As the news spread round the borough, crowds poured into the streets. The people themselves posted guards at the house of the 27 other councillors threatened with arrest, and announced that they would permit no arrests after dusk.[21]

As arrests followed, day after day, feelings grew intense. On the day when the women councillors were taken, the streets were so densely packed with protesting people that those who had assembled in Poplar town hall for a meeting were for some time unable to get out.

Trade Union banners were brought out, a band appeared, and the women councillors were triumphantly escorted to the borough boundary. Next day 15,000 people marched to Holloway Gaol to cheer the women prisoners.[22]

As Annie Lansbury recalled, the street spectacle of 'Poplarism' reached its pinnacle with the public arrest of the five women councillors—Nellie Cressall, Minnie Lansbury, Susan Lawrence, Jennie Mackay, and Julia Scurr—at the Poplar town

[19] Key, *Red Poplar*, pp. 17–19.
[20] The main account of the Poplar Rates Rebellion is Branson, *Poplarism*, but see also P. Ryan, '"Poplarism", 1894–1930 in P. Thane (ed.), The Origins of British Social Policy (1978), pp. 56–83. 'The Poplar Story' reached the stage in B. Keefe, *Better Times: A Play* (1985). See also J. Shepherd, 'Poverty and Poplar Rebellion', *B.B.C History Magazine* (Oct. 2001), pp. 20–22.
[21] *Daily Worker*, 7 May 1951.   [22] Ibid.

hall at 3 p.m. on 6 September. The day before, Minnie Lansbury had challenged critical press coverage of the dispute:

We have taken every ordinary course open to us in the processes of the law, and not a few extraordinary (*sic*); we have employed the most skilful legal aid; and we have appeared in Court after Court precisely to have our action vindicated and to avoid going to gaol. The only step we have not taken, and will not take, is to leave 12,000 unemployed people to starve—for that is the alternative.[23]

On the day of their arrest, an equally defiant Susan Lawrence arrived at the town hall from Cardiff an hour early to meet the sheriff's officer. To the large crowd of her supporters she declared: 'I am going if I have to walk all the way to Holloway. We are here representing a principle which we have a right to defend as well as the men.'[24]

However, 'Poplarism' had its opponents, as well as its supporters. In addition to the Lloyd George Coalition government, a hostile press, and the Poplar Borough Municipal Alliance in East London, 'Poplarism' brought George Lansbury and his colleagues into direct conflict with the leadership of the Labour party. The moderate Ramsay MacDonald would have no truck with the unconstitutional methods of a Labour local authority. J. H. Thomas underlined the point that illegal action, such as a rates rebellion, could seriously damage Labour prospects as a party of government.[25]

MacDonald endeavoured to reassure those who feared this particular socialist bogey: 'It cannot be over-emphasized that public doles, Poplarism, strikes for increased wages, limitation of output, not only are not Socialism, but may mislead the spirit and policy of the Socialist movement.'[26]

The fundamental differences between Lansbury and MacDonald over 'Poplarism' revealed a direct clash of socialist faiths and methodologies—the revolutionary versus the evolutionary—that had surfaced earlier in 1911 over the National Insurance Bill. The Rates Dispute provided the Labour councillors with the opportunity to demonstrate socialism in action. While MacDonald and other Labour leaders strove to demonstrate that their respectability and moderation made them fit to hold high office, the populist Lansbury envisaged a different type of Labour party, pledged to replace capitalism and imperialism with socialism:

Sooner or later the Labour Party must face all the implications of administrative responsibility. The workers must be given tangible proof that Labour administration means something different from Capitalist administration, and in a nutshell this means diverting wealth from wealthy ratepayers to the poor. Those who pretend that a sound Labour policy can be pursued nationally or locally without making the rich poorer should find another party.[27]

Powerful opposition also came from Herbert Morrison who looked with disdain

---

[23] *The Times*, 5 Sept. 1921.   [24] Ibid. 6 Sept. 1921.
[25] J. H. Thomas's remark was quoted by George Lansbury in 'Poplar and the Labour Party: A Defence of Poplarism', *Labour Monthly* (June 1922), p. 383.
[26] J. R. MacDonald, *Socialism: Critical and Constructive* (1924 [*c*.1921] edition), p. vii.
[27] Lansbury, 'Poplar and the Labour Party', p. 388.

at the public spectacle that took place in nearby Poplar during his mayoralty in Hackney.[28] Moreover, such independent action by the Poplar councillors, who sought help in Stepney, Woolwich, and Bermondsey, threatened the electoral machine Morrison was building as secretary of the London Labour Party. Morrison feared that direct defiance of the law opened up the possibility of the central government appointing commissioners to run the Borough Council's business. He later recalled that:

The London Labour Party Executive did not feel able to advise other Labour boroughs to follow the Poplar Council, and I found myself in a row at the next annual conference of the Party, with John Scurr running against me for the secretaryship and Major C. R. Attlee . . . delivering at me a needle-pointed and rather superior lecture, in the manner of major to private.[29]

Not surprisingly, Morrison co-operated with other local Labour leaders to end the Poplar dispute and to secure the release of the Poplar councillors from prison to attend the Whitehall conference convened by the Minister of Health, Sir Alfred Mond, to seek a settlement.[30]

In East London, as anticipated, there was a hostile reaction from the PBMA of local employers, shopkeepers, and opposition politicians concerned about the rise of municipal socialism in the East End. As we have seen, the Municipal Alliance had secured the appointment of the Davy Local Government Board Inquiry into the local administration in the pre-war era. The Alliance was well organized with committees in each of Poplar's fourteen wards and fought local elections—though with a singular lack of success.[31]

The Representation of the People Act of 1918 had removed the disqualification of paupers from voting in municipal and parliamentary elections. As a result, this group played an important part in local contests, as guardians usually decided cases for poor law relief from their own wards. In many cases, a significant part of the electorate consisted of compound householders who paid their rates as part of their rent. In this respect, increases in their payments appeared to be the responsibility of their landlords, rather than the local council. In Poplar, where the pauper vote was significant, many of the local ratepayers were shopkeepers and owners of firms who largely dwelt outside the borough.[32] In fact, the Lansbury family sawmill and timber yard—now run by Lansbury's sons Edgar and William—was one of the few local businesses with resident employers surviving since the 1880s. Isaac Brine, George, Edgar, and William Lansbury all lived with their families among their local workforce and had first-hand experience of East End life.

[28] According to his biographers, Herbert Morrison scorned ceremony, always seemed to wear a brown Harris tweed suit, red tie, and brown brogue shoes, and followed George Lansbury's example of not wearing mayoral robes of office. See B. Donoughue and G. W. Jones, *Herbert Morrison: Portrait of a Politician* (1973), p. 45.

[29] Lord Morrison, *Herbert Morrison* (1960), pp. 86.   [30] Ibid.

[31] D. Englander, *Landlord and Tenant in Urban Britain, 1838–1983* (Oxford, 1983), pp. 106–9.

[32] A. Deacon and E. Briggs, 'Local Democracy and Central Policy: The Issue of Pauper Votes in the 1920s', *Policy and Politics*, 2 (1974), pp. 347–64.

In carrying out the arrests over several days, the Sheriff added to the popular commotion in the East End and handed George Lansbury and the Poplar councillors a valuable opportunity to publicize their cause. To the consternation of the PBMA, the spectacle of popular elected Labour representatives going to gaol attracted considerable media attention of an unwelcome kind. Newsreel film captured the fate of several councillors about to be plucked from tranquil domestic surroundings—including the mayor, Sam March, a respected Justice of the Peace, two other local stalwarts, Julia and John Scurr, and Nellie Cressall, heavily pregnant and surrounded by her young family. George Lansbury was also depicted at his home surrounded by children, while his daughter-in-law, Minnie, gathered a nosegay in the garden. However, Lansbury was centre stage in 'Red Poplar'—a significance the film director did not miss as he identified him as the 'Benevolent Bolshie' in the film caption.[33]

These dramatic scenes in the East End now made the plight of Poplar a subject of national attention and brought an angry protest from the Alliance:

For the past six days this Borough has been in a condition of ferment and upheaval and why those in charge of the Sheriff's Department could not in the exercise of their duties have arrested these persons if not in one body at least on one day passes our comprehension. The course pursued has been one to give a cheap advertisement and notoriety to those responsible for the present condition of affairs, with the consequent result that the passions of their followers have been inflamed and aggravated; and a feeling of much disgust occasioned in the minds of those entirely opposed to their unconstitutional procedure.[34]

As the Poplar Borough Council defied the order of the High Court, the *Daily Herald* mounted its last campaign before the paper passed into official ownership of the Labour party. Huw Richards has pointed out that 'Poplarism' had all the characteristics of a favourite *Daily Herald* story, as Labour councillors struggled against an uncaring authority on behalf of their oppressed and dispossessed local community.

During these dramatic weeks the newspaper reported the 'Poplar Story' as it unfolded, giving detailed coverage in eight consecutive issues of the arrest and imprisonment of the thirty councillors. On 1 September the *Daily Herald* devoted the front page to the Poplar councillors' last meeting. In his page-one article George Lansbury outlined the Poplar case and told his readers: 'Today with my colleagues I await arrest. Putting us in prison may suit Sir Alfred Mond [Minister of Health] and the Government. They are sowing dragons' teeth'.

There was an interesting sidelight to the pending imprisonment of the Poplar councillors. The editorial staff of the *Daily Herald* had commissioned a young artist, John Flanaghan, to produce a portrait in oils of George Lansbury 'as a sort of riposte to our anti-Bolshevik friends who think he ought to be boiled in oils!'. In a desperate bid to finish the portrait before his subject was incarcerated in prison,

---

[33] This historic film footage still survives: 'Farcical "revolution" which may be serious if it spreads', Topical Budget 523–2, 5 Sept. 1921, British Film Institute, National Film and Television Archive.

[34] Secretary of the PBMA to Home Secretary, 6 Sept. 1921, PRO, HO 45/112, 33/423 652.

Flanaghan explained how he had attempted to capture Lansbury's personality. He declared, 'whether his political views be right or wrong, there is no getting away from the fact that he possesses extraordinary force of character and, what is rather rare these days, intense sincerity. This and his obvious idealism makes him a unique personality, as interesting to the painter as to the politician.'[35]

The portrait was ready on time and it is now in the private possession of the Lansbury family.[36] Eventually, at least two other public likenesses of George Lansbury were fashioned: in 1930 the official plaque by 'Lansbury's Lido' on the Serpentine in Hyde Park and, six years later, Sylvia Grosse's oil painting for the National Portrait Gallery.

On 2 September 1921 the *Daily Herald* carried the front-page headline: 'POPLAR COUNCILLORS GAOLED FOR JUSTICE', and denounced the initial arrests as the thirty councillors went to prison. On 5 September the *Daily Herald* headline, 'OUR EDITOR IN GAOL FOR JUSTICE', announced the arrival of George Lansbury in Brixton Prison. Lansbury, when he had not been taken on the first day, phoned the Sheriff offering to make an appointment for the arrest of himself, his son, Edgar, and daughter-in-law, Minnie![37] This shrewd stage-management meant that pictures of the plucky threesome with the Sheriff appeared in the press the next day.

Of the thirty Labour councillors, the twenty-five men were dispatched to Brixton prison and the five women councillors imprisoned in Holloway. In fact, during the legal action that precipitated the crisis, mysteriously not all of the Poplar councillors had been served with writs. Thirty-one of the forty-nine councillors and aldermen, including five of the six non-Labour members, had writs taken out by the LCC, whereas the Metropolitan Asylums Board served writs on twenty-nine councillors. As a result Jack Wooster, chairman of the Works' Committee and Charles Key, chairman of the Public Health Committee, who had moved the defiant resolution not to levy the rate, never ended up in Brixton.[38] Key, who was Lansbury's successor as the MP for Poplar, Bow, and Bromley in 1940, remained at large to co-ordinate the campaign outside prison.[39]

Once inside, the thirty Poplar councillors issued their manifesto to explain the reasons for their action:

Thirty of us, members of the Poplar Borough Council, have been committed to prison. This has been done because we have refused to levy the rate on people of our borough to meet the demands of the LCC and the other Central authorities.

We have taken this action deliberately, and shall continue to take the same course until the Government deals properly with the question of unemployment, providing work or full maintenance for all, and carries into effect the long promised and much overdue reform of equalisation of the rates.[40]

---

[35] *Daily Herald*, 1 Sept. 1921.
[36] I am most grateful to the late Esme Whiskin Lansbury and to Kate Lansbury for generous assistance and access to their Lansbury collection. For the official portrait as First Commissioner, see plate 20.
[37] *Daily Herald*, 1–2 Sept. 1921.   [38] Branson, *Poplarism*, pp. 43–5.
[39] For this contemporary account, see Key, *Red Poplar*.   [40] *Daily Herald*, 3 Sept. 1921.

In Brixton George Lansbury, Poplar councillor and editor of the *Daily Herald*, became prisoner no. 7004.[41] With his fellow inmates he successfully broke prison regulations and disrupted routine by complaining about the unwholesome diet and other harsh aspects of prison life. As a group, led by George Lansbury and Sam March, the Labour councillors exerted considerable influence over the conditions of their imprisonment, negotiating improvements in their situation with the governor.

However, prison life had many grim features for the Poplar councillors, particularly the early death of the thirty-two-year-old Minnie Lansbury within weeks of gaining her freedom. Less detail is known about the treatment of the five women in Holloway, except that Nellie Cressall, who was seven months' pregnant on arrest, secured an earlier release than her fellow prisoners. George Lansbury, who suffered spells of sickness and diarrhoea but refused hospital treatment, recalled their prison experience and its merciless toll on the councillors. He remembered: 'I have no doubt in my own mind that the lives of Mrs Scurr and Minnie Lansbury were shortened by the imprisonment; neither have I any doubt that [Charlie] Sumner, [James] Rugless and [Joseph] Callaghan also shortened their lives by going to prison at the time.'[42]

While in Brixton George Lansbury was denied the opportunity to edit the *Daily Herald*, though he cited the famous precedents of John Wilkes and W. T. Stead from the eighteenth and nineteenth centuries. However, Lansbury penned regular articles for the *Daily Herald* on prison life, prison food, and the Brixton Chapel that clearly rattled the authorities. In particular, the official files reveal that the prison governor, Captain Haynes, went to some lengths to deny that the Poplar councillors had undermined discipline in his establishment.[43]

Edgar Lansbury also had his application refused to run his timber business while alongside his father in Brixton Prison.[44] On 5 September Minnie Lansbury telegraphed the authorities protesting that the treatment in prison of her husband and father-in-law was 'from pure political spite'. Two days later, seventeen of the councillors petitioned the Brixton governor to be treated under the rules for prisoners of the First Division, as well as pressing for improved facilities such as the provision of daily newspapers. This request was eventually granted, but not before the Governor was advised: 'I think newspapers had better not be conceded. They would all take the *Daily Herald* which would encourage them to persist in their contumacious conduct in disobeying the order of the Court.'[45]

The councillors, their families, and their tireless supporters, mainly East End unemployed who sang the 'Red Flag' outside Brixton and Holloway, caused the prison authorities a number of problems. One difficulty the Poplar councillors caused—and which the prison authorities were unable to deal with—was the

[41] '7004 George Lansbury', 15 Sept. 1921, PRO, HO 45/11233/423652.
[42] Lansbury, *My Life*, p. 157.
[43] For the prison reports on the Poplar councillors, see PRO, HO 45/1123/46937.
[44] Edgar Lansbury, 1 Sept. 1921, to prison governor with reply 2 Sept. 1921, PRO, HO 45/11233/423652.
[45] 'Governor of Brixton Prison', 'Rt. Hon. J. R. Clynes', 5, 15 Sept. 1921, ibid.

constant stream of visitors, politicians, and TUC representatives, as well as family members, friends, or those on council business. Most famously, the Poplar councillors successfully petitioned the Home Office to meet as a group and thereby held thirty-four Borough Council meetings with the town clerk and other council staff in official attendance in Brixton.

By this stage there was considerable support for the councillors. The 'Poplar Revolt' had become a public embarrassment for the Lloyd George Coalition government and especially for the new Minister of Health, Sir Alfred Mond, who was under pressure to find a solution from the group of eleven Labour mayors from the metropolitan boroughs. In East London a tenants' defence league threatened a rent and rates strike if an attempt was made to levy payment by other means. George Lansbury wrote to *The Times* from Brixton to demand rate equalization and to oppose Mond's plan to give the LCC power to raise their own rate. Lansbury warned: 'But before the House of Commons agrees to any such proposal, members will surely try to understand that such legislation will only transfer the dispute from the councillors to the ratepayers—from 30 to more than 30,000.'[46]

On 7 October, Sir Alfred Mond, the Minister of Health, urged the Cabinet to settle the matter of the imprisoned Poplar councillors, owing to the possibility of similar action by other London boroughs including Bethnal Green and Stepney. On 13 September, Clem Attlee had successfully moved a resolution on the Stepney Borough Council threatening such action unless the Poplar councillors were released. After considerable negotiations with Mond, the Poplar councillors, advised by their solicitor and treasurer, W. H. Thompson, a former imprisoned conscientious objector, applied to the High Court for their release. Freedom was secured for the Poplar councillors from Brixton and Holloway on Wednesday, 12 October 1921. Five days later, a tense conference of borough representatives held at the Ministry of Health followed by a committee of rich and poor boroughs—with George Lansbury representing Poplar—paved the way for the Local Authorities (Financial Provisions) Act that was passed for twelve months. By its main measure—the equalization of outdoor relief throughout the LCC area through the Metropolitan Common Poor Fund—in 1921 Poplar gained increased poor relief to a staggering sum of £400,000. However, a prescient John Scurr noted, 'the victory was great . . . all who shared in the fight can feel proud of their achievement' but 'we have to gird up our loins for the next struggle'.[47] As we shall see, George Lansbury and his fellow councillors had fought only the first battle on behalf of their local community rather than the war. 'Poplarism' raged on for several more years.

The remarkable feature of the events in Poplar during the turbulent summer and autumn weeks of 1921 was the extent to which large numbers of ordinary people were involved in the Borough Council's conflict with the authorities. Any explanation of this phenomenon requires an analysis of the local political culture dominated by the Poplar Labour Party from 1919 and the prevailing economic and social structures of the East London borough.

---

[46] *The Times*, 26 Sept. 1921.   [47] J. Scurr, *The Rate Protest of Poplar* (1922).

As Gillian Rose has shown, Poplar's political culture—consisting of class loyalty, community values, local religiosity, and the appeal of street melodrama—combined to produce 'a participatory form of politics'. As political institutions were opened up to working-class control, with an increased franchise after 1918, the Poplar Labour Party built a powerful local electoral machine that dominated municipal politics in the inter-war years and beyond. However, any attempt to explain the phenomenon of the Poplar Rates Rebellion must recognize marked differences to other labour heartlands where working-class unity and the development of Labour politics were normally derived from the strength of the trade union movement and a factory- and chapel-based culture.

James Gillespie has stated that, even in the post-First World War years, the dominant characteristics of the East End economy remained different: 'a massive casual labour market, founded upon a chronic oversupply of labour and exacerbated by the instability of the demand for dock workers, combined with the small scale of London industries based on workshop production and outworking rather than steam technologies and the factory.' However, trade unionism was relatively weak in working-class Poplar, which was instead a stronghold for left-wing and revolutionary socialist groups. As a result, 'Poplarism' was 'founded on a series of alliances between groups sharing a common political interest in the control of institutions of local government'.[48]

Father St John B. Groser, who took up his ministry in Poplar shortly after the release of the Poplar councillors, noted the 'essentially religious nature of the revolt'. As evidence, he pointed to their pamphlet, *Guilty and Proud of It* (1922) with its opening Biblical quotation: 'Pure religion and undefiled before God and the Father is this, to visit the Fathers.'[49]

What Father Groser noticed was the special relationship of the Labour councillors and the people they represented. 'Poplarism' was 'deeds not words'—local democracy in action as the councillors sought to inform and consult their local community. As John Scurr observed, at the height of the 'Rates Protest' every occupier received a letter from the mayor explaining their action, and twelve meetings were held in various parts of the borough from 22 to 31 August, at which the position was explained. In particular, the Labour councillors—mainly manual workers—drew immense strength, popularity, and pride from the fact that they lived in the same streets as those who had elected them. In answer to their critics, 'Poplarism' worked. In March and April 1922 the Labour candidates for the LCC elections and the guardians' elections stood firmly for the principle of 'work or maintenance' and secured four County Council seats in Bow and Bromley and South Poplar. The number of Labour representatives on the local Board of Guardians also increased

---

[48] For more on these themes, see G. Rose, 'Locality, Politics and Culture: Poplar in the 1920s', *Environment and Planning D: Society and Space*, 6 (1988), pp. 151–68; id., 'Imagining Poplar in the 1920s: Contested Concepts of Community', *Journal of Historical Geography*, 16 (1990), pp. 425–37; J. Gillespie, 'Poplarism and Proletarianism: Unemployment and Labour Politics in London, 1918–34', in D. Feldman and G. S. Jones (eds.), *Metropolis London: Histories and Representations since 1800* (1989), pp. 163–88.

[49] St J. B. Groser, *Politics and Persons* (1949), p. 22.

from sixteen to twenty-one out of twenty-four members. In Bow West, George Lansbury was returned with J. H. Banks and Edgar Lansbury headed the poll in Bow North.

Edgar Lansbury, who became chairman of the board of guardians in 1923 and later mayor of Poplar, considered that his father's leadership of his fellow council-lors during the Poplar Rates Dispute was his best piece of business as a public ser-vant. The brilliant stage-management of the Poplar Rates Rebellion once again demonstrated Lansbury's political flair and his instinctive regard for democratic values enshrined in his unflagging belief in service to his community.

He was probably the first to note that in 1921, in defending their working-class community, the largely unknown Labour councillors added a new word to the English language, which was soon celebrated beyond the confines of the East End municipal borough of Poplar.[50] In their willingness to go to gaol for their political beliefs, George Lansbury and the Labour councillors left an important legacy in local government relations with central authority. 'Poplarism' readily became the symbol of all those who would put up a determined struggle to use the law on behalf of the poor and underprivileged in British society. In 1925 Lansbury argued that:

Our crime . . . is that we have refused to believe in the necessity of starvation. We have taught our people that it is no more wrong for a workman's widow and family to receive from the community the means of life than for a king's widow and family to receive sums varying from £10,000 to £70,000 a year.[51]

It was a theme he continued to hammer away at in the inter-war years, whether in Parliament to which he was returned at the 1922 general election—more evidence that 'Poplarism' did not deter his voters—or in different parts of Britain.

---

[50] See George Lansbury's foreword to Key, *Red Poplar*, pp. 3–4.   [51] Ibid.

12

First Labour Government, 1924

On 22 January 1924 King George V made a famous observation in his diary on the first occasion he asked Ramsay MacDonald to form a government: 'Today 23 years ago dear Grandmama died. I wonder what she would have thought of a Labour Government!' His note reflected the panic and despondency in governing circles in this country in 1924 at the prospect of a Socialist administration full of revolutionaries led by a Prime Minister who had never held even junior ministerial office.[1] Cautiously, MacDonald chose moderate Labour politicians and trade unionists in assembling his first Cabinet, including as well some former Liberals and Conservative peers. However, there was no place in the first Labour Cabinet in Britain for George Lansbury, the most prominent representative of the political Left in 1924.

During 1922–3 Labour had established itself as the second party in British politics to become His Majesty's Opposition in Parliament. The 1922 general election was also an important landmark in shaping the Labour leadership for nearly a decade: among those back at Westminster were Ramsay MacDonald and Philip Snowden, who joined the re-elected J. R. Clynes and J. H. Thomas. Only Arthur Henderson was missing from 'Labour's Big Five'—defeated at Widnes—but within weeks he was returned in the first by-election of the new Parliament to represent his home base of Newcastle, where George Lansbury had joined him in the campaign.[2]

Bonar Law had won the 1922 general election—his 344 Tory MPs provided a sizeable and considerable majority over his combined opponents. However, it was Labour's result that was significant. The 142 Labour MPs represented a credible 29.7 per cent of the total vote cast instead of 20.8 per cent four years before, with the Liberals pushed into third place with 115 members.

In East London, George Lansbury's victory, ten years after his dramatic by-election defeat, gave him a considerable margin over a new Conservative opponent, G. E. Dureen—15,402 votes (64.1 per cent) to 8,626 (35.9 per cent), a majority of 6,776. As the member for Poplar, Bow and Bromley, Lansbury held an invincible position and power-base for the next eighteen years. In the neighbouring constituency of Poplar, South Poplar, Sam March saw off the sitting MP and National Liberal, Sir A. W. Yeo. In 1922 their two parliamentary victories turned Poplar into the Labour heartland of East London.

Also noticeable in 1922 was the changing social and political composition of the Parliamentary Labour Party. While over half of its members—eighty-five MPs—

---

[1] H. Nicolson, *King George V: His Life and Reign* (1984), p. 384.
[2] Wrigley, *Arthur Henderson*, p. 139.

1. At the seaside: Bessie and George Lansbury and their children, *c*.1889.

2. After baby Bessie Haverson's christening, *c*.1900. Lansbury family, left to right: front row: Doreen, Connie. Middle row: Daisy, Bessie Lansbury, Bessie Haverson (*née* Lansbury) with baby Bessie Haverson, George Lansbury, Nelly. Back row: William, Edgar, Annie, Harry Haverson, Dorothy. Children not in photograph: George (deceased); Violet, Eric (unborn).

3. George Lansbury (centre of second row, with tie). With the workforce at his sawmill and timber yard, St Stephen's Road, Bow, late 1890s.

4. George Lansbury (centre, with cape). With Poplar comrades, Victoria Park, East London c.1905.

29. Bessie and George Lansbury's granddaughter, Angela Lansbury and her actress mother, Moyna (MacGill) Lansbury, early 1930s.

30. Screen and stage legend in her lifetime, Angela Lansbury.

31. A happy trio before the Labour Party Conference, Bournemouth 1937. (Left to right) George Lansbury, Clem Attlee, and Lord Arthur Ponsonby.

were still sponsored by trade unions, the Socialist societies provided thirty-four MPs, virtually all belonging to the ILP. Labour was now a political party with some national appeal. Included among its ranks was a sprinkling of MPs who were products of a public school and university education. Middle-class and upper-class recruits included C. P. (later Sir Charles) Trevelyan, great-nephew of the historian Macaulay, and Arthur Ponsonby, whose father had been Queen Victoria's secretary. Both MPs became staunch allies of the pacifist George Lansbury.[3] As Catherine Ann Cline has shown, Trevelyan and Ponsonby were among a prominent group of around seventy disillusioned Liberals, mainly MPs or former MPs attracted by Labour's stance on war and peace, who shifted their political allegiances during the period 1914–31.[4] At Westminster, George Lansbury found that his new colleagues included Clem Attlee, A. V. Alexander, Arthur Greenwood, Tom Johnston, and Sidney Webb—all newcomers in 1922 and destined to serve alongside Lansbury in the second Labour Cabinet.

Another group of class warriors with whom George Lansbury was closely associated was the 'Red Clydesiders', an important left-wing presence at Westminster in the 1920s. They had won twenty-one of the twenty-eight seats in the Clydeside area. David Kirkwood—to whose autobiography Lansbury later contributed a preface—exclaimed to the ecstatic thousands who cheered him and his fellow Clydeside MPs off at St Enoch's Station: 'when we come back, this station, this railway, will belong to the people!'[5]

Also important in Labour's changing profile was the growth of the new women's sections in certain parts of Britain after 1918.[6] In Poplar, Southwark, and Woolwich, working-class women had a long history of political activity, playing important roles in building local Labour parties. As noted, Poplar was the scene for the Match Girls' Strike, suffragette militancy, and trades council campaigns, as well as the Poplar Rates Rebellion that mobilized local women. Nearby, across the Thames, there was a total of over 1,000 women party members in the two post-First World War Woolwich constituencies.[7]

Labour's political progress also reflected important changes in the party's organizational development and its successful advance in British local politics. With its socialist Constitution and policy statement *Labour and the New Social Order*, newly adopted in June 1918, Labour had built up a network of 527 Divisional or Local Labour Parties and Trades and Labour Councils in the post-war years. Important election gains had been made in the industrial areas of Scotland, South Wales, Northumberland, Yorkshire, and parts of London. However, the rise of Labour was somewhat uneven in parliamentary terms with, for example, Labour winning only sixteen seats out of a total of seventy-two contested in Greater London.

[3] For Charles Trevelyan, see A. J. A. Morris, *C. P. Trevelyan, 1870–1958: Portrait of a Radical* (1977); for Arthur Ponsonby, see R. Jones, *Arthur Ponsonby: The Politics of Life* (1989).
[4] C. A. Cline, *Recruits to Labour: The British Labour Party, 1914–1931* (Syracuse, N.Y., 1963).
[5] Taylor, *English History* (1975), pp. 198–9.
[6] G. D. H. Cole, *A History of the Labour Party from 1914* (1948), pp. 141–3.
[7] K. Y. Stenberg, 'Working-Class Women in London Politics, 1894–1914', *Twentieth Century British History*, 9 (1998), p. 337 n. 47.

In East London an extremely optimistic George Lansbury saw the exciting prospect of the advent of a Labour government in Britain. In 1922, as he returned to a House of Commons with a strong Socialist presence, he contemplated what could be achieved to banish unemployment and improve the lot of ordinary people:

I am looking forward with real joy to sitting amongst such a jolly band as will forgather on the Labour benches: Davie Kirkwood, Josh Wedgwood, Neil Mclean, E. Shinwell, Jack Jones, Clement Attlee, Will Thorne and Walter Newbold and lots of others . . . one question for us which overshadows all others is the 'Condition of the People' question . . . [O]ur business is to put the poverty problem before the nation on every occasion.[8]

In 1922, Lansbury's election victory had been a personal triumph and a vindication of his defiance on the women's question ten years before. As he readily confessed: 'ten years ago I lost Bow and Bromley during the struggle for women's freedom. It makes me very proud to know that women have sent me back with a record majority.'[9]

Six days after polling day, another significant event took place that shaped Labour fortunes for the next decade and beyond, as the PLP chose its first leader. Ramsay MacDonald narrowly defeated the sitting chairman, J. R. Clynes, for the newly designated post, probably owing his narrow victory of 61 to 56 votes to significant support from the new contingent of Clydesider MPs. Even in 1922 there was a lurking suspicion about the suitability of the aloof MacDonald as leader.[10] Lansbury, critical of MacDonald's cosy relationship with the Liberals in the pre-war Parliament, did not want MacDonald to stand. On the day of the election, the *Daily Herald* warned accordingly: 'Only one thing need be said about today's elections of leaders of the Labour Party in Parliament. They must be unanimous. Any contest, any pressure of opposing claims, would only give the enemy cause to exult; it might lead to an unfortunate fissure in the Party itself.'[11]

The following day the *Daily Herald* was on a back foot. The paper, forced to acknowledge MacDonald's virtues—particularly his knowledge of foreign affairs—observed that Clynes had earned 'the compliment of re-election', but, with MacDonald's victory, appealed for 'the most loyal and hearty support' for the new leader and his deputy.[12] Despite this belated expression of unity, MacDonald never forgot that the *Daily Herald* had backed Clynes, particularly as the Labour party and the TUC had salvaged the ailing newspaper in 1922 by taking it into ownership.[13]

Lansbury contributed to the debate on the King's Speech that opened the 1923 session. Unemployment was his chosen theme but, for good measure, there was first an outright assault on anti-German prejudice prevailing in government circles. He declared to the House of Commons:

---

[8] *Daily Herald*, 18 Nov. 1922.   [9] Ibid.
[10] C. Wrigley, 'James Ramsay MacDonald, 1922–31,' in K. Jeffreys (ed.), *Leading Labour: From Keir Hardie to Tony Blair* (1999), p. 28. See also Marquand, *Ramsay MacDonald*, pp. 285–7.
[11] *Daily Herald*, 21 Nov. 1921.   [12] Ibid. 22 Nov. 1922.
[13] On the change of ownership of the *Daily Herald*, see Richards, *The Bloody Circus*, pp. 43–8.

Until a few years ago they were saying that the Germans had everything to teach us in the way of life . . . I would have cut my right hand off had I been King of this country before I would have changed my name at the bidding of the late Hon. Member for South Hackney [Horatio Bottomley][14]

In the following weeks he regularly took up the cudgels on a multiplicity of causes: ex-servicemen, paupers and the unemployed, pensioners, municipal workers, civil servants, and hunger Marchers. No stone was left unturned in 1923, as Lansbury queried Tory government policy on the bombing of Iraqi villages, Anglo-Russian relations, and lack of self-determination for India and Ireland.

Within months, Labour soon faced the second of three general elections in the years 1922–4, as Stanley Baldwin, who had replaced the terminally ill Bonar Law as Prime Minister in 1923, went very early to the country on a programme of Protection in an attempt to unite his party. In consequence, the Liberals came together on a 'Free Trade versus Tariff' platform and increased their representation from 116 to 159 seats.[15]

Not surprisingly, the general election of 1923 produced an indecisive overall result—Conservatives 258, Labour 191, Liberals 158—and a political *impasse* with no party possessing a clear majority in the House of Commons. Within this three-party system, only a new coalition government of the warring talents of Asquith, Baldwin, and Lloyd George (a format seen as rejected at the 1922 general election), or a minority administration dependent on the support of another party, was possible. Though roundly defeated at the polls with the lowest Tory number of MPs since 1906, the Prime Minister, Stanley Baldwin, stayed on in government and chose to resign only when defeated in the new Parliament.

In December 1923 George Lansbury had romped home once more in Poplar, Bow and Bromley, against a new Conservative candidate. The result was Lansbury 15,336; Albery 6,941; and the majority 8,395. Characteristically, Lansbury had raised a Christian battle cry to those who toiled by 'hand and brain' to 'build Jerusalem in England's fair and pleasant land . . . and the establishment of Christ's kingdom of peace and goodwill among all the nations of the world'. 'Tariffs, Free Trade and Protection' were rejected as the worn out shibboleths of the nineteenth century. Instead, an alternative choice for Lansbury's electors promised an 'International Commonwealth of all nations' to promote trade, the nationalization of industry and agriculture, as well as programmes of social reconstruction to end unemployment and bad housing.[16] At Westminster, two veterans of the Poplar Rates Rebellion joined Lansbury and March. John Scurr was elected for Mile End, Stepney, and East Ham North returned Susan Lawrence, the first woman Labour MP.

The dominant question within the Labour movement was whether or not the Party should assume office without an overall majority once the Baldwin administration had fallen. Since Labour had been the official opposition since 1922, it was

---

[14] *Hansard*, 13 Feb. 1923, cols. 84–8.
[15] J. Charmley, *A History of Conservative Politics, 1900–1996* (1998), pp. 70–2.
[16] G. Lansbury, *Socialism versus Protection: The Battle Cry of the Election* (1923).

difficult for MacDonald to be seen to refuse. He had worked hard to portray his party as the alternative government. Even so, George Lansbury was one of a small number of left-wing MPs—including Robert Smillie, David Kirkwood, and Frederick Pethick Lawrence—who took the view that Labour should only take office with a clear majority.[17] Others on the left, such as James Maxton, wanted Labour to take office to bring in a socialist parliamentary programme and, when defeated, to seek an improved mandate by going to the country. However an adamant George Lansbury would have no truck with 'accommodation or arrangements', a position he held throughout the inter-war years:

If the King's Government cannot be carried on without a coalition, let those who, though divided in name, are in fact but two expressions of the same principles, once again come together and carry on as best as they may. We of the British Labour Movement will, as ever, keep ourselves clear of that unholy thing which now masquerades as Liberalism.[18]

Lansbury fully realized that his principled stand of waiting for an outright victory at the polls would delay the advent of political power for the Labour movement. He concluded that he would rather die 'without seeing our triumph than see any arrangement, open or secret, made with the party that has as its leaders Lord Grey, Asquith, Winston Churchill and Lloyd George'.[19]

By 15 December, when Ramsay MacDonald departed for Christmas to his Scottish home at Lossiemouth, the Labour National Executive and the TUC General Council had decided that MacDonald should mount the challenge to end Baldwin's government in the new Parliament. If the king sent for him, the Socialist leader should assume office—if only for a period of six to eight months.[20] At Lossiemouth, MacDonald started forming his government, which included 'Labour's Big Five': Philip Snowden (Chancellor of the Exchequer), J. H. Thomas (Colonial Secretary), and J. R. Clynes (Lord Privy Seal). Arthur Henderson, who returned to Parliament in an early by-election, became Home Secretary—but only after MacDonald had failed to persuade him to remain as party secretary to prepare the party for the next general election. The group became an inner circle of moderate politicians which Lansbury, the socialist East Ender, owing to MacDonald's personal dislike, never joined.

While MacDonald kept the Foreign Office portfolio for himself, he looked outside the Labour party to recruit two Conservative peers—Parmoor and Chelmsford—and four ex-Liberals—Lord Haldane (who became Lord Chancellor and advised on the Conservative appointments), Noel Buxton, Charles Trevelyan, and Josiah Wedgwood.[21] Margaret Bondfield turned down the opportunity to be the first woman Cabinet minister—a post she accepted five years later—to accept a

---

[17] For Lansbury's view, see *Workers' Weekly*, 21 Dec. 1923. See also Klugmann, *History of the Communist Party of Great Britain*, i, p. 245.

[18] *Daily Herald*, 8 Dec. 1923.   [19] Ibid.

[20] *Manchester Guardian*, 12, 13, 14 Dec. 1923. See also *Diary of Beatrice Webb*, ed. Mackenzie and Mackenzie, iii (entries for 12, 18 Dec. 1923), pp. 430–3.

[21] Taylor, *English History* (1975), pp. 209–10.

junior position in the government. In a Labour Cabinet of twenty men, according to most accounts there was only one out-and-out left-winger—John Wheatley, one of the Clydesiders, widely acknowledged later as a successful Minister of Health. However, the Cabinet also included three associates of George Lansbury: Sidney Webb and Charles Trevelyan, both of moderate left-wing or radical sympathies, and the pre-war stalwart of municipal socialism, Fred Jowett, who was appointed to the Office of Works. MacDonald had selected a conservative Cabinet to balance the interests of the unions in different parts of the country. Above all, it was 'fit to govern' the nation.

According to the sixty-five-year-old Sidney Webb, appointed President of the Board of Trade one year after first becoming an MP, the name of George Lansbury was the most glaring omission on the list of MacDonald's Cabinet appointments. Webb recorded his views in a contemporary memorandum not published until nearly forty years later.[22] In early 1924, Lansbury had responded with enthusiasm when Arthur Henderson first sounded him out about the possibility of Cabinet office. As he told Henderson, for nearly forty years he had been trying to help in the work of getting such a government established.[23] The way should have been clear for the member for Poplar, Bow and Bromley to join the First Labour Cabinet in Britain. As will become clear, under the new editorship of Hamilton Fyfe, the future of the *Daily Herald* had been secured by a take-over by the Labour party nearly two years before—with Lansbury remaining as general manager until 1925. This position also provided him with an important weekly Saturday column for his mainly dissenting views on politics and religion.

Why in 1924 did MacDonald find no Cabinet post for Lansbury? The main reason appeared to be that, although he seemed to have an entirely free hand over appointments, MacDonald's power and authority was not free from the influence and concerns of others. He was uneasy; the MP for Poplar was unpredictable. Uppermost in MacDonald's mind, as revealed in his diary, was the attitude of the monarch, George V, towards Lansbury's public utterances and his undisguised association with Bolshevik Russia. 'Another long talk. Referred to Russia. Hope I would do nothing to compel him [George V] to shake hands with the murderers of his cousins [Nicholas and Alexandra Romanov and their family]', MacDonald noted, after an early audience with the king.[24]

However, 1924 was an important landmark in working-class history—the first Labour government in office, if not in power. Without a majority in the House of Commons, the new administration required all the support it could muster from its phalanx of 142 members. On 8 January 1924 George Lansbury was alongside MacDonald, Henderson, and other Labour leaders on the platform at the Albert Hall for the Labour Victory Rally. MacDonald pledged a Labour government that would uphold the British constitution. Lansbury's speech was popular, inspirational, and

---

[22] S. Webb, 'The First Labour Government', *Political Quarterly*, 32 (1961), pp. 13–14.
[23] George Lansbury to Arthur Henderson, 15 Jan. 1924, LP, vol. 28, fo. 162.
[24] Diary entry, 22 Jan. 1924, JRMP, PRO 30/69/1753.

reflected the abundant optimism in Labour circles that the parliamentary road to the Socialist New Jerusalem was in sight:

They in Britain, because of all the sacrifices that had been made and all the work that had been done, had the God-given chance of leading from the inferno of capitalism to the co-operative commonwealth . . . he believed that the British Labour movement could give it that [new] life if its members were true to the best that was in them.[25]

Yet, three days before at Shoreditch town hall, George Lansbury had scuppered any remaining chance of Cabinet office. In a widely reported speech, he referred directly to the conniving in political circles to attempt to ensure that the king would prevent the formation of a Labour government. In no uncertain terms George V was given a timely reminder of the fate that had befallen his ancestors, Charles I and James II:

a few centuries ago one King who stood up against the common people of that day lost his head—lost it really (laughter and cheers). Later one of his descendants was told to get out as quickly as he could. Since that day kings and queens had been what they ought to be if you had them. They never interfered with ordinary politics and George V would be well advised to keep his finger out of the pie now.[26]

This was not the first time there had been tensions between the monarch and the left in British politics. In 1907, as Prince of Wales, a worried George V had complained to his Secretary of State for India, John Morley, about the civil disorder in India. The future king blamed the unrest on the 'evil doings' of Keir Hardie who was visiting the country on a world tour. In 1912, George V still resented the Order of Merit that his father had awarded to the socialist and naturalist, Dr Alfred Russel Wallace.[27]

In 1924 when George V formally asked MacDonald to form a government, he soon voiced his fears to the Labour leader about Lansbury's Shoreditch speech. Lord Stamfordham, George V's private secretary, noted the reaction of the king, who was also unhappy that the strains of the 'Marseillaise' and the 'Red Flag' had been heard at Labour's Albert Hall victory rally:

The King referred to recent utterances of Mr Lansbury, in which he went out of his way to express a threat and a reminder of the fate which had befallen King Charles I. His Majesty was not affected by these personal attacks, but did take exception to Mr Lansbury basing his remarks upon the idea of intrigues at Court.[28]

George Lansbury and threats against the 'existing Monarchy' were somewhat familiar territory. In 1917, the Albert Hall rally—chaired by Lansbury—which celebrated the overthrow of the Tsarist régime in Russia had produced some paranoia among the political establishment. Shortly after Lansbury's meeting, a reassuring

---

[25] *Forward*, 19 Jan. 1924; *The Times*, 9 Jan. 1924.
[26] *Manchester Guardian*, 7 Jan. 1924.
[27] For this recently discovered royal correspondence, see *The Times*, 9 Aug. 2000.
[28] 'Memorandum by Lord Stamfordham', RA, GV K1918/164. See also Nicolson, *King George V*, p. 384.

report about the event was compiled for the King in the hope of assuaging any fears of the likelihood of a similar occurrence in Britain.[29]

What may not have been noticed was the letter George Lansbury had dispatched in January 1924 to *The Times* to allay any fears of middle England about a Labour government. He opened in promising style by pointing out how Labour had loyally served the nation in municipal office. The Labour movement had played a full part in the affairs of the country and contributed to the development of popular democracy. Britain was the only country where 'it is possible to change fundamentally the existing social and industrial order without the horrors of a "bloody" revolution', he added. A Labour government was entitled to use the full powers of the constitution to introduce change. However, as a known class-warrior, Lansbury was less wise in hinting that if Labour was defeated—'by any other means than by a straightforward vote of the House of Commons'—extra-Parliamentary action might result. Moreover, his reference to Lenin, even if Lansbury added that 'our British Labour Movement was different' had no place in a letter to *The Times* in January 1924.[30]

The business of excluding Lansbury from the Cabinet was speedily settled, notwithstanding his notorious Shoreditch speech. MacDonald offered the member for Bow and Bromley only the lowly post of Minister of Transport. It was relatively light in departmental duties in 1924 and certainly did not carry Cabinet status, as it had done in the Lloyd George Coalition administration. Lansbury's reply was brief and to the point: 'As to the position you suggest to me is one which does not carry Cabinet rank, and would, therefore, involve no participation in the formation of general policy or responsibility for that policy, I cannot accept.'[31]

Marquand's account of MacDonald's Cabinet-making does not mention George Lansbury.[32] The political relationship between MacDonald and Lansbury was important, and the extent to which Ramsay MacDonald disliked and even loathed 'the John Bull of Poplar' and his 'Poplarism' has been largely underestimated. As Sidney Webb put it, Ramsay MacDonald might tolerate Lansbury in his government, but would go no further. MacDonald told Webb that: 'Lansbury was always speaking so wildly and indiscreetly at meetings that he would injure the government.' MacDonald also rejected an alternative proposal of the Office of Works— to which Lansbury was appointed five years later. Lansbury could not be trusted to be in charge of any big administrative office and a defensive MacDonald insisted that 'Lansbury flatly refused to accept anything outside the Cabinet'. In fact, after Henderson's soundings, MacDonald knew Lansbury would turn down a junior post—owing to the consequent loss of political independence. Labour's first Prime Minister was well aware of Lansbury's reputation as a political dissenter over the years: SDF organizer, independent socialist at Middlesbrough, a combative opponent of the National Insurance Bill, editor of the pacifist *Herald*, and chief advocate

---

[29] 'Notes on Meeting Held in Albert Hall on Saturday Mar. 31ˢᵗ. To Celebrate The Recent Russian Disturbance', 10 Apr. 1917, RA, GV O 1106/9, 10.
[30] *The Times*, 9 Jan. 1924.
[31] George Lansbury to Ramsay MacDonald, 18 Jan. 1924, LP, vol. 28, fo. 163.
[32] Marquand, *Ramsay MacDonald*, pp. 299–304.

of 'Poplarism'. However, the calculation that it is safer to have a parliamentary rebel firmly within the political tent, rather than outside it, was not part of the first Labour Prime Minister's judgement in 1924.

Webb's memorandum also confirms that the attitude of the King was a serious consideration in MacDonald's thinking. Webb observed that 'MacDonald believed the King would object: I could see that his [Lansbury's] admission to it was very difficult, for one reason or another; but I felt his exclusion to be a mistake, and so did Henderson, who also criticised it to MacDonald, and so it proved.'[33]

Other factors weighed heavily against Lansbury with his avowed public sympathies for Bolshevik Russia. In 1924 two members of Lansbury's family belonged openly to the newly founded Communist Party of Great Britain. His son, Edgar, publicly warned the Labour Prime Minister, within days of MacDonald taking up residence at 10 Downing Street, that 'all England will be Poplarised. Of course, we mean to Poplarise the House of Commons and the British Empire'.[34] His younger sister, Violet, a most staunch adherent of Communism, had been working for the Russian Trade Delegation as a shorthand typist.[35] A year later she departed to Moscow for a sojourn of ten years, where she lived with a Russian professor and later married C. P. Dutt, the brother of the Marxist intellectual, Rajane Palme Dutt. The British Foreign Office listed her there as one of a small group of resident British citizens.[36] In 1926 Bessie and George visited their daughter in Soviet Russia, where Lansbury publicly praised the improvements he witnessed after an absence of six years. Officially, the British authorities responded by summarily dismissing his views as the 'subconscious dithyrambs' of the typical visitor.[37]

In the Lansbury household Communist sympathies competed with the strains of republicanism. At the 1923 Labour party conference Lansbury's son-in-law, Ernest Thurtle, had seconded the resolution: 'that the Royal Family is no longer necessary as part of the British Constitution'. Lansbury, as a member of the National Executive Committee, dismissed the question as of 'no vital importance' and therefore not worthy of consideration—this was the last time that the Labour party conference debated this issue in the twentieth century.[38]

Shortly after the formation of the first Labour government, George Lansbury addressed a crowded meeting of his electors at Bow Baths. A firm believer in public accountability, he explained he had declined a post outside the Labour Cabinet. He explained it would have meant the sacrifice of his political independence, thereby denying him an opportunity to share in national and international policy-making. Instead, he declared 'he was going to support the government as strongly as he

[33] Webb, 'First Labour Government', pp. 13–14.   [34] *Workers' Weekly*, 15 Feb. 1924.

[35] M. Berzin to Under-Secretary of State for Foreign Affairs, 16 Aug. 1922, PRO, FO 371/8151.

[36] 'List of British Subjects Resident in Moscow and the rest of the Soviet Socialist Republics except Petrograd and Vladivostock', 27 June 1927, PRO, FO 371/1990.

[37] Sir R. Hodgson to Sir Austen Chamberlain, 6 Sept. 1926, enclosing *Once More in Soviet Russia* ('Summary of article by Mr George Lansbury. From "Isvestiya" of Aug. 29th [1926]') PRO, FO 371/4245. See also V. Lansbury, *An Englishwoman in the USSR* (1940).

[38] C. McCall, 'Free Thought and the Monarchy: The Mystique of the Monarchy', *Freethinker* (Oct. 1997), p. 5. I am grateful to Pat Perry for this reference.

possibly could'.[39] Of course, it is doubtful whether many of Lansbury's East End constituents attached much weight to this declaration from their popular and independent-minded champion.

Though only briefly at Westminster before the First World War, George Lansbury nevertheless became notorious as the parliamentary rebel *par excellence*. The member for Bow and Bromley—whose 'bleeding heart ran away with his bloody head'—was remembered as the MP whom Speaker Lowther ordered from the House of Commons in 1912, when he shook his fist in Asquith's face over injustice to imprisoned suffragettes. Ten years on, those who witnessed the return in 1922 of the East Ender with the thunderous voice soon saw that his parliamentary reputation had lost nothing in the intervening years.

The record of MacDonald's first government has largely been forgotten or dismissed, but there were some important and practical achievements in domestic legislation and foreign policy. Wheatley's 1924 Housing Act funded the first substantial scheme of local council house building that lasted until 1934. After the short-lived post-war boom the number of registered unemployed was hardly ever below 10 per cent. With 1.4 million out of work as Labour took office, a special Cabinet unemployment committee planned rural electrification and the building of a national grid. Unemployment benefits were also improved and extended to more recipients under the 1911 Insurance Act. At the Board of Education, Trevelyan oversaw the building of new schools and set up the influential Hadow Committee, which reported in 1926. As Chancellor of the Exchequer, Snowden marginally improved working-class living standards by reducing both direct and indirect taxation in his first budget in March 1924. In easing tensions in international relations, MacDonald achieved some success, principally in the negotiations at the Dawes Conference over the withdrawal of French troops from the Ruhr and changes to German reparation payments that led to the Dawes Plan.[40]

During these months of Labour minority rule, one measure of the Government's relative popularity in the country was reflected in two memorable by-election victories. Not only did Arthur Henderson take Burnley on 28 February with an increased majority, but nearly three months later the Toxteth constituency in Liverpool was prised away from the Conservatives.

During this time, Lansbury remained an active Labour MP and a popular member of Labour's NEC, regularly heading the poll at the party conference during the 1920s. In February 1924 he became vice-chairman of a special Labour committee of backbenchers and ministers—including Clynes, Henderson, and Ben Spoor—to keep the rank and file of the party in touch with the government. However, the committee was incapable of preventing the difficulties that arose within weeks, when the Labour government used the Emergency Powers Act (1920) in response to a series of strikes by dockers and London tram and underground workers. Lansbury expressed his concern about government complacency. 'We are doing nothing that

[39] *The Times*, 28 Jan. 1924.
[40] T. Wright and M. Carter, *The People's Party: The History of the Labour Party* (1997), pp. 36–9; A. Thorpe, *A History of the British Labour Party* (1997), pp. 58–60.

is any worth', he wrote to Beatrice Webb. He added: 'MacDonald is more adept at intrigue and word twisting and word spinning than even Lloyd George himself.' [41]

Outside Parliament, Lansbury also continued his celebrated role as itinerant propagandist, preaching revolutionary socialism, pacifism, and anti-imperialism. However, on all these questions, his stance meant possible conflict with the Labour leadership. At certain times, criticism from the left-wingers on the back-benches could occasionally flair up into open revolt against the MacDonald government.

Lansbury recognized that his personality and his political principles would often distance him from the mainstream of the Labour party and could set him on an unavoidable collision course with the party leadership. How he behaved at Westminster was always a political and moral dilemma to trouble his Christian conscience. After nearly three months of Labour government he confessed that:

> There is always the temptation to glory in being one alone and apart. All my life it has been my lot to find myself separated in action from some whose goodwill and respect has been of the utmost value and concern to me . . . In the House of Commons, however, this [the right course of action] is not at all an easy thing to accomplish . . . all questions contain a great mixture of good and evil, and consequences are not always clear and certain . . . I know some people think it an heroic thing to vote against one's Party. Others consider such actions as one of treachery and disloyalty . . . People like myself, who are often found in a minority, need every day to pray for that sort of guidance which will lead us right away from self and make us only think of what is impersonal and of benefit to others.[42]

However as party leader, MacDonald's main concern in taking office in 1924 was to show that Labour was 'fit to govern' and that he led a party of national standing rather than one that was solely class-based. George V was reassured as Labour ministers famously wore court dress, accepted royal social invitations, and received honours. Labour was a patriotic party that endorsed the monarchy, loyally governed the British Empire, and played by the rules of the parliamentary game at Westminster. In fact, the British brand of socialism as advocated by the MacDonald government owed more to the utopian tradition of Robert Owen than to Karl Marx.[43]

By contrast, while Lansbury readily acknowledged that the Labour party was a broad church and had been established in 1900 as a federation of local Labour organizations, socialist groups, and trade unions, his ideals of socialism and political democracy differed from the modest gradualism practised by the MacDonald Government. Labour's new constitution in 1918 had included the celebrated commitment in 'Clause Four'—the 'common ownership of the means of production and the best obtainable system of popular administration and control of each industry or service'. George Lansbury belonged to the Labour party because he believed in this parliamentary road to socialism and was determined to establish a new social order to replace capitalism. The precise mechanism to achieve this

---

[41] George Lansbury to Beatrice Webb, 14 Mar. 1924, PP, Sect II 4h9.

[42] *Daily Herald*, 24 Mar. 1924. For Lansbury's protests over the RAF bombing of Iraq, see ibid., 11 July, 14, 16 Aug. 1924.

[43] P. Ward, *Red Flag and Union Jack: Englishness, Patriotism and the British Left* (1998), *passim*.

objective was somewhat vague. But Lansbury and his left-wing colleagues advocated an immediate programme of nationalization to secure the communal ownership and reorganization of the major industries: principally coal, agriculture, and the railways in the first instance. Through the provision of national social services, the scourge of destitution, poverty, unemployment, and similar social ills could be prevented and eradicated from the British landscape.[44]

In 1924 no Labour back-bencher was more loyal than George Lansbury, but his loyalties were not always to the first Labour government. While MacDonald and his ministers compliantly wore ceremonial dress, Lansbury doubted whether 'the Labour Party fulfils its mission by proving how adaptable we are and how nicely we can dress and behave when we are in official, royal, or upper class circles'.[45] Lansbury's loyalties were to a different set of principles and convictions, rooted in his first-hand experience of Poplar, his working-class constituents and the local Labour party that had sent him back to Parliament. In 1924 the latest battle in the Poplar conflict proved to be one of the immediate issues to confront the new Labour government at Westminster.

One of John Wheatley's first acts as Minister of Health was to rescind the so-called Mond Scale of 1922, which the Poplar guardians had always ignored. Mond and his successors had been unable or unwilling to enforce this scale. It prescribed amounts of poor law relief (the maximum figure was 10s. below a labourer's wage) which struck particularly at large families and involved a detested family means test. Wheatley's action provoked a strong reaction in Parliament from Asquith and others, thereby almost ending the tenure of the first Labour government before it had begun. However, abolishing the Mond Scale did bring to an end the continuing tensions between the Poplar guardians and Whitehall officials that had marked the previous Coalition and Tory administrations.

The Poplar Rates Dispute had rumbled on after the thirty councillors had been released in October 1921. In March 1922 the Cooper Report compiled for the Ministry of Health accused Poplar of extravagance to the annual tune of £100,000. It provoked the famous pamphlet by Lansbury and his fellow guardians, *Guilty and Proud of It!* In June 1922 the Ministry endeavoured to withhold an advance from the Metropolitan Common Fund, only to be outwitted by a Poplar deputation skilfully led by Edgar Lansbury, now chairman of the Poplar Board of Guardians.[46] Next, the District Auditor surcharged all expenditure above the Mond Scale, as well as excessive municipal wages, but Lansbury and his colleagues ignored the penalties.[47] Further unsuccessful attempts included a personal surcharge on George Lansbury

---

[44] G. Lansbury, 'The Policy of the Left Wing', in H. B. Lees-Smith (ed.), *The Encyclopaedia of the Labour Movement*, ii (1928), pp. 191–4.

[45] Lansbury, *My Life*, p. 268.

[46] Charles W. Key to George Lansbury, 28 June 1922, LP, vol. 28, fos. 127–33; 'Shorthand Notes of a Deputation from the Poplar Board of Guardians Received by the Minister of Health on Tuesday, 20th June 1922', ibid. fos. 132–41; 'Shorthand Notes of a Deputation from the Poplar Board of Guardians received by the Minister of Health on Wednesday the 28th June 1922', ibid. fos. 147–54.

[47] Postgate, *Lansbury*, pp. 223–4.

in 1926 of £43,000.[48] In July–August 1923 the Poplar Guardians paid relief to local dockers in their national strike against an official pay-cut agreed by Ernest Bevin's TGWU—though the *Daily Herald*, no longer edited by George Lansbury, eventually sided with the union officials.[49] In a letter to *The Times*, Lansbury deprecated a bitter dispute that had divided the TGWU and the Stevedores' Union, as well as individual Poplar Guardians.[50] The Poplar Guardians, with a financial crisis and declining local wage levels, were compelled to reduce poor relief scales. At the guardians' meeting a demonstration organized by Sylvia Pankhurst's Unemployed Workers' Organisation turned ugly and resulted in George Lansbury summoning the police.[51]

In February 1924, the debate on abolition of the 'Poplar Order' provided the occasion for Wheatley to distinguish himself as an outstanding parliamentary debater. 'I do not think there is the least chance of that administrative act receiving the countenance or approval of the House of Commons', was Asquith's outright attack. Lansbury's sterling contribution further undermined the former Liberal Prime Minister by highlighting the inadequacies of the Cooper investigation two years before, as well as exposing his woeful understanding of the poor law regulations.[52]

In these early post-war years Lansbury had used the *Daily Herald* not only to publicize the continuing feud with the authorities over 'Poplarism', but also the activities of a young Communist tool-maker, Wal Hannington, who was organizing the unemployed. The National Unemployed Workers' Movement (NUWM) was the most prominent organization to campaign on behalf of the unemployed in inter-war Britain. However, in the early 1920s Lansbury's close connections with Hannington's organization—regarded by the authorities as a Communist-front organization—set him apart from a Labour party that outwardly adopted respectability and moderation as MacDonald and his colleagues prepared to be the next government. From 1920, the *Daily Herald* had reported the activities of NUWM and had given the fledgling organization vital support. Lansbury addressed NUWM demonstrations and, by acting as an intermediary for Hannington's organization in its dealings with the government, became identified with the hunger marchers' cause fifteen years before the famous Jarrow Crusade of 1936. As early as June 1921, the NUWM organized the first long-distance march of the unemployed from London to Brighton—now largely forgotten as the pioneer hunger march.[53] Lansbury addressed the NUWM marchers on Brighton beach and

[48] A. Roberts, District Auditor to George Lansbury, 20 Jan. 1926, LP, vol. 28, fo. 177.
[49] Richards, *The Bloody Circus*, pp. 54–6.   [50] *The Times*, 15 Aug. 1923.
[51] For more on these events, see Branson, *Poplarism*, ch. 12.
[52] *Hansard*, 13 Feb. 1924, cols. 863–923; *Daily Herald*, 14, 16 Feb. 1924.
[53] Excerpt from W. Hannington, *Never on our Knees* (1967) by Ron Horton (with photograph of marchers on Brighton beach), in Dick Penniford Papers, ESRO AMS 6375/1/71, 6375/1/2/56. Dick Penniford, former conscientious objector, was President of Brighton Trades Council in 1921 and took part in the march. See D. Penniford, 'Talk Given to the Literature Group Teachers' Training Department, Brighton College of Art, about 1960' (transcribed from tape-recording by Margaret Horton), ibid. ESRO AMS/6375/1/69.

persuaded reluctant Labour party organizers to allow Wal Hannington and his associates to address the annual party conference at the Brighton Dome.[54]

In 1924 the formation of the first British Labour government coincided with the announcement on 22 January of the death of Lenin.[55] Four days later, the Communist Party of Great Britain (CPGB) held a packed memorial service at Poplar town hall with the Russian funeral march played on the piano. George Lansbury shared his memories of the dead leader with those present, and recalled his first meeting with Lenin at the Southgate Road Brotherhood church in 1907, as well as their famous encounter in the Kremlin only four years before Lenin's death:

He was sitting in a plain room, wearing an ordinary suit, and treated me in such a way that I at once felt he was my comrade. When I came back from Russia I said that Lenin stood head and shoulders above the heads of all the men I had met in my lifetime.[56]

The Labour administration was the first British government to recognize Soviet Russia and to resume economic and diplomatic relations, in the belief that an easing of international tensions would improve international trade and create employment in Britain. In March 1924, George Lansbury, with R. C. Wallhead, Ben Turner, and Rob Smillie, pressed the government to apply the Trade Facilities Acts to the Soviet Union to promote commerce between the two countries. When the talks—which started in April over a commercial loan to Russia and the payment of Tsarist debts—collapsed Lansbury was one of a group of left-wingers in Parliament who rescued the negotiations that eventually concluded in three Anglo-Russian treaties.[57]

Ramsay MacDonald had been on the platform at the Leeds Convention of 1917, but only to celebrate the overthrow of the detested Tsarist régime. Three years later, a war-weary British labour movement had united in the 'Hands off Russia' campaign to prevent renewed conflict in Europe. Despite their unity over these events, there were fundamental differences between George Lansbury and Ramsay MacDonald in their attitude towards Soviet Russia. Nothing separated them more. Lansbury travelled to Russia twice to see at first hand a socialist government in action and to celebrate its achievements. MacDonald saw the Bolshevik régime as

---

[54] George Lansbury's association with the NUWM again alerted the British Secret Service. When, representing the NUWM, Lansbury sought an interview with the Prime Minister, Andrew Bonar Law, certain newspapers were provided with Special Branch records containing information on the 'communist character and record of the leaders of the unemployed marchers'—together with evidence of Lansbury's connections with the NUWM. In Parliament, Lansbury moved an adjournment to reveal that the material had been leaked to certain newspapers, but not the *Daily Herald*. He also complained about excessive police surveillance at political meetings and robustly defended maligned hunger marchers who had fought in the Great War. See extracts from *Daily Mail*, 22 Nov. 1922; *Morning Post*, 22 Nov. 1922; *Daily Herald*, 23 Nov. 1922 (including marginalia denying the criminal allegations) in PRO, HO 45/11275/438775. See also *Hansard*, Fifth Series, 27 Nov. 1922, cols. 389–424.

[55] *Daily Herald*, 23 Jan. 1924.

[56] George Bernard Shaw endorsed Lansbury's judgement. In an interview with the London correspondent of *Isvestia*, the Irish playwright predicted that a statue of Lenin would be set up in London alongside George Washington, who had been equally vilified in his time. *Daily Herald*, 28 Jan. 1924.

[57] George Lansbury, R. C. Wallhead, Ben Turner, and Robert Smillie to Ramsay MacDonald, n.d. [28 Mar. 1924], PRO, FO 371/10469/2753.

an alien form of socialism—totally different from the English version—and one that could only discredit his Labour party in governing circles and among the wider electorate. Moreover, as far as the Labour Prime Minister was concerned and for many others in the Labour party, Moscow directed the newly founded CPGB. Mac-Donald worked hard and effectively to outlaw all Communists from the British Labour Party.[58]

More tensions arose between the Labour government and its left-wing critics when the administration continued the defence policy of its Tory predecessor. In defending the estimates for the armed forces, MacDonald and his colleagues faced the moral and political dilemmas that would confront future Labour governments over defence and disarmament later in the twentieth century.

Labour took up the Baldwin administration's plans for naval construction by agreeing to build five cruisers and two destroyers. 'Was this decision to be taken as a great moral gesture to the world?' Ernest Thurtle—Lansbury's son-in-law— asked in a pointed parliamentary question. Fourteen defiant Labour MPs went into the opposition division lobby to vote against the Navy Estimates.

Thurtle—a serving officer in the First World War—was mainly on the right wing of his party. Yet, on the Army Estimates he seconded a pacifist amendment put forward by the Quaker and Labour MP, W. H. Ayles, to reduce the Army from 160,000 to 10,000. It attracted only thirteen votes. In the debate Lansbury intervened to declare that 'this country should lead the way in the matter of disarmament. Our duty . . . was to resort to arbitration and not to poison gas'. Lansbury also proposed that soldiers should be permitted to contract out of any service connected with industrial disputes, but was defeated by 236 to 67 votes. Finally, Thurtle endeavoured to abolish the death penalty in court martial cases without success (207 to 136 votes).[59]

British foreign policy and the defence of Britain and her Empire were also questions that distanced George Lansbury from the Labour leadership, particularly once the first Labour government had taken office. MacDonald, who to his cost had honourably opposed the Great War as a member of the UDC, was anxious to demonstrate that the defence of the realm was safe in Labour hands. It was a difficult position to reconcile in government, as strong strands of pacifism existed traditionally within his party's ranks.

To reconcile pacifist principles with the defence of the nation, Lansbury instead argued that Britain should give a moral lead to the world by the renunciation of its weapons accompanied by the abandonment of imperialism. 'So far, no nation has yet shown itself willing to give up its reliance on armaments. I am certain that if our country did so, and at the same time gave up all exclusive right to own or dominate other parts of the world, other nations would follow', was Lansbury's declaration of faith.[60]

---

[58] For a discussion of George Lansbury and Labour–Communist relations, see below, pp. 230, 240, 241–3.

[59] R. W. Lyman, *The First Labour Government, 1924* (1957), pp. 211–12.

[60] *Daily Herald*, 15 Mar. 1924.

The horrific carnage of the First World War had deepened Lansbury's Christian pacifism. He never deviated from his central conviction—derived from Christ's teaching in the Sermon on the Mount—that war was strictly forbidden between nations.[61] In the 1920s the number of anti-war organizations proliferated and, as the newly elected chairman of the 'No More War Movement', Lansbury was in constant demand to address pacifist meetings. In January 1924—with the Labour government about to take office—his message at the Memorial Hall in London was loud and clear to all: the removal of the causes of war 'would abolish armies and navies from the face of the earth'.[62]

The First World War, in which large numbers of troops from the Empire had fought in the British armed forces, had also transformed Indo-British relations and given rise to a militant upsurge of Indian nationalism. However, in terms of its imperial policy, the first Labour government, without the benefit of a long period in office to implement new ideas, largely pursued the path of its Tory predecessor. On taking office, MacDonald (who had visited India in 1910 and on his return published a perceptive account, *The Awakening of India*) disillusioned Indian nationalists by his Cabinet appointment to the Admiralty of Lord Chelmsford—a previous Viceroy of India and an unyielding Tory—and the exclusion of the sympathetic Josiah Wedgwood.[63]

India became another leading cause for left-wing critics of the MacDonald government, particularly as Indian politicians had regularly toured Britain since the end of the Great War. In the 1920s Lansbury, who saw imperialism as indissolubly linked to capitalism, was vehemently anti-imperialist and took up nationalist causes abroad and at home. In 1916 he had been the founder-chairman in Britain of The Home Rule for India League (British Auxiliary), one of a number of organizations working for various forms of Indian self-government and independence. Lansbury had been introduced to the politics of the Indian continent through his friendship with Annie Besant and her political secretary, David Graham Pole, a future Labour MP who became one of his close friends.[64]

As Rosemary Dinnage has written, Annie Besant, former socialist and feminist, had turned to the spiritual philosophy of theosophy and adopted India as her home and headquarters in 1894.[65] There she worked ceaselessly for religious, educational, and social causes before campaigning for self-government and eventual Dominion status for India. In 1916, the year in which Gandhi returned to India with his political philosophy of passive resistance, Annie Besant established the Home Rule

---

[61] 'Blessed are the peacemakers; for they shall be called the children of God' (Matt. 5: 9). See also, S. Briscoe, *The Sermon on the Mount: Daring to be Different* (1996), ch. 4.

[62] *The Times*, 21 Jan. 1924.

[63] Lyman, *The First Labour Government*, p. 124. For MacDonald's views on India, see Marquand, *Ramsay MacDonald*, pp. 117–18.

[64] For the important Lansbury–Pole friendship, see below, Ch. 12.

[65] Annie Besant continued to visit Britain. In 1911 she brought a 16-year-old Indian youth, Krishnamurti—who theosophists saw as a future charismatic Messiah—and his brother to study in Britain. They enjoyed the considerable hospitality of Muriel De La Warr, a committed theosophist, and her family. Krishnamurti met Lansbury and assisted him during his parliamentary election in 1918. For Krishnamurti, see M. Lutyens, *Krishnamurti: the Years of Awakening* (1997).

League but, as a result of her political agitation, she was briefly interned by the British authorities. In 1917, aged sixty-nine and at the height of her personal popularity, she had become the President of the Indian National Congress, only soon to quarrel and fall out with the Congress leaders.[66] Sympathetic British Labour and socialist figures were recruited to the Indian cause by establishing a British auxiliary to the League. Of these Lansbury—with his campaigning *Daily Herald*—and Pole were among the most prominent, both at Westminster and beyond during the inter-war years. In the House of Commons, Lansbury was indefatigable in raising Indian issues and acting as a parliamentary spokesman.[67]

Following the debate on Home Rule for Scotland in May 1924, Lansbury revealed how far his views differed from the Labour party and the Labour movement over imperial matters. First, though a fervent supporter of Irish independence, he considered it an anomaly that Irish MPs sat at Westminster. Instead, he proposed a fundamental constitutional reform of Parliament that also embraced India and other British colonial territories:

The present Parliament does not, and cannot, effectively manage or control either national or international affairs . . . due to the party and Cabinet systems, but . . . also . . . to the fact that no Parliament can ever be able at one and the same time to deal effectively with national, international and local government . . . what I want to see are National Councils for Wales, England and Scotland, each with full powers over local affairs . . .[68]

His proposal advocated the abolition of the Westminster Parliament, to be replaced by a fully empowered Commonwealth Assembly:

to which should come representatives of Britain and Ireland, India, the Dominions and Colonies. To this Parliament should be given full powers over all matters which concern them all . . . this will involve complete self-government for India, which I am confident must be conceded unless we are to lose all connection with that great people . . . on this question the will of the people of India must prevail. We must treat them in such a manner as will ensure their willingness to accept partnership with us. Such a policy would also remove the last vestige of a claim for a divided Ireland.[69]

Lansbury continued to pursue these ideas, though the first Labour government had only a short time remaining in office.[70]

As Postgate recalled, despite the welcome action over 'Poplarism', his father-in-law shared in the general disenchantment over the record of the first Labour government. In the autumn the Attorney-General, Sir Patrick Hastings, made the

---

[66] R. Dinnage, *Annie Besant* (Harmondsworth, 1986), pp. 106–10. For the India Home Rule League, see also H. F. Owen, 'Towards Nation-Wide Agitation and Organisation: The Home Rule Leagues, 1915–1918', in D. A. Low (ed.), *Soundings in Modern South Asian History* (1968), pp. 159–95.

[67] Annie Besant also became General Secretary of the Indian National Convention, which produced a moderate parliamentary Bill 'to establish within the British Empire a Commonwealth of India'. Though Gandhi, Nehru, Jinnah, and other Indian leaders did not back it, Lansbury brought it forward at Westminster as a private Member's measure that secured only a first reading in Dec. 1925. A. Taylor, *Annie Besant: A Biography* (Oxford, 1992), pp. 319–21. For Lansbury's campaigning on India, see *Daily Herald*, 3, 23 Feb. 1924.

[68] *Daily Herald*, 17 May 1924.   [69] *Daily Herald*, 14 June 1924.

[70] For more on George Lansbury and India, see below, Ch. 13.

ill-advised decision to prosecute the acting editor of the *Workers' Weekly*, a veteran war hero, J. R. Campbell, for a 'Don't Shoot' article that the minister considered seditious. Old crusading spirits of syndicalist days were instantly revived, as Lansbury joined others on the left in an outpouring of outrage at Westminster. An embarrassed government withdrew the prosecution, but was defeated in the Commons by the combined Tory and Liberal opposition. MacDonald chose this occasion to go to the country, and Labour had to fight its third election campaign in three years.[71]

Three weeks before polling day, Lansbury issued a rallying-cry to return a Labour government to power, as more had been achieved in 'Labour's term of office than ever before in the history of Parliament'. He also appealed for increased sales of the *Daily Herald* and for financial contributions to party funds.[72]

In East London, Lansbury fought another straight fight against a Conservative opponent and held Poplar, Bow and Bromley in December 1924 with a reduced majority on the largest turn-out at the polls recorded there in the inter-war years—72.1 per cent, up from the 63.7 per cent of a year before. The voting figures were: G. Lansbury 15,740 (61.6 per cent), Capt. H. A. Hill 9,806 (30.6 per cent). Lansbury's own election victory took place amid the disappointment of overall Labour losses across the country. While Labour campaigned on its achievements in foreign policy, the *Daily Mail* published the notorious Zinoviev letter encouraging the British Communist Party to prepare to spread Leninism and armed insurrection in Britain. Subsequent newspaper headlines whipped up virulent anti-Communism in the last weeks of the election campaign. The document was discredited later as a forgery, but MacDonald's critics believed the episode—badly handled by MacDonald—had cost the party the general election. While Labour's vote was 5.5 million—an increase of 1.5 million—the Tories (including twelve Constitutionalists) won 419 seats, Labour was reduced to 151 MPs, and the Liberals down to only 40. Baldwin formed his second government and was in office for nearly five years.

A dejected George Lansbury attempted to put a brave face on Labour's defeat as part of a cause that 'marches forward irrespective of electoral results . . . a movement which slowly, but surely, is enshrining itself as a religion in the hearts and lives of men and women the wide world over'.[73] Shortly afterwards, with John Wheatley, he addressed a crowded ILP meeting in Glasgow full of the rhetoric of the class war and his memories of Lenin. He ended with a flourish on pacifism and imperialism:

You can only get rid of war, by getting rid of the system of exploitation which enslaves the whole world . . . it is just as unchristian to kill black men as it is to kill white men, and the war whether it be in Egypt or in the Sudan, is every bit as bad as war in Europe . . . It is because I am against all wars, that I am in favour of settling our quarrels by peaceful methods, I believe human life to be sacred.[74]

In concluding, the 'wild man of Poplar'—as he described himself at the end of 1924—had struck a perennial theme and one that he was to return to constantly in his speeches ten years later.

[71] Postgate, *Lansbury*, pp. 226–7.   [72] *Daily Herald*, 11 Oct. 1924.
[73] Ibid. 1 Nov. 1924.   [74] *Forward*, 27 Dec. 1924.

The fall of the Labour government fuelled the disquiet about MacDonald's leadership among senior party members and trade union leaders. Now in opposition, MacDonald faced a serious threat of an attempt by either the left or the right in the party to remove him from the leadership.[75] Lansbury was dissatisfied with MacDonald's leadership and sought meetings with Clifford Allen, Brailsford, and E. D. Morel about the future of the party.[76] Bevin and Snowden saw Henderson as MacDonald's natural replacement, but Henderson remained firmly loyal until the collapse of the second Labour government in August 1931.[77] MacDonald considered Wheatley a possible challenger from the left wing of the party.

When neither candidature materialized at the first meeting of the PLP after the election defeat, Maxton put forward George Lansbury's name for the leadership. However, Lansbury declined to accept a nomination he had only heard about shortly before the meeting and declared that a change of leader 'would be most inopportune in the circumstances'.[78] In the event MacDonald was re-elected with only five votes cast against him. It is difficult to know why Lansbury, who was disenchanted with MacDonald's moderate politics in office and with his cosiness with the Liberals, refused the nomination. Four years later, in his autobiography he still maintained a discreet silence, and twenty years later Postgate had nothing to say about these events. However, Lansbury possessed no leadership ambitions and had been genuinely taken by surprise at Maxton's proposal. Earlier he confessed to Clifford Allen: 'I am however certain I should make a very bad chairman of any organization because I am so strong an individualist.'[79] Even when he finally became leader of the rump of forty-six Labour MPs, after the disastrous 1931 election defeat that left him as the only surviving Cabinet minister from the 1929–31 second Labour government, Lansbury was to display a very different and unassuming style of leadership from that of his predecessor.

Nevertheless, during the 1920s Lansbury remained one of MacDonald's most consistent critics, particularly with the launching in 1925 of his new newspaper, *Lansbury's Labour Weekly*, founded after he finally left the *Daily Herald*. In 1922 the Labour party and the TUC had taken over the control and financial management of the *Daily Herald*. Lansbury had realized only this course of action could prevent the extinction of the newspaper. Despite the post-war rise of Labour, the fortunes of the newspaper had slumped to a point where George Lansbury and the informal board of trade unionists running the independent Labour daily paper since the 1919 relaunch could keep it afloat no longer.

---

[75] Marquand, *Ramsay MacDonald*, pp. 390–2.

[76] George Lansbury to Clifford Allen, 18 Nov. 1923, E. D. Morel to George Lansbury, n.d. [Nov. 1923], CAP. Marwick, *Clifford Allen*, pp. 93–4.

[77] Wrigley, *Arthur Henderson*, pp. 154–5.

[78] *Daily Herald*, 4 Dec. 1924. For the Labour party leadership contest in the 1920s, see R. Mackenzie, *British Political Parties: The Distribution of Power within the Conservative and Labour Parties* (1963), pp. 306–7, 347–52; on George Lansbury and the leadership election in 1924; W. Knox, *James Maxton* (Manchester, 1987), pp. 53–5.

[79] George Lansbury to Clifford Allen, 7 Feb. 1923, CAP.

As Huw Richards has commented, the fate of the *Daily Herald* itself was the best story carried by the newspaper during these post-war years. The restoration of racing news in 1919, public appeals for support, and a new debenture issue failed to reverse declining sales and large-scale losses. By Christmas 1921, the *Daily Herald* board and debenture holders offered the ownership and control of the paper to the Labour party and the TUC.[80]

Crucially, the phrase 'the only paper Labour had got' summed up the paper's future. In an era before modern broadcasting, the paper remained a vital source of information on post-war policy as Labour gained increased representation on local authorities.[81] Lansbury had tried to press the two national organizations to take control by replacing the *Daily Herald* board with Arthur Henderson, C. W. Bowerman, General Secretary of the TUC, and himself as the shareholders.[82] Eventually, Henderson, responsible for the important reconstruction of Labour party organization, had encouraged the Labour party and the TUC to take on this new challenge, despite the chastening experience of the *Daily Citizen*. By August 1922 a new board of eleven directors, including Lansbury, was in operation.

However, it was no longer feasible for an opponent of the Labour leadership to edit the Labour daily now under official party control. George Lansbury resigned and was replaced by fifty-three-year-old Henry Hamilton Fyfe, a professional journalist with extensive experience on the *Mirror, Morning Advertiser*, and *Mail*. By arrangement, Fyfe's appointment was kept secret for four months.[83] Lansbury told his readers: '[M]y resignation is voluntary. I desire the new owners to be perfectly free to appoint who they please.'[84] As the paper was shifted onto the centre-ground of Labour politics, Lansbury said little about the controversial changes Fyfe introduced and the consequent dissent in the staff office. Instead, in a passionate appeal to the 1923 party conference that invoked the *Herald* rebel spirit, Lansbury reminded the delegates 'that in the *Daily Herald* there was the life-blood of tens of thousands of poor men and poor women, some of whom had sacrificed everything . . . for the workers to have a daily paper'.[85]

Lansbury did not depart immediately, remaining as general manager for two years and assisted by his daughter, Daisy Postgate, as his personal secretary—a role she undertook throughout his parliamentary career.[86] In 1923 as part of an internal

---

[80] Richards, *The Bloody Circus*, p. 43; 'Daily Herald Newspaper. Report on the position of *Daily Herald* submitted to Joint Meeting of General Council TUC, the Labour Party Executive, and the *Daily Herald* Directorate, Jan. 1923', LPLF, LP/DH/163.

[81] Prof. Philip Bagwell recalled that his father, an Isle of Wight newsagent who sold the *Daily Herald*, was elected to the Ventnor Urban District Council on a similar programme to the Poplar councillors: pers. com., 1 Aug. 2001.

[82] George Lansbury to Arthur Henderson, 2 Mar. 1922; Arthur Henderson to George Lansbury, 3 Mar. 1922; Ethel Snowden to Arthur Henderson, 4 Mar. 1922, LPLF, LP/DH/63–65.

[83] For the Labour party–TUC take-over of the *Daily Herald*, see Richards, *The Bloody Circus*, pp. 43–64; R. McKibbin, *The Evolution of the Labour Party, 1910–1924* (1983), pp. 221–34.

[84] *Daily Herald*, 29 July 1922.

[85] Labour Party, *Report of the Twenty-Third Annual Conference* (1923), pp. 209–10.

[86] Lansbury's weekly wage was £8. 13s. 2d. Daisy Postgate received £6. 18s. 9d. per week.

programme of economies he offered his resignation.[87] On 3 January 1925, after citing 'the best year in its (*Daily Herald*'s) existence, and . . . no question of leaving a sinking ship', George Lansbury resigned and finally left the paper.[88]

Even during his final two years on the *Daily Herald*, the paper's columns provided George Lansbury with a regular political platform. His writings—akin to a weekly sermon to the nation—reflected the issues he raised in Parliament. Each Saturday, Lansbury hammered away at a number of major themes: unemployment, poverty, the Poplar case, pacifism, and the struggle against imperialism.

In the months following the fall of the first Labour government, the Labour party and the TUC experienced a shift to the left. From 1925–7, George Lansbury's Socialist Club, based on *Lansbury's Labour Weekly*, played an important part in debates on the political left on Labour party policy and strategy in the critical times ahead.[89] In 1925, however, one issue in domestic politics continually filled the pages of *Lansbury's Labour Weekly*—the struggle of the British miners. During the ensuing months, George Lansbury and his new weekly paper were directly involved with the threatening crisis in the coal industry that in 1926 resulted in the British General Strike.

[87] A. E. Holmes, '*Daily Herald* Report' 8 Oct. 1923, LPCF, LP/DH/248.

[88] George Lansbury, 'Memorandum re the *Daily Herald & Victoria House Printing Co*', 19 July 1924; George Lansbury to *Daily Herald* Board, 3 Jan. 1925, LPCF, LP/DH/358; 405i–ii.

[89] G. Brown, *Maxton* (Edinburgh, 1986), pp. 172–3.

13
Backbench Rebel, 1925–1927

On Saturday 1 May 1926 over 800 delegates, representing more than 140 unions, gathered at a Special Conference of Trade Union Executives at the Memorial Hall in London. On that celebrated May Day they voted overwhelmingly by 3,653,529 to 49,911 to empower the TUC to call a national shut-down if the coal owners' lock-out of almost 1 million British miners did not end within two days. On 3 May, the General Strike of 1926—the most famous industrial conflict in twentieth-century Britain—started at one minute to midnight. Over 1.5 million 'first-line' workers in transport, printing, iron and steel, power, building, and chemicals answered the TUC General Council's summons to halt work.[1]

During the nine-day stoppage, large numbers of activists were directly involved on both sides in one of the few national events that bitterly divided social classes in Britain during the twentieth century.[2] On 6 May, Stanley Baldwin denounced the General Strike as: 'a challenge to Parliament and . . . the road to anarchy and ruin'. On the following day, the TUC retaliated: 'the General Council does not challenge the Constitution . . . the sole aim is to secure for the miners a decent standard of living. The Council is engaged in an industrial dispute.'

Since July 1925 the Baldwin administration had revived and strengthened well-laid government anti-strike preparations first established by the post-war Lloyd George coalition government. These contingency plans had not been disbanded when Labour held office in 1924. Unofficial organizations and right-wing political groups, such as the Organisation for Maintenance and Supplies (OMS), the Chambers of Commerce, the *Fasciti*, and the Crusaders had also begun to recruit volunteers.[3] By contrast, the trade union leadership was unprepared for a national dispute until just before the strike when the TUC belatedly became involved with the abortive negotiations to resolve the mining dispute.

Various images of those who participated on both sides in the 'Great Strike' of May 1926 remain in the folklore of working-class history. Mainly middle-class and upper-class strike-breakers—or 'volunteers'—rallied to the government's summons

---

[1] There is an extensive literature on the General Strike. See esp. K. Laybourn, *The General Strike: Day by Day* (Stroud, 1996) and *The General Strike of 1926* (Manchester, 1993); see also M. Morris, *The General Strike* (1976); G. A. Phillips, *The General Strike: The Politics of Industrial Conflict* (1976); P. Renshaw, *Nine Days in May: The General Strike* (1976); C. Farman, *The General Strike, May 1926* (St Alban's, 1974).

[2] After the TUC called off the national action, accounts of the effects of 'Great Strike' in different localities soon appeared. See e.g. E. Wilkinson, J. F. Horrabin, and R. W. Postgate, *A Workers' History of the Great Strike* (1927).

[3] For these preparations, see Morris, *The General Strike*, ch. 8.

to the civil colours to thwart the stoppage by keeping essential services running. Outside Parliament, Lady Astor, George Lansbury's feisty Tory opponent at Westminster, stiffened aristocratic sinews. Her 'society' ladies billeted civil servants conveniently close to Whitehall and served tea and sympathy to fellow volunteers at the enormous government food and distribution centre in Hyde Park. Not all, however, were of the same social milieu as Viscountess Astor and her *grandes dames*— nor from the ranks of the hundreds of bank clerks, former army officers, and university students who put aside their books in Cambridge and Oxford to don Fair Isle jerseys and plus-fours and eagerly man the railways, act as temporary dock workers, or enrol as special constables. Some were from working-class origins. Remarkably, twenty-five-year-old Ernest Seeley, a future trade union general secretary and later doyen of the Progressive League, drove one of the 300 'pirate' London General Omnibus Company vehicles crewed by volunteers at the start of the dispute.[4]

Overall, the Great Strike appeared relatively peaceful—symbolized by the celebrated football match on 10 May in Plymouth, where the wife of the local Chief Constable kicked off and the strikers' team narrowly defeated the police side by a 2–1 score-line. However, on the same day, the *Flying Scotsman* carrying 300 passengers was deliberately derailed outside Edinburgh. Violent clashes occurred during the dispute with mounted police setting about the strikers with batons. There were around four thousand arrests, including that of the Communist MP for Battersea, Shapurji Saklatvala, imprisoned for two months for a seditious speech at the May Day Rally.

Standing on his native Bow Road, George Lansbury watched with dismay as troops and armoured cars moved into the East End, where the docks came to an immediate standstill on the first day of the strike. 'The whole East End of London is a great silent city, even quieter and more peaceful than on Sunday. Not a workshop, factory, or commercial concern of any kind is doing business', commented the *British Worker*.[5] In Parliament, Lansbury complained bitterly about the Baldwin government's employment of troops against his constituents, a provocative act against a local community largely free from civil disorder:

Not a blunderbuss has been discovered, not an old horse pistol has been discovered; there has not been found even a box of bullets given by some Tory member's secretary, not even that and yet we got thousands of fully-armed and fully-equipped troops dumped on us, and I want to know what for . . .[6]

The events of May 1926 were no surprise to the Member for Bow and Bromley, who could do little except mount a vigorous defence of his constituents in

---

[4] Dr Ernest A. Seeley (1900–89) was born in working-class North London, where he attended Gillespie Road Elementary School in Highbury. After a career as Head of Science at Bournemouth Technical College, he became General Secretary of the Association of Teachers in Technical Institutes for over ten years. For the Progressive League's left-wing programmes, see its journal, *Plan*. I am grateful to Dr Janet Shepherd (Ernest Seeley's daughter) for this information.

[5] Quoted in Laybourn, *The General Strike*, pp. 78–9.

[6] *Hansard*, 10 May 1926, col. 776.

Parliament by attacking the government's handling of the dispute. George Lansbury had a long and close involvement with the origins of the industrial dispute. During 1925–6 his venture, *Lansbury's Labour Weekly*, remained almost a lone voice in the industrial wilderness—alongside local councils of action—warning of a forthcoming massive industrial struggle.

In 1925 George Lansbury had left the *Daily Herald* to the accompaniment of H. H. Fyfe's tribute: 'As long as the *Daily Herald* lives its name will be coupled in thoughts of the workers with the name of the great leader who made it.' However, Lansbury's resignation was a complete breach. His regular Saturday column ended and afterwards there was only the occasional article and support with publicity. With the assistance of an old friend, David Graham Pole, Lansbury had immediately launched *Lansbury's Labour Weekly*, which ran from February 1925 to July 1927. To publish the paper, Palace Publications Limited was formed—with Pole, Lansbury, and the Countess De La Warr as its directors.

Lansbury disliked the use of his name in the title of the new publication, but the *Daily Herald* vetoed his use of the *Weekly Herald*. Five members of the *Daily Herald* staff accompanied him to the new weekly, with a sixth, company secretary Philip Millwood, joining shortly afterwards.[7] Once again, Lansbury gathered together a group of talented writers and intellectuals that included G. D. H. Cole, Norman Ewer, Gerald Gould, and Margaret Cole. Ellen Wilkinson contributed a regular parliamentary column, illustrated by J. F. Horrabin. A newcomer, Herbert Farjeon, joined as dramatic critic. As assistant editor, Raymond Postgate became increasingly influential.

The first of 123 issues of *Lansbury's Labour Weekly* appeared on 28 February 1925. It proclaimed 'What We Stand For'—a detailed declaration of Lansbury's personal testimony based on an end to capitalism and its replacement by socialism, democracy, and pacifism. 'We shall stand then with the workers in Parliament or out of Parliament, in every struggle great or small, for a higher standard of life, till the day dawns when Socialism is triumphant', was the message that characterized the new crusading journal.[8] The paper's close identification with the struggle of the British miners continued the support given by the *Daily Herald* in the post-war years.

The immediate origins of the General Strike have been well discussed in terms of the chronic economic difficulties in the British coal industry after the First World War and the miners' struggle to resist wage cuts.[9] Though, in 1919, the Majority Report of the Sankey Commission had recommended nationalization as the solution to the industry's financial problems, on 31 March 1921 the Lloyd George Coalition government returned the mines to the coal-owners. Industrial conflict in the coalfields resulted in the débâcle of the Triple Alliance on 15 April 1921—'Black

---

[7] Huw Richards suggests that Lansbury resigned the day after he misinformed the Labour Executive about a £400 payment from the General Council, which would have been raised at the next directors' meeting. Richards, *The Bloody Circus* (1997), pp. 68–70.

[8] *Lansbury's Labour Weekly*, 28 Feb. 1925.

[9] For a valuable summary of these debates, see Laybourn, *The General Strike*, pp. 1–7.

Friday'—when the National Union of Railwaymen and the National Transport Workers' Federation failed to back the miners' strike action and led to substantial wage cuts and cries of betrayal.

In forming his Tory government in November 1924, Stanley Baldwin had appointed an old opponent of Labour as Chancellor of the Exchequer. Winston Churchill, in accepting high office in April 1925 restored Britain to the gold standard with the English pound overcharged at parity with the American dollar. The effect on British exports produced a crisis in the coal industry and led to the most famous dispute of the TUC and the Tory government in the 1926 General Strike. It was the major confrontation in British Labour history during the last century and one that George Lansbury and his newspaper had been predicting for months.

On 30 July 1925, Stanley Baldwin, Prime Minister, announced the need for reductions in the wages of the working class at a time when the number of registered unemployed was nearly 1 million. The first assault was on the vanguard of the Labour movement. The miners were threatened by the coal-owners (anxious to offset the 13 per cent wage rises of 1924) with a lock-out, if they did not agree to a reduction in wages and a longer working day. However, among the labour movement, there was widespread sympathy and support for the miners, particularly as their defeat was regarded as the prelude to an employers' attack on workers in general. In July 1925 the Railwaymen and the Transport Workers—at the prompting of the TUC General Council—placed an embargo on the movement of coal to offset the large stockpiles of coal. On 31 July 1925—'Red Friday'—the government postponed the critical industrial situation by granting a nine-month subsidy to the coal-owners and appointing the Samuel Commission to make recommendations for the future of the coal industry. At the same time, the government prepared contingency plans to deal with an industrial strike.

Even after the apparent success of 'Red Friday', *Lansbury's Labour Weekly* advised working people: 'the victory gained must only provide us with a breathing space and time to prepare our forces for the next great conflict.'[10] George Lansbury warned the TUC that the previous three years of relative industrial tranquillity were an illusion.[11]

Throughout its relatively short-lived existence, *Lansbury's Labour Weekly* campaigned tirelessly for miners and their communities in this country. Lansbury devoted a series of articles to defend the cause of British miners, as he had done regularly in the post-war years in the *Daily Herald*. He predicted an imminent clash with capitalism and the dangers of an unprepared working-class movement. On the eve of 'Red Friday', *Lansbury's Labour Weekly* had published a detailed analysis of the economic condition of the coal trade to demonstrate that the nationalization of the mines under workers' control could prove an effective remedy to the industry's chronic problems.[12] Typical of the newspaper's crusade was the publication of the following stark facts: 'the number of miners killed and injured in one year would form a procession in single file thirty-nine miles long. In the place of every

[10] *Lansbury's Labour Weekly*, 8 Aug. 1925.   [11] Ibid. 4 July 1925.   [12] Ibid. 1 Aug. 1925.

fourteenth man there would be a stretcher for the seriously maimed, and in every 62nd place a coffin.'[13]

The newspaper also jibed at the unbalanced composition of the Royal Commission appointed to investigate the coal industry with no representatives of the miners or coal-owners. The Samuel Commission—as it became known—comprised a group of well-heeled Liberal politicians, all unconnected with the mining industry. The Rt. Hon. Sir Herbert Samuel, PC, GBE, educated at Balliol College, Oxford, previously Postmaster-General (1910–14) and subsequently Governor of Palestine headed the roll-call. His fellow commissioners included the former wartime Chief of Staff, General the Hon. Sir Herbert Lawrence, managing partner of the bankers, Glyn, Mills, and Co., and a director of seven other prominent banking, railway, and ship-building companies. The remaining members were the Balliol-educated civil servant, Sir William Beveridge, director of the London School of Economics, and Kenneth Lee, chairman of the textile manufacturers, Tootal, Broadhurst, Lee, & Co. As Chairman of the Royal Commission—which held thirty-three public meetings taking evidence from nearly eighty witnesses, inspected twenty-five collieries in person with assistants visiting forty others—Samuel described his task as 'the most strenuous six months' work I have ever done'.[14]

Published on 10 March 1926, the 300-page *Report* of the Samuel Commission recommended the nationalization of mining royalties and amalgamation of the coal companies, as well as a reduction in wages. *Lansbury's Labour Weekly* exposed the inadequacies of the Commission's report, arguing that the coal industry was a symbol of capitalist decay: 'In sum, there is no constructive proposal made whose fulfilment under private enterprise can be guaranteed or whose benefits are likely to reach the miners.'[15] The miners' complete opposition to the Commission's proposal was captured in the memorable slogan 'Not a penny off the pay, not a second on the day!'[16]

During the months before the General Strike, Lansbury also played an important part in the opposition to the Government's political assault on the left wing of the Labour movement. In October 1925, after police raids on their headquarters, twelve leading Communists—including Albert Inkpin, Harry Pollitt, Wal Hannington, and Robin Page Arnot—were arrested for unlawfully conspiring to publish seditious libels and to incite others to commit breaches of the Incitement to Mutiny Act of 1797. After a trial at the Old Bailey they were found guilty and sentenced to periods of six and twelve months' imprisonment.[17] In the public outcry at these prosecutions, George Lansbury immediately offered bail for those arrested and played a significant part in the public protests surrounding their imprisonment after their trial.

At this time, Lansbury was closely identified with the British section of the

---

[13] Ibid. 6 Feb. 1926.
[14] For the Samuel Commission, see Wasserstein, *Herbert Samuel*, ch. 10; Farman, *The General Strike*, ch. 5.
[15] *Lansbury's Labour Weekly*, 20 Mar. 1926.   [16] Laybourn, *The General Strike*, p. 8.
[17] Morris, *The General Strike*, pp. 162–3.

International Class War Prisoners' Aid (ICWPA), an international body established to defend free speech and assist the families of those imprisoned in the class
struggle.[18] As treasurer of the Free Speech and Maintenance Fund, Lansbury was a
leading figure in the ICWPA demonstrations demanding the release of the imprisoned Communists. In December 1925, with A. J. Cook, he addressed a crowded
Essex Hall meeting off the Strand: 'He was under no illusion. Either the workers
would find their salvation through constitutional action or they would by other
means,' was Lansbury's warning.[19] As the agitation for the prisoners' release grew,
he organized another mass Albert Hall rally—booking the venue in his name—
where Margaret Pollitt presented him with an address acknowledging his endeavours on behalf of the Communists. Lansbury also led large-scale marches from
Clapham to Wandsworth Prison, where the twelve were incarcerated, with all the
theatrical razzmatazz reminiscent of the Poplar Rates Rebellion.[20] However, he
went further in his challenge to the authorities. At each of these public gatherings
Lansbury orchestrated thousands of those present to repeat after him the 'Don't
Shoot' appeal for which the Communist party leaders had been imprisoned.
Lansbury was part of a broad left coalition of support for the imprisoned Communists. However throughout 1925 and 1926, the Communist press constantly
attacked him and poured disdain on the flawed ideology of *Lansbury's Labour
Weekly*.[21] As we shall see, George Lansbury's sympathy for British Communism in
the 1920s and his participation in its ancillary organizations—such as the ICWPA—
limited his influence in the Labour movement and contributed to the tensions
between his position as a back-bencher and the Labour party leadership at
Westminster.

On 22 June 1925, Beatrice Webb noted the disunity between the TUC and the
PLP, which she attributed to disenchantment within the Labour movement with
MacDonald's leadership. One result was a swing to the left in Labour politics. 'Certainly the Liberals must be smiling in very broad smiles over the revolutionary
speeches of Smillie, Maxton, Lansbury and Cook', she added in her diary.[22] Two
months later, she detected greater evidence of revolutionary socialism and its
source: 'Maxton, Wheatley, Lansbury and Cook are the four leaders of this revolutionary Socialism, and judged by their public utterances they have really convinced
themselves that the capitalist citadel is falling.'[23]

However, though in Parliament George Lansbury formed part of the left-
wing opposition—including James Maxton and the Clydeside MPs—who were
critical of MacDonald's leadership, particularly after the fall of the first Labour
government, he was not always on the closest terms with this group. Arthur
Woodburn observed 'how hurt he [Lansbury] sometimes felt when the
Scottish MPs banded together to fight for socialism all by themselves and

---

[18] For more on this organization, see *Geo. Lansbury's Speech to the Meeting of the Executive of the
I.C.W.P.A., Moscow, 29 July 1926*, published as a pamphlet.
[19] *Workers' Weekly*, 18 Dec. 1925.   [20] Ibid. 5 Mar. 1926.
[21] For examples, see *Workers' Weekly*, 2, 16 Oct. 1925; 15 Jan.; 13 Aug. 1926.
[22] *Beatrice Webb's Diaries, 1924–1932*, ed. Cole (1952), p. 65.   [23] Ibid. entry for 22 June 1925.

excluded English comrades who were as energetic, as able and as willing as themselves'.[24]

According to Postgate, outside Westminster, Lansbury's period of greatest influence with the British trade union leadership coincided with his relatively brief time as editor of *Lansbury's Labour Weekly*. Among his associates were the textile workers' leader, Ben Turner, and a powerful left-wing trio on the General Council of the TUC: George Hicks of the Bricklayers, A. A. Purcell of the Furniture Workers, and Alonzo Swales of the Engineers.[25] The columns of his newspaper remained open to trade union leaders and included the Communist miners' leader A. J. Cook among the contributors.

The dominance of the left wing on the TUC General Council was relatively short lived, particularly once the able thirty-six-year-old Walter Citrine rose from acting general secretary to general secretary just before the General Strike and placed his decisive imprint on the national organization.[26]

In May 1926, George Lansbury played no part in central direction of the nine-day strike, which remained firmly in the hands of the General Council of the TUC at the Ecclestone Square headquarters it had shared with the Labour party in Belgravia until earlier in the year. Along with most of the British press, *Lansbury's Labour Weekly* was not published during the dispute, though George Lansbury's staff walked into their central London office from the suburbs. According to Postgate, Lansbury stayed in his East End constituency, where his role was limited to running off his local strike bulletin on a duplicator, like many trades council secretaries in different parts of Britain.[27] The proceeds of £25. 10s. from the ten-day production were handed over to the miners' relief fund.[28]

It is possible to add considerably more detail—from Raymond Postgate himself—about George Lansbury's day-to-day activities during the General Strike, which extended beyond Bow and Bromley. Postgate was politically active in the dispute and afterwards wrote a general account of the main events.[29] Also, for the only time in his life, he kept a diary of his activities during the historic nine days, which was published later in an American paper.[30]

What can be gleaned from this useful source is that on Saturday 1 May 1926, amid considerable public speculation about the possibility of a strike, members of the Lansbury family assembled on the Victoria Embankment ready to march in the traditional May Day procession to Hyde Park. Edgar Lansbury had walked to Bouverie Street in an unsuccessful attempt to obtain a newspaper. Only when his younger brother, Eric, arrived with a copy of the *Standard* did they discover in the 'Stop Press' that the TUC had announced a general strike. Eventually, Postgate bought

---

[24] *Labour Standard*, 17 Dec. 1925, newscutting in Arthur Woodburn Papers, quoted in Brown, *Maxton*, pp. 172–3.

[25] Postgate, *Lansbury*, pp. 228–31.

[26] R. Taylor, *The TUC: From the General Strike to New Unionism* (Basingstoke, 2000), ch. 1.

[27] Postgate, *Lansbury*, pp. 239–40.   [28] *Lansbury's Labour Weekly*, 5 June 1926.

[29] Postgate, Wilkinson, and Horrabin, *A Workers' History of the Great Strike* (1927).

[30] R. W. Postgate, 'Diary of the British Strike', *New Masses*, Sept. 1926. Detailed extracts from Postgate's diary were published in Postgate and Postgate, *Life of Raymond Postgate*, pp. 127–36.

another newspaper in Oxford Street that confirmed the strike deadline of midnight on 3 May 1926. After returning from the Hyde Park festivities, he wired his father-in-law, who had been speaking in Devon and Cornwall over the weekend, to return from Newton Abbott immediately. After playing bridge at Dorothy and Ernest Thurtle's home that evening, Postgate noted, 'What a May Day!'

At the Memorial Hall meeting on that Saturday, Ramsay MacDonald had brought cheers from the union delegates with his assault on the Baldwin government as responsible for the current situation, but as leader of the Labour party he was most anxious to avoid the pending industrial conflict. The use of a general strike—for political purposes or to avert international conflict—had been part of working-class history since William Benbow and the Chartists in the 1830s and 1840s. Nearly a century later, under Lansbury's editorship, the *Herald* had called for such direct action against 'the Washout Parliament' after the disappointment of the 'Coupon election' of 1918 that re-elected the Lloyd George Coalition government. Unable to sleep on 4 May, Beatrice Webb condemned the General Strike as the death gasp of 'workers' control' and blamed Lansbury among others for the national stoppage. 'An absurd doctrine ... introduced into British working class life by Tom Mann and the Guild Socialists and preached incessantly, before the War, by the *Daily Herald* under George Lansbury', she recorded at 4.00 a.m.[31] Whatever its origins, now that the possibility of a general strike had become political reality, Raymond Postgate shared the views of many on the political left who doubted the capacity and determination of the TUC to carry it out in May 1926. On hearing the news, he noted on Sunday, 2 May:

After writing continually to urge the workers to stand together—wondering whether they will ever be determined enough for a general strike—has it come at last? . . . Has [the TUC Headquarters at] Eccleston Square any plans? Enough guts? It is like asking for an elephant or a dragon, not expecting to receive it, and lo, here it is walking up the garden path.[32]

During the next nine days regular communication and news about the conflict became extremely difficult, since most of the daily newspapers ceased production. The General Strike was an important stage in the development of the fledgling BBC into a public institution. The Corporation broadcast five daily bulletins, which were monitored by a government determined to control the airwaves. An appeal for industrial peace by the Archbishop of Canterbury was vetoed and no trade union leader was allowed to broadcast. However, the Director-General, John Reith, by keeping the nation informed about the industrial conflict, carefully maintained the BBC's independence and thereby prevented a government takeover, as desired by the Cabinet hardliners, Churchill and Birkenhead.[33] At 39 Bow Road the Lansbury family owned one of the new valve radio sets that constituted part of the listening nation in May 1926. On Sunday evening, Raymond Postgate called on his mother-in-law, Bessie, 'to cheer up Mrs L and hear the wireless'. 'No settlement yet,

    [31] *Beatrice Webb's Diaries*, ed. Cole, p. 92.   [32] Postgate, 'Diary'.
    [33] A. Crisell, *An Introductory History of British Broadcasting* (1997), pp. 18–19; J. Curran and J. Seaton, *Power without Responsibility: The Press and Broadcasting in Britain* (1997), p. 119.

it says . . .', he learned from one of the government sources that monopolized the radio during the next nine days.[34]

With most of the national newspapers ceasing production, the General Council of the TUC made a tactical error in not allowing the *Daily Herald* to publish during the days of the General Strike. It also denied Lansbury's application for permission to continue printing *Lansbury's Labour Weekly*. Instead, the *British Worker*, edited by Hamilton Fyfe at the *Daily Herald* office in Gray's Inn Road, was brought out by the TUC within twenty-four hours in response to the Government's *British Gazette*. This propaganda newspaper was produced by Baldwin's former PPS, J. C. Davidson, edited by the belligerent Winston Churchill and printed at the *Morning Post* building by staff from the *Mail* and the *Express*, and artificers from the Royal Navy.[35]

Though the government and the TUC endeavoured to reach an agreement based on the Samuel Report on Sunday 2 May, negotiations proved fruitless. Neither the miners nor the coal-owners would compromise—and the whole business ended in the infamous incident of the NATSOPA printers' refusal to set up the leader article on 'King and Country' in the *Daily Mail*. Under pressure from right-wingers in his Cabinet, Baldwin had his pretext to call off the negotiations.

On Monday 3 May, as the possibility that the strike would take effect loomed, Postgate, on advice from the Journalists' Union, sent the latest edition of *Lansbury's Labour Weekly* to the printers. He consulted George Lansbury at the House of Commons in the evening and was told that: 'the *Mirror* and the *Sketch* have been stopped. The *Daily Mail* was stopped this morning, by the NATSOPA [the printing union] because they would not print a violently anti-Labour appeal. He says the *Mail* is running with a blackleg staff.'

Lansbury was a spectator to the main debate in the House of Commons that revealed the divisions among the main political parties to the forthcoming conflict. He also witnessed the desperate last-minute attempts to settle the dispute by J. H. Thomas loathed for his betrayal over 'Black Friday' in 1921 and his opposition on the General Council to the strike call. 'GL comes out [of Parliament]: he says Thomas is almost in collapse. He is making frantic efforts, with Henderson and [Ramsay] MacDonald, to "find a formula". They are meeting the Cabinet again. There is no settlement,' was Postgate's note of this hurly-burly.

Tuesday 4 May was the first full day of the General Strike. In East London there were outbreaks of social disorder. Crowds stopped car-drivers from using the Blackwall Tunnel and four cars were burnt in Poplar. Bitter class divisions and high emotions engendered by the strike can be seen in one account by the right-wing press on the activities of the Poplar Strike Committee:

When matters were at their worst, a body which styled itself the 'Strike Committee' strove to seize control of affairs. For a time the members of this little self-appointed group exerted

---

[34] By 1926 the Post Office issued about 2 million licences, though there were around five times as many unlicensed sets. Postgate's account suggests that the Lansbury home, which had a telephone (East 3247), had a new valve wireless (cost £5) with a loudspeaker for group listening, rather than the rudimentary crystal set that required headphones.

[35] Renshaw, *The General Strike*, ch. 21.

authority in various directions . . . Orders were issued right and left, and business people and others were provided with a taste of what government by such a tyrannous autocracy is like.[36]

On Wednesday 5 May Raymond Postgate penned details of social unrest in the East End and a mysterious note that his father-in-law had not been arrested:

met G.L. at the office and heard news. G.L has not been arrested. Four policemen have not been killed in Bow, though about twelve have been roughly handled. The East End is absolutely tied up. They are not even trying to get the roads open there. There are a few private cars and food lorries with permits running only. Several lorries were overturned and some ostentatious private cars.[37]

With no national press, as most of the print unions refused to handle production, there was an explosion of unofficial strike bulletins produced during the nine days of the General Strike. The Labour Research Department later discovered that about seventy trade unions and local councils of action produced these news sheets during the stoppage, though Lansbury's publication is not named in the published list.[38] His cyclostyled 'Bulletin' provides some valuable insights into his attitude to the industrial dispute. He consistently urged strikers to exercise civil restraint and exemplified the Christian virtues of passive resistance. A typical passage included this exhortation:

Keep in mind the fact that the Son of Man, the Christ who lived and was executed by the government of His day, was a great leader, and leader of the common people. It was his great message of Love and Brotherhood which brought him to his death. He knew the poor of the earth were oppressed by the rich and the wealthy, and in scathing terms denounced the money changers and all those who defiled the Temple and brought suffering to starving humanity.[39]

Outside Bow and Bromley, George Lansbury was active in Parliament throughout the General Strike. On 5 May 1926, Lansbury was one of a number of members who intervened in attempts to amend the use of emergency powers by the government. In a parliamentary clash with the Attorney General, Lansbury denounced the Baldwin government's action as a deliberate attack on wages and the trade unions.[40]

On the following day Lansbury was part of Labour's back bench attack on the Government's emergency powers. 'I want to challenge the whole theory that in objecting to these kind of penal regulations we are actuated by any motive against the community', he declared as he moved to delete regulation 21. This gave the government sweeping powers to combat the fostering of mutiny, sedition, and disaffection among the armed forces and to enter premises to search for documents.[41]

The following day in Parliament, Sir John Simon unexpectedly made his celebrated declaration on the illegality of the General Strike. Late at night, with few MPs

---

[36] *Daily Telegraph*, 19 May 1926.
[37] Postgate, 'Diary' (entry of May 1926); *New Masses*, Sept. 1926.
[38] For unofficial strike bulletins, see E. Burns, *General Strike, May 1926: Trades Councils in Action* (1975). Nearby Stepney is listed on p. 177.
[39] *Strike Bulletin*, May 1926.   [40] *Hansard*, 5 May 1926, cols. 373, 381–2.
[41] Ibid. 6 May 1926, cols. 471–7.

present at Westminster, he told the House of Commons: 'the Resolution which was arrived at the Memorial Hall last week, or at any rate, the decision of the Council of the Trade Union Executive to call out everybody, regardless of the contracts which those workmen had made, was not a lawful act at all . . .'[42]

Twenty-fours hours later, there was still no official response from the Labour leadership to the intervention by the Member for Spen Valley and former Liberal Attorney-General—Sir Henry Slesser later revealed that Ramsay MacDonald had stopped him from speaking.[43] Simon had advanced a legal interpretation of the General Strike—including the liability of trade union officials to damages from personal finances as well as union funds—not even put forward by the government's own law officers. Not until the 10 May was Simon challenged by Slesser, Solicitor-General in the 1924 Labour government, who had represented the Poplar councillors in 1921 and defended eight of the Communist leaders four years later. Slesser maintained that the General Strike was lawful, as it could be seen as sympathetic action. A day later, Mr Justice Astbury of the High Court in granting an application from the Seamen's leader, Joseph Havelock Wilson, for an injunction to stop members of his union being called out, also declared *en passant* that the General Strike was illegal.[44]

However, in the immediate aftermath of Simon's sensational pronouncement on the third day of the General Strike, it remained for George Lansbury immediately to take up the cudgels in the House of Commons. Lansbury, who had addressed a vast rally of strikers in his constituency only hours before, opposed Simon's declaration as the only legal interpretation of the General Strike:

I represent in this House one of the poorest constituencies in the metropolis, and I would be unworthy to be their representative if in these days when rich men and the rich man's government is trying to crush and break and destroy the Labour movement, I did not say that all of us, whether in this House or out of it, will stand four-square whatever the consequences. Another lawyer, for a fee, would say exactly the opposite of what has been said. The idea that what a learned counsel says must be true is nonsense. We are not willing that the speech of the Right Hon. and Learned Member for Spen Valley should be printed alone, but we are willing that the whole of the facts should be printed.[45]

In 1941 Slesser commented that the adverse legal interpretation of the General Strike brought about its rapid end, with the TUC capitulating at 12 noon on Wednesday, 12 May 1926. However, it was a confrontation that most of the General Council had never wanted. They readily accepted the opportunity to make the car journey from Eccleston Square to 10 Downing Street to be allowed in only after confirmation of the ending of the strike had been given. Six days before, Samuel had returned from Italy and, driven by motoring-ace Major Segrave at a speed of

[42] C. E. B. Roberts, *Sir John Simon: Being an Account of the Life of John Allsebrook Simon, G.C.S.I., K.C.V.O., K.C., M.P.* (1938), pp. 220–2.

[43] Sir H. Slesser, *Judgment Reserved: The Reminiscences of the Right Honourable Sir Henry Slesser* (1941), p. 156.

[44] Morris, *The General Strike*, p. 255.   [45] *Hansard*, 7 May 1926, cols. 647–8.

85 m.p.h, had reached Pall Mall in one hour and ten minutes.[46] Samuel's unofficial intervention reopened negotiations with the TUC Negotiating Committee and led eventually to the General Strike being called off without any settlement of the mining dispute.[47]

Jack Jones, General Secretary of the TGWU 1969–78, who at the age of thirteen biked messages around Liverpool for the local council of action in May 1926, recalled the utter dismay and sense of betrayal felt by strikers at the TUC surrender. His father and brothers took part in the General Strike and his uncle suffered in the miners' lockout of 1926.[48] At the time, *Lansbury's Labour Weekly* returned to the fray with a twenty-page strike number. 'In these pages *Lansbury's* tells the secret history of the greatest strike of the British workers since 1834. It is a history, first of all, of magnificent solidarity', it declared, to raise spirits and to boost morale.[49]

Yet, surprisingly, in his autobiography only two years after the General Strike, George Lansbury said nothing about the nine days of May 1926, though some brief views were expressed nine years later in his *Looking Backwards and Forwards*. In 1935 Lansbury defended the General Strike as an industrial action against the coal-owners, and the Baldwin government that had supported them. The action taken by the TUC had no potential for political revolution that, in Lansbury's view, could be achieved only by parliamentary means:

> our first effort at a general strike was a tremendous success . . . Of course, all the power of the State was mobilised on the side of the employers. If I am asked what beat us, when the masses were so unanimous, I think the answer is . . . such a strike must turn into a revolution . . . But [it] . . . has got to come through Parliament.[50]

After the TUC called off the General Strike, the locked-out miners continued their struggle for a further six months until, beaten by starvation within their communities, they were forced to return to work on the coal-owners' terms of wage reduction and longer working hours. *Lansbury's Labour Weekly* continued to crusade for the miners' cause with national relief appeals and fund-raising rallies.

With the General Strike at an end, the Albert Hall was now the scene for another huge rally as an immediate expression of solidarity with the miners. This enthusiastic gathering was typical of the large-scale events staged by Lansbury in the years after 1917. How it was convened and assembled so speedily demonstrates his political flair in mobilizing large numbers in support of a multiplicity of popular causes during these years, from suffragism and 'Don't Shoot' campaigns to pacifism and solidarity with Russian workers.

Within less than a week, Lydia Smith and other staff on *Lansbury's Labour Weekly* had brought together a range of Labour supporters and other left-wing groups—

---

[46] Farman, *The General Strike*, p. 265.

[47] For more on the ending of the General Strike, see Laybourn, *The General Strike*, pp. 106–21; Wasserstein, *Herbert Samuel*, ch. 10.

[48] I am most grateful to Jack Jones for an interview at the TGWU Head Office on his recollections of Labour pioneers in the inter-war years.

[49] *Lansbury's Labour Weekly*, 22 May 1926.

[50] Lansbury, *Looking Backwards and Forwards*, pp. 59–62.

including the Plebs League, the friends of the International Class War Prisoners' Aid, the Communist party, and the *Sunday Worker*—to organize the event. Packed out, colourful, and emotional, the feverish atmosphere was reminiscent of those earlier gatherings at the Albert Hall arranged under the auspices of the *Daily Herald*.

Rutland Boughton and the London Choral Union provided the musical programme with 'our brave singing comrades from South Wales'. Hilda Saxe 'as usual without hesitation' played piano selections. The actress and former suffragette, Moyna MacGill (described as 'Mrs Edgar Lansbury'), read extracts from Shelley's *Masque of Anarchy*.[51] Among the speakers joining Lansbury on the platform were A. J. Cook, Ellen Wilkinson, Dr Marion Phillips, and Lady Cynthia Mosley. Only John Wheatley, delayed in Ireland, was not present. Lansbury's account provides a fascinating insight into his ability at fund-raising:

> I started out to get people to give sums of £2, and also desired whoever could do so, should give us a £100; Cynthia Mosley and Frank Horrabin at once weighed in £100 each, which, with £100 already received and sent to Wales made a nice start of £300. Very soon, however, golden sovereigns, half sovereigns, watches, penknives, necklaces, bangles, wedding rings, engagement rings, dress rings, and other articles came rolling in, and I found myself selling articles several times over . . . I had no idea of values, indeed, one ring alone, I am informed, is worth over 80 guineas . . . Meantime, a comrade from Hammersmith has offered us for sale a *King George Snuff Box over 100 years old*. Who will give me a bid. Do it now.'[52]

About £1,200 was raised at the Albert Hall rally on that evening in June 1926.[53]

Lansbury's fund-raising activities also took him to other parts of Britain, including Manchester where he addressed another large gathering at the Free Trade Hall on 2 July. His speech, which almost resulted in his prosecution, was a vehement attack on the Baldwin government and a passionate defence of locked-out miners and imprisoned Communists:

> I think it is a perfect disgrace that the Government should be so mean as to lock up poor men who are not known and not lock up people like myself, Wheatley and others . . . During the General Strike I did my best to spread disaffection and I am doing my best tonight . . .[54]

Lansbury joined those Labour MPs who had denounced the government as 'murderers' for its Miners' Eight Hours Bill. Lansbury's response brought him dangerously close once more to prosecution, probable conviction, and a prison sentence:

> I look upon Mr Baldwin as a cold calculating humbug . . . Here he is posing as a friend of the workers . . . and yet his Government has blundered in unemployment and the imprisonment

---

[51] I am grateful to Angela Lansbury for an interview, 15 Aug. 1989, and access to family papers. For Moyna Macgill, Edgar Lansbury, and their daughter, the award-winning actress, Angela Lansbury, see M. Gottfried, *Balancing Act: The Authorized Biography of Angela Lansbury* (1999), pp. 20–52; R. Edelman & A. E. Kupferberg, *Angela Lansbury: A Life on Stage and Screen* (Secaucus, N.J., 1997), pp. 3–20.

[52] *Lansbury's Labour Weekly*, 5 June 1926 (orig. emph.).

[53] *Geo. Lansbury's Speech to the Meeting of the Executive Committee of the I.C.P.W.A., Moscow, 29 July 1926*.

[54] 'Commissioner of Police: Disturbance: George Lansbury MP: Forwards notes of a speech at the Free Trade Hall, Manchester, 2nd July 1926', PRO, HO 410/194/12.

of 1500 men . . . Mr. Neville Chamberlain who is doing his best to make his Ministry a Ministry of Death, is cutting off the last avenue of poor relief . . . If they had their deserts you would do to them what Mr. A. M. Samuels said ought to be done with the Liberals; take them out and hang them to the lamp posts . . . friends if anybody deserves hanging on lamp posts, it is those who pass legislation for the murder of miners . . .[55]

The authorities took the view that Lansbury could have been successfully convicted but, as he was 'out for martyrdom', no proceedings were started.

While he remained out of prison himself, Lansbury redoubled his efforts to free those who had been imprisoned such as trade council leaders and Labour JPs. He led a deputation to the acting Home Secretary, Lord Birkenhead, to secure the release of Welsh Miners' leader and later Labour MP, Arthur Jenkins.[56]

In the summer of 1926 George Lansbury returned to Russia for a second time, on this occasion accompanied by Bessie. Disembarking from the SS *Dago*, they were met at the quayside by their youngest daughter, Violet, who worked as a secretary in Moscow. While the main purpose of Lansbury's stay was ostensibly to take a cure for his stomach problem at Essentuki in the Caucasus, he also made careful notes on the successful development of Russia six years after his previous visit. As he commented cheerily on departure: 'we shall see the Red flag still flying! The Workers' Government still in power. Other governments in Europe may come and go—the Soviet Government remains.' Lansbury's belief in public accountability meant that he wrote long letters home and kept his constituents fully informed through the columns of his newspaper. In Leningrad he toured former palaces—now educational institutes—inspected at first hand Soviet industrial training, as well as addressing the Leningrad Trades Council. He reported that the knowledgeable Russian workers' interest in the plight of the British miners was overwhelming.[57]

Nor was George Lansbury far from the gaze of the British Intelligence Services. While *Lansbury's Labour Weekly* received regular dispatches from the Lansburys in Russia, the British Foreign Secretary was kept equally informed by his own secret sources of Lansbury's arrival in Leningrad by steamer and his public speeches.[58] Russian workers had sent large sums of money to support the locked-out British miners. The British secret service also noted Lansbury's interview with *Isvestia* about the General Strike and the miners' continuing lock-out in Britain.[59]

Some unique glimpses of Bessie Lansbury—probably an even more enthusiastic supporter of the Soviet régime than her husband—survive from this visit to Russia. Bessie and Violet spent a considerable amount of time together, often in the

---

[55] Ibid.

[56] Arthur Jenkins was the father of the Gladstone biographer, Roy Jenkins, Labour MP and Cabinet Minister, one of the four founders of the short-lived SDP and President of the European Commission.

[57] *Lansbury's Labour Weekly*, 24 July; 7, 14 Aug. 1926.

[58] See e.g. Hodgson to Chamberlain, July 1926, PRO, 371/11788/3689.

[59] 'Extract from "Isvestia" of 23rd July, 1926. No. 167 (2798) interview with Lansbury'; 'Extract from Isvestia of 24th July, 1926 No. 168 (2799) Report of the British Strike'; 'Extract from Isvestia of 27.7 1926. No. 170 (2801) Arrival in Moscow of G. Lansbury, Member of the British Labour Party'. PRO, HO 410194/13.

Moscow museums and art galleries—a rare opportunity for mother and daughter to make up for lost time in a busy family life. Violet observed:

being the youngest daughter of a large family, I had never really known my mother . . . I had merely looked upon her as somebody in authority . . . who perpetually pulled me up for dirty shoes, no gloves, and my habit of never wearing a hat. There in Moscow I saw her differently . . . she put all her freed energy [from the endless burden of running a house] into watching, trying to understand, shedding her sweetness and charm on all and sundry.[60]

However, Lansbury's thoughts were never far from the struggle of everyday life at home. A visit to the former Tsarist palace at Tsarskoe Seloe built on the proceeds of 'misery and suffering' took him back to the miners' lock-out in Britain: 'The miners' struggle is awakening issues which will not be settled today . . . but capitalism is doomed—so also are all those who pin their faith to the unholy thing.'[61]

Nevertheless, according to Raymond Postgate, the disaster of the General Strike finally ended any remaining belief his father-in-law held in syndicalism or direct action. 'Political action through the slow and often exasperating parliamentary machine was now the only hope [since nobody really believed in armed revolt]', he observed in his biography in 1951.

Despite his avowed admiration for Lenin, George Lansbury always totally rejected the path of armed revolution in Britain. Yet the events of May 1926 had confirmed the weakness of the Labour leadership in the face of a 'Government [that] had decided to use all the forces of the capitalist state to crush it [a limited strike within the framework of capitalism]'.[62] His final efforts during the General Strike had been restricted to supplying *Lansbury's Labour Weekly* newsprint to the *British Worker* and to protesting with his son-in-law, Ernest Thurtle MP, about the *British Gazette*'s partisan omission of the Archbishop of Canterbury's message for industrial peace.[63] Outside Parliament, Lansbury believed it was time for re-doubling of his efforts in socialist propaganda and, at Westminster, a renewal of the pressure group tactics.

As a keen observer of parliamentary life, George Lansbury had always been impressed by the tactics that Charles Stewart Parnell and his group of Irish Nationalists had adopted in the House of Commons to bring the Irish Question to the forefront of Westminster politics. By hampering day-to-day business at Westminster in the late nineteenth century, the Irish Nationalists had been responsible for the introduction of parliamentary procedures—the Closure and the Guillotine. In November 1925 Lansbury had taken a leaf from their book: 'I intend on every possible occasion to obstruct, hold up, and in every way hinder the progress of business, he declared'. Within the PLP, Lansbury joined Josiah Wedgwood in an unsuccessful proposal that groups of thirty MPs be organized to hold up government business 'save such as may be considered by the party as tending to reduce unemployment'.

---

[60] V. Lansbury, *An Englishwoman in the USSR*, p. 123. See also *Daily Mirror*, 14 Aug. 1947; *Morning Star*, 14 Mar. 1972.
[61] *Lansbury's Labour Weekly*, 7, 14 Aug. 1926.
[62] Ibid. 22 May 1926.   [63] *The Times*, 11 May 1926.

'The Labour Front Bench is anxious to get through business . . . a sham fight . . . Lansbury and I and others are determined to fight whatever the Front Bench may arrange', Wedgwood disclosed to Fenner Brockway.[64]

The most spectacular example of the tactics of parliamentary obstruction occurred when thirteen Labour MPs delayed the voting on the government's Economy Bill. Lansbury and his colleagues defeated Neville Chamberlain's attempt to use the Closure by sitting down in the division lobbies and thereby extending the debate of the Tory Economy Bill from 2.45 p.m. on Wednesday, 14 April to 9.07 a.m. on Thursday, 15 April. At 5.30 a.m. an exasperated Speaker—summoned from his slumbers—promptly suspended the thirteen members from the House of Commons.[65] This was not an isolated instance of the successful obstruction of parliamentary business. By June 1926 Ramsay MacDonald publicly disowned Lansbury and other Labour rebels who caused disorder at Westminster—on this occasion in relation to the Miners' Eight Hours Bill, part of the anti-union legislation implemented after the General Strike.[66] In a special press release, Lansbury responded firmly by disassociating himself from MacDonald's censure of Labour members. 'He considered that the Labour Party had a better right to use every form of the House of Commons, every traditional right and privilege which members in the past had assumed in order to block and defeat this Bill', was his trenchant rebuke to the party leader.[67]

While Lansbury remained on the NEC, he still retained an independent stance on various issues—Russia, Communist affiliation, pacifism—and remained a thorn in MacDonald's side. In February 1926 Lansbury had left the 'free air' of the backbenches to descend to the Opposition Front Bench in the House of Commons. The following day he encountered Stanley Baldwin in the lobby at Westminster. The Prime Minister remarked, 'You look like an old watch dog brought into the drawing room.'[68]

It is possible, however, to see this episode as some kind of turning-point—or partial adoption of a *modus vivendi* with the Labour leadership—for the back-bench rebel. Along with Wheatley and Kirkwood, George Lansbury had reversed his decision in early 1926 not to stand for the National Executive Committee after the intervention of Arthur Henderson.[69] At the time he openly shared his thoughts and commented on the perennial dilemma that has confronted socialists battling for socialism within the Labour party during the last century:

Last December I certainly felt the time had come either to break away or give up. The latter for me is not possible. I have given too many pledges to my own conscience ever to think of retiring while health and strength remain to me. As to breaking away: where can any of us who are Socialists go, other than to the working-class movement?[70]

As a member of the NEC, at the annual party conferences, George Lansbury was

---

[64] Quoted in Brown, *Maxton*, pp. 178–9.   [65] *Lansbury's Labour Weekly*, 16 Apr. 1926.
[66] *Hansard*, 30 June 1926, col. 1,117.   [67] *The Times*, 2 July 1926.
[68] *Lansbury's Labour Weekly*, 22 Feb. 1926.
[69] Brown, *Maxton*, p. 176.   [70] *Lansbury's Labour Weekly*, 27 Feb. 1926.

regularly required to propose official resolutions on behalf of the Labour leadership or occasionally speak against those proposed from the left wing of the party. In October 1926 he secured the successful defeat of proportional representation.[71] However, the Margate Labour party conference witnessed stormier political weather over the selection of its parliamentary candidates.

In 1926 Lansbury became involved in the public wrangling over the selection of the popular Communist candidate for West Birmingham, Dr Robert Dunstan, who had contested the seat against Austen Chamberlain in 1924 with the open support of local Labour parties. Birmingham became one of the centres of the National Left Wing Movement, associated with the *Sunday Worker*, and founded in December 1925 with a strong Communist membership. About fifty divisional and borough Labour parties, including the Edgbaston and Moseley Labour parties in Birmingham which backed Dr Dunstan, supported the new left-wing movement's aim to sway the national Labour party 'back to its proper sphere of working-class politics and activity'. Lansbury did not join the National Left Wing Movement, though Poplar was one of its heartlands. His support for Robert Dunstan, who he had first met on the 'Hands off Russia Committee' was a political mistake—though entirely consistent with his sympathies for Communists in Labour politics.

Throughout the 1920s, George Lansbury's support for the Communists in Britain was a constant source of friction with the Labour party leadership, especially as Lansbury was a member of the NEC.[72] No issue distanced George Lansbury from the right-wing leadership of the Labour party as much as his conciliatory attitude towards British Communism and its fellow adherents in various ancillary organizations, such as the National Unemployed Workers' Committee Movement (NUWCM) and the ICWPA. While MacDonald, Henderson, and Thomas condemned the Communist Party of Great Britain (CPGB) as dominated and driven by Moscow, Lansbury had no difficulty in maintaining his association with an alien country.

None the less, Lansbury never joined the CPGB—unlike those members of his family—Violet, Edgar, and Minnie, as well as Raymond Postgate, who were all active members for a time. As we have seen, in the early 1920s Lansbury's sympathies for the Bolshevik Revolution, clearly displayed in the *Daily Herald*—as well as his public admiration for Lenin—were well known in political circles, especially after his first visit to Russia.

After the CPGB was founded on 31 July 1920 by representatives from the British Socialist Party, the Socialist Labour Party, Workers' Socialist Federation, Plebs League, and other left-wing groups in British politics, Lenin encouraged the fledgling CPGB to affiliate to the Labour party. But MacDonald made certain that the CPGB's formal applications were rejected at Labour party conferences from 1920 to 1924.[73] However, throughout the 1920s Lansbury was prepared to entertain the

---

[71] *The Times*, 16 Oct. 1926.   [72] Postgate, *Lansbury*, pp. 237–8.
[73] K. Laybourn and D. Murphy, *Under the Red Flag: A History of Communism in Britain, c.1849–1991*, (1991), pp. 42–57. In Aug. 1920 the first application was declined on the grounds that the Communist and Labour parties had different principles, constitutions, and programmes. When the CPGB again applied

affiliation of the CPGB to the Labour party, with the proviso that its standing orders and other procedures were accepted. At the 1925 Liverpool party conference, where MacDonald and the right-wing leadership secured overwhelming anti-Communist majorities that banned individual Communists from membership and imposed a three-year-ban on further applications for party affiliation, Lansbury voted against the leadership.[74] However, he also expressed his antipathy to the Labour party machine which dominated the proceedings—reminiscent of the National Liberal Federation (NLF) at Manchester in 1890 that had kept the young Radical from London off the platform.[75]

In 1926, the selection of O. G. Wiley as the official Labour candidate for the division in opposition to Dunstan led to a bitter two-year-long fray between the Birmingham Borough Labour Party and local left-wingers. Dunstan exposed the political machinations in the Birmingham caucus in two open letters to the press.[76]

At the Labour party conference in Margate in 1926, Joseph Southall, one of the founders of the NLWF and chairman of the local Labour Left-Wing Group in Birmingham, had attempted unsuccessfully to refer back the section of the Executive Committee's report on the adoption of parliamentary candidates to publicize the case of Robert Dunstan. At one stage, Southall, chairman of the Edgbaston Divisional Party, had himself been expelled from the Birmingham Borough Labour Party. After Josiah Wedgwood had spoken in support at the conference, George Lansbury intervened. 'He thought the Labour movement was taking a line in regard to the Communists which would lead the movement to disaster', was Lansbury's uncompromising view. Lansbury told the Margate Conference that: 'He did not take the view that the Communists were the enemies. For him the philosophy of the Communist Party was sacred, although he did not agree with their methods. (Cries of 'Ah!')'[77]

This episode at the Margate Labour Party Conference was a microcosm of the difficulties George Lansbury encountered over his views on Communist–Labour relations. 'Southall put up a splendid case against this splitting of the working-class vote in Birmingham, and Lansbury bound as he was by the decision of the delegation that had sent him, and his own membership of the E.C. made his position clear in a speech from the platform,' was how Ellen Wilkinson and J. F. Horrabin reported the position Lansbury had put himself in.[78]

The matter did not rest there. In 1928 the NEC appointed a committee of inquiry

---

for affiliation, George Lansbury represented the Labour party at a joint meeting in Dec. 1921 alongside Arthur Henderson, F. W. Jowett, R. J. Davies, and Sidney Webb. At the 1924 Conference, where the Communist party's application for affiliation was again rejected by 411,500 to 224,000, the Labour party added a rule to its official standing orders banning such applications for the next three years. The first Labour government also came under attack from the CPGB, particularly over its attitude to strikers in 1924 and for continuing British imperialism in India. In Apr. 1924 Lansbury challenged the Labour government in the House of Commons about the clandestine activities of two police spies at the Ben Greet Academy in Bedford Street near the Strand during the London District Congress of the Communist Party. Klugman, *History of the Communist Party*, pp. 170, 276–7.

[74] *Lansbury's Labour Weekly*, 10, 17 Oct. 1925.   [75] Ibid. 10 Oct. 1925.
[76] *Workers' Weekly*, 6 Aug., 10 Sept. 1926.
[77] *The Times*, 12 Oct. 1926.   [78] *Lansbury's Labour Weekly*, 16 Oct. 1926.

consisting of Labour party secretary, Arthur Henderson, F. O. Roberts MP, assistant national agent G. R. Shepherd, and George Lansbury, chairman of the NEC. After an official investigation in Birmingham, this four-member committee recommended the disaffiliation of the Edgbaston and Moseley Labour Parties. Lansbury received considerable criticism, principally from Joseph Southall, for his role in this internecine dispute and his withdrawal of support for Dr Dunstan.

On 19 September 1926 the *Sunday Worker* had carried an interview with George Lansbury in which he had denounced the adoption of an official Labour candidate against Dunstan:

I would be glad to support Dr. Dunstan's candidature at any time. The Communists are not our enemies, but our friends. I have not changed my attitude on political action, but I want the same thing as the Communists—the replacement of capitalism by Socialism. The movement is bigger than individuals, and, therefore, I cannot take part in or support any division of forces. Dunstan was the first man in the field in West Birmingham, and received and should continue to receive, the support of the workers in the district.[79]

After the Margate conference, George Lansbury withdrew his promise to speak for Robert Dunstan at a protest meeting. Instead, in a letter to Dunstan, which Lansbury published, he explained his disagreement with the West Birmingham Labour party's action and made clear the conflict of loyalties that led to his decision:

This vote of the Conference has changed the situation for me . . . and I am only sorry that circumstances connected with my membership of the Labour Party and the loyalty which such membership involves prevents me carrying out my promise. To do so now would be to flaunt, not the decision of the local party but the decision of the Conference, and that I am not prepared to do.[80]

During 1927, rapidly declining sales of *Lansbury's Labour Weekly* finally forced a merger with the *New Leader*. Effectively, it was the end after an existence of two and a half years, though Lansbury wrote each week in the new paper. There were other contributions from Ellen Wilkinson and the artist Frank Horrabin, as well as an international review by George Young and occasional pieces from G. D. H. Cole and Raymond Postgate. The Ginger Bookshop, part of the belated attempt to revitalize *Lansbury's Labour Weekly*, was absorbed by the ILP Publications Department.[81]

At 2*d.* per week *Lansbury's Labour Weekly* had achieved the creditable circulation figure of 172,000 copies—some seven times that of the six-penny *New Statesman*. With falling sales, the newspaper had consistently lost money, particularly after the Communist party launched a rival production backed by greater resources, including a small army dedicated to selling the new paper.[82] With the appearance of the Communist *Sunday Worker*, Lansbury took the wholly unrealistic view 'that

[79] This section draws heavily on the entry on Joseph Southall (1861–1944), a leading figure in the National Left Wing Movement in Bellamy, Saville, and Martin (eds.), *Dictionary of Labour Biography*, ix, pp. 200–2.

[80] *Lansbury's Labour Weekly*, 13 Nov. 1926.   [81] *New Leader*, 15 July 1927.
[82] Postgate, *Lansbury*, pp. 230–1.

there is room for quite a number of papers in our movement' and even spoke optimistically of *Lansbury's Labour Weekly* reaching 250,000 in sales. Nor was his ill-fated paper assisted by his editorial decision to carry advertisements proclaiming its competitor.[83]

The closure of *Lansbury's Labour Weekly* in 1927 also interrupted Postgate's career as a journalist for over ten years. He had assisted his father-in-law to produce a history of the *Daily Herald* and also helped Lansbury prepare his autobiography, published in 1928. However, the demise of *Lansbury's Labour Weekly* after two and a half years was no surprise. When Postgate contacted an old Oxford friend, David Blelloch, about the possibility of employment in the International Labour Office in Geneva, he told him that lack of advertising revenue, as well as competition from the *Sunday Worker*, had killed off the paper.[84]

In 1927 the *New Leader* trumpeted its merger with *Lansbury's Labour Weekly* as an attempt 'to produce a challenging and constructive expression of the demand for "Socialism in Our Time"'—a reflection of contemporary policy debates on the political left.[85] During November and December 1926, Lansbury had published in *Lansbury's Labour Weekly* a twelve-point draft programme for the next Labour government, based on approved Conference decisions.[86] Particular attention was given to the means a future Labour Government would use to secure and retain the political power necessary to construct a Socialist Britain. Described as 'thought out by a group of class-conscious Socialists', 'Socialism in Our Time' ('SIOT') had been compiled at the Ecclestone Square headquarters by four senior Labour officials—according to Postgate, all anonymous or forgotten except for the chief women's officer, Dr Marion Phillips.[87]

There were many similarities between the programme advocated in *Lansbury's Labour Weekly* and a similarly named policy of 'Socialism in Our Time'. The latter incorporated the idea of the 'Living Wage' and was developed by H. N. Brailsford and James Maxton. 'Socialism in Our Time' was adopted in April 1926 by the ILP as the under-consumptionist remedy of J. A. Hobson for mass unemployment but rejected by a hostile Ramsay MacDonald and the trade unions as potential state interference in wage negotiations.[88] As Gordon Brown has written:

in the 1920s he [Maxton] offered British Socialism an alternative course and direction. *Socialism in Our Time*, the programme that he championed, was a proto-Keynesian programme to banish unemployment and poverty, and to create socialism quickly and without catastrophe. Socialists had predicted a crisis of capitalism, a point at which there would be no alternative to a move towards a socialist society. But most would be frightened into action by the economic hurricane that would sweep Britain between the wars.[89]

In the *New Leader* Lansbury's weekly articles included a number of familiar

---

[83] Postgate, *Lansbury*, pp. 241–2.
[84] Postgate and Postgate, *Life of Raymond Postgate*, pp. 115–17, 138–40.
[85] *New Leader*, 15 July 1927.   [86] *Lansbury's Labour Weekly*, 20, 27 Nov., 4 Dec. 1926.
[87] Postgate, *Lansbury*, p. 243.
[88] R. E. Dowse, *Left in the Centre: The Independent Labour Party, 1893–1940* (1966), pp. 130–41.
[89] Brown, *Maxton*, pp. 19–20.

post-war themes: pacifism, the poor law, and public health, as well as his general assaults on capitalism and commentaries on socialist politics. To mark a forthcoming weekend of war resistance demonstrations throughout Britain, Lansbury called for a general refusal to fight and attacked the growth of armaments at a time of talk about disarmament. 'Those who desire "No More War" must refuse to fight in any war by whomsoever it is undertaken, and together work to establish peace by means of national and international co-operation,' he declared.[90]

George Lansbury also commented on the rumours and press articles about the position of the Labour party in a 'hung Parliament' after the next election. As a member of the Executive of the PLP and vice-chairman of the NEC, he maintained that the matter had not been discussed officially. He made clear his own implacable opposition to any 'Lib–Lab Coalition'—a position he resolutely upheld in public as chairman of the Labour party as the 1929 general election approached. 'The only reason for a Socialist Government is that it shall put into operation a Socialist policy,' was his unequivocal stance on this question.[91]

As the spectre of 'Poplarism' continued to haunt the government's corridors of power, the Baldwin administration took further action under the Guardians' Default Act by appointing officials to take over the administration of the poor law in certain recalcitrant Boards of Guardians that dared to follow in Poplar's footsteps. An unrepentant George Lansbury rallied to defence of the Labour guardians of West Ham and others by attacks in his column on the 'Ministry of Death' at Whitehall:

Some comrades object to poor law relief, and talk as if it were a crime to assist the poor. Some talk in the language of the COS [Charity Organisation Society] and suggest that the Labour guardians in West Ham, Poplar, Durham, Bedwelty, and other places create the poor. This is nonsense: poverty and pauperism are the result of social conditions. Nobody thinks poor-law relief is the true remedy, but every baby's life saved, every mother rescued from the thral-dom of suffering and death, every aged, infirm and sick person brought out of the vortex of destitution, and every widow and orphan saved from the terrible consequences of starvation and semi-starvation, all are a tribute to the humanity and rightness of the policies pursued by Labour guardians.[92]

By this stage, George Lansbury had been a poor law guardian for over thirty years. In the 1890s Henry Mayers Hyndman had told the young Lansbury that first-hand experience in municipal politics was a crucial training-ground for a potential revolutionary. Now, in 1927, Lansbury in turn recommended the office of guardian as the ideal apprenticeship for all aspiring MPs and quoted the Victorian Radical, Sir Charles Dilke in his support.[93]

The *New Leader* marked its acquisition of George Lansbury as a regular columnist with a striking pen-and-ink portrait of 'GL' by the cartoonist 'Brill' [Reginald Brill], soon to be the winner of the *Prix de Rome*.[94] By the end of the 1920s, the paper

---

[90] *New Leader*, 22 July 1927.
[91] Ibid. 29 July 1927. See also Lansbury's 'No Pact with Liberals' article in ibid. 28 Sept. 1928.
[92] Ibid. 5 Aug. 1927.   [93] Ibid. 26 Aug. 1927.   [94] Ibid. 22 July, 21 Oct. 1927.

was also continuing to utilize Lansbury's prominence in the British Labour movement in various associated trading ventures. Originally, George Lansbury had been
opposed to the appearance of his surname in the newspaper's title. As the circulation of *Lansbury's Labour Weekly* fell, various sidelines were tried. The paper mar-
keted a series of commercial left-wing gramophone records banned by record
companies.[95] On 21 December 1926 *Lansbury's Labour Weekly* issued recording
number 6, 'The March of the Workers' and 'A Talk by George Lansbury', in a series
of Labour Gramophone Records. *Lansbury's Labour Weekly* also issued *Rebel Song-
books* of words and music, and a *Portfolio of Portraits* of Labour leaders. In 1951 Postgate recalled that the *Labour Gramophone Records* had to be labelled—often
inaccurately—at the newspaper's office, as the 'frightened firm' that produced
them wished to remain anonymous. Consequently, readers sometimes discovered
they had received the 'Red Flag' instead of 'A Talk by George Lansbury'.[96]

In 1927 the paper carried ILP bookshop advertisements for these Labour
records—10 inch double-sided, price 3s. (postage 6d.) and the complete set in a fine
red album for £3. 1s., post free. Record No. 1 was the 'Red Flag' and the 'International', Record No. 6 included the item by Lansbury. There were also talks by Mac-
Donald and Maxton in the series. Also on offer to readers at '5s only' was 'A Plaster
Portrait of George Lansbury'—a 4"×6" wall-plaque finished in relief with a background of ivory colour with facsimile of Lansbury's signature.[97] George Lansbury
had hardly become a cult figure, but the use of his image by others around him indi-
cates his popularity and the prominence accorded to him as a politician and
journalist.

George Lansbury's election as chairman of the Labour party for 1927–8 was a
measure of his personal popularity and the celebrity he had achieved within the
Party. In the inter-war years few Labour politicians were so well known and recog-
nizable among the rank and file throughout Britain in an era before the advent of
global radio and television. The rudimentary state of twentieth-century mass communications is well illustrated in the same issue of the *New Leader* that published
Lansbury's appeal to his fellow comrades to join him in building an educated
democracy in Britain. Alongside Lansbury's article, the paper carried an advertisement for 'a great wireless invention' that had been 'the sensation of this year's Radio
Exhibition at Olympia'. For 'an all-in price' of £12 (or 20s. down and 20s. per month
for twelve months) (about the equivalent of one month's wages for those
employed), the General Radio Company, of 235 Regent Street, London W. 1.,
announced for sale a new wireless set 'of advanced design', featuring the 'Filinator',
which the listener recharged periodically by dropping in compressed tablets
supplied by the manufacturer at 1s. per charge.

---

[95] I am grateful to Prof. Philip Bagwell for sharing his rare collection of *Labour Gramophone Records*
with me, and to Terry Monaghan for his assistance, which allowed me to hear George Lansbury's voice
for the first time. For an extract of George Lansbury's broadcast in 1933 opposing German rearmament,
see *Great Political Speeches* (Hodder Headline Audiobooks: London, 1996), HH660. Film and sound
recordings of George Lansbury currently available in British archives are listed in the bibliography.

[96] Postgate, *Lansbury*, pp. 240–1.   [97] *New Leader*, 19 Aug. 1927.

Despite the infancy of radio technology, Lansbury's prominence spread beyond Britain. During 1927, George Lansbury faced a conflict of loyalties similar to that surrounding his links with Communism over his association with the League Against Imperialism. The February 1927 Brussels International Congress against Colonial Oppression was an important landmark for Jawaharlal Nehru, the only Indian delegate appointed as one of the Presidium. Nehru spent several days there and later recalled that he 'could not but be influenced by some of the men and women he met there', including Lansbury. At the Congress George Lansbury was elected President, mainly to discount rumours of Communist influence. Lansbury also accepted the Presidency of the International League Against Imperialism, where Nehru joined him on the executive with Mme Sun Yat-Sen, Romain Rolland, and Albert Einstein. A later recruit was the Vietnamese revolutionary, Nguyen-Ai-Quoc, later known to the Western world as Ho Chi-Minh. However, Lansbury did not remain President for long and resigned after pressure from the Labour party.[98]

Throughout the 1920s, George Lansbury's personal friendship with Maj. David Graham Pole, later Labour MP for South Derbyshire, was the important foundation for Lansbury's championship of Indian nationalism.[99] The two men enjoyed a political association that lasted nearly thirty years and was clearly influential in both their lives. Surprisingly, Pole is hardly mentioned in George Lansbury's writings and not at all in Postgate's biography of his father-in-law.[100] While Pole's short autobiography contains some important references to their friendship, it is his surviving papers that throw new light on different episodes in Lansbury's political career, as well as his family life, in the late 1920s. Rhoda Vickers, who joined Pole's office as his secretary in April, 1926, sorted out his letters after his death and left a typed summary of Pole's correspondence with George Lansbury—though, as she noted, 'with all the surviving files, there are many unexplained gaps'. In many cases Rhoda Vickers made a hand-written copy of the original correspondence.

A Scottish solicitor by training, Pole, who was Annie Besant's secretary and an expert on Indian and Burmese politics, encouraged Lansbury to join the Theosophical Society in 1915.[101] In turn, Lansbury was responsible for Pole, previously a Conservative supporter, joining the Labour party and standing for Parliament in 1918. Pole's war service in France had brought him into contact with Northumberland coal-miners serving in his battalion. Lansbury provided valuable guidance on constituencies and spoke at Pole's election campaigns. In 1929 Pole was elected for the first time for Derbyshire South, after previous contests in East Grinstead,

[98] S. Gopal, *Jawaharlal Nehru: A Biography*, i, *1889–1947* (1975), pp. 100–1; M. Edwardes, *Nehru: A Political Biography* (1971), p. 60.

[99] I am most grateful to Prof. Chris Wrigley for bringing the Pole Papers to my attention. See also Pole, *War Letters and Autobiography*.

[100] Pole's name does not appear in the index of Lansbury's autobiography, despite his significance in encouraging Lansbury to join the Theosophical Society. Pole's importance as an authority on Indian nationalism and his parliamentary committee work with Lansbury, including the Commonwealth Labour Group of MPs, are briefly acknowledged. See Lansbury, *My Life*, pp. 4, 7, 272.

[101] Lansbury, *My Life*, p. 7.

South Cardiff, East Cardiff, and in North Edinburgh, where Lansbury notably filled the large Usher Hall to capacity.

During these years, Pole provided an important source of financial assistance for George Lansbury, particularly in rescuing the *Daily Herald*—he raised £100,000 for the paper's relaunch as a daily in 1919—during its many financial crises by becoming the principal shareholder of the printing company. He was also instrumental in establishing *Lansbury's Labour Weekly*.

Both men worked closely together in the Commonwealth Labour Group which Lansbury formed at Westminster with Dr Haden Guest, Tom Johnston, Harry Snell, and others to discuss economic and political policy with representatives from India and other colonial and dominion countries.[102] After the Home Rule League was wound up in 1920, Lansbury then organized the India Parliamentary Committee at Westminster with Pole its most influential source of advice as a result of his frequent visits to India.[103]

1928 and 1929 were important years in the life of George Lansbury and in the part he played in the history of the Labour party. As the decade moved to its close, as we have seen, Lansbury became chairman of the Labour party conference held in Birmingham in 1928. After the 1929 general election, he was appointed First Commissioner of Works in Ramsay MacDonald's second Labour government 1929–31. It was to be a remarkable transformation in the political fortunes of one of Ramsay MacDonald's sternest critics especially, as has never been revealed before, George Lansbury had been privately contemplating resignation from parliamentary life only a few months before.

In 1928 Lansbury was engulfed by one of those periodic personal crises in his life, on this occasion caused by the bankruptcy of William and Edgar Lansbury's family firm in Bow. With their father increasingly absorbed by his political activities, Lansbury's two sons had taken over the sawmill and timber yard in St Stephen's Road in 1914. Nevertheless, by the late 1920s the business was suffering from the serious effects of the recession in world trade. Writing fifty years later, Raymond Postgate said nothing about these unhappy events, although he must have been aware of the family misfortune.

The bankruptcy of William and Edgar understandably caused their father considerable personal and private distress. Furthermore, the bankruptcy had revived political memories of the earlier scandal surrounding the funding of the *Daily Herald*. Lansbury wrote to Pole, who was in India, explaining how the press had raked up the story of the Russian jewels just after the war: 'It was rather a scare business for the evening and morning press, but as far as the jewels were concerned it was a rehash of the whole business years ago.'[104]

In 1928 the affairs of the bankrupt Lansbury firm came before the Official Receiver. David Graham Pole himself was one of the creditors in the public

---

[102] Lansbury, *My Life*, pp. 169–72. For the work of this Commonwealth Labour Group, see P. S. Gupta, *Imperialism and the British Labour Movement, 1914–1964* (1975).

[103] For Lansbury, Pole, and Indian politics, see pp. 264–5.

[104] George Lansbury to David Graham Pole, 21 Dec. 1927, DGPP, UL 5/1.

bankruptcy proceedings, but as the Official Receiver appealed against his claim, matters were delayed until Pole's return from India. In turn, this brought Lansbury further anxiety: 'It is all a rotten business now, because they [William and Edgar] will need that money very badly—and I don't quite see where they will get it from. Still, we must just leave it as it is till you get back,' he acknowledged.

The evidence in the Pole Papers suggests that Lansbury's solicitor, Enever, was incompetent. 'A most unsuitable choice!', according to George Lansbury, though his family continued to instruct him because, as the bankruptcy proceedings revealed, he had become part-owner of the business. Enever's advice—that an earlier case be contested and not settled out of court—resulted in considerable costs of £5,000. However, on this occasion the Lansburys prevailed and matters were settled somewhat expensively but without recourse to a costly appeal.[105] Fortunately, Pole was a most sympathetic creditor, who made certain any money he received from the financial crash was returned to the Lansbury family.[106] As a result, George Lansbury prevented the sale of furniture and other domestic items.[107] Not for the first time had David Graham Pole demonstrated the worth of his long-standing friendship. He had helped out before when the firm was in similar financial difficulties. In 1920 Lansbury wrote: 'I can never forget all the trouble you took to get me out of the 1914 mess and how helpful you have been a thousand times since . . .'[108]

At nearly seventy, the bankruptcy of his two sons in 1928 also had a devastating effect on George Lansbury in terms of his public life and political work. He confessed to Pole:

It has been a regular nightmare of a business from a thousand points of view . . . Nobody, either at meetings or away from meetings, has ever said a syllable, except of sympathy on one or two occasions to me. In fact, most people seem to have come to a sort of tacit understanding not to mention it, which has been awfully good of them. And as to my meetings, they all seem more enthusiastic than ever. It is only our own self-consciousness, I suppose, coupled with self-criticism, that makes us feel unhappy about such happenings, especially when you have no sort of responsibility for them.[109]

In 1928 the family bankruptcy was not the only reason that caused George Lansbury to consider his retirement from parliamentary politics. A totally disillusioned and bereft Lansbury told Pole of his complete disenchantment with Labour politics. Lansbury felt unable to remain on the Opposition Front Bench. What he saw all around him were 'such meanness, half truths and lies that I feel I am losing my self respect or what is left of it'. As before, only his strong sense of loyalty and personal duty to those who depended upon him sustained him in his political endeavours. As the possibility of office in the next Labour government beckoned, George Lansbury could not forget the financial sacrifices of those who helped to fund his party agent and constituency expenses. However, his innermost feelings and self-doubt, which

[105] George Lansbury to David Graham Pole, 19 Jan. 1928, ibid. UL 5/1.
[106] Rhoda Vickers, 'The Lansbury Sons Bankruptcy', n.d., ibid. UL 5/1.
[107] George Lansbury to Rhoda Vickers, 27 Jan. 1928, ibid. UL 5/1.
[108] George Lansbury to David Graham Pole, 20 Mar. 1920, ibid. UL 5/1.
[109] George Lansbury to David Graham Pole, 19 Jan. 1928, ibid. UL 5/1.

he poured out to Pole, reveal Lansbury's inability to handle the Labour party caucus and to effect the compromises necessary in British political life:

Old as I am it seems to me I am once more at a crisis in my political life. It is not possible for
my peace of mind to remain on the Parliamentary Executive . . . I should have given up long
ago but for you and our friends. For all my whole political livelihood depends on their
money. I could not keep going down here with agent & other expenses without them & I do
know our friend thinks I shld hang on & get into the next Govt. I feel it is impossible to do
this . . .[110]

At this point Constable published George Lansbury's autobiography which
covered his career of over forty years in British politics. In part, the appearance of *My
Life* was the product of straitened financial circumstances, particularly in the aftermath of the family bankruptcy. Throughout his career George Lansbury suffered
from personal financial difficulties. Despite his salary of £400 as a back-bench MP,
he gave most of his disposable income away and often took no expenses for the vast
number of speaking engagements in different parts of the country. Lansbury admitted openly: 'I have written this book, first (of course!) because I hope to make a
little money through the sales'. 'A fairly generous cheque' from the publishers
averted the onset of serious debt caused by Lansbury's generous nature as the head
of a large family.

Lansbury also put pen to paper to record his memories of fellow socialist pioneers, as he was most anxious to defend the history of socialist action that underpinned 'Poplarism'. Perhaps there was an additional undisclosed reason. At the age
of almost seventy—'nearing the allotted span of three score years and ten', as he put
it—George Lansbury was seriously considering leaving public life as he felt his
political career was over.[111]

The book was hardly an autobiography, more a collection of reminiscences. The
Yorkshire Post gave the publication of *My Life* only a lukewarm reception. Lansbury's life was described as of extreme interest and never dull—'irrespective of his
views'. Overall the paper's reviewer, disappointed by the lack of political analysis,
concluded that the rambling and uncritical style amounted to 'mainly an interesting miscellany of facts and observations'.[112]

None the less, those on the political left welcomed the story of Lansbury's life as
a tract for the times. The pacifist Labour MP, Wilfred Wellock, praised *My Life*, calling it an inspirational text on how to fight for hopeless causes for the poor and
downtrodden.

George Lansbury walks through this book as he walked through life, the embodiment of
democracy . . . Peasant, peer and prince will ever find in him a comrade and a friend, but a
toady, never. George Lansbury has never betrayed the cause of the depressed, whether of a
class or a race . . . . To read this book is to be encouraged and inspired . . .

was one of the glowing tributes the book received.[113]

[110] George Lansbury to David Graham Pole, 19 Jan. 1928, *loc. cit.*
[111] Lansbury, *My Life*, pp. 1, 275, 285–6. See also Postgate, *Lansbury*, p. 243.
[112] *Yorkshire Post*, 17 Oct. 1928.   [113] *Bradford Pioneer*, 19 Oct. 1928.

After parts of the book had been serialized in the *New Leader*, J. R. Clynes gave it a good review in the left-wing journal:

History, romance, comedy, tragedy abound in its pages, and as soon as you begin to read it you have walked into prison with the writer, who found his way there as though it were his natural home and because he had done something or other for the people of Poplar.[114]

In *My Life*, George Lansbury, chairman of the Labour party, 1927–8, and NEC member, took the opportunity to reflect on the current state of the British Labour Party. He was extremely critical of what he saw: hob-nobbing with a view to social advancement on a day-to-day basis and the development of the machinery of party politics that overrode political independence:

I cannot think the Labour Party fulfils its mission by proving how adaptable we are and how nicely we can dress and behave when we enter official, royal or upper circles. It seems to me we could do better to try and order our lives on the same lines as before we became Members of Parliament. I cannot feel I am better or worse because some people have elected me as their MP, and it is certain neither evening dress, court dress, nor indeed any particular set of clothes, adds either to my ability or integrity.[115]

Lansbury's disenchantment went further than his dismay at the social and political attitudes of the Labour leadership that were reflected in the conventional dress codes MacDonald and his colleagues subserviently adopted on public occasions. After fifty years of close observation of life at Westminster, Lansbury was convinced that the party machine had wiped out political independence. The early pioneers believed that socialists should capture Parliament to achieve social reconstruction and revolution. To achieve this Lansbury advanced a programme of constitutional reform to overcome the power of the political caucus: 'The Labour Party has forged a huge machine which is rapidly becoming a caucus which, because of its size and the work it must do, ruthlessly crushes individual initiative and expression. This is not democracy.'

Lansbury's solution was to return to those proposals for constitutional reform that he had adopted before the First World War as an alternative to the servile state:

Somehow we must find a way whereby individual thought will be allied with organization. The one sure way by which this can be accomplished is by the establishment of the Initiative, Referendum and Recall. With an educated nation, every man and woman entitled to vote on equal terms, it is possible to reduce the status of elected persons and use them as servants carrying out the will of the people, instead of as now, imposing their will upon the nation. The details of such a scheme cannot be worked out here, but in some homes in America and in Switzerland the voice of the people is heard in a direct manner when laws are made. This method would be easily adaptable if we reformed Parliament as proposed above.[116]

In the 1920s George Lansbury was not without his critics in the Labour movement. In 1932 John Scanlon published a strong critique of the Labour party, alleging that, under Ramsay MacDonald's leadership, it had failed to introduce socialism on

---

[114] *The New Leader*, 5 Oct. 1928.   [115] George Lansbury, *My Life*, p. 268.
[116] Ibid. p. 274.

gaining office three years before. He included George Lansbury, who by the time of the second Labour government, Scanlon regarded as a conformist reformer rather than the independent rebel who had re-entered parliament after the 1922 general election.[117]

It was not surprising that George Lansbury, on approaching his seventieth birthday, had considered retiring from public life. The turbulent decade of the 1920s had seen his imprisonment and exclusion from the first Labour government, the loss of his two newspapers, turmoil in Communist–Labour relations, and the disaster of the General Strike. However, election as chairman of the Labour party for 1927–8 gave him a new lease of life and the refreshing opportunity to contribute to Labour politics in his own way with the return of a Labour government.

[117] J. Scanlon, *Decline and Fall of the Labour Party* (1932).

14
Second Labour Government, 1929–1931

On Monday, 10 June 1929, the Prime Minister, Ramsay MacDonald, was filmed on the terrace of 10 Downing Street presenting the nineteen members of his new Labour administration to the nation before the first Cabinet meeting. To make this first 'talkie' at Whitehall, there was an extraordinary collection of cameras among the rhododendrons bordering the lawn, as well as two film-production vans parked outside in Downing Street.[1] Ironically, only an American agency using German equipment responded to the Government's invitation to record this notable occasion.[2] No one else spoke as MacDonald announced his Cabinet colleagues in turn. He introduced his First Commissioner of Works—'our old friend, George Lansbury'—and declared that the Member for Bow and Bromley, besides looking after historic buildings and royal parks, also had an important role in the government's plans for tackling unemployment in Britain.[3]

In 1929, the MacDonald government took office with considerable optimism, despite its minority position and a figure of 1.2 million registered out of work in Britain. To conclude naval disarmament talks with America, MacDonald made the first visit of a British Prime Minister to the United States, where he was honoured with a traditional ticker-tape parade in New York. However, world depression soon followed the Wall Street Crash of October and November 1929 with fatal implications for the British economy. Until recently, historians have concentrated more on the collapse of the Second Labour government in August 1931, and the dramatic financial crisis that brought its downfall, than the day-to-day history of an administration that lasted only twenty-six months.[4] For many years Robert Skidelsky's account remained the only scholarly study of the MacDonald government.[5] Although A. J. P. Taylor described 'Lansbury's Lido' on the Hyde Park Serpentine as the second Labour government's only memorable achievement—an epitaph that has crossed the generations—little attention has been given to the part played by George Lansbury at the Office of Works during 1929–31.[6]

Despite the misgivings that almost led to his resignation in 1927, Lansbury had

[1] *Manchester Guardian*, 11 June 1929.

[2] R. G. Leigh to Sir Robert Vansittart, 20 June 1929, JRMP, PRO 30/69/247.

[3] *Daily News and Westminster Gazette*, 11 June 1929.

[4] For recent accounts of the second Labour government, see N. Riddell, *Labour in Crisis: The Second Labour Government, 1929–1931* (1999); P. Williamson, *National Crisis and National Government: British Politics, the Economy and Empire, 1926–1932* (Cambridge, 1992).

[5] R. Skidelsky, *Politicians and the Slump: The Labour Government of 1929–1931* (1970).

[6] Taylor, *English History* (1970), p. 343. See also E. H. J. N. Dalton, *Memoirs: Call back Yesterday, 1887–1931* (1953), pp. 759–60; C. L. Mowat, *Britain between the Wars, 1918–1940* (1955), p. 354.

worked hard to return Labour to office and was one of the few major Labour politicians who commanded large audiences in Britain.[7] His position, on the left of the
party, was important to the leadership. At the 1927 Blackpool Conference Lansbury
loyally seconded the NEC resolution moved by MacDonald to draw up a programme for the forthcoming election.[8] The member for Bow and Bromley also had
little time now for former allies in the schismatic ILP, which had become a hostile
grouping within the Labour party. 'I write therefore to say how hurt and sorry I felt
you raised your manifesto without saying a word to me during our discussion of the
paper on Tuesday,' he informed James Maxton after the appearance of the
Cook–Maxton Manifesto calling for 'an unceasing war against capitalism'.[9]

Later in 1928, Lansbury's pre-Labour party conference message as chairman,
when he warmly acknowledged the radical ancestry of the host-city, Birmingham,
revealed how far he had come to accept the gradualist approach to socialism. 'Do
not tell me I am writing as an apostle of gradualness: no, I am an old man in a
hurry . . . but I am conscious of the fact that progress is only gradual,' he admitted.[10]
At this annual conference, Lansbury's appeal for party unity underpinned a ringing
endorsement of *Labour and the Nation*, the new policy document that replaced the
ten-year-old *Labour and the New Social Order*. In Cabinet he was to battle with
little success to get some of it implemented.

As Chris Wrigley has shown, the party secretary, Arthur Henderson, had been
the influential driving-force behind the formulation of this lengthy statement of
Labour's aims, with a tireless campaign as party secretary to broaden Labour's
appeal in the years between the two Labour governments. There were few direct
commitments to bind an incoming Labour administration and little was said about
specific future strategy in the new document.[11] Compiled largely by R. H. Tawney,
Ramsay MacDonald, and Philip Snowden, *Labour and the Nation* made the gradualist case for a socialist commonwealth. Public ownership of land, coal, power,
and transport, control of the Bank of England, as well as improved social services,
were part of Labour's new programme.

As chairman, Lansbury joined MacDonald and Henderson in putting his weight
behind these new proposals, despite constant sniping from the party's left at the
conference. James Maxton opened the attack on the lack of socialism: 'This is no
programme of action for the next Labour government. What you are doing here . . .
is giving a free hand to the next Labour government to define any programme it
pleases.' John Wheatley complained that it would take Labour forty years to implement such an omnibus programme. Lansbury's response was that minorities had to
accept a majority decision in a political democracy. 'I am the last person in the
world who would support unfair treatment of a minority, because most of my life
has been spent as a rebel acting with minorities, struggling to become a majority,' he

---

[7] Taylor, *English History*, p. 408.
[8] Labour Party, *Report of the Annual Conference* (1927), p. 182.
[9] George Lansbury to James Maxton, June 1928, Maxton Papers.
[10] G. Lansbury, 'All Aboard for Birmingham', *Labour Magazine*, Oct. 1928.
[11] Wrigley, *Arthur Henderson*, pp. 156–62.

declared in his chairman's address. But Lansbury was firmly associated with the party leadership. Far from frightening middle England, he now fought off the attacks from the left.

On polling day, 30 May 1929, as part of Labour's election campaign, Lansbury rounded off a series of daily articles in the *Daily Herald* by leading Labour figures. J. R. Clynes recalled 'the wonderful months' of the 1924 first Labour government and Ellen Wilkinson spelt out why women voters—many only recently enfranchised in 1928—should vote Labour. Characteristically, a brazen J. H. Thomas explained how the Tories had brought about the 1926 General Strike.[12]

Lansbury's clarion-call was loud and clear. Poverty in Britain could only be conquered eventually by the state ownership of the nation's major industries. After Winston Churchill's budget in April 1929, he had observed that 'when our day of power comes Providence will provide us with a Chancellor of the Exchequer with the same spirit of courage and determination to break down worn-out economic shibboleths'. He added: 'We have reached the end of our journey along what might be described as the "Palliative Highway".'[13] Faced with the prospect of a minority ministry, however, he promised social reform rather than the introduction of socialism. 'No, our palliatives will pave the way for the day when we shall reorganise industry on a basis of social co-operation so as to bring the benefits of industrial re-organisation and rationalisation to the service of the whole community.' There was 'a vital difference between us and the other parties', who preserved 'the right of the few to become inordinately rich', he added.[14]

At the general election of 1929, the three political parties each fielded over 500 candidates. Labour became the leading party in the new Parliament, but again without a clear majority over the united opposition of Conservatives and Liberals. Labour had 287 seats, the Conservatives 260, and Liberals 89, whereas the Conservatives had a slight edge in terms of the share of the votes cast: Conservatives 8,656,225 (38.1 per cent); Labour 8,370,417 (37.1 per cent); and 5,349,000 (23 per cent) for the Liberals.

In East London, Lansbury's return had been confidently predicted—only the size of his majority was open to question. He achieved a very comfortable victory over his Tory opponent by almost doubling his majority in Bow and Bromley. (George Lansbury 20,119; A. W. Goodman, 8,852: majority 11,267).[15] '*In my own case, my victory will be due mainly to the women*' was the reason given by Lansbury during his campaign.[16]

To celebrate the success of the 1929 election, the London Labour Party, now boasting thirty-six MPs compared to two members in 1918, held a victory rally. Lansbury told those present in the Queen's Hall: 'the present years were going to make or mar the party for a very long time'. He welcomed Wedgwood Benn's appointment at the India Office—'a man whose whole life had been devoted to the

---

[12] *Daily Herald*, 6, 7, 13 May 1929.   [13] *New Leader*, 19 Apr. 1929.
[14] *Daily Herald*, 30 May 1929.   [15] *Daily News and Westminster Gazette*, 1 June 1929.
[16] *Daily Herald*, 24 May 1929 (orig. emph.).

principle of national liberty was now at the head of the India Office'—before launching a trenchant attack on the problem of poverty and unemployment faced by the second Labour government.[17]

The return of George Lansbury—and the promise of a Labour government—brought forth a shoal of congratulations. 'We are particularly encouraged to know that peace and disarmament played such an important part in your election campaign,' declared Lucy Cox, General Secretary of the No More War Movement.[18] Percy Bartlett, of the Fellowship of Reconciliation, who would accompany George Lansbury on his world peace mission eight years later, looked forward to 'disarmament and to a constructive peace programme'.[19] 'Hurrah! Hurrah! Hurrah! . . . [G]o on and prosper—may they have the sense to offer you office,' an ecstatic Margaret Cole wrote from Oxford.[20]

Raymond Postgate recalled that his father-in-law thought a Cabinet appointment most unlikely. 'The Nabobs would rather not have me . . . If they were really sensible they would send me to Russia, as Ambassador,' Lansbury noted dryly.[21] However, at seventy years old, he was too important and senior a figure in the British Labour movement to be overlooked again in the distribution of Cabinet posts.

Despite difficulties over appointments, especially Henderson at the Foreign Office instead of his choice of Thomas, MacDonald assembled his second Labour government within a week. On 1 June, he secured agreement from Henderson, Snowden, Thomas, and Clynes—the party's weightiest leading figures. Three days later, Baldwin met MacDonald in London to assure him of a 'fair chance'. By 8 June, the new Prime Minister had met an indisposed King—who received him at Windsor in his Chinese dressing-gown—and announced his Cabinet with nineteen ministers, two fewer than in his 1924 administration, and apparently no royal query about the Bolshevik sympathizer, George Lansbury.[22]

In distributing these Cabinet portfolios, MacDonald had on this occasion consulted his inner circle of ministers. Of this group, Snowden remains the principal source of information on Lansbury's inclusion in the second Labour Cabinet, though he revealed only part of the story:

What to do with Lansbury was something of a problem. He had been kept out of the previous Labour Cabinet, but we all agreed that some Cabinet office would have to be found for him in the new Government. But we also agreed that he could not be put in as head of an important Department. Merited or unmerited, the stigma of 'Poplarism' still clung to him. I suggested that he might be given the Office of Works. I thought this post would suit him admirably. He would not have much opportunity for squandering money, but he would be able to do a good many small things which would improve the amenities of Government buildings and the public parks.[23]

[17] *The Times*, 1 July 1929.   [18] Lucy Cox to George Lansbury, 6 June 1929, LP, vol. 9, fo. 70.
[19] Percy Bartlett to George Lansbury, [probably] 7 June 1929, ibid. fo. 73.
[20] Margaret Cole to George Lansbury, 6 June 1929, ibid. fo. 69.   [21] Postgate, *Lansbury*, p. 245.
[22] Morgan, *Ramsay MacDonald*, pp. 149–50; Marquand, *Ramsay MacDonald*, pp. 489–95.
[23] Snowden, *An Autobiography*, p. 760.

Snowden published his memoirs after the fall of the government and his comments were probably added with hindsight. There had been no mention of any radical plans for the Office of Works and no minister had made any remarkable impact in this post, traditionally regarded almost as a sinecure. Lansbury's usefulness to the leadership owed much to his popularity on the left of British politics.

G. D. H. Cole was convinced that Lansbury's inclusion was a sop to the left-wing of the party.[24] In 1929 MacDonald was adamant that Clydesider, John Wheatley—one of the successes in his 1924 Cabinet—would not be in his new administration and, as one of six changes, omitted him. Lansbury therefore became the only recognized left-winger (with the possible subsequent exception of Charles P. Trevelyan, the former Liberal, who went to the Board of Education). David Marquand, in his official biography of MacDonald, took a similar view of Lansbury's appointment, as well as mentioning his advisory role on unemployment.[25]

Once again, the 'Big Five' of 1924 dominated the new government: Ramsay MacDonald (Prime Minister); Philip Snowden (Chancellor of the Exchequer); Arthur Henderson (Foreign Secretary); J. R. Clynes (Home Secretary), and J. H. Thomas (Lord Privy Seal). Pressure from Henderson kept J. H. Thomas out of the Foreign Office. MacDonald, who retained a close interest in Anglo-American affairs, instead persuaded Thomas to take the post of Lord Privy Seal to tackle unemployment with a co-opted team of civil servants and a small inter-departmental group of ministers, including George Lansbury.

Now largely forgotten, the composition of the second Labour government had some significant aspects. Of the promoted junior ministers, Margaret Bondfield, former chairman of the TUC General Council, was appointed Minister of Labour and became the first woman Cabinet minister and Privy Councillor in Britain. MacDonald's selection of one of his law officers from outside his party caused a political upset, as the new Attorney General, William Jowitt, had only just been elected as the Liberal MP for Preston. He was subsequently returned once more as the Labour candidate at the first by-election in the town.

In July 1929, the social structure of the second Labour government was subjected to the keen scrutiny of Beatrice Webb and the newly ennobled Sidney Webb, who became Lord Passfield and combined the posts of Colonial and Dominions Secretary. Sidney and Beatrice Webb's three-fold classification (old governing class, lower middle class, and working class) placed Lansbury among the '*Ci-devant* manual workers mostly represented by Trade Unions'—along with Arthur Henderson, J. R. Clynes, Tom Shaw, William Adamson, and J. H. Thomas. Lansbury was not one of 'the *brains* of the Party [that] are in the lower middle class section', according to Beatrice Webb, a category comprising Arthur Greenwood, William Graham, Philip Snowden, and Ramsay MacDonald, along with her husband, Sidney. Also, she saw her former associate on the 1905–09 Royal Commission on the Poor Law as no longer a 'professional profit-maker'. 'Lansbury retired from business some time ago', she noted.[26]

---

[24] Cole, *History of the Labour Party.*   [25] Marquand, *Ramsay MacDonald*, p. 492.
[26] B. Webb, Diary, 27 July 1929, PP.

The new Cabinet members travelled to Windsor Castle to receive their seals of office from George V. 'A black frock coat or a black tailcoat will be worn, with silk hat', was the unmistakable command as to dress code. In 1919 Lansbury had refused to don municipal robes as mayor of Poplar. Ten years later, he wore the 'Prince Albert-like black frock coat' and added a dignified top hat. However, MacDonald insisted on knee breeches and then full evening dress—anathema to a class warrior like George Lansbury. This opening clash became inflamed into internecine Cabinet warfare as the First Commissioner of Works often found reason after reason for avoiding official dinners and *levées* for which full dress was *de rigueur*.[27]

In the evening, MacDonald broadcast from the radio station 2Lo via the BBC at Sandy Hill promising that the problems of unemployment and national reconstruction would be given priority.[28] 'Mr Thomas has been placed at the head of an organization which will survey and tackle with energy the most practical means of dealing with unemployment . . . not only by relief works but by . . . national reconstruction,' MacDonald declared in a flourish of showmanship.[29]

Victory in the 1929 General Election raised expectations of the second Labour government which would be judged by its supporters on how successfully the administration tackled unemployment and poverty. Lansbury recognized the opportunity to exercise power on behalf of ordinary people. 'Like many of my friends I go to Parliament representing very poor people, whose sole chance of a decent existence is to raise their standard of life by legislative and administrative action,' he acknowledged. There was no doubt in his mind what had to be accomplished. He added: 'these poor people who pinned their faith to our leaders, our programme and our Party will expect us to deal immediately with unemployment, old age and widows' pensions, slums and housing.'[30] An incoming Labour government did not lack for economic guidance, particularly from the left. 'I realise that the Government does not possess a mandate for "Socialism in our Time", but I and a very large section of the Labour Party in Parliament have such a mandate,' James Maxton told *New Leader* readers.

What MacDonald had in mind was a Cabinet committee on unemployment headed by the arch-moderate 'Jimmy' Thomas. MacDonald thought Lansbury's light load at the Office of Works would give him free time to take on an advisory role. Tom Johnston, former editor of the Glasgow socialist paper, *Forward*, and the Chancellor of the Duchy of Lancaster, Sir Oswald Mosley were added to the team. The charismatic Mosley brimmed with ideas, drive, and burning ambition—he had wanted to be Foreign Secretary.[31] 'The rich and ambitious son of a Tory baronet, with white teeth, metallic charm and a Douglas Fairbanks' smile,' Postgate scoffed on hearing of Lansbury's new collaborator.[32]

In the 1920s, J. H. Thomas had been a leading trade union and Labour figure, at

---

[27] Postgate, *Lansbury*, p. 247.   [28] *The Observer*, 9 June 1929.
[29] *Manchester Guardian*, 10 June 1929.   [30] *New Leader*, 14 June 1929.
[31] For Mosley, see R. Skidelsky, *Oswald Mosley* (1975).
[32] Postgate, *Lansbury*, pp. 252, 259.

one point even seen by some as a possible successor to MacDonald.[33] However, Jennie Lee, a recent addition to the ILP parliamentary group, thought Thomas's role as an 'emergency Minister of Action' on unemployment as 'some puckish whim' on MacDonald's part. 'When I met him in the evenings bulging out of his dress shirt I could never help grinning,' she recalled. 'He looked so exactly like the caricatures of himself that you had to prod him to see if he were real'.[34] According to Herbert Morrison, this miscellany of ministers was no accident—not one of 'the Prime Minister's many stalling devices'—but a deliberate concoction calculated by MacDonald to produce some constructive outcomes.[35]

Once assembled, this mismatched team encountered implacable opposition to increased public expenditure from the mandarins of the Treasury and the Bank of England. Internal divisions between the Lord Privy Seal and his lieutenants became apparent during an unhappy and brief coexistence as Thomas brushed aside proposal after proposal. For several weeks, Scottish Office minister Tom Johnston was unable to confirm whether he was a full member of the committee and suspected MacDonald had deliberately engineered an ill-composed consortium that could achieve little under the right-wing Lord Privy Seal. Initially, Thomas rushed everywhere arranging endless meetings with civil servants, businessmen, and scientists. But his energetic globe-trotting, that easily fooled his biographer, failed to unearth any new answers to British unemployment. Blaxland wrote approvingly: 'The projects that seethed in his mind ranged from a bridge over the Zambesi river to a traffic circus at the Elephant and Castle'.[36] Those who had to work with Thomas took a more realistic view of his capabilities. Johnston and others recalled a farcical meeting in Whitehall on Thomas's return from an abortive six-week jaunt in Canada concerning a brown paper parcel on the mantelpiece in the Treasury Chambers. In Johnston's words:

Then the fun began . . . Thomas said he had been surprised at one or two things brought to his notice since his return . . . he had asked a chief officer from the Post Office to be present . . .

'Well,' said Thomas. 'You see the wooden boxes with the two little bells on them that's in every telephone kiosk?'

'Where do we get the wood from?'

'From Sweden, sir!'

'Just so,' said Thomas. '. . . and how much does each box cost?'

'About 10s. 6d., sir.'

'Well,' said Thomas triumphantly . . . 'That box is not made of foreign wood, but of British steel, made by British labour, and it didn't cost 10s. 6d . . . but only 4s. 6d. Now what have you to say for yourself?'

'Well, sir,' replied the Post Officer, 'My box has two bells on it, and machinery inside it, and yours has none!'

[33] For Thomas and the unemployment committee, see Skidelsky, *Oswald Mosley*, ch. 9.
[34] J. Lee, *Tomorrow Is a New Day* (1939), pp. 148–9.
[35] Ibid.; Morrison, *Herbert Morrison*, p. 221.
[36] G. Blaxland, *J. H. Thomas: A Life for Unity* (1964).

Johnston noted that 'Lansbury in glee kicked my ankle beneath the table, but Thomas never batted an eyelid . . . he declared he would go farther into this matter . . . That was the end of the unemployment committee as such.'[37] In fact, the ministers joined an interdepartmental committee 'in a sort of semi-dungeon high up in the Treasury offices . . . surrounded by the reputed *elite* of the Civil Service' and headed by Thomas, but only after the Treasury had already decided unemployment policy at two earlier meetings.[38]

On 29 June 1929 Thomas appointed a sub-committee (Lansbury, as chairman; Mosley; and Johnston) to enquire into retirement pensions for industrial workers and raising the school-leaving age, both important pledges in Labour's 1929 election campaign, as possible ways forward. Dubbed the 'Old and Young Committee' by Mosley, its membership was overburdened with civil servants from the Treasury, the Ministries of Health, Labour, and Education, and the Scottish Office, as well as the Government Actuary.[39] As he later wrote, this experience did nothing to change his attitude towards 'experts':

There were four ministers and again about two dozen civil servants. Not a single one of these latter was in favour of Labour's policy to extend pensions and raise the school-leaving age . . . this is just where the whole policy of a Labour Government, depending on Civil Service experts to determine whether Socialist policy is right or wrong, must break down.[40]

The prospects for government action looked extremely slim. Lansbury told Dalton that the Lord Privy Seal was 'wobbly on pensions and the school leaving age' and failed to consult his three advisory colleagues.[41]

During the next two years of the Labour government, Lansbury made a number of attempts to take action on unemployment, a role that he considered far more important than his work as First Commissioner of Works. In particular, Lansbury pressed for 'work or maintenance', which had been traditional Labour policy since 1907, as he told the House of Commons in the debate on the King's Speech.[42] His major contribution comprised various ideas for land-settlement that echoed strongly his interest in farm colonies nearly thirty years before.

On 22 July 1929 Lansbury forwarded his ideas in a memorandum to J. H. Thomas to ask the Minister of Agriculture to: 'formulate plans for utilising labour at present unemployed in mining and other areas for the purpose of re-establishing and developing every form of forestry and agriculture . . .'[43]

The Ministry of Agriculture turned down his scheme to use 'many, many miles of Crown land' in this way. Schemes for co-operative farming on Danish lines, work for former miners on French soil, as well as the feasibility of resettling 10,000 British colliers in Western Australia were all advanced with enthusiasm. Emigration was

---

[37] T. Johnston, *Memories* (1952), pp. 105–6.

[38] G. Lansbury, *My England* (1934), pp. 142–3.

[39] Skidelsky, *Politicians and the Slump*, pp. 113–14.   [40] Lansbury, *My England*, p. 144.

[41] *The Political Diary of Hugh Dalton, 1918–40, 1945–60*, ed. B. Pimlott (1987), entry for 24 June 1929, pp. 57–9.

[42] *Hansard*, 4 July 1929, cols. 287–94.

[43] For Lansbury's memorandum of 27 July 1929, see LP, vol. 19, III d 87 ff.

important to the Commonwealth as well as to Britain.[44] 'I am convinced that if . . . we cannot develop our own resources in this country, including agriculture . . . the most important of all—or develop the land lying idle in the Dominions, the end of the British Empire is not very far off,' he later told MacDonald.[45] Sir Horace Wilson investigated the Australian proposal and declared the land unfit for wheat growing. However, Sir James Mitchell, the Prime Minister of Western Australia, offered to 'pump prime' the scheme, until MacDonald warned Lansbury of the perils of Australian domestic politics.[46]

In October 1929 George Lansbury became the first Labour minister to speak at the Cambridge Union, where he defended the Government's record in the debate on the motion: 'That this House has little or no confidence in the policy of His Majesty's Government to conquer unemployment or to promote industrial prosperity.'

His opponents included Capt. Anthony Eden, Conservative MP and future Foreign Secretary and Prime Minister. 'It was promised [before the election] that something should be done "immediately", and that word had never been so stretched before', the Conservative MP for Warwick complained. Lansbury's spirited reply—sufficient to win the debate—was that Labour had achieved more in four months than any other government in forty months with work schemes and assistance for the heavy industries.[47] 'In the last resort there was only one thing to do, they must increase the spending powers of the worker. This was the problem of modern civilisation,' Lansbury concluded.

However, Lansbury knew he had lost the argument—'*from their point of view* [they] really smashed us up', he wrote hastily to 'Jimmy' Thomas.[48] Labour had failed to act on its manifesto pledges to raise the school-leaving age and introduce retirement pensions. Lansbury forecast that proposals being prepared by Mosley, Johnston, and himself would reduce the number of unemployed by 220,000 to 310,000. They had been working 'night and day for weeks past' on a scheme costing around £20 million.[49]

Thomas told Philip Snowden—to whom he sent Lansbury's note—that the Cabinet should 'consider any measures of social legislation which they have in mind not in isolation but in strict relation to the present economic position of industry'. Being 'driven into panic measures by any criticisms of our opponents', he deplored. 'Has now the time come therefore when it is essential that we should pause to consider where we are going?' he wondered.[50]

After more than two months' work during August and September, the 'Retirement Committee' (the 'Raising of the School Leaving Age' was being handled separately as an educational issue) presented two reports from the civil servants and the

[44] For Lansbury's memorandum of *c*.29 Nov. 1929, see ibid. vol. 19, fos. 277–81.
[45] George Lansbury to Ramsay MacDonald, 9 May 1930, ibid. vol. 20, ibid. fo. 355.
[46] MacDonald to Lansbury, 10 May 1935, LP, vol. 20, fo. 356. Skidelsky, *Politicians and the Slump*, (2nd edn., 1994), pp. 400–2.
[47] *Cambridge Independent Press*, 25 Oct. 1929.
[48] George Lansbury to J. H. Thomas, 23 Oct. 1929, Thomas Papers, U1625, C78 (orig. emph.).
[49] Ibid.   [50] J. H. Thomas to Philip Snowden, 24 Oct. 1929, ibid. U1625, C134.

ministers on 21 and 22 October 1929. Lansbury urged Thomas's support in Cabinet for the Ministers' 'scheme C'. For a cost of £21.6 million in the first year, reducing to £10.5 million in the fifth year, this proposal provided a weekly retirement pension at sixty for insured men of £1 (and 10 shillings for a wife) and would create estimated job vacancies 'ranging from 220,000 up to 310,000'.[51]

None the less, Thomas opposed the proposals Lansbury brought to Cabinet and contemporaries noted the dismal failure of Thomas's efforts to tackle unemployment. Beatrice Webb commented on the clash of personalities and on Thomas's poor health owing to stress and drink:

Oswald Mosley and Lansbury, his lieutenants, report that Thomas does not see them, but that he is in the hands of that arch-reactionary, Horace Wilson—my old enemy—whom he calls 'Orace' and obeys implicitly; that he refuses to sit down and study the plans proposed and therefore cannot champion them in the House . . .[52]

By the end of 1929 the Labour government had done little to alter the unemployment situation. While the number of registered unemployed in Britain had reached nearly 1.5 million (12 per cent), the government's strategy was to rely on a general improvement in world trade. Oswald Mosley's decision to compile a portfolio of proposals, which became known as the 'Mosley Memorandum' brought forward a radical programme to deal with unemployment on quasi-Keynesian lines. Writing after the Second World War, Postgate understandably consigned Mosley to a subordinate role as draftsman and described Lansbury as the instigator of the Memorandum:

In the spring of 1930 he decided, in consultation with Mosley and Johnston, to assemble the most obviously useful of them into one document and force it on his colleague's attention. Mosley, the least occupied and the best writer was the draftsman . . . Lansbury used his position as Cabinet minister to put it [the Memorandum] on the table himself.[53]

In fact, the 'Mosley Memorandum' was correctly named, as it was largely the work of the Chancellor of the Duchy of Lancaster—with a contribution from his Private Parliamentary Secretary, John Strachey. Mosley mentioned the document to MacDonald as early as December 1930 and assembled it briskly during the Christmas vacation. If adopted, the Memorandum would have put the nation on a war footing, with a high-powered 'General Staff', headed by the Prime Minister and backed by expert advisers, to do away with the scourge of inter-war unemployment. The 'Mosley Memorandum', based on the various proposals its author had put forward during the previous months, comprised four sections: the machinery of government; long-term economic reconstruction; short-term work plans; and finance and credit policy. Lansbury and Johnston, though they fully supported the Memorandum when it was before the Cabinet, were only directly associated with the public works programme in section three that created employment for

---

[51] Skidelsky, *Politicians and the Slump*, pp. 95–9.
[52] *Beatrice Webb's Diaries*, ed. Cole (entry for 28 July 1929), pp. 212–13.
[53] Postgate, *Lansbury*, pp. 256–7.

300,000 unemployed over three years at a cost of £300 million. The three advisory ministers had two sessions with the Cabinet group set up to vet the proposals.

Oswald Mosley's Memorandum ran into the three-sided opposition of Snowden, Thomas, and Herbert Morrison, the Minister of Transport antagonistic to his proposal to build a network of motorways—'national highways'—across Britain to improve communications and ease unemployment. The Cabinet sub-committee chaired by Philip Snowden with Arthur Greenwood (Health), Margaret Bondfield (Labour), and Tom Shaw (War) roundly criticized Mosley's ideas on the grounds of cost and the imposition of a central bureaucracy on the democratic traditions of local government.

When the full Cabinet finally rejected his proposals, Mosley left the second Labour government. He delivered a powerful resignation speech to the House of Commons lasting over an hour on 28 May 1930, while Lansbury (along with Johnston) remained silent. Only two weeks before Labour had lost the Fulham West by-election, the first seat recaptured by the Conservatives in the 1929–31 Parliament. Now, in a 'very private' letter, MacDonald accordingly expressed his appreciation for Lansbury's demonstration of collective responsibility at a difficult time in the middle of the Nottingham Central by-election campaign:

I must say how very much obliged I, and, I am sure, all my colleagues are to you for the line you have taken in the Mosley affair. I think it is a most deplorable piece of bad judgment and of narrow views. It is not Mosley himself we have now to deal with but a very serious situation, not only for the Government but for the whole party.[54]

Significantly, neither Lansbury nor Johnston had resigned with Mosley. In Lansbury's case, he had become somewhat suspicious of the former Chancellor of the Duchy of Lancaster. Arthur Horner remembered a strained silence between the two Labour ministers when they visited the ailing A. J. Cook in the Manor House Hospital in 1930.[55]

Mosley defended his Memorandum on the second day of the annual party conference, held at Llandudno in October 1930. However, Mosley's speech was overshadowed by the sombre and tragic news from France that dominated the opening of the conference. On 5 October the British airship HM R101, which had departed for India from its home base at Cardington in Bedfordshire, crashed in a fierce storm and was destroyed in an inferno at Beauvais near Paris. Forty-six passengers and crew perished, including the Secretary of State for Air, Lord Thomson of Cardington.[56] As the news of the terrible disaster swept Britain, one Labour politician realized he had had a remarkable escape. George Lansbury had declined his friend Lord Thomson's invitation to join him on the ill-fated flight to India.[57]

Thomson had been a leading pioneer of British airships and was a personal friend of Ramsay MacDonald, himself an early flying enthusiast, who put him in his

[54] Ramsay MacDonald to George Lansbury, 21 May 1930, LP, vol. 9, fo. 253.
[55] A. Horner, *Incorrigible Rebel* (1960), p. 107.
[56] For more on the R101, see P. G. Masefield, *To Ride the Storm: The Story of the Airship R101* (1982).
[57] *Daily Herald*, 7 Oct. 1930.

1924 government and made him one of Labour's leaders in the House of Lords. Thomson envisaged a global network of air communications linking the British Empire, as well as profitable routes across the Atlantic. However, by the time of the second Labour government, the German *Graf Zeppelin* had already completed sixty flights. On 26 April 1930 this rival airship flew from Friedrichshafen to Cardington—the British airship base—in 11 hours and 13 minutes, casting an ominous shadow *en route* over Wembley Stadium during the second half of the FA Cup Final between Arsenal and Huddersfield Town.[58]

Thomson had arranged test flights for British MPs to promote British airships, including the flagships R100 and R101, built at the astonishing cost of £2,396,948 over six and a half years.[59] In a spectacular move, just as the Imperial Conference opened in London, the Labour Cabinet minister planned to fly to India—his birthplace—and to address the conference on his return, thereby consolidating his claim to be the next Viceroy of India.[60]

Lansbury, who was more fortunate than his tragic colleague Thomson, was therefore at Llandudno to hear Mosley's defiant and rousing speech challenge the government's lacklustre economic performance:

They must go to Parliament with an unemployment policy . . . If their proposals were thrown out, they must go to the country and fight their opponents on the question of unemployment and a revision of Parliament. At the best, they would have their majority, at the worst they would go down.

Mosley narrowly lost the vote—no trade union leader supported him—polling 1,046,000 against 1,251,000, after George Lansbury had replied on behalf of the NEC. At Llandudno, Lansbury played a vital part for the NEC in deflecting attacks from the left wing of the party over Communist affiliation, India, and unemployment policy.

On Communist affiliation, Lansbury defended the official ban that required party members to cease all connections with various proscribed organizations—including the League Against Imperialism, the NUWM, and the ICWPA with which he had been closely associated. This additional embargo on Communist activity within the Labour party was accepted on a show of hands after Lansbury had defeated the motion to refer back. Some felt that the poacher had turned gamekeeper. However, in 1951, Raymond Postgate explained Lansbury's change of attitude towards British Communism: 'He had had a bellyful of Communist tactics; he answered their demand for affiliation with the round statement that they were in favour of violence.'[61]

Similarly, on India, Lansbury worked closely with Wedgwood Benn, Secretary of State for India, in supporting Labour's plans for self-government. As a result, the

---

[58] For a photograph of this historic encounter, see P. Soar and M. Tyler, *Arsenal, 1886–1986* (1986), p. 11.

[59] Masefield, *To Ride the Storm*, p. 537.

[60] Ibid. p. 137. See also J. R. MacDonald, 'Introduction', in C. B. Thompson, *Smaranda* (1931), pp. viii–ix, xxviii.

[61] Postgate, *Lansbury*, p. 258.

first of three round-table conferences was held under the aegis of the second Labour government. As Chairman of the British Committee on Indian and Burman Affairs, Lansbury continued to champion the extension of Indian self-government, loyally assisted by his old ally, David Graham Pole. Pole was a regular visitor to India and an important source of information via Lansbury for the Labour leadership.[62] At Llandudno, in response to the ILP resolution critical of the Labour government's policy in India following the Simon Commission moved by Fenner Brockway, David Graham Pole came to Lansbury's assistance to defeat the resolution.[63]

Moreover, put in an embarrassing position by the NEC to defend the Cabinet over the Mosley Memorandum that he himself supported, Lansbury took a totally different tack in a speech of some political dexterity and guile that has been largely neglected by historians. To all present, Lansbury made clear that the proposals enjoyed his continued support. 'Further, Mosley, Johnston and himself very much together,' he added, 'the three of them came to the same conclusions which were in the Memorandum. The major part of the Memorandum was, of course, prepared by Mosley himself,' he told the delegates.

Then, an assertive Lansbury denied that the Memorandum had not been considered. 'There was only one reason at present why it had not been published . . . because it became a Cabinet document, and . . . it was not usual to publish such a document,' he explained to the assembled delegates. In fact, parts of the Memorandum were still under consideration and he challenged Mosley to 're-write his views' and to turn them into a public document. Lansbury's son-in-law was rightly impressed with this performance:

the Minister on the platform, in fact, was deliberately throwing the cards across the hall into the lap of the critic, sitting Byronically among the rank and file with folded arms. But they were not picked up: Mosley was not the sincere and ardent Socialist he seemed, but was already embryonically the Fascist leader.[64]

After detailing the government's relief programme for the unemployed, Lansbury readily admitted: 'He was much too old a Socialist to stand there and say that under the prevailing conditions anything that any government could do in the shape of public works would more than tickle the situation'.

To conclude, there was a characteristic appeal for unity to achieve socialism: 'therefore let them educate, agitate and organise—sweep the present Cabinet out and put themselves in, if that would help—until they got the teeming millions of their people imbued with Socialist ideals, and when they got that, they would not want anybody's Memorandum to bring about Socialism'.

Despite his defeat, Mosley was hardly the politician to remain silent or inactive and he continued to campaign on his proposals. On 13 December 1930 he published

[62] Ramsay MacDonald to George Lansbury, 12 Jan. 1928; George Lansbury to Ramsay MacDonald, 15 Jan. 1928, JRMP, PRO 30/69/1173. See also P. S. Gupta, 'British Labour and the Indian Left, 1919–1939', in B. R. Nanda (ed.), *Socialism in India* (1972), pp. 69–121.

[63] Labour Party, *Report of the Thirtieth Annual Conference* (1930), pp. 216–20.

[64] Postgate, *Lansbury*, pp. 125–59.

Mosley's Manifesto—which included a few changes to his earlier Memorandum—'as an immediate plan to meet an emergency situation'. It had the support of seventeen Labour MPs, but Lansbury was not a signatory.[65] The Mosley Manifesto had nothing to do with the introduction of socialism. Its author was now on a different political trajectory. He was expelled as a Labour MP on forming his New Party and was defeated in the October 1931 general election, before drifting off into British fascism in the 1930s.

The early optimism of the Labour government quickly dissolved as the harsh realities of the 'economic blizzard'—in MacDonald's phrase—hit Britain in 1930 to 1931. The world slump cruelly exposed the shortcomings of the Labour administration's economic performance and its failure, seen in the Cabinet's rejection of the 'Mosley Memorandum', to develop any fresh ideas on tackling unemployment.

On taking office, the second Labour government had instituted a series of investigations into the structural reorganization of coal, iron and steel, and cotton. Lansbury encountered early Treasury opposition to any hint of public control, when his Prime Minister rebuked him for an incautious speech to his Bow and Bromley constituents on the future of the coal industry. 'I have had requests to say whether your pronouncement or mine on the coal situation is the official one,' MacDonald wrote disapprovingly. 'Do pray remember every word you now say about policy is studied as the pronouncement of a Cabinet minister.' Now bound by Cabinet collective responsibility, Lansbury could only apologize and promise, 'you shall not have cause to write again. Throw me to the wolves if necessary when Parliament meets.'[66]

In January 1930, MacDonald had established the ineffectual Economic Advisory Council to bring together experts on industry and economics, such as J. M. Keynes and G. D. H. Cole, though Lansbury, Mosley, and Johnston, grappling with the practical problems of unemployment, were not invited to attend. The new economic thinking of J. M. Keynes that underpinned government management of the vicissitudes of the British economy lay in the future. In 1929 Lloyd George had produced his proposals in *We Can Conquer Unemployment*, a programme of large-scale public works to be funded by the state through deficit financing—similar to Franklin Roosevelt's *New Deal* in the United States in the 1930s. But in 1929–31 the Labour government did not respond with a similar expansionist programme to create jobs—'any fool can spend money' Thomas chided Lansbury—and also dismissed the possibility of abandoning Free Trade in favour of protective tariffs to safeguard British industry.

Instead, symbolized by its 'Iron Chancellor', Philip Snowden, the second Labour government remained wedded to Victorian financial orthodoxy of balanced budgets and classical economics. Snowden's traditional policy of deflation endeavoured to reduce the budget deficit by expenditure cuts, including the startling rise in unemployment benefit costs on which the Labour Cabinet eventually ran aground in August 1931.

[65] *The Political Diaries of Hugh Dalton, 1918–40, 1945–60*, ed. B. Pimlott (1986), p. 134.
[66] George Lansbury to Ramsay MacDonald, 12 Sept. 1929, JRMP, PRO 30/69/1174, fo. 68. However, MacDonald did respond, 'Be easy. No throwing to wolves. Only let us be careful.'

Difficult times, reflected in a decline in Labour votes at by-elections, brought increasing acrimony in the Cabinet. The Labour government was also under constant challenge, particularly on unemployment, from a reinvigorated Lloyd George, full of ideas from the Liberal's *Britain's Industrial Future*. Dependent on Liberal votes in Parliament, MacDonald sought a Lib–Lab deal of franchise reform in exchange for Liberal support at Westminster. Talks that had started in February 1930 proved fruitless, especially once Labour's National Executive had ruled out the introduction of the alternative vote. Desultory inter-party discussions continued on agriculture and employment throughout 1930, with Lloyd George even airing the possibility of Coalition government. By early 1931 MacDonald, still highly suspicious of Lloyd George, needed Liberal backing to avoid an early general election. At Westminster a considerable snarl-up in parliamentary bills prevented legislation on the repeal of the 1927 Trade Union Act, electoral reform, consumers' councils, and agriculture.

Remarkably, in a letter of 13 February 1931, probably written without MacDonald's knowledge, Lansbury put behind him previous hostility to any concordat with the Liberals. He encouraged Lloyd George to bring his dynamic energy into the Labour party. 'Your help would be invaluable, *as one of us*', Lansbury wrote warmly to the former Premier.[67] Not surprisingly, Lloyd George—'seventeen years [of office] is just as much as anyone can put up with'—declined an offer containing the possibility of senior office. 'As to the best method of ensuring cooperation . . . "coming over" is not the best way to help. It would antagonize millions of Liberals with hereditary party loyalties . . . I am sure I can render more effective assistance to a government of energetic action by remaining where I am.'[68] After Lansbury's initiative, Lib–Lab relations improved in 1931, once the government had abandoned its trade union legislation.

In the two years of government, Lansbury could do little to relieve the misery of mounting unemployment by way of his brief as one of three advisory ministers. However, his Cabinet post as First Commissioner of Works afforded him an unlikely opportunity which he took, in customary fashion, to bring some much-needed joy and brightness to the metropolis amid the gloom and doom that inexorably settled over the second Labour government. Universally renowned before entering Cabinet office, Lansbury's innovations as First Commissioner of Works increased his public popularity with media coverage that at times rivalled that of Henderson or Snowden.

His Majesty's Office of Works, overlooking the lawns of St James's Park, had a history stretching back to the reign of Edward I. During this time, the Office had accumulated an odd collection of public duties and services, including the upkeep of the royal parks and palaces, as well as the maintenance of other official buildings and institutions in this country and abroad. Lansbury's department undoubtedly

---

[67] For Lib–Lab relations in the 1920s and 1930s, see C. Wrigley, 'Lloyd George and the Labour Party after 1922', in J. Loades (ed.), *The Life and Times of David Lloyd George* (1991), pp. 49–69. See also, Postgate, *Lansbury*, pp. 264–6.

[68] David Lloyd George to George Lansbury, 16 Feb. 1931, LP, vol. 10, fos. 7–8.

undertook important work in the conservation of the nation's heritage. The establishment of the Ancient Monuments Branch in 1913 placed nearly 300 historic buildings and sites in its charge by the time of the second Labour government. However, little was heard of Lansbury's predecessors at the Office of Works, who included Fred Jowett in the 1924 Labour Government. Repairing the drains in St James's Palace or protecting the flowering paulownia of Green Park were rarely the stuff of domestic high politics.[69]

Lansbury appeared to hold the least important post in the Cabinet, but his zest and imagination amazed civil servants more accustomed to time-honoured Victorian administration at Storey's Gate. The urbane Permanent Secretary, Sir Lionel Earle, recalled how he soon changed his mind about the East End socialist whose appointment at first 'filled him with dismay': 'I soon recognised my conception of his character was quite wrong, and looking back over twenty years of experience with First Commissioners, I regard him as one of the best Ministers I have ever served in that office.'[70]

In the Office of Works at Storey's Gate, besides his official Private Secretary, Mr R. Auriol Barker, two members of the Lansbury family joined the new First Commissioner. His daughter, Daisy Postgate, was his personal private secretary for many years. The Labour MP, Ernest Thurtle—a future junior Labour whip—became his Parliamentary Private Secretary. Thurtle had married another Lansbury daughter, Dorothy, later London County councillor and mayor of Shoreditch.[71] In the 1920s Ernest Thurtle, a former First World War army officer and champion of unemployed servicemen, had campaigned strenuously with other radical backbenchers for the abolition of the military death penalty for cowardice and desertion, a reform he finally achieved with his pacifist father-in-law's support in the 1930 Army Act.

Nevertheless, unlike some of his contemporaries, the acquisition of Cabinet office did not alter the new First Commissioner's simple lifestyle. As Labour party leader, Ramsay MacDonald was criticized for his friendship with Lady Londonderry and embarrassed by the public furore over the 'knighthood-for-a-Daimler-car' scandal involving biscuit manufacturer, Sir Alexander Grant.[72] 'Jimmy' Thomas became notorious for his social pretensions and stock exchange speculations as a Cabinet minister. Lansbury's ordinary home in Bow remained the centre of his socialist activities and continued to be so throughout his political life. Jack Jones, future General Secretary of the Transport and General Workers' Union (TGWU), who had moved from Liverpool to find work in the East End around 1930, remembered seeing Lansbury's familiar figure on the streets of Poplar as the

---

[69] For the Victorian history of the Office of Works, see M. H. Port, 'A Contrast in Styles at the Office of Works. Layard and Ayrton: Aesthete and Economist', *Historical Journal*, 27 (1984), pp. 151–76.

[70] Sir L. Earle, *Turn over the Page* (1935), pp. 212–13.

[71] For Daisy Postgate, see Postgate and Postgate, *Life of Raymond Postgate*; for Ernest Thurtle: E. Thurtle, *Time's Winged Chariot: Memories and Comments* (1945); for Dorothy Thurtle: 'Thurtle, Dorothy 1890(c)-?' (sic), in O. Banks, *The Biographical Dictionary of British Feminists*, ii, A Supplement, 1900–1945 (1990), pp. 203–5.

[72] Morgan, *J. Ramsay MacDonald*, p. 225; Wrigley, 'James Ramsay MacDonald', p. 31.

friendly First Commissioner regularly took the underground or bus to Whitehall each day.[73]

Lansbury himself provided a glimpse of his working day as a Cabinet minister:

Every day, at quarter past seven, my daughter brings tea, the newspapers and letters to me. I begin work from that moment. I arrive at this office between 10 and 10.15 in the morning and work here for five or six hours. Generally I travel to and fro by Underground, and occasionally, just for a change, by bus. When I am at home, however, work does not stop . . . My house in Bow has always been an open house. People come in to see me at breakfast; they come at supper; and on Sundays they never stop coming in. Some of them come to talk, some for advice about money, rent or old-age pensions.

Characteristically, little had changed about the septuagenarian Cabinet minister, still deeply influenced by Tolstoyan ascetic ideals. 'Money is worthless' and '£40 a week but he cannot save' were the headlines Lansbury attracted in response to press questions about the compatibility of a £2,000 Cabinet salary and his socialist convictions. In fact, he and Bessie had a large family to support, although Lansbury gave most of his income as always to deserving causes and rarely took a fee for his public speaking.[74] To the crowds who heard the East End socialist at Labour gatherings or now saw him on *Pathé News* at the cinema, Lansbury remained 'good old George'. 'He is 70. Fluffy white hair, white moustache and thistledown side-whiskers confirmed the fact, but there was a young man's power in his broad shoulders, emphasised by the navy-blue reefer jacket and the smile in his eyes was ageless,' observed one journalist who interviewed the First Commissioner at his Office of Works. He remembered the unmistakable bass richness of the Lansbury voice with 'a laugh like the rumble of the sea in a cave'.

One of Lansbury's first duties at the Office of Works took him in August 1929 to distant prehistoric Skara Brae, on the Bay of Skail on the main island of the Orkneys, to inspect the recent excavation of the Neolithic village around 5,000 years old.[75] In 1927 the Office of Works had taken over Skara Brae after its Chief Inspector of Ancient Monuments recommended that the previously excavated but storm-ravaged site needed urgent protection. Vere Gordon Childe, an Australian pre-historian newly appointed as the first Abercromby professor of archaeology at Edinburgh University, had been commissioned to take over the restoration.

On this official visit, the First Commissioner scrambled through the uncovered complex of six subterranean stone houses, passageways, and outhouses accompanied by his son-in-law, Raymond Postgate, one of Childe's closest university friends. At Oxford, Postgate—imprisoned as a conscientious objector—and Childe had been active in university anti-war activities with Rajane Palme Dutt, the future leading intellectual of the CPGB.[76] By 1929, the Marxist Childe was better known for his involvement in Australian politics, particularly after the publication of his

[73] Interview with Jack Jones, 24 Oct. 2000.   [74] *Evening Standard*, 13 Jan. 1931.

[75] I am grateful to Peter Gathercole, Emeritus Fellow of Darwin College, Cambridge, for bringing George Lansbury's visit to Skara Brae to my attention.

[76] Postgate and Postgate, *Life of Raymond Postgate*, pp. 37, 75.

renowned study of left-wing politics, *How Labour Governs*.[77] His excavation in Orkney was the start of a long and distinguished international career in archaeology and anthropology.[78] The inspection of Skara Brae became a regular annual outing for First Commissioners and, to this day, part of the celebrated excavation is known as the 'Lansbury Gallery'.[79]

Eight months later, at a more famous ancient site also far from London, the First Commissioner found himself faced with one of the most difficult decisions at the Office of Works. In April 1930 he toured Hadrian's Wall in Northumberland to investigate the threat of a proposed stone quarry in the hillside. The surface rights had been bought in the neighbourhood of Shields-on-the-Wall, Pele Cray, and Housesteads for conversion of Great Whin Sill into tar macadam at the rate of 200,000 tons per annum and the resultant waste into concrete pipes.

While the quarry-owner, Mr J. F. Wake of Roman Stone Ltd., claimed that his operations would provide work for 500 men without endangering the ancient site, Lansbury received protests from local antiquarian and archaeological societies, as well as questions in Parliament.[80]

The First Commissioner wrote directly to the Prime Minister outlining the environmental issues raised by quarrying at Hadrian's Wall and the dilemma for a Labour government that would have to pay compensation for the £20,000 already expended by the quarrying company: 'More serious still, the quarrying as it progresses will tend to create a meaningless cliff on the southern side . . . out of all relation to the natural features.'[81] Part of Lansbury's dilemma was that the quarrying would create sorely needed employment in the district and the local Labour party was among those making strong representations. As he informed MacDonald: 'The latest resolution that I have received from them is to the effect that "We urge the Government to give immediate consent for employment, believing as we do that the principal portions of the Wall can be preserved without danger by quarrying operations".'[82]

On 2 June 1930 Lansbury announced in Parliament a compromise proposal, first mentioned in his letter to MacDonald, to confine the quarrying to a limited area to preserve the ground between Hadrian's Wall and the *vallum* to the south.[83] Earlier, at a National Trust dinner, faced by an old opponent, Lord Crawford and Balcarres, Lansbury had revealed that his Office of Works had prepared a bill currently before the Cabinet to protect historic sites and buildings.[84] Introduced into the House of Lords, the Ancient Monuments Bill—Lansbury's one and only Act of Parliament—eventually became law on 11 June 1931.[85]

---

[77] V. G. Childe, *How Labour Governs: A Study of Workers' Representation in Australia* (1923).

[78] For Childe, see P. Gathercole, T. H. Irving, and G. Melleuish, *Childe and Australia: Archaeology, Politics and Ideas* (1995); S. Green, *Prehistorian: A Biography of V. Gordon Childe* (1981).

[79] V. G. Childe, *Skara Brae: A Pictish Village in Orkney* (1931), pp. 47–8.

[80] Grey of Fallodon (Chancellor of Oxford University) *et al.* to George Lansbury, 28 Apr. 1930, copy in *The Times*, 3 May 1930; *Daily Mail*, 24 Apr. 1930; *Leeds Mercury*, 24 Apr. 1930.

[81] George Lansbury to Ramsay MacDonald, 9 May 1930, PRO, WORK 14/1257/184682.

[82] Ibid.   [83] *The Times*, 3 June 1930.   [84] Ibid. 29 Nov. 1930.

[85] *Hansard*, 11 Dec. 1930, cols. 526–34; 3 Feb. 1931, cols. 747–58; Postgate, *Lansbury*, pp. 264–5.

Besides the long-running saga of Hadrian's Wall, George Lansbury's time was taken up with his plans for a 'Brighter London', announced soon after he took command of the Office of Works overlooking the smooth lawns of St James's Palace. Among his proposals were mixed bathing in the Serpentine, improved leisure and sports facilities in the Royal Parks, sunbathing and experimental open-air drama. Besides increased playing areas for children, Lansbury wanted to develop the large open space opposite the Knightsbridge Barracks, the historic site of the Great Exhibition of 1851, for football, tennis, athletics, and putting. However, in some circles, Lansbury's infamy had few bounds as his attention next turned to pulling down the iron railings round the parks of London to provide greater access for working people. This was only the beginning, according to the indomitable First Commissioner: 'But the development of bathing facilities in the Serpentine is only a tiny fraction of what I hope to do . . . at Bushey Park, Petersham Park, Regents Park and Greenwich Park, there are actually no shelters for children. These will now be provided . . .'[86]

Once again, George Lansbury was innovative in fund-raising to finance this development of social amenities, especially the provision for children. After a newspaper appeal, generous donations rolled in from Sir Arthur du Cros, Mrs Van der Bergh, Mr Grage, Mr L. Barr, and some anonymous sponsors—all to be matched pound for pound by the British Treasury. In retrospect, Philip Snowden, Labour's flinty Chancellor of the Exchequer, probably did not appreciate the implications of this early financial concession. The First Commissioner of Works had brought one telling talent to his new post. 'He had greater power for getting money for worthy causes than anyone I have ever known,' Sir Lionel Earle noted shrewdly.[87] At least one generous donation came from a former Tory parliamentary opponent.

Around this time, *Punch* depicted the Labour Cabinet as a Shakespearean troupe with Ramsay MacDonald as Macbeth, Arthur Henderson as Mark Antony, Philip Snowden as Henry V, J. H. Thomas as Hamlet, and George Lansbury as a Winged Ariel from *The Tempest* standing by a 'Serpentine Mixed Bathing' notice.[88] To this day, Lansbury's presence survives on a commemorative plaque depicting his profile placed on the Serpentine pavilion wall.

Despite widespread enthusiasm among the general public, Lansbury's proposals for the Royal Parks provoked an extraordinary reaction in some quarters, especially his most famous project for mixed bathing on the Serpentine in Hyde Park. After angry representations and moral protests from bodies such as the London Public Morality Council and the London Free Church Federation, as well as outraged individuals, he told one interviewer: 'I have had people with horror in their voices and almost tears in their eyes who told me of the most frightful moral and physical evils that would result when we permit mixed bathing.'[89]

For two weeks the letters columns of *The Times* bulged with the protests. The outraged Lord Crawford and Balcarres became a regular correspondent:

The playground policy (football, bowling, cricket) means cutting up the parks . . . [I]n spite of

---

[86] *Everyman*, 14 Nov. 1929.   [87] Ibid.   [88] *Punch*, 4 Nov. 1929.
[89] *Everyman*, 14 Nov. 1929.

60 miles of roadway and footpaths, the openness of Hyde Park and Kensington Gardens is unexcelled and makes a profound impression on foreign visitors . . . But for the real health of London, the spaciousness of the parks, their remoteness, the quiet, the distances and the long views . . . all compose health-giving and restful attributes which are unequalled in great cities.[90]

The Times grew increasingly agitated about Lansbury's changes to the park landscapes: 'The tendency in the London parks today is more and more to destroy their peace and beauties and to restrict the freedom of those who use them.' It also queried Lansbury's motives: 'There is also probably the natural ambition of every new Minister to set his mark on the work of his Department . . . nothing more than change for the sake of change.'[91]

This leader brought down a chorus of protest and derision on the head of the First Commissioner of Works. Philip Guedalla of nearby Hyde Park Street observed that Lansbury's ideas avoided parliamentary control—'one of his wealthier acquaintances defrays the cost; and by this genial blend of autocracy and capitalism no vote comes before the House of Commons'. All of this amounted to public gloom and doom: 'we are promised a perpetuation of the carillon which, housed in a cardboard lighthouse, ennobles the central spaces of Hyde Park with music that reminds some of Belgium, and others of a demented kitchen maid, playing upon tin trays.'[92]

Not only was mixed bathing in the Serpentine considered a sin, but it was thought that the rural beauty of the parks would be destroyed with plans for increased recreational and leisure facilities. Postgate came to his father-in-law's defence and revealed his ideas for improving the metropolis. Postgate noted that there was 'only one place [a so-called "roof garden") in which one can get a dinner in the open air in London even in the hottest weather'. In the view of the future editor of the *Good Food Guide*: 'There is certainly no place like the Paris restaurants in the *Bois de Boulogne* and the park at Belleville.' He appealed for the opening of restaurants in the Hyde Park, Kensington Gardens, St James's Park, or Green Park with indoor facilities for dancing in the winter.[93] Lansbury sanctioned licensed restaurants—despite his own teetotalism and protests from church groups.

During his two years at the Office of Works, George Lansbury became hugely popular for his schemes of improvement to the Royal Parks in London, in particular the building of 'Lansbury's Lido' on the Serpentine in Hyde Park where there was mixed bathing for the first time in the summer of 1930. His grandson, Oliver Postgate, remembered being lost in the crowds that swarmed around the Serpentine at the official opening.[94] For Lansbury's critics, the introduction of improved leisure and sporting facilities made him, according to *The Times*, 'the Caliban of the Parks'. However, even his doughty opponent in Cabinet was moved to put pen to paper in praise of the cost-effective pleasure the First Commissioner had brought to

---

[90] *The Times*, 10 Feb. 1930.   [91] Ibid. 7 Feb. 1930.   [92] Ibid. 8 Feb. 1930.
[93] *The Listener*, 6 Nov. 1929.
[94] For other family reminiscences of the First Commissioner, see O. Postgate, *Seeing Things: An Auto-biography* (2000), pp. 12–15.

countless Londoners. Philip Snowden wrote: 'I have seen a little of the gorgeous beauty of the Parks. We cannot estimate the wonderful influence all this as (*sic*) on the character of the people . . . and you are showing how cheaply it can be done compared with the incalculably blessings it brings (*sic*).'[95]

What the Chancellor of the Exchequer recognized was Lansbury's almost unique ability to strike a common chord with immense numbers of people, clearly demonstrated earlier in the First Commissioner's Christian response to the deepening depression. In January 1931 Lansbury had written passionately to the *News Chronicle*, following Hugh Redwood's articles that exposed appalling social conditions in the South Wales mining valleys, to advocate social ownership for the problems of the coalfields. His letter—printed prominently on the front page—initiated a largely sympathetic public correspondence that lasted weeks. 'The fact is we do not believe God is our father and *all of us* are brothers and sisters . . . our minds are still moving along the old individualist lines which teach that industry without profits, rents and dividends is useless and evil', Lansbury declared. Lord Brentford, formerly Sir William Joynson-Hicks, a fervent evangelical and hostile opponent of the miners and Communists in the 1926 General Strike, censured Lansbury for mixing up 'party politics with religion . . . [T]here is a great gulf between Karl Marx and Jesus Christ.' Lansbury agreed with 'Jix': 'He that will not work shall not eat,' he told an audience in Kent, except that the First Commissioner applied that doctrine to all social classes, unlike the former Conservative Home Secretary.[96] Shortly afterwards, at Smethwick, he repeated his Christian socialist message that 'the modern Labour movement . . . was pledged to revolutionise modern capitalism and bring it into line with those Christian morals preached but not practised in this and other Christian countries'.[97] These pronouncements reflected the personal faith of the First Commissioner of Works who, now more than ever since his days in the Church Socialist League, sought a Christian answer to the world's problems. In 1931 Lansbury became President of the Christian Socialist Crusade, a new body instrumental in reviving Christian Socialism of the 1930s. The Crusade, active throughout Britain with meetings and publicity, included twenty-four other Labour MPs and aimed to secure the spiritual and economic emancipation of all people and an international socialist order on earth.[98]

Lansbury's stint at the Office of Works also brought him into contact with the head of the Church of England in his official capacity as Chief Warden of the Royal Parks. King George V, unhappy at the thought of George Lansbury as a Cabinet minister five years before, now found their official meetings harmonious and friendly. Apparently, both elderly men happily avoided any lofty discourse on socialism and monarchy and instead recounted stories of their operations.[99] However, in the Cabinet crisis of August 1931 the king was to play a far more significant

---

[95] Philip Snowden to George Lansbury, 1 June 1931, LP, vol. 10, fo. 64.
[96] *News Chronicle*, 14, 15, 17 Jan. 1931.   [97] *Daily Herald*, 26 Jan. 1931.
[98] C. Bryant, *Possible Dreams: A Personal History of British Christian Socialists* (1996), pp. 238–41.
[99] This is mentioned by Postgate (*Lansbury*, pp. 251–2), but there is no reference in Harold Nicolson's biography: *King George V*.

role than that of sharing cosy reminiscences about hospital scars with the First Commissioner of Works.

As the world economic depression deepened after the New York stock market crash in 1929 and the recall of American loans to Europe, the number of those registered jobless in Britain reached over 2.5 million at the end of 1930. By July 1931 the figure surpassed 2.75 million. An international crisis in the European banking system, combined with a deficit in the British domestic budget, brought about a major political crisis in this country and the collapse of the minority second Labour government in August 1931.

On 11 May 1931 Austria's largest bank, the Credit Anstalt, failed and, despite various international efforts to stave off the growing crisis, eventually in turn toppled the German Danat (Darmstadter und National) Bank with severe effects on assets across Europe. By 22 July, with a panic run as investors sold sterling, the Bank of England suffered dramatic losses of £22 million in gold and foreign currency and had to secure credits from France and New York. In 1931 financial orthodoxy made it axiomatic that Britain remain on the international gold standard, which required the Chancellor of the Exchequer to maintain a balanced budget.[100]

During this serious international situation, any moratorium and exchange controls that might prevent bankruptcies in Britain were considered incompatible with the maintenance of the gold standard. In these critical circumstances, rumours of a 'national government' circulated in governing circles and in the British press. Crucially, confidence in Britain's financial stability was shaken further by the ill-timed findings of a government-appointed inquiry into the British economy. On the 31 July 1931 the report of the May Committee, which predicted a possible budget deficit of £120 million by April 1932, recommended additional taxation of £24 million per year and a reduction in expenditure of £96 million—to be achieved by a 20 per cent cut in unemployment benefit; a 10 per cent reduction in the salaries of civil servants and in the pay of teachers, servicemen, and the police.

The leading economist John Maynard Keynes called the May Report 'the most foolish document I have ever read', but an Economic Committee of the Cabinet (ECC), consisting of MacDonald, Snowden, Thomas, Henderson, and Graham, was established to consider these recommendations. The Bank of England and other banks, as well as the opposition parties, accepted the report but, significantly for the Labour Cabinet, the TUC and Labour movement rejected the bankers' view of the budgetary crisis. At this point the Cabinet dispersed for the holiday season. The ECC was not scheduled to meet until 25 August. However, in early August the Deputy Governor of the Bank of England, Sir Ernest Harvey (the Governor, Montagu Norman, was convalescing in Canada) warned of a collapse in sterling. MacDonald returned to London and recalled his Cabinet after further losses totalling £66 million in a fortnight made additional foreign loans inevitable.

From 19–24 August the political crisis in Britain centred on the meetings of the

---

[100] For details of this European financial crisis, see C. L. Mowat, *Britain between the Wars, 1918–1940* (1966), pp. 378–82.

second Labour Cabinet in Whitehall. On 19 August the report of the ECC was presented at an all-day meeting lasting nearly nine hours. Faced with a severe economic and budgetary crisis, the ministers discussed the feasibility of large cuts in government expenditure, direct tax increases, and the possibility of opposition support for a package of emergency measures. The introduction of a revenue tariff was also considered but rejected by the free traders in the Cabinet, Philip Snowden indicating that he would resign if this policy was adopted.

On Thursday, 20 August MacDonald held a three-party conference with Conservative and Liberal opposition leaders, at which an increased figure of economies totalling £78 millions was mentioned. However, the most important meeting that day took place at 3 p.m. in the Council Chamber of Transport House between the ECC and the TUC General Council and the Labour party National Executive. These representatives of the trade union and labour movement, influenced by Ernie Bevin, the powerful general secretary of the TGWU, rejected any notion of cuts in unemployment insurance and public service incomes (apart from judges and government ministers) and suggested alternative revenue-increasing measures. On Friday, 21 August at another Cabinet meeting lasting nearly four hours, the ministers considered cuts of up to £56 million before dispersing for the weekend. But, at a meeting with opposition leaders, MacDonald and Snowden were informed that greater cuts of over £78 million would still be insufficient.

During the final weekend of the second Labour government on the 22–3 August, the Cabinet debated whether a reduction of at least 10 per cent in unemployment benefit would restore the confidence of the international bankers. On Sunday, 23 August the Cabinet waited all day, only to receive a confused telephone reply late in the evening from New York via the Bank of England in London. By this stage, a significant minority of nine Cabinet ministers was totally opposed to the 10 per cent cut in the rates of unemployment benefit, thereby making it impossible to continue. MacDonald informed the king during the evening of the situation, as well as the opposition leaders, Baldwin and Samuel (who was deputizing for the unwell Lloyd George). That night it appeared to Neville Chamberlain, as well as Labour ministers such as Snowden and Lansbury, that Baldwin would be asked to form a Tory administration. The following morning, Monday, 24 August 1931, an overwrought Prime Minister took the resignations of his Cabinet to George V at Buckingham Palace. At noon MacDonald returned to announce to his astonished ministers that he had accepted the King's appeal to head a National government during the crisis by taking in the leading Conservative and Liberal figures. Only Snowden, Thomas, and Sankey of the Cabinet were invited to take up Cabinet office in the National government, which carried through the emergency economies and, six weeks later, won a landslide victory in the October 1931 general election.

For the Labour movement, MacDonald's defection was the 'Great Betrayal': and not only for his role in bringing about the end of the second Labour government. Though the first National government was announced as a temporary 'co-operation of persons and not a coalition of parties' to deal with the immediate emergency (and possibly non-contentious measures such as the London Passenger

Transport Bill), the new administration won a landslide victory at the October 1931 general election. Thereafter, as the second and third National governments, these, in effect, Conservative administrations remained in power until 1940 brought the next national emergency of wartime. MacDonald, consorting with political opponents who were seen as the class enemy, had opened the way for nearly a decade of reviled National governments, bitterly associated with the means test and appeasement of the 1930s. In 1945 the British electorate gave its verdict in the Labour landslide that returned the Attlee Government.

No twentieth-century party leader has been more hated than Ramsay MacDonald for his part in the historic events of August 1931. For many contemporaries in the British Labour Movement, his unacceptable action gave credence to the long-standing myth that MacDonald cynically plotted the overthrow of his administration and its replacement by a National government led by himself.[101] In 1938, the publication of *The Tragedy of Ramsay MacDonald* by his former Parliamentary Private Secretary, with its damnation of MacDonald's conduct, reflected a widespread sense of betrayal among many rank-and-file Labour supporters, especially in the constituency parties.[102] At the same time, it was widely believed that a 'bankers' ramp' had also deliberately undermined the second Labour government—a capitalist conspiracy by international financiers to replace the Labour ministry with a Conservative government. Both myths were subsequently revised in the second half of the twentieth century.

Following the collapse of the second Labour government, there were bitter recriminations between MacDonald, Snowden, and Thomas and their former Labour Cabinet colleagues, now in opposition. Accusation and counter-accusation were brandished as to what actually happened during the last days of the Labour ministry. George Lansbury played a decisive part in that political crisis, and no minister was more committed to setting the record straight.

During the debate on the National Economy Bill, Lansbury continually harried MacDonald, Snowden, Thomas, and Sir Herbert Samuel about their version of the events a month before. He pressed for the publication of the official Cabinet minutes although he knew they were bound by the fifty-year rule.[103]

Within days, Lansbury wrote his own account of the Cabinet crisis, as he was determined that the inside story of the second Labour government should eventually be told. 'Whoever writes about this business must read not only Cabinet papers but reports of committees, experts and ministers,' Lansbury advised in September 1931.[104] He later handed over to Raymond Postgate, his future biographer, various private papers and official documents, including a full set of the Cabinet papers he had deliberately kept on leaving office in August 1931.[105]

---

[101] Wrigley, 'James Ramsay MacDonald', pp. 32–4.
[102] L. M. Weir, *The Tragedy of Ramsay MacDonald* (1938).
[103] *Hansard*, 8, 11, 14, 17 Sept. 1931, cols. 128–30; 423–6; 451–4; 483–90; 547–50; 627–38; 1013–21.
[104] 'The Cabinet Crisis of 1931', n.d. [Sept. 1931], LP, vol. 25, fo. 17.
[105] Postgate, *Lansbury*, p. 321.

At the time, it was normal practice for retiring Cabinet ministers to retain their papers, if they wished. In Lansbury's case, when he was leader of HM Opposition in 1934, possession of his old Cabinet papers was to put his son, Edgar, in court, charged with offences under the Official Secrets Act. After Lansbury's death in 1940, the authorities removed thirty boxes of Lansbury papers from Postgate's house on the understanding that only the 1929–31 Cabinet documents would be extracted. However, none of Lansbury's private papers were ever returned to Raymond Postgate, not even when the Attlee government came to power in 1945. Cabinet papers were closed under the fifty-year rule (reduced to thirty years in 1967), and Postgate wrote *The Life of George Lansbury* in 1951 without seeing the missing material.[106]

Postgate did have the benefit of Lansbury's document on the 1931 Cabinet crisis, in which his father-in-law gave his version of the downfall of the second Labour government. Throughout the minority administration, Lansbury resisted the policies pursued by Snowden and the Prime Minister who supported him. Now, in his commentary on the Cabinet crisis, he laid the blame squarely at the door of the British Treasury, the Bank of England, and the Federal Bank of New York. In Lansbury's view, the origins of the 1931 Cabinet crisis went back to the beginnings of the MacDonald administration. It lay in the government's failure to tackle unemployment, owing to 'sinister' Treasury influence that limited expenditure to 'revenue producing schemes'—a policy that almost brought early resignations from some Cabinet members. From the outset, there was a Cabinet fault-line on policy between the MacDonald and Snowden circle, on the one hand, and, on the other, Lansbury and his colleagues who were anxious to try different strategies on unemployment. Remarkably, besides Mosley's exodus as a junior government minister in 1930, MacDonald lost only Charles P. Trevelyan, the Education Minister, who resigned over the failure to raise the school-leaving age—though not without a biting denunciation of the premier and his policies prior to his departure.[107]

Lansbury had pointed out the futility of government policy in a memorandum as early as August 1929. He denounced the well-held belief that British trade would improve once *détente* had been achieved in international relations. In supporting the Mosley Memorandum, Lansbury had challenged its nonsensical rejection of the work creation proposals put forward by the Cabinet sub-committee. In his own memorandum, he warned the Cabinet of the historical lesson of the Liberal party, 'driven from the counsels of the nation because it failed to live up to its declared policy and programmes'. 'It makes me ask myself whether we should not tell the nation without reservation that the statements in "Labour and the Nation" and in our election Manifest concerning unemployment, were ill-thought out and not worth the paper they were written on,' he added bitterly.[108]

Lansbury believed firmly that the history of the second Labour government was

[106] For the prosecution of Edgar Lansbury for infringement of the Official Secrets Act, and for the missing Lansbury Papers, see below, Ch. 16.
[107] Morris, *C. P. Trevelyan*, pp. 178–9.
[108] 'Unemployment Policy (1930), Committee: Memorandum by the First Commissioner of Works', 6 May 1930, CP 145(30), PRO, CAB 21/391/48536.

a succession of attempts to curtail social expenditure, including the replacement of Labour's traditional policy of 'work or maintenance' by putting people in receipt of transitional benefit onto the poor law. According to Lansbury, this plan was so controversial, that the typed documents circulated in Cabinet were collected in by officials. There was also a fierce struggle in the Cabinet over the recommendations of the Holman-Gregory Commission set up to investigate the problems of the bankrupt Unemployment Revenue Fund. Lansbury was also convinced that the May Committee, appointed without Cabinet approval, was a conspiracy—'the May Report was a report of the British Treasury against the Government that employed it,' he wrote. 'I am convinced that the whole procedure was a "frame-up" to stampede the Government.' He judged the timing and impact of the May Report fatal— 'certainly no time or guidance was given the Cabinet to consider the effect on our Movement or on the finances of the country of the publication of this report in the middle of the German crisis.'

On 17 October, during the 1931 election campaign, Snowden's radio broadcast included his famous condemnation of the financial proposals in the Labour manifesto as 'Bolshevism run mad'. Lansbury responded with one of the first public accounts of the break-up of the Labour government and a direct attack on the former Chancellor of the Exchequer. Lansbury's newspaper article reiterated many of the critical points contained in his 'Cabinet Crisis of 1931' document about Treasury influence on Snowden's financial policy. He reminded the former Labour Chancellor that on the fateful days of 19–24 August he had promised no cuts in unemployment benefit at the meeting with trade union and Labour party representatives. Although, with the rest of the Cabinet, Lansbury agreed that Britain had to stay on the gold standard, he added damningly:

In addition, all the time the Chancellor, acting for the bankers and on behalf of the Treasury officials, insisted no matter what economies we effected, no matter what scheme we proposed for taxing the rich, nothing would get the Bank of England the gold it needed unless the unemployed were victimised, and education, housing and other social services expenditure stopped. This is where we broke with the Chancellor, the Treasury and the Bankers.[109]

As the only left-winger initially in the Cabinet, George Lansbury was an implacable opponent of cuts in social service expenditure. As early as February 1931, he had submitted alternative proposals to the Cabinet to solve the unavoidable rise in expenditure on unemployment relief, in part through work creation and emigration schemes. 'All the same, I am compelled to give my view ... whether [to] raise contributions or lower benefits. I am against both, but if I must choose ... [I] favour an increase in contributions,' he commented. His main proposal was for a gesture of 'sacrifices all round' that would demonstrate to the whole world that the British nation wanted to face liabilities and restore trade:

Instead of starting with the weak and helpless—that is, the unemployed and the down and outs—let us start at the top ... go to the House of Commons and say that, in order to cope with

---

[109] *Daily Herald*, 23 Oct. 1931.

the situation, great national effort and sacrifice is needed from us all. We propose an emergency tax, on all incomes above £500 net . . . I am sure it would yield very much more than 10 per cent on unemployment pay . . . as a Labour Government, [we] would be carrying out our policy of putting the burden where it ought to be placed.[110]

During the days of 19–24 August, as the political crisis unfolded, Lansbury's large room at the Office of Works became the centre for meetings of the various ministers who joined him to resist the reductions in expenditure proposed by MacDonald and Snowden. According to Postgate, at first there were only three dissentient ministers but before the last meeting of the Cabinet there were ten out of twenty-one. He observed that 'the great shift in opinion occurred, as ever, when Henderson changed his mind'.[111]

On the morning of 24 August, Lansbury was as surprised and shaken as his colleagues to hear MacDonald's announcement of the formation of a National government. Despite some varied accounts of how the Labour Cabinet ended, Lansbury's biographer captured the mood as the Cabinet finally broke up:

As he left the meeting, Lansbury looked white enough and haggard, but the face of his most powerful ally was ghastly . . . Henderson seemed shrivelled and bowed, and his usual ruddy face was yellow. Disloyalty was a thing he could not understand. He had given his most unswerving support to the handsome, eloquent leader who had helped him build up the movement . . . he [Henderson] looked like a man who had been given a mortal wound.[112]

The words came from the pen of Raymond Postgate who, of course, was not present—the voice was unmistakably that of George Lansbury.

In 1951, on publication of *The Life of George Lansbury*, Postgate confirmed 'the widespread belief that it was the King, who stepping away from the traditional neutrality of the Crown, was responsible for MacDonald's astonishing action'.[113] Since then, the crisis of August 1931 has attracted considerable attention from historians. Seventy years later, few believe that MacDonald deliberately engineered the National government in 1931 or that a conspiracy of international bankers set out to overthrow the second Labour government. Both myths have been laid to rest by recent historical scholarship.[114] In particular, Ramsay MacDonald's role in deliberately plotting these events has been greatly revised, principally in the large-scale biography by David Marquand based on the extensive MacDonald papers. His revisionist account used MacDonald's diary and the testimony of Malcolm MacDonald to the effect that his father indicated his forthcoming resignation and intention to depart from public life in a telephone conversation on the evening of 23 August.

[110] 'Unemployment Insurance: Memorandum by the First Commissioner of Works', 6 Feb. 1931, UP (30) 61, PRO, CAB 21/391/48536.

[111] Postgate, *Lansbury* (1951), p. 269.   [112] Ibid. pp. 271–2.   [113] Ibid. p. 261.

[114] For a reappraisal of MacDonald's role, see Marquand, *Ramsay MacDonald*, ch. 25; R. Bassett, *Nineteen Thirty-One: Political Crisis* (1986). For a revision of 'the banker's ramp' theory, see P. Williamson, 'A "Bankers" Ramp? Financiers and the British Political Crisis of Aug. 1931', *English Historical Review*, 99 (1984), pp. 770–806. On the Cabinet crisis of 1931 and the formation of the National government, see also V. Bogdanor, '1931 Revisited: The Constitutional Aspects', *Twentieth Century British History*, 2 (1991), pp. 1–25; P. Williamson, '1931 Revisited: The Political Realities', ibid. pp. 328–38; V. Bogdanor, '1931 Revisited: Reply to Philip Williamson', ibid. pp. 339–43.

To MacDonald's contemporaries in the Labour movement, who saw his actions as a betrayal, the role of the international bankers was also a crucial part of the conspiracy which overturned the Labour government. The myth of a 'bankers' ramp' ending the Labour government had its origins in the lunch-time meeting of the outgoing ministers held in George Lansbury's room at the Office of Works immediately after the last Cabinet meeting. Such an idea was also in the minds of the members of the General Council of the TUC.[115] On 25 August the *Daily Herald* carried the headlines 'Mr MacDonald Forming New Cabinet' and 'Dictation from U.S. Bankers' and alleged that the Federal Reserve Bank gave the outgoing Labour Government an ultimatum to the effect that credits would only be forthcoming if specific and considerable economies were made in unemployment insurance benefits.[116]

Understandably, George Lansbury certainly held this view and, in blaming the Federal Bank of New York for dictating terms that brought down the government, may have been the source for the *Daily Herald* stories. As he explained, on the evening of Sunday, 23 August 1931:

the Cabinet waited for an hour while the Bank of England people were getting a telephone message across from America as to whether the terms were acceptable or not. (Unless the Prime Minister was lying there can be no doubt about this). This message is very cleverly drafted and from it you would gather that the final decision was put by the Federal Bank on to the Bank of England. But the fact remains that the Federal Bank had to be communicated with. The whole business had to be discussed over with them and the Bank of England was the medium through which this was done.[117]

Originally numbered among the majority of the outgoing ministers, Lord Passfield was one of the first of the former Labour Cabinet to go on record over 'what will rank as the most remarkable happening in modern British political history'.[118] Writing in 1931, his account laid the basis for future versions of the plot theory. According to Beatrice Webb, George Lansbury also provided some of the evidence that MacDonald was considering the possibility of the National government well in advance. Only two days after the formation of the new administration she noted:

[Lord] Arnold reports that Lansbury told him that J.R.M. spoke to him casually at the end of July after the issue of the May report, as to the desirability of a National Government if the financial position became serious. Lansbury rejected the notion as impossible and J.R.M. dropped the question.[119]

Nevertheless, Beatrice Webb rejected any suggestion of intentional plotting by MacDonald but wrote instead:

I don't believe that Mac. deliberately led the Cabinet into a trap . . . *tried* to get them into

---

[115] A. Thorpe, 'Arthur Henderson and the British Political Crisis of 1931', *Historical Journal*, 31 (1988), p. 122.

[116] *Daily Herald*, 25 Aug. 1931. [117] Ibid. 23 Oct. 1931.

[118] S. Webb (Lord Passfield), 'What Happened in 1931: A Record', *Political Quarterly*, 3 Mar. (1932), pp. 1–17.

[119] B. Webb, Diary, 27 Aug. 1931, PP.

agreeing to economies in the process of bargaining with the U.S.A. financiers, all the time intending to throw his colleagues over and form a National Government—but he *drifted into doing it*, largely because he is secretive—he never can be frank—yet will let the cat out of the bag . . . even [to] an enemy like Lansbury . . .[120]

Though in the main Lansbury had maintained cordial relations with the Prime Minister during the lifetime of the MacDonald administration, Lansbury had been highly critical of his leadership throughout the 1920s. After 1931 he revealed his true feelings. In 1932, after a long journey to appeal to MacDonald about his old friend, the imprisoned Communist, Tom Mann, a disillusioned George Lansbury wrote to Stafford Cripps: 'He [MacDonald] is a terrible mixture of sanity, cowardice, and utter lack of principle. He is like a rudderless vessel, just drifts, does not attempt to see an argument.'[121]

The events of August 1931 were an important watershed in the political history of the Labour party. What followed in the weeks of September and October was a critical realignment of the main political parties. Indeed, the unexpected outcome of the October 1931 election placed George Lansbury at the helm of his party and in direct opposition to Ramsay MacDonald at the head of the National government.

[120] Ibid.
[121] George Lansbury to Stafford Cripps, 31 Dec. 1932, Cripps Papers; E. Estorick, *Stafford Cripps: A Biography* (1949), p. 120.

15
Party Leader: Domestic Politics, 1931–1933

The general election of 1931 was the greatest electoral landslide in twentieth-century political history and by far Labour's greatest defeat. The National government secured 67 per cent of the poll and a gargantuan total of 554 out of 615 seats. Only a rump of forty-six Labour MPs remained to survey the parliamentary scene. To capture the dramatic election result, two people were photographed scaling a pair of colossal ladders outside the main office of a daily newspaper. The National government figure had virtually disappeared from sight high in the sky while his Labour opponent was barely off the first rung.[1]

After this catastrophic defeat, the Christian pacifist George Lansbury became party leader at Westminster, simply because there appeared to be no other choice. The only Cabinet Minister of the 1929–31 government among HM Opposition to survive the 1931 election, the septuagenarian Lansbury took over the helm of a parliamentary party reduced to rubble and at the nadir of its political fortunes. Arthur Henderson, who had lost at Burnley by 8,200 votes, remained the national leader, as well as party secretary and treasurer, in the expectation that he would return to Parliament once a suitable by-election occurred. But a year later, with the ailing Henderson not only outside Parliament but often away in Geneva as President of the World Disarmament Conference, Lansbury succeeded him as party leader after the annual party conference at Leicester. Until recently, historians have mostly ignored the years of Lansbury's leadership; only his dramatic confrontation with Ernie Bevin and resignation over foreign policy and rearmament after the 1935 Labour party conference at Brighton has attracted any interest.[2] Overshadowed by the longevity of MacDonald and Attlee in the twentieth-century history of the British Labour party, Lansbury's period of office has been overlooked or dismissed, since it was secured by default in the absence of more prominent party politicians. Some mistakenly judged Lansbury as little more than a parliamentary figurehead, with Henderson retaining effective power within the party even after 1932.[3] However, in the dark days that followed 1931, as Britain faced world depression, mass unemployment, and the rise of international fascism, no one was better fitted than the inspirational George Lansbury of Poplar to represent the ranks of the disadvantaged and the dispossessed. His value to his party throughout the country, as well as at Westminster, made him an irreplaceable figure. On the rare occasions (as at Cardiff in 1933), when Lansbury was unable to appear, the public meeting was

[1] *Manchester Guardian*, 29 Oct. 1931.
[2] For a recent study, see Thorpe, 'George Lansbury 1932–35'. See also Shore, *Leading the Left*, pp. 17–34.
[3] For this view of Lansbury, see *Diary of Beatrice Webb*, iv, ed. Mackenzie and Mackenzie, p. 308.

immediately postponed. 'The reason why it [the postponement] was worded this way is that of course no one can take Mr Lansbury's place at a meeting', the organizers explained.[4]

In terms of the number of MPs, it is worth recalling that the extent of the Labour rout in 1931 was unprecedented. Before the election only fifteen Labour MPs had joined Ramsay MacDonald, Philip Snowden, J. H. Thomas, and Lord Sankey to support the National government, leaving the Labour Opposition led by Henderson with 246 MPs. But on polling day on 27 October 1931, the Tories lost not a single seat and Labour did not gain one.[5] Apart from former Cabinet ministers who threw in their lot with the National government, virtually the whole of the second Labour government suffered defeat at the hands of the electors, a total of fourteen Cabinet members and twenty-one other ministers and party whips. Among a generation of figures prominent in Labour politics in the 1920s, some of whom never returned to Parliament after 1931, notable Labour casualties included ex-Cabinet Ministers Arthur Henderson, Christopher Addison, J. R. Clynes, Arthur Greenwood, Tom Johnston, A. V. Alexander, William Graham, Wedgwood Benn, Tom Shaw and Herbert Morrison as well as junior ministers Hugh Dalton and Susan Lawrence.[6]

Labour suffered its heaviest defeats in the Midlands and in Scotland, where the party was reduced from a total of eighty-four MPs to six. Labour even failed to hold strongholds such as Bermondsey (where the 1929 majority had been 42.3 per cent), Sheffield Attercliffe (40.8 per cent), and Morpeth (39.2 per cent).[7] In 1929 there were nine women Labour MPs, but not one of its thirty endorsed women candidates was returned to Westminster in 1931. In Greater London forty-five seats were lost. Outside the Metropolis there was not a single Labour MP in the South of England. Only the former Solicitor-General, Stafford Cripps, survived as the solitary Labour representative in the West at Bristol East. Even the East End Labour heartland of Poplar produced a swing of 11.1 per cent to the Tory candidate D. L. Guthrie at Bow and Bromley. George Lansbury, who contested the National government's campaign for 'a Doctor's Mandate' as 'no remedy for trade depression and therefore no cure for unemployment', saw his majority cut from 11,267 to 4,664, his lowest winning margin in the five elections of the inter-war years.[8]

Clem Attlee, the ex-Postmaster-General, who scraped home in Stepney, Limehouse with a majority of 551, remembered Henderson's hand as party organizer and secretary in controlling the election of the PLP chairman and deputy in October 1931. 'On going to the first Party meeting after the election, I had a message from Arthur Henderson that George Lansbury would be proposed as Leader and myself as Deputy. These nominations went through without opposition,' he recalled.[9]

---

[4] Secretary [Rhona Vickers] to Daisy Postgate, 24 Mar. 1933, DGPP, UL5/6/5.

[5] In addition, there were the 5 unendorsed ILP MPs and Josiah Wedgwood, who stood as an independent. The best study of the 1931 election is A. Thorpe, *The British General Election of 1931* (1991).

[6] Williamson, *National Crisis and National Government*, p. 456.

[7] Thorpe, *The British General Election of 1931*, p. 255.

[8] *Election Address of George Lansbury*, Oct. 1931 (copy in THLLH&A).

[9] C. R. Attlee, *As It Happened* (1954), p. 75.

Lansbury's elevation as PLP chairman was not perhaps totally *faute de mieux*, as has been suggested.[10] 'Apparently the choice for leadership in the Commons will lie between you and Lansbury,' Lord Marley, Labour's Chief Whip in the Lords, told Sir Stafford Cripps.[11]

During the dual Labour leadership of 1931–2, Henderson, who was in failing health, became unable to fulfil the post. He had been appointed President of the World Disarmament Conference (when Foreign Secretary in May 1931) and against medical advice loyally continued with his new role—for which he won the Nobel Prize for Peace in the autumn of 1934. Half of 1932 was spent presiding over the Conference in Geneva where it was feared he might die in the chair.

Lansbury increasingly took on the mantle of party leadership within the country and campaigned continuously to bolster the British Labour movement. 'Few movements could have stood the desertion of some of its chief leaders . . . in spite of unparalleled difficulties, the Labour organisation remained intact,' he reassured the annual conference of Labour women.[12] His regular pronouncements on the world situation included the condemnation of indemnities, reparations, and war debts. 'The world knows that the day of reparations, and indemnity is over. You cannot take out of that nation and try to ruin that nation without ruining ourselves at the same time', he declared in a speech at Bow.[13] On India he welcomed the reopening of negotiations—'there could be no peace in India without the Congress. Conferences without Gandhi were like the play without Hamlet.'[14] On the crisis in the Far East between China and Japan, Lansbury looked to the League of Nations 'to settle the dispute peaceably and amicably'.[15] At home, a Christian appeal to the nation's religious leaders to end 'twelve years of ever-increasing degradation, starvation, penury and destitution' in a long letter to *The Times* brought a stern response in the form of a leader in the paper: 'Mr Lansbury is guilty of that hysteria which he himself deplores when he pictures the coming winter in advance as a period of hunger riots and baton charges.' Lansbury had threatened that if subjected to such a starvation ordeal he 'might forget [his] pacifist principles and throw bricks or take any means which seemed to offer a way of escape.'[16]

Despite his work in Geneva, Henderson remained party secretary (until May 1934) and part-time treasurer. Nevertheless, he was a shadow of his former self. At the annual party conference at Leicester in October 1932 he had difficulty in securing a hearing from the delegates when, on behalf of the NEC, he unsuccessfully opposed Trevelyan's resolution to commit a future Labour government to a radical programme of socialist legislation. It was no surprise, therefore, when Henderson resigned shortly afterwards—and recommended Lansbury as the national leader. Henderson had previously notified his constituency party of his reluctance to

[10] Williamson, *National Crisis and National Government*, p. 456.

[11] Lord Marley to Stafford Cripps, 31 Oct. 1931, quoted in S. Burgess, *Stafford Cripps: A Political Life* (1999), p. 73.

[12] *The Times*, 16 June 1932.   [13] Ibid. 16 Jan. 1932.   [14] Ibid. 11 Jan. 1932.

[15] Ibid. 1, 4 Feb. 1932.   [16] Ibid. 11 Oct. 1932.

contest a by-election to return to Westminster while the World Disarmament Conference continued.[17]

From his Northumberland estate, where he had retired after the 1931 débâcle, Sir Charles Trevelyan had been fearful about his country's prospects. 'A puzzled, deceived and rather frightened nation has played for safety. I am afraid it will have a bitter period to repent in.' But he struck a more confident tone on the prospect of the Labour leadership under George Lansbury. 'My fine friend, this later work of yours, which seems to have been thrust upon you, may be the greatest you have ever had to do,' he prophesied.[18] Ben Tillett agreed with this verdict: 'At a time and age, when men are to lay their tasks to rest; you have been chosen by fate to lead the party, the people you have always served so well,' he observed.[19] In retrospect, Lansbury regretted not resigning from the Labour Cabinet in August 1929. 'It is hard to determine though had I done so then the National Government would not have been born, at least not as we now see it', he replied to Trevelyan.[20]

Typically, George Lansbury remained defiant about Labour's future. 'As a matter of fact . . . I honestly believe the movement is going to be purer and stronger for the very heavy defeat we have sustained', he later told Trevelyan.[21] In public Lansbury was soon challenged on whether the 1931 result meant the end of the Labour party after their Conservative opponents had secured large majorities, even in working-class quarters of London. 'Most emphatically I do not believe that this means the smashing of the Labour Movement,' Lansbury responded immediately. 'I have lived through too many terrible defeats of Labour to despair. After the election of 1906 the Tories were reduced, I think, to 130 members, but they soon revived again. So will it be with us.'[22]

As Labour leader, Lansbury was right to strike a note of optimism about Labour's popular vote. The vagaries of the British electoral system had delivered vast serried ranks of National government MPs at Westminster who crowded the government benches and spilled over to the Opposition side of the Commons. But in 1931 Labour had received 6.5 million votes (31 per cent)—which compared favourably with the party's 1923 election performance. Whereas Labour's poll share in 1923 returned 158 members, eight years later the same percentage of the vote produced only a tiny Opposition group of 46 Labour MPs, mainly older trade union figures from the Yorkshire and South Wales coalfields sponsored by the Miners' Federation of Great Britain. After Parliament reassembled in 1931, in an early broadside on the National government, Lansbury declared that 'a reasonable electorate system' would have yielded Labour at least 180 MPs—a claim that brought nods of approval from the Liberal leader, Sir Herbert Samuel.[23]

---

[17] For this period of dual leadership, see Wrigley, *Arthur Henderson*, pp. 179–83; F. M. Leventhal, *Arthur Henderson* (Manchester, 1989), pp. 201–14.

[18] Charles Trevelyan to George Lansbury, 29 Oct. 1931, LP, vol. 9, fos. 172–3.

[19] Ben Tillett to George Lansbury, 21 Feb. 1932, LP, vol. 10, fo. 212.

[20] George Lansbury to Charles Trevelyan, 30 Oct. 1931, Trevelyan Papers, CPT 98.

[21] George Lansbury to Charles Trevelyan, 5 Jan. 1932. Ibid. CPT 145.

[22] *Manchester Guardian*, 29 Oct. 1931.

[23] *News Chronicle*, 11 Nov. 1931. The young Aneurin Bevan, re-elected unopposed as the MP for

Instead, the size of the challenge that confronted George Lansbury and his Labour colleagues can be seen in the composition of the 1931–5 Parliament. Of the 554 MPs who composed the massed numbers behind the National government, 470 were Conservative members. The Liberal contingent was divided between the 35 Liberal Nationals led by Sir John Simon and the 33 Liberals under the official leadership of Herbert Samuel. There were only 13 National Labour and 4 National MPs.[24]

Over seventy years after the 1931 catastrophe, it is difficult to imagine the depth of disappointment and disillusion experienced by rank-and-file members of the Labour movement, as well as by most of the leading figures in the Labour party. Antagonism and a sense of betrayal soon followed the break up of the 1929–31 Labour Cabinet. Constituency parties throughout Britain rejected MacDonald, Snowden, and those who followed them into the National Labour Party and participated in the National governments that dominated the next decade of British politics. There was a deep distrust of intellectuals within the Labour movement, particularly on the part of the trade union leadership.[25]

There could have been no better leader for the Labour party at the collapse of its political fortunes in 1931 than George Lansbury—a universally popular choice, and a source of immediate inspiration among Labour ranks. As appropriate testimony, Postgate cited Lord Ponsonby's remarks on becoming Labour Leader in the House of Lords: 'Could I ask for anything more than to be quit of those people [Mac-Donald and Snowden] and to have Lansbury as my chief?'[26] 'If George Lansbury had left us I should have doubted Christ himself,' was how miners' leader and Parliamentary Secretary to the Ministry of Labour 1929–31, Jack Lawson, underlined Lansbury's value to the Labour party.[27]

A measure of George Lansbury's remarkable personal popularity that has never been matched by any other Labour party leader can be seen during the last weeks of his leadership in 1935 at the Durham Miners' Gala, a gathering numbering more than 100,000 miners and their families. Ecstatic cheering 'that lasted for over two hours' accompanied Lansbury's appearance on the balcony of the Royal County Hall and brought the vast procession below to a standstill until the police requested he retire for public safety. 'Lansbury obviously is the idol of all these workers and their women-folk. He has moved, in his time, in proud places. But his heart remains with the people,' observed Hannen Swaffer, the *Daily Herald* columnist, a speaker at the Gala who witnessed the scene.[28]

Compared to the Olympian leadership previously displayed by the weary Ramsay MacDonald, George Lansbury cut a different political figure. 'Old in the

Ebbw Vale briefly became George Lansbury's Parliamentary Private Secretary. Michael Foot, *Aneurin Bevan* (1962), p. 164 n. 1.

[24] For the National government, see N. Smart, *The National Government, 1931–1940* (1999); for the Liberal party: Wasserstein, *Herbert Samuel*, ch. 13.

[25] See A. Bullock, *The Life and Times of Ernest Bevin*, i, *Trade Union Leader, 1881–1940* (1960), ch. 19.

[26] Postgate, *Lansbury*, p. 277.

[27] 'George Lansbury by Jack Lawson' (typescript n.d. [May 1940]), Lawson Papers, Box 5.

[28] *Daily Herald*, 29 July 1935; H. Beynon and T. Austin, *Masters and Servants: Class and Patronage in the Making of a Labour Organisation* (1994), pp. 354–6.

workers' cause, yet as young as the youngest in outlook and enthusiasm . . . [H]is name is a banner, and his simplest sentence a message,' proclaimed Jack Lawson.[29] Deeply rooted in the life of East London among fellow working-class residents, Lansbury did not associate with dukes, or chase duchesses, thus avoiding 'the aristocratic embrace'—associated with Ramsay MacDonald and the extravagant lifestyle, right-wing politics, and stock exchange dealings of Jimmy Thomas. In a time of political crisis, his contemporaries recognized the personal attributes of honesty and humility that Lansbury brought to the leadership of the party. The former Labour Minister of Agriculture, Christopher Addison, noted the size of the audiences the Christian pacifist attracted to his meetings at which he attacked the scourge of unemployment and the futility of war. 'They see an old man full of energy, very much alive and possessed of an unquenchable zeal, breathing love and kindliness, and yet all the time a fighter, vehement and determined', he observed.[30]

George Lansbury not only provided a new type of leadership but one based firmly on his ideas of working-class participation in a political democracy. 'Leaders may be necessary,' he added, 'but the best kind of leader is one who leads from the centre of those he speaks for, in fact, it is not possible for me to imagine the need for leadership within an educated democracy.'[31]

One of the clearest expressions of this philosophy can be seen in his 1934 address to the annual party conference at Southport, where Lansbury underlined his concept of leadership as acting as the main representative or spokesman of the party. Characteristically, he told the Labour delegates:

I never dreamed in my wildest imagining that I would ever be called upon to act as the spokesman. I have never considered myself leader—but as spokesman of my colleagues in the House of Commons. I am proud to have been one of that little band. I am proud to have been chosen to speak for them when it was necessary for me to speak on behalf of the Party . . . It was an accident that put me there—the accident of the last General Election—and I am only there for as long as my colleagues think it wise for me to be there. When they think a change is needed, then I shall go . . .[32]

At Westminster, Clem Attlee and Stafford Cripps joined George Lansbury in the parliamentary leadership to form a socialist triumvirate in the Commons. The threesome, who had come together by chance, shared the HM Opposition leader's official room behind the Speaker's chair and worked closely and happily as a team to restore the morale of the PLP in the face of considerable odds. Both Attlee and Cripps possessed a special affection for Lansbury, the beloved, warm-hearted, sentimental, and rampageous champion of the under-privileged and far from the terrible agitator of 'Poplarism' depicted in the press. Another admirer was the fellow life-long pacifist, Lord Ponsonby, the socialist aristocrat whose position at this time as Labour leader in the Lords is scarcely mentioned by historians.[33] In their different ways, all three men were destined to play important roles during this period of

[29] J. Lawson, *A Man's Life* (1932), p. 127. [30] *Clarion*, 7 Jan. 1933. [31] *Forward*, 19 Dec. 1931.
[32] Labour Party, *Report of the Annual Conference* (1934), p. 146.
[33] For Lord Ponsonby, see Jones, *Arthur Ponsonby*.

leadership, though their various backgrounds were remarkably different from that of George Lansbury.

In 1931 Clem Attlee was a largely unknown national figure, despite serving in both Labour governments. Elected mayor of Stepney in 1919 after honourable military service in the First World War, Major Attlee was prominent with Lansbury in organizing the London unemployed in the post-war years. Unlike his fellow East End mayor, Attlee's background was comfortable Victorian middle class—public school at Haileybury and University College, Oxford. First-hand experience as an East End social worker at Toynbee Hall sharpened Attlee's political awareness and growing socialist conscience. As he recalled, his stint in Stepney from 1903 brought personal contact with George Lansbury and Will Crooks and soon enrolled him in the socialist ranks. Attlee joined the local ILP branch at the age of twenty-five and became its chief organizer. There were also other common bonds with George Lansbury.[34] Attlee's pacifist brother, Tom, a former conscientious objector during the First World War, had been a local party worker on Lansbury's Bow and Bromley election campaigns in 1910. Kathleen Attlee (Tom's wife) was the first woman elected to Poplar Council at the time Lansbury led the Labour group.[35]

By contrast, the wealthy city lawyer Richard Stafford Cripps's political apprenticeship was far shorter and more meteoric. A Wykehamist, Cripps was the youngest son of Lord Parmoor, Lord President of the Council in the second Labour government. Within eighteen months of joining the Labour party in 1929, Cripps had become Solicitor-General and afterwards entered Parliament for a safe Labour seat at the 1931 Bristol by-election.[36] Cripps was also a nephew of Beatrice Webb, who advised him of the difficulties of combining a professional career with leadership in the House of Commons. 'I am afraid you must be feeling lonely on that Opposition bench, though Lansbury seems to be doing well and creating a certain impression of directness and honesty as well as good humour,' she added.[37] Despite an age-gap of some thirty years Lansbury and Cripps shared a particularly close friendship based on their common Anglican faith. The Crippses' home—Goodfellows—on the Oxfordshire–Gloucestershire borders provided a political retreat for the leadership trio. There a future leader of the Labour party, Michael Foot, who joined the party in 1933, first met George Lansbury through his friendship with the Cripps family.[38]

In 1931, Arthur Augustus William Harry Ponsonby became Labour leader in the Lords. A son of Queen Victoria's Principal Private Secretary and one of Her Majesty's pages, Ponsonby had been born in Windsor Castle and educated at Eton and Balliol College, Oxford. Despite his patrician lineage, he was widely acknowledged as a champion of the underdog and one 'not dazzled by his proximity to the

---

[34] For Clem Attlee, see K. Harris, *Attlee* (1982).
[35] For Kathleen and Tom Attlee, see P. Attlee, *With a Quiet Conscience: A Biography of Thomas Simms Attlee, 1880–1960* (1995), pp. 35–8.
[36] For Stafford Cripps, see Burgess, *Stafford Cripps*, esp. ch. 7.
[37] Quoted in C. Bryant, *Stafford Cripps: The First Modern Chancellor* (1997), pp. 94–5.
[38] Interview with Michael Foot, 7 Aug. 1991.

throne'. Prominent in the UDC—and later in the Peace Pledge Union (PPU)—he was also one of those former Liberals who moved over to the Labour party at the time of the Great War. Though an accomplished diplomat and a Labour MP with unrivalled expertise in international affairs, he held only junior office under Mac-Donald in the 1920s. 'He had not offered quite enough incense on his leader's altar,' Harold Laski observed. In 1930 Ponsonby's elevation to the peerage took him to the House of Lords where he eventually became Leader of the small group of Labour peers after the 1931 election.

As Labour leader George Lansbury faced the immediate problem of further defections and losses from his party arising from the rapidly deteriorating relationship between the Labour party and the ILP over the question of party discipline and the observation of the PLP's standing orders. Labour had already been weakened by the earlier departures of Mosley and MacDonald and their supporters in 1930 and 1931, but there was little Lansbury could do to prevent the breakaway of the ILP in 1932.

In the 1929–31 Parliament, 142 Labour MPs had been ILP members, of whom the ILP sponsored 37, but in 1931 only 5 ILP MPs (Maxton, Wallhead, McGovern, Kirkwood, and Buchanan) were returned out of 19 ILP candidates not endorsed by the Labour party. In the new Parliament, the Speaker recognized the 5 ILP MPs as a separate political party. In a shrewd, but unsuccessful move, Lansbury invited Maxton—the left's most outstanding and charismatic orator at Westminster—to join him on the Opposition front bench. A messy squabble then ensued over the occupancy of Opposition rooms in the Commons. In the end, Lansbury had to concede the inevitability of losing the handful of remaining ILP MPs. In exasperation he wrote to Trevelyan: 'I want very much unity with the ILP, and especially unity in this House—but I am now convinced that this is hopeless with the four members who represent the ILP.'[39]

In the pre-1914 years Lansbury had been a leading member of the ILP and in the 1920s was often associated with James Maxton and the 'Clydesider' MPs in their criticism of the MacDonald leadership. During the second Labour government the left wing of the ILP was in open revolt against party discipline and was regarded by Arthur Henderson as a 'party within a party'.

Increasingly disenchanted with the government's performance, the Clydesiders within the ILP under Maxton's leadership frequently flaunted PLP standing orders. They objected to the rigidity of party discipline that required voting for parliamentary bills not sanctioned by the PLP or the annual party conference. The standing orders did not permit an individual MP to vote against the party line, but the ILP wanted the right to instruct its MPs to vote in accordance with ILP policy decisions.

Not all of the ILP MPs supported the action of the Maxton group, but at the 1930 ILP Birmingham Conference the ILP National Council declared openly against the 'rigid discipline preventing liberty of action on matters of deep conviction'. In July

---

[39] George Lansbury to Charles Trevelyan, 5 Jan. 1932, Trevelyan Papers, CPT 145.

1930 Lansbury was a member of the Labour party negotiating team—with Arthur Henderson and Susan Lawrence—that unsuccessfully attempted to achieve a *modus vivendi* with Maxton's deputation on ILP–Labour party relations. From 1930, the Labour party executive refused to endorse any candidate unwilling to accept party discipline. At the Labour party conference in October 1931 the NEC was empowered to enforce the Standing Orders and Fenner Brockway's motion to refer back the matter was defeated.

In 1931–2 Lansbury stood like Canute against the ILP waves breaking over his embattled party. Of Maxton's and his colleagues' refusal to accept the Labour party's standing orders he observed: 'If the rules and regulations in this place, made by the Party, are not what we want them to be—surely they can come in and help change them.'

During intense negotiations with the Labour leadership, Fenner Brockway took over as ILP leader from Maxton and journeyed to the East End to meet Lansbury, possibly expecting a favourable discussion, in view of their earlier friendship within the ILP. But Brockway found the former member of the ILP intransigent—firmly convinced that the ILP should either remain within the Labour party, subject to party discipline and majority decisions on voting, or remain outside. 'There was no place for a Party within a Party,' Brockway was told.[40] George Lansbury had travelled some distance himself since his time in the ILP, when he clashed passionately with the Labour party leadership over his independent stance on women's enfranchisement in 1912. In particular, he had departed from the position of his former ally, Fred Jowett, who now opposed the PLP's standing orders in favour of independent socialist action.

In March 1932 at the ILP Conference at Blackpool the die was finally cast for the largest socialist society to leave the Labour party, since the conference decision—in favour of conditional affiliation and further negotiations with the Labour leadership—held no prospect of a solution to the conflict between the two parties. As Keith Laybourn has explained, after a fierce internal debate over disaffiliation on 30–1 July 1932, the ILP took the momentous and foolhardy decision to secede from the Labour party at its special conference in Jowett Hall, Bradford, where the party had been founded in 1893.[41]

Although the Labour Opposition was outgunned by a twelve to one ratio in the Commons, Lansbury still declined to contemplate any parliamentary pact or alliance with the Liberals or electoral scheme for proportional representation. After 1931 there was chronic speculation about a realignment of progressive forces in British politics—even talk of MacDonald returning to the Labour party after the *Clarion* in January 1932 reported an unlikely meeting between Lansbury and the

    [40] F. Brockway, *Inside the Left: Thirty Years of Platform, Press, Prison and Parliament* (1942), p. 238.
    [41] K. Laybourn, '"Suicide during a Fit of Insanity or the Defence of Socialism?" The Secession of the Independent Labour Party from the Labour Party at the Special Conference at Bradford, July 1932', *The Bradford Antiquary*, 3rd ser. no. 5 (1991), pp. 41–53. See also G. Cohen, 'The Independent Labour Party: Disaffiliation, Revelation and Standing Orders', *History*, 86 (2001), pp. 200–21.

Prime Minister.[42] In public speeches Lansbury killed rumours of any such deal with the Lloyd George Liberals—his earlier overtures to Lloyd George to join Labour were conditional upon any Liberals who switched accepting socialism. 'No combination will persuade us to cut down or belittle in anyway the programme endorsed last October at the Scarborough Conference of the Labour Party', he announced.[43] Two years later, former Cabinet colleague Christopher Addison, helped by Lansbury in his endeavours to return to Parliament, acted as an intermediary in further abortive attempts to secure an electoral understanding with Lloyd George before the next general election.[44]

After 1931, the years of the Lansbury leadership must be considered in the context of a significant period of re-examination of Labour policy and political strategy. MacDonald's defection in 1931 to the class enemy made a profound impact on the Labour party and the Labour movement. While the triumvirate of Lansbury, Attlee, and Cripps in the Commons was in general to the left of the parliamentary party, the early 1930s witnessed an emerging alliance between moderates in the political and industrial wings of the Labour movement.

The growing influence of the trade unions in Labour circles on domestic and international questions was reflected by the personalities and stance adopted by Ernie Bevin, the pugnacious Transport and General Workers' leader, and Walter Citrine, the urbane General Secretary of the TUC. Determined efforts were made to strengthen trade union leverage on the party organization particularly through the revived National Joint Council (NJC) (later renamed the National Council of Labour). The failure of the second Labour government, and the defection of Mac-Donald, Snowden, and other Labour ministers to the National government, caused a strong distrust of left-wing Labour intellectuals within trade union circles and a determination by Bevin and Citrine to mould the policy and style of a future Labour administration. In December 1931 the NJC, the consultative body with representatives from the TUC General Council, the Parliamentary Executive, and the National Executive, was reorganized with greater duties and powers and gave the trade union movement a majority of the membership.[45]

As Ben Pimlott has argued, after 1931 the balance of power shifted in the Labour Party to a new and younger generation of politicians, with only Lansbury and Henderson (absent from Parliament until 1933) left of the pioneers. In reality there were two centres of power, at Transport House and at Westminster, often in conflict over the development of party policy. Outside Parliament the NEC became dominant over Transport House. Unlike the decade after the First World War, in the period

---

[42] For the reference to the *Clarion*, see B. Pimlott, *Labour and the Left in the 1930s* (1977), pp. 144–5; but David Marquand and Raymond Postgate do not mention this encounter in their biographies.

[43] *Daily Herald*, 11 Dec. 1931.

[44] K. Morgan and J. Morgan, *Portrait of a Progressive: The Political Career of Christopher, Viscount Addison* (1980), pp. 215–17; *Lloyd George: A Diary by Frances Stevenson*, ed. A. J. P. Taylor (1971), pp. 290, 292, 295.

[45] J. Shepherd, 'Labour and the Trade Unions: George Lansbury, Ernest Bevin and the Labour Leadership Crisis of 1935', in C. Wrigley and J. Shepherd (eds.), *On the Move: Essays in Labour and Transport History Presented to Philip Bagwell* (1991), pp. 210–12.

1931–5 the parliamentary membership of the NEC declined to an average of three. One of Lansbury's difficulties as party leader was that he was the only MP on the NEC. At Westminster the parliamentary party, with a leadership to the left, often took a stance independent of that of the NEC.

In December 1931 the NEC, where Hugh Dalton and Herbert Morrison were dominant, established a new Policy Committee to oversee future policy-making in key areas, such as finance and trade, industrial reorganization, local government, and social services. These sub-committees provided opportunities for co-operation and consensus between the moderate politicians, such as Dalton and Morrison, and trade union leaders. This collaboration was strengthened by dual exchanges between the NEC Policy Committee and the TUC economic committee.[46]

After 1931 an important part of the reaction on the left to Ramsay MacDonald's defection and the gradualist philosophy of the 1929–31 Labour government was to push the Labour party firmly leftwards in terms of policy and strategy. In October 1932, the Socialist League was formed by an amalgamation of the Society for Socialist Inquiry and Propaganda (SSIP) and those members of ILP who refused to accept the Bradford decision to disaffiliate from the Labour party.

Also disillusioned with the Labour government's slow progress towards implementing socialism, G. D. H. Cole in June 1931 had established the SSIP group, known as 'the loyal grousers', which was also connected to the New Fabian Research Bureau. Unlike the ILP dissidents, both bodies remained loyal to the Labour party as research and propagandist groups working towards a distinct future socialist programme. Lansbury was numbered among the SSIP supporters, who also included Raymond Postgate, Clem Attlee, Ellen Wilkinson, and R. H. Tawney, among others. They gathered at a number of weekend conferences organized by George and Margaret Cole at the exotic and palatial Easton Lodge, the home of the Labour sympathizer, the 'Red' Countess of Warwick at Dunmow, Essex. Besides the Coles, the most important member was Ernest Bevin, the truculent General Secretary of the Transport and General Workers' Union, who became SSIP chairman.[47]

Unfortunately for George Lansbury as Labour leader, Bevin was no longer on board when the Socialist League was founded at Leicester immediately before the Labour party Conference of 1932. During the negotiations, G. D. H. Cole opposed amalgamation and eventually left the League; Bevin had nothing to do with the new organization. The manoeuvres of the ILP faction, that secured appointment of Frank Wise as the founding chairman, enraged Bevin and only confirmed his distrust of left-wing intellectuals—among whom he apparently numbered George Lansbury. As was to become clear at the 1935 Brighton conference, Ernie Bevin, the outstanding Minister of Labour in Churchill's war-time government and British Foreign Secretary in Attlee's 1945 Labour administration, could certainly throw his weight around when displeased.

    [46] Pimlott, *Labour and the Left in the 1930s*, pp. 17–20.
    [47] Ibid. pp. 41–58. For the SSIP, see also M. Cole, 'The Society for Socialist Inquiry and Propaganda', in A. Briggs and J. Saville (eds.), *Essays in Labour History, 1918–1939* (1977), pp. 190–201.

When in March 1933 Bevin tried to exert the control of the NJC over the party leader when Lansbury agreed to speak without NJC permission at an Albert Hall rally organized by the Socialist League, Lansbury dealt firmly with the criticism:

When I feel it is impossible to state the Party's own view I shall of course resign, not merely from the leadership but from membership; but I do maintain my right to put the Party's case . . . and I do not think I am called upon to ask permission from anybody to do this—and certainly have no intention of doing so.[48]

The neo-Marxist Socialist League became the guardian of the socialist conscience of the Labour party for most of the 1930s. After the death of Frank Wise in November 1933, the League was particularly associated with Stafford Cripps who was elected as chairman until 1936. William Mellor, former editor of the *Daily Herald* and associate of George Lansbury, then took over. By March 1934 the League organization encompassed seventy-four branches, a National Council, headquarters staff, annual conference, and regional committees, as well as various publications including the *Socialist Leaguer*—eventually replaced by *Tribune* in 1937.[49] Until its estrangement from the mainstream of the Labour party and eventual disbandment in 1937, most of the leading left-wing intellectuals were among a membership of around 3,000. For a while the League's influence on policy was felt at the annual Labour party conferences, though the organization never remotely reached the scale and position in Labour politics previously occupied by the ILP.

At the 1932 Leicester conference, which considered the first four reports of the policy sub-committees, Wise successfully moved an amendment to the NEC resolution on the public ownership of the Bank of England to include the joint stock banks, despite the opposition of Ernie Bevin and others. A resolution in favour of workers' control of the nationalized industries was also passed.

At the 1933 Hastings Conference, where Attlee supported Trevelyan's resolution—carried without a card vote despite Arthur Henderson's opposition—to commit the next Labour government to enact 'definite Socialist legislation', the Socialist League was less successful. The conference debated a new policy statement, 'Socialism and the Condition of the People', which included proposals for nationalization and a National Investment Board. Cripps's amendment for the immediate abolition of the House of Lords and the passage of an Emergency Powers Act—as well as other changes to parliamentary procedures and an economic plan—to enable the next Labour government to effect an immediate transition to full-blooded socialism was delayed for twelve months by Lansbury's intervention on behalf of the NEC. After this, despite the considerable efforts of William Mellor at the 1934 Southport Conference, the Labour party did not accept any resolution advanced by the Socialist League.[50]

Historians remain divided about the general political, intellectual, and strategic

---

[48] Quoted in Postgate, *Lansbury*, p. 288.
[49] P. Seyd, 'Factionalism within the Labour Party: the Socialist League, 1932–1937', in A. Briggs and J. Saville (eds.), *Essays in Labour History, 1918–1939* (1977), pp. 205–11.
[50] Interview with Baroness Barbara Castle, 13 Jan. 1994.

background to George Lansbury's term of office—the early years of the 'Devil's Decade' of Jarrow, Guernica, and Munich. In recent writing about the remaking of Labour policy that underpinned the rehabilitation of the Labour party, greater emphasis has been placed on the intellectual drive of Hugh Dalton and the administrative expertise of Herbert Morrison. Dalton's influence can be seen in the promotion of a new crop of young left-wing academic economists and politicians, especially Hugh Gaitskell, Douglas Jay, Evan Durbin, and others, and bodies such the XYZ group and the New Fabian Research Bureau, that led to the 1937 *Interim Programme*.[51]

Even so, by holding his party together, Lansbury played a key role in the beginnings of its period of renaissance. As he had demonstrated in the pre-war suffragette days and during his time as the editor of the *Daily Herald*, Labour's 'Grand Old Man' not only had a personal rapport with the rank and file but also had an uncanny ability to work with differing figures, often with strong and flamboyant personalities who led the labour and women's movements. Labour has always been a broad church; in the 1930s its Leader moved successfully across the political spectrum from Stafford Cripps to Arthur Henderson, including even co-operation with Ernie Bevin (to whom Lansbury offered to show confidential Cabinet documents).[52] No one came forward to challenge Lansbury, despite the intrigues of Dalton, Bevin, and others. In March 1932 an official NEC statement quickly scotched press speculation about a change of leadership before Arthur Greenwood's successful election at the Wakefield by-election.[53] As can be witnessed in the day-to-day dealings of Labour politics, George Lansbury remained as popular as party leader as he was in his East End constituency—and remarkably unassailable.

With the considerable burden of parliamentary business, the months until December 1933 were among the busiest and most hard working of his career. Lansbury's first task was to maintain the morale of the forty-six MPs returned to Westminster at the 1931 election. When Parliament re-assembled he penned a personal appeal to each member of the PLP to keep up attendances, votes, questions, and speeches, despite 'the overwhelming numbers arrayed against us'. Lansbury told his party 'that as sure as the sun rises, victory, full and complete, will in the near future come to the Cause we represent'. He also reminded the Labour members of the voters who had sent them back to Westminster and who relied on them in the aftermath of 1931, and that they had to work loyally together to 'convince the masses of our people that we are worthy descendants of those who founded our Movement, that our faith is unshaken and that the principles on which our Party was founded not merely will live but are the inspiring motives of our lives and actions.'[54]

At Westminster the enormous task of coping with parliamentary affairs,

---

[51] Interview with Lord Douglas Jay, 15 Sept. 1995. See also K. O. Morgan, *Labour People: Leaders and Lieutenants, Hardie to Kinnock* (1987), pp. 107–8; B. Pimlott, *Hugh Dalton* (1985), ch. 14.

[52] Ernest Bevin to George Lansbury, 12 May 1933; George Lansbury to Ernest Bevin, 18 May 1933; [Daisy Postgate] to Ernest Bevin, 25 May 1933, LP, vol. 12, fos. 275, 277, 279.

[53] *New Clarion*, 7 Jan. 1932.   [54] *Daily Herald*, 9 Nov. 1931.

especially the debates on national and international policy, fell directly on Lansbury, Attlee, and Cripps. In reality, only about thirty of the forty-six Labour MPs were effective parliamentary performers. 'We have been having a very strenuous time in the House. I have to spend hours on the Bench. The Govt are very cheap in their arguments especially N Chamberlain & Hore Belisha,' Attlee told his brother Tom.[55]

The trio of parliamentary leaders arranged their schedules so that one of them was always on duty to lead the Opposition. Lansbury ended the remoteness of the MacDonald era by ensuring his Executive team planned strategy before each Question Time and met the PLP at least once a week.[56] Lansbury was omnipresent, chivvying and harrying the government on all occasions and ensuring his small Labour group marshalled its limited resources to participate in the normal business of the House. In the Commons, those drafted in to speak on behalf of Labour were not alone against the massed forces of the National government. Invariably, they found Lansbury alongside them in support—'Speak up. Put your chin up, X, put your *chin* up'—mentoring tones that sometimes could be heard in the press gallery.[57]

Under Lansbury's leadership, his diminished foot-soldiers put up a stout resistance against the battalions of the National government. In November 1931, the Labour Opposition moved an amendment to the King's Speech advocating public ownership of the main basic industries and as a protest against expenditure cuts in the public services. Attempts were made to avoid changes to the Town and Country Planning Bill; opposition was mounted to the seven-and-a-half-hours clause in the Coal Mines Bill, as well as motions against the means test; coercion in India, and in support of Henderson's work at the World Disarmament Conference.[58]

As a result, as the House rose at the end of the 1931 parliamentary session, Lansbury reported that Labour was 'holding the fort' after delivering unyielding opposition, even if the Government had introduced tariff restrictions. 'We have definitely been an effective voice in the House, making clear where the "National" Government is leading us,' Lansbury congratulated his Labour members.[59] The new President of the Board of Trade, Walter Runciman, had introduced the Abnormal Importations bill to impose a temporary tariff on a wide range of imports. By September 1932, both Snowden and the Samuelite Liberals had left the National government, when it became clear that Protection was the permanent policy. As expected after a major election defeat, Labour started an overhaul of the party machine—starting with Henderson's survey of the 1931 defeat and including drives to improve party finances and recruit a million members.[60] Partial success was reached with these targets. Under Lansbury's leadership, Labour fought a number of parliamentary by-elections gaining ten seats during 1931–5, notably at Wakefield (April 1932), Wednesbury (July 1932), Rotherham (February 1933), and Fulham

[55] Clem Attlee to Tom Attlee, 29 Feb. 1932, Attlee Papers, fo. 46.
[56] Harris, *Attlee*, pp. 102–3.   [57] Postgate, *Lansbury*, pp. 27–79.
[58] Cole, *A History of the Labour Party*, pp. 273–4.   [59] *Daily Herald*, 11 Dec. 1931.
[60] T. Stannage, *Baldwin Thwarts the Opposition: The British General Election of 1935* (1980), ch. 2.

East (October 1933). Valuable advances were also achieved in municipal elections, including control of the LCC under the leadership of Herbert Morrison in 1934.

At the opening of Parliament on 23 November 1932 Lansbury launched a spirited attack on the government with unfavourable comparisons between lords in their jewels and shoeless children in his constituency. According to Robert Bernays, this only brought a tirade from MacDonald. 'Ramsay was terrible. The moment he had stopped shouting at Lansbury, for he has made the same speech a hundred times, he became almost totally obscure,' the Liberal MP for Bristol (North) observed.[61]

At the same time there were a number of tussles—that raised Labour morale— with another celebrated parliamentarian who no longer enjoyed ministerial office. Winston Churchill had been left out of the National government and now stalked Westminster as an increasingly lone voice in the political wilderness. On 26 May 1932, the Leader of HM Opposition admonished his intoxicated opponent, who had ambled into the Chamber late at night to disrupt the Finance Bill debate. 'He usurps a position in this House, as if he had the right to walk in, make his speech, walk out, and leave the whole place as if God almighty had spoken.' Lansbury remonstrated to the Commons about 'the contemptuous manner that the Right Hon. Gentleman the Member for Epping has treated it'.[62] But his reprimand only elicited a feeble response from the former Chancellor of the Exchequer, who denounced Lansbury's rebuke as 'the perfect cataract of semi-incoherent insults from the so-called leader of the so-called opposition'. Following this heated encounter, it was not surprising that some evasive action was required in the future when both men wished to speak at the same time. Baldwin told MacDonald during the India debate that 'As Winston looked as if he was going to hit Lansbury over the head with the mace, I suggested that if Lansbury sat down before half-past-ten, I would give Winston the intervening time.'[63]

'When the history of that Parliament is written, see that Lansbury gets his due' was the mark of Stanley Baldwin's respect for George Lansbury's contribution that kept 'the flag of Parliamentary Government flying in the world'.[64] Clearly, this sentiment was not shared by some Tories, nor by MacDonald, the Prime Minister who now stood at the dispatch box opposite his former First Commissioner of Works. MacDonald remained scornful of his Labour opponents and their leader. He noted 'the sad plight into what (*sic*) the Labour Party has been brought shown today by Lansbury's lead (*sic*)', during the debate on the King's Speech. Later he described the Leader of HM Opposition as 'more incompetent than ever & the remnant of the brawling East End vestryman'.

For MacDonald, the revered George Lansbury, who led the 1921 Poplar Rates Rebellion to the discomfort of the Labour establishment, was now in charge of the

[61] *The Diaries and Letters of Robert Bernays, 1932–1939: An Insider's Account of the House of Commons*, ed. N. Smart (1996), p. 19 (diary entry for 23 Nov. 1932).

[62] *Hansard*, 26 May 1932, cols. 683–7.

[63] Stanley Baldwin to Ramsay MacDonald, 1 July 1932, quoted in M. Gilbert, *Winston S. Churchil*, v, *The Wilderness Years, 1929–1935* (1981), pp. 448–89.

[64] K. Middlemas and J. Barnes, *Baldwin: A Biography* (1969), pp. 694–5.

political party to which he could never return. It must have been a bitter pill to swallow, hardly cloaked by MacDonald's acid comment that the party he had built from 1900 'was as far removed from Poplarism as the present party is drowned in it'.[65] From the opposite side of the House, Clem Attlee witnessed MacDonald's decline into incompetence and sensed what was irritating his former political chief: 'I fear J.R.M. has completely gone. He revels in titled friends. He will have a rude awakening soon I think.'[66] Later Attlee wrote: 'What I think annoys him is that G.L. has taken his place entirely with the masses of the people and is also popular with a House of Commons which is entirely indifferent to him.'[67]

From outside Parliament, Hugh Dalton recorded his own remarks on the Labour parliamentary leadership, though he did not disguise the personal axe he had to grind:

The Parliamentary Party is a poor little affair, isolated from the National Executive, whose only MP is George Lansbury. Attlee is the Deputy Leader of the Parliamentary Party. He and Cripps, who are in close touch with Cole, sit in Lansbury's room at the House all day and all night, and continually influence the old man. With none of these are Henderson's relations close or cordial.[68]

Historians often use this well-known extract from Dalton's memoirs as direct evidence of the ineffectiveness of the PLP and the frailty of the Lansbury leadership during 1931–5.

The talented Dalton, previously Under-Secretary at the Foreign Office, had seen his leadership prospects dashed in the electoral rout that accounted for over 200 Labour MPs, and did little to hide his displeasure. In 1931 he had lost by fewer than a thousand votes in the Durham mining constituency of Bishop Auckland where he had succeeded his wife, Ruth, in 1929. Meanwhile Cripps and Attlee, who made it back to Westminster and were rapidly elevated to leading positions, had not previously been members of the NEC or the PLP executive. 'I should almost certainly have become Deputy Leader of the parliamentary Labour Party in place of Attlee and succeeded Lansbury in 1935, or earlier. In that case I might well have continued as leader from 1935,' he noted bitterly. According to Dalton's order of precedence— of Labour figures, all absent from the parliamentary scene after 1931—Lansbury had no right to the position of party leader.[69]

In his correspondence with his brother, Tom, Clem Attlee wrote in somewhat similar vein about the PLP, but with a very different interpretation:

I had a very strenuous time during the session, having to speak on something or other every day almost. GL makes an excellent leader. He has far more idea of teamwork than JRM ever had. We are quite a happy family. GL, Cripps and I inhabit the leader of the opposition's room, and get on excellently.[70]

[65] Diary entries, 10 Oct. 1931, 5 Mar. 1933, 23 Feb. 1934, JRMP, PRO 30/69 /1753.
[66] Clem Attlee to Tom Attlee, 18 Dec. 1931, Attlee Papers, fo. 45.
[67] Clem Attlee to Tom Attlee, 15 Feb. 1933, ibid. fo. 56.
[68] Diary entry, 8 Oct. 1932, Dalton Papers.
[69] H. Dalton, *The Fateful Years: Memoirs, 1931–1945* (1957), pp. 20–1.
[70] Clem Attlee to Tom Attlee, 18 Dec. 1931, Attlee Papers, fo. 45.

Clem Attlee acknowledged that a number of the mining contingent 'could not contribute much beyond their votes'. He later recalled the sterling work of certain individuals such as the Yorkshire miners' representative, Tom Williams, Labour's spokesman on agriculture. The hard-working Williams, who was an ally of Krishna Menon on India affairs and also knowledgeable on Palestine, was reminded by a lobby correspondent that in the 1932 parliamentary session he 'filled no fewer than 274 columns of *Hansard* . . . asked 607 oral questions and 67 written ones'.[71] Help came from an unexpected quarter across the House. 'We get some support for our views from the YMCA group Macmillan, Boothby & co who are in pretty strong enmity to the Diehards', Attlee readily acknowledged.[72]

Six months and ninety-three speeches later, Attlee's opinion of Lansbury's leadership had not diminished. He readily agreed that

our fellows have done extraordinarily well, especially our miners George Hall, Tom Williams and David Grenfell. The last two especially promoted to the front bench have risen to the occasion and have made themselves conversant with all kinds of subjects . . . GL has been splendid all through and Stafford Cripps a tower of strength.[73]

During this time, George Lansbury remained heavily engaged with the struggles of the organized working class in different parts of Britain. Tom Mann's imprisonment in early 1932, along with Emrhys Llewellyn, brought an instant response from the Labour party and the trade union movement. The National Joint Council also pressed the BBC to allow George Lansbury to reply to the Prime Minister's radio broadcast on 'The Nation and the Unemployed'.[74]

On 29 December 1932, George Lansbury led a small deputation to Lossiemouth in the north of Scotland to see the Prime Minister concerning the release of the imprisoned Tom Mann and Emrhys Llewellyn, the treasurer and secretary of the NUWM. They had been imprisoned for two months on 18 December for failing to enter into recognizances or find sureties to keep the peace and be of good behaviour, the offence that had put George Lansbury in Pentonville Prison nearly twenty years before.[75]

After a 'convivial conversation of over three hours', Lansbury issued a statement to the effect that the Prime Minister 'received the memorial on the subject, and has promised to put the whole verbatim report of our recommendations. He asked us to leave the matter there for the present.'[76] The outcome proved futile; privately, Lansbury could only record his fury with MacDonald and his betrayal of socialism. 'But I came away terribly distressed that a man with his mentality should have led us all for so many years. He could never have believed in civil liberty or socialism. His whole mind is one web of tortuous conservatism,' he confided to Stafford Cripps.[77]

---

[71] See C. R. Attlee, 'Foreword', in Lord [Tom] Williams of Barnburgh, *Digging for Britain* (1965), pp. 7–8; see also ibid. ch. 6.

[72] Clem Attlee to Tom Attlee, 29 Feb. 1932, Attlee Papers, fo. 46.

[73] Clem Attlee to Tom Attlee, 15 July 1932, ibid. fo. 48.   [74] *The Times*, 22 Dec. 1932.

[75] Ibid. 29, 30 Dec. 1932.   [76] Ibid. 30 Dec. 1932.

[77] Quoted in Estorick, *Stafford Cripps*, p. 120.

This was not the first time George Lansbury had opened up his heart to his younger disciple on matters of politics and religion. Previously, emotionally exhausted by the weight of his responsibilities as party leader, he had confessed to a horrified Cripps that he had 'felt like joining the Communists'. In explanation, Lansbury returned to a constant theme in his life: what propelled onward was his Christian belief and duty that the multitudes of working people he served expected that he would, and could, bring about democratic change and improvement in their lives. It was a trust and faith that meant his period as party leader was also a search for a form of 'Practical Christianity' to help 'the hard-driven, stricken and underpaid workers, the unemployed and all the other victims of our social and industrial life'.[78] After one of his regular visits to Goodfellows, he wrote to Cripps that he believed 'the world, and our people especially, need a purely religious message . . . there are days when my want of faith both in our actions and our courage and discretion worries me to distraction.' He confessed that he tried to 'keep a stout heart in the hills of difficulty as is possible, but often my heart fails and my soul seems to cry out within me whether I am spending my old age in the way that is best'.[79]

More than ever at this time, Lansbury's political outlook was inspired by his simple Christian faith. Any misgivings he revealed to Cripps did not diminish his efforts to work towards a Christian solution to world social and economic problems. It was no surprise that Lansbury was the moving force behind attempts to rejuvenate Christian Socialism and link it directly with the Labour movement. In June 1932, George Lansbury became President of the Socialist Christian League (SCL)—an amalgamation of the smaller Society of Socialist Christians and the Christian Socialist Crusade—a revivalist organization composed mainly of parliamentarians that was affiliated for a while to the Labour party.[80] Robust appeals were also made in the press to shake up the hierarchy of the established Church in the face of the mounting problems of world depression that afflicted Britain.[81]

After seeking 'a doctor's mandate' in the 1931 general election to carry through measures necessary for the British economy, the financial cuts introduced by the National government in 1931 included reductions in the salaries of teachers, government employees, and servicemen, which provoked the teachers' protest marches and the 'Invergordon Mutiny' in the Royal Navy. The National government was forced to abandon the gold standard in Septembeer 1931 and also introduced protectionist tariffs in 1931–2 that compelled Snowden and the Samuelite Liberals to leave the divided Cabinet.

In Parliament, Lansbury challenged MacDonald directly: 'It was said that the last election gave the Government a doctor's mandate, but it was not a mandate for fiscal quackery.'[82]

---

[78] George Lansbury to Revd John Charles Carlile, 22 Jan. 1931, LP, vol. 10, fo. 3.
[79] George Lansbury to Stafford Cripps, 17 July 1932, Cripps Papers. Estorick, *Stafford Cripps*, pp. 117–19.
[80] *The Times*, 9 June 1932. See also Bryant, *Possible Dreams*, pp. 239–41.
[81] For an example of Lansbury's appeals to Church leaders, see *Daily Herald*, 12 Oct. 1932.
[82] *Daily Herald*, 19 Oct. 1932.

Outside Westminster there were national agitations against the government's savage reductions in public expenditure and the worsening of conditions in the public services. In October 1932, Wal Hannington's NUWM organized a new Hunger March with around 1,500 men and women marching from different regions in Britain to take a petition with 1,000,000 signatures to London. The prime target for the protests of the unemployed was the introduction of the detested means test.[83]

In the 1930s no measure attracted more public odium in the inter-war years, or has persisted longer in the folk memory of ordinary people in this country, than the means test. Among the families of the unemployed, it became the most emotional symbol of the Depression in Britain.

In October 1931 two orders-in-council cut the rates of unemployment benefit and introduced a new means test. By the second order, statutory unemployment benefit was limited to twenty-six weeks and to claimants with thirty contributions in the previous two years. For those excluded—about a million claimants—a new relief called 'transitional payments' was made subject to a household means test carried out by the local Public Assistance Committees. The means test became hated for its callous intrusion into family homes to investigate any form of income, including pensions, earnings of other family members, and even savings and household possessions. Claimants were prosecuted for not disclosing income details of any family member and had these amounts either deducted from their meagre benefit or were denied any payment whatsoever.[84] Its savage effects on working-class families—including its heartless administration that broke up families and caused suicides—was graphically depicted in Walter Greenwood's *Love on the Dole* and George Orwell's *The Road to Wigan Pier*.

Unemployment and the means test also formed the main dramatic themes of a two-reel film, *The Road To Hell*, produced by Rudolf Messel and Raymond Postgate for the Socialist Film Council. The novelist Naomi Mitchison and Daisy Postgate were in the cast. George Lansbury gave his support to this new venture in socialist propaganda by becoming the Council's president and allowing indoor scenes to be shot at 39 Bow Road with a 16 mm. ciné camera borrowed from Stafford Cripps.[85]

Yet, extraordinarily, in his public statements as Labour leader, George Lansbury, the champion of the unemployed and downtrodden, appeared to support the imposition of the new means test—a position that disturbed the Labour rank and file and brought correspondence from bewildered party supporters throughout the country, as well as providing his opponents with a political stick to beat him.

---

[83] R. Croucher, *We Refuse to Starve in Silence: A History of the National Unemployed Workers Movement, 1920–1946* (1987), ch. 6.

[84] J. Stevenson and C. Cook, *The Slump: Society and Politics during the Depression* (1979), pp. 67–8.

[85] For Lansbury's involvement with the Socialist Film Council, see S. G. Jones, *The British Labour Movement and Film, 1918–1939* (1987), ch. 6; J. Postgate, 'Raymond Postgate and the Socialist Film Council', *Sight and Sound*, 68 (1990–1), pp. 19–21; Postgate and Postgate, *Life of Raymond Postgate*, pp. 175–9. I am grateful for an interview with Prof. John Postgate on 12 Nov. 1999.

Incredibly, George Lansbury appeared out of line with his own party on one of the burning issues of the day and also muddle-headed, as his critics took pleasure in pointing out. Perhaps not unexpectedly, noisy scenes were reported during the 1932 municipal election campaign at several Labour meetings in the East End, with a mixed reception for Lansbury at a Mile End Municipal Baths rally. Intermittent booing disrupted the singing of the *Internationale* and 'He's a jolly good fellow'.[86] Shortly afterwards, addressing a meeting of local unemployed at Shoreditch, Lansbury was forced once again to explain that though 'he was against giving benefit to the individual unemployed man who had means of his own . . . the means of that man's family ought to be taken into account'. By this time the public reaction to his views was such that he had to emphasize that 'all unemployed men, whether insured or uninsured, should be taken away from the Poor Law administration, and he was going to press for the complete abolition of the Means Test'.[87] The Labour leader, George Lansbury, was forced to defend his position in the East End. How had he got himself in this predicament?

In a heated exchange in the Commons on 13 November 1931, Lansbury had responded to his opponents' constant taunt that the last Labour Cabinet had favoured imposing a means test. The Holman Gregory Report on the National Insurance fund recommended it among the measures to cope with those unemployed who had exhausted their statutory benefit. Cabinet secrecy stopped Lansbury from answering this criticism in full, but he told one correspondent 'at no time did the Cabinet, as a Cabinet, agree to the imposition of a means test to be operated through the Public Assistance Committees'. He added a postcript: '*Never at anytime* did the Cabinet agree to place any unemployed person under the Poor Law or take into a/c any income other than the income of the person applying for transitional benefit.'[88]

Unfortunately, in Parliament on 13 November 1931 he went on to state his own view that he was not against a means test for an *individual*—'that is to say that if a person has gone out of ordinary benefit and has means of his own to maintain himself, I am not prepared to pay him state money'. There lay the confusion of Lansbury's own making. He had described his usual practice as a poor law guardian over four decades. The application of a means test for public assistance had existed from the beginning of the Victorian poor law system and earlier. But now the term was applied to a vastly different *household* means test with a far more sinister meaning. It was a test to decide whether claimants were destitute before being granted any relief. The unemployed applying for transitional benefit now applied to the Public Assistance Committees that had replaced the guardians and were in effect part of the stigmatized poor law.

In addition, Lansbury's position was even more complicated as he was out of line with the Labour party policy of opposition to any form of means test. He had to acknowledge to a confused Susan Lawrence the serious political implications of

---

[86] *The Times*, 31 Oct. 1932. [87] Ibid. 7 Nov. 1932.
[88] George Lansbury to William Tait, 30 Nov. 1931, LP, vol. 25 sect. III, fo. 3.

his error in stating his position publicly in the way he did. 'Our [party] policy is *no* means test whatsoever . . . so that is our declared *official* policy. At public meetings—at Enfield, Birmingham and Swindon, I have been challenged as to my statement in the House,' he admitted.[89]

Speaking in Bow, Lansbury later confirmed that the Opposition would co-operate in bringing in revised means test legislation in order to persuade the government 'to take the unemployed away from the Poor Law altogether'.[90] However, even though he admitted his mistake, the damage was done. Edgar Lansbury later wrote: 'So far as the unemployed are concerned father now takes his stand with the majority of the Labour Party. He stands for work or maintenance, whether the unemployed is destitute or a millionaire.'[91] But political opponents took full advantage of George Lansbury's error—even deliberately misquoting his remarks or taking them out of context.

As a result, Lansbury constantly had to clarify his position for the rest of his leadership—particularly to Labour candidates under attack about the views of the party leader. In 1933 he replied to the prospective Labour candidate for Whitehaven that there was no sense in trying to challenge his political opponent, the local MP, who was citing *Hansard* to show that the Labour leader favoured a personal means test. Lansbury added:

But the National Executive and the Parliamentary Party met and decided the resolution passed at Scarborough [Labour party conference, October 1931] meant that in no circumstances should there be an enquiry into a person's means, either individual means or family means. The statement was made by me in the House of Commons, and that has been the attitude of the Party ever since. But I want you to understand, comrade, that I do not as an individual depart from the original statement . . . But the Party has decided to oppose any means test and of course I accept its decision.[92]

In the end, George Lansbury's unrivalled popularity and a universal reputation for personal sincerity survived his muddle-headedness over the means test. In some cases supporters saw it as the work of his opponents: 'we all undoubtedly know to a certain extent how the Tory factions can hoodwink and Bluff the Electors to suit their own ends and Purposes (*sic*)', William Gully wrote on behalf of the Wednesbury unemployed.[93] As party leader, Lansbury had more success with the medium of public broadcasting which, during these years, enhanced his reputation in this country and abroad.

One of George Lansbury's last acts as First Commissioner of Works had been to broadcast to the United States.[94] His fifteen-minute talk on 'Parks and Open Spaces' brought an immediate and warm response: '*It did my heart good.* Altho' we were 6,000 miles away we heard every word distinctly,' G. S. Brett wrote from

[89] George Lansbury to Susan Lawrence, 16 Mar. 1932, ibid. vol. 25, fo. 112.
[90] *The Times*, 24 Oct. 1932.   [91] E. Lansbury, *George Lansbury*, p. 192.
[92] George Lansbury to Frank Anderson, 15 May 1933, LP, vol. 25, fo. 114.
[93] William Gully to George Lansbury, 14 Mar. 1932, ibid. vol. 25, fo. 48.
[94] 'Transatlantic Broadcast: 19 July 1931', copy, ibid. vol. 10, fos. 78–82.

California.[95] James W. Erwin of 142 Ransome Street, San Francisco, agreed: 'In fact, I regard it as one of the very best of numerous London broadcasts I have had the pleasure to listening to.'[96] A class warrior from the distant days of the *Daily Herald* sent similar congratulations. 'You spoke of St James' Park and Kensington Gardens, but I wanted to be reminded of Victoria Park, Hampstead Heath and Peckham Rye,' William Seed wrote from Chicago.[97] According to Raymond Postgate, on the radio George Lansbury possessed 'a technique almost as good as King George's—the most "fatherly" broadcaster of the thirties'.[98]

Despite his apparent success, Lansbury remained wary of the new medium. The opening of the new Daventry transmitter had brought an end to the era of the crystal sets of 1920s, but broadcasting remained in its infancy as far as British politics was concerned. As leader of the Opposition, Lansbury was suspicious about bias in the news service and pressed the issue of the allocation of radio broadcasts for the Labour party.[99] He first met Reith in October 1932 over the transmission of the resignation speeches of Snowden and Samuel.[100] In the same year, the BBC carried Lansbury's appeal to the nation to support the War Loan Conversion scheme recently launched by the National government. The opportunity was not lost to ask the allies of capitalism—bankers, solicitors, and stockbrokers—to demonstrate their patriotism by waiving their commission. 'I know many people to whom the thirty shilling a year reduction in interest on one hundred pounds investment will mean a real sacrifice,' he observed.[101]

In 1933, Stanley Baldwin's broadcast on the record of the National government brought a trenchant reply from the leader of HM Opposition. Lansbury made one of his finest broadcasts, with powerful themes that reached back forty years. His message, hammered out over the airwaves in the 1930s, had a familiar resonance with that preached at SDF meetings on street-corners and in distant village halls in the 1890s. 'I may, however, remind listeners that riches and poverty, millionaires and paupers, slums and palaces, unemployment, destitution and crime, are the inevitable outcome of a social system based on usury, rent and private profit,' he argued. Now the voice of the Christian Socialist leader was also heard, loud and clear, in denunciation of the National government's 'futile, senseless policy of economy, restricting expenditure, erecting trade barriers, and by every means in its power striving to turn abundance into scarcity'. Lansbury ended with a timeless, universal truth: 'Christ calls to us across the centuries "Choose ye this day whom you will serve; you cannot serve God and Mammon". And quite simply I repeat His challenge. Socialism is the opposite of Mammon-worship and to me means putting into practice the gospel of love, peace and joy.'[102]

His broadcast demonstrated his unfailing ability to strike a common chord.

---

[95] G. S. Brett to George Lansbury, 19 July 1931, ibid. vol. 10, fo. 89.

[96] James W. Ermin to George Lansbury, 19 July 1931, ibid. vol. 10, fo. 95.

[97] William H. Seed to George Lansbury, 20 July 1931, ibid. vol. 10, fo. 129.

[98] Postgate, *Lansbury*, p. 282.   [99] J. Reith, *Into the Wind* (1949), pp. 172–3.

[100] *The Reith Diaries* (1975), ed. C. Stuart, p. 112 (entry for 11 Oct. 1932).

[101] *The Listener*, 20 July 1932.   [102] Ibid. 18, 25 Oct. 1933.

Postgate quoted Lord Ponsonby's comment in 1933: 'My sister writes to me that she nearly cried over your broadcast.'

As Labour leader, George Lansbury also remained closely identified with the cause of Indian nationalism in the 1930s, including the long drawn-out constitutional conflict that led to the Government of India Bill in 1935. With Tom Williams, Lansbury was a prominent member in Britain of the India League which was transformed by Krishna Menon from the Commonwealth of India League to lobby for Indian independence.

Surprisingly, considering his links with Indian politicians such as Annie Besant and his long friendship with her secretary—the Labour MP David Graham Pole—Lansbury never visited India, despite some encouragement by his daughter and son-in-law, Dorothy and Ernest Thurtle who toured the sub-continent in 1928.[103]

In 1931, George Lansbury met Mahatma Gandhi, the political and spiritual leader of India and one of the outstanding practitioners of non-violent civil disobedience, who stayed in Bow at the home of Muriel Lester during the Round Table Conference in London.[104] Amid the considerable press interest in Gandhi's visit that took him to his famous encounter with the cotton factory workers of Lancashire, Lansbury was photographed outside the House of Commons with him after Gandhi had addressed a meeting of Labour MPs.[105]

Earlier in the year George Lansbury suffered the first of a series of devastating personal blows that was to seriously affect him in the years 1933 to 1935. On 23 March 1933, Bessie Lansbury died at their home at 39 Bow Road at the age of seventy-two. 'My wife was always my sweetheart, my friend, and my comrade in all my doings', a grief-stricken Lansbury declared.[106] The importance of their marriage to Lansbury's political career cannot be stressed enough. Deeply committed to building the New Jerusalem, Bessie Lansbury had supported her husband through every vicissitude of radical and revolutionary politics, from their troubled emigration to Australia in the 1880s to his turbulent years as Opposition leader in the 1930s. During this time, Bessie and George Lansbury had twelve children—ten of whom survived to adulthood. Their large family played an important part in many of the events of these years. In Bow and Bromley, the Lansbury household, to which Lansbury returned from his frequent travels on behalf of British socialism was a byword in local politics and a haven of warmth and loving support.[107] The loss of Bessie was immeasurable and widely recognized at home and abroad. 'Lloyd George said he had never known such a wave of sympathy in the House and the country,' Attlee told his brother Tom.[108] By the end of the year George Lansbury had suffered his second misfortune—a near-fatal accident that put him out of action as party leader for seven months.

In December 1933 Lansbury was in Gainsborough to address an evening meeting

---

[103] Dorothy Lansbury to George and Bessie Lansbury, 21 Feb. 1928, LP, vol. 28, fos. 307–9.
[104] M. Lester, *Entertaining Gandhi* (1932), pp. 93, 125.
[105] *Daily Sketch*, 16 Sept. 1931.   [106] *Daily Herald*, 24 Mar. 1933.
[107] For Lansbury home and family life, see below, Ch. 18.
[108] Clem Attlee to Tom Attlee, 3 Apr. 1933, Attlee Papers, fo. 58.

of the local Labour party. In the afternoon, after opening a bazaar in the town hall, he fell several feet when he missed his step on leaving an ante-room to the main hall. He was seriously hurt and was taken to the John Coupland Hospital in Gainsborough, where Dr Ervin reset his fractured thigh. His son, William, caught the mail train to Doncaster and arrived by car at the hospital at 1.30 a.m. Nine hours later, he accompanied his seventy-four-year-old father to the Manor House Hospital in North London, where the senior surgeon, Sir Ambrose Woodall, operated on the Labour leader.[109]

News of Lansbury's accident spread quickly in Britain and abroad. In the East End, constituents inundated his Bow home. Hundreds of messages were received, including telegrams from the Viceroy of India, and from Gandhi, who cabled: 'Hope accident not serious may God spare you.' From Paris, Henry Harben summed up the tone of the many messages which flooded in: 'I hope that your own vigour and the genuine sympathy of your many real friends will pull you through pretty quickly and restore you to your ordinary life and work as little damaged as may be.'[110]

Early statements that Lansbury would remain in hospital for about two months were sadly wrong, and the mishap had important implications for the Labour leadership. Lansbury was in hospital for over six months, until the following July. As the distressed officials of Gainsborough Labour party declared shortly after the accident: 'The past twenty hours have been a nightmare to us . . . It is a tragedy for our glorious cause that it should have happened at all, especially when so great a part of the Party's responsibility is resting on your shoulders.'[111]

Arthur Henderson, who had returned to Parliament in the Clay Cross by-election in September 1933, was extremely busy with his European disarmament work and in poor health. Clem Attlee, who had been elected deputy chairman of the parliamentary party in November, took over the leadership. Though Lansbury was present at the 1934 Annual Conference at Southport he played little part in the proceedings, and was out of effective action for nine months.[112]

Unwilling to leave his successful legal practice, Stafford Cripps gave £500 to the Labour party towards Attlee's salary as acting leader when Attlee felt unable to continue in early 1934. Lansbury's absence provided a valuable opportunity for Attlee to step into the role of caretaker leader at a crucial time in domestic and European affairs and opened up his future career as Labour leader and Prime Minister.[113]

From his hospital bed in 1934, as we shall see, Lansbury remained in contact with the Labour party and also spent a great deal of time in meditation. His daughter

---

[109] *Gainsborough Evening News*, 12 Dec. 1933; *The Times* reported that Edgar Lansbury, not William, had accompanied his father from Gainsborough to hospital in London: *The Times*, 11 Dec. 1933.

[110] *Gainsborough Evening News*, 12 Dec. 1933. Imperial and International Communications Ltd, Gandhi to Rt Honorable George Lansbury, 11 Dec. 1933; Henry D. Harben to George Lansbury, 11 Dec. 1933, LP, vol. 13, fos. 231, 237.

[111] Hilda and Edwin Pittwood to George Lansbury, 10 Dec. 1933, ibid. vol. 13, fos. 177–80.

[112] Wrigley, *Arthur Henderson*, pp. 182–3.

[113] Stafford Cripps to George Lansbury, 3 Jan. 1934, Cripps Papers; Harris, *Attlee*, pp. 110–11; R. Pearce, *Attlee* (1997), p. 54.

Daisy, who was also his secretary, was frequently at the Manor House Hospital dealing with the considerable amount of correspondence that arrived regularly. His son-in-law recalled the effect this period had on Lansbury's life and how he changed in the next year or two. Postgate noted that 'the diffidence which had intermittently plagued him almost disappeared. He seemed satisfied that he had a duty to do, and assured he was able to do it.'[114]

A year earlier at Kingsley Hall, Bow, shortly before Armistice Day, George Lansbury had once again condemned widespread destitution and poverty and outlined Labour ideas for economic regeneration—adding that 'part of the task of recreating Britain included the avoidance of another world war'. When the Christian pacifist George Lansbury returned to take up his duties after his accident, he faced irreconcilable issues of foreign policy and the international Fascism that would challenge and eventually bring about his downfall as Labour leader.[115]

---

[114] Postgate, *Lansbury*, p. 291.   [115] *The Times*, 7 Nov. 1932.

16
Party Leadership Crisis, 1934–1935

In 1934, while George Lansbury was still in the Manor House Hospital, his son, Edgar, published a book—*George Lansbury: My Father*—that told the life-story of the exuberant seventy-five-year-old Labour leader and gave some fascinating glimpses into his family life in the East End. One scene evoked echoes of E. Nesbit's *The Railway Children*, as Edgar remembered the Great Eastern expresses that thundered past near the Lansbury home at Bow, with their father waving his large red flag to his watching children as he journeyed to preach socialism the length and breadth of Britain.[1]

To all intents and purposes, Edgar Lansbury's account was a typical memoir full of anecdotes and sketches about his parents, Bessie and George, their large brood of children, and the joys and tribulations of late Victorian domesticity.[2] However, within days of publication, this apparently harmless book brought its author before Bow Street Magistrates' Court charged with offences under the Official Secrets Act.

A member of a large and highly visible political family, Edgar Lansbury was well qualified to write about his father and East End life. With his first wife, Minnie, Edgar had been prominent in the women's movement before and during the First World War. Both were briefly members of the Communist Party of Great Britain in 1920, but subsequently left it. From 1921 they had been at the centre of the Poplar Rates Dispute and imprisoned with the other Labour councillors. Tragically, Minnie had died shortly after her release from Holloway Prison. Today her memory is commemorated by the large electric clock installed in the 1920s above the parade of shops in Bow Road. In 1924, Edgar Lansbury married the leading actress and former suffragette, Moyna MacGill.[3] In 1925 Edgar, who had become prominent as a local councillor and chairman of the board of guardians, became mayor of Poplar. During these years he and his wife remained close, both politically and personally, to George Lansbury.

When reviews of Edgar Lansbury's book appeared in 1934, it was not surprising that the authorities soon realized that the author had seen secret Cabinet documents in his father's possession. On resigning Cabinet office in August 1931, as was standard practice at the time, George Lansbury took with him copies of his Cabinet papers including those marked: 'This document is the property of His Britannic

---

[1] E. Lansbury, *George Lansbury*, p. 34.

[2] See Jack Lawson's review, 'Lansbury of Bow', in *The Listener*, 25 Apr. 1934. For the Lansbury family, see below, Ch. 18.

[3] For further details, see Gottfried, *Balancing Act*. I am grateful to Chris Sumner for showing me his pre-publication copy of Edgar Lansbury's book given to his mother, Doris Sumner.

Majesty's Government. Secret. To be kept under lock and key.' With the bitter recriminations among former Labour ministers that followed the formation of the National government, Lansbury was determined that the inside story of the second Labour government should eventually be told.

Though Edgar quickly absolved his father of responsibility for any illegalities connected with the book, it is a reasonable assumption that George Lansbury was involved with its preparation, especially as the chapters on the family's emigration to Australia in 1884–5 occurred before Edgar's birth. Moreover, this was not the only occasion that Lansbury made Cabinet documents available to others.[4]

Edgar Lansbury quoted *verbatim* from two Cabinet memoranda to reveal his father's role in attempting to change social policy during the second Labour government.[5] 'In view of statements made by Mr. Ramsay MacDonald and other members of the Labour Cabinet, that my father agreed with unemployment [benefit] and other cuts I was determined that the truth should be made known,' he admitted.[6] The National government, faced with the question of rearmament, had worried about a series of newspaper leaks for sometime.[7] Lansbury was suspected of being the source for stories in the *Daily Herald*, his former paper, during the August 1931 crisis. Though the book was withdrawn hastily while six pages were rewritten over a weekend, the National government debated as to whether it should make an example of those concerned, including the publisher and the newspapers which printed the extracts.[8] In the end, on 20 March 1934, only Edgar Lansbury found himself at Bow Street Magistrates' Court, where he answered two allegations that he had: 'Unlawfully received certain information . . . contained in a certain secret [Cabinet] memorandum . . . having reasonable ground to believe that the said information had been communicated in contravention of the Official Secrets Act, 1911, contrary to Section Two (2) of the said Act.'[9]

In 1911 the Official Secrets Act had been hurriedly passed through Parliament with minimal debate during a period of pre-war 'German spy fever'. But its real origins lay in the concern of the state in the late nineteenth century to maintain official secrecy in an age of increasing state bureaucracy. Section 2 of the Act had a 'catch-all' characteristic, making all information that a Crown Servant learns 'official'. It could be said that a menu in the civil service canteen was 'official information'![10]

The government decision in 1934 to prosecute only Edgar Lansbury is an

---

[4] For an offer to Ernie Bevin, see above, p. 294 n. 52. Though Postgate said that he had only looked at some of the official papers 'casually', he later wrote 'that the documents on India alone which Lansbury left for his biographer are a pile 24 inches high'. Postgate, *Lansbury*, pp. vi, 281.

[5] Edgar Lansbury quoted extensively from 'Unemployment Policy (1930) Committee: Memorandum by the First Commissioner of Works', 6 May 1930 C.P. 145 (30), and 'Unemployment Insurance: Memorandum by the First Commissioner of Works', 6 Feb. 1931, U.P. (30) 61, PRO, CAB 21/391/48536.

[6] *News Chronicle*, 9 Mar. 1934.

[7] 'Leakages of Information', 19 Mar. 1934, PRO, CAB 21/391/48536.

[8] *News Chronicle*, 9 Mar. 1934; 'Biography of Mr George Lansbury', 5 Mar. 1934, PRO, CAB 21/391/48536.

[9] *Daily Telegraph*, 21 Mar. 1934.

[10] A. Rogers, *Secrecy and Power in the British State: A History of the Official Secrets Act* (1997), pp. 16–24.

interesting one. His father (and his publisher) must have known that the use of the two official Cabinet memoranda would be a breach of the Official Secrets Act. George Lansbury was one of the few MPs to vote against the bill in 1911. In 1934 the Cabinet was advised that George Lansbury had probably breached his oath as a Privy Councillor, as well as infringed the 1911 Act. However, his serious injury, as well as his universal popularity, may have made it politically insensitive to prosecute the septuagenarian leader of HM Opposition.[11]

The Attorney-General, Sir Thomas Inskip, opened the prosecution and had little trouble in demonstrating that the author had seen and quoted directly from official Cabinet papers. He argued that it was a misdemeanour rather than a felony. But Edgar Lansbury had little defence. When summoned, he was quoted as saying, 'I am very sorry it has happened. I did not know it was an offence at the time, but . . . I should not have made the use I did of the documents.' His counsel, Mr C. H. Pearson, called no witnesses but simply argued that no secrets had really been disclosed, since George Lansbury's views on social policy were well known.

The Director of Public Prosecutions, Sir Tindal Atkinson, was present in court to hear the Stipendiary Magistrate, Sir Rollo Graham Campbell, decide that the Official Secrets Act had been contravened. He declared that official documents had been communicated to Edgar Lansbury, who knew his father had been a Cabinet minister. The magistrate also observed that the prosecution had been brought to establish that Cabinet documents were confidential and not to be disclosed to any persons other than Cabinet ministers. Found guilty on both counts, Edgar Lansbury was fined a total of £20 with 25 guineas' costs, though the court made no direction about the return of the documents.[12]

That was not the end of the story. After the court case, the Director of Public Prosecutions and the Cabinet Secretary, between them, managed to lose one of the copies of the confidential documents supplied to the court for the legal proceedings.[13] More importantly, the Government quickly changed the ruling about the retention of Cabinet papers by former ministers.[14] The Cabinet Office tried hard to retrieve papers from various politicians. In all, papers were recovered in seventy-seven out of a total of eighty-seven cases, but the remaining ten cases included papers in the possession of David Lloyd George, Winston Churchill, and George Lansbury.[15] The Labour leader declared: 'he was still determined not to return

---

[11] 'Mr Edgar Lansbury's Life of Mr. George Lansbury. Cabinet Leakage', 7 Mar. 1934, PRO, CAB 21/391/48536. For other prosecutions at this time under the Official Secrets Act, see D. Vincent, *The Culture of Secrecy: Britain, 1832–1998* (Oxford, 1998), pp. 170–8. One small indication of the status and reputation of the leader of HM Opposition was his appearance in wax in Madame Tussaud's, albeit placed incongruously in the parliamentary gallery between Lloyd George and Lady Astor. *Madame Tussaud's Catalogue* (1934), pp. 36–7.

[12] W. Barker (Chief Inspector) to Acting Superintendent, 24 Mar. 1934, PRO, MEPO 3/1106/64092.

[13] R. B. Howarth to E. H. Tindal Atkinson, 20 Mar. 1934; E. H. Tindal Atkinson to Rupert Howarth, 20 Mar. 1934, PRO, CAB 21/391/48536.

[14] CC 11 (34) 5, 21 Mar. 1934, PRO, CAB 23/78; CC 51 (35) PRO, CAB 23/82.

[15] CP 218 (35), PRO, CAB 24/257. For Churchill's reasons for not returning his Cabinet papers, see Winston Churchill to Rupert P. Howarth, 19 Nov. 1934, PRO, CAB 21/2393/64092.

voluntarily any documents in his possession.' Nor would he call a meeting of ex-Ministers to discuss the matter.[16]

After George Lansbury's death in May 1940, the authorities pressed his family to return the Cabinet papers. His son-in-law, Raymond Postgate, Lansbury's literary executor and biographer, finally gave in to increasing official pressure in wartime. About thirty boxes were collected by van from Postgate's Finchley home on the understanding that, once the Cabinet papers were extracted, other material would be returned. But, Postgate never got them back—not even when the Attlee Labour government came to power in 1945. 'I think there can be no doubt that these papers are Crown property which the Cabinet Office were entitled to recover after Lansbury's death,' Attlee replied with some coolness.

At the time, Cabinet papers remained closed to scholars under the fifty-year rule (altered to thirty years in 1967). Access to these documents was promised to Postgate to defend his father-in-law's reputation against contemporary criticism, but only if the author could convince the Cabinet Secretary of this necessity.[17] As reviewers noted in 1951, Postgate published his book—*The Life of George Lansbury*—without the benefit of seeing the papers.[18] The loss of these important documents—which Postgate was badgered into surrendering—started the saga of 'the Missing Lansbury Papers', causing rumours of conspiracy and subterfuge by the state against a prominent left-wing politician. As late as June 1994, Lord Jenkins of Putney raised the matter again in the House of Lords without any success.[19]

The serious injury that George Lansbury sustained at Gainsborough in December 1933 kept him in the Manor House Hospital at Hampstead until July 1934. At first, he believed that the accident had brought him close to death. Later, often in great pain, he feared he might never walk again; some photographs of his prolonged stay in the trade union hospital show he was very ill during this time.[20] That he recovered to resume the Labour leadership, followed by his remarkable participation in British and international politics until his death in 1940, attests to an astonishingly indomitable spirit and an extraordinary commitment to the ideals of public service, despite grievous personal and family difficulties. However, despite

---

[16] *The Times*, 9 Oct. 1934. On 22 July 1934 at a parliamentary Lobby dinner with a remarkable cross-party gathering to welcome Lansbury on his return after illness, the Leader of HM Opposition was in typically jovial mood. He 'derided Cabinet secrets—had, he felt sure, told many simply because he hadn't realized that they were secrets . . . one day when Ramsay in his heavy way had enjoined on the Cabinet . . . not to say anything . . . when, he, Lansbury left No. 10, he saw a newspaper bill revealing the whole story'. *Fleet Street, Press Barons and Politics: The Journals of Collin Brooks, 1932–1940*, ed. N. J. Crowson (1998), pp. 64–5. The authorities continued to monitor Lansbury's political activities, subjecting his views on Cabinet government in *My England* (1935) to close scrutiny: 'really very little is contained in it respecting the period when Mr. Lansbury was a Cabinet Minister in 1929–31.' R. W. Howarth to Ramsay MacDonald, 1 Oct. 1934, MacDonald Papers, PRO 30/69/681/417–19.

[17] Clem Attlee to Raymond Postgate, 29 Nov. 1946, PRO, CAB 21/2393.

[18] For the correspondence between the Cabinet Office and Raymond Postgate, see PRO, CAB 21/2393. See also J. F. Naylor, *A Man and an Institution: Sir Maurice Hankey, the Cabinet Secretariat and the Custody of Cabinet Secrecy* (1984), pp. 212–14; Rogers, *Secrecy and Power*, pp. 21–4, 34.

[19] *Hansard*, 26 June 1994, WA 34. Cf. Fred Peart's intervention over forty years earlier in the House of Commons: ibid. 5 Dec. 1951, col. 2396.

[20] *Clarion*, 14 Apr. 1934; see also Pl. 24.

some perceptive observations by his first biographer, in the main historians have disregarded Lansbury's spell in hospital. In some cases, his absence from the party leadership has not been mentioned.[21]

George Lansbury's enforced stay in hospital raised the important question of the party leadership. Clem Attlee was an early visitor at the Manor House Hospital. 'I saw G.L. last Friday and found him very cheerful and going on well, but it will be a long job,' he told his brother, Tom.[22] Five weeks after his accident, Lansbury had no doubts about continuing as party leader when he recovered. He told a press reporter: 'If I recover sufficiently I shall continue to carry on my work as Parliamentary leader if the party wish me to do so. Let me emphasize again that no one has raised this question.'[23]

During these months, with Clem Attlee as acting leader, George Lansbury kept in touch with national politics and party business with the assistance of his secretary, Daisy Postgate. Besides his family, regular visitors included the Speaker of the House of Commons.[24] Lansbury declined to comment on Stafford Cripps's speech at the University Labour Federation conference at Nottingham on 7 January which included injudicious remarks about Buckingham Palace that provoked pandemonium in the press. Cripps predicted the imminent end of the National government and declared what Labour had to do on taking office. 'They must act rapidly and it will be necessary to deal with the House of Lords and the influence of the City of London. There is no doubt that we shall have to overcome opposition from Buckingham Palace and other places as well,' he warned. Despite Cripps's denials, George V thought he meant sinister influence on the part of the Crown rather than the royal footmen. Dalton complained bitterly about Cripps's ill-advised observations on the monarchy: 'Cripps seems quite unable to see the argument that he is damaging the party electorally.'[25] Lansbury quietly told the press that the Labour party remained one of 'the biggest defenders of the Constitution'.[26]

There was also direct advice from the Labour leader to his friend Cripps on how to deal with foreign policy in the light of the Sino-Japanese crisis in the Far East. Ever distrustful of the National government, Lansbury wrote: 'I must write & say how much I hope you will dot Simon in the eye about Eden's proposal re Paraguay & Bolivia for the embargo on arms . . . Why don't we stop arms & money for Japan & not wait for others . . . I just boil over when I hear and read the "make believe" of most Govt spokesmen.'[27]

On 22 February 1934 Lansbury celebrated his seventy-fifth birthday in the Manor House Hospital surrounded by members of his family. Though the patient was making 'good progress', the hospital bulletin stated 'he is not expected to be able to leave his bed for at least a fortnight'.[28]

[21] See Shore, *Leading the Left*, p. 30.
[22] Clem Attlee to Tom Attlee, 1 Jan. 1934 [wrongly dated 1933]. Attlee Papers, fo. 52.
[23] *The Times*, 15 Jan. 1934.   [24] Ibid. 25 July 1934.
[25] Diary entry for 19 Jan. 1934, *Political Diary of Hugh Dalton*, ed. Pimlott, p. 181.
[26] *News Chronicle*, 8 Jan. 1934.
[27] George Lansbury to Stafford Cripps, 17 May 1934, Cripps Papers, A1.
[28] *The Times*, 22 Feb. 1934.

Regular announcements from his bedside included messages for all Labour candidates fighting election contests. On the eve of the important London County Council elections Lansbury asked the voters for a Labour victory that would 'enable London to take its place with Leeds, Sheffield and other great centres in creating the enthusiasm and devotion to the cause of human progress which is so much needed everywhere'.[29] Once again, Lansbury also ruled out any formal alliance with the Liberal party.[30]

George Lansbury also put this time in hospital to good use with a productive burst of writing. Within the next year he published two books—a second set of memoirs, *Looking Backwards and Forwards,* and *Labour's Way with the Commonwealth,* one of a series of eight monographs by prominent Labour politicians.

The enforced idleness of seven months gave Lansbury an almost unique opportunity to think deeply not only on personal issues but also on the future of the Labour party. As a busy politician he was given a chance—rarely afforded to political figures—to reflect at length on his political beliefs and outlook. As a result, his new Christian socialist manifesto for the British people appeared in a series of exclusive newspaper articles he penned in 1934. 'Mr George Lansbury has thrown overboard some of his old beliefs . . . he has forged new convictions out of his reflection, his idealism—a new message for Britain, for the common people, in their crusade for a finer world,' the *Clarion* proclaimed with great enthusiasm.[31] For these front-page pieces, Postgate negotiated a cheque for £1,000 that had to be forced upon a reluctant Lansbury.[32] A year later, his book *My England,* based on these articles, was published while he was still Labour leader.

As outlined in the *Clarion,* the Christian basis of George Lansbury's new gospel was clear: 'Our Movement is in urgent need of being born again'; 'We may gain the world of office and lose our souls', he declared. It was a message still couched in simple Christian teaching 'Love thy neighbour as thyself'. Lansbury told his readers: 'Whatever else I may write in these articles, the most important and undying truth will be that without love all our efforts at building Jerusalem will fail'.[33] In this respect, George Lansbury was saying little different—with some exceptions—from what he had expounded on political platforms and the pages of the *Daily Herald* in previous years. As a Christian socialist, the difference now was that he restated his political position with greater urgency and with the utmost conviction that he was right and had to succeed.

Part-utopian and part-pragmatic, the vision George Lansbury described for the future of his country was laid out with renewed religious fervour. Among the themes he explored during the next three months was how Labour would govern the next time it held office. The socialist programme he sketched included the modernization of parliamentary procedure, the enhancement of educational provision, house-building, and land-reclamation, as well as vital measures to control industry, banking, and finance. Raising the school-leaving age, with allowances paid from

[29] *The Times,* 7 Mar. 1934.   [30] Ibid. 7 May 1934.   [31] *Clarion,* 7 Apr. 1934.
[32] Postgate, *Lansbury,* p. 291.   [33] *Clarion,* 14 Apr. 1934.

national funds, increased pensions, and a reduction of the working week to thirty-six hours were among the steps that the Labour leader saw as part of future party policy.[34] 'The Labour government of a new England ... would reconstruct the whole life of the nation,' he announced.[35] Few stones were left unturned. As the former First Commissioner of Works, his successful plans for a 'Brighter Britain' were now extended to valuable support for increased leisure and recreation. Seventy years later, one or two of these ideas appear ludicrous and out of touch with everyday reality. In all seriousness, he proposed—with abolition of war in Britain—to turn the British Navy and Air Force over to the Board of Education for educational cruises. Lansbury explained: 'I would tell them [the Admirals] that hence forward, with dismantled guns, their duty was to enable the children of this country to see the world.'[36]

Lansbury's 'sick-bed vision of Labour's need' was a remarkable effort for a seventy-five-year-old politician who, close to death shortly before, none the less possessed the physical courage and strength of character to review the whole of his political outlook. Lansbury firmly intended to return to the Labour leadership and actively contemplated the possibility of a future Labour government, either under his leadership or that of Stafford Cripps, his choice as his successor. An instinctive democrat, Lansbury had already determined that a future socialist administration should not suffer the insurmountable difficulties that had overwhelmed the Labour Cabinet he had served in during 1929–31. The reform of Parliament—including the introduction of the Referendum, Initiative, and Recall, measures he had first advocated before the First World War—was essential to achieve democracy. 'So we ask for a big majority, which means power ... No obstruction, either from Lords or Commons will stop us in our march forward. No Treasury officials will order our actions; no bank managers will tell us what we may or may not do,' he declared.[37]

In these *Clarion* articles, the most remarkable statement was the admission by the class warrior George Lansbury that he no longer saw the strike as an essential weapon in the workers' struggle for emancipation from capitalism. The former National Secretary of the Marxist SDF confessed: 'I backed the General Strike whole-heartedly, and joined with those who said we should, if necessity arose, do the same thing again.'[38] Now Lansbury envisaged that once socialism had replaced capitalism by parliamentary means, the abolition of class differences would end strikes and industrial conflict. He predicted: 'by doing so [gaining parliamentary and municipal power] we shall abolish the causes which produce the class war and strikes.'

For Lansbury the introduction of socialism meant the end of class war 'with all its horrible starvation and bitterness of strikes and lock-outs'. In these circumstances, he believed, the trade union movement should be expected to support a future socialist administration. 'A properly organised blackleg proof trade union movement should feel it an honour and privilege to associate with Socialist authorities in giving the very best service possible to the community.'[39]

[34] *The Times*, 30 Apr. 1934.   [35] *Clarion*, 21 Apr. 1934.   [36] Ibid. 23 June 1934.
[37] *The Times*, 7 Mar. 1934.   [38] *Clarion*, 5 May 1934.   [39] Ibid.

By April, Lansbury had been in hospital for more than eighteen weeks. 'He is to be fitted with an instrument with which he will practise walking for two or three weeks. He will later go to the seaside to recuperate,' the hospital announced optimistically.[40] But it was not until 5 June that the Labour leader could briefly attend a meeting of the PLP, where he received a warm welcome from Clem Attlee and in return paid tribute to his work as deputy leader in his absence.[41] Only after seven months in hospital and a nursing home, did George Lansbury finally arrive home quietly on 2 July 1934.[42] There, the Labour leader issued a simple Socialist message: 'I want to be with men and women of all ages and all classes, united selflessly in a great and onward movement for Co-operation, Peace and Brotherhood.'[43]

Restored to the leadership, George Lansbury soon took up his duties with a renewed enthusiasm and determination. In August 1934 he was present at the four-day national centenary celebrations organized by the TUC in memory of the six Dorsetshire agricultural labourers transported to Australia a hundred years before. Among the programme of festivities, the central event on the Friday was the opening ceremony for the six modern cottages built by the TUC at Tolpuddle as a permanent memorial to George Loveless and his fellow 'Tolpuddle Martyrs'.

Afterwards, propped up on two walking sticks, Lansbury unveiled a memorial stone—carved by Eric Gill—at the grave of James Hammett, with the trade union pioneer's son and niece in the large crowd in the village churchyard. In a moving address, Lansbury declared that 'what the six men did in their day was one of the most heroic things poor men could do . . . they stood up to the ignorance and irreligion of the possessing class of their time'.[44] None of the Lansbury charisma, or his natural rapport with large gatherings, had been diminished by his prolonged illness. Conducting the great crowd, Lansbury's voice boomed out above those present as they sang 'England Arise'. According to Walter Citrine, TUC General Secretary, two local Tories abandoned their Conservatism at the centenary celebrations, after witnessing Lansbury's graveyard address and the performance of the play, *Six Men of Dorset*, written by Harry Brooks and Miles Malleson.

During his political life, George Lansbury probably appeared at more Labour rallies and similar gatherings than any other contemporary figure. But his association as Labour leader with the Tolpuddle centenary commemoration had a greater symbolic significance for the labour movement in this country and beyond. Twelve years earlier, Arthur Henderson's dedication of the Martyrs' Arch outside the village Methodist Chapel had a wider meaning for Nonconformity in Britain. For two years, Walter Citrine had personally supervised the TUC planning of the 1934 commemoration, designed to inspire the ailing movement in the difficult years of post-1931 Britain. Each July, the annual 'Tolpuddle Sunday' rally has remained one of the foremost events in the national Labour calendar. The six memorial cottages—and a museum that until recently contained some magnificent photographs of George Lansbury at the Tolpuddle Centenary celebrations—have acquired an almost

---

[40]   *The Times*, 10 April 1934.   [41] Ibid. 6 June 1934.   [42] Ibid. 3 July 1934.
[43]   *Daily Herald*, 2 July 1934.   [44] *The Times*, 1 Sept. 1934.

shrine-like status.[45] The events of August 1934 did not go unnoticed by members of trade union and labour movements abroad who were being attacked and exterminated by Fascist régimes in Europe. At Tolpuddle, Lansbury took up the theme of the survival of democracy: 'We in the Labour Movement have no guns or poison gas, but we have the intelligence that God has given us, and if we only use it we can change the world.'[46] This theme remained at the heart of his political outlook as a Christian pacifist for the remainder of his Labour leadership. The threat of international Fascism, and the problems of foreign policy, increasingly dominated British domestic politics until the crisis of the Italian invasion of Abyssinia brought about his downfall as leader in 1935.

Raymond Postgate was the first to point to the prolonged stay in the Manor House Hospital as a decisive turning-point in George Lansbury's life. On a personal note, he observed a mellowing in his father-in-law's normal behaviour. The Labour leader now admitted to a liking for the luxury of cold lobster.[47] After he left hospital, he was also prepared to use the comfort of a private car—often driven by his youngest son, Eric—rather than public transport.[48] But there were deeper and far more important changes in his personality and outlook.

During his time in hospital, George Lansbury's religious faith was totally reaffirmed and renewed. On leaving hospital he announced his 'profound sense of gratitude for my recovery and . . . the conviction that I have been spared only because there is work for me to do'. He believed he could influence the Christian churches to undertake a crusade to eradicate social evils and to achieve a just and fair society. But for the remainder of his life, Lansbury possessed an even more imperative mission—to devote himself to an unremitting fight to secure the abolition of Fascism, imperialism, and war.[49]

Up to the early 1930s there was greater unity in the Labour party over foreign issues than domestic politics. The main aims of the party's foreign policy had been to abolish the combined evils of capitalism, imperialism, and war and to achieve world peace and socialism. Within the party, there was broad agreement that these aims could be accomplished through the rejection of secret diplomacy and alliances; by resistance to militarism and rearmament; and by support for the League of Nations to provide international security and achieve general disarmament.

Yet after 1931 the serious deterioration in the international situation threatened the post-war order, based on internationalism and collective security through the League of Nations. The rise of Fascist régimes in the Far East and in Europe exposed the weakness of the League as a peace-keeping organization, as well as British foreign policy based on appeasement. In September 1931, the Japanese invasion of Manchuria, and establishment there of the puppet régime of Manchukuo in 1932,

---

[45] *Daily Herald*, 1 Sept. 1934; *The Times*, 1 Sept. 1934. For the Tolpuddle centenary commemoration, see C. Griffiths, 'Remembering Tolpuddle: Rural History and Commemoration in the Inter-War Labour Movement', *History Workshop Journal*, 44 (1997), pp. 145–99.

[46] *News Chronicle*, 1 Sept. 1934.   [47] Postgate, *Lansbury* (1951), pp. 291–2.

[48] Interview with Angela Lansbury, 15 Aug. 1989.   [49] *Daily Herald*, 4 June 1934.

provoked a major international crisis in the Far East. The Sino-Japanese conflict eventually led to Japan's withdrawal from the League of Nations. In 1933 the demise of the Weimar Republic and Hitler's rise to power resulted in German rearmament and the withdrawal of Germany from the League of Nations and from the World Disarmament Conference, which collapsed shortly afterwards. As Henry Winkler has shown, the world depression and the rise of international Fascism swept away the bases of Labour foreign policy of the 1920s, developed by both MacDonald and Henderson around the international security of the League of Nations, despite their differences on the final means of settling disputes.[50]

Labour party foreign policy went through a period of re-examination of pacifism and rearmament during the 1930s, in which the trade union leadership of Bevin and Citrine played the key role with Labour moderates such as Dalton. While, in the main, the overall aims of achieving world peace and socialism were maintained, there were divisions as to whether Fascist régimes and their aggressive imperialism should, and could, be checked by economic sanctions backed, if necessary, by the use of military force rather than through pacifism and disarmament.[51]

Lansbury's return to active political duty coincided with these developments and changes in Labour policy. His pacifist convictions, deepened by his experience during the First World War in pacifist societies such as the NCF, and later as Chairman of the War Resisters International, were no longer shared by large sections of the labour movement and the Labour party.

The differences can in part be explained by the changes in the use of the term 'pacifism'. In the late nineteenth century the longer and etymologically correct version of the term was 'pacificism', which meant opposition to militarism and the attempt to achieve peace through the arbitration and the settlement of international disputes. By the 1930s, the shortened form of 'pacifism' was in common usage: it embraced not only pacifism but, in its absolute form, the belief that any resort to war and the use of force in any circumstances was morally indefensible and wrong. At the same time, as definitions developed and altered, people's sympathies also changed on this question. By 1935 Dalton, who moved the NEC resolution at Brighton, for example, no longer held those views displayed by his membership of the pacifist No More War Movement in the late 1920s.[52]

Against this background, for almost the first time, foreign policy became an important concern of the Labour party at the annual party conference. In 1931, the Japanese attack on Manchuria received relatively little attention within the Labour ranks. Demands for an arms embargo proliferated as the Sino-Japanese crisis developed. In February 1932, Lansbury put his name to the tripartite NJC manifestos pressing the British Government to act through the League of Nations and in

---

[50] H. Winkler, *Paths not Taken: British Labour and International Policy in the 1920s* (Chapel Hill, NC, 1994); S. Howe, 'Labour and International Affairs', in D. Tanner, P. Thane, and N. Tiratsoo (eds.), *Labour's First Century* (2000), pp. 128–9.

[51] J. W. Young, 'Idealism and Realism in the History of Labour's Foreign Policy', *Bulletin of the Society for the Study of Labour History*, 50 (1985), pp. 14–19.

[52] Ibid.

association with the USA. 'No arms, no money, no trade', he declared at Bristol later that month; though critics of Labour foreign policy have pointed to Lansbury's inconsistencies in various speeches, as the Labour leader wavered as to how an export ban would be applied.[53] By 1933 the delegates at the Hastings conference carried Charles Trevelyan's anti-war resolution including the proposition of a general strike by the working class against international conflict in the future. The Hastings conference was the first skirmish between the Labour left and the trade union leaders. Bevin opposed Trevelyan's resolution on the grounds of 'Who and What is There to Oppose?', since the Fascists had wiped out organized trade unionism in Germany and Italy.

By the summer of 1934 the Labour leadership had renounced Trevelyan's pacifist resolution, in favour of resisting aggression through the collective peace system of the League of Nations. After the 'Three Executives' (the General Council of the TUC, the NEC, and the PLP) had discussed the matter, Arthur Henderson produced the memorandum, 'War and Peace', for the National Executive Committee. From his considerable experience of international affairs and his management of the party machine, Henderson was able to establish a workable consensus on foreign policy between the TUC and the Labour party. This rejected a workers' general strike against war for the collective peace-keeping machinery of the League. As a result, this stance became part of party policy in the 'For Socialism and Peace' document at the Southport conference in 1934 where the ailing Henderson bravely made one of the longest speeches delivered at a party conference. In opening the 'War and Peace' debate, he declared that 'the executive is not putting forward a new policy . . . We are restating Labour's aims and Labour's policy, and indicating the method by which we hope that policy may be applied'.[54]

Henderson's speech provided a comprehensive and detailed commentary on the responsibilities and obligations of British membership of the League of Nations. Labour's policy was to work through the collective security system of the League to abolish war, to support international peace-keeping, and to promote the peaceful settlement of disputes. Article X of the League Covenant pledged member states to refrain from aggression against fellow members. Under Article XI the League was bound to take any action to safeguard the peace of nations. Members of the League had to fulfil all the obligations, including those of sanctions. By this provision, if the member states comprising its council agreed, the League could impose economic sanctions and take military action following Italy's invasion of the territory of a fellow member of the League, Abyssinia.[55]

'For Socialism and Peace' in 1934 was the final outcome of meetings of the 'Three Executives'. The policy was also put to, and endorsed by, the Annual Congress of the TUC, which met the month before the Labour party annual conference. While

---

[53] See R. Bassett, *Democracy and Foreign Policy: The Sino-Japanese Dispute: A Case History* (1932), pp. 150–4, 211, 329.

[54] Labour Party, *Report of the Thirty-Fourth Annual Conference* (1934), pp. 152–3.

[55] For the weakness of the League of Nations as an international peacekeeping organization, see P. Raffo, *The League of Nations* (1974).

'For Socialism and Peace' was being written Lansbury was ill in hospital. He did attend the 1934 Southport conference shortly after his return but made no direct contribution to the debate. Shortly before the conference, in a personal letter to the new Labour party secretary, Jim Middleton, Lansbury explained his views on international policy:

I feel strongly that those who have drafted the chapters [of 'For Socialism and Peace'] should be in charge and will be quite satisfied if the whole thing is taken up without me . . . I think we have been all wrong for centuries. The only path to peace is not to fight . . . our people must give up all right to hold any other country, renounce all Imperialism and stand unarmed before the world. She will then become the strongest nation in the world, fully armed by justice and love.[56]

At the Brighton conference, and since, one of the criticisms made of Lansbury's leadership was that he kept silent about his position in relation to this latest policy document. In fact, from the beginning of his leadership, his views as a convinced pacifist, against all forms of violence and war were well known. As he readily explained: '[I]n 1931, when I became leader of the Labour Party, I was up against the difficulty of squaring my pacifist principles with the policy of the party.'[57] Lansbury acted as spokesman speaking on behalf of Labour party policy—where he was mostly in agreement, except for the obligation to support military sanctions under the Covenant of the League of Nations.

In the months leading up to the Brighton conference, Lansbury made his position clear at many speaking engagements throughout the country; at Stafford in March 1935, he urged the churches to act for peace in resisting preparations for war. Two days later, at the Norwich by-election, he revealed his plans for a world economic conference as a preliminary step towards disarmament and peace. The following month Lansbury addressed a gathering of over 3,000 in a 'Victory for Socialism' campaign at Ipswich, where he admitted: 'If I had my way I would stand up before the world unarmed. But that I am told and I know is not the result of a show of force but because of the spirit of good behaviour which is in the heart of everyone.'[58]

In May 1935 George Lansbury suffered another overwhelming personal loss when his son, Edgar, was taken seriously ill and admitted to hospital with inoperable cancer. During the defence debate in the House of Commons Lansbury rushed to his son's bedside and remained in the hospital until the end. Edgar Lansbury died on 28 May.[59] Once more George Lansbury was inundated with tributes and messages of sympathy, many reflecting on this further loss less than two years after his wife Bessie's death. Arthur Henderson wrote: 'Our hearts go out to you in this further bereavement.' Lloyd George telegraphed that he 'felt sure that the sympathy of the nation without distinction of party will be extended in his sorrow to one whose personality it holds in high esteem'.[60] 'The King and Queen feel much for you in this

---

[56] George Lansbury to Jim Middleton, 9 Aug. 1934, Middleton Papers, MID 54.
[57] Lansbury, *My Quest for Peace*, p. 16.   [58] *Daily Herald*, 11, 13 Mar.; 6 Apr. 1935.
[59] Gottfried, *Balancing Act*, pp. 23–39.
[60] Lloyd George to George Lansbury, n.d. [probably 29 May 1935], LP, vol. 15, fo. 270.

further sorrow you have been called upon to bear,' was the simple message from Their Majesties at Buckingham Palace.[61] This loss gave even greater urgency to his remaining mission in life to bring about the pacific settlement of world conflict.

Prior to the Brighton conference there was little doubt about the personal position of the leader of the Labour party. On 19 August, Lansbury had written a famous letter to *The Times*, entitled 'Mr Lansbury's Plea for a Truce of God', in which he called on the Pope and the Archbishops of Canterbury and York to summon a convocation in the Holy Land of all religions to seek world peace through a 'Truce of God'. While expressing sympathy with the spirit behind Lansbury's Christian action in calling for this initiative, the Archbishop of Canterbury urged Christians to support their government in taking such action as would give support to the Covenant of the League. The next day Lansbury responded with a statement to the Press Association in which he claimed that his call for a world economic conference had not been understood: 'Let us remove the causes which lead to armaments.' On 9 September, speaking in a critical by-election in Dumfries, Lansbury made his position clear on the international crisis. At the same time in a press interview he explained:

During the whole period I have been serving as leader of the Labour party I have made it quite clear that under no circumstances could I support the use of armed force, either by the League of Nations or by individual nations. However anomalous the position may appear to be, it has been accepted by the Parliamentary Party and by the National Executive of the Labour Party.[62]

Lansbury's statement sums up the dilemma he faced, especially in the weeks before the Brighton conference, when two of his closest friends and supporters made clear their attitude to Labour policy. During September, the pacifist Arthur Ponsonby, who had been a long-standing associate with Lansbury in the peace movement in the inter-war years, gave up the leadership of the Labour peers in Parliament.[63] Ponsonby wrote to Lansbury: 'I cannot wait any longer—so here goes. After careful consideration I have thought it best to make the move before Brighton. I am sending a copy of my letter to the press.'[64] At the same time, Stafford Cripps decided to resign from the NEC. At the meeting that discussed Cripps's resignation, Lansbury raised his own position as leader in relation to the Labour party's attitude towards the Italo-Abyssinian dispute. He was told that it was a matter for the parliamentary party, but that 'in the opinion of the National Executive Committee, there is no reason why he should tender his resignation'.[65]

Only a few days before Lansbury had been compelled to attend the TUC congress at Margate as the fraternal delegate of the Labour party. There, before the congress, Lansbury was present at the meeting of the 'Three Executives' that agreed a joint declaration condemning Italian aggression and supporting any action by the

[61] Clive Wigram to George Lansbury, 29 May 1935, ibid. vol. 15, fo. 239.
[62] *Manchester Guardian*, 9 Sept. 1935.
[63] For Lansbury's support of Ponsonby's Peace Letter in 1926, see Jones, *Arthur Ponsonby*, pp. 165–6.
[64] Ponsonby to Lansbury, 17 Sept., LP, vol. 28, fo. 208.   [65] NEC, *Minutes*, 19 Sept. 1935.

League to enforce peace. At the Congress Lansbury was distressed to hear Walter Citrine, the General Secretary of the TUC, tell the delegates that to reject the joint resolution 'will be turning down the deliberate and considered policy of this move-ment . . . *It will mean turning down George Lansbury* [emph. added]'. After this, Citrine had great difficulty in persuading Lansbury, who was by now suffering from a grave crisis of conscience, to address the congress as party leader without dissent-ing from official policy.[66] Afterwards, no longer able to reconcile his conscience with his political position, in a private letter to the new party secretary, J. S. Middle-ton, Lansbury appealed:

This note is to say the position at conferences and meetings . . . is quite impossible . . . the question of possible war and preparations for war cannot be dodged or avoided and so we are forced to contradict each other in a friendly though painful way. Someone should break the circle. Everybody publicly and . . . privately urges me to continue. My own mind never wavers. I should resign . . . cannot they [the NLC] pass a friendly resolution saying the situa-tion is one which must be resolved the party cannot go into a general election with a leader who disagrees with them on so fundamental a question of policy. I should take action myself were it not for the request at meetings and from my colleagues to remain.[67]

Lansbury also told Middleton that he was going to call a meeting of the PLP at the annual conference to settle his position. At this point, the party leader made his views clear to the press on military sanctions and prepared to speak out about party policy at the Brighton conference.[68]

Hugh Dalton opened the morning session of the Italy and Abyssinian debate by moving the five-paragraph resolution of the NEC. It is worth examining this reso-lution in some detail, since its main provision of support for any kind of action by the League of Nations lay at the heart of the leadership crisis at Brighton. First, the resolution condemned the Italian Fascist imperial aggression towards Abyssinia, and Mussolini's defiance of the League of Nations. In its third and main paragraph it called on the British government and other nations 'to use all the necessary meas-ures provided by the Covenant [of the League of Nations] to prevent Italy's unjust and rapacious attack upon the territory of a fellow member of the League'.[69] Firm support by the Brighton conference was pledged for 'any action consistent with the principles and statutes of the League to restrain the Italian Government and to uphold the authority of the League in enforcing Peace'.

In addition, the resolution also proposed that the League should summon a world economic conference to discuss the international control of the sources and supply of raw materials and their more equitable use for all nations. This was a

---

[66] For Citrine's speech and for Lansbury's fraternal address, in which he repeated his call for a world economic conference to settle the Italo-Abyssinian dispute, see *Report of Proceedings at the Sixty-Seventh Annual Trades Union Congress* (1935).

[67] Lansbury to Middleton, n.d. [Sept.] 1935, Middleton Papers, MID 54.

[68] For a private memorandum on his position, see 'A Page of History by GL' (n.d. [prob. Oct. 1935]), LP, vol. 28, fos. 209–19.

[69] All quotations from the speeches of Dalton and the other delegates at the Brighton Conference are drawn from Labour Party, *Report of the Thirty-Fifth Annual Conference* (1935).

deliberate concession to include George Lansbury's singular attempt since he became Labour leader to summon a new world conference to discuss the causes of war.[70]

In speaking in support of the resolution, Dalton pointed out that world attention was focused on the outcome of the proceedings at the Brighton conference. Aware of the divisions over foreign policy within the Labour leadership, which the debate was to reveal, Dalton paid tribute to the work of both Lansbury and Bevin in pioneering the proposal for a world economic conference. Socialists and trade unionists in other countries were standing firm behind the League of Nations. Above all, Dalton reminded the delegates, support for collective security through the League of Nations was a long-standing tenet of Labour foreign policy: a position which had been recently endorsed by Lansbury and Stafford Cripps. According to Dalton, only a few weeks before, Lansbury had declared in the House of Commons that

the Labour party will support the Government by every means in its power so long as the Government stand quite firmly by their obligation under the Covenant of the League ... ever since the League was formed the Labour party has pinned its faith to the League for the preservation of peace and law and order.[71]

Dalton finished his speech by interpreting the League of Nations Union Peace Ballot as a popular mandate for the Labour party's foreign policy on the collective security of the League of Nations.[72] By contrast he accused the National government over its conduct of foreign affairs, in particular over the failure of Ramsay MacDonald and Sir John Simon to take the necessary initiatives at the World Disarmament Conference and at the Stresa meeting with Mussolini on the reduction of armaments and on the settlement of the Abyssinian question.

Dalton was followed by Stafford Cripps, who argued that the successful endorsement of the NEC resolution by the Brighton conference would only strengthen their opponents in the Conservative party who dominated the National government:

I cannot rid my mind of the sordid history of capitalist deception. The empty and hollow excuses of 1914 ... echo through the arguments today ... Can we trust the Conservative Party ... backed by the great industrialists and capitalists who today control the National Government—can we trust them with the lives of the British workers?[73]

For Cripps, war was the direct product of the economic conflict generated by

---

[70] Lansbury, *My Quest for Peace*, p. 55. For Lansbury's project for a world economic conference, see Ch. 17.

[71] *Annual Conference Report* (1935), p. 154.

[72] In June 1935, the League of Nations Union published the results of its private Peace Ballot—the largest survey ever conducted by a British peace organization—in which over 11.6 million people between autumn 1934 and summer 1935 were asked about British membership of the League, multilateral disarmament, private manufacture and sale of arms, and the abolition of military and naval aircraft. Nearly 90 per cent of those polled supported economic sanctions against aggressor states, though fewer than 60 per cent approved of military measures. J. Hinton, *Protests and Visions: Peace Politics in 20th-Century Britain* (1989), pp. 94–9.

[73] *Annual Conference Report* (1935), p. 156.

international capitalism and imperialism that could only be resisted by the unity and co-operation of socialists throughout the world. As a result, at the Brighton conference, Cripps, who had originally supported the concept of the League of Nations, argued that the organization was the creation of capitalist governments and an integral part of capitalism and imperialism. Any support for economic or military sanctions by the League against Italy would only commit workers in different countries to a capitalist war machine. Cripps defended the change of views that had brought about his resignation from the NEC: 'I have been accused of changing my views on this topic. I have changed them, because events have satisfied me that now the League of Nations, with three major Powers outside, has become nothing but the tool of the satiated imperialist powers.'[74]

In this way, Cripps clearly told the conference that the endorsement of the NEC resolution would only put the weapon of sanctions in the hands of imperialist governments over which the working class had no control. Even if the Italian Fascist dictator was defeated by this strategy, he believed that 'in all probability Mussolini will drive a satisfactory bargain with his fellow-members of the international burglar's union even though they had momentarily turned policemen'. Instead, Cripps could only advocate that the labour movement channel its efforts into replacing the National government with a British socialist government.[75]

By this time, the scene was set for the two sides in the debate to present their arguments for and against the NEC resolution. John Marchbank, of the National Union of Railwaymen, noted that Cripps had presented an eloquent critique of capitalism and imperialism that bore little resemblance to current events in international affairs. Marchbank argued that, from the foundation of the League of Nations, British support for the League Covenant and the public enforcement of sanctions always carried the possibility of the use of armed force and war. In making this point he demonstrated that, two years before, Cripps had advocated the use of sanctions against Japan over the invasion of China. He also quoted the following from Lansbury at that time:

Some people may think that Great Britain signed the Covenant of the League and did not mean it. I think we did mean it. If we did not mean that we were going to use these means of stopping or preventing war, I do not know why we signed the Covenant.[76]

The NEC position was supported by several other speakers: trade union leaders, Charles Dukes (National Union of General and Municipal Workers), Rhys J. Davies (Distributive and Allied Workers), and John Williams (Miners' Federation of Great Britain), as well as Charles P. Trevelyan and Clement Attlee. Trevelyan admitted that the obligation to support sanctions against Mussolini was the inescapable outcome of membership of the League and might entail war. Speaking directly for the National Executive and its policy of support for collective security through the machinery of the League, Attlee argued that in the final analysis

---

[74] Ibid. p. 157.
[75] For Cripps, see C. Cooke, *The Life of Richard Stafford Cripps* (1957); Burgess, *Stafford Cripps*.
[76] *Annual Conference Report* (1935), p. 159.

maintenance of the rule of law in a civilized society depended on the use of force. Aware that Lansbury was still to speak, he acknowledged his great respect for Christian pacifists and their ideals but added 'we are in favour of the proper use of force for ensuring the rule of law. Non-resistance is not a political attitude, it is a personal attitude. I do not believe it is a possible policy for people with responsibility.'[77]

In his speech, Attlee referred to the main speakers who had presented the pacifist case before Lansbury addressed the conference. Dr Alfred Salter, MP for Bermondsey, proposed the application of Christian pacifist principles of non-resistance and moral persuasion as an alternative to the futility of force and violence. Instead of sanctions, Salter suggested the British government offer to surrender immediately its colonial possessions to an international régime, as a concrete demonstration to Italy of the peaceful method of settling imperialist disputes. In a classic defence of pacifism he told the Brighton delegates:

The Executive's policy means almost certain and inevitable war . . . You start to fight Italy, and before you know where you are you may be in the middle of a general European, or even a World War . . . and if that happens . . . this Labour Party will have part responsibility if you commit yourself to military sanctions.[78]

At the Brighton conference, only three women had the opportunity to participate in the debate: Dorothy Woodman of the Wood Green and Southgate Labour party, and Lucy Cox and Helen Bentwich who were, respectively, the prospective parliamentary candidates for Pudsey and Otley and for Harrow. Dorothy Woodman emphasized that pacifist principles could no longer be applied to a world changed by the rise of the Fascist dictators. Instead, support for the League of Nations and sanctions provided an excellent opportunity for the Labour party to campaign for international solidarity with socialists throughout the world. Helen Bentwich took up this theme: three weeks before she had been present in Geneva at the League when the British Foreign Secretary, Sir Samuel Hoare, had made his famous speech committing the Conservative-dominated National government to the League of Nations, which, she declared, not only stole Labour's policy but was the best piece of electioneering propaganda any government could have. On the other side, in opposing the Executive policy, Lucy Cox poured scorn on the notion that Mussolini was a megalomaniac. Instead she saw the dispute as an economic problem associated with capitalism and the effects of the First World War:

Those of us who represent the pacifist point of view at this conference ask now that we should take the opportunity of using the League of Nations to solve those economic questions that are not only the question of Japan or the question of Italy; but are questions of the whole world.[79]

Late on the Tuesday afternoon, to the accompaniment of loud and prolonged applause and the singing of 'For He's a Jolly Good Fellow', George Lansbury addressed the conference with an impassioned and honest speech on his dilemma as a Christian pacifist and leader of the Labour party. From the outset he admitted

[77] Ibid. p. 173.   [78] Ibid. p. 167.   [79] Ibid. p. 165.

his difficulties on a major and fundamental point of policy. Lansbury readily agreed that, in these circumstances, his deeply held convictions were irreconcilable with his position as party leader:

My only difficulty, and it is a real one, is my relationships with the Party . . . I agree with the position of those of my friends who think that it is quite intolerable that you should have a man speaking as Leader who disagrees fundamentally on an issue of this kind . . . And I want to say that I should not consider an expression of opinion [by the Brighton Conference] hostile to my continuance as Leader as anything more than natural and perfectly friendly. I hope that statement will make it absolutely clear where I stand . . .[80]

Lansbury also dealt directly with his 'Jekyll and Hyde position', explaining that he had always attempted to represent the views of the party when speaking as leader, as for example, to the Foreign Secretary, Sir Samuel Hoare. The remainder of his speech was a clear statement of the pacifist views he had held since boyhood. He found it morally indefensible to advocate peaceful methods to the labour movement in domestic politics but to support the use of force in foreign affairs: 'I believe that force never has and never will bring permanent peace and permanent goodwill in the world . . . I have no right to preach pacifism to starving people in this country and preach something else in relation to people elsewhere.'[81]

As an absolute Christian pacifist, Lansbury gave as his reason that his religion taught that those 'who lived by the sword, shall perish by the sword'. His experience demonstrated that the First World War and the Treaty of Versailles had not ended the horror of total war, nor made the world safe for democracy by the reduction of the level of armaments. As an alternative, to serve as the moral example of practical Christian values to the rest of the world, Lansbury brought forward his remarkable proposition that, as well as disarming unilaterally, this country should renounce imperialism by placing its colonial resources under the control of an international commission. 'I would go to them [at Geneva] and say . . . that Great Britain—the great imperialist race—led by the common people of our race were [sic] finished with imperialism,'[82] he told the delegates.

In this respect Lansbury clearly answered the critics who claimed he was inconsistent in his views. Inside and outside Parliament, he had always been passionately anti-imperialist, supporting nationalist causes in Ireland, Egypt, India, and elsewhere in the world against the tyranny of colonialism. In announcing the programme he was to campaign on following his return to the leadership, he had emphasized to the British people: 'There must be no mistake about this [the abolition of imperialism]. If we are to have peace in the world Imperialism must go and be replaced by a Commonwealth of brothers.'[83]

At Brighton, Lansbury stressed to his audience the essential connection between the ending of imperialism and the securing of world peace. He also suggested that his days were numbered as party leader: 'It may be that I shall not meet you on this platform any more. [cries of "No"] . . . It may well be that in carrying out your

---

[80] *Annual Conference Report* (1935), p. 175.   [81] Ibid. p. 176.   [82] Ibid. p. 177.
[83] *Daily Herald*, 4 June 1934.

policy, I shall be in your way.' Finally, Lansbury answered the charge that he had acted irresponsibly as party leader, in the line he had taken, by a simple restatement of his Christian pacifism:

If mine were the only voice in the conference, I would say, in the name of the faith I hold, the belief that God intends us to live peacefully and quietly with one another. If some people do not allow us to do so, I am ready to stand as the early Christians did, and say, this is our faith, this is where we stand, and, if necessary, this is where we will die.[84]

Immediately after Lansbury had finished, Bevin, who always sat with his trade union delegation in the main body of the conference hall, walked directly to the platform. The *New Statesman and Nation* noted that his bulky figure and aggressive manner had long made him a conspicuous personality at Labour party conferences. His reply was in stark contrast to Lansbury's speech, which Bevin could see had been received in the Dome with great popularity.[85] Seething with rage, Bevin immediately launched into Lansbury's conflict of loyalties—between personal conscience and political party—by accusing him of betrayal. According to the official party conference report, Bevin accused Lansbury as follows: 'it is placing the Executive and the Movement in an absolutely wrong position to be *taking your conscience* round from body to body asking to be told what to do with it'.[86] It has always been described as a scathing attack on Lansbury's pacifism—the trigger that drove him from the Labour leadership—with Bevin's precise phraseology subject to debate ever since.

The official conference record probably toned it down by misreporting the actual words used by the TGWU leader. At the time, where the accusation was directly reported, most of the major newspapers printed a similar version to the official report except, on the following weekend, the *Observer* quoted the phrase '*hawking your conscience*'.[87] Those delegates present—who were close to the platform—such as the Socialist Leaguer, J. T. Murphy, agreed this was what Bevin had uttered.[88] Esme Whiskin, Lansbury's granddaughter, who travelled expressly to Brighton to support her grandfather, remembered the high drama of the 1935 conference, with Bevin's scathing assault accompanied by hailstones that thundered down on the roof of the dome.[89] The journalist, Trevor Evans, recalled the highly emotional occasion in detail. Lansbury stood behind him to the back of the hall wringing his hands in disbelief and anguish at his attacker's use of 'hawking your conscience'.[90]

It was one of the most infamous and cruel taunts heard at a Labour conference

---

[84] Ibid. (1935), p. 177.

[85] *The New Statesman and Nation*, 5 Oct. 1935; *Annual Conference Report* (1935), p. 178.

[86] *Annual Conference Report* (1935), p. 178 (emph. added).

[87] *The Observer*, 6 Oct. 1935 (emph. added).

[88] J. T. Murphy, *Labour's Big Three: A Biographical Study of Clement Attlee, Herbert Morrison and Ernest Bevin* (1946), p. 184.

[89] In interviews with the author in 1989–90 Esme Whiskin recalled Bevin's words '*hawking* your conscience', but also pointed to the possibility—suggested by others—of '*carting* your conscience' (emph. added).

[90] T. Evans, 'Peace Issue at the 1935 Labour Conference', *BBC Sound Archives*. I am grateful to Ivan Howlett of BBC Radio 4 for a copy of this recording.

and caused uproar among the delegates because Bevin's attack on the Christian pacifist leader went beyond an uncompromising difference over policy. His insult had an odious dimension totally unworthy of British democratic politics. In using 'hawking your conscience', the pugilistic Ernest Bevin—no stranger to hard-hitting language—meant 'selling for money'. As those assembled knew, nothing was further from the truth, as far as their icon, George Lansbury, was concerned. The thirty-year-old Lionel Elvin, one of the Socialist League delegates who spoke at Brighton, definitely heard these words and never forgot the moment.[91]

At the time, Bevin's colleague, Citrine, was out of the country on a private visit to Russia, *en route* to Kharkov in the Ukraine.[92] Later, he accurately summed up the charge of 'hawking his conscience': 'It was a cruel . . . unnecessarily brutal assault on a man who was certainly no hypocrite and had served the Labour movement well.'[93]

Behind Bevin's invective was the seething sense of outrage of a man who had spent a lifetime in the labour movement fighting for, and keeping, agreements. He thundered angrily that the trade unions had been betrayed by the leadership shown by Lansbury in his failure to abide by decisions in the policy document, 'For Socialism and Peace', and his public declaration of dissent, late in the day, made directly to the Press Association: 'When you work on a Committee and you have to take collective responsibility, there is a standard in the Trade Union Movement which we all follow. In this world loyalty to a decision gives less publicity than disloyalty under certain circumstances.'[94]

Bevin explained how the policy on war and peace had been the product of joint collaboration in the NCL between the TUC and the Labour party and endorsed by the meeting of the 'Three Executives' at Margate, but at no point had unilateral disarmament been mentioned. He chided those who had opposed the NEC resolution at Brighton for not speaking out the previous year at the Southport conference. In this respect, a key part of Bevin's attack was directed at Stafford Cripps, whom he castigated for failing to turn up at the main meeting of the 'Three Executives' at Margate and for resigning just before the conference. He thundered:

People have been on this platform talking about the destruction of capitalism. The middle classes are not doing too badly as a whole under capitalism and Fascism. The thing that is being wiped out is the Trade Union Movement . . . It is we who are being wiped out and who will be wiped out if Fascism comes here.[95]

Bevin's speech went to the heart of the historic relationship between the trade union and labour movement and the political leadership of the Labour party. Since its foundation, as the LRC, the Labour party had always been a broad alliance but it

---

[91] Shortly afterwards he contested the 1935 general election as the Labour candidate for Cambridge University. George Lansbury was a friend of his father, Herbert Elvin, General Secretary of the National Union of Clerks and Administrative Workers, and from the 1920s had been one of many Labour visitors to the family home in Southend. I am grateful to Prof. Lionel Elvin for an interview (30 May 2001) about Labour politics in the 1930s and his recollections of the historic 1935 debate at Brighton.

[92] W. Citrine, *I Search for Truth in Russia* (1938), pp. 168–9.

[93] Lord Citrine, *Men and Work: an autobiography* (1964), p. 352.

[94] *Annual Conference Report* (1935), p. 178.   [95] Ibid. p. 179.

had been essentially a trade union party which socialists joined. In a famous, often-quoted remark, Bevin reminded the delegates of this: 'I want to say this to our friends who have joined us in this political movement, that our predecessors formed this party. It was not Keir Hardie who formed it, it grew out of the bowels of the Trades Union Congress.'[96]

Bevin ended his speech on the theme of loyalty, by recalling the contribution of the TUC in serving on the NCL. By contrast he linked the actions of Lansbury, Cripps, and the other dissenters to that of Ramsay MacDonald in 1931 and urged the delegates to give an almost unanimous vote for the NEC resolution on the next day. Lansbury tried to respond but, with the microphones switched off, he could only shout a few brief points.[97]

The strength and tone of Bevin's speech had effectively ended the debate on the first day. An unrepentant Bevin was reported as glowering in equally unpleasant terms: 'Lansbury's been dressed in saint's clothes for years waiting for martyrdom. All I did was set fire to the faggots.'[98] Although several delegates participated on the second day, which included an impressive speech by Philip Noel Baker, the parliamentary candidate for Coventry, it was left to Morrison to wind up for the NEC with a conciliatory speech, in which he revealed that he had opposed the First World War. Morrison was, however, no different from virtually every delegate who had supported the NEC resolution, which was carried overwhelmingly at the end of the two-day debate. Nearly all had previously held some kind of pacifist position, either in the First World War or in the years before the Brighton conference. Only Lansbury and the small group of supporters who shared his views on war and peace had not altered their position by the mid 1930s.

The following week, Lansbury offered his resignation at the meeting of the PLP that he had called before the Brighton conference. Remarkably, even then, as Parliament reassembled for the new session, his fellow MPs refused at first to allow him to relinquish the leadership by thirty-eight votes to seven with five abstentions, until Lansbury finally insisted.

Virginia Woolf felt she was unable to attend any more conference sessions after Bevin's devastating attack on Lansbury reduced her to tears.[99] Leonard Woolf mistakenly commented that, 'the show-down . . . at the Labour party conference in 1935' was where Bevin 'battered the poor man to political death', as 'Lansbury afterwards resigned the leadership'.[100] However, what finally destroyed the Labour leader was the fact that, after Bevin's onslaught, no member of the NEC went to his rescue; only Herbert Morrison sympathetically (according to Raymond Postgate) said to

---

[96] Ibid. p. 180.

[97] The official report said nothing about Lansbury's difficulty in replying to Bevin. Instead, it noted his point of order that he was in hospital when *For Socialism and Peace* was drafted and that he had always stated the Party's view in Parliament and elsewhere, as well as 'his own view on the question of sanctions', *Annual Conference Report* (1935), p. 180.

[98] F. Williams, *Nothing So Strange: An Autobiography* (1970), p. 139.

[99] *The Diary of Virginia Woolf*, ed. A. O. Bell and A. McNellie (1982), (entry for 2 Oct. 1935), p. 345. I am grateful to Dr Mary Joannou for this reference.

[100] L. Woolf, *Downhill All the Way: An Autobiography of the Years 1919–1939* (1967), pp. 244–5.

him on leaving the platform, 'Stand by your beliefs, George'.[101] With Bevin and other major trade union leaders holding huge card votes in their pockets, the outcome of the debate was never in doubt. Before October 1935, Lansbury had attempted to resign as party leader on more than one occasion, only to be requested to continue by his colleagues. Labour's most loved party leader had long recognized that his beliefs as a Christian pacifist would eventually be irreconcilable with his role in leading the party.[102]

Lansbury's resignation did not bring to an end his long and eventful political career. As we shall see, he remained an active politician identified with the peace movement inside and outside Parliament. As a prominent member of the PPU, Lansbury was elected president following the death in 1937 of its founder, Dick Sheppard. Though nearly eighty years of age, he devoted himself in his last years to a major international crusade to prevent the outbreak of war by peace journeys to the USA and Europe, including personal visits to Hitler and Mussolini.[103]

Nor did the Brighton conference immediately settle the matter of the Labour leadership or difficulties within the party over defence and foreign policy. Fifteen days later, Stanley Baldwin seized the opportunity to call the 1935 general election, which the Labour party fought with Attlee as a caretaker leader. At Bow and Bromley, Lansbury achieved a resounding victory, polling 19,064 votes to his Conservative opponent's 5,707. In the new House of Commons, the Labour Opposition to the Conservative-dominated National government increased to 154 MPs, including the return of prominent individuals, such as Dalton, Morrison, and Clynes.

In the ensuing election contest between Attlee, Morrison, and Greenwood, Attlee finally won on the second ballot.[104] Yet while the Labour party had elected a new leader, it was still bedevilled by policy divisions, especially in its attitude to rearmament. New threats to international peace were posed by Hitler's remilitarization of the Rhineland and the outbreak of the Spanish Civil War. The Brighton conference had given unambiguous and clear support to the League of Nations, including the use of military force if necessary, but the PLP continued to oppose Conservative arms estimates in the Commons. Not until July 1937 did the PLP, by a narrow majority of forty-five votes to thirty-nine, decide to abstain on the arms estimates. At the Labour party conference in Bournemouth, Lansbury was again part of a small minority who opposed the statement on international policy and defence, prepared by Dalton for the National Council of Labour and endorsed both by the TUC and by the 1937 Labour party conference. By this vote, the Labour party finally gave a clear signal that it supported a policy of rearmament to face the threat of war in Europe.[105]

---

[101] Postgate, *Lansbury*, p. 304.
[102] Lansbury, 'A Page of History', fos. 213–14.
[103] For his account of his two peace journeys to Hitler and Mussolini, see *Tribune*, 30 April, 23 July 1937, and below, Ch. 17.
[104] Harris, *Attlee*, pp. 120–2.
[105] Interview with Michael Foot, 7 Aug. 1991. For the role of Dalton and Bevin in changing Labour policy on rearmament, see Pimlott, *Hugh Dalton*, pp. 234–5, 241–2; H. Pelling, *A Short History of the Labour Party* (1972), pp. 81–2.

17
Pacifism, 1935–1940

Following his resignation as Labour leader after the Brighton party conference, George Lansbury was convinced that his association with the Labour party was over and that he would never hold any kind of office in the national organization again. Financially, he was in desperate straits and needed his son, Bill, to help clear up his election expenses with a temporary loan of £100. 'I can't ask the party for money. I am really finished with them. Most of the men and women at the centre have never accepted me as leader and have just used my influence with the masses for their own ends,' he claimed bitterly to his son. Deserted by faithful followers at Brighton, Lansbury was scathing and contemptuous about 'the loyalty of that little band' of friends and supporters who in the end had 'fallen in with the top dogs', as well as those who opposed him in the leadership crisis.[1]

In his account of the Brighton conference, he wrote that 'no single one of the colleagues who had urged me to remain as leader, or anyone else, said a word in my defence'.[2] On the issue of peace and war, he remained true to his principles in the years before the Second World War. Despite his differences, he was not prepared to split the Labour party at the 1935 general election by campaigning against those who had opposed him at the party conference. 'Were I like them I could have toured the country against them on the issue of "Peace".' But that would have been treachery to the movement. 'Some day the masses will understand and clear them all out,' he declared. Instead, he responded to many appeals for speaking engagements during the election contest.

It was clear that, after the loss of the Labour leadership, Lansbury was determined to stay on as a Member of Parliament to advocate the gospel of peace. He avowed he would 'be happier still standing alone among the crowd at Westminster'. His only consolation at this time of desolation and desertion in 1935 was that Bessie and Edgar had not witnessed it all.[3]

Lansbury's son-in law, Ernest Thurtle, recognized that Lansbury's resignation in 1935 was 'a bitter pill to swallow', though one the Labour leader accepted as inevitable with the ascendancy of the war and armaments issue. There was no going back on his unshakable and deeply held pacifist conviction.[4]

However, after 1935, Lansbury's pacifism took him away from mainstream Labour politics to become the leading figure in a remarkable peace campaign in

---

[1] George Lansbury to William Lansbury, n.d. [probably Oct. or Nov., 1935], EWP.
[2] Lansbury, 'A Page of History', fo. 214.
[3] George Lansbury to William Lansbury, n.d. [probably Oct. or Nov., 1935], EWP.
[4] Thurtle, *Time's Winged Chariot*, p. 121.

which he visited the USA and most of Europe in a single-minded attempt to prevent the drift to war. As a result, during these years, the Member for Bow and Bromley played little part in Britain in important ventures on the Labour Left, such as the attempt to form a united front against the National government in 1937 or a Popular Front in the late 1930s to mobilize democratic opinion against international fascism.[5] Postgate recalled that his father-in-law at first disagreed with him over the origins of the Spanish Civil War, in which many individual Britons fought in the International Brigades for the republic against General Franco while the British government maintained a policy of non-intervention. Later, Lansbury condemned the Fascist bombing and openly sympathized with the Republican cause to the extent he confessed he might have taken up arms himself as a younger man.[6]

Those who saw him regularly provide a distinctive portrait of the elder statesman during these remaining years of his life. As we have seen already, according to Raymond Postgate, Lansbury was physically, as well as psychologically, a changed man. Although he suffered less from stomach and heart problems, he now wore spectacles all the time and walked with a stick. None the less, his granddaughter, Esme Whiskin, who remembered him well during the late 1930s, confirmed that his voice and spirit remained strong and convincing throughout these years.[7]

Lansbury's absolute conviction, that only pacifism could achieve world peace, is why he is probably remembered as the politician whose heart ruled his head. Raymond Postgate remarked on his 'unwillingness to see facts which obstructed his hopes, a disinclination to follow out arguments that pointed in a direction he disliked, and a habit of repeating general statements (such as that war was supremely evil) as if they were contributions to the discussion, and not platitudes'.[8]

Postgate's explanation was that, as an elder statesman with a worldwide reputation by this time, George Lansbury had few close associates, particularly among the Labour ranks, who could influence him in his remaining years. He considered only Dr Alfred Salter a possible exception in this respect, but was somewhat dismissive of Lansbury's fellow pacifist.[9]

In the 1935 general election, George Lansbury's election address was an appeal for peace based squarely on the pacifist convictions he had advanced in his conference speech at Brighton: 'Send me to Parliament with a mandate to call the nation to one ... supreme effort for peace. If peace is to be saved ... At Geneva we must renounce imperialism, call upon all nations to ... endeavour to abolish the causes of war ...'[10]

---

[5] For Lansbury's proposal to reform the Labour Party as an 'all-in party organisation' to keep it as a broad church for socialism, see *Tribune*, 22 Jan., 5 Feb. 1937. For the Unity Campaign and the Popular Front in Britain, see D. Blaazer, *The Popular Front and the Progressive Tradition* (1992).

[6] For the Spanish Civil War, see T. Buchanan, *Britain and the Spanish Civil War* (1997); J. Jones, *Union Man* (1986), pp. 55–81; Postgate, *Lansbury*, pp. 308–9. In an interview with the author in 1989, Peter Thurtle confirmed the story about his grandfather's sympathies for the Spanish republic, but, for Lansbury's earlier pronouncement that he would not have fought in Spain, see his article, 'Peace at any Price', *Tribune*, 9 July 1937.

[7] Interview with Esme Whiskin, 2–3 Sept. 1989.

[8] Postgate, *Lansbury*, p. 308.   [9] Ibid. p. 310.

[10] *Parliamentary General Election, 1935: To the Electors of Bow and Bromley*, copy in LP, vol. 15, fos. 361–2.

Though no longer party leader, Lansbury attended the annual conferences between 1936 and 1939 as a delegate of his local party at Bow and Bromley. This provided him with an opportunity to speak on peace and disarmament issues. In 1936 he challenged the Labour party to support disarmament by promising, when next in office, to surrender armaments. He told the annual conference at Edinburgh:

... I am convinced that once war starts in Europe it will be a world war. I have been asked through ... the Fellowship of Reconciliation to go to America and to five capitals in Europe, and I have not met a President, Prime Minister, Foreign Minister, or any other responsible man either at home or abroad, but who is convinced that if this catastrophe takes place it will be the end of civilisation.[11]

Lansbury's unyielding pacifism remained a likely source of future tension for him as a senior figure within the party, especially in terms of voting at Westminster on issues such as the defence estimates. He made clear that the peace question was a matter of conscience, similar to religion and temperance. After the Edinburgh conference, Lansbury observed that the delegates found their own point of view in the widely drawn resolution.

My own position remains unchanged. I am an unrepentant Pacifist, who will oppose the armaments race whenever the subject is before the House of Commons, and I get my chance to speak. I shall only be able to vote against any decision of the Party, if my colleagues allow myself and those with me to exercise the conscience clause of the Party's constitution. . . . No member is compelled to vote against his conscience . . .[12]

In October 1937, in his last major address to the annual party conference, at seventy-eight years George Lansbury made one of his finest speeches in defence of his pacifist principles. During the debate on international policy and defence, Clynes opened for the NEC by calling for the endorsement of its report supporting rearmament in the face of international Fascist aggression by Japan, Italy, and Germany. He declared: 'We cannot safely conclude that there is no risk the Fascist states attacking democratic Britain. We cannot therefore leave every preparation for resistance until attacks actually begin.'

At the Bournemouth conference, Lansbury moved the reference back to the report. His main argument was that no previous war had made the world safe for democracy nor ensured a permanent peace. He cited Churchill, Baldwin, and Eden from among his opponents who believed that another world war would mean the destruction of European civilization.

In the last war I heard many recruiting speeches, and every speech was to the young men to come out and defend democracy, to come out and destroy militarism . . . Now, less than 20 years afterwards, what is going to be the slogan for the young men who are to fight in the new war?[13]

Condemning Fascism and imperialism, Lansbury appealed again for Britain to

---

[11] Labour Party, *Report of the Thirty-Sixth Annual Conference* (1936), p. 187.
[12] *Sunday Sun*, 18 Oct. 1936.
[13] Labour Party, *Report of the Thirty-Seventh Annual Conference* (1937), p. 199.

provide a moral lead by renouncing armaments and convening a new world conference to resolve conflict over territories, raw materials, and markets. Otherwise, he added: 'I have it burned in my soul that if the Labour Party supports this expenditure you may at any moment find yourselves plunged into a war of absolute destruction about which you have no option but to see it through.'[14]

After the 1935 general election he had covered Britain, speaking on behalf of the pacifist cause at meetings organized by the Fellowship of Reconciliation, the Women's Co-Operative Guild, trade union and labour organizations, and a new organization, the PPU.[15] Now, in his late-seventies, for the next four years Lansbury embarked on a remarkable international peace crusade to campaign for a conference of world powers that would remove the financial, economic, and territorial inequalities that caused international conflict and war.

This proposal for a world summit had been his main goal above all in foreign policy as Labour leader from the early 1930s. He recalled:

When in 1931 I became leader of the Labour Party, I tried my utmost to direct the thoughts and actions of the Party in relation to foreign affairs along one line . . . [that] the British Government should either itself or through the League of Nations . . . summon a world conference for the purpose of discussing the causes of war.[16]

Lansbury's various peace journeys were recounted in his book, *My Quest for Peace*, in which he gave an insight into those influences which determined his view of world affairs.[17] For Lansbury, the basis of appeal that informed his peace mission was Christian doctrine based on the life and teaching of Jesus Christ—that killing was wrong, whether by individuals or by governments. Lansbury rejected the Christian concept of a 'Holy War' derived from St Thomas Aquinas that justified war by the state in certain circumstances. Instead, 'forgive us our trespasses as we forgive them that trespass against us' and 'do unto others as you would they should do unto you' were among the prevailing precepts of an enduring Christian faith that underpinned his attitude to the question of war and peace.[18]

For most of his life Lansbury also believed in, and practised without compromise, a philosophy associated with St Francis, Tolstoy, and Gandhi, the doctrine of passive non-resistance, the central core of his absolute pacifism. 'I confess that when I first learned about St Francis and his life, and read the teaching of Tolstoi I wished to live like them,' he wrote.[19]

---

[14] Labour Party, *Report of the Thirty-Seventh Annual Conference*, p. 201.
[15] Lansbury, *My Quest for Peace*, pp. 12–13.   [16] Ibid. p. 55.
[17] Lansbury continued to write for various papers, including a regular column in 1937 for *Tribune*, which his old friend, Stafford Cripps, had launched. Lansbury also joined Margaret Cole, Rudolph Messel, Francis Meynell, and others on the editorial board of a socialist publication, *Fact*, under the general editorship of Raymond Postgate. Lansbury contributed number 7 in the series of new sixpenny monographs published on the 15th of each month—*Why Pacifists Should Be Socialists*, which gave him a platform for his ideas on promoting world peace. However, he played no part in the influential *Left Book Club* (LBC), established the previous year by the publisher Victor Gollancz with the support of John Strachey and Harold Laski. The LBC, which issued many significant left-wing books and backed the campaign for a popular front, built up a membership of 57,000 and a network of social and political activities.
[18] Ibid. pp. 14–15.   [19] Lansbury, *My Life*, pp. 8–9.

In British political life, there were always practical considerations that even an idealist, such as George Lansbury, had to consider. As a Cabinet minister he had felt compelled to support Labour's defence strategy and foreign policy. Now, no longer bound by the doctrine of 'collective responsibility', he confessed that he regretted his role as a member of a government that had not abandoned armaments. As a senior statesman political questions were matters of conscience which weighed heavily with him, particularly as he contemplated the world situation. Always he returned to his Christian pacifist position. 'It is the duty of Christians in all countries to oppose war and take no part in furthering such horrors,' he wrote in answer to the question, 'Should a Christian go to war?'[20] At Westminster he gathered a group of like-minded Labour MPs around him to form the Parliamentary Pacifist Group.[21]

The beginnings of his public campaign for a world conference can be seen in the long letter he penned to *The Times* in 1935 on the futility of war and the certainty of a crash into ruin, if that path was followed. His solution was a Christian appeal to religious leaders to 'call a Truce of God'. In this letter, he announced his plan for a conference of world leaders to share economic resources to avert war for the single purpose: 'of discussing how the vast stores of natural resources and the tremendous unsatisfied markets of the world can be organised and regulated for the service of mankind.'[22]

This idea became the main project he strove for, ardently and singularly, as a Christian pacifist and to which he returned time and time again in these final years. On 5 February 1936 he brought forward his scheme in a resolution in the House of Commons requesting the British government to organize a world economic conference through the League of Nations.

Despite support from Lloyd George, this initiative was defeated by 228 votes to 137, largely on the grounds that the timing was inappropriate.[23] Lansbury was to travel across the United States and throughout Europe to put forward his proposal, which he later argued for, even after war between Britain and Germany had been declared on 3 September 1939.

In the spring of 1936 George Lansbury accepted the invitation of the Society of Friends and the Emergency Peace Campaign in the USA to return there on a speaking tour. He had previously visited in 1913 campaigning for women's suffrage, Irish Home Rule, and socialism.

This venture arose after Lansbury failed to secure the permission of the Governor of the BBC to broadcast a Peace Appeal to the USA. Lansbury had sought the assistance of Dr Alfred Salter, the Socialist MP for Bermondsey, and Cecil Wilson, the Quaker MP, to arrange the broadcasts that would take his peace message beyond

---

[20] G. Lansbury, 'Should a Christian Go to War?', *John Bull*, 28 Mar. 1936; see also id., 'The Politician and his Conscience', ibid. 23 May 1936.

[21] Copy of Report of National Convention of the Parliamentary Pacifist Group, 18 Sept. 1937, in PPU Archives.

[22] *The Times*, 19 Aug. 1935.

[23] *Hansard*, 5 Feb. 1936, cols. 209–16. See also Lansbury, *This Way to Peace* (1940), pp. 28–9.

Britain.[24] Lansbury was anxious to involve the USA in peace-making with Britain and France, particularly as he felt these nations had a responsibility to redress the punitive Versailles Treaty that continued to inflame the current European situation. 'President Roosevelt . . . appreciated what America did during the Great War . . . the penal terms inflicted on the defeated nations in defiance of [President] Wilson's 14 points. He knew also the catastrophe facing Europe . . . [that] would engulf America and the rest of the world,' he warned in a public meeting at Battersea.[25]

At a farewell meeting on 6 April 1936 arranged by the Revd 'Dick' Sheppard—who founded the PPU a month later—at Friends House, George Lansbury proclaimed the Christian pacifist basis of his peace mission to the United States. He explained he was going to America to rouse public opinion against war in a great peace campaign. He added: 'We who are pacifists are not dreamers. We are trying to be true-hearted followers of the Prince of Peace, who was crucified because He preached the only realist way of life. His message to the world has stood the test of time.'[26]

On 15 April, with his daughter Daisy Postgate, who travelled as his secretary, and his fellow pacifist Dr Alfred Salter, Lansbury sailed to America on the Cunard White Star liner, *Berengaria*, from Southampton via Cherbourg. They were seen off from Waterloo by a large gathering of friends and associates including 'Dick' Sheppard and J. S. Middleton, secretary of the Labour party.[27] Even on the Atlantic crossing, where Lansbury left the deck-tennis and quoits to others in order to rest his injured leg, his humanitarianism resulted in his presiding at a successful fund-raising event for the dependants of sick or lost seafarers.[28]

On arrival outside New York, Lansbury—who was not prepared to fly anywhere on this tour—was plucked off the liner early and whisked by train to Washington to address a large gathering of Senators, Congressmen, and public figures arranged by the National Peace Council of America. The Emergency Peace Campaign of the United States, who funded the trip with the slogan 'Keep America out of War', included other American church leaders and peace-makers—not all of them out-and-out pacifists—besides their luminary from Britain.[29]

This was the start of a whirlwind tour of rallies, meetings, and public broadcasts in America and Canada with all the razzmatazz of an American presidential election campaign. Dr Salter addressed fifty-nine meetings across the middle-West to the Pacific, and also broadcast five times. Given his age, Lansbury also took on a gruelling schedule, visiting twenty-seven cities in six weeks nation-wide, starting in Washington and New York and including two or three meetings in Pittsburgh, Philadelphia, Cleveland, Milwaukee, Detroit, St Louis, and Chicago, besides other locations. The mayor of Philadelphia rang the famous 'Liberty Bell'. At other demonstrations carrier pigeons—each with an individual peace message—were

---

[24] F. Brockway, *Bermondsey Story: The Life of Alfred Salter* (1949), pp. 196–8; Lansbury, *My Quest for Peace*, ch. 3.
[25] *The Times*, 9 Mar. 1936.   [26] Ibid. 7 Apr. 1936.   [27] Ibid. 16 Apr. 1936.
[28] For the Emergency Peace Campaign, see Lansbury, *My Quest for Peace*, ch. 3.
[29] 'Memorandum of an agreement between the Emergency Peace Campaign . . . and the Right Honourable George Lansbury MP', LP, vol. 16, fos. 9–10.

released. Lansbury also addressed gatherings of young students and women who were demanding government pensions in advance of the next war.[30] It was a punishing schedule—particularly as Lansbury prepared a different speech for each occasion. He also broadcast a number of times, though the planned radio transmission with Eleanor Roosevelt went ahead without the President's wife and with her speech read by a friend.[31] At key points, the campaign was filmed under ferocious 'Klieg-lights', a totally new occurrence for the former Labour leader. 'My home experience had been limited to pictures taken of me in hospital, small talkies for the Board of Agriculture and one or two political and social talks in my own garden—lasting just a few minutes,' he recalled.[32]

Audiences ranged in size from a few hundred to several thousand at the mall rallies in the American cities, the largest at the New Municipal Auditorium in Kansas City with 6,000 people. In Washington he told the audience at the National Peace Conference dinner:

What's the matter with the world? The power of production is so great we are too stupid to use it. If men of affairs were brought around the council table they would think out how to get all the nations of the world the materials they need and to distribute all the goods they produce. That is the root problem.[33]

Lansbury also hammered away at his central message that international peace and security would be achieved, not through weapons of destruction, but by eliminating the economic inequalities between nations in terms of natural resources and world markets. He informed his American audience: 'get your minds away from the idea of attaining security through poison gas and guns and . . . talk instead of economic problems and a square deal in regard to the world's resources.'

The New York Times remained unconvinced, conceding Lansbury's stature as the most prominent Christian statesman in British politics but adding: 'This faith, too, without works is dead. It is easy to whip up a great fervour of emotion against war, but to take practical steps against it is another and much harder affair.'[34]

On the next day, at the Carnegie Hall, Lansbury pursued the same theme, though his presentation had a fresh perspective, as he reminded an audience of 2,000: 'We haven't paid for the Crimean War yet, or for Waterloo yet, and we never will. But did anyone say they settled anything?'[35]

The Emergency Peace Campaign closed with a big rally in Boston. But before this last event, and accompanied by the British ambassador, Sir Ronald Lindsay, Lansbury finally met President Roosevelt and his Secretary of State, Cordell Hull. The meeting was private and secret. All that was publicized was Lansbury's proposal for the Americans to invite Hitler, Mussolini, Stalin, Chamberlain, and representatives from France, China, and Japan to a round table conference—free from the world's

---

[30] Postgate, *Lansbury*, pp. 312–13.

[31] Ray Newton to George Lansbury, 28 Feb. 1939, and copy of press statement, 1 Mar. 1936, LP, vol. 16, fos. 31, 34–6.

[32] Lansbury, *My Quest for Peace*, pp. 64–5.   [33] *New York Times*, 22 Apr. 1936.   [34] Ibid.

[35] Ibid. 23 Apr. 1936.

media—in the Azores. In fact, Lansbury believed that Roosevelt had promised to summon a world summit, provided he could be convinced that the European leaders would answer his appeal. On his return, in the hope that the British Prime Minister would take up the initiative as well, Lansbury told Stanley Baldwin of the enthusiastic response his peace proposal had received throughout the USA, as well as the standpoint of the American President. All that remained—in Roosevelt's words—was a 'peg on which to hang an appeal to Europe'. Here was the spur for Lansbury's international peace crusade in his remaining years. His steadfast conviction that a conference of world leaders could be achieved, allied to a dogged belief that even Hitler, Mussolini, and Stalin grasped the costs of a futile and ruinous war, drove the British pacifist to embark on a succession of peace journeys across Europe in a final endeavour to escape the inevitability of international conflict.[36]

Landing in Southampton on 4 June 1936, Lansbury remained optimistic about American interest in a world summit, provided Britain and the other imperialist powers were prepared to renounce colonialism.[37] To Jim Middleton, Lansbury wrote with enthusiasm from the United States about his peace journey across the world and the well-attended meetings. He told him: 'The churches are well represented: Jews and Catholics, Protestants of all brands and ethical people.' However, Lansbury detected a strong feeling against war in Europe that reflected American isolationism. 'I am certain they will never be persuaded to send men, money or materials to Europe again', he added.[38]

During Lansbury's absence in America the PPU was formally launched in Britain by his friend, the remarkable cleric and influential pacifist, 'Dick' Sheppard, whose twelve-year ministry as vicar of St Martin-in-the-Fields and pioneering religious broadcasts made him a universally popular and beloved figure in the 1920s. Educated at Marlborough and Trinity Hall, Cambridge, Hugh Richard Lawrie Sheppard was a charismatic figure whose early career was spent in social work in East London and as secretary to Cosmo Lang, bishop of Stepney, before his own ordination in 1907. Despite being plagued by recurrent ill health, this witty and rebellious priest—later dean of Canterbury and canon of St Pauls—transformed St Martin-in-the-Fields and attracted thousands to the restored church. During the Great War his devastating experience as chaplain to the Australian Field Hospital on the Western Front left him with a lasting abhorrence of war that converted him to pacifism and made him one of the leading figures in the British peace movement.[39]

The PPU soon became the largest pacifist organization in British history and continues to this day. Its origins lay in the letter sent to the press in October 1934 by Sheppard asking people to join him in making an individual pacifist pledge. 'We renounce war and never again, directly or indirectly, will we support or sanction

---

[36] George Lansbury to Stanley Baldwin, 27 Aug. 1936, Baldwin Papers, vol. 129, fos. 79–83; Lansbury, *My Quest for Peace*, pp. 82–5.

[37] *The Times*, 5 June 1936.

[38] George Lansbury to Jim Middleton, 6 May 1936, Middleton Papers, MID 58, fo. 66.

[39] For 'Dick' Sheppard, see R. K. Roberts, *H. R. L. Sheppard: His Life and Letters* (1942); C. Scott, *Dick Sheppard* (1977).

another' was an expression of personal commitment that produced a remarkable response. About 50,000 men sent in their personal pledge within a few days, thus overwhelming the local post office. Lansbury's own card survives to this day in the PPU archives. 'HRL Sheppard's Peace Movement', a non-party organization, came into existence, though its convenor had no further plans at the time. The PPU eventually took shape with permanent offices and staff, after a packed rally at the Albert Hall some months later. By February 1937 the PPU had taken over the No More War Movement, founded in 1921, and had become the British section of the War Resisters' International. By April 1940 its membership peaked at 136,000.[40] In 1936 the new organization attracted the support of religious figures, politicians, and writers as sponsors, including Canon Stuart Morris, Aldous Huxley, Revd Maude Royden, Vera Brittain, and the young Methodist minister, Donald Soper, as well as Lansbury himself.[41]

On 20 June 1936 George Lansbury travelled by train to Dorset to take part in a remarkable peace rally on the outskirts of Dorchester. Probably as many as 10,000 people from different peace groups in the south of England gathered in the Roman amphitheatre of the Maumbury Rings in sweltering heat to hear George Lansbury, Canon 'Dick' Sheppard, Donald Soper, and Vera Brittain. The chairman was the novelist and dramatist, Laurence Housman. Vera Brittain described the scene:

On the raised platform, scintillating with heat, the speakers addressed their listeners from beneath a striped umbrella. George Lansbury followed the chairman; shrewd and benign, sturdily erect in his black alpaca coat, he appeared in spite of his seventy-six years to be the only person unaffected by the temperature. At the end of the row sat Dick Sheppard in his customary informal attire. As he listened to George Lansbury he inhaled oxygen from a rubber apparatus which he carried to relieve his chronic asthma.[42]

Raymond Postgate did not mention the rally in his biography, but among Donald Soper's memories of that hot summer day was the impact that George Lansbury made—'it was the deep sincerity of what he said that was so powerful'—as he spoke in compelling terms to those gathered on the grassy banks:

What endeared me to him was that I learnt that you cannot have socialism without pacifism and pacifism without socialism . . . it was a very simple faith but not a simplistic view of Lansbury that came across . . . his was the complete political and social vision and pacifist vision and his pacifism was one aspect of an all inclusive concept.[43]

Lansbury said that what was needed was a new League of Nations cut adrift from the Versailles Treaty and prepared to tackle the questions of territory, raw material, and the use of the resources of the world. He added: 'We must have a League whose primary duty should be to remove the causes of war rather than hide them'.[44]

---

[40] M. Ceadel, *Pacifism in Britain, 1914–1945: The Defining of a Faith* (Oxford, 1980), ch. 12.

[41] For the PPU, see also S. Morrison, *I Renounce War: The Story of the Peace Pledge Union* (1962). See also Roberts, *Sheppard*; Scott, *Sheppard passim*.

[42] V. Brittain, *Testament of Experience: An Autobiographical Story of the Years 1925–1950* (1979), pp. 164–7. See also P. Berry and M. Bostridge, *Vera Brittain: A Life* (1995), pp. 355–7.

[43] Interview with Lord Soper, 4 Aug. 1988.   [44] *The Times*, 22 June 1936.

Freed from the leadership of the Labour party, in 1936 George Lansbury was invited to become the chief ambassador for the new venture—the 'Embassies of Reconciliation' that were established at a conference of the International Fellow-ship of Reconciliation (IFOR) in July 1936 to strengthen the world-wide activity of the Christian pacifist movement. Among the leading figures in the group were: the Revd Canon Charles E. Raven, Chairman of the British Fellowship of Recon-ciliation, and the Revd Henry Carter, Joint Chairman of the Council of Christian Pacifist Groups. Particularly prominent was an English Quaker, Percy Bartlett, formerly treasurer of the National Peace Council in 1924, general secretary of the British section of IFOR in 1925 and finally secretary in 1937. Barrow Cadbury, of the chocolate business, provided the finance and was treasurer.[45]

While the original plan envisaged sponsored visits by well-known people from different countries to various parts of the world, in the end Lansbury himself undertook the main peace missions during the next three years. In 1936 he travelled abroad to interview Leon Blum, prime minister of France, and the premiers of the Scandinavian countries. In Belgium, he met the Liberal leader, M. Van Zealand, who later produced a similar set of proposals to Lansbury's after a study of world economic conditions for the British and French governments.[46]

On 30 April 1937 *Tribune* readers were provided with a first-hand account of George Lansbury's visit to Germany some ten days before, entitled 'Why I Saw Herr Hitler'. Lansbury went as a private individual and not the representative of the British government. His venture was therefore seen as a personal peace mission rather than conventional diplomacy.

Before he departed to see Hitler in 1937, George Lansbury consulted the Foreign Secretary, Anthony Eden, and told him he did not wish to interfere with the govern-ment's endeavours in foreign policy and would appeal for an agreement on arms limitation and international economic co-operation. However, the British ambas-sador in Berlin thought little of Lansbury's venture, which he described as 'worse than useless'. Lansbury also visited the German embassy in London and the German ambassador, von Ribbentrop, was probably instrumental in arranging the visit.[47]

Lansbury travelled to Berlin with Percy Bartlett and Corder Catchpool, a Quaker pacifist once arrested by the Gestapo as an enemy of the régime, but in favour of improved Anglo-German relations; Catchpool could also act as an interpreter, if needed.

Lansbury prepared a memorandum for the interview in which he outlined his disagreements with Hitler, but advanced his ideas for a new world conference to tackle the major causes of war. Characteristically, he opened with a Christian message: 'that millions of people are daily working, longing and praying for peace, a peace based upon the great saying of Jesus Christ, "Do to others as you would that they should do to you"'. He added: 'I come to you with the same message.

[45] For Percy Bartlett, see *The Friend*, 1 Feb. 1980, pp. 123–5.

[46] Postgate, *Lansbury*, p. 316.

[47] For Lansbury's peace journeys in 1937, see D. Lukowitz, 'George Lansbury's Peace Missions to Hitler and Mussolini in 1937', *Canadian Journal of History*, 15 (1980), pp. 67–82.

You and I disagree fundamentally as to methods of government, but I am quite sure this fact will not prevent your giving full consideration to the message that it is my purpose to deliver.'

Lansbury willingly conceded that the Treaty of Versailles had caused grievances that had to be remedied. He therefore proposed that

an entirely new world conference should be summoned, a conference at which all nations must be represented and all attend as equals. I have asked President Roosevelt to summon such a conference . . . I am convinced that every leading man I have talked with, has agreed such a conference should be called.[48]

Lansbury identified the purpose of the conference was to halt armaments and deal with the causes of war. He added, 'there is a general recognition of the fact that imperialism as a national policy is finished'.

In his *Tribune* article he explained his mission in terms of Hitler being the *de jure* government of Germany. He recalled his earlier visits to Ireland in 1887, to France and Belgium in 1905, the Soviet Union in 1920 and 1926 in these terms: 'You see, it is in my blood to try and bring peace between warring factions.'[49]

The interview took place on 19 April 1937 and lasted two hours and a half, with Paul Schmidt acting as interpreter. To Lansbury's surprise, Hitler did not indulge in any customary outbursts and indicated he was willing to participate in a world conference, if convened by some other statesman, such as Roosevelt.

After Lansbury's interview, the *News Chronicle* published 'an exclusive message' from the British politician in Berlin. Lansbury declared that he was 'convinced that Germany does not want to go to war'.[50]

In fact, all that was issued after the two and a half hours meeting was a brief agreed statement: 'Germany will be very willing to attend a conference and take part in a united effort to establish economic cooperation and mutual understanding between the nations of the world if President Roosevelt or the head of another country will take the lead in calling such a conference.'[51]

Lansbury reminded the British public of the limited aim of his journey to Berlin to see the German Chancellor. 'My sole purpose in seeing Herr Hitler was to secure his support for a world conference that would be expressly called to remove the causes of war.'[52]

The *News Chronicle* gave a cautious welcome to the 'first direct offer to attend a world conference which Germany has made since she walked out of the League [of Nations]'.[53] However, in government circles reaction was mixed, owing to doubts about Hitler's intentions after his withdrawal from the World Disarmament Conference. Vernon Bartlett reported that Lansbury's visit was received with 'mingled relief and anxiety in well-informed British circles'.

---

[48] 'Memorandum by Mr. George Lansbury for the Information of Herr Hitler in connection with the interview proposed for Monday, Apr. 19th, 1937', in 'Visit of Mr George Lansbury, M.P. to Berlin', 20 Apr. 1937, PRO, FO 371/20745/35228.

[49] *Tribune*, 30 Apr. 1937.   [50] *News Chronicle*, 20 Apr. 1937.

[51] *Manchester Guardian*, 20 Apr. 1937.   [52] *Daily Herald*, 20 Apr. 1937.

[53] *News Chronicle*, 20 Apr. 1937.

Paul Schmidt, Hitler's official interpreter, later recalled the encounter as part of a varied programme that included the visits of the Duke of Windsor to Obersalzberg and Sir Oswald Mosley, as well as negotiations between Hitler and Lord Fairfax at Berchtesgaden.[54]

On the day before the German Chancellor's birthday, Schmidt recalled that a distracted Hitler was 'a man pale from sleeplessness, his complexion almost grey with somewhat puffy features, whose absent-minded expression clearly showed that he was brooding on other things'. Schmidt felt that Lansbury did not realize that 'a practising pacifist would [hardly] have any effect' on the Fascist dictator. 'I almost felt sorry for the old gentleman from England. Again and again he advanced his pacific plans with great enthusiasm and persistence. He seemed wholly unaware of Hitler's lack of interest, being obviously delighted with his replies, vague though they might be.'[55]

On his return George Lansbury met a number of Labour MPs at Westminster. As a new Labour MP, miners' leader James Griffiths, who was present at this gathering, later provided a different perspective on Lansbury's encounter with Hitler.[56] In this account, the interview comprised prepared questions and answers, after which Lansbury ended with 'one further question'. Lansbury requested the reluctant Schmidt to ask Hitler 'if he can give me a message I can take back to them [Lansbury's Jewish constituents] which will offer some hope that the treatment of their people in Germany will be changed'. If the report is accurate, what happened next does not suggest that Hitler deceived Lansbury: 'When Schmidt came to the word "Jud" (Jew), Hitler jumped to his feet and, giving the Nazi salute, poured out a torrent of words, whereupon George said to Schmidt: "You need not trouble to translate—I know what the answer means".'

Afterwards, Lansbury revealed little about his interview with Hitler, as the German Chancellor had bound him to secrecy in return for a possible future amnesty for Nazi victims. Postgate recorded that Lansbury thought the interview 'a triumph' and that he told Clifford Allen, 'He will not go to war, unless pushed into it by others.' He saw Hitler as 'a distressed and lonely man'. Lansbury's biographer made no other comment, though the peace mission was generally well received by the British press. The British government and its Foreign Office officials saw it differently. The British ambassador in Berlin cabled home a summary of Lansbury's interview. 'Apart from Herr Hitler's publicly indicated readiness to participate in a conference, this two and a half hour interview threw no new light on his views or designs', was the sceptical note on the official file.[57]

Immediately after his meeting with Hitler, Lansbury broadcast from the Berlin studios. The BBC relayed this transmission to Britain, in which he confined himself to a public statement about his objective of German participation in a world conference to remove international differences that led to war.[58]

[54] P. Schmidt, *Hitler's Interpreter* (1951), p. 61.

[55] Ibid. pp. 61–2.   [56] J. Griffiths, *Pages from Memory* (1969), pp. 60–1.

[57] 'Visit of Mr. George Lansbury, M.P., to Berlin', 20 Apr. 1937, PRO, FO 371/20745/35228.

[58] *Manchester Guardian*, 21 Apr. 1937.

Lansbury later elaborated on his meeting with Hitler, including the admission that 'it seemed to me that he could listen to reason and, I felt strong enough to believe that Christianity in its purest sense might have a chance with him.'[59] This belief suggests *naïveté*, and even a degree of arrogance, on the part of the British pacifist to the point that he was deceived by Hitler's charm.

His journey to Germany was followed later in 1937 with a visit to Rome to see the Italian dictator, Benito Mussolini, and his foreign secretary, Count Ciano. Lansbury told *Tribune* readers that Mussolini was a 'mixture of Stanley Baldwin, Lloyd George and Winston Churchill'. At first Mussolini turned down Lansbury's proposal for a world conference, but at their second interview on 12 July he indicated he had changed his mind. On the controversial issue of the Spanish Civil War, Lansbury noted that Mussolini 'desired friendship with Great Britain and peace with the world' and that Italian intervention in Spain 'was in defence of religion and civilisation'. Lansbury later commented that both the Italian dictator and his foreign secretary 'used the same arguments as members of Lloyd George's coalition government and the French and American governments used when defending their blockade of Soviet Russia and supply of men, money and armaments to Wrangel, Kolchak and Denikin for the purpose of destroying the Bolshevik Government'.[60]

Lansbury's visits to the two European dictators in 1937 brought considerable criticism at the time—and since—to the effect that he had been taken in by the Fascist leaders who had no intention of seeking a peaceful resolution of international disagreements. Typically, the *Daily Worker* accused him of diverting attention from what was happening in Europe. 'While Hitler talked peace to Lansbury, he was getting ready his bombing squadrons to blast Guernica and Durango off the map,' his Communist opponents declared.[61]

In retrospect, it is easy to dismiss 'Lansbury's peregrinations' as the idealism of an aged pacifist who was out of touch and ingenuous about the evil régimes that threatened the world. His explanations for his actions were difficult to understand in the language in which they were sometimes couched.[62] However, Lansbury, who was fully aware of the nature of the Fascist brutality, which he always condemned, was only one of a number of British politicians and diplomats who hurried to Germany and Italy to return with favourable or optimistic reports about the international future.[63] By the 1930s, in Britain, the popular mood for peace was overwhelming and it was against this background, as well as against his memories of the carnage of the Great War, that Lansbury undertook his—often misunderstood—peace missions.[64]

---

[59] G. Lansbury, *My Quest for Peace*, p. 141.

[60] *Tribune*, 23 July 1937. See also Lansbury, *My Quest for Peace*, ch. 7.

[61] *Daily Worker*, 10 July 1937.

[62] See e.g. 'My Talk with Mussolini by George Lansbury M.P.', *Reynolds News*, 18 July 1937.

[63] For the positive reactions of Lloyd George, Lansbury, and other politicians after visits to Hitler in the 1930s, see I. Kershaw, *Hitler: 1936–45: Nemesis* (2000), pp. 28–30.

[64] By the 1930s, indications of a growing popular mood for peace were seen in the explosion of anti-war writing and memoirs about the First World War (1929–30), such as R. C. Sherriff's play, *Journey's End*, the famous 1933 Oxford Union resolution—'this House will not fight for King and Country'—and

Not only in Europe did George Lansbury have to face the menace of Fascism. During the 1930s the East End of London witnessed some of the worst episodes of anti-Semitism, violence towards opponents, and political street disturbances associated with organized Fascist activity in Britain. Two events—the 'Olympia' Rally of 7 June 1934 and 'the Battle of Cable Street' of 4 October 1936—symbolized the rise of Fascism and those on the political left who opposed the threat from the right.[65]

In 1932 Sir Oswald Mosley founded the British Union of Fascists (BUF), following the defeat of the twenty-five candidates in his New Party in the 1931 general election. By late 1932, a BUF branch was launched in Bow Road in a basement café beneath the Poplar Borough Electricity Works Building, though it did not last and a second branch was opened four years later at 9 Medway Road, Bow. These early attempts, and those in south Poplar, proved less successful than the recruitment achieved by the BUF in the neighbouring boroughs of Bethnal Green, Stepney, and Hackney. The BUF itself acknowledged the strength of the local Labour party in the inter-war years and the personal popularity of George Lansbury, which meant the organization was 'facing a hard struggle in Lansbury's strong-hold'.[66] However this did not prevent BUF participation in municipal elections in East London and large rallies such as that in Victoria Park in July 1936.

Postgate largely ignored Lansbury's involvement in domestic politics after he was no longer party leader, even quickly passing over his election as mayor of Poplar for the second time in 1936.[67] However, Lansbury was still active. He opposed the growing Fascist threat at home with questions in Parliament on the government's attitude towards violence against the Jewish population. In 1935 he wrote on the topic of anti-Semitism in the East End denouncing 'the coming of the "Blackshirts" with the terrible hatred of Jews as Jews'.[68] At the time of the 'Battle of Cable Street', in alliance with four other East London mayors Lansbury attempted, unsuccessfully, to persuade Sir John Simon, the Home Secretary, to maintain peace and order by redirecting Sir Oswald Mosley's BUF march away from Aldgate and High Street, Whitechapel. Lansbury was left to declare: 'What I want is to maintain peace and order, and I advise those people who are opposed to Fascism to keep away from the demonstration.'[69] Many others took a similar line to Lansbury, including other Labour leaders and the Board of Deputies of British Jews. However, today the wall mural in Cable Street commemorates the hundreds of Labour and Jewish activists who ignored Lansbury's appeal and turned out on the barricades to thwart Mosley's attempt to march through the heart of the East End.

the success of the pacifist candidate, John Wilmot, at the Fulham by-election of 1933. In 1935, the results of the League of Nations Peace Ballot were published and, three years later, the immediate reaction in Britain to the Munich Agreement was highly favourable.

[65] R. C. Thurlow, 'The Straw that Broke the Camel's Back: Public Order, Civil Liberties and the Battle of Cable Street', in T. Kushner and N. Valman (eds.), *Remembering Cable Street: Fascism and Anti-Fascism in Britain* (2000), pp. 79–83.

[66] T. P. Lineham, *East London for Mosley: The British Union of Fascists in East London and South-West Essex, 1933–40* (1996), pp. 59–61, 92–5.

[67] Postgate, *Lansbury*, p. 307.   [68] Lansbury, 'Anti-Semitism in the East End', pp. 133–4.

[69] *The Times*, 1 Oct. 1936; The Cable Street Group, *The Battle of Cable Street* (1995).

At the end of 1936, the National Government introduced the Public Order Bill, which became law on 1 January 1937. Its chief provision was a ban on the wearing of political uniform, principally aimed at the Blackshirts. Other aspects of the Act, such as the regulation of meetings and processions, disturbed those on the left, who felt that a future government could use the measure against their organizations. Lansbury spoke on the third reading to this effect: 'I think everybody will agree with the Hon. Speaker [James Maxton] in disliking and distrusting the effect of this Bill. The reason why we are going to allow the Bill to go through is solely because of the circumstances . . .'

Lansbury admitted he was one of those who had pressed the Home Secretary to take action after the disturbances in the East End and explained the reasons he would reluctantly support him. Though there had been disturbances at public meetings throughout his life in the East End, he now acknowledged: 'Today we are up against something entirely different where men come from other parts of London and pursue vindictive policy or racial and so-called religious hatred which is foreign to anything I have ever experienced in the East of London or anywhere else.' Drawing on his own political experience he concluded: 'The speeches made in Bow, Poplar and Bethnal Green by the Fascists, if made by Communists or Socialists, or as in the days of the suffragette agitation, by people such as myself, would have caused proceedings to have been taken against them.'

In December 1937 Lansbury visited Czechoslovakia, where he met President Benes, and also Poland and Austria, where he outlined his peace plans which now included a £1,000 million international development fund to be raised as a proportion of armaments expenditure. On his return, he continued to press the British and American governments for action and, at the age of seventy-nine, wrote a book about his peace journeys. Raymond Postgate helped him prepare it for publication in 1938. As someone who had renounced his pacifism of the Great War years, Postgate found his father-in-law, whose belief was 'based more on religion than ever before', would brook no criticism of his stance on the international situation. 'I have got my mind settled about the book,' he told Postgate resolutely, 'I know you cannot understand how it is possible to hold my faith. The fact is it has hold of me quite firmly.'[70]

In the second half of 1938, there were further peace journeys as the indefatigable Lansbury visited Romania, Yugoslavia, and Hungary, where he had interviews with crowned heads of state and their chief ministers. In London he met King Boris of Bulgaria in the Ritz Hotel.

This frenetic travelling all took place against the background of the worsening situation in Europe as Hitler annexed his homeland of Austria and then made his territorial demands on Czechoslovakia as Britain prepared to mobilize for war. By now George Lansbury had become President of the PPU on the death of 'Dick' Sheppard in 1937. Like many in Britain at the time, Lansbury welcomed the Munich Agreement of September 1938. He sent telegrams to Hitler, Mussolini, and (in 1939)

---

[70] Postgate, *Lansbury*, pp. 315–16.

to the Pope, asking him to call a peace conference for Easter Day on the Mount of Olives. There was little that George Lansbury could do to affect events in Europe.

As his peace crusade with its extensive network of journeys demonstrated, George Lansbury's pacifism was not passivity. From 1933 he was directly involved in work to help those fleeing from Nazi tyranny. He was appeal chairman of the Polish Refugee Fund that, in conjunction with other charitable organizations, arranged for the rescue and care of Jewish children from Europe and their care in Britain by guarantors.[71]

A year earlier, Lansbury had participated in an emergency conference at Woburn House in Bloomsbury to arrange for a Jewish day of public protest, meditation, and self-denial in connection with the Nazi treatment of Jewish citizens. He hoped that the proposed day of sacrifice would at least enable them to rescue the 600 children stranded in the 'no man's land' between the Jewish and Polish frontiers.[72]

In early 1940 George Lansbury was nominated for the Nobel Peace Prize for his efforts for peace from the Boer War onwards, and especially for his marathon peace journeys since 1935. His nominees included Lord Sankey, Sir William Jowitt, Colonel Josiah Wedgwood, and William Wedgwood Benn.[73]

On 3 September 1939 Neville Chamberlain made his historic broadcast to the nation. Since then, his ominous concluding words—that Britain was now at war with Germany—have echoed down the twentieth century. At Westminster, George Lansbury rose on behalf of his fellow pacifists to declare:

The cause that I and a handful of friends represent is this morning apparently going down to ruin. But I think we ought to take heart and courage from the fact that after two thousand years of war and strife, at least even those who enter upon this colossal struggle have to admit that force has not settled and cannot settle anything. I hope that out of this terrible calamity will arise a spirit that will compel people to give up the reliance on force . . .'[74]

According to Professor John Postgate, his grandfather was devastated by Britain's declaration of war. Towards the end, many in Lansbury's family had not agreed with his peace journeys but respected the senior statesman's utter determination to pursue his mission to its limit.[75] This meant, for example, a few weeks later speaking up in Parliament against the continuation of the war as the leaders of the three main parties rejected the vague 'peace proposals' made in the Führer's speech of 6 October.

During this period, of the so-called 'phoney war', George Lansbury still thought a cessation of hostilities possible and set out his hopes for a permanent peace in a little-noticed book started six weeks after the outbreak of war and published in early 1940. In this monograph, he foresaw the coming of the United Nations but, in what was his final testament of pacifism, he called for Britain to disarm. Remarkably, he wrote: 'I am also quite certain that the first great nation that declares its willingness

[71] *The Times*, 16 Feb. 1939. See also Lansbury's letter, ibid. 6 Jan. 1939.
[72] Ibid. 19 Dec. 1938.   [73] Ibid. 23 Jan. 1940.   [74] *Peace News*, 8 Sept. 1939.
[75] Prof. Postgate had been a member of the PPU but turned away from pacifism at the start of the Second World War. Interview with Prof. John Postgate, 12 Nov. 1999.

to share the world's resources, territories and markets and also disarms will be the safest in the world.'[76]

But, by now, little time remained. Postgate noted that his father-in-law's heart and stomach troubles returned after he had been rushed down to an underground shelter during a false alarm in the last weeks of 1939. Lansbury continued to attend at the House of Commons, but spoke infrequently, and he was also too ill to go to the annual conference of the PPU in 1940. Instead, as President, he sent a letter to be read out on the role of pacifists in wartime, which included his appeal to the PPU to abandon picketing the Employment Exchanges when men were registering for military service. 'We are not playing fair with Government or Parliament. We possess rights and privileges such as no other nation allows pacifists in war-time,' he declared.[77]

After the difficult winter, in early March 1940 it was reported that George Lansbury was suffering from bronchitis and had been advised to take a complete rest from public duties for a few weeks.[78] Lansbury, who had been seeing a heart specialist, spent a short while recuperating with his old friends, David Graham Pole and his wife, Jessie, at 'The Shack', their Canadian log-house on a pine-clad hill a few miles from Farnham, Surrey.[79] At this retreat, Lansbury was partly restored to his old *bonhomie*. He read thrillers, biographies, tuned into Syd Walker, his favourite radio star, and even took the occasional glass of wine for medicinal purposes.

But press photographs showed the true picture—a gaunt George Lansbury, who after a few days collapsed suddenly and was ordered by a local doctor to the Manor House Hospital in London.[80] There Lansbury's doctors diagnosed stomach cancer—the disease that had claimed his son, Edgar, five years before—and decided not to operate. Lansbury, who had worried about the condition of his heart, was probably unaware of how ill he was. 'I *am* better but fluctuate very much. Some nights very good. Some days ditto. Some rather mad, this is nature's way,' he told Jessie and David Graham Pole.[81] On St George's Day, he managed to write to them again, hoping that he might visit them in the near future.[82]

Remarkably, during his last days, the eighty-one-year-old Member for Bow and Bromley compiled a final article comprising his enduring thoughts about life. He handed it over to Raymond Postgate who, as editor of *Tribune*, published the article on 25 April 1940. Lansbury's idealism remained undiminished. 'As for myself, I remain an unashamed, solid-as-a-rock-of-granite pacifist. There is no half-way house for any of us.' But he also showed his unfailing tolerance towards others and a lasting belief in a world based on co-operation not division. His youngest son,

---

[76] George Lansbury, *This Way to Peace* (1940), p. 126.

[77] Postgate, *Lansbury*, pp. 321–33.   [78] *The Times*, 5 Mar. 1940.

[79] George Lansbury to David Graham Pole, 29 Mar. 1940, DGPP, UL/5/6/9.

[80] *Daily Express*, 5 Apr. 1940.

[81] Rhona Vickers's undated notes, George Lansbury to Jessie and David Graham Pole, n.d. [*c.* Apr. 1940], DGPP, UL/5/6/9.

[82] George Lansbury to Jessie and David Graham Pole, 23 Apr. 1940. Ibid.

Eric, who did not share his pacifism, had written to him about a 'future when this ghastly slaughter will end—a future not of victors or vanquished because . . . there will be neither'.[83] In his *Tribune* article, Lansbury concluded with a reference to his Christian faith: 'I hold fast to the truth that this world is big enough for all; that we are all brethren, children of one Father . . . I beg all my readers to join, not in creating a new British World, but a new world wherein will be practised the true way of life. "Each for all and all for each".'[84] Postgate recalled taking the published article to the hospital—his father-in-law 'thanked the editor with his unvarying kindness, but did not look at the paper'.[85] By now, Lansbury knew he was dying and had one last task—to provide for the future of his daughter, Annie, who had been running his home at 39 Bow Road since the death of Bessie in 1933. He wrote a 'very, very private' letter to David Graham Pole to ask him to attempt to secure a civil list pension for her.[86] On 7 May 1940, after his family had been called urgently to the hospital, George Lansbury died peacefully in his sleep with his children William, Dorothy, and Annie by his bedside.[87]

[83] David Graham Pole reassured Eric Lansbury, who had joined the Royal Engineers as a driver, that his father would have understood his position: 'When he was staying with us, during his last weeks, in the course of a conversation with my wife on pacifism, he said he wasn't at all sure that had he been a young man, he would not have joined up.' Eric Lansbury to David Graham Pole, 18 Dec. 1940; David Graham Pole to Eric Lansbury, 27 Dec. 1940. DGPP, UL/5/6/9.

[84] *Tribune*, 26 Apr. 1940.

[85] Postgate, *Lansbury*, p. 324. See also G. Lansbury, 'Christ or Chaos', *Fortnightly*, 147 (June 1940), pp. 614–18.

[86] George Lansbury, 20 Apr. 1940 to David Graham Pole, DGPP, UL/5/6/9. For the failure of this attempt, see also below, Ch. 18.

[87] *Daily Herald*, 8 May 1940.

18
Home and Family, 1881–1940[1]

The important part played in the public careers of prominent politicians by their families is often given little attention by historians, unless perhaps close scrutiny reveals scandal or similar indiscretion. Even then, it is the public figure that predominates, rather than the private life of the subject. In many memoirs and biographies, the male politician's wife and family remain 'hidden from history'.[2] Rarely are the women forward and centre-stage.[3]

George Lansbury's home and family life contributed enormously to his record of public service in municipal and national politics. The demands on Lansbury's time—as a widely travelled propagandist for socialism, a local politician who held every elective office and was later an MP at Westminster—were enormous and endless. Yet, despite his frequent absences from home, he enjoyed a happy and secure marriage and family life. Lansbury was the first to recognize the part played by his wife, Bessie, who, by remaining at home to care for their family, made her contribution to the socialist cause. Their son, Edgar, also described the pivotal role of his mother 'who in her heyday played a great and noble part in his life'. He noted her 'enthusiasm, courage, thrift, skill in the management of household affairs and above all, [her] capacity for taking a back seat without fretting or nagging'.[4]

Publication of his memoirs in 1935 provided Lansbury with an opportunity to write this tribute to his wife: 'through all our long years of courtship and married life [Bessie] shared all my joys and sorrows, my failures and successes and . . . knew me for what I really am, as only a lover and wife could'.[5] They had been sweethearts since their days at St Mary's School—the beginning of a lifetime partnership of over fifty years.[6] When Bessie and George celebrated their golden wedding anniversary in 1930, Lansbury was a household name and, among the

[1] This chapter is based mainly on personal information derived from interviews with those who knew Bessie and George Lansbury and members of their family, as well as material in the George Lansbury Papers and Esme Whiskin Papers.

[2] For two recent exceptions, see K. O. Morgan, *Callaghan: A Life* (1997), ch. 7; R. Martin, *The Lancashire Giant: David Shackleton, Labour Leader and Civil Servant* (2002), ch. 9.

[3] For an excellent exception, see P. Yalland, *Women, Marriage and Politics, 1860–1914* (1986).

[4] E. Lansbury, *George Lansbury*, p. 85.

[5] Lansbury, *Looking Backwards and Forwards*, pp. 129–30.

[6] The Lansbury marriage was always strong. During his long political career, Lansbury was never accused of any personal wrongdoing or sexual impropriety in connection with either his well-known fund-raising or his close association with the women's movement. There is no evidence to support the story that Lansbury and Muriel, Countess De La Warr had an extra-marital affair. See E. Crawford, *The Women's Suffrage Movement: A Reference Guide, 1866–1928* (1999), pp. 165, 334; but also E. Lansbury, *George Lansbury*, pp. 81–2.

many messages of congratulations the couple received, was a note from the King and Queen.[7]

The Lansburys had twelve children—eight girls and four boys—ten of whom survived into adulthood. In his biography, Raymond Postgate provided a genealogical tree, which has been added to subsequently by his son, John, and other members of the Lansbury family.[8] Bessie and George's children were:

Bessie	1881–1909
Annie	1882–1952
George	1884–9
William	1885–1957
Edgar	1887–1935
Dorothy	1890–1973
Daisy	1892–1971
Nellie	1896–1980
Doreen	1899–1902
Constance	1899–1983
Violet	1900–72
Eric	1905–69

As was normal in late Victorian Britain, all the Lansbury children were born at home, probably without any professional medical care for Bessie. Thirty-seven years later, Edgar recalled when 'mother was ill' during the night, his father sent him and William to fetch Mrs Waterhouse from a nearby street to assist at the birth of the new arrival (probably their sister Nellie). 'With an outsize in reputations as a midwife', this 'tiny, wizened old lady' remained at the family home as nurse to Bessie and the newborn baby, as well as surrogate mother to the family—an example of a neighbourhood network at work. 'The first few days were a novelty, but we were glad when she packed her box and departed,' Edgar recalled.[9]

Like many late Victorian and Edwardian families, the joys and tribulations of family life were well represented in the Lansbury household. Bessie had to weather the trauma of almost endless pregnancies, as well as the dangers of childbirth, that commonly afflicted women of her generation. None the less, personal tragedy was never far away. Two of their children died very young (George at five years in 1889 and the twin Doreen at three years in 1902). Besides these early bereavements, which would have been sadly familiar to working-class families accustomed to infant mortality and the loss of young children, in 1909 their eldest child Bessie died in the London Hospital at twenty-eight from a perforated gastric ulcer and general peritonitis.[10] Thirty years later, one of George's last acts—in declining health himself—was to encourage his thirteen-year-old grandson, Terry, recovering in hospital from the same illness.[11]

[7] For official royal messages to George Lansbury in the 1930s, see RA, GVPS 54594.

[8] For the Lansbury family tree, see Postgate, *Life of George Lansbury*.

[9] E. Lansbury, *George Lansbury*, pp. 150–2.

[10] Certificate of Registry of Death, 17 June 1909.

[11] Holman, *Good Old George*, p. 163.

In the 1930s Lansbury was devastated first by the loss of his wife, Bessie, in 1933, then two years later by the death from cancer of his popular son, Edgar, who, at forty-eight, left a wife and young family of three children. Lansbury had been summoned from a House of Commons debate to the hospital and spent a continuous vigil of over twenty-four hours at his son's bedside.[12] Angela Lansbury, Edgar and Moyna's daughter, who later became the world-famous Hollywood, Broadway, and television actress, was only nine years' old when her father died. She recalls her bewilderment and shock following his sudden death but also the support and comfort she received from her extended family.[13] Angela remembers her father with great affection as a gentle and placid man who worshipped, but was never intimidated by, his more famous parent, George.[14]

The arrival of the twelve children born to Bessie and George Lansbury spanned the twenty-four years from 1881–1905, when Bessie was aged between nineteen and forty-three. The Lansbury children attended local Board schools in East London during the late Victorian period, when mass elementary schooling became compulsory. Daisy Postgate recalled her days at Wrights Road School, where her attendance was affected by opthalmia, the unpleasant eye disease, as well as similar afflictions, such as rampant head lice, from which poor children suffered at the time. Daisy never forgot how her mother strove to keep her children's hair clear of lice and their beds free from fleas

by the continuous use of insect powder and careful scrutiny each morning . . . [and by using] a small-toothed comb dipped in a solution of carbolic acid and methylated spirit each Saturday morning, ignoring our squeals and wriggles as the strong fluid stung our scalps and rolled down into our smarting eyes.[15]

In producing such a large family, the Lansburys clearly did not practise any of the more effective methods of birth-control that were increasingly available by the late nineteenth century to middle-class and upper-class parents and, to some extent, to the skilled working class.[16] Postgate observed that his father-in-law 'had a typically Victorian unwillingness to discuss sex, and the mechanics of contraception disgusted him'.[17] No specific reasons were suggested for this attitude—such as the Lansburys' membership of the Anglican Church, which may well have influenced their attitude to marriage and sex. It is not clear whether Lansbury, while a member of the SDF, shared his fellow Marxists' general hostility to birth-control on the

---

[12] Earlier, there had been three family misfortunes in 1927. George Lansbury's brother, James, was killed mysteriously one January morning on the railway line near his home at Forest Gate station, just three weeks after the loss of his daughter. The coroner recorded a verdict of 'death in a state of temporary insanity'. The year closed with the declared bankruptcies of Lansbury's sons, Edgar and William.

[13] Moyna and Edgar Lansbury also had twins, Edgar Jnr and Bruce. Interview with Angela Lansbury, 15 Aug. 1989 and pers. com. Gottfried, *Balancing Act*, pp. 40–1.

[14] Ibid. p. 36.   [15] D. Postgate, 'A Child in George Lansbury's Home', *Fortnightly*, pp. 390–1.

[16] On birth-control, see A. McClaren, *Birth Control in Nineteenth-Century England* (1978); J. Martin, *The Politics of Motherhood: Child and Maternal Welfare in England, 1900–1939* (1980), ch. 7; R. Ledbetter, *A History of the Malthusian League, 1877–1927* (1976), ch. 4.

[17] Postgate, *Lansbury*, p. 242.

grounds that it diverted attention from solving the true causes of poverty and unemployment.[18]

No explanation was also offered for the dramatic change in George Lansbury's views on the subject in the 1920s except that, according to Postgate, he was convinced 'that women should be allowed to control what happened to their own bodies'.[19] Clearly, Lansbury's participation in the women's movement had been decisive in altering his thinking on this crucial issue. The *Daily Herald*, under Lansbury's editorship, had a strict policy of no advertisements for birth-control, but these featured regularly in his *Lansbury's Labour Weekly* during the period 1925–7.[20] In 1920 there was an early hint of changing attitudes in Lansbury's public statement when he visited Denmark. 'I could not help wondering when men will become honest and above-board about the question of sex relationship,' he declared.[21]

After the First World War, attitudes towards artificial contraception changed, in part owing to the work of the birth-controller and eugenicist Marie Stopes. H. G. Wells noted that birth-control had replaced the vote as the symbol of the inter-war women's movement.[22] The First World War was an important agent of change which influenced attitudes towards personal relations; it is clear also that George Lansbury's new thinking on contraception reflected developments in Labour party social policy in the 1920s. In particular, members of his family had been actively involved with women's rights for a number of years.

In the 1920s Dorothy Lansbury and her husband, Ernest Thurtle, were highly visible in the campaign within the Labour party for rate-aided birth-control assistance at welfare centres. With her older siblings, Dorothy had been politically active from an early age, selling *Justice* and *Merrie England* in Victoria Park on Sunday afternoons in the 1890s, while her father had attempted to persuade his audience of the merits of socialism. All the Lansbury children were caught up in the suffragette movement in East London in the pre-war years, with Dorothy joining the Women's Freedom League and the Women's Labour League. Fenner Brockway also remembered the lively Dorothy for her trade union work in the National Union of Clerks with her future husband, Ernest Thurtle.[23] Rowland Kenney, Labour editor of the *Daily Herald*, recalled she commemorated his fading youth on his twenty-eighth birthday with a copy of Hilaire Belloc's *Verses* inscribed: 'Rowland Kenney, in commiseration from Dorothy Lansbury, 28 November 1910'.[24] In 1912 Dorothy and Ernest married and they subsequently had two children, a daughter, Helen, and a son, Peter, who worked at Westminster in his grandfather's parliamentary office in the 1930s.[25] Dorothy

---

[18] McLaren, *Birth Control in the Nineteeth-Century*, ch. 9.   [19] Ibid.

[20] Henry Harben, 'confidential memorandum', 13 Nov. 1948, LP, vol. 28, b. ii, fo. 4.

[21] *Daily Herald*, 7 Feb. 1920.

[22] R. Soloway, *Birth Control and the Population Question in England, 1877–1930* (Chapel Hill, NC, 1982), p. 287.

[23] Brockway, *Inside the Left*, pp. 26–7. See also S. D. Pennybacker, *A Vision for London, 1889–1914: Labour, Everyday Life and the LCC Experiment* (1995), pp. 42–3, 60.

[24] Kenney, *Westering*, p. 168.

[25] After George Lansbury resigned the party leadership in 1935, Peter Thurtle remained at Westminster as an assistant to Clem Attlee. Interview with Peter Thurtle, 1 Aug. 1989.

Thurtle had pursued a distinguished career in municipal politics in Shoreditch, while Ernest Thurtle joined his father-in-law in the House of Commons in 1923.[26] By this time, the Thurtles were prominent members of the Workers' Birth Control Group (WBCG), together with Dora Russell and Frida Laski, and campaigned for the public dissemination of birth-control information to working-class women.[27] Ernest's entry to Parliament gave him the opportunity to act as a spokesman for the growing birth-control lobby within the Labour party.

In 1924, the first Labour government—concerned about alienating its Roman Catholic voters in industrial areas—was wary of the birth-control issue. In July 1924, Thurtle and Dorothy Jewson, the Labour MP for Norwich, raised the issue of illegal and dangerous abortions with the Catholic John Wheatley, Minister of Health, only to receive the reply that parliamentary legislation was required.

As a vice-president of the WBCG, Ernest Thurtle became the key figure in the parliamentary campaign at Westminster. The WBCG had taken the campaign to the 1925 Labour party conference at Liverpool where they were thwarted by the NEC making birth-control an issue of individual conscience. In February 1926, Thurtle introduced a Bill to empower local authorities to provide information on birth-control methods to married women. Limited to only ten minutes, he argued for the measure on grounds of gender and class equality but was defeated by 167 votes to 81.[28] George Lansbury was among the Labour MPs who supported the measure—although the Conservative members who also went into the 'ayes' lobby outnumbered them. Of the four women MPs in 1926, only Dorothy Jewson turned up to vote.

Dorothy Thurtle, aided by her husband, remained a pioneer of birth-control and women's welfare for the rest of her life. She served on the Executive Committee of the National Birth Control Council (later the Family Planning Association) and, in the late 1930s, as a member of the Birkett Inter-Departmental Committee on Abortion, was the author of the Minority Report to the Ministry of Health and Home Office.[29] Ahead of her time, Dorothy Thurtle's views were not implemented until David Steel's Abortion Act of 1967.[30]

Bessie and George Lansbury lived most of their married life in Bow, first at 105 St Stephen's Road, and from *c.*1916, at 39 Bow Road, where their house became a political haven for all kinds of callers and those who needed assistance.[31] Terry

[26] Dorothy Thurtle gained election to the Shoreditch Borough Council in 1925, became mayor in 1936, alderman in 1953, and was granted the freedom of the borough in 1960. After unsuccessfully standing for Parliament in 1918, Ernest Thurtle became Labour MP for Shoreditch in 1923, losing the seat in 1931 but regaining it in 1935. He was a Lord Commissioner of the Treasury 1930–1 and Parliamentary Secretary to the Minister of Information from 1941–5.

[27] Family Planning Association, Correspondence and newscuttings A/14/93; Workers' Birth Control Group, Box 293 A8/10. See also, D. Russell, *The Tamarisk Tree*: i, *My Quest for Liberty and Love* (1985).

[28] *Hansard*, 9 Feb. 1926, cols. 849–56.

[29] B. Brookes, *Abortion in England, 1900–1967* (1988) pp. 87, 107, 111, 122–5.

[30] *Hackney Gazette*, 2 Mar. 1973.

[31] Two excellent studies of working-class life in late 19th-cent. London are E. Ross, *Love and Toil: Motherhood in Outcast London, 1870–1918* (1993) and A. Davin, *Growing Up Poor: Home, School and Street in London 1870–1914* (1996).

Lansbury recalled visits as a young grandson in the early 1930s to '39 Bow Road'—
as it was known—and although ever a place of vibrant activity: 'George and Bessie
[my grandparents] always seemed relatively quiet. "GL" was always busy in what we
now called "surgery". I remember [my aunt] Annie marshalling unscheduled sup-
plicants while Bessie was busy making soft drinks and biscuits for us all in the background'.[32]

Living in Bow in the 1930s was very different from the poor rural accommodation and unemployment the Lansburys had suffered in Queensland during their
emigration at the start of their married life. Their Australian experience in 1884–5
'bore heavily', particularly on Bessie. 'Often I have heard her scolding the girls at
home for grumbling over the domestic work . . . reminding them of the days when
she did the washing, helped with the farm work, reared three or four children, and
did all the cooking, under the broiling heat of the Australian sun,' Edgar Lansbury
recollected.[33]

After their return from Australia, the Lansburys found temporary accommodation at Tottenham before moving to East London. 'Our house was a tiny four
roomed cottage, two up and two down, with a small wash-house', Lansbury
recalled of the accommodation that housed their family of six in Bow.[34]

The laundry for a large and growing family was immense and wearing. Edgar
captured the washday scene in the Lansbury household:

It recalls like a stab in the heart a picture of mother, hands crinkled and white by the action of
soda, water and soap, face dripping with perspiration, digging and pounding masses of
clothes in the boiling copper or wash tub, wringing them out first roughly in her hands, and
then passing them on to us.[35]

Eventually, Lansbury asked his friend Wait Sewell for a loan for the purchase of a
washing-machine. Hire purchase was out of the question, 'Bessie wants a washing
machine like Alice, it will cost 50 shillings I believe. I suppose if we paid the shop so
much a week it would cost 55 shillings', Lansbury complained to Sewell.[36] Financial
circumstances were difficult for the Lansburys with a growing family. Seven
children had arrived in twelve years by this time. Lack of money again meant refusing Wait Sewell's invitation to go on holiday. 'One of the difficulties is to make
20 shillings stretch to 22 shillings or more', Lansbury admitted. To which he added
gloomily:

I wish for Bessie's sake very often it were otherwise . . . she had me for better or for worse & that
as far as money is concerned *it has been all worse and no better* . . . one ought not to have principles at all in this age they all ways (*sic*) come in the way in a most inconvenient manner.[37]

Marion Coates Hansen befriended Bessie, about whom she often expressed concern, during a long and influential friendship that extended beyond her political
association with George Lansbury. She had no children herself, but was not slow to

---

[32] Terry Lansbury, letter to author, 20 Aug. 2001.
[33] E. Lansbury, *George Lansbury*, 82.   [34] Lansbury, *My Life*, p. 63.
[35] E. Lansbury, *George Lansbury*, p. 84.
[36] George Lansbury to Wait Sewell, 1 Apr. 1892, LP, vol. 1, fo. 48.   [37] Ibid. (orig. emph.).

offer friendly advice as revealed in her invitation—sent while inspecting work-houses in Denmark—for Bessie to holiday in Middlesbrough. 'The boys can look after the children and the girls can cook dinner and Mr Lansbury can darn his socks, and you can take the baby [Eric] with you, if you wish though a week or two without his royal highness would not hurt you,' she commanded.[38]

In her account of life in Britain during the First World War, as we have seen Sylvia Pankhurst made some critical observations about the Lansbury household.[39] However, Sylvia Pankhurst does not appear to have said much at the time; her observations were made over a decade later.[40]

Instead, in East London, the Lansbury family remained active and loyal support-ers of the various causes associated with Sylvia Pankhurst and her Federation.[41] In February 1915 the establishment of a League of Rights, for Soldiers' and Sailors' Wives and Relatives to empower East End women and their families to protect and defend working-class living standards, was one result of this political alliance. The new organization, with Lansbury and Joe Banks as prominent office-holders, fought valiantly for the various pensions and allowances denied to the dependants of armed forces personnel by the bungling of an inefficient, if not hard-hearted, state bureaucracy. Sylvia Pankhurst used Lansbury's political connections in an attempt to secure the support of the trade union and labour movement.

None the less, Sylvia's account of her work for the League of Rights based at 400 Old Ford Road contains some swingeing comments on what she regarded as Lans-bury's token participation in the new organization. Sylvia noted dismissively: 'Lansbury protested that he could not give his time to these small gatherings. Where real spade-work was being accomplished . . . he was too much occupied and merely gave his name . . . [H]appily in after years Lansbury was pleased to recall his associ-ation with the League of Rights.'

Prominent in the relief work at this time was Minnie Lansbury (*née* Glassman) who, on Sylvia's invitation, gave up her East End teaching-post to become the hon-orary secretary of the ELFS. Sylvia had earlier suggested Bessie for the post of hon-orary secretary of the League, but was not surprised to learn she would be unable to even sign a letter or attend a committee meeting. The suffragette leader roundly condemned Bessie's domestic situation that prevented her participation in local politics:

In my knowledge of her she was far too much overwhelmed, depressed by her housework, her excessively large family. And the long-standing varicose ulcers, from which so many working mothers suffered a martyrdom, to the disgrace of our so-called civilised standards. Indeed she was one of the sort of women who made women of my sort suffragettes; hers to stint, suffer, and work in silence, enduring all the hardships of participation in pioneer causes, without the breath of the exhilaration.[42]

---

[38] Marion Coates Hansen to George Lansbury, 20 Feb. 1905, LP, vol. 2, fos. 34–5.
[39] See above, pp. 165–6.   [40] Pankhurst, *The Suffragette Movement*, p. 198.
[41] For Sylvia Pankhurst's campaigns in the East End, see also Winslow, *Sylvia Pankhurst*, ch. 4.
[42] Pankhurst, *The Home Front*, p. 131.

Sylvia Pankhurst's scorn was directed mainly towards George, rather than Bessie—Lansbury's socialist politics left little time, according to the suffragette activist, for sharing the burden of domestic duties with his wife. In this respect, Bessie and George Lansbury conformed to traditional Victorian roles that separated the world of work—mainly inhabited and controlled by men—from the domestic sphere to which women were relegated as wives and mothers.

Lansbury was aware of this unsatisfactory state of affairs. His immense public commitment as a male socialist propagandist, that elevated social and economic justice for the women as a political issue, was also matched by his private misgivings about the demands of his political activities on his personal and family situation.[43] But for Lansbury, striving to achieve his political ideals, politics and the world of work would always come first.

Yet this did not diminish him as a caring person, particularly in connection with his family. All three children—Edgar, Violet, and Daisy—who published memories of their family life, wrote warmly of their parents and their upbringing in East London. Daisy gave this insight of her realization that her father was also a notable local figure: 'not that he was an extremely affectionate and interested father, but rather he belonged to the people as well as to us and that we were part of something much bigger than the mere family.'[44] After secretarial training at Clark's College and working for Edgar in the family business, Daisy joined George as his private secretary for more than twenty years.[45]

George Lansbury later recalled that in 1913 six of his family were in prison or in danger of going there owing to their political activities, particularly in connection with the militant women's movement. Lansbury himself suffered imprisonment twice in 1913 and 1921—all of which placed a huge burden on Bessie as wife and mother. Ernest Thurtle wrote to his mother-in-law to sympathize with the effect of enforced separation of political campaigning and the imprisonment of her husband and children which made 1913 an '*annus horribilis*' for her. He commented that:

It is not cheerful to be left alone, I know, and of course Mr Lansbury is a wandering agitator *par excellence*, but I fancy you are rather glad of it, when you think of how he does agitate and what he agitates for . . . By this time you will have one of your gaol birds out of the cage, and the other won't have much longer to stay . . . It is hard to see how it will all end. Just now it looks as if the different martyrdoms will all be in vain.[46]

Living with George Lansbury and his open-hearted approach to all who called at their door must at times have been difficult for Bessie, the home maker. Recently, Terry Lansbury recalled that his father, Bill, paid tribute to Bessie's strength of character and fortitude:

She sacrificed her own well being and happiness to provide the support and stable domestic life George needed. Her achievement in rearing 13 (*sic*) demanding children as well as

---

[43] See George Lansbury, 'Our Wives' [drafts *c*.1910], LP, vol. 1, fos. 314–18.

[44] D. Lansbury, 'A Child in George Lansbury's House', p. 393.

[45] Postgate and Postgate, *Life of Raymond Postgate*, p. 102. For Lansbury's earlier difficulty in employing Keir Hardie's secretary, Maggie Symons, see C. Benn, *Keir Hardie* (1992), pp. 293–4.

[46] Ernest Thurtle to Bessie Lansbury, 21 Mar. 1913, LP, vol. 7, fo. 30.

bearing the vicissitudes of a foundering family business, the ostracism arising from her husband's noisy association with [then] unpopular causes and a constant struggle to make ends meet, despite having a husband who gave no priority to personal earnings, cannot be overstated.[47]

Of all the strong-minded and independent Lansbury women, Violet, the youngest of Bessie and George's six daughters, became an ardent Communist. She worked for the Russian Trade Delegation in London before moving to Russia in 1925.[48] There she stayed for ten years, setting up home initially with a Russian professor with whom she had two children. In the early years they were unable to marry, because Violet would not then have been allowed re-entry 'to visit her father in England'.[49] Bessie and George Lansbury were, however, able to travel to Russia. They were invited to Leningrad to 'visit all they could manage to see' by the Central Council of Trade Unions of the Soviet Union. Violet met her parents at the Leningrad docks and was immediately struck by her mother's demeanour: 'Mother, despite her years, tripped down the gangway for all the world like a Victorian miss . . . [her] face was radiant with expectancy—so different she seemed from the harassed mother I had always known, worried about the vagaries of her numerous children and the fate of her agitator-husband.'

After the First World War, once her large family had eventually grown up, Bessie was able to give a little more time to issues that had first fired her enthusiasm so many years before. On the Russian trip she gently remonstrated with Violet, who was concerned that the endless political discussions were tiring for her mother:

You forget, Violet, that I used to go economics classes with your father at the old Ethical Society in South Place. In those days before you were born I used to take part in discussions of this sort. I find it all very interesting to be in it all again (*sic*).[50]

In fact, Bessie Lansbury returned from the Soviet Union 'a staunch supporter' of the new régime, and in the early 1930s was possibly a more enthusiastic internationalist than her husband.[51]

For most of their marriage, however, Bessie's role was to support from the sidelines and she often tended to be overlooked. East End socialist, Walter Southgate, who joined the SDF in 1905, and later married into the Lansbury family, writes of George, rather than of his closer relation, Bessie: 'His pioneering work on behalf of the poor and downtrodden, particularly in his beloved borough of Poplar, was inspiring. My future mother-in-law was his wife's sister, so later I was to have a family connection with him. I looked upon him as a great man with a heart of gold.'[52] However, as Terry Lansbury commented, 'without Bessie Brine there might never have been a "Good old George"'.[53]

[47] Terry Lansbury, pers. com., 20 Aug. 2001.
[48] V. Lansbury, *An Englishwoman in the USSR*, p. 18.
[49] Unnamed newscutting, 14 Aug. 1947, Daily Mirror Newscuttings Collection. For Violet Lansbury in Moscow, see also E. Trory, *Soviet Trade Unions and the General Strike* (Brighton, 1975).
[50] V. Lansbury, *An Englishwoman in the USSR*, pp. 150–1.   [51] Ibid. p. 150.
[52] W. Southgate, *That's the Way It Was: A Working Class Autobiography, 1890–1950* (1982), p. 105.
[53] Terry Lansbury, pers. com., 20 Aug. 2001.

In addition to the vitality and excitement of politics, the Lansbury household also had its fair measure of family joy and home-spun entertainment, especially centred on Sunday musical evenings with Lansbury's 'resonant baritone voice', accompanied by Bessie playing the family 'American Organ', in renderings of 'Queen of the Earth' and similar popular ballads.[54] The fact that George and Bessie Lansbury were absolute teetotallers from their days in the Whitechapel Band of Hope, and also rarely attended the cinema or theatre, might suggest a different picture of home life in East London. Such a conclusion would be entirely wrong—as testified by outsiders, as well as younger members of the family. Senior civil servant, R. Auriol Barker, readily admitted that the socialist First Commissioner was the last person to impose his personal abstinence from alcohol on others. As his Private Secretary at the Office of Works, he accompanied his minister to Hadrian's Wall, Canterbury, Edinburgh, Stirling, Inchmahone on the Isle of Meneith and beyond. 'One of the things that struck me was that though a teetotaller himself he would never, if he could avoid it, have a meal on unlicensed premises,' Auriol Barker noted.[55] Lansbury also broke 'the hitherto inviolable rule' that banned the sale of intoxicants in any of the Royal Parks and created a new precedent, despite protests, by licensing the Tilt Yard restaurant at Hampton Court.[56]

By the inter-war years there were a large number of Lansbury grandchildren who regularly gathered at 39 Bow Road, particularly for the annual Christmas family party. Though a busy politician, George Lansbury kept in touch with all members of his family.[57] At the height of his leadership of the parliamentary Labour party in 1933, Lansbury nevertheless found time to reply to a letter from his granddaughter Esme:

It is always good to see you and hear of you. I hope you are well and as happy as possible in your job. Wherever we are life is never all 'Beer and Skittles'. There is always a sort of fly in the honey and this will remain so till we are all better people.[58]

In 1933 'time's winged chariot' pressed the leader of HM Opposition. The letter arrived postmarked '11.30 p.m.'. 'I am up to my neck with work if it were not so life would fade away into nothingness even if I did not actually die', he told his granddaughter. On her birthday he sent 'love and good wishes. I hope your mother, Nigel [Esme's son] and Terry [Esme's brother] and of course yourself will enjoy a lovely day together.' He also sent Esme an official key presented to him at the opening of new homes in Redcar. 'It is for you to keep for "Nigel" on his birthday—a kind of heirloom', he wrote. These examples of his personal care extended to all his children and growing number of grandchildren and great-grandchildren.[59]

---

54 E. Lansbury, *George Lansbury*, pp. 104–5.

55 'Memorandum by R. Auriol Barker', n.d. [*c*.1948], LP, vol. 28.

56 E. Lansbury, *George Lansbury*, 12.

57 In 1929, George Lansbury wrote to thank their 4-year-old grandchild, Angela—'My darling Bidsie'—for 'your nice long letter'. He ended: 'Now I must stop because a lot of people are here waiting to see me.' George Lansbury to Angela Lansbury, 17 Sept. 1929, Angela Lansbury Papers.

58 George Lansbury to Esme Whiskin, 3 Nov. 1933, EWP.

59 George Lansbury to Esme Whiskin, 14 Aug. 1938, EWP.

In the midst of his international peace campaign, George Lansbury remembered to pen some kind lines to a close relative only recently out of hospital. 'When you are about we will fix up a tea or a lunch all on our own. So get well quicker, so that [I] am not away in Poland or some other outlandish place', he wrote to Kitty Thurtle. But the current political situation was never far from his thoughts. In the same letter Lansbury made clear his hatred of dictatorship:

Yes people *are* a bit mad they curse the 'Japs' and yet prepare to do a thousand times worse in Europe. I think, however, in spite of the Labour Party and others we shall escape. I hate Dictatorships of any kind. This however does not prevent me understanding, that, even those men know war will bring them nothing but ruin.[60]

Even after his interview with Hitler, only five months before, Lansbury still clung to his belief that Fascism did not mean world conflict.

George Lansbury's prominence in British politics meant that members of his family were never far from the attention of the press. By the 1930s, the arrival of yet another Lansbury grandchild usually received media coverage. In 1934, the press greeted 'Mr Lansbury's nineteenth grandchild [in some newspapers it was 'G.L.'s 20th grandchild'] born to his youngest son Eric and his wife, Emily'.[61]

On a more serious note, Edgar Lansbury was cited as co-respondent when the actor and theatrical producer, Reginald Denham, petitioned for the dissolution of his marriage with his wife, Charlotte, known in the theatrical world as the leading actress, Moyna MacGill. The local newspapers published in full Moyna's letter to her husband on her departure to live with Edgar.[62] In times of great personal difficulty, the Lansbury children found their devoted parents not judgemental, but caring and supportive—as can be seen in some of the correspondence published in family biographies.[63]

Comparisons between father and son were perhaps inevitable with two active politicians in East London such as George and Edgar Lansbury. 'There is not much resemblance between Councillor Edgar Lansbury and his father, the famous George, except perhaps, in his ready flow of speech', announced *The East London Advertiser* in a pen portrait of 'probably the tallest man on the Poplar Borough Council'.[64] Over two years later, however, Edgar, who was one of the Poplar councillors and guardians imprisoned during the Poplar 1921 Rates Rebellion, had established himself in his own right. His famous father was merely listed among the councillors present as Edgar Lansbury, watched by Moyna, the new mayoress, was elected mayor. On taking office, he continued in the family tradition and donned no mayoral robes as the Labour councillors joined in singing 'The Red Flag'.[65]

---

[60] George Lansbury to Kitty Thurtle, 2 Oct. 1937, Peter Thurtle Papers.
[61] Undated and unnamed newscutting, Daily Mirror Newscuttings.
[62] *East End News*, 22 Feb. 1924.
[63] See E. Lansbury, *George Lansbury*, pp. 154–6; Postgate and Postgate, *Life of Raymond Postgate*, pp. 163–4.
[64] *East London Advertiser*, 13 May 1922.   [65] Ibid. 15 Nov. 1924.

Though George Lansbury was an important public figure with many years of service as an MP, Cabinet minister, and leader of HM Opposition, he had given away the bulk of his income. He had lived his life in terms of his Christian principles, but was always aware of the practicalities of providing for his family. 'How Mrs Lansbury kept eight on 30 shillings a week' was among the headlines of newspaper articles about the Lansbury's golden wedding anniversary in 1930 outlining their married life. 'My wages at the [Brine] works were 30 shillings and the house rent free. How my wife managed to feed and clothe us all I don't know, except that she worked early and late at her job,' Lansbury declared.[66]

On first entering Parliament, Lansbury had drawn on this personal experience in the debates on the National Insurance Bill in 1911.

Personally, I have a great deal of experience of a 30s. income, and I know just how far it goes in keeping a man and his family in anything like decency . . . I want to tell those that all the talk which we hear about poor people wasting their money who earn only 30s. a week in London is the sheerest nonsense . . .

he told the House of Commons. He added that he never drank, smoked, or went to the theatre as virtually every penny went to keeping his family. 'I spent practically all my money at home, and yet I had to run out of the Hearts of Oak Society because I could not make up the payments to that Society . . . when I hear of what people can do on 30s., I go back on my experience,' he concluded.[67] It was a constant concern that was never far from his thoughts as he tried to balance principles against practicalities.

Towards the end of his life, Lansbury became very concerned about the financial predicament his daughter Annie would face after his death. After Bessie died, Annie Lansbury—in her fifties—took a firm command of 39 Bow Road and continued to look after her father who was still busy with his international peace crusade and many public duties.

In April 1939, at 80, Lansbury drafted an appeal to the Prime Minister for a civil list pension for his daughter after his death:

But my financial position is due to a large extent to the necessary claim made upon me by those in need around me and my total inability to say No. Annie is not responsible for her father and has given a good many years service to her Mother and me.[68]

He left the document with his old friend, David Graham Pole, who contacted Clem Attlee, Lord Simon and others to no avail. The official reply from the Prime Minister was that 'a very strict rule . . . was always observed . . . Civil List pensions [were not] for the poor relations of politicians'.[69]

Lansbury was probably right to be concerned about his family finances, which had always been straitened. In the late 1930s his son, Bill, ran the family firm—

---

[66] *Daily Herald*, 28 May 1930.   [67] *Hansard*, 31 Oct. 1911, cols. 725–6.

[68] George Lansbury to David Graham Pole, 20 Apr. 1939 (enclosing 'To whoever is Prime Minister when I pass away', Apr. 1939), DGPP, UL 5/6/9.

[69] David Graham Pole to Clement Attlee, 15 May 1940; David Graham Pole to Lord Simon, 29 May 1940, 25, 28 Apr. 1941; Lord Simon to David Graham Pole, 28 May 1940, 25 Apr. 1941, ibid.

now based at Stratford—and was a continuing source of financial support for his father's political activities.[70] In fact, George Lansbury did not die penniless, as he previously had thought and wished. He left £1,695 (net £916)—still a relatively modest sum for a public figure and less than that of many contemporary Labour politicians.[71] Worldly possessions and material assets had not been important to Bessie and George Lansbury. For, in making their way in the world, they believed firmly that 'fellowship is life'.

[70] Terry Lansbury, pers. com., 21 Aug. 2001.

[71] In 1937, Ramsay MacDonald left an estate valued at just over £25,000; two years before, Arthur Henderson's estate was £5,417; and in 1943 John Burns's estate was worth £15,137, excluding his book collection, which sold for over £25,000.

19

George Lansbury's Legacies

After George Lansbury's death, tributes world wide poured in—letters, telegrams, and messages—so numerous it was impossible for his family to acknowledge them individually.[1] At Westminster, the debate on the Nazi invasion of Norway was interrupted for Neville Chamberlain, in one of his last acts as Prime Minister, to pay an official tribute to Lansbury's contribution to parliamentary life—particularly his leadership of HM Opposition in 1931–5.[2] Clem Attlee followed with the perfect accolade: 'He was a great Londoner and a great Englishman and a Socialist who practised and preached the brotherhood of man. He was a sincere and devoted Christian who strove to follow in the footsteps of his Master.'[3]

For a week, George Lansbury's body lay at 39 Bow Road where hundreds passed by to pay their last respects. On 14 May, before a packed congregation that included the Russian ambassador, Mr Maisky, and Mr Quo Tai-chi, the ambassador of the Chinese Republic among the family members and Labour representatives, the rector of St Mary's, George Lansbury's parish church, conducted a short funeral service before the cremation at Ilford Crematorium accompanied by the strains of 'The Red Flag'.[4] Five days later, Clem Attlee, who was now Deputy Prime Minister and Lord Privy Seal in the Churchill Coalition government, was the principal speaker at the memorial meeting at Poplar town hall. On 23 May 1940, the nation paid tribute at the Memorial Service at Westminster Abbey. The choir sang 'Jerusalem' and, for once, there were no air-raid sirens over London. Later, Bill Lansbury mixed his wife Jessie's ashes with those of his parents, and scattered them over the sea off Land's End in accordance with his father's last written request to mark his internationalism.[6]

To this day, the memory of George Lansbury lives on in various streets and housing developments in Britain named after him. To commemorate his life, Laurence Housman and Councillor Nellie Cressall headed an appeal fund after the Second World War that established a stained glass window by the Belgian artist, Eugène Yoors, in the Kingsley Hall at Bow.[7] Another famous testimonial to the champion of East London was the construction of the Lansbury Estate in Poplar as 'living architecture'—part of the Attlee government's Festival of Britain in 1951. Today, the estate continues to house the local populace, albeit close by towering Canary

---

[1] *The Times*, 16, 22 May 1940.   [2] *Hansard*, 8 May 1940, cols. 1233–5.
[3] Ibid. cols. 1235–7.   [4] Postgate, *Lansbury*, pp. 325–6.   [5] *The Times*, 21, 24 May 1940.
[6] Ibid. 16 May 1940; Terry Lansbury, pers. com., 20 Aug. 2001.
[7] For the appeal fund, see 'George Lansbury Memorial Window Committee' material in the Vera Brittain Papers.

Wharf, the Docklands' monument to late twentieth-century capitalism in the heart of the East End.[8]

George Lansbury believed in, and worked for, the time when Labour would secure a majority in power and introduce socialism by parliamentary means. The Attlee government that took office after the 1945 electoral landside introduced the Welfare State, secured the public ownership of the major industries and services in Britain and pursued a policy of full employment. Only after the Second World War were workhouses—the hated symbol of the poor law—finally abolished, although the buildings often became hospitals and retirement homes for the elderly. Eradicating the misery and degradation associated with the poor law in ordinary people's lives always remained high on Lansbury's political agenda. He would have identified with the historic *Beveridge Report* and its attack upon the five evils of Want, Disease, Ignorance, Squalor, and Idleness; the free National Health Service brought in by Nye Bevan, as well as with the various measures of nationalization that helped 'to build Jerusalem in Britain's green and pleasant land' in the post-war years. Similarly, Lansbury would have welcomed the Establishment of the United Nations Organisation and rejoiced that the post-war Labour Government had started decolonization by granting independence to India and Pakistan.

Over fifty years later, in a new political era, it is not a straightforward task to place George Lansbury within any specific Labour tradition. In 1951, in publishing *The Life of George Lansbury*, Raymond Postgate explained: 'I have not concluded this *Life* with a formal estimate of George Lansbury's place in history.' As his son-in-law, Postgate was very close to his subject—particularly after his own father's death—and considered '1951 was too early in time'.[9]

George Lansbury does not fit easily into the 'socialist intellectual' or 'trade union' wings of the twentieth-century Labour party in which he spent the majority of his political life. He certainly must be numbered among a remarkable and varied generation of working-class leaders that included Keir Hardie, John Burns, Will Crooks, Mary Macarthur, Will Thorne, Arthur Henderson, and other Labour pioneers who sacrificed time and unfaltering spirit to their cause. Lansbury's own political trajectory was also typical of his generation who, in many cases, moved—often in disillusion—from Liberalism to Labour in the late nineteenth and early twentieth centuries. As an apostle of socialism who inspired so many others, particularly among the ordinary people of Britain, Labour's 'best-loved leader' of the early 1930s has a firm place in the Christian Socialist tradition—though he was very different from the middle-class figures usually associated with Christian Socialism.[10]

Gladstonian Liberalism first captured and aroused Lansbury's political interest. The Marxism of the SDF and, afterwards, his regained Christianity inspired his political faith and the ethical and moral perspectives that underpinned his feminism, socialism, pacifism, and internationalism. In the pre-First World War years

---

[8] For the Lansbury estate, see S. Porter (ed.), *Survey of London*, xliii, *Poplar, Blackwall and the Isle of Dogs* (1994), pp. 212–47.

[9] Postgate, *Lansbury*, p. v.

[10] For Christian Socialism, see N. Dennis and A. H. Halsey, *English Ethical Socialism* (1988).

(and beyond) his militant involvement in the women's movement was an important catalyst in the development of his political outlook. There was no greater or more effective propagandist in his time, whose personal qualities carried his message with sincerity and conviction. Lansbury believed that capitalism and imperialism in India, Ireland, and elsewhere were inherently wrong and had to be replaced by socialism and democracy.

As an idealist, Lansbury believed in the perfectibility of people. Part of his heritage as a Victorian radical can be seen in his demand in the 1930s that Britain should provide a moral lead over disarmament and the peaceful settlement of international disputes which echoed Gladstone's principled stand on foreign policy over subject peoples. As late as 1940, Lansbury recalled with pride Gladstone's settlement of the *Alabama* dispute by international jurisdiction.[11]

During most of Lansbury's career, Labour was a party of popular protest that, gradually and hesitatingly, became a party of national government. For most of this time, he was, essentially, a political rebel and a thorn in the side of the Labour leadership. Associated with so many minority causes and different political groups, historians wrongly point to Lansbury's propensity for resignation and the search for his true political home. In 1912 he made his biggest mistake by resigning his seat to fight the Bow and Bromley by-election. It was a decision he always regretted and was determined not to repeat. But, as the political crisis of 1931 revealed, George Lansbury never forgot his loyalties nor trimmed his principles. Despite the landmarks in his political life of 1912 and 1935, he was no inveterate resigner. Lansbury eschewed resignation, even when international developments preceding the 1935 party conference made his personal position impossible. In the inter-war years he remained one of the few commanding figures within his party, particularly among the rank and file who revered him.

George Lansbury remained an extraordinary politician of the people whose legendary reputation was derived from an instinct for democracy and selfless service to the wider community. Living with his family—who played an important role in his political life—in the heart of the East End, 'Good Old George', as he was popularly acclaimed, was a larger-than-life figure of generosity and joviality, whose private character mirrored his public image. Lansbury had found his eventual political home in the Poplar Labour Party—the political party that dominated municipal politics in the inter-war years and whom he represented in Parliament from 1910–12 and 1922–40. His flair for political organization, allied to his uncanny ability to mobilize popular support, was reflected in his greatest political success during the Poplar Rates Rebellion of 1921.

'No brains to speak of' was the remorseless Beatrice Webb's verdict on her poor law commissioner colleague. To all intents and purposes, George Lansbury was no great innovative thinker or planner like those who refashioned Labour policy in the later 1930s. Yet his speeches, especially in the House of Commons, often contained a depth of historical and literary reference. Intellectuals like Harold Laski admired

---

[11] G. Lansbury, *This Way to Peace*, pp. 119–20.

him and enjoyed his company. Politicians and journalists often wrongly accused him of being 'muddle-headed' and sentimental—all captured in the oft-quoted phrase that 'his bleeding heart ran away with his bloody head'.

However, this said more about Lansbury's consummate passion for the righting of social injustice than his political ability as a practical politician. The young Liberal agent, who masterminded three outstanding election victories, could still be seen in the septuagenarian parliamentarian who ably led HM Opposition after the political hurricane had depleted the Labour ranks in 1931. His accomplishment, in founding and maintaining the outstanding *Daily Herald*, demonstrated shrewd business acumen and a style of leadership that gave early opportunities to a host of younger intellectuals of the political left.

In an era of 'New Labour', it seems unlikely that George Lansbury could find a place in a political party that has reconstituted itself, discarded 'Clause Four', and abandoned its traditional links with the trade unions in favour of those with 'Big Business'. Yet, despite his own personal code of a simple lifestyle and avoidance of 'the aristocratic embrace', Lansbury also understood the practical realities of politics. As a staunch Christian in a capitalist world, he always recognized the necessity of securing a living for himself and his family. There was no more effective fundraiser than the East End socialist, as his association with the plutocratic fellow radical, Joseph Fels, demonstrated. Despite the stories associated with the 'foreign funding' of the *Daily Herald*, large sums of money passed through Lansbury's hands directly and safely to worthy causes and public campaigns with not the slightest rumour of personal impropriety or scandal.

Most of the burning issues on which Lansbury campaigned—those of differences in social class, gender, and race, as well as environmental problems—are still current today. Above all, George Lansbury fought for the dispossessed and downtrodden in Britain. He understood that merely alleviating poverty would not obliterate structural inequalities in society or produce an irreversible shift in power and wealth to ordinary people. In 1940 he left a vital legacy for any Labour politician—exemplified in his own political life—the conviction that people matter.

Bibliography

CLASSIFICATION

A. UNPUBLISHED SOURCES

1. Lansbury papers
2. Other private papers
3. Family papers
4. Official sources
5. Labour party sources
6. Independent Labour party sources
7. Other collections

B. PUBLISHED SOURCES

1. British Parliamentary Papers
2. Reports by local authorities and other institutions
3. Miscellaneous reports

C. GEORGE LANSBURY'S WRITINGS

1. Books
2. Pamphlets
3. Articles

D. SECONDARY SOURCES

1. General studies
2. Biographies and memoirs
3. Edited diaries, letters, and writings
4. Articles
5. Biographical dictionaries
6. Plays and novels

E. NEWSPAPERS AND PERIODICALS

F. THESES

G. FILM AND SOUND ARCHIVES

1. British Film Institute

2. BBC

3. Other sound recordings

A. UNPUBLISHED SOURCES

1. Lansbury papers

George Lansbury (British Library of Political and Economic Science)
George Lansbury (Tower Hamlets Libraries Local History and Archives)

2. Other private papers

Clifford Allen (University of South Carolina Library)
Clement Attlee (Bodleian Library)
Stanley Baldwin (Cambridge University Library)
William Beveridge (British Library of Political and Economic Science)
Charles Booth (British Library of Political and Economic Science)
John Burns (British Library)
Vera Brittain (McMaster University)
Winston Churchill (Churchill Archives, Cambridge)
Walter Citrine (British Library of Political and Economic Science)
Jane Cobden (Bristol University Library)
G. D. H. Cole (Nuffield College Library)
Stafford Cripps (Nuffield College Library and courtesy of Professor Peter Clarke)
Hugh Dalton (British Library of Political and Economic Science)
R. C. K. Ensor (Bodleian Library)
Joseph Fels (The Historical Society of Pennsylvania)
E. Hughes (National Library of Scotland)
J. Gainford (Nuffield College)
David Lloyd George (House of Lords Record Office)
J. B. Glasier (University of Liverpool Library)
Arthur Greenwood (Bodleian Library)
H. D. Harben (British Library)
Charles Key (Bodleian Library)
Harold Laski (University of Hull Library)

James Maxton (Strathclyde Regional Archives)
J. R. MacDonald (Public Record Office)
Violet Markham (British Library of Political and Economic Science)
Catherine Marshall (Cumbria Record Office)
J. Middleton (Ruskin College Library)
Henry Nevinson (Bodleian Library)
E. Sylvia Pankhurst (International Institute of Social History)
Passfield S. and B. Webb (British Library of Political and Economic Science)
Dick Penniford (East Sussex Record Office)
Frederick Pethick-Lawrence (Trinity College, Cambridge)
David Graham Pole (Borthwick Institute of Historical Research)
Lord Ponsonby (Bodleian Library)
Royal Archives (Windsor)
Lord Sankey (Bodleian Library)
H. R. L. ('Dick') Sheppard (Lambeth Palace Library)
Lord Simon (Bodleian Library)
The Theosophical Society Archives (Adyar, India; London)
J. H. Thomas (Kent Record Office)
C. P. Trevelyan (Newcastle University Library)

3. Family papers (in private possession)

Angela Lansbury (by courtesy of Angela Lansbury)
Raymond Postgate (by courtesy of Professor John Postgate)
Peter Thurtle (by courtesy of the late Peter Thurtle)
Esme Whiskin (by courtesy of the late Esme Whiskin, Kate Geraghty, Alison Higgs, and
 Terry Lansbury)

4. Official sources

 i. Public Record Office
 BT 31
 CAB 21
 FO 371
 FO 395
 HO 45, 144
 MEPO 2, 3
 MH 53, 63, 68, 79
 WORK 14, 16
 ii. Home Office
 HO 144
 iii. Queensland State Archives
 Immigration Passenger Lists, 1883–5
 Immigration Department, Z 1961
 Letter Book of the Agent-General from Queensland, AGE/G623

5. Labour party sources

Labour Representation Committee Correspondence Files/Labour Party Letter Files,
 1900–1939

National Executive Committee, Minutes, 1900–35
Cambridge Constituency Labour Party, Minutes, 1920–35
Woolwich Constituency Labour Party, Minutes, 1905–20

6. Independent Labour party sources

Independent Labour Party, Minutes, 1910–13
Middlesbrough Independent Labour Party, Minutes, 1900–14

7. Other Collections

Daily Mirror Newscuttings Collection (Cambridge University Library)
Women's Freedom League, Minutes (The Women's Library)
Abortion Law Reform Assn.; Family Planning Assn.; Workers' Birth Control Group
    Collections (Wellcome Institute Library)
PPU Archive (Peace Pledge Union)

B. PUBLISHED SOURCES

1. British Parliamentary Papers

Papers relating to the Emigrants' Information Office, *Parliamentary Papers*, lvii, 1887
    (Accounts and Papers, 9) (C. 5078).
Report of the Royal Commission on the Aged Poor, *Parliamentary Papers*, xiv, 1895 (Reports
    from Commissioners, Inspectors and Others, 1) (C. 7684).
Report to the President of the Local Government Board on the Poplar Union, by J. S. Davey,
    Parliamentary Papers, civ, 1906 (Accounts and Papers, 40) (Cd. 3240).
Return of charges made to Candidates at the General Election of 1895 in Great Britain, and
    Ireland by Returning Officers, specifying the Total Expenses of each Candidate, *Parlia-
    mentary Papers*, lxvii, 1896 (Accounts and Papers, 19) (HC 145).
Second report (on Afforestation) of the Royal Commission appointed to inquire into . . .
    Coast Erosion, the Reclamation of Tidal Lands, and Afforestation in the United King-
    dom, ii, pt. 1, *Parliamentary Papers*, xiv, 1909 (Reports from Commissioners, Inspectors
    and Others, 6) (Cd. 3240).
Third report from the Select Committee on Distress from Want of Employment. Proceed-
    ings, Minutes of Evidence, Appendix, *Parliamentary Papers*, ix, 1895 (Reports from
    Committees, 3) (HC 365).

2. Reports by local authorities and other institutions

East London Ethical Society, 1890–1900
Independent Labour Party, 1900–20
Labour Representation Committee and Labour Party, 1900–39
*Report of Working Colonies Committee for the period covering 12th December 1905 to 30th June
    1907*, Central (Unemployed) Body.

3. Miscellaneous reports

*Report of the Debate on the Poor Law Minority Report between Geo. Lansbury, LCC, and
    H. Quelch (Editor of Justice), 20–21 September 1910*.

British Labour and the Russian Revolution: The Leeds Convention: A Report from the Daily Herald, with an Introduction by Ken Coates (Nottingham [n.d.]).

C. GEORGE LANSBURY'S WRITINGS

1. Books

Your Part in Poverty (1917).
These Things Shall Be (1920).
What I Saw in Russia (1920).
The Miracle of Fleet Street: The Story of the Daily Herald (n.d. [1925]).
My Life (1928).
My England (1951).
Looking Backwards and Forwards (1935).
Why Pacifists Should Be Socialists (1937).
My Quest for Peace (1938).
This Way to Peace (1940).

2. Pamphlets

The Principles of the English Poor Law (1897).
London for Labour (1909).
Unemployment: The Next Step (1909).
Socialism for the Poor: the End of Pauperism (1909).
The Chief Need of the Labour Movement (1911).
My Impression of Soviet Russia (1920).
Jesus and Labour (1924).
Socialism versus Protection: The Battle Cry of the Election (1923).
Speech to the Meeting of the Executive of the ICWPA, Moscow (29 July 1926).
Strike Bulletin (May 1926).
The Futility of the National Government ([n.d.]).

3. Articles

Only certain periodical articles have been listed. George Lansbury's extensive writings can be found in the *Daily Herald/Herald, Lansbury's Labour Weekly, Clarion, John Bull, Reynolds' News, Tribune*, and other papers.

'A Socialist View of the Government', *The National Review*, 25 (June 1895), pp. 564–70.
'The Principles of the English Poor Law', read at the Central Poor Law Conference (1897).
'Why I Returned to Christianity', *Clarion* (29 July 1904), p. 5.
'Hollesley Bay Colony', *Commonwealth* (7 July 1907), pp. 196–9.
'Hollesley Bay', *Socialist Review* (1 May 1908), pp. 220–33.
'How I Became a Socialist', *Labour Leader* (17 May 1912), pp. 315–16.
'Poplar and the Labour Party: A Defence of Poplarism', *Labour Monthly* (2 June 1922), pp. 383–9.
'The Policy of the Left Wing', in H. B. Lees-Smith (ed.), *The Encyclopaedia of the Labour Movement*, ii (1928), pp. 191–4.
'All Aboard for Birmingham', *Labour Magazine* (October 1928).

'Anti-Semitism in the East End', *Spectator*, 157 (24 July 1936).
'Christ or Chaos', *Fortnightly*, 147 (June 1940), pp. 614–18.

D. SECONDARY SOURCES

1. General studies

The place of publication is London unless otherwise stated.

Addison, P., *The Road to 1945* (1975).

Adelman, P., *The Rise of the Labour Party, 1880–1945* (1972).

Alberti, J., *Beyond Suffrage: Feminists in War and Peace* (New York, 1898).

Aldred, G., *No Traitors Gate* (1956).

Allen, V. L., *Trade Union Leadership: Based on a Study of Arthur Deakin* (1957).

Anderson, G. D., *Fascists, Communists and the National Government: Civil Liberties in Great Britain, 1931–37* (Columbia, 1983).

Andrew, C., *Secret Service: The Making of the British Intelligence Community* (1992).

Arnot, R. P., *The Miners* (1949).

Arnstein, W. L., *The Bradlaugh Case: Atheism, Sex and Politics among the Late Victorians* (Columbia, 1983).

Attlee, C. R., *The Labour Party in Perspective* (1937).

—— *As It Happened* (1954).

Bagwell, P., *The Railwaymen: The History of the National Union of Railwaymen* (1963).

—— *Outcast London: A Christian Response: The West London Mission of the Methodist Church, 1887–1987* (1987).

Baines, D., *Migration in a Mature Economy: Emigration and Internal Migration in England and Wales, 1861–1900* (1985).

Ball, S., *Baldwin and the Conservative Party: The Crisis of 1929–31* (1988).

Banks, J. A., and Banks, O. (1964), *Feminism and Family Planning in Victorian England* (Liverpool, 1964).

Banks, O., *Faces of Feminism: A Study of Feminism as a Social Movement* (Oxford, 1986).

—— *Dictionary of British Feminists, 2: A Supplement, 1900–1945* (1990).

Barker, M., *Gladstone and Radicalism: The Reconstruction of Liberal Policy in Britain, 1885–1894* (1975).

Barnes, A. (in conversation with K. Harding and C. Gibbs), *Tough Annie: From Suffragette to Stepney Councillor* (1980).

Barrow, L., and Bullock, I. (eds.), *Democratic Ideas and the British Labour Movement, 1880–1914* (Cambridge, 1996).

Bassett, R., *Democracy and Foreign Policy: A Case History—The Sino-Japanese Dispute, 1931–1933* (1952).

—— *Nineteen thirty-one: Political Crisis* (1958).

Bealey, F., and Pelling, H., *Labour and Politics, 1900–1906* (1958).

Bean, J. M. W. (ed.), *The Political Culture of Modern Britain: Studies in Memory of Stephen Koss* (1987).

Bellamy, M., Saville, J., and Martin, D. E. (eds.), *Dictionary of Labour Biography* (1993).

Benewick, R., and Smith, T. (eds.), *Direct Action and Democratic Politics* (1972).

Berkeley, H., *The Myth that Will not Die* (1978).

Beveridge, Lord, *Power and Influence* (1953).

Beynon, H., and Austin, T., *Masters and Servants: Class and Patronage in the Making of a Labour Organisation* (1994).

Biagini, E. F., *Liberty, Retrenchment and Reform: Popular Liberalism in the Age of Gladstone* (Cambridge, 1992).

Biagini, E. F., and Reid, A. J. (eds.), *Currents of Radicalism: Popular Radicalism, Organised Labour and Party Politics, 1850–1914* (Cambridge, 1991).

Bilankin, G., *Maisky: Ten Years Ambassador* (1944).

Binyon, G. C., *The Christian Socialist Movement in England* (1931).

Blaazer, D., *The Popular Front and the Progressive Tradition* (Cambridge, 1992).

Blake, J., *Memories of Old Poplar* (1977).

Bland, L., *Banishing the Beast: English Feminism and Sexual Morality, 1885–1914* (1995).

Blewett, N., *The Peers, the Parties and the People: The General Elections of 1910* (1972).

Blythe, R., *The Age of Illusion: Glimpses of Britain between the Wars, 1919–1940* (1986).

Booth, C. (ed.), *Life and Labour of the People of London*, i, *East, Central and South* (1904).

Borman, W., *Gandhi and Non-Violence* (New York, 1986).

Branson, N., and Heinemann, M., *Britain in the Nineteen Thirties* (1971).

—— *Poplarism, 1919–1925: George Lansbury and the Councillors' Revolt* (1979).

Braunthal, J., *History of the International, 1864–1914* (1966).

Briggs, A., and Saville, J. (eds.), *Essays in Labour History*, ii, *1886–1923* (1971).

—— and —— (eds.), *Essays in Labour History*, iii, *1918–1939* (1977).

Briscoe, S., *The Sermon on the Mount: Daring to be Different* (1996).

Brivati, B., and Heffernan, R. (eds.), *The Labour Party: A Centenary History* (Basingstoke, 2000).

Brookes, B., *Abortion in England, 1900–1967* (1988).

Brown, K. D., *Labour and Unemployment, 1900–1914* (Newton Abbott, 1971).

—— (ed.), *Essays in Anti-Labour History: Responses to the Rise of Labour in Britain* (1974).

—— (ed.), *The First Labour Party, 1906–1914* (1985).

Bryant, C., *Possible Dreams: A Personal History of British Christian Socialists* (1996).

Buchanan, T., *Britain and the Spanish Civil War* (Cambridge, 1997).

Burns, E., *The General Strike, May 1926: Trades Councils in Action* (1975).

Bush, J., *Behind the Lines: East London Labour, 1914–1919* (1984).

Cable Street Group, The, *The Battle of Cable Street* (1995).

Campbell, J., *Nye Bevan and the Mirage of British Socialism* (1987).

Carsten, F. L., *War against War: British and German Radical Movements in the First World War* (1982).

Ceadel, M., *Pacifism in Britain, 1914–1945* (Oxford, 1980).

Chadha, Y., *Rediscovering Gandhi* (1997).

Challinor, R., *The Origins of British Bolshevism* (1977).

Charmley, J., *A History of Conservative Politics, 1990–1996* (1998).

Childe, V. G., *How Labour Governs: A Study of Workers' Representation in Australia* (1923).

—— *Skara Brae: A Pictish Village in Orkney* (1931).

Chinn, C., *They Worked All Their Lives: Women of the Urban Poor in England, 1880–1939* (Manchester, 1988).

Clark, D., *We Do Not Want the Earth: The History of the South Shields Labour Party* (Whitley Bay, 1992).

Clarke, P. F., *Lancashire and the New Liberalism* (1971).

Clarke, P., *A Question of Leadership: Gladstone to Thatcher* (1991).

—— *Hope and Glory: Britain, 1900–1990* (Harmondsworth, 1996).

Clegg, H. A., Fox A., and Thompson, A. F., *A History of British Trade Unionism since 1889*, 1 (1964).

—— *A History of British Trade Unionism since 1889*, ii, *1911–1933* (Oxford, 1985).

Cline, C. A., *E. D. Morel* (Belfast, 1980).

Cline, C. A., *Recruits to Labour: The British Labour Party, 1914–1931* (Syracuse, 1963).

Coates, K., and Topham, T., *The Making of the Labour Movement: The Formation of the TGWU, 1870–1922* (Nottingham, 1994).

Cole, M., *Makers of the Labour Movement* (1948).

—— *A History of the Labour Party from 1914* (1948).

—— *Growing up into Revolution* (1949).

—— *The Story of Fabian Socialism* (1961).

Collette, C., *For Labour and for Women: The Women's Labour League, 1906–1918* (Manchester, 1989).

Collins, H., and Abramsky, C., *Karl Marx and the British Labour Movement* (1965).

Cowling, M., *The Impact of Labour, 1920–1924* (1971).

—— *The Impact of Hitler* (1975).

Craig, F. W. S., *British Parliamentary Election Results, 1885–1918* (1974).

—— *British Parliamentary Election Results, 1918–1949* (1977).

Crick, M., *The History of the Social-Democratic Federation* (Keele, 1994).

Crisell, A., *An Introductory History of British Broadcasting* (1997).

Cross, C., *Phillip Snowden* (1966).

Croucher, R., *We Refuse to Starve in Silence: A History of the National Unemployed Workers' Movement, 1920–1946* (1987).

Curran, J., and Seaton, J., *Power without Responsibility: The Press and Broadcasting in Britain* (1997).

Dale, G., *God's Politicians: The Christian Contribution to 100 Years of Labour* (2000).

Dangerfield, G., *The Strange Death of Liberal England* (1961).

Davin, A., *Growing Up Poor: Home, School and Street in London, 1870–1914* (1996).

Dennis, N., and Halsey, A. H., *English Ethical Socialism* (1988).

Dowse, R. E., *Left in the Centre: The Independent Labour Party, 1893–1940* (1966).

Durbin, E., *New Jerusalems: The Labour Party and the Economics of Democratic Socialism* (1985).

Earle, Sir L., *Turn over the Page* (1935).

Edwards, B., *The Burston School Strike* (1974).

Englander, D., *Landlord and Tenant in Urban Britain, 1838–1983* (Oxford, 1983).

—— and O'Day, R. (eds.), *Retrieved Riches: Social Investigation in Britain, 1840–1914* (1995).

Ensor, R. C. K., *England 1870 to 1914* (1936).

Erickson, C., *Invisible Immigrants: The Adaptation of English and Scottish Immigrants in Nineteenth-Century America* (1972).

Eustance, C., Ryan, J., and Ugolini, L. (eds.), *A Suffrage Reader* (2000).

Fairley, A., *Bucking the Trend: The Life and Times of the Ninth Earl De La Warr, 1900–1976* (2001).

Farman, C., *The General Strike, May 1926* (St Albans, 1972).

Farrar, M. J., *News from the Front: War Correspondents on the Western Front, 1914–1918* (1990).

Feldman, D., and Stedman Jones, G. (eds.), *Metropolis, London: Histories and Representations since 1800* (1989).

Fishman, W. J., *East End, 1888: A Year in a London Borough among the Labour Poor* (1988).

Fitzpatrick, D., *Oceans of Consolation: Personal Accounts of Irish Migration to Australia* (1994).

Frow, R., and Frow, E., *The Communist Party in Manchester, 1920–1926* (Manchester, n.d.).

—— *The General Strike in Salford in 1911* (1990).

Gallacher, W., *Revolt on the Clyde* (1936).

Gander, M., *After These Many Quests* (1949).

Gardner, P., *The Lost Elementary Schools of Victorian England* (1984).

Garner, L., *Stepping Stones to Women's Liberty: Feminist Ideas in the Women's Suffrage Movement, 1900–1918* (1984).

Gathercole, P., Irving, T. H., and Melleuish, G., *Childe and Australia: Archaeology, Politics and Ideas* (1995).

Gibson-Wilde, D. M., *Gateway to a Golden Land: Townsville to 1884* (Townsville, 1984).

Gooch, M., and Goody, S., *The People of a Suffolk Town: Halesworth, 1100–1900* (Halesworth, 1999).

Graham, J. W., *Conscription and Conscience* (1965).

Graham, T. N., *The Life of the Rt Hon. Willie Graham* (1948).

Graubard, S. R., *British Labour and the Russian Revolution, 1917–1924* (1956).

Graves, P., *Labour Women: Women in British Working-Class Politics, 1918–1939* (1994).

Groser, St J. B., *Politics and Persons* (1949).

Groves, R., *Sharpen the Sickle: The History of the Farm Workers' Union* (1981).

Gupta, P. S., *Imperialism and the British Labour Movement, 1914–1964* (1975).

Hall, L., *et al.*, *Let Us Reform the Labour Party* (1910).

Hamilton, M. A., *Arthur Henderson* (1938).

—— *Remembering My Good Friends* (1944).

Hannington, W., *Unemployment Struggles, 1919–36: My Life Struggles amongst the Unemployed* (1977).

Hardy, D., *Alternative Communities in Nineteenth Century England* (1979).

Harris, J., *Unemployment and Politics: A Study in English Social Policy, 1886–1914* (Oxford, 1972).

Harrison, B., *Separate Spheres: The Opposition to Women's Suffrage in Britain* (1978).

—— *Prudent Revolutionaries: Portraits of British Feminists between the Wars* (Oxford, 1987).

Helmstadter, R. J., Lightman, B. (eds.), *Victorian Faith in Crisis: Essays on Continuity and Change in Nineteenth Century Religious Beliefs* (1990).

Higdon, T. G., *The Burston Rebellion* (1984).

Hinton, J., *The First Shop Stewards Movement* (1973).

—— *Labour and Socialism: A History of the British Labour Movement, 1867–1974* (1983).

—— *Protests and Visions: Peace Politics in Twentieth Century Britain* (1989).

Hobsbawm, E. J., *Labouring Men* (1964).

—— *Industry and Empire* (Harmondsworth, 1975).

—— *Uncommon People: Resistance, Rebellion and Jazz* (1998).

—— *The New Century* (2000).

Hollis, P., *Ladies Elect: Women in English Local Government, 1865–1914* (Oxford, 1987).

Holton, R., *British Syndicalism, 1910–14* (1976).

Holton, S. S., *Feminism and Democracy: Women's Suffrage and Reform Politics in Britain, 1900–1918* (Cambridge, 1986).

—— *Suffrage Days: Stories from the Women's Suffrage Movement* (1996).

Howarth, T. E. B., *Cambridge between Two Wars* (1978).

Howell, D., *British Social Democracy* (1980).

Hunt, K., *Equivocal Feminists: The Social Democratic Federation and the Woman Question, 1884–1911* (Cambridge, 1996).

Jalland, P., *Women, Marriage and Politics, 1860–1914* (Oxford, 1986).

Jefferys, K. (ed.), *Leading Labour: From Keir Hardie to Tony Blair* (1999).

John, A. V., and Eustance, C. (eds.), *The Men's Share: Masculinities, Male Support and Women's Suffrage in Britain, 1890–1920* (1997).

Jones, G. S., *Outcast London: A Study in the Relationship between Classes in Victorian Society* (1971).

Jones, S. G., *The British Labour Movement and Film, 1918–1939* (1987).

Jupp, J., *The Radical Left in Britain, 1931–1941* (1982).

Kendall, W., *The Revolutionary Movement in Britain, 1900–21* (1969).

Kennedy, T. C., *The Hound of Conscience: A History of the No-Conscription Fellowship, 1914–1919* (1918).

Kenney, R., *Westering: An Autobiography* (1939).

Kent, S. K., *Sex and Suffrage in Britain, 1860–1914* (1990).

Key, C. W., *Red Poplar: Six Years of Socialist Rule* (1925).

Kingsford, P., *The Hunger Marchers in Britain, 1920–1940* (1982).

Klugmann, J., *History of the Communist Party of Great Britain*, i, *1919–1924*; ii, *1925–1927* (1980).

Koss, S., *The Rise and Fall of the Political Press in Britain* (1990).

Kushner, T., and Valman, N. (eds.), *Remembering Cable Street: Fascism and Anti-Fascism in British Society* (2000).

Lansley, S., Goss, S., and Wolmar, C., *Councils in Conflict: The Rise and Fall of the Municipal Left* (1989).

Lawrence, J., *Speaking for the People: Party, Language and Politics in England, 1867–1914* (Cambridge, 1998).

—— and Taylor, M. (eds.), *Party, State and Society: Electoral Behaviour in Britain since 1820* (Aldershot, 1997).

Laybourn, K., *The Labour Party, 1881–1951* (Gloucester, 1988).

—— *The Rise of Labour* (1988).

—— *The General Strike of 1926* (Manchester, 1993).

—— *The General Strike: Day by Day* (Stroud, 1996).

—— *The Rise of Socialism in Britain* (Stroud, 1997).

—— *Modern Britain Since 1906* (1999).

—— *A Century of Labour: A History of the Labour Party, 1900–2000* (Stroud, 2000).

—— and James, D. (eds.), *'The Rising Sun of Socialism': The Independent Labour Party in the Textile District of the West Riding of Yorkshire between 1890 and 1914* (Wakefield, 1991).

—— and Murphy, D., *Under the Red Flag: A History of Communism in Britain, c.1849–1991* (Stroud, 1999).

—— and Reynolds, J., *Liberalism and the Rise of Labour, 1890–1918* (Bradford, 1984).

Ledbetter, R., *A History of the Malthusian League, 1877–1927* (1976).

Lee, F., *Fabianism and Colonialism: The Life and Political Thought of Lord Sydney Olivier* (1988).

Lees-Smith, H. B., *The Encyclopaedia of the Labour Movement*, ii (1928).

Lenin, V. I., *On Britain* (London and Moscow, 1941).

—— *British Labour and British Imperialism* (1969).

Lester, M., *Entertaining Gandhi* (1932).

Liddington, J., and Norris, J., *One Hand Tied Behind Us: The Rise of the Women's Suffrage Movement* (1984).

Lineham, T. P., *East London for Mosley: The British Union of Fascists in East London and South-West Essex*, 1933–40 (1996).

Lovell, J., *Stevedores and Dockers: A Study of Trade Unionism in the Port of London, 1870–1914* (1969).

Low, D. A., *Soundings in Modern South Asian History* (1968).

Lutyens, M., *Krishnamurti: The Years of Awakening* (Boston, 1997).

Lyman, R. W., *The First Labour Government, 1924* (1957).

McBriar, A. M., *Fabian Socialism and English Politics, 1884–1918* (1966).

—— *An Edwardian Mixed Doubles: The Bosanquets versus the Webbs: A Study in British Social Policy, 1890–1929* (Oxford, 1987).

McCarthy, T. (ed.), *The Great Dock Strike, 1889* (1988).

McClaren, A., *Birth Control in Nineteenth-Century England* (1978).

MacDonald, J. R., *Socialism: Critical and Constructive* (1924 edition).

MacFarlane, L. J., *The British Communist Party* (1966).

McKenzie, R., *British Radical Parties* (1963).

McKibbin, R., *The Evolution of the Labour Party, 1910–1924* (Oxford, 1983).

McLean, I., *The Legend of Red Clydeside* (Edinburgh, 1983).

McLeod, H., *Religion and the Working Class in Nineteenth Century Britain* (1984).

McWilliam, R., *Popular Politics in Nineteenth-Century England* (1998).

Mace, R., *Trafalgar Square: Emblem of Empire* (1976).

Macintyre, S., *Little Moscows: Communism and Working Class Militancy in Inter-War Britain* (1980).

Mackenzie, N., and Mackenzie, J., *The Fabians* (New York, 1977).

Mackenzie, R., *British Political Parties: The Distribution of Power within the Conservative and Labour Parties* (1963).

Macneill Weir, L., *The Tragedy of Ramsay MacDonald* (1938).

Maddox, W. P., *Foreign Relations in British Labour Politics* (Cambridge, Mass., 1934).

Malleson, C., *After Ten Years: A Personal Record* (1931).

Marcus, J. (ed.), *Suffrage and the Pankhursts* (1987).

Marsh, J., *Back to the Land: The Pastoral Impulse in Victorian England from 1880 to 1914* (1982).

Martin, D. E., and Rubinstein, D. (eds.), *Ideology and the Labour Movement* (1979).

Martin, J., *The Politics of Motherhood: Child and Maternal Welfare in England, 1900–1939* (1980).

Marwick, A., *A History of the Modern British Isles, 1914–1999* (Oxford, 2000).

Masefield, P. G., *To Ride the Storm: The Story of the Airship R101* (1982).

Mason, A., *The General Strike in the North East* (Hull, 1970).

Matthew, H. C. G., *The Liberal Imperialists: The Ideas and Politics of a Post-Gladstonian Elite*, (Oxford, 1973).

Mernick, P., and Kendall, D., *A Pictorial History of Victoria Park London E3* (1996).

Middlemas, R. K., *The Clydesiders* (1965).

Miliband, R., *Parliamentary Socialism: A Study in the Politics of Labour*, 2nd edn. (1972).

Minkin, L., *The Labour Party Conference: A Study in the Politics of Intra-Party Democracy* (Manchester, 1980).

Mitchell, D., *Women on the Warpath* (1966).

Morgan, J., *Conflict and Order: The Police and Labour Disputes in England and Wales, 1900–1939* (Oxford, 1987).

Morgan, K. O., *The Age of Lloyd George* (1971).

Morgan, K. O., *Consensus and Disunity: The Lloyd George Coalition Government, 1918–1922* (Oxford, 1986).

Morris, M., *The General Strike* (Harmondsworth, 1976).

Morrison, S., *I Renounce War: The Story of the Peace Pledge Union* (1962).

Mowatt, C. L., *Britain between the Wars, 1918–1940* (1966).

Nanda, B. R., *Socialism in India* (1972).

Naylor, J. F., *Labour's International Policy: The Labour Party in the 1930s* (1969).

Newsome, S., *The Women's Freedom League, 1907–1957* (1957).

Owens, R. C., *Smashing Times: A History of the Irish Women's Suffrage Movement, 1889–1922* (Dublin, 1984).

Palmer, A., *The East End: Four Centuries of London Life* (1989).

Pankhurst, Dame C., *Unshackled: The Story of How We Won the Vote* (1987).

Pankhurst, E. S., *The Suffragette Movement: An Intimate Account of Persons and Ideals* (1931).

—— *The Home Front: A Mirror of Life in England during the First World War* (1932).

Pankhurst, R. K. P., *Sylvia Pankhurst: Artist and Crusader* (1979).

Pankhurst, S., *Soviet Russia as I Saw It* (1921).

Paton, J., *Proletarian Pilgrimage* (1935).

Peak, S., *Troops in Strikes: Military Intervention in Industrial Disputes* (1984).

Pelling, H., *The Origins of the Labour Party, 1880–1900* (1954).

—— *The British Communist Party: A Historical Profile* (1958).

—— *Popular Politics and Society in Late Victorian Britain* (1967).

—— *Social Geography of British Elections, 1885–1910* (1968).

—— *A Short History of the Labour Party* (1972).

—— *A History of British Trade Unionism* (Harmondsworth, 1974).

—— (with Bealey, F.) *Labour and Politics, 1900–1906: A History of the Labour Representation Committee* (1958).

Pennybacker, S. D., *A Vision for London, 1889–1914: Labour, Everyday Life and the LCC Experiment* (1995).

Philipps, G. A., *The General Strike: The Politics of Industrial Conflict* (1976).

Pierson, S., *British Socialists* (Harvard, 1979).

Pimlott, B., *Labour and the Left in the 1930s* (Cambridge, 1977).

Piratin, P., *Our Flag Stays Red* (1978).

Poirier, P., *The Advent of the Labour Party* (1958).

Pollard, A. J., *Middlesbrough: Town and Community, 1830–1950* (1996).

Ponting, C., *Secrecy in Britain* (Oxford, 1990).

Porter, S. (ed.), *Survey of London*, xliii, *Poplar, Blackwall and the Isle of Dogs* (1994).

Postgate, R. W., *The Builders' History* (1923).

Poulson, C., *Victoria Park: A Study in the History of East London* (1978).

Powell, D., *The Edwardian Crisis: Britain, 1901–1914* (Basingstoke, 1996).

Price, R., *An Imperial War and the British Working Class: Working Class Attitudes and Reactions to the Boer War* (1972).

Pugh, M., *Electoral Reform in War and Peace, 1906–1918* (1978).

—— *The Pankhursts* (2001).

Pugh, P., *Educate, Agitate, Organise: 100 years of Fabian Socialism* (1984).

Purvis, J., *Women's History: Britain, 1850–1945* (1995).

Rae, J., *Conscience and Politics: The British Government and the Conscientious Objector to Military Service, 1916–1919* (1970).

Raffo, P., *The League of Nations* (1974).

Ratcliffe, S. K., *The Story of South Place* (1955).

Renshaw, P., *Nine Days in May: The General Strike* (1975).

Reynolds, G. W., and Judge, T., *The Night the Police Went on Strike* (1968).

Richards, E., Reid, R., and Fitzpatrick, D., *Visible Immigrants: Neglected Sources for the History of Australian Immigration* (1989).

Richards, H., *The Bloody Circus: The Daily Herald and the Left* (1997).

Richman, G., *Fly a Flag for Poplar* (n.d.).

Riddell, N., *Labour in Crisis: The Second Labour Government, 1929–31* (1999).

Rodgers, W. T., and Donoughue B., *The People into Parliament* (1966).

Rogers, A., *Secrecy and Power in the British State: A History of the Official Secrets Act* (1997).

Rosen, A., *The Militant Campaign of the Women's Social and Political Union, 1903–1914* (1974).

Ross, E., *Love and Toil: Motherhood in Outcast London, 1870–1918* (1993).

Rover, C., *Women's Suffrage and Party Politics in Britain, 1866–1914* (London, 1967).

Rowbotham, S., *A New World for Women: Stella Browne, Socialist and Feminist* (London, 1977).

—— *Hidden from History: 300 Years of Women's Oppression and the Fight against It* (1985).

Sassoon, D., *One Hundred Years of Socialism: The West European Left in the Twentieth Century* (1994).

Scanlon, J., *Decline and Fall of the Labour Party* (1932).

Schmidt, P., *Hitler's Interpreter* (1951).

Schneer, J., *London, 1900: The Imperial Metropolis* (New Haven, Conn., 1999).

Scurr, J., *The Rate Protest of Poplar* (1922).

Seldon, A. (ed.), *The Blair Effect: The Blair Government, 1997–2001* (2001).

Sellwood, A. V., *Police Strike, 1919* (1978).

Shen, P., *The Age of Appeasement: The Evolution of British Foreign Policy in the 1930s* (Stroud, 1999).

Shore, P., *Leading the Left* (1993).

Skelley, J. (ed.), *The General Strike, 1926* (1976).

Skidelsky, R., *Politicians and the Slump: The Labour Government of 1929–1931* (Harmondsworth, 1970).

Slessor, H. H., *Judgement Reserved* (1941).

Slocombe, G., *The Tumult and the Shouting* (1935).

Smart, N., *The National Government, 1931–40* (1999).

Snell, H., *Men, Movements and Myself* (1936).

Soar, P., and Tyler, M., *Arsenal, 1886–1986* (1986).

Soloway, R. A., *Birth Control and the Population Question in England, 1877–1930* (Chapel Hill, NC, 1982).

Stafford, D., *Churchill and the Secret Service* (1997).

Stannage, T., *Baldwin Thwarts the Opposition: The British General Election of 1935* (1980).

Stansky, P. (ed.), *The Left and the War* (1969).

Stevenson, J., and Cook, C., *The Slump: Society and Politics during the Depression* (1977).

Strauss, S., *'Traitors to the Masculine Cause': The Men's Campaigns for Women's Rights* (1982).

Swanwick, H. M., *Builders of Peace* (1924).

Swartz, M., *The Union of Democratic Control* (Oxford, 1971).

Swift, J., *Labour in Crisis: Clement Attlee and the Labour Party in Opposition, 1931–40* (Basingstoke, 2001).

Symons, J., *The General Strike* (1957).

Tanner, D., *Political Change and the Labour Party, 1900–1918* (Cambridge, 1990).

—— Thane, P., and Tiratsoo, N. (eds.), *Labour's First Century* (Cambridge, 2000).

Taylor, A. J. P., *English History, 1914–1945* (Oxford, 1970).

Taylor, R., *From the General Strike to New Unionism* (Basingstoke, 2000).

Taylor, R., *In Letters of Gold: The Story of Sylvia Pankhurst and the East London Federation of the Suffragettes in Bow* (Stepney, 1993).

—— and Lloyd, C., *Britain in Old Photographs: Stepney, Bethnal Green and Poplar* (Stroud, 1995).

Tebbutt, M., *Making Ends Meet: Pawnbroking and Working Class Credit* (Leicester, 1983).

Templewood, Viscount, *Nine Troubled Years* (1954).

Thane, P. (ed.), *The Origins of British Social Policy* (1978).

—— *Foundations of the Welfare State* (1982).

Thompson, P., *Socialists, Liberals and Labour: The Struggle for London, 1885–1914* (1967).

Thomson, C., *Air Facts and Problems* (1927).

Thorpe, A., *A History of the British Labour Party* (1997).

—— *The British General Election of 1931* (Oxford, 1991).

Thorpe, B., *Colonial Queensland: Perspectives on a Frontier Society* (St Lucia, Queensland, 1996).

Tickner, T., *The Spectacle of Women: Imagery of the Suffrage Campaign, 1907–1914* (1987).

Troy, E., *Soviet Trade Unions and The General Strike* (Brighton, 1975).

Tsuzuki, C., *H. M. Hyndman and British Socialism* (1961).

Vellacott, J., *Bertrand Russell and the Pacifists of the First World War* (Oxford, 1940).

Vincent, D., *Poor Citizens: The State and the Poor in Twentieth Century Britain* (1991).

—— *The Culture of Secrecy: Britain, 1832–1998* (Oxford, 1998).

Waites, B., *A Class Society at War: England, 1914–18* (Leamington Spa, 1987).

Waley, D., *British Public Opinion and the Abyssinian War, 1935–1936* (1975).

Ward, P., *Red Flag and Union Jack: Englishness, Patriotism and the British Left* (1998).

Wedgwood, C. V., *The Last of the Radicals* (1951).

Weller, K., *'Don't Be a Soldier!' The Radical Anti-War Movement in North London, 1914–1918* (1985).

White, S., *Britain and the Bolshevik Revolution* (New York, 1979).

Wilkinson, A., *Dissent or Conform: War, Peace and the English Churches, 1900–1945* (1986).

—— *Christian Socialism: Scott Holland to Tony Blair* (1998).

Wilkinson, E., Horrabin, J. F., and Postgate, R. W., *A Workers' History of the Great Strike* (1927).

Williams, A., *Labour and Russia: The Attitude of the Labour Party to the USSR, 1924–34* (Manchester, 1989).

Williams, E. T., and Nichols, C. S. (eds.), *The Dictionary of National Biography, 1961–1970* (Oxford, 1981).

Williams, F., *Nothing so Strange* (1961).

Williams, Lord, *Digging for Britain* (1965).

Williamson, P., *National Crisis and National Government: British Politics, the Economy and the Empire, 1926–1932* (Cambridge, 1992).

Wilson, H., *The Governance of Britain* (1976).

Winkler, H. R., *Paths not Taken: British Labour and International Policy in the 1920s* (Chapel Hill, NC, 1994).

Winslow, B., *Sylvia Pankhurst: Sexual Politics and Political Activism* (1996).

Woodcock, H. R., *Rights of Passage: Emigration to Australia in the Nineteenth Century* (1986).

Wright, T., and Carter, M., *The People's Party: The History of the Labour Party* (1997).

Wrigley, C. (ed.), *Warfare, Diplomacy and Politics* (1986).

—— *Lloyd George and the British Labour Movement: Peace and War* (1979).

—— *Lloyd George and the Challenge of Labour: The Post War Coalition, 1918–1922* (Hemel Hempstead, 1990).

—— and Shepherd, J. (eds.), *On the Move: Essays in Labour and Transport History Presented to Philip Bagwell* (1991).

Yalland, P., *Women, Marriage and Politics, 1860–1914* (1986).

Yeo, S. (ed.), *New Views of Cooperation* (1988).

2. Biography and memoirs

'Ephesian' [C. E. Bechofer Roberts], *Philip Snowden* (London, 1929).

Ackroyd, P., *London: The Biography* (2000).

Aldred, G. A., *No Traitor's Gate* (1955).

Attlee, C. R., *As It Happened* (Kingswood, 1954).

Attlee, P., *With a Quiet Conscience: A Biography of Thomas Simms Attlee, 1880–1960* (1995).

Bagwell, P. S., and Lawley, J., *From Prison Cell to Council Chamber: The Life of Philip William Bagwell, 1885–1958* (1994).

Bell, A. O., and McNeillie, A. (eds.), *The Diary of Virginia Woolf* (1982).

Benn, C., *Keir Hardie* (1992).

Berry, P., and Bostridge, M., *Vera Brittain: A Life* (1995).

Besant, A., *Annie Besant, An Autobiography* (1893).

Blake, J., *Memories of Old Poplar* (1977).

Blaxland, G., *J. H. Thomas: A Life for Unity* (1964).

Boyle, A., *Montagu Norman: A Biography* (1967).

Brittain, V., *Pethick-Lawrence: A Portrait* (1963).

—— *Testament of Youth* (1978).

—— *Testament of Experience: An Autobiographical Story of the Years, 1925–1950* (1979).

Broadhurst, H., *Henry Broadhurst, MP: Told by Himself* (1901).

Brockway, F., *Inside the Left: Thirty Years of Platform, Press, Prison and Parliament* (1942).

—— *Socialism over Sixty Years: The Life of Jowett of Bradford* (1946).

—— *Bermondsey Story: The Life of Alfred Salter* (1949).

Brown, G., *Maxton* (Edinburgh, 1986).

Brown, K. D., *John Burns* (1977).

Bryant, C., *Stafford Cripps: The First Modern Chancellor* (1997).

Bullock, A., *The Life and Times of Ernest Bevin*, i, *Trade Union Leader, 1881–1940* (1960).

Burgess, S., *Stafford Cripps: A Political Life* (1999).

Burke, K., *Troublemaker: The Life and History of A. J. P. Taylor* (New Haven, 2000).

Burridge, T., *Clement Attlee* (1985).

By His Friends, *Dick Sheppard* (1938).

Caldwell, J. T., *Come Dungeons Dark: The Life and Times of Guy Aldred, Glasgow Anarchist* (Barr, 1988).

Campbell, J., *Nye Bevan and the Mirage of British Socialism* (1987).

Carlton, D., *Anthony Eden* (1981).

Castle, B., *Sylvia and Christabel Pankhurst* (Harmondsworth, 1987).

—— *Fighting all the Way* (1993).

Champness, E. I., *Frank Smith: Pioneer and Mystic* (1943).

Charmley, J., *A History of Conservative Politics, 1900–1996* (Basingstoke, 1998).

Citrine, W., *I Search for Truth in Russia*.

—— *Men and Work: An Autobiography* (1964).

Clark, D., *Victor Grayson: Labour's Lost Leader* (1985).

Clynes, J. R., *Memoirs, 1869–1937* (2 vols.; 1937).

Cole, M. (ed.), *Beatrice Webb's Diary, 1912–24* (1952).

—— *The Life of G. D. H. Cole* (1971).

Cooke, C., *The Life of Richard Stafford Cripps* (1957).

Crowson, N. J. (ed.), *Fleet Street, Press Barons and Politics: The Journals of Collin Brooks, 1932–1940* (1998).

Dalton, E. H. J. N., *Memoirs: Call Back Yesterday, 1887–1931* (1953).

Dalton, H., *The Fateful Years: Memoirs, 1931–1945* (1957).

Darlington, R., *The Political Trajectory of J. T. Murphy* (Liverpool, 1998).

Davies, P., *A. J. Cook* (Manchester, 1987).

Davis, M., *Sylvia Pankhurst: A Life in Radical Politics* (1999).

Dinnage, R., *Annie Besant* (Harmondsworth, 1986).

Dodd, K. (ed.), *Sylvia Pankhurst* (Manchester, 1993).

Donoughue, B., and Jones, G. W., *Herbert Morrison: Portrait of a Politician* (1973).

Dudden, A. P., *Joseph Fels and the Single-Tax Movement* (1971).

Eastwood, G., *Harold Laski* (1977).

Edwardes, M., *Nehru: A Political Biography* (1971).

Estorick, E., *Stafford Cripps: A Biography* (1949).

Fels, Mary, *Joseph Fels: His Life and Work* (1920).

Feuchtwanger, E. J., *Gladstone* (1975).

Fischer, L., *The Life of Mahatma Gandhi* (1982).

Foot, M., *Aneurin Bevan*, i, *1897–1945* (1962).

Fox, R. M., *Smokey Crusade* (1937).

Fyfe, H., *My Seven Selves* (1935).

Gandhi, M. K., *An Autobiography or the Story of My Experiments with Truth* (Harmondsworth, 1982).

Gilbert, M., *Plough My Own Furrow: The Story of Lord Allen of Hurtwood as Told through His Writings and Correspondence* (1965).

—— *Winston S. Churchill*, v, *The Wilderness Years, 1929–1935* (1981).

Gobat, M., *T. C. Gobat: His Life, Work, and Teaching* (1938).

Gopal, S., *Jawaharlal Nehru: A Biography*, i, *1889–1947* (1975).

Gottfried, M., *Balancing Act: The Authorized Biography of Angela Lansbury* (New York, 1999).

Greaves, C. D., *The Life and Times of James Connolly* (1986).

Green, S., *Prehistorian: A Biography of V. Gordon Childe* (1981).

Grigg, J., *Lloyd George: the people's champion* (1978).

—— *Lloyd George: From Peace to War* (1985).

Griffiths, J., *Pages from Memory* (1969).

Hamilton, M., *Arthur Henderson* (1938).

Hannington, W., *Unemployed Struggles, 1919–1936* (1977).

Hamer, D. A., *John Morley: Liberal Intellectual in Politics* (Oxford, 1968).

Harris, J., *William Beveridge: A Biography* (Oxford, 1977).

Harris, K., *Attlee* (1982).

Hattersley, R., *Blood and Fire: William and Catherine Booth and Their Salvation Army* (1999).

Haw, G., *From Workhouse to Westminster: The Life Story of Will Crooks, M.P.* (1907).

Hobson, S. G., *Pilgrim to the Left* (1938).

Hollis, P., *Jennie Lee: A Life* (Oxford, 1997).

Holman, B., *Good Old George: The Life of George Lansbury* (Sutherland, 1990).

Horner, A., *Incorrigible Rebel* (1960).

Hyndman, H. M., *The Record of an Adventurous Life* (1911).

—— *Further Reminiscences* (1912).

Jay, D., *Change and Fortune: A Political Record* (1980).

Jenkins, R., *Asquith* (1964).

Johnston, T., *Memories* (1952).

Jones, J., *My Lively Life* (1928).

Jones, M., *Michael Foot* (1994).

Jones, R. A., *Arthur Ponsonby: The Politics of Life* (1989).

Harris, K., *Attlee* (1982).

Kenney, A., *Memories of a Militant* (1924).

Kent, W., *John Burns: Labour's Lost Leader* (1950).

Knapp, Y., *Eleanor Marx: The Clouded Years, 1884–1898* (1976).

Knox, W., *James Maxton* (Manchester, 1987).

Kramnick, I., and Sheerman, B., *Harold Laski: A Life on the Left* (1993).

Lansbury, E., *George Lansbury, My Father* (1934).

Lansbury, V., *An Englishwoman in the USSR* (1940).

Larkin, E., *James Larkin: Irish Labour Leader* (1965).

Lawley, J., and Bagwell, P. S., *From Prison Cell to Council Chamber: The Life of Philip William Bagwell* (York, 1994).

Lawson, J., *A Man's Life* (1932).

Laybourn, K., *Philip Snowden, A Biography, 1864–1937* (1988).

Lax of Poplar, *The Story of a Wonderful Quarter of a Century* (1930).

—— *Lax His Book: The Autobiography of Lax of Poplar* (1937).

Laybourn, Keith, *Philip Snowden: A Biography, 1864–1937* (Aldershot, 1988).

—— and James, D. (eds.), *Philip Snowden: The First Labour Chancellor of the Exchequer* (Bradford, 1987).

Lee, J., *Tomorrow Is a New Day* (1939).

—— *My Life with Nye* (1980).

Leventhal, F. M., *The Last Dissenter: H. N. Brailsford and His World* (Oxford, 1985).

—— *Arthur Henderson* (Manchester, 1989).

Lewis, G., *Eva Gore Booth and Esther Roper: A Biography* (1988).

Liddington, J., *The Life and Times of a Respectable Rebel: Selina Cooper, 1864–1946* (1984).

Linklater, A., *An Unhusbanded Life: Charlotte Despard: Suffragette, Socialist and Sinn Feiner* (1980).

Loades, J. (ed.), *The Life and Times of David Lloyd George* (Bangor, 1991).

Lockhart, J. G., *Cosmo Gordon Lang* (1949).

MacCarthy, F., *William Morris: A Life for Our Times* (1994).

MacLean, I., *Keir Hardie* (1974).

Mahon, J., *Harry Pollitt: A Biography* (1976).

Maisky, I., *Memoirs of a Soviet Ambassador, 1938–1943* (1967).

Malleson, C., *After Ten Years: A Personal Record* (1931).

Marquand, D., *Ramsay MacDonald* (1977).

Martin, R. M., *The Lancashire Giant: David Shackleton Labour Leader and Civil Servant* (Liverpool, 2000).

Marwick, A., *Clifford Allen: The Open Conspirator* (1964).

Matthew, H. C. G., *Gladstone, 1878–1895* (Oxford, 1995).

McMullen, R., *Will Dyson: Cartoonist, Etcher and Australia's Finest War Artist* (1984).

Meynell, F., *My Lives* (1971).

Middlemas, K., and Barnes, J., *Baldwin: A Biography* (1969).

Milton, N., *John Maclean* (1973).

Mitchell, D., *The Fighting Pankhursts* (1966).

—— *Queen Christabel: A Biography of Christabel Pankhurst* (1977).

Mitchell, G. (ed.), *The Hard Way Up: The Autobiography of Hannah Mitchell, Suffragette and Rebel* (1977).

Mitchison, N., *You May Well Ask—A Memoir, 1920–1940* (1979).

Montefiore, D., *From a Victorian to a Modern* (1927).

Moorehead, C., *Bertrand Russsell* (1992).

Morgan, A., *J. Ramsay MacDonald* (Manchester, 1987).

Morgan, K. O., *Keir Hardie: Radical and Socialist* (1975).

—— *Labour People: Leaders and Lieutenants, Hardie to Kinnock* (Oxford, 1989).

—— *Callaghan: A Life* (Oxford, 1997).

—— and Morgan, J., *Portrait of a Progressive: The Political Career of Christopher, Viscount Addison* (Oxford, 1980).

Morgan, K., *Harry Pollitt* (Manchester, 1993).

Morrison, H., *An Autobiography* (1960).

Morley, A., with Stanley, L., *The Life and Death of Emily Wilding Davison* (1988).

Morley, J., *The Life of William Ewart Gladstone*, i, *1809–1879* (1905); ii, *1872–1898* (1906).

Morris, A. J. A., *C. P. Trevelyan, 1870–1958: Portrait of a Radical* (Belfast, 1977).

Morris, H., Lord, *Herbert Morrison* (1960).

Murphy, J. T., *Labour's Big Three: A Biographical Study of Clement Attlee, Herbert Morrison and Ernest Bevin* (1948).

Naylor, J. F., *A Man and an Institution: Sir Maurice Hankey, the Cabinet Secretariat and the Custody of Cabinet Secrecy* (1984).

Nield Chew, D., *The Life and Writings of Ada Nield Chew* (Virago, 1982).

Newman, M., *Harold Laski: A Political Biography* (1993).

Nicolson, H., *King George V: His Life and Reign* (1984).

O'Neill, G., *My East End: Memories of Life in Cockney London* (Harmondsworth, 2000).

Pankhurst, E., *My Own Story* (1914).

Pankhurst, E. S., *The Life of Emmeline Pankhurst: The Suffragette Struggle for Women's Citizenship* (1935).

Paton, J., *Left Turn! The Autobiography of John Paton* (1936).

Pearce, R., *Attlee* (1997).

Pethick-Lawrence, E., *My Part in a Changing World* (1938).

Pethick-Lawrence, F. W., *Fate Has Been Kind* (1943).

Pimlott, B., *Hugh Dalton* (1986).

Pole, D. G., *War Letters and Autobiography* (1961).

Postgate, J., and Postgate, M., *A Stomach for Dissent: The Life of Raymond Postgate* (Keele, 1994).

Postgate, O., *Seeing Things: An Autobiography* (2000).

Postgate, R., *The Life of George Lansbury* (1951).

Preston, P., *Tired and Emotional: The Life of George-Brown* (1993).

Pugh, M., *The March of the Women: A Revisionist Analysis of the Campaign for Women's Suffrage, 1866–1914* (Oxford, 2000).

—— *The Pankhursts* (2001).

Purcell, W., *Portrait of Soper: A Biography of the Reverend the Lord Soper of Kingsway* (1972).

Rae, S., *W. G. Grace: A Life* (1998).

Ray, G. N., *H. G. Wells and Rebecca West* (London, 1975).

Reckitt, M., *As It Happened* (1941).

Reid, F., *Keir Hardie: The Making of a Socialist* (1978).

Reith, J., *Into the Wind* (1949).

Riley, J. R., and McHugh, J., *John Maclean* (Manchester, 1989).

Roberts, C. E. B., *Sir John Simon: Being an Account of the Life of John Allsebrook Simon, G.C.S.I., K.C.V.O., K.C., M.P.* (1938).

Roberts, R. E., *H. R. L. Sheppard: His Life and Letters* (1942).

Romero, P. E., *Sylvia Pankhurst: A Portrait of a Radical* (New Haven, 1986).

Rosen, E. B., *The Philadelphia Fels, 1880–1920: A Social Portrait* (2000).

Russell, D., *The Tamarisk Tree: My Quest for Liberty and Love*, i (1975); *My School and the Years of War*, ii (1980); *Challenge to the Cold War*, iii (1985).

Samuel, Viscount, *Memoirs* (1945).

Schneer, J., *Ben Tillett: Portrait of a Labour Leader* (1982).

—— *George Lansbury* (Manchester, 1990).

Scott, C., *Dick Sheppard: A Biography* (1977).

Service, R., *Lenin: A Biography* (2000).

Shinwell, E., *Conflict without Malice: An Autobiography* (1955).

Sisman, A., *A. J. P. Taylor: A Biography* (1995).

Skidelsky, R., *Oswald Mosley* (1975).

Slesser, Sir H., *Judgement Reserved: The Reminiscences of the Right Honourable Sir Henry Slesser* (1941).

Smillie, R., *My Life for Labour* (1924).

Smith, J., and McShane, H., *Harry McShane: No Mean Fighter* (1978).

Snell, Lord, *Men, Movements and Myself* (1936).

Snowden, P., *An Autobiography*, i–ii (1934).

Southgate, W., *That's the Way It Was: A Working Class Autobiography, 1890–1950* (1982).

Stanley, L., and Morley, A., *The Life and Death of Emily Wilding Davison* (1988).

Sutherland, J., *Mrs Humphry Ward* (Oxford, 1991).

Sylvester, A. J., *The Real Lloyd George* (1947).

Symons, J., *Horatio Bottomley* (1955).

Tahmankar, D. V., *Lokamanya Tilak: Father of Indian Unrest and Maker of Modern India* (1956).

Taylor, A. J. P., *A Personal History* (1983).

Taylor, A., *Annie Besant: A Biography* (Oxford, 1992).

Thomas, J. H., *My Story* (1937).

Thompson, E. P., *William Morris: Romantic to Revolutionary* (1977).

Thorne, W., *My Life's Battles* (1925).

Thurtle, E., *Time's Winged Chariot: Memories and Comments* (1945).

Torr, D., *Tom Mann and His Times*, i (1950).

Tsuzuki, C., *H. M. Hyndman and British Socialism* (Oxford, 1961).
—— *Life of Eleanor Marx, 1855–1898: A Socialist Tragedy* (1967).
Wallis, J., *Mother of World Peace: The Life of Muriel Lester* (Enfield Lock, 1993).
Warwick, F., Countess of, *Afterthoughts* (1931).
Wasserstein, B., *Herbert Samuel: A Political Life* (Oxford, 1992).
Webb, B., *My Apprenticeship* (1926).
—— *Our Partnership* (1948).
Wedgwood, J. C., *Memoirs of a Fighting Life* (1941).
Weinbren, D., *Generating Socialism: Recollections of Life in the Labour Party* (Stroud, 1997).
Wertheimer, E., *Portrait of the Labour Party* (1929).
Wheen, F., *Karl Marx* (1999).
Williams, F., *Ernest Bevin* (1952).
—— *A Prime Minister Remembers: The War and Post-War Memories of the Rt Hon. Earl Attlee* (1961).
—— *Nothing so Strange: An Autobiography* (1970).
Williams, P. M., *Hugh Gaitskell* (Oxford, 1982).
Wilson, A. N., *Tolstoy* (1988).
—— *Hilaire Belloc: A Biography* (1997).
Winslow, B., *Sylvia Pankhurst: Sexual Politics and Political Activism* (1996).
Woolf, L., *Downhill All the Way: An Autobiography of the Years, 1919–1939* (1967).
Wolpert, A., *Tilak and Gokhale* (Berkeley, 1962).
Wood, I., *John Wheatley* (Manchester, 1990).
Wright, A., *G. D. H. Cole and Socialist Democracy* (Oxford, 1979).
—— *R. H. Tawney* (Manchester, 1987).
Wrigley, C., *Arthur Henderson* (Cardiff, 1990).
—— *Lloyd George and the Challenge of Labour: The Post-War Coalition 1918–1922* (1990).
—— *Lloyd George* (Oxford, 1992).
Young, J. D., *John Maclean: Clydeside Socialist* (Clydeside, 1992).

3. Edited diaries, letters and writings

[Allen of Hurtwood, Lord], *Plough my Own Furrow: The Story of Lord Allen of Hurtwood as Told through his Writtings and Correspondence*, ed. M. Gilbert (1965).
[Amery, L. S.], *The Empire at Bay: The Leo Amery Diaries, 1929–1945*, ed. J. Barnes and D. Nicholson (1988).
[Asquith, H. H.], *H. H. Asquith: Letters to Venetia Stanley*, ed. M. Brock and E. Brock (Oxford, 1982).
[Bernays, R.], *The Diaries and Letters of Robert Bernays, 1932–1939: An Insider's Account of the House of Commons*, ed. N. Smart (1996).
[Billington-Grieg, T.], *The Non-Violent Militant: Selected Writings of Teresa Billington-Grieg*, ed. C. McPhee and A. Fitzgerald (1987).
[Brooks, C.], *Fleet Street, Press Barons and Politics: The Journals of Collin Brooks, 1932–1940*, ed. N. J. Crowson (1998).
[Chamberlain, A.], *The Austen Chamberlain Diary Letters*, ed. R. C. Self (Camden 5th ser., 5; Cambridge, 1995).
[Dalton, H.], *The Political Diary of Hugh Dalton, 1918–40, 1945–60*, ed. B. Pimlott (1986).
[Headlam, C.], *Parliament and Politics in the Age of Churchill and Attlee: The Headlam Diaries, 1935–1951*, ed. S. Ball (Cambridge, 1999).

[Jones, T.], *Thomas Jones: Whitehall Diary*, i, *1916–1925*; ii, *1926–1930*, ed. K. Middlemas (1969).

[Lloyd George, D.], *Lloyd George: A Diary by Frances Stevenson*, ed. A. J. P. Taylor (1971).

[MacDonald, R.], *Ramsay MacDonald's Political Writings*, ed. B. Barker (1972).

Nicolson, H., *Diaries and Letters, 1939–1945* (1967).

—— *Diaries and Letters, 1945–1962* (1970).

[Reith, Lord], *The Reith Diaries*, ed. N. Smart (1975).

[Sanders, Sir R.], *Real Old Tory Politics: The Political Diaries of Sir Robert Sanders, Lord Bayford, 1910–1935*, ed. J. Ramsden (1984).

[Webb, B.], *Beatrice Webb's Diaries, 1912–1924*, ed. M. I. Cole (1977).

[——] *Beatrice Webb's Diaries, 1924–1932*, ed. M. I. Cole (1952).

[——] *The Diary of Beatrice Webb*, i, *1873–1892, Glitter around and Darkness within*; ii, *1892–1905, All the Good Things of Life*; iii, *1905–1924, The Power to Alter Things*; iv, *1924–1943, The Wheel of Life*, ed. N. Mackenzie and J. Mackenzie, (1982–5).

[—— and Webb, S.], *The Letters of Sidney and Beatrice Webb*, i, *Apprenticeship, 1873–1892*; ii, *Partnership, 1892–1912*; iii, *Pilgrimage, 1912–1947*, ed. N. Mackenzie (Cambridge, 1978).

[Wilson, W. T.], *The Papers of Woodrow Wilson*, ed. A. S. Link *et al.* (Princeton, N. J., 1988).

4. Articles

Bagwell, P., 'The Triple Industrial Alliance, 1913–1922', in A. Briggs and J. Saville (eds.), *Essays in Labour History, 1886–1923* (1971), pp. 96–128.

Ball, S., 'The Conservative Party and the Formation of the National Government: August 1931', *Historical Journal*, 29 (1986), pp. 159–82.

Barker, B., 'Anatomy of Reformism: The Social and Political Ideas of the Labour Leadership in Yorkshire', *International Review of Social History*, 18 (1) (1973), pp. 1–27.

Baston, L., 'Labour Local Government, 1900–1999', in B. Bavati and R. Heffernan (eds.), *The Labour Party: A Centenary History* (2000), pp. 449–85.

Bedarida, F., 'Urban Growth and Social Structure in Nineteenth-Century Poplar', *London Journal*, 1 (November, 1975), pp. 159–88.

Blewitt, N., 'The Franchise in the United Kingdom', *Past and Present*, 32 (1965), pp. 27–56.

Bogdanor, V., '1931 Revisited: The Constitutional Aspects', *Twentieth Century British History*, 2 (1991), pp. 1–25.

—— '1931 Revisited: Reply to Philip Williamson', *Twentieth Century British History*, 2 (1991), pp. 339–43.

Booth, A., 'How Long are Light Years in British Politics? The Labour Party's Economic Ideas in the 1930s', *Twentieth Century British History*, 7 (1996), pp. 1–26.

Brown, J., 'Athercliffe 1894: How One Local Liberal Party Failed to Meet the Challenge of Labour', *Journal of British Studies*, 14: 2 (May 1975), pp. 48–77.

Brundage, A., 'Reform of the Poor Law Electoral System, 1834–94', *Albion*, 7 (1975), 206–11.

Bullock, I., 'Review of Patricia W. Romero, *Sylvia Pankhurst: Portrait of a Radical*', *History Workshop Journal*, 26 (1988), pp. 204–7.

Camm, J., 'The Hunt for Muscle and Bone: Emigration Agents and Their Role in Migration to Queensland during the 1880s', *Australian Historical Geography*, 2 (1981), pp. 7–29.

Ceadel, M., 'The First Communist Peace Society: The British Anti-War Movement, 1932–1935', *Twentieth Century British History*, 1 (1990), pp. 58–86.

Cohen, G., 'The Independent Labour Party, Disaffection, Revelation, and Standing Orders', *History*, 86 (2001), pp. 200–21.

Cole, M., 'The Society for Socialist Inquiry and Propaganda', in A. Briggs and J. Saville (eds.), *Essays in Labour History, 1918–1939* (1977), pp. 190–201.

Collett, C., 'Socialism and Scandal: The Sexual Politics of the Early Labour Movement', *History Workshop Journal* (1987), pp. 103–11.

Cowan, K., 'A Party between Revolution and Peaceful Persuasion: A Fresh Look at the United Suffragettes', in M. Joannou and J. Purvis (eds.), *The Women's Suffrage Movement: New Feminist Perspectives* (1998).

Davin, A., 'Imperialism and Motherhood in History', *History Workshop*, 5 (1978), pp. 9–65.

Deacon, A., and Briggs, E., 'Local Democracy and Central Policy: The Issue of Pauper Votes in the 1920s', *Policy and Politics*, 2 (1974), pp. 347–64.

Dore, R., 'British Labour, the National government and the National interest, 1931', *Historical Studies* (1979), pp. 345–64.

Dudden, A. P., and von Laue, T. H., 'The RSDLP and Joseph Fels: A Study in Intercultural Contact', *American Historical Review*, 61 (1955–6), pp. 21–47.

Duffy, A. E. P., 'Differing Policies and Personal Rivalries in the Origins of the ILP', *Victorian Studies*, 6 (1962–3), pp. 43–65.

Englander, D., 'Troops and Trade Unions, 1919', *History Today* (March 1987), pp. 8–13.

Fleay, C., and Sanders, M. L., 'The Labour Spain Committee: Labour Party Policy and the Spanish Civil War', *Historical Journal*, 28 (1985), pp. 187–97.

Fletcher, I. C., ' "Prosecutions . . . Are Always Risky Business": Labor, Liberals and the 1912 "Don't Shoot" Prosecutions', *Albion* 28: 2 (Summer 1996), pp. 251–78.

Gillespie, J., 'Poplarism and Proletarianism: Unemployment and Labour Politics in London, 1918–34', in D. Feldman and G. S. Jones (eds.), *Metropolis London: Histories and Representations since 1800* (1989), pp. 163–88.

Golant, W., 'The Emergence of C. R. Attlee as Leader of the Parliamentary Labour Party in 1935', *Historical Journal*, 13 (1970), pp. 318–32.

Griffiths, C., 'Remembering Tolpuddle: Rural History and Commemoration in the Inter-War Labour Movement', *History Workshop Journal*, 44 (1997), pp. 145–99.

Gupta, P. S., 'British Labour and the Indian Left, 1919–1939', in B. R. Nanda (ed.), *Socialism in India* (1972), pp. 69–121.

Harding, K., 'The "Co-operative Commonwealth": Ireland, Larkin and the *Daily Herald*', in S. Yeo (ed.), *New Views of Co-Operation* (1988), ch. 6.

Harrison, R., 'The War Emergency: Workers' National Committee, 1914–1920', in A. and J. Saville (eds.), *Essays in Labour History* (1971), pp. 211–59.

Hobsbawm, E. J., 'Hyndman and the SDF', in id., *Labouring Men* (1971), pp. 231–8.

—— 'Birth of a Holiday: The First of May', in C. Wrigley and J. Shepherd (eds.), *On the Move: Essays in Labour and Transport History Presented to Philip Bagwell* (1991), pp. 104–22.

Holton, S. S., 'Manliness and Militancy: The Political Protest of Male Suffragists and the Gendering of the "Suffragette" Identity', in A. V. John and C. Eustance (eds.), *The Men's Share? Masculinities, Male Support and Women's Suffrage in Britain, 1890–1920* (1997), pp. 110–34.

Holton, R. J., 'Daily Herald v. Daily Citizen, 1912–1915', *International Review of Social History*, 19 (1974), pp. 360–1.

Howard, C., 'Expectations Born to Death: The Local Labour Party Expansion in the 1920s', in J. Winter (ed.), *The Working Class in Modern British History: Essays in Honour of Henry Pelling* (Cambridge, 1983), pp. 65–81.

Howe, S., 'Labour and International Affairs', in D. Tanner, P. Thane, and N. Tiratsoo (eds.), *Labour's First Century* (2000), pp. 119–50.

Keating, P. J., 'Fact and Fiction in the East End', in H. J. Dyos and M. Woolff (eds.), *The Victorian City: Images and Reality*, ii (1999), pp. 585–602.

Laski, H., 'Why I Am a Marxist', *Nation*, 14 Jan. 1939, pp. 59–61.

Lawrence, J., 'Popular Radicalism and the Socialist Revival in Britain', *Journal of British Studies*, 31 (1992), pp. 175–7.

Lawson, R., 'Class or Status? The Social Structure of Brisbane in the 1890s', *Australian Journal of Politics and History*, 17–18 (1971–2), pp. 344–59.

Laybourn, K., 'Suicide during a Fit of Insanity or the Defence of Socialism? The Secession of the Independent Labour Party from the Labour Party at the Special Conference at Bradford (July 1923)', *The Bradford Antiquary*, 3rd ser. no. 5, pp. 41–53.

—— 'The Failure of Socialist Unity in Britain, 1893–1914', *Transactions of the Royal Historical Society*, 6th ser., 4 (1994), pp. 153–75.

—— 'The Rise of Labour and the Decline of Liberalism: The State of the Debate', *History*, 80 (1995), pp. 207–26.

Leventhal, F. M., 'Seeing the Future: British Left-Wing Travellers to the Soviet Union, 1919–32', in J. M. W. Bean (ed.), *The Political Culture of Modern Britain: Studies in Memory of Stephen Koss* (1987), pp. 209–27.

Lewis, R., 'The Evolution of a Political Culture: Middlesbrough, 1850–1950', in A. J. Pollard (ed.), *Middlesbrough: Town and Community, 1830–1950* (1996), pp. 103–25.

Lightman, B., 'Robert Elsmere and the Agnostic Crisis of Faith', in R. J. Helmstadter and B. Lightman (eds.), *Victorian Faith in Crisis: Essays on Continuity and Change in Nineteenth-Century Religious Belief* (1990), pp. 283–307.

Lukowitz, D., 'George Lansbury's Peace Mission to Hitler and Mussolini in 1937', *Canadian Journal of History*, 15 (1980), pp. 67–82.

MacFarlane, L. J., 'Hands off Russia: British Labour and the Russo-Polish War, 1920', *Past and Present*, 38 (December 1967), pp. 126–52.

Malament, B. C., 'Philip Snowden and the Cabinet Deliberations of August 1931', *Society for the Study of Labour History*, 41 (1980).

Martin, D., 'Ideology and Composition', in K. D. Brown (ed.), *The First Labour Party, 1906–1914* (1985), pp. 17–37.

Matthew, H. C., McKibbin, R. I., and Kay, J. A., 'The Franchise Factor in the Rise of the Labour Party', *English Historical Review*, 91 (1976), pp. 723–52.

McCall, C., 'Free Thought and the Monarchy: The Mystique of Monarchy', *Freethinker* (1997).

McKibbin, R., 'James Ramsay MacDonald and the Problem of the Independence of the Labour Party', *Journal of Modern History*, 42: 2 (June 1970), pp. 216–35.

—— 'The Economic Policy and the Second Labour Government, 1929–1931', *Past and Present*, 68 (August 1975), pp. 95–123.

McWilliam, R., 'Radicalism and Popular Culture: The Tichborne Case and the Policies of Fair Play, 1867–1886', in E. F. Biagini and A. J. Reid (eds.), *Currents of Radicalism: Popular Radicalism, Organised Labour and Party Politics in Britain, 1850–1914* (1995), pp. 44–64.

Mitchell, D., 'Ghost of a Chance: British Revolutionaries in 1919', *History Today*, 20 (November 1970), pp. 753–61.

Morel, E. D., 'The Employment of Black Troops', *Nation*, 27 Mar. 1920, p. 893.

Morgan, K. O., 'Riding the Wave of War Frenzy', *BBC History Magazine* (Dec. 2001), 22–5.

Murray MacDonald, J. A., 'The Case for An Eight-Hour Day', *Nineteenth Century*, 27 (April 1890), pp. 553–65.

—— 'The Liberal Party and Imperial Federation', *Contemporary Review*, 77 (1900), pp. 644–55.

Naylor, T. E., 'Life-Story of the "Daily Herald": A Drama of Newspaper Production', *Daily Herald*, 15 April 1913.

Nelson, K. L., 'The "Black Horror on the Rhine": Race as a Factor of Post-War I Diplomacy', *Journal of Modern History*, 42 (1970), pp. 606–27.

Owen, H. F., 'Towards Nation-Wide Agitation and Organisation: The Home Rule Leagues, 1915–1918', in D. A. Low (ed.), *Soundings in Modern South Asian History* (1968), pp. 159–95.

Panayi, P., 'Anti-German Riots in London, 1914–1918', *German History*, 7 (1989), pp. 184–203.

Pelling, H., 'Governing without Power', *Political Quarterly*, 32 (1961), pp. 45–61.

Port, M. H., 'A Contrast in Styles at the Office of Works. Layard and Ayrton: Aesthete and Economist', *Historical Journal*, 27 (1984), pp. 151–76.

Postgate, D., 'A Child in George Lansbury's House', *The Fortnightly*, Nov. and Dec. 1948.

Postgate, J., 'Raymond Postgate and the Socialist Film Council', *Sight and Sound*, 68 (1990–1), pp. 19–21.

Postgate, R. W., 'Diary of the British Strike', *New Masses* (September 1926), pp. 13–15.

—— 'A Socialist Remembers, 1', *New Statesman*, 9 Apr. 1971, p. 495.

Purdue, A. W., 'George Lansbury and the Middlesbrough Election of 1906', *International Review of Social History*, 18 (1973), pp. 333–52.

—— 'The Liberal and the Labour Party in North East Politics', *International Review of Social History*, 36 (1981), pp. 333–52.

Rheiners, R. C., 'Radicalism on the Left: E. D. Morel and the "Black Horror on the Rhine"', *International Review of Social History*, 13 (1968), pp. 1–28.

Richards, E., 'Annals of the Australian Immigrant', in E. Richards, R. Reid, and D. Fitzpatrick, *Visible Immigrants: Neglected sources for the History of Australian Immigration* (1989), pp. 7–22.

Rose, G., 'Locality, Politics and Culture: Poplar in the 1920s', *Environment and Planning: Society and Space*, 6 (1988), pp. 151–68.

—— 'Imagining Poplar in the 1920s: Contested concepts of Community', *Journal of Historical Geography*, 16 (1990), pp. 425–37.

Ryan, P., '"Poplarism", 1894–1930', in P. Thane (ed.), *The Origins of British Social Policy* (1978), pp. 56–83.

Seyd, P., 'Factionalism within the Labour Party: The Socialist League, 1932–1937', in A. Briggs and J. Saville (eds.), *Essays in Labour History, 1918–1939* (1977), pp. 205–11.

Shefftz, M., 'The Impact of the Ulster Crisis (1912–1914) on the British Labour Party', *Albion*, 5 (1973), pp. 169–83.

Shepherd, J., 'Labour and Parliament: The Lib.–Labs. as the First Working-Class MPs, 1885–1906', in E. F. Biagini and A. Reid (eds.), *Currents of Radicalism: Popular Radicalism: Organised Labour and Party Politics in Britain, 1850–1914* (1991), pp. 187–213.

—— 'Labour and the Trade Unions: George Lansbury, Ernest Bevin and the Labour Leadership Crisis of 1935', in C. Wrigley and J. Shepherd (eds.), *On the Move: Essays in Labour and Transport History Presented to Philip Bagwell* (1991), pp. 204–30.

—— 'A Pioneer, by George', *Tribune* (12 May 2000).

—— 'Poverty and Poplar Rebellion', *BBC History Magazine* (Oct. 2000), pp. 20–2.

Stenberg, K. Y., 'Working-Class Women in London Politics, 1894–1914', *Twentieth Century British History*, 9 (1998).

Tanner, D., 'The Parliamentary Electoral Reform System, the Fourth Reform Act and the Rise of Labour in England and Wales', *Bulletin of the Institute of Historical Research*, 56 (1983), pp. 205–19.

Tanner, D., "Ideological Debate in Edwardian Politics', in E. F. Biagini, and A. J. Reid (eds.), *Currents of Radicalism: Popular Radicalism, Organised Labour and Party Politics in Britain, 1850–1914* (1991), pp. 271–93.

Thane, P., 'The Working Class and State "Welfare" in Britain, 1880–1914', *Historical Journal,* 27 (1984), pp. 877–900.

—— 'Labour and Local Politics: Radicalism, Democracy and Social Reform', in E. F. Biagini and A. J. Reid (eds.), *Currents of Radicalism: Popular Radicalism, Organised Labour and Party Politics* (1991), pp. 148–252.

Thorpe, A., 'Arthur Henderson and the British Political Crisis of 1931', *Historical Journal,* 31 (1988), pp. 117–39.

—— 'George Lansbury, 1932–35', in K. Jeffreys (ed.), *Leading Labour: From Keir Hardie to Tony Blair* (1999), pp. 61–79.

Thurlow, R. C., 'The Straw that Broke the Camel's Back: Public Order, Civil Liberties and the Battle of Cable Street', in T. Kushner and N. Valman (eds.), *Remembering Cable Street: Fascism and Anti-Fascism in Britain* (2000), pp. 74–94.

Tsuzuki, C., 'The "Impossibilist Revolt" in Britain', *International Review of Social History,* 1 (1956), pp. 377–97.

Vernon Jensen, J., 'Clement Atlee and Twentieth Century Parliamentary Speaking', *Parliamentary Affairs,* 23 (1969–70), pp. 277–85.

Ward, S. R., 'Intelligence Surveillance of British Ex-Servicemen, 1918–20', *Historical Journal,* 26 (1973), pp. 179–88.

Webb, S. [Lord Passfield], 'What Happened in 1931: A Record', *Political Quarterly,* 3 (January–March 1932), pp. 1–17.

—— 'The First Labour Government', *Political Quarterly,* 32 (1961), pp. 6–44.

White, S., 'Labour's Council of Action, 1920', *Journal of Contemporary History,* 9 (1974), pp. 99–122.

—— 'Soviets in Britain: The Leeds Convention of 1917', *International Review of Social History,* 19 (1974).

Williamson, P., '1931 Revisited: The Political Realities', *Twentieth Century British History,* 2 (1991), pp. 328–38.

Williamson, R., 'A "Bankers' Ramp"? Financiers and the British Political Crisis of August 1931', *English Historical Review,* 99 (1984), pp. 770–806.

Woolock, H., 'Immigrant Health and Reception Facilities', in Brisbane History Group (eds.), *Brisbane in 1888: The Historical Perspective* (1988), pp. 71–82.

Wrigley, C., 'Liberals and the Desire for Working-Class Representatives in Battersea', in K. D. Brown (ed.), *Essays in Anti-Labour History: Responses to the Rise of Labour* (1974), pp. 126–58.

—— 'May Days and After', *History Today,* 40 (June 1990), pp. 35–41.

—— 'Lloyd George and the Labour Party after 1922', in J. Loades (ed.), *The Life and Times of David Lloyd George* (Bangor 1991), pp. 19–40, 49–69.

—— 'James Ramsay MacDonald, 1922–31', in K. Jeffreys (ed.), *Leading Labour: From Keir Hardie to Tony Blair* (1999), pp. 19–40.

—— 'William Morris, Art and the Rise of the British Labour Movement', *The Historian* (Fall 2000), pp. 4–10.

Yeo, S., 'A New Life: The Religion of Socialism in Britain, 1883–1896', *History Workshop Journal,* 4 (autumn 1977).

Young, J. W., 'Idealism and Realism in the History of Labour's Foreign Policy', *Bulletin of the Society for the Study of Labour History,* 50 (1985), pp. 14–19.

5. Biographical dictionaries

The names of authors of articles on George Lansbury have been placed in square brackets.

Bellamy, J. M., and Saville, J. (eds.), *Dictionary of Labour Biography*, 10 vols. (Basingstoke, 1971–2000), pp. 214–23 [M. Cole].

Dictionary of National Biography, 1931–1940 (Oxford, 1949), pp. 524–6 [M. A. Hamilton].

Leventhal, K. M. (ed.), *Twentieth-Century Britain: An Encyclopaedia* (New York, 1955), pp. 438–40 [J. Schneer].

New Dictionary of National Biography (forthcoming) [J. Shepherd].

Ramsden, J. (ed.), *The Oxford Companion to 20th-Century British Politics* (Oxford, 2002), pp. 366–7 [J. Shepherd].

Robbins, K. (ed.), *The Blackwell Biographical Dictionary of British Political Life in the Twentieth Century* (Oxford, 1990), pp. 250–4 [G. Studdert-Kennedy].

Rosen, G. (ed.), *Dictionary of Labour Biography* (2001), pp. 345–8 [P. Richards].

6. Plays and novels

Allen, J., *Days of Hope* (1975).
Keefe, B., *Better Times* (1985).

E. NEWSPAPERS AND PERIODICALS

Bradford Antiquary
Bradford Pioneer
Call
Cambridge Independent Press
Carlisle Express and Examiner
Christian Commonwealth
Church Socialist Quarterly
Clarion
Cockermouth Free Press
Coming Times
Commonwealth
Daily Chronicle
Daily Herald/Herald
Daily Mail
Daily Mirror
Daily News
Daily Sketch
Daily Telegraph
East End News and Shipping Chronicle
East London Observer
Eastern Post and City Chronicle
Echo
English Labourer's Chronicle
Evening Standard
Fortnightly

Forward
Freethinker
Gainsborough Evening News
Graphic
Hackney Gazette
Justice
Labour Leader
Labour Magazine
Lansbury's Labour Weekly
Leeds Mercury
The Listener
Manchester Guardian
Morning Star
Nation
National Review
New Witness
News Chronicle
Nineteenth Century
North Eastern Daily Gazette
Pall Mall Gazette
Peace News
People's Press
Reynolds Newspaper
Social Democrat
Socialist Review
South London Press
Star
Suffragette
Sunday Sun
The Times
Todmorden Advertiser and Hebden Bridge Newsletter
Tribune
Votes for Women
West Cumberland Times
Woman's Dreadnought
Woolwich Pioneer
Worker
Workers' Dreadnought
Workers' Weekly
Yorkshire Post

F. THESES

Bush, J., 'Labour Politics and Culture: Poplar in the 1920s', Ph.D. thesis (London, 1988).
Ellen, E., 'Women's Suffrage and the Labour Party: George Lansbury's By-Election at Bow and Bromley', MA thesis (Warwick, 1982).

Gillespie, J. A., 'Industrial and Political Change in the East End of London during the 1920s', Ph.D. thesis (Cambridge, 1984).

Goodfellow, I., 'The Church Socialist League, 1906–1923: Origins, Development and Disintegration', Ph.D. thesis (Durham, 1983).

Janeway, W. H., 'The Economic Policy of the Second Labour Government, 1929–31', Ph.D. thesis (Cambridge, 1971).

Johnson, G., 'Social Democratic Politics in Britain 1881–1911: The Marxism of the Social Democratic Federation', Ph.D. thesis (Hull, 1988).

Lewis, M., 'George Lansbury and the Labour Party' (Colgate, 1974).

Livingstone, J. E., 'Pauper Education in Victorian England: Organisation and Administration within the New Poor Law, 1834–1880', Ph.D. thesis (London, Guildhall, 1993).

Morris, D., 'Labour or Socialism? Opposition and Dissent within the ILP with Special Reference to the Lancashire Division', Ph.D. thesis (Manchester, 1982).

Rabinovitch, V., 'British Marxist Socialism and Trade Unionism: The Attitudes, Experiences, and Activities of the Social-Democratic Federation 1884–1901', D.Phil thesis (Sussex, 1977).

Rose, G., 'Locality, Politics and Culture: Poplar in the 1920s', Ph.D. thesis (London, 1988).

Rowlett, J. S., 'The Labour Party in Local Government: Theory and Practice in the Inter-War Years', D.Phil. thesis (Oxford, 1979).

Shepherd, E., 'The Foundation and Early Social History of Woolwich Arsenal Football Club, 1886–1913', BA diss. (Salford, 1999).

G. FILM AND SOUND ARCHIVES

1. British Film Institute

Pathé Gazette, 'London: The Suffragette Election' (26 November 1912).

Pathé, 'The Peaceful Years' (1920s).

Topical Budget, 'Farcical "Revolution" which may be Serious if it Spreads' (5 September 1921).

British Pathé, 'Scrapbook for 1922' (1922).

British Pathé, 'Scrapbook for 1933' (1933).

Peace Pledge Union, 'Rt. Hon. George Lansbury P.C. MP' (1937).

Gaumont British News, 'Mr Lansbury Leaves on a Peace Tour' (1938).

British Paramount News, 'George Lansbury's 80th Birthday' (1939).

2. BBC

Attlee, Lord, 'Leading the Opposition, 1931' (1960).

Bond, J., 'East London Street Meetings during The Boer War' (1960).

Cresswell, N., 'Imprisonment of Poplar Council, 1921' (1960).

Evans, T., 'Peace Issue at the 1935 Labour Conference' (1960).

Lansbury, G., 'The Disarmament Situation' (19 Oct. 1933).

—— 'The Debate Continues' (19 Oct. 1933).

—— 'India' (1 Feb. 1935).

—— 'Birthday Message' (22 Feb. 1939).

Sheridan, L., 'Early Days of the Daily Herald' (1960).

Stansgate, Lord, 'Indian Question, 1929' (1960).

3. Other sound recordings

Labour Gramophone Records (issued by *Lansbury's Labour Weekly* c.1927) (courtesy of Professor Philip Bagwell).

British Pathé News, 'Rise Up Women! The Suffragette Campaign in London' (Museum of London, 1992), PAL VHS.

Great Political Speeches (Hodder Headline Audio Books, 1996).

Index